WITHDRAWN

Feline Infectious Diseases

Niels C. Pedersen, DVM, PhD
Professor, Department of Medicine
School of Veterinary Medicine
University of California
Davis, California

Book Editor: Paul W. Pratt, VMD
Associate Editor: Susan E. Aiello, DVM
Production Manager: Elisabeth S. Stein
Cover Design: Elizabeth R. Mason

American Veterinary Publications, Inc.
5782 Thornwood Drive, Goleta, CA 93117

© **1988** Niels C. Pedersen. Copyright under the International Copyright Union. All rights reserved. This book is protected by copyright. No part of it may be reproduced, stored in a retrieval system, or transmitted in any form or by any means, electronic, mechanical, photocopying, recording or otherwise, without written permission from the publisher.

While every effort has been made to ensure the accuracy of information contained herein, the publisher and author are not legally responsible for errors or omissions.

Library of Congress Catalog Card Number: 88-72173

ISBN 0-939674-20-3

Printed in the United States of America

Dedication

This book is dedicated to Christian Pedersen and Bede Morris. One helped me to become a man, the other a scientist. They were intimidating and exacting taskmasters, as different from each other as a Danish countryside tradeschool, the vast Nevada desert, the Emu plain, Oxford, and the hauntingly rugged Australian Monaro. They have gone ahead to a more perfect place. Although I could not say it then, I love and miss them.

Preface

I was raised on a poultry farm, where we had more than our share of cats. They were working members of our family, repaying our kindness of shelter and food by being companions and mousers. My fondest memories are of "MoMo" (mother cat in a child's language). She was my constant companion for the first 12 years of my life. True to her name, MoMo had many kittens during those years, and it was my duty to see that each found a good home. Many a customer of our farm went home with a few dozen eggs and a new cat. For my part, I was often a quarter or fifty cents richer, sometimes from the customer and sometimes from my parents. This was money well spent to ease the heavy heart of a small boy who had to part with something so special.

My first years in veterinary school were as a budding large animal practitioner. This turned out to be a fickle choice. Those old memories returned as I went through classroom and clinics. "What about cats?," I kept saying to myself and to my instructors. We knew them, but oh so little! For sure, there were the Cellos, Holzworths, Otts and other pioneering feline clinicians like them. They became my idols. My first real research project as a student was on feline infectious peritonitis, a disease of then-unknown etiology and unique clinical manifestation. I was hooked!

The writing of books is something I had always avoided. I thought it was better to physically discover new diseases than to mentally rediscover old ones. After writing numerous chapters for other people's books, almost always on the same 2 or 3 diseases, I rebelled. I felt like the actor who was always sought out to play the same type of character. Out of frustration, I set out to explore the whole world of feline infectious diseases. At first, it was for myself. After reading hundreds of interesting and sometimes obscure accounts that never saw the inside of a textbook, I began to entertain a thought. "It's a shame that all of this work should go unheralded!" Here were insightful accounts written by numerous practitioners and academicians. They were also saying, "What about cats?"

Beginning a book is one thing; finishing it is another. The list of diseases grew, as did the information on each. What started out as a handbook ended up as a rather large textbook. There were so many interesting facts, statistics, hypotheses and experiments. My scientific training got the best of me. The result may be viewed by some as overblown, by others as too scientific. Remember, this book is for the cats and for the many people that have written about them and care for them. It is these people's thoughts that are presented in these pages.

Like all books, it is not definitive. A few diseases have been left out and numerous worthwhile references remain in the literature; to these authors I offer an apology. I also thank Mrs. Patricia Landon for her work on the early drafts, and Mrs. Yvonne Garrett for the monumental task of getting the manuscript into final form. I am also deeply appreciative to my publisher, Dr. Paul Pratt, and his staff for allowing me to work on the manuscript right up to the time of publication and for transforming a collection of words and pictures into a book. I hope that everyone will learn as much from this book as I did from writing it.

Niels C. Pedersen

Contents

Introduction 1

Section I
Viral Diseases

Chapter		Page
1	Pox Virus Infection	11
2	Feline Panleukopenia	15
3	Feline Herpesvirus Type-1 Infection	21
4	Pseudorabies	29
5	Rabies	33
6	Feline Enteric Coronavirus Infection	41
7	Feline Infectious Peritonitis	45
8	Feline Calicivirus Infection	61
9	Feline Reovirus Infection	69
10	Feline Astrovirus Infection	71
11	Feline Rotavirus Infection	75
12	Feline Syncytium-Forming Virus Infection	77
13	Feline Leukemia Virus Infection	83
14	Feline Sarcoma Virus Infection	107
15	Feline Immunodeficiency Virus Infection	115

Section II
Bacterial Diseases

16	*Pseudomonas* Infection	127
17	Campylobacteriosis	129
18	*Streptococcus* Infection	133
19	*Staphylococcus* Infection	137
20	Listeriosis	141
21	Clostridial Infections	145
	Tetanus	145
	Miscellaneous Clostridial Infections	147
22	Bacillary Infections	149
	Anthrax	149
	Tyzzer's Disease	150
	Miscellaneous Bacillary Infection	151
23	Bordetellosis	153
24	Pasteurellosis	155
25	Tularemia	159
26	Anaerobic Bacterial Infections	161
27	Salmonellosis	165
28	*Yersinia* Infections	169
	Plague	169

Chapter		Page
	Pseudotuberculosis	172
29	*Escherichia coli* Infection	175
30	Leptospirosis	179
31	Nocardiosis	183
32	Dermatophilosis	187
33	Mycobacteriosis	189
	Systemic Mycobacteriosis	189
	Feline Leprosy	194
	Atypical Mycobacteriosis	197
34	Actinomycosis	201
35	Miscellaneous Bacterial Infections	203
36	Unclassified Bacterial Infections	205
	EF-4 Infection	205
37	Cat Scratch Disease	209

Section III
Mycoplasmal, Rickettsial, Chlamydial and L-Form Diseases

38	Mycoplasmosis	215
39	Q Fever	221
40	Hemobartonellosis	225
41	Chlamydiosis	231
42	Cell Wall-Deficient Organism (L-Form) Infection	237

Section IV
Fungal Diseases (Mycoses)

43	Coccidioidomycosis	243
44	Histoplasmosis	247
45	Blastomycosis	251
46	Cryptococcosis	255
47	Dermatomycosis	263
48	Sporotrichosis	273
49	Chromomycosis	277
50	Aspergillosis, Mucormycosis, Candidiasis and Penicilliosis	281
51	Mycetomas	285
52	Protothecosis	289
53	Miscellaneous Fungal Infections	291

Section V
Parasitic Diseases

54	Roundworm Infections	295
	Toxocariasis	295
	Miscellaneous Ascarid Infection	298

Chapter		Page
	Heartworm Disease (Dirofilariasis)	299
	Lungworm Infection	305
	Nasal Worm (Gapeworm) Infection	309
	Trichurid Worm Infection	311
	Trichinellosis	315
	Hookworm Infection	317
	Stomach Worm Infection	319
	Large Intestinal Worm Infection	326
55	Flatworm Infections	331
	Paragonimiasis (Lung Fluke Infection)	331
	Platynosomiasis (Liver Fluke Infection)	334
	Pancreatic Fluke Infection	336
	Miscellaneous Liver and Pancreatic Fluke Infections	338
	Tapeworm Infection	339
56	Thorny-Headed Worm Infection (Acanthocephaliasis)	345
57	Arthropod Infestations	347
	Ear Mite Infestation	347
	Cheyletiellosis	349
	Chigger Mite Infestation	351
	Demodectic Mange	352
	Notoedric Mange	354
	Miscellaneous Mange Mite Infestation	356
	Fur Mite Infestation	357
	Pediculosis (Lice Infestation)	358
	Flea Infestation	359
	Stick-Tight Flea Infestation	366
58	Protozoal Infections	367
	Coccidiosis	367
	Toxoplasmosis	372
	Cryptosporidiosis	380
	Babesiosis	383
	Cytauxzoonosis	386
	Giardiasis	389
	Trypanosomiasis	392
	Leishmaniasis	397
	Encephalitozoonosis	399
	Hepatozoonosis	399
Index		401

Introduction

Introduction

Domestic cats suffer from a variety of infectious diseases. At times, they seem to suffer inordinately, as compared to other species of animals. Cats are not immunologic cripples, however. They belong to one of the most successful families of carnivores that has ever evolved on the earth. Cats and their wild relatives are found on many continents and climates. In their own environment, and under usual conditions of population density and pressure, cats handle infectious diseases very well.

Cats are not intrinsically sensitive to infectious disease, but seem so as a reflection of their modern environments. These environments are often totally different from the environments in which cats evolved. The concept that environment is one of the most important factors in determining incidence and severity of disease is not only applicable to cats, it is one of the pillars of our understanding of infectious diseases. Infectious agents usually do not kill or incapacitate a significant number of their hosts. To do so would deprive them of the environment essential to their own survival. Therefore, when disease occurs, it must be the exception rather than the rule.

The term "infection" is not synonymous with the term "disease." Infection occurs when the microbe invades the body. Disease is the pathologic state caused by the invading microbe or the host's own attempts to contain and destroy the infectious agent. Many infectious agents of cats cause mild or inapparent disease. For instance, most cats infected with corona-, calici-, parvo-, rota-, herpes- and feline leukemia viruses do not demonstrate disease following infection. If factors are favorable, however, these same agents can cause severe and often fatal disease. Therefore, control and prevention of infectious "disease" rests with understanding co-factors of infection that favor disease.

Factors Influencing Disease

As veterinarians, we are frequently confronted with infectious diseases manifested in many ways. Unfortunately, we are usually only aware of the most severe form of a given infection that is most often described in textbooks as being the "classic" or "typical" presentation. In truth, the severe form of the disease is not the most common form occurring in nature. All animals have evolved with their diseases to the point that when exposed to a disease agent under normal conditions, a mild self-limiting or clinically inapparent illness usually occurs. When host and environmental factors are unfavorable, the primary illness is apt to be severe, the proportion of animals developing persistent infections increases, aberrant or chronic forms of the disease are more frequent, and the overall death rate is higher.

Consider the following situation in which a young kitten is born to a family cat. As in most households, the queen is the sole cat, only about one-third of the houses in the neighborhoods have cats and very few of these cats produce kittens. So, very few young kittens are in the neighborhood at

---

Table 1. Factors that influence the outcome of infection.

Host Factors

- Developmental and heritable anomalies of the immune system
- Undefined heritable resistance factors
- Maternal immunity (passive systemic, passive local)
- Age at time of exposure
- Intercurrent illness
- Nutritional state

Environmental Factors

- Population density
- Sanitation
- Ventilation
- Accumulation of excretions
- Interchange of animals from one population to another

Agent Factors

- Virulence
- Dose
- Route of inoculation

---

any time. When this young kitten is 6-9 weeks old, it is adopted by a person down the street who has no other cats. The kitten is vaccinated for panleukopenia and dewormed, and lives in the home for years without apparent illness. When the cat is 3 years old, a blood sample reveals antibodies against all of the common viruses of cats. You might then ask yourself, how can this be? The cat has never been sick a day in its life!

Contrast this to a kitten born in a large cattery, where 25 adult breeding animals and numerous kittens of varying ages are raised together in several rooms. The odds are great that this kitten will have a series of diseases, starting as early as 4-6 weeks of age. Many other kittens in the cattery may die before they are 16 weeks of age and some of the surviving animals manifest chronic disease. The likelihood of this cat's developing a FeLV-related disease or fatal feline infectious peritonitis (FIP) is much greater than for the first kitten described. What so drastically altered the course of disease in the second kitten? This question can only be answered by a study of factors that influence the course of infection (Table 1).

Heritable or developmental anomalies of the immune apparatus can greatly influence the course of infection. These anomalies cause the host to be deficient in cell-mediated immunity, deficient in the ability to make all or certain immunoglobulins, or combinations of both. Fortunately, such defects are rare in cats, but they have disastrous consequences when they occur. Most affected cats die before they reach 4 months of age.

Far more important than developmental anomalies of the immune system are the *undefined genetic factors* that influence host resistance. In this situation, a group of animals is born with immune systems that seem intact and the animals are normal and equal by every conceivable test of immune competence. In spite of their apparent normalcy, one of the group may react to an infectious agent very differently than another. Some animals in the group suffer severe or fatal disease, while others show virtualkly no signs to the same infection. There are a large number of such examples in the animal kingdom. About half of the puppies exposed to canine distemper virus produce sufficient immunity within the first 10 days to abort the infection and show mild and transient signs.[1] In contrast, the remaining half of the puppies fail to mount an effective immune response within the first 10 days, and the infection progresses into its secondary stage, when respiratory, enteric and CNS signs are seen. Most of these puppies eventually die. Cat breeds of Siamese origin appear to have inordinate problems with chronic nasal infections following herpesvirus infection. Abyssinian cats appear to have more gum disease than other breeds. Very little is known about these undefined genetic factors that influence resistance to infection. However, their importance is very apparent.

As important as these undefined genetic factors are in determining resistance to infection, most animal breeders totally ignore disease resistance when selecting breeding stock. Breeders are more interested in other traits, many of which are of benefit to the beholders rather than the animals. Unfortunately, in selecting for such traits as coat color, body confirmation, size, etc, breeders are forced to inbreed. Inbreeding limits genetic diversity and is one means of decreasing resistance of a breed or species. All animals carry many lethal or sublethal alleles of normal genes. If the genetic backgrounds of the parents are diverse, the likelihood of matching up 2 of the same deleterious genes is low. If the gene pool is similar, however, chances are high.

Maternal immunity is an important factor for infectious diseases occurring in kittens between 4 and 16 weeks of age. Maternal immunity provides protection for the kitten from infectious diseases during this critical period when the kitten's own immune system is developing. Maternal immunity is of 2 types: passive systemic and passive local. *Passive systemic immunity* is derived from antibodies a kitten gets from its dam *in utero* (10%) and from the first milk or colostrum (90%). Passive systemic immunity wears off after birth and ultimately, the young animal is left to combat infection on its own. Fortunately, maternal immunity does not disappear until the young animal's immune system is nearly mature. Maternal immunity in kittens may last as long as 14-16 weeks. Situations that prevent adequate transfer of maternal antibodies to the young *in utero* and in the colostrum cause the young animal to be prematurely susceptible to infection. Since the bulk of passive systemic immunity is derived from the colostrum during the first 12-24 hours of life, adequate nursing at birth is essential. Failure of kittens to receive sufficient colostrum can contribute to severe or fatal infections in the neonatal period.

Passive local immunity is provided continually as long as the kitten nurses and is vital for prevention of infections resulting from ingestionof pathogenic microbes. Local antibodies coat receptors on the surface of the pathogens that are responsible for their attachment and penetration of host cells. Passive local immunity may also have a direct killing effect and is provided by ingestion of IgG and IgA antibodies in the milk. The IgG class of antibodies is largely degraded by stomach acids and intestinal enzymes, and is probably more important in preventing infection in the upper digestive tract (tonsils and lymphoid aggtregates in theoropharynx), where such degradation is less likely to occur. Since many infections begin in lymphoid tissues (tonsils) of the oropharynx, IgG immunity is still beneficial. The IgA class of antibodies is much more resistant to proteolytic destruciton by digestive enzymes and prevents infection by coating the entire intestinal tract. For passive local immunity to be protective, it must be: specific for the agent, *ie*, if the queen has no antibodies to rotavirus in the milk, then the young will not be protected against rotavirus; present in adequate levels; and present more or less continuously in the milk. It is available only as long as the kittens nurse and is obviously, terminated at weaning. Also, not all queens provide adequate levels of antibodies in the milk for the entire nursing period. Relatively high levels of antibodies may be secreated into the mild for the first weeks or so, but low levels thereafter.

Age resistance is a very important phenomenon. One of the best exammples of its importance has been documented for feline leukemia virus (FeLV) infection (see Chapter 13). Feline leukemia virus infection differs greatly in severity, depending on age of the animal when exposed. Almost all neonatal kittens develop a progressively fatal infection when inoculated with FeLV. There is both a high morbidity and mortality. In contrast, only about 50% of 12- to 16- week-old kittens develop a chronic persistent infection, and the rest recover rapidly without becoming ill. Kittens of this age that remain infected usually survive for a much longer time than infected neonates. Adult cats are even more resistant to the virus. How does age influence the course of infection? One can only suppose that full immunologic competence develops slowly over many weeks or months after birth.

Intercurrent illness, whether from infectious or noninfectious causes, can greatly influence host resistance. Disease saps the body of necessary nutrients. Some infections, such as from human measles, canine distemper, feline and canine parvovirus, FeLV and feline lentivirus, can directly suppress the host's immune system. In other cases, one microorganism sets up an environment that allows other organisms to invade and cause disease. For instance, herpesvirus infection of cats can damage the nasal mucosa and allow secondary invasion of bacteria and mycoplasma that normally inhabit surfaces of the nasal passages (see Chapter 3). The mortality of panleukopenia virus infection in cats can be greatly enhanced by concurrent with calicivirus infection.[2]

The *nutritional state* of an animal is very important in determining its resistance to infection.[3] Products of the immune response are proteins produced by healthy well-nourished tissues. Nutritional problems are particularly common in young animals. Caloric requirements per unit weight of young animals are several times greater than requirements of adults. Specific nutrient needs, such as protein, vitamins and minerals, are also much different for young animals. Unfortunately, malnutrition is common in enterprises where large numbers of young animals are being reared. Kittens are at the lower end of the social order, must compete more for food, and are often drained of energy and nutrients by kittenhood diseases.

Population density is one of the most important factors in determining the course of a particular disease within a population and among individuals of that population. A high population density increases spread and severity of an infection by increasing: the number of carriers of the agent; proximity of susceptible to contagious animals; environmental contamination *eg*, food, water, air and soil; the dose or amount of infectious agent passed from contagious to susceptible animals; stress of undefined nature; and competition for food.

Effects of increased population density can be counteracted in part by improving ventilation (to dilute airborne contamination) and excrement removal. Unfortunately, these steps become more time- consuming and expensive as population density increases. Most kennels, catteries, farms, feedlots, etc, fail to realize the problems caused by increased population density and cannot or will not spend the money or time to make adjustments.

Increased population density has an interesting interrelationship with other factors. For instance, in a normal urban situation, only every third or fourth household has a cat and very few of these cats are breeding queens. Kittens born in such households usually have no contact with cats other than their dam until they are 4 months of age or older. Then, they begin to socialize with cats out of their immediate environment. Even so, exposure to other cats is usually fleeting and the chance for infection is low. In contrast, kittens born in a cattery or multiple-cat household are exposed to other animals immediately and become infected almost as soon as their maternal immunity wears off (6-12 weeks of age). In addition to being exposed at a young age, the degree of exposure is likely to be high. Kittens born in urban environments have much less illness (older at time of exposure and exposure is less severe), while kittens born in catteries have more serious illness (younger at time of exposure and exposure is more severe).

The *interchange of animals* between populations is important in disseminating disease, especially when it occurs between high-density populations. Each population has its own viral, bacterial, parasitic and protozoal flora. Because of the severity of disease in such environments, many older animals from high-density populations are carriers of the very agents they suffered so much from as kittens. Due to the nature of infection and immunity, cats within a given cattery or area are the most resistant to pathogens to which they are continuously exposed. They may have very little exposure to strains and types of agens found in another isolated population. Interchange of animals between high-density populations is a common practice, especially for breeding purposes. Animals taken from one population to another are more likely to spread new strains and types of infectious agents into the second population, and are exposed themselves to myriad new microorganisms. Once a new type of infection is introduced into such a population, unfavorable environmental and host factors ensure rapid spread. The new infection first appears as an epizootic. As the population develops immunity to the new pathogen, the disease becomes enzootic.

Environmental temperatures and humidity are significant factors in infection. Certain species of animals have optimum temperature and humidity requirements for good health. Acute fluctuations in temperature and humidity can sometimes be as deleterious as static unfavorable temperature and humidity. Outbreaks of respiratory and enteric disease in people and animals are often related to climatic changes. Temperature mnay influence disease by directly stressing the local immunity or by other more subtle means. For instance, animals and people are often brought together in cramped, poorly ventilated quarters (cattle brought into barns or corrals, people staying indoors, cats penned inside) during sudden changes in temperature or humidity. Optimum temperatures and humidities might also favor build-up of one organism more than another. For example, warm and humid climates are favorable for flea growth, while cold and dry climates are inhibitory (see Chapter 57).

Stress is a nebulous term and difficult to measure, though there is no doubt it can contribute to disease. Shipping fever pneumonia of calves is a prime example of how stress interacts with other factors to enhance disease. Calves that are widely dispersed on ranges with their dams are suddenly weaned, congregated at a common site in preparation for shipping, put in trucks or trains and often shipped long distances. They are suddenly introduced to a feedlot containing animals of may different ages and sick animals. Conditions are crowded and the calves undergo a drastic change in diet. Given these circumstances, sickness is inevitable. How much different is the weaning, sale and shipment of kittens? What about the stress cats must undergo in preparation for and transportation to and from shows? Another more subtle example of how stress influences disease is seen in specific-pathogen-free (SPF) mice that are experimentally housed at different population densities. As population density increases, reproductive performance and longevity decrease dramatically. Contagion is not an experimental factor, so how does this occur? What about raising cats, which are naturally solitary free-roaming creatures, in close confinement with large numbers of other cats?

Besides host and environmental factors, features of the infectious agent also influence disease. The *virulence of the organism* is very important and refers to the ability of an organism to cause disease. As an example, there are numerous strains of feline caliciviruses; some cause severe disease and others are virtually nonpathogenic. Dose of the agent to the host is also important. Age-related resistance to many infectious agents can be overcome by giving largere and larger doses. Providing all other factors are equal, a larger dose of infectious agent leads to a higher infection rate, more severe disease and greater mortality. Cats in close proximity to animals shedding high levels of pathogenic microbes are more likely to be exposed to large numbers of organisms than cats leading a more solitary existence.

Besides dose and virulence of the agent, *route of infection* is important, probably more so for experimental then natural disease. As an example, herpesvirus does not produce illness when inoculated IM into cats (see Chapter 3). However, if herpesvirus is put on the conjunctival or nasal membranes, illness occurs. This particular phenomenon occurs because herpesvirus does not replicate at the core body temperature, but only at the slightly cooler temperatures of the superficial mucous membranes of the eyes and nasal passages.

Proper and Improper Immunization

Infectious diseases are more serious and common in young animals, so this is the obvious age group requiring immunizations. Unfortunately, maternal immunity (passive systemic immunity) interferes with vaccination for the first 4-6 weeks of life. Between 6 and 16 weeks of age, this inhibitory effect gradually disappears. However, the exact age of disappearance varies greatly among individuals.

Maternal immunity is the main reason why young kittens receive a series of immunizations given at intervals. The last immunization in the series is given at 12-16 weeks of age, when 95% or more of the kittens have lost their inhibiting maternal immunity. If only one properly timed vaccination at 12-16 weeks of age can immunize most kittens, why is it necessary to give additional vaccinations earlier in life? By so doing, the period during which animals are susceptible to natural infection is markedly reduced. For instance, if a particular kitten loses all of its maternal immunity at 7 weeks of age, and is not immunized until 14 weeks of age, it is unprotected for 7 weeks. If the kitten had been vaccinated at 8 weeks of age, then it would only be unprotected for one week.

The inhibitory effect of maternal immunity disappears earlier for virulent than for vaccine-induced infections; most young animals can be infected a week or more earlier by a virulent organism than they can be successfullly immmunized by an avirulent one. If the agent is in the environment and co-factors favor infection virulent infection always precedes the time of successful vaccination. This is why many vaccines fail in catteries where disease agents are rampant and co- factors favor disease.

The period between immunizations is decided by cost and biology of the immune response. A secondary, or booster, immune response is not likely to occur if a vaccine ius given sooner than 2-3 weeks after the preceding one. Cost also dictates as few vaccinations as possible. This usually translates to 3 immunizations at 3- to 4-week intervals. The first vaccination should not be given before 6 weeks of age and the last not before 12-16 weeks of age.

Before undertaking a study of individual infectious diseases, it is important to understand some useful terms. An *epizootic* refers to a sudden or explosive occurrence of infection within a susceptible population. Since none of the animals has been infected previously, they have no acquired immunity. *Epizootics*, or *epidemics* in human terminology, usually are associated with rapid spread of the pathogen through the population, a high incidence of disease or *morbidity* and a relatively high death rate or *mortality*. Disease tends to occur in all age groups. As the infected population adjusts immunologically and genetically to the new pathogen, a high level of resistance develops among survivors. This resistance is passed on to the newborn through maternal immunity and genetic factors (offspring of survivors are genetically selected for resistance). Development of genetic and immunologic resistance in a population does not necessarily translate to a loss of the infectious agent from the environment. Many agents persist very well in resistant populations and in fact, have reached the ideal host-parasite relationship. Though infection rate may still be high in resistant populations, morbidity is low. Once an infectious agent becomes established in a population, it is said to be *enzootic*. The term *endemic*, which applies to people, is often used interchangeably for this type of animal infection. Enzootic disease is more sporadic and less severe, and tends to affect mainly younger animals. Older animals are immune to infection.

Sporadic disease refers to clincial infections that occur from time to time in individuals or small groups of animals. It often appears and disappears with no apparent reason. Sporadic diseases, such as FIP, usually occur in the background of an enzootic infection. *Incidental, accidental* or *spurious diseases* usually involve individual animals only and occur when the host animal accidentally contacts a reservoir of the agent. *Nosocomial infections* refer to disease that occurs from exposure to hospital pathogens that are often highly drug resistant. Since most animals are hospitalized due to illness, they are also more susceptible to infections. This is why nosocomial infections are often so life threatening. *Zoonotic diseases* refer to infections that can be transmitted from animals to people.

Most pathogens spend all or par to their life cycle on the species in which they cause disease or in the host's environment. Therefore, cats are the biggest source of their own infections. Cat-to-cat transmission occurs when animals shedding organisms are put in contact with *susceptible animals* (animals without prior exposure or immunity). Cats that shed organisms more or less continuously in an intact and infectious form are called *active carriers* or *active shedders*. Calicivirus and dermatophyte carriers are of this type. Some cats shed pathogens intermittently even though they are continuously infected with the agent. For example, cats infected with herpesvirus are intermittent carriers. Herpesvirus remains dormant in the nasal mucosa and turbinates of many recovered cats (see Chapter 3). When these animals are stressed, their local immunity is temporarily depressed and active virus expression occurs for a short time. Animals that carry the disease agent in a hidden form and do not shed the agent are called *latent carriers*. In herpesvirus infections, active and latent carrier states interchange considerably.

Active shedding of microorganisms is not necessarily associated with disease signs. For instance, healthy active FeLV carriers shed as much virus as clincially ill FeLV-infected cats. In herpesvirus and dermatophyte infections, cats showing disease signs from either primary or secondary flare-ups of infection probably shed more organisms than healthy active carriers. *Environmental diseases*, or *occupational diseases* in human terminology, occur when susceptible hosts come into contact with pathogenic microorganisms that inhabit their environment. Most mycobacterial and deep mycotic infections are of this type. Th agents have free-living niches do not require infection of cat

Opportunistic infections usually occur in immunocompromised hosts. Opportunistic diseases are almost always associated with microbes that are not considered pathogenic in healthy hosts. Opportunistic organisms may be part of the normal flora of the cat or reside in the environment. Periodontitis caused by normal mouth bacteria in feline immunodeficiency virus (FIV) infection or FeLV-immunosuppressed cats is an example of opportunistic infection due to resident bacteria (see Chapters 13, 15). Cryptococcosis in an immunocompromised animal is an example of an infection by a normally nonpathogen that lives off the cat (see Chapter 46).

Disease transmission generally occurs by one of 4 routes: ingestion, penetration via fomites (needles, thorns, bites, scratches), inhalation or animate vectors. Ingestion is by far the most common route of exposure. The agent may be taken in with food or water, or deposited on hair and ingested during grooming. Mutual grooming may also be a common means of oral transmission. Grooming of kittens by queens is thought to be a route of transmission for many common diseases of kittens. Inhalation, though widely touted as a means of transmission, is probably one of the least common routes. For infection to occur by this route, the disease agent must be incorporated in particles small enough to be aspirated into the lower air passages. It is unusual for such aerosols to occur, and most airborne pathogens are either deposited on hair or never make it past the oropharynx or nasal passages. This is essentially the same as ingestion, because pathogens deposited in these areas are ultimately swallowed. True airborne transmission associated with primary pulmonary infection has been described for deep mycotic infections and some cases of tuberculosis. Transmission by penetrating wounds is the predominant route of infection for a number of common and rare diseases, such as atypical mycobacteriosis and feline leprosy. Atypical mycobacteria reside in the environment and enter the body through wounds caused by sharp vegetation or contamination of scratch or bite wounds with hair-bound organisms during grooming. Feline leprosy probably results from the bite of an infected rodent or is initiated by the cat grooming itself after having fed on an infected rodent. Feline leukemia virus infection is efficiently transmitted through cat bites. The same is true of cat-bite abscesses and FIV infection.

Vectors are species of lower animals that transmit pathogens to susceptible hosts. Vectors may actually be important in the life cycle and transmission of the infectious agent, as in the case of mosquitoes and heartworm infection. Many vectors are efficient transmitters of infectious agents because they are natural prey species of the cat. Fluke infections occur in this manner (see Chapter 55). Finally, the vector may play no part in the life cycle of the disease agent, but merely transport the organism mechanically to the cat. This is seen with paratenic transmission of *Toxocara cati* from mice to cats (see Chapter 54).

References

1. Appel M: Pathogenesis of canine distemper. *Am J Vet Res* 30:1167-1182, 1969.

2. Bittle JL et al: Serologic relationship of new feline cytopathogenic viruses. *Am J Vet Res* 21:547-550, 1960.

3. Sheffy BE: Nutrition, infection, and immunity. *Comp Cont Ed Pract Vet* 7:990-997, 1985.

Section I

Viral Diseases

Viruses are small particles (20-400 nm in diameter) containing a single type of nucleic acid; RNA viruses contain ribonucleic acid and DNA viruses contain deoxyribonucleic acid. The nucleic acid, whether DNA or RNA, is found either in a single- or double-stranded form and is linear or coiled. The viral nucleic acid is surrounded by a protective protein coat, and together they are referred to as the nucleocapsid. Some viruses possess an additional outer protective coat or envelope that is comprised both of virus-specific proteins, usually glycoproteins, and host cell-membrane proteins. Viruses possessing this outer membrane are called enveloped viruses, while viruses lacking the outer membrane are called nonenveloped viruses.

Viruses do not possess the essential enzyme systems required for independent survival. Therefore, they are parasites of living cells. The viral nucleic acid commandeers host-cell ribosomes to produce viral proteins.

Virus infection occurs through attachment of the virus onto susceptible cell membranes. This attachment is usually species- and host-cell-specific, involving interaction of receptor proteins on the virus envelope or nucleocapsid and the host-cell membrane. The cell membrane-bound particles are then taken into the cell by endocytosis; the envelope or nucleocapsid proteins dissolve and the nucleic acid is freed. In some RNA viruses, such as caliciviruses and coronaviruses, the viral RNA serves as a messenger RNA that directs viral protein synthesis on host-cell ribosomes. Large RNA viruses, such as reoviruses and rhabdoviruses, convert their RNA to a complementary strand of cellular RNA, which then acts as a messenger RNA to direct viral protein synthesis. Retroviruses, a group of single-stranded RNA viruses, form messenger RNA in a unique manner. Retroviruses possess an RNA-directed DNA-polymerase enzyme (reverse transcriptase) that causes the cell to make a DNA copy of the viral RNA. This DNA copy is incorporated into the viral genome, where it exists as proviral DNA. Cellular messenger RNA is made from the proviral DNA. Deoxyribonucleic acid viruses have a more straightforward synthetic pathway. The viral DNA is converted to messenger RNA through a DNA-dependent RNA polymerase. Except for retroviruses, synthesis of viral proteins is directed by extragenomic viral nucleic acid either in the nucleus or cytoplasm. Though retroviruses utilize cytosolic messenger RNA, control of viral synthesis resides within genomic proviral DNA.

Once viral protein is synthesized and the viral nucleic acid is replicated, viral proteins and nucleic acid come together within the cell to produce new virus particles. In DNA viruses, viral synthesis usually takes place in the nucleus. The intranuclear inclusion bodies of parvovirus and herpesvirus are, in reality, sites of virus production. In RNA viruses, viral production is outside the nucleus either on aggregates of ribosomes (eg, in calicivirus, reovirus), within internal profiles of smooth endoplasmic reticulum (eg, in coronavirus), or on the cell membrane itself (*eg*, in retroviruses). Viruses formed on cell membranes or within internal profiles of endoplasmic reticulum are produced by a budding process. Viruses that do not form as buds usually form crystalline arrays within the cytoplasm (*eg*, in reovirus, calicivirus).

Release of virus from infected cells is either by cytolysis, in which virus-laden cells burst and spew out virus particles, or through the budding process. Virions budding off outer cell membranes are released directly into the surrounding interstitial fluid. Viruses formed within the endoplasmic reticulum are eventually secreted through the Golgi apparatus. Not all budding viruses are noncytolytic, however, and in some cases both cytolysis and budding serve as means for virus particles to leave cells.

Viruses are initially classified as RNA viruses or DNA viruses, depending on the type of nucleic acid present in their nucleocapsids. They are then further subdivided according to family characteristics. Various families of viruses are important causes of disease in domestic cats (Table 1).

Table 1. Classification of viruses that cause disease in domestic cats.

DNA Viruses

Poxviridae
    Rodent poxvirus?
Parvoviridae
    Feline panleukopenia virus (FPL)
Herpesviridae
    Feline herpesvirus, Type 1 (FHV-1)
    Pseudorabies virus

RNA Viruses

Rhabdoviridae
    Rabies virus
Coronaviridae
    Feline enteric coronavirus (FECV)
    Feline infectious peritonitis virus (FIPV)
Picornaviridae
    Feline calicivirus (FCV)
    Feline astrovirus
Reoviridae
    Feline reoviruses, Types 1 and 3 (FRV-1, FRV-3)
    Feline rotavirus
Retroviridae
    Spumavirinae
        Feline syncytium-forming virus (FeFSV)
    Oncornaviridae
        Feline leukemia virus (FeLV)
        Feline sarcoma virus (FeSV)
    Lentiviridae
        Feline immunodeficiency virus (FIV)

Chapter 1

Pox Virus Infection

Etiologic Agent

Thomsett and co-workers were the first to describe pox virus infection in a domestic cat.[7] Similar case reports by Baxby and co-workers, Schönbauer and associates, Martland and co-workers, and Gaskell and associates followed.[1,2,5,6] Pox virus infection was recognized earlier, however, in wild Felidae.[4]

Pox viruses are ubiquitous among most animal species and considerable cross-species infection occurs. However, some types of animals are much more susceptible to infection than others. In a large pox virus outbreak at the Moscow zoo in 1977, Felidae and Edentata (anteaters) were much more susceptible than other types of animals.[4] Feline isolates have either resembled cowpox or have been of an unidentified type.[1,6,7] Pox virus isolates of Thomsett and associates grew well in vero cells, producing hemorrhagic lesions on chorioallantoic membranes (CAM) of chicken embryos.[7] Growth on the CAM differentiated this feline isolate from mousepox and vaccinia virus. Such growth characteristics are similar to those of cowpox virus. The isolate of Schön-bauer and co-workers appeared as a typical pox virus on electron microscopy but did not propagate either in cell culture or on the CAM, so its identity was not determined.[6] Pox viruses are among the largest, being 200-400 nm in length (Fig 1).

Pathogenesis

Domestic cats possibly acquire pox virus infection from interaction with normal reservoir hosts.[2,6,7] Small rodents would be one possible source. In support of this, a serious pox virus outbreak in lions and giant anteaters was traced to the feeding of rats.[3] The rats were from a rodent farm that had lost up to 50% of its animals 2 months earlier from what retrospectively turned out to have been a pox virus infection. Pox virus isolated from the rats was identical to that isolated earlier from the zoo animals, and turned out to be a cowpox variant. Cowpox itself may be a misnomer because cows are probably not the natural reservoir host, but are infected incidentally.

Fig 1. Typical pox virus as seen on an electron microscopic view of negatively stained material. (Courtesy of Dr. Malcolm Bennett, University of Bristol, England)

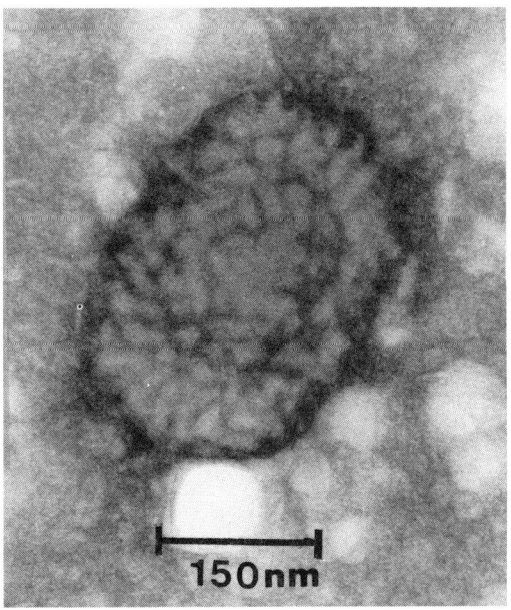

Fig 2. Raised, ulcerated pox virus lesions on the ears of a cat. Smaller secondary lesions are evident near the larger primary sores. (Courtesy of Dr. Malcolm Bennett, University of Bristol, England)

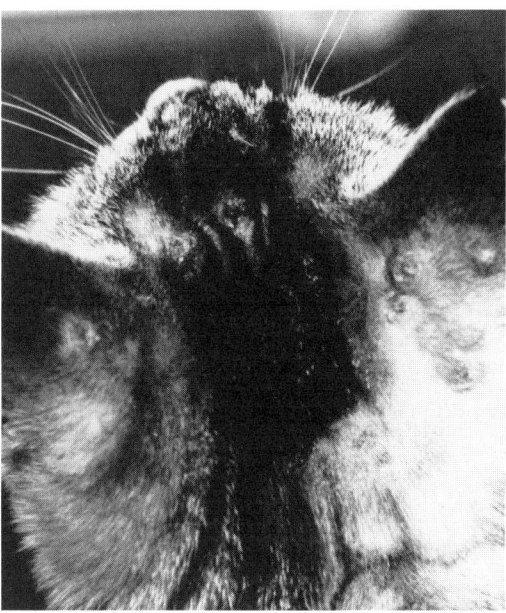

The primary route of infection in cats is unknown. Ingestion of infected rats was the primary route of infection in the Moscow zoo outbreak.[3] Both dermal and pulmonary forms of the disease occurred, indicating that virus disseminated widely throughout the body and that skin was secondarily involved. It was possible, however, that pox virus spread directly to the facial skin and limbs by grooming. Such animals as cats frequently have minute abrasions around the head and legs; virus can easily be transferred from saliva to skin during feeding and grooming.

In experimental situations, virus placed into scarified skin of domestic cats caused some inappetence, but the main lesion occurred in the skin at the inoculation site. However, when pox virus was given IV to kittens, severe generalized edema, profound depression and death resulted.[2]

Clinical Features

Pox virus infection tends to occur naturally in young to middle-aged cats. Recorded cases have involved animals that were 10 weeks, 5 months, 11 months, and 7 and 8 years of age.

Pruritic non-healing sores, with raised indurated borders on the face or limbs, are the most common presenting sign (Fig 2).[2] Skin lesions can be localized or generalized. Severely affected animals may have ulceroproliferative lesions on the muzzle and tongue, and even in mucosal linings of the pharynx and upper digestive tract.[4] Pneumonia with or without exudative pleuritis has also been seen in domestic cats.[6,7] Pneumonic signs in domestic and wild cats can occur by themselves or simultaneously with mild or severe dermal lesions.[4,6,7] Pox virus infection can become more severe when glucocorticoids are used to treat infected animals.[2] Inadvertent corticosteroid treatment is a potential problem because pox virus skin lesions do not respond readily to topical or systemic antibiotic treatment and can be mistaken for corticosteroid-responsive feline dermatopathies.

Pox virus infection of domestic cats can be progressive and fatal, especially if the animals are young or corticosteroid therapy is instituted. Solitary or less-defined lesions may resolve spontaneously after several weeks.

Pathologic Features

Pox lesions, especially when on dermal or mucosal surfaces, start out as reddened, raised papules. Vesicles may appear within these papules, but they are transient and easily ruptured. With time, skin lesions become more ulcerative and covered with scabs (Fig 2). Edges of the lesions tend to be more raised than the centers. Lesions exude a considerable amount of serum or blood, especially if the scabs are disrupted. Pneumonic involvement may appear as reddened atelectatic lesions in the lungs. Pleural inflammation with fibrinous exudates may be associated with more extensive pulmonary disease.

Histopathologic descriptions of pox virus lesions in domestic cats and wild Felidae have been given by Gaskell and co-workers, Marennikova and associates, and Schönbauer and co-workers.[2,4,6] Dermal lesions are characterized by hemorrhage and edema. Edema and ballooning degeneration of epithelial cells are present in areas where skin or mucosa is still intact. In other areas, the epithelial or mucosal cell lining may be absent and the craters covered with a fibrinous inflammatory exudate. Dense, homogeneous, eosinophilic cytoplasmic inclusion bodies (type A) are easily identified in involved epidermis and mucosa. Type-B inclusions (Guarnieri bodies) are also seen in these same tissues, but are less noticeable. In widespread disease, necrotizing inflammatory foci may appear in the CNS, kidneys, spleen, liver or other organs.

Pulmonary disease is typically bronchopneumonia or bronchoalveolar pneumonia. Exudative pleuritis may result as an extension of the underlying pneumonia. Hemorrhage, edema and acute inflammatory cell infiltrates can be widespread in the respiratory tract. More discrete and typical pox lesions can also be seen in mucosal linings.

Clinicopathologic Features

Virus can be readily identified by immunofluorescent antibody in tissue sections. Types-A and -B inclusion bodies are also easily demonstrated on routine histopathologic examination. Most pox virus isolates from cats have resembled cowpox and readily grow in tissue culture and on the CAM of chicken embryos.

Treatment and Prevention

Treatment of cats with pox virus infection is supportive. Open wounds should be kept clean and secondary bacterial infections treated with antibiotics. Topical and systemic glucocorticoid therapy should be avoided. Cats with a few superficial lesions and in good flesh frequently recover, whereas cats with more generalized lesions usually die.

Outbreaks are sporadic and often involve single animals. Therefore, control procedures are unnecessary. Moreover, without knowing the natural reservoirs of pox viruses, a proper control program cannot be implemented. In large outbreaks, such as at the Moscow zoo, infected animals were isolated or destroyed.[4] The source of the infection was identified and the possibility for reinfection from outside was eliminated. Even after such procedures, coupled with disinfection and repainting of quarters, a second outbreak occurred 11 months later in a new generation of pumas.[4]

Infection and Immunity

The course of pox virus infections in cats is reminiscent of vaccinia virus infection in people. Most people immunized with vaccinia virus develop a localized pustular disease. A few unfortunate individuals develop a disseminated and frequently fatal infection. This disseminated disease is similar to generalized pox virus infections of cats. It is also significant that younger cats and cats treated with glucocorticoids are more likely to develop the disseminated form of illness.

Animal and Public Health Considerations

Pox virus infections of cats originate from infections of other species of animals. It is not possible to identify all possible host species for any given cat isolate. The Moscow zoo outbreak involved wild cats and anteaters, and apparently originated in rodents.[4] An earlier outbreak traced to the same source involved elephants and okapis. Cat isolates have often resembled cowpox virus, which is infectious to people. It is logical to assume that people can be infected by some strains of pox virus that infect cats. Indeed, a Moscow zoo attendant that handled sick animals also developed a diffuse self-limiting skin rash.[4]

References

1. Baxby D and Gaskell RM: Cowpox in cats. *Vet Record* 111:132, 1982.

2. Gaskell RM *et al*: Natural and experimental pox virus infection in the domestic cat. *Vet Record* 112:164-170, 1983.

3. Marennikova SS and Shelukhina EM: White rats as a source of pox infection in carnivora of the family Felidae. *Acta Virol* 20:442, 1976.

4. Marennikova SS *et al*: Outbreak of pox disease among carnivora (Felidae) and edentata. *J Infect Dis* 135:358-366, 1977.

5. Martland MF *et al*: Pox virus infection in a domestic cat. *Vet Record* 112:171-172, 1983.

6. Schönbauer M *et al*: Pox infection in a domestic cat. *Zentralbl Veterinarmed B* 29:434-440, 1982.

7. Thomsett LF *et al*: Cowpox in the domestic cat. *Vet Record* 103:567, 1978.

Chapter 2

Feline Panleukopenia

Etiologic Agent

Outbreaks of fatal enteritis have been recognized in kittens since the turn of the century. Zschokke suggested *Escherichia coli* as a possible cause.[38] The disease was recreated several decades later in healthy cats using Berkfield candle filtrates of tissue from affected animals, thus refuting the role of bacteria.[37] The etiologic agent of feline enteritis was confirmed to be a virus in the early 1930s.[10,36] Johnson first described the disease reproduced with tissue culture-grown virus.[11] The name panleukopenia, derived from the very low WBC count of infected cats, was coined by Hammon and Enders.[9]

Feline panleukopenia virus (FPLV) is hexagonal and about 22-24 nm in diameter.[17,33] The FPLV virion has a calculated molecular weight of 5900 Kd; 28.5% is made up of a single linear strand of 23s DNA and 71% is protein. The 2 major viral proteins are 60.3 and 73.1 Kd and comprise 86% and 10%, respectively, of the total protein. About 3-6% of the protein is found as a 36.9-Kd moiety.

Feline panleukopenia virus is very hardy, and withstands heating to 60 C for 30 minutes.[18] Infectivity decreases only 100-fold after being heated to 75 C for 30 minutes.[12] Partially purified virus has been known to survive for 30 minutes at 80 C. Poole recorded no drop in viral infectivity after storage at 4-25 C for 13 months and a 100-fold decrease after storage at 32 C for 6 months.[26] Infectivity of FPLV is not affected by chloroform or acidity (pH of 3).[12,14,33] The virus is resistant to trypsin and most disinfectants, but can be inactivated by 0.5% formalin or 1:32 dilution of commercial hypochlorite solution.[31]

Feline panleukopenia virus isolates agglutinate rhesus and swine RBCs to varying degrees.[2] Agglutination is most apparent at a pH lower than 6 and weak or inapparent at pH of 6.8 or greater. Hemagglutination is one major differentiating feature between feline and canine parvoviruses. Canine parvovirus hemagglutinates over a wide pH range (agglutinates at pH 7.2), whereas FPLV does not.[2]

Six strains of FPLV have been identified.[13] Serologically, FPLV is virtually identical to mink enteritis (MEV) and raccoon parvovirus (RPV).[13,25,35,42] Restriction enzyme analysis of viral DNA revealed no consistent differences between isolates of FPLV and RPV, while canine parvovirus (CPV) and MEV isolates were readily distinguished from other parvovirus types.[42] However, Trachschin and co-workers found a difference of only 1 of 79 restriction sites that were mapped in MEV and FPLV.[35] Canine parvovirus and FPLV have 80% identity on restriction enzyme mapping. The CPV and FPLV can be differentiated by agar gel immunodiffusion, serum neutralization and hemagglutination.[2,6,21,25]

Feline panleukopenia virus grows in feline, mink and ferret cells but not in bovine, dog, monkey or human cells. Cell monolayers infected with large amounts of virus show some degree of roughening, thinning and clumping.[12,23,32] Lower dilutions of virus produce very little cytopathic effect. Intranuclear inclusion bodies appear in cells about 12 hours after infection and are associated with a dramatic increase in intracellular virus.[13] Free virus reaches peak levels by 48 hours after infection. Virus production almost ceases when cells in the monolayer reach confluency and stop dividing, thus establishing the requirement of viral DNA for an activated cellular DNA and protein synthetic apparatus.

Pathogenesis

Feline panleukopenia virus both infects and causes disease in most species of Felidae. It infects Mustelidae, such as mink and ferrets, but causes only mild or inapparent disease in these species.[39,42] Procyanidae, including raccoons and coatimundi, are susceptible to both infection and disease.[8,14,39,42] Feline panleukopenia virus replicates poorly in dogs and does not cause disease.[42] The red fox and skunk are resistant to infection with FPLV.[39] All other species are also resistant.

Feline panleukopenia virus is shed in the feces during acute illness and for several weeks after clinical signs abate. Low-grade chronic shedding by asymptomatic carriers, probably from the oropharynx, appears likely.[3] Unlike most other viruses of cats, FPLV survives for months or years off the host. Therefore, prolonged or direct exposure between infected and susceptible cats is not needed for infection.

Infection occurs in 2 basic forms: fetal and postnatal. Postnatal infection is usually by the oral route, though almost any route will suffice.[20] The incubation period is 2-10 days.[1,11,20,22,27,34] An initial fever spike occurs during the initial viremic phase. A second fever spike is often seen several days later when the white cell count drops. Virus replication probably initiates in the oropharynx and spreads systemically to target organs. Though virus can replicate in virtually any body tissue, cells with high mitotic rates, such as intestinal epithelium of the crypts of Lieberkuhn, bone marrow stem cells and lymphoid cells, are the principal targets.

Fetal infection usually occurs midgestation. Virus enters the fetus from the maternal circulation, but the precise way this occurs is unknown. Queens giving birth to affected kittens are rarely clinically ill during pregnancy, suggesting the fetuses are infected by an inapparent primary, secondary or latent maternal infection.

Classic postnatal FPLV infection usually occurs in kittens 6-14 weeks of age.[7] Clinical signs become progressively less severe as cats get older. Because of widespread vaccination, the disease is less prevalent than in the past. Nowadays, FPLV infection is more likely to occur in unvaccinated cats from certain environments. Infection in rural cats often follows local population increases that generate large numbers of susceptible young animals. Conditions in pounds are also ideal for the disease; many unvaccinated older cats and weanling kittens are in close contact with carrier or clinically ill cats and younger susceptible kittens. High exposure, coupled with weaning, environmental and social stresses and concurrent diseases, ensure that weanling kittens develop severe disease.

Clinical Features

Feline panleukopenia virus infection results in inapparent, acute or subacute disease.[7] Subclinical infections are probably common, particularly in older kittens and adult cats.[11] Peracute disease is characterized by sudden death 4-9 days postexposure and is usually observed in kittens. Infected animals are apparently healthy and then moribund a few hours later. This form is most often mistaken for poisoning. Diarrhea and vomiting are infrequent, but severe abdominal pain may be elicited on palpation. Fever usually goes undetected, and by the time clinical signs are manifested, shock is advanced and the temperature is often subnormal. Death usually ensues within hours. Acute illness is manifested by colic, fever, depression, anorexia and vomiting of a frothy bile-tinged fluid. Abdominal palpation elicits pain. Diarrhea, usually fluid and fetid, follows several hours to a day later. Untreated cats dehydrate rapidly and most die of shock within 24-96 hours. Subacute disease is often manifested by mild depression and diarrhea lasting several days. Chronic diarrhea lasting several weeks to months or more has been observed postrecovery in a small proportion of cats and is due to extensive bowel damage and secondary fibrosis and not to persistent infection.

The course of the disease in fetal infections differs dramatically from that described for postnatal disease.[12,18,19,34] Fetal infection results in almost selective destruction of the Purkinje cell layer of the cerebellum, and to a lesser extent, the retina. Infected fetuses can be aborted, but are usually born alive. Characteristic ataxia is noticed when infected kittens begin to walk. Ataxia is associated with hypermetria, dysmetria and incoordination. Kittens with cerebellar hypoplasia are otherwise normal and many become affectionate and functional pets. Retinal involvement is usually of no clinical significance.

Pathologic Features

Gross lesions are observed mainly in the gut and bone marrow.[40] In mild cases, the bowel is fluid filled and the jejunal and ileal mucosa is reddened. Mesenteric lymph nodes are enlarged, edematous and occasionally hemorrhagic. In severe cases, the mucosa is hemorrhagic and covered with fibrinous exudate. The bowel wall may be so severely affected that fibrinous exudate can be seen on serosal surfaces. The bone marrow may be gelatinous and liquid. The stomach and esophagus in vomiting animals are reddened and bile stained.

Microscopic changes are mainly seen in the mucosa of the small intestine, bone marrow and lymphoid tissues.[40] Necrosis of the intestinal mucosa, beginning in the crypt epithelium, is most prominent in the jejunum and ileum. In severe cases, the mucosa sloughs and is replaced by a fibrinous diphtheritic membrane. Epithelial cells within the crypts of Lieberkuhn are in various stages of damage, ranging from hydropic degeneration to lysis. Eosinophilic intranuclear inclusion bodies are seen within some infected cells. Inclusion bodies are more evident when tissue is fixed in Bouin's or Zenker's fixatives than in formalin. Bone marrow shows varying degrees of myeloid destruction. Lymphoid tissue can be totally depleted of lymphocytes but show evidence of reticuloendothelial hyperplasia. Leukocytes are almost totally absent in peripheral blood.

Clinicopathologic Features

Leukopenia is a consistent feature of FPLV infection. The drop in the peripheral WBC count parallels the second fever spike and starts as early as 4-6 days postinfection. Cells remaining in the peripheral blood are predominantly lymphocytes. Disease severity tends to parallel the WBC count. Counts above 7000 cells/μl are infrequently associated with clinical signs, while counts of 500-2000 cells/μl are associated with severe disease.

Feline panleukopenia virus can be detected in feces by antigen-detection enzyme-linked immunosorbent assay (ELISA) and electron microscopy. Virus shedding is detected before onset of signs and for a week or more after signs disappear.

Treatment and Prevention

Cats with clinical FPLV infection should be treated supportively and vigorously. Food and water are withheld, especially if colic, vomiting and diarrhea are severe. A balanced fluid and electrolyte solution should be given IV as a continuous drip while clinical signs are present. Fresh whole blood should be given if plasma protein levels fall below 4 g/dl or WBC counts fall below 2000 cells/μl. Broad-spectrum antibiotics should be given parenterally to prevent sepsis and temporarily decrease bacterial overgrowth in the damaged bowel. Supportive treatment decreases mortality by 50% in severe infections.

Vaccination has proven very effective in controlling FPLV infection.[7] Attenuated live-virus vaccines produce rapid immunity in kittens. Killed-virus vaccines are somewhat slower in producing immunity, are more apt to be blocked by low levels of maternal immunity and induce lower neutralizing antibody titers. In practice, however, killed-virus vaccines provide adequate protection and remain the mainstay of most immunization procedures.

Starting at 6-10 weeks of age, 2-3 doses of vaccine should be given at 3-week intervals. Vaccination should not be ended before 12 weeks of age because of the presence of interfering maternal antibodies in younger kittens. For maximum protection, a final immunization at 16 weeks of age has been recommended.[30] The need for booster immunizations is debatable. Though yearly boosters have been recommended by some groups, experience with disease in the field does not indicate a need for such intensive revaccination.[7] Older cats are much less susceptible to clinical disease, and most cats with access to the outdoors are probably naturally boosted by field exposure.

Infection and Immunity

Maternal antibodies prevent infection in kittens for 6-14 weeks. Maternal FPLV antibodies have a half-life of 9.7 days, and there is a good correlation between passive titers of the kittens and the serum titer of the queen.[32] Passive immunity interferes with the immunizing ability of both live and inactivated FPLV vaccines.[5,24,32] Scott found that 89% of kittens without maternal FPV antibodies responded to vaccination and that only 12% of kittens with maternal titers greater then 1:10 responded. Modified-live FPV vaccines are more likely to overcome low maternal titers than inactivated-virus vaccines.[30]

Antibodies that inhibit viral infection and hemagglutination appear within 5-7 days of vaccination or infection.[41,43] The titer of these antibodies rises rapidly and reaches extremely high levels as compared to that for other infectious agents. Lymphocyte-mediated killing that is both major histocompatibility complex restricted and unrestricted can be detected in the blood after a second immunization with inactivated FPLV vaccine, and following infection.[43] Natural killer lymphocytes, active against FPLV-infected cells, are in the blood of immunized and unimmunized cats.[43]

Feline panleukopenia virus infection can have an immunosuppressive effect on kittens. Kittens infected in midgestation are often born with cerebellar hypoplasia, but are normal otherwise. These kittens continue to harbor and shed virus for extended periods after birth.[34] Fetal infection, therefore, induces a form of tolerance to the virus. Fetuses infected at 35 days of gestation have depressed T-lymphocyte-mediated immunity, as measured by prolonged survival of allogenic skin grafts placed on the fetuses later in gestation.[29] Infection at 45 days of gestation has no such effect. Infection of adult cats leads to a transient decrease in response of blood lymphocytes to T-lymphocyte mitogens.[29] A similar transient inhibitory effect on conA-induced lymphocyte blastogenesis occurs after vaccination.[43] This effect does not appear to have any clinical relevance, however.

Feline panleukopenia virus produces fever, leukopenia and lymphoid lesions when inoculated into germ-free cats, but very little enteritis and no mortality.[27] The mitotic activity of the crypt epithelium of germ-free cats is apparently lower than in conventional cats, thus providing the virus with fewer target cells. It is likely that many mild intestinal pathogens of kittens can increase the mitotic index of the crypt epithelium and predispose kittens to FPLV-induced disease.

Animal and Public Health Considerations

Feline panleukopenia virus is only infectious to Felidae, Mustelidae and Procyanidae. It is not a human pathogen.

References

1. Bentinck-Smith J: Feline panleukopenia (feline infectious enteritis). A review of 574 cases. *No Am Vet* 30:379-384, 1949.

2. Carmichael LE *et al*: Hemagglutination by canine parvovirus: serologic studies and diagnostic applications. *Am J Vet Res* 41:784-791, 1980.

3. Csiza CK *et al*: Immune carrier state of feline panleukopenia virus-infected cats. *Am J Vet Res* 32:419-426, 1971.

4. Csiza CK et al: Feline viruses. XIV. Transplacental infections in spontaneous panleukopenia of cats. *Cornell Vet* 61:423-439, 1971.

5. Fastier LB: Feline panleukopenia: a serological study. *Vet Record* 83:653-655, 1968.

6. Flower RLP et al: Antigenic differences between canine parvovirus and feline panleukopenia virus. *Vet Record* 107:254-256, 1980.

7. Gillespie JH and Scott FW: Feline viral infections. *Adv Vet Sci Comp Med* 17:163-200, 1973.

8. Gorham JR et al: Studies on cell culture-adapted feline panleukopenia virus-virus neutralization and antigenic extinction. *Vet Med* 61:35-40, 1966.

9. Hammon WD and Enders JF: A virus disease of cats, principally characterized by leucocytosis, enteric lesions, and the presence of intranuclear inclusion bodies. *J Exp Med* 69:327-352, 1939.

10. Hindle E and Findlay GM: Studies on feline distemper. *J Comp Pathol* 45:11, 1932.

11. Johnson RH: Feline panleukopenia. I. Identification of a virus associated with the syndrome. *Res Vet Sci* 6:466-471, 1965.

12. Johnson RH: Feline panleukopenia virus. IV. Methods for obtaining reproducible *in vitro* results. *Res Vet Sci* 8:256-264, 1967.

13. Johnson RH: Feline panleukopenia virus: *in vitro* comparsion of strains with a mink enteritis virus. *J Small Anim Pract* 8:319-323, 1967.

14. Johnson RH: A search for parvoviridae (Picornaviridae). *Vet Record* 84:19-20, 1969.

15. Johnson RH and Cruickshank JG: Problems in classification of feline panleucopenia virus. *Nature* 212:622-623, 1966.

16. Johnson RH et al: Identity of feline ataxia virus with feline panleukopenia virus. *Nature* 214:175-177, 1967.

17. Johnson RH et al: Characteristics of feline panleukopenia virus strains enabling definitive classification as parvoviruses. *Arch Ges Virusforsch* 46:315-324, 1974.

18. Kilham L and Margolis G: Viral etiology of spontaneous ataxia of cats. *Am J Pathol* 48:991-1011, 1966.

19. Kilham L et al: Cerebellar ataxia and its congenital transmission in cats by feline panleukopenia virus. *JAVMA* 158:888-901, 1971.

20. Lawrence JS et al: The viruses of infectious feline agranulocytosis. II. Immunological relations to other viruses. *J Exp Med* 77:57-64, 1943.

21. Lenghaus C and Studdert MJ: Relationships of canine panleukopenia (enteritis and myocarditis) parvoviruses to panleukopenia virus. *Aust Vet J* 56:152-153, 1980.

22. Lucas AM and Riser WH: Intranuclear inclusions in panleukopenia of cats. A correlation with the pathogenesis of the disease and comparsion with inclusions of herpes, B-virus, yellow fever and burns. *Am J Pathol* 21:435-465, 1945.

23. Lust SJ et al: The occurrence of intranuclear inclusions in cell cultures infected with infectious feline panleukopenia virus. *Am J Vet Res* 26:1163-1166, 1965.

24. O'Reilly KJ et al: The persistence in kittens of maternal antibody to feline infectious enteritis (panleukopenia).*Vet Record* 84:376-378, 1969.

25. Parrish CR et al: Antigenic relationships between canine parvovirus Type 2, feline panleukopenia and mink enteritis virus using conventional antisera and monoclonal antibodies. *Arch Virol* 72:267-278, 1982.

26. Poole GM: Stability of a modified live panleukopenia virus stored in liquid phase. *Appl Microbiol* 24:663-664, 1972.

27. Rohovsky MW and Griesemer RA: Experimental feline infectious enteritis in the germ-free cat. *Path Vet* 4:391-410, 1967.

28. Schofield FW: Virus enteritis in mink. *No Am Vet* 30:651, 1970.

29. Schultz RD et al: Effect of panleukopenia virus infection on development of humoral and cellular immunity. *Cornell Vet* 66:324-332, 1976.

30. Scott FW: Comments on feline panleukopenia biologics. *JAVMA* 158:910-915, 1971.

31. Scott FW: Virucidal disinfectants and feline viruses. *Am J Vet Res* 41:410-414, 1980.

32. Scott FW et al: Feline viruses. IV. Isolation and characterization of feline panleukopenia virus in tissue culture and comparison of cytopathogenicity with feline picornavirus, herpesvirus and reovirus. *Cornell Vet* 60:165-183, 1970.

33. Studdert MJ and Peterson JE: Some properties of feline panleukopenia virus. *Arch ges Virusforsch* 42:345-354, 1973.

34. Syverton JT et al: The virus of infectious feline agranulocytosis. I. Characters of the virus: Pathogenicity. *J Exp Med* 77:41-56, 1943.

35. Tratschin JD et al: Canine parvovirus: Relationship to wild-type and vaccine strains of feline panleukopenia virus and mink enteritis virus. *J Gen Virol* 61:33-41, 1982.

36. Urbain A: Contribution a l'etude de la gastroenterite infectieuse des chats. *Ann Inst Psteur* 51:202-214, 1933.

37. Verge J and Christoforoni N: La gastro-enterite infectieuse des chats estelle due a un virus filtrable?: *Compt Rend Soc Biol* (Paris) 312-314, 1928.

38. Zschokke E: Uber coli-bacillare Infektionen. *Schweiz Arch Tierheilk* 42:20-30, 1900.

Additional References

39. Barker IK et al: Response of mink, skunk, red fox, and raccoon to inoculation with mink virus enteritis, feline panleukopenia and canine parvovirus and prevalence of antibody in wild carnivores in Ontario. *Can J Comp Med* 47:199-197, 1983.

40. Langheinrich KA and Nielsen SW: Histopathology of feline panleukopenia: A report of 65 cases. *JAVMA* 158:863-872, 1971.

41. Johnson RH: Serologic procedures for the study of feline panleukopenia. *JAVMA* 158:876-884, 1971.

42. Parrish CR et al: Comparisons of feline panleukopenia virus, canine parvovirus, raccoon parvovirus, and mink enteritis virus and their pathogenicity for mink and ferrets. *Am J Vet Res* 48:1429-1435, 1987.

43. Tham KM and Studdert MJ: Antibody and cell mediated responses to an inactivated panleukopenia virus vaccine. *Zbl Vet Med B* 34:701-712, 1987.

Chapter 3

Feline Herpesvirus Type-1 Infection

Etiologic Agent

Feline herpesvirus, type 1 (FHV-1), was first isolated from nasopharyngeal and conjunctival secretions of a group of 5- to 10-week-old kittens with upper respiratory disease.[12] It was originally called feline rhinotracheitis virus by Crandell and Despeaux in reference to the disease it caused.[9] Most viruses produce a number of clinical syndromes; descriptive names are misleading and sometimes inaccurate, and have fallen out of favor.

Feline herpesvirus, type 1, is a double-stranded DNA virus.[5,6,11,14,15] The virus is inactivated by ether, chloroform, deoxycholate, and almost all common commercial disinfectants, antiseptics, sanitizers and detergents.[1,29,44,46] Infectivity is maintained at 4 C for 154 days or more, but is lost within 33 days at 25 C, 3 hours at 37 C and 4-5 minutes at 56 C.[36] The virus stores well at subzero temperature and withstands lyophilization.

Feline herpesvirus, type 1, is composed of 162 hollow, elongated capsomeres 10 nm long and 25 nm wide. Intranuclear particles have an average diameter of 95 nm and consist of a dense central core surrounded by a clear zone and an outer membrane (Fig 1).[15] Intracytoplasmic particles have an average diameter of 148 nm and are sometimes enveloped in a double membrane. Extracellular particles are usually enveloped and have an average diameter of 164 nm.

The overall protein and glycoprotein composition of FHV-1 is in general agreement with that of other herpesviruses. Feline herpesvirus, type 1, is made up of 23 proteins, 6 of which are glycoproteins.[19] The 23 proteins range in size from 15,000 to 300,000 daltons. By comparing the electrophoretic profile of whole virus and nucleocapsid, it has been found that most viral proteins are envelope associated.[19] Though Fargeaud and associates have found similarities in the structure of FHV-1 and other mammalian herpesviruses, FHV-1-immune sera do not cross-react with herpes simplex, pseudorabies, infectious bovine rhinotracheitis virus, or equine herpesviruses 1, 2, 3 and 4.[19,40]

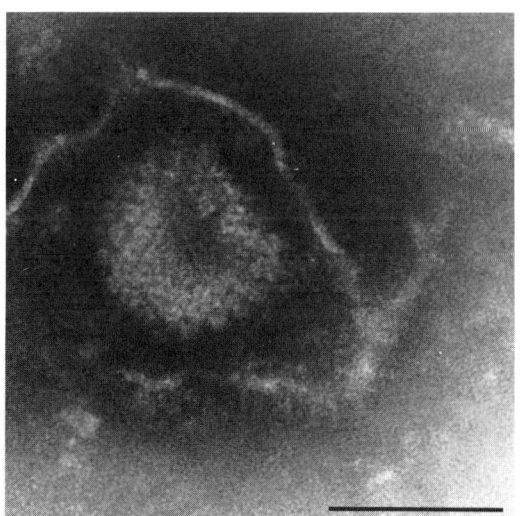

Fig 1. Electron micrograph of a negatively stained herpesvirus particle isolated in cell culture from a sand cat. The virion is about 111 nm in diameter and made up of numerous capsulomeres. The bar at the bottom of the photograph is 100 nm long. (Courtesy of Dr. Anthony E. Castro, University of California, Davis)

Only one antigenic type of FHV-1 exists in nature.[1,4,7,10,15,31,33] All isolates studied so far have been identical to the prototype strain designated C-27.[40] Various isolates may differ somewhat in virulence.[8]

Feline herpesvirus, type 1, grows best in various feline cell lines.[34] Cells infected *in vitro* round up, become refractile and detach from the monolayer.[12] Rounded cells are often connected to each other by protoplasmic bands, giving the appearance of small clusters of grapes. Multinucleated cells can also be seen. Cytopathic effect may rapidly spread through the culture, resulting in diffuse monolayer disruption. Infection of cultures with smaller amounts of virus may produce plaque-like areas of cytopathic effect, sometimes with syncytium formation. Infected cell cultures do not usually yield much free virus for at least 18-24 hours.[16] Virus titers in culture supernatants rise rapidly thereafter and peak by 3-4 days postinoculation. Acidophilic intranuclear inclusion bodies are seen at the same time as infectious extracellular virus. Cytopathic changes without formation of infectious virus have been observed in lion kidney cells.[8] Similar abortive infections have been demonstrated in human embryonic lung cells.[46] However, cells of other species are usually refractory to FHV-1 infection.[8,34]

Pathogenesis

Feline herpesvirus, type 1, is found throughout the world and infects only domestic and closely related wild Felidae.[8] Healthy-appearing carrier cats and cats with clinically active infections are the principal sources of virus. Carrier cats are either latently or actively infected, with considerable interconversion between the 2 states. Latent carriers maintain the viral genome in tissues of the nasal passages, but do not shed infectious virus.[20,21,23] Under situations of stress or corticosteroid administration, the genome can be activated and intact virus shed.[18,20-22] In a study of over 200 healthy cats in Australia, Ellis found that 1.5% were actively shedding FHV-1 and 25.8% were latent carriers.[17]

Kittens are infected from 2 major sources: the queen or other cats in the environment. Virus is infectious when placed on almost any mucous membrane, but is not infectious when injected IM.[40] It seems the virus does not replicate at the higher core temperature of the body. Latently infected queens may become transient virus shedders because of the stress of gestation, parturition or lactation.[23] Infection of kittens can occur *in utero*, neonatally or between the ages of 6 and 12 weeks, when maternal immunity wanes. Asymptomatic or clinically ill kittens and older animals in the same environment constitute a second reservoir of virus. Social and environmental stresses in catteries, multiple-cat households and animal shelters lead to a high level of shedding in resident cats. Conversely, these same stresses lead to decreased resistance in newly introduced animals and make them more susceptible to infection from resident virus shedders.

Contrary to earlier beliefs, infection requires intimate contact between shedding and susceptible cats. Licking, grooming, and eating and drinking from the same food dishes appear to be more important than aerosol exposure in spreading the infection. Airborne spread via large droplets occurs only over short distances, and sentinel cats that share the same airspace but different quarters as virus shedders are infrequently infected.[23]

Virus can be recovered from the nasal passages and oropharynx within 24 hours, following intranasal and conjunctival sac inoculation.[47] Recovery of virus from these sites diminishes between days 11-14, and ceases by day 15. The virus can be recovered from mononuclear cells in peripheral blood around day 8 postinfection.[47] Feline herpesvirus, type 1, infection has been experimentally reproduced by a number of researchers.[12,13,20-22,25-27,35] Clinical signs usually appear within 2 days in experimentally inoculated cats and persist for 10-14 days. Fever in germ-free cats occurs by the second day postinfection and disappears by the fourth day. A second fever spike follows in natural infections, probably as a result of complicating secondary bacterial involvement.[13,35,39,45]

Clinical disease is more common in environments where there is a high density of kittens and where stress and other exposure factors are unfavorable. High-incidence environments include catteries, boarding facilities, multiple-cat households, animal pounds and humane shelters. Clinical disease is much less common among relatively free-roaming, solitary, household and yard cats.

Clinical Features

At least 7 naturally occurring clinical syndromes are attributed to FHV-1 infection: abortion; neonatal disease; classic rhinotracheitis in kittens; chronic conjunctivitis and keratitis; recurrent disease in older cats; chronic sinusitis; and miscellaneous syndromes.

The first report of abortion due to FHV-1 was by Johnson and Thomas.[31] Hoover and Griesemer alluded to the occurrence of abortion in queens spontaneously infected with FHV-1.[25] The role of FHV-1 in abortion in queens was confirmed by experimental studies in which pregnant queens were inoculated IV with infectious virus.[25] Virus was found in the junctional zone of the placenta and uterine vessels 6-9 days later. Virus was demonstrated at day 26 in the fetal liver and chorioallantoic membrane. Though abortion was seen occasionally in pregnant queens that had been intranasally infected, no virus was detected in the uterus, placenta or fetuses.[25] Abortion after intranasal inoculation was attributed to nonspecific debilitating effects of the infection. Gaskell and Povey were also unable to show *in-utero* transmission following maternal infection.[23]

Neonatal disease seems to be associated with queens that either fail to provide maternal immunity or infect their young at birth or shortly thereafter. Bittle and Peckham observed high neonatal mortality among kittens born to queens that had been infected intravaginally with FHV-1 late in gestation.[2] Some of these kittens were born with respiratory disease and the clinical ap-

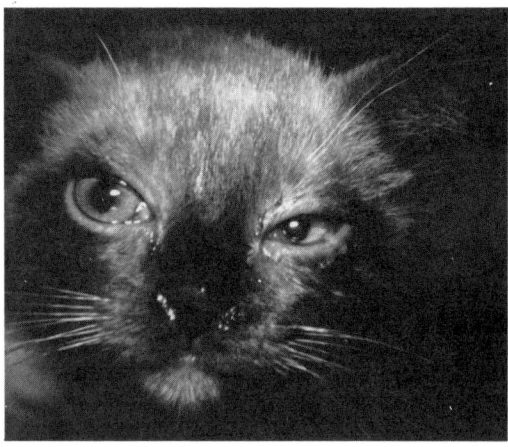

Fig 2. Rhinitis and keratoconjunctivitis in a kitten with herpesvirus type-1 infection. The serous oculonasal discharges often becomes purulent after several days. Squinting indicates painful eyes.

pearance was reminiscent of canine herpesvirus infection. Kittens infected during this neonatal period usually "faded away" and died over several days.

Classic FHV-1 infection occurs in kittens 6-12 weeks of age, when maternal immunity has waned. Severity of signs varies greatly from outbreak to outbreak and animal to animal. Inapparent infections are common.[23] The most consistent manifestation is rhinitis with sneezing and nasal ex-

Fig 3. Mild recurrent rhinitis, characterized by a slight serous nasal discharge, in an adult cat with herpesvirus type-1 infection. The eyes and mouth are unaffected. Sneezing and nasal exudation lasted about 1 week before resolving.

udation. Sneezing is particularly pronounced in the early stages of infection. The nasal exudate is serous initially but rapidly becomes purulent and sometimes blood tinged (Figs 2-4). Kittens that manifest mainly rhinitis may have a low-grade fever but usually continue to eat. Clinical signs usually disappear in 7-14 days. A few kittens in an outbreak manifest rhinitis, pharyngitis, glossitis, tracheitis, high fever, depression, anorexia, open-mouth breathing and drooling (Fig 4). Pneumonia may be seen at necropsy. Mortality, when it occurs, is usually among this latter group of animals. Recovery often takes 2 weeks or more. Contrary to clinical descriptions of the disease, conjunctivitis is less common in FHV-1 infection than rhinitis. When conjunctivitis does occur, it can be mild to severe, and is bilateral (Fig 2). Minimal serous discharge is seen early in the infection, but can become more copious and purulent with time. Photophobia, or squinting, is particularly characteristic of FHV-1 keratoconjunctivitis and is due to involvement of the corneal epithelium and possibly the associated nerves (Fig 5). Chronic low-grade conjunctivitis and rhinitis can persist for weeks or months in some cats.

Fig 4. A young cat with herpesvirus type-1 infection. The eyes are unaffected, but the nares are encrusted with exudate. Glossitis and pharyngitis cause drooling. (From *Virus Infections of Carnivores*, courtesy of Elsevier Science Publishing)

Herpetic ulcers can also be a troublesome complication of FHV-1 infection.[37] Corneal lesions are either acute or chronic. Corneal ulcers occurring during the acute stage of illness are often large, superficial and very painful (Fig 4). Chronic lesions are less painful and consist of clusters of small whitish plaques in the central cornea. Limbal blood vessels invade the area in an attempt to heal the ulcer, and pigment is deposited along their paths. Acute herpetic ulcers sometimes enlarge rapidly and perforate the cornea, especially if lesions are secondarily infected with bacteria, and corticosteroids are used topically.

Recurrent disease in older cats is infrequent. It occurs either as a result of reinfection in the face of waning or short-lived primary immunity or from stress-activation of a latent infection. Recurrent disease can be brought about by corticosteroid injections, social stress associated with cat shows or new environments, surgical stress, chronic debilitating diseases, or the immunosuppressive effects of disease, such as FeLV or FIV infections (see Chapter 13, Fig 6). Recurrent disease resembles primary disease but is much milder and does not last as long. However, severe refractory chronic FHV-1 infection can occur in debilitated or immunosuppressed cats.

Chronic rhinitis and sinusitis can be sequelae of severe upper respiratory infections. Turbinate necrosis and damage to the mucosal linings caused by FHV-1 may render the nasal passages permanently prone to chronic infections with bacteria and mycoplasma that normally reside in the area.[26,35] Turbinate atrophy with nasal deformity and chronic epiphora from tear duct obstruction are other uncommon sequelae.

Several miscellaneous disorders have been associated with FHV-1 infection. The virus has been recovered from the brain of kittens, and has been implicated as a cause of CNS disease in experimentally and naturally infected kittens.[8,27] Ulcerative glossitis and skin ulcers due to FHV-1 have been observed in cats without respiratory signs.[30] Severe pancreatitis and pneumonia in a kitten have been associated with FHV-1 infection.[50]

Pathologic Features

Following intranasal infection, the virus causes rapid cytolytic infection of the nasal epithelium, with secondary spread to the conjunctival sac, oropharynx, trachea, bronchi and bronchioli. The earliest changes consist of mucosal edema, hyperemia and serous exudation. Focal necrosis of the mucosa follows and the discharges become mucopurulent. Regional lymph nodes and tonsils become enlarged, and small areas of atelectasis may be seen in the lungs.

Microscopic changes in infected epithelial cells resemble those described in cell cultures. Intranuclear inclusion bodies appear in epithelial cells in such areas as the nasal septum, turbinates, bronchi, bronchioli, tongue, conjunctiva and cornea. This is followed by disruption of the epithelium and secondary bacterial invasion. The submucosal tissues become edematous and infiltrated with polymorphonuclear cells. Lymphoid-cell infiltration follows during the recovery stage.

Bone necrosis has been described in kittens inoculated IV with FHV-1.[26] Adult cats do not demonstrate bone lesions following IV challenge, suggesting that growing bone is more susceptible to infection than mature bone. Bone lesions in intranasally infected kittens are limited to the nasal turbinates.[35] Atrophy of the turbinates and gross facial bone deformities may be sequelae in rare instances.

Clinicopathologic Features

Feline herpesvirus infection should be suspected in outbreaks of respiratory disease where rhinitis and sneezing are the prominent signs. Conjunctivitis as the only clinical sign is more apt to be due to *Chlamydia* or *Mycoplasma*, especially if it initially affects only one eye. Oral ulcers in the absence of nasal and conjunctival involvement are more likely to be due to calicivirus.

Feline herpesvirus, type 1, can be easily isolated from nasal exudates, conjunctival swabs or oropharyngeal swabs from clinically affected animals. Such material contains large amounts of virus. A characteristic herpesvirus cytopathic effect is usually seen in cell cultures within 48-96 hours. Intranuclear inclusion bodies can also be readily seen in epithelial cells in fluorescent antibody-stained scrapings from inflamed conjunctival membranes. Typical herpesvirus intranuclear inclusion bodies can also be identified by conventional hematoxylin and eosin staining of tissue sections made from inflamed mucous membranes.

Cats that have positive virus-neutralizing antibody titers should be considered active or latent carriers. Some latent carriers, however, may not have appreciable antibody titers. The latent carrier state can be detected by treating cats with corticosteroids for several days and culturing oropharyngeal secretions 4-10 days later.[23]

Leukocytosis with absolute neutrophilia is common in the first week of infection. Lymphocytosis may occur in the immediate postrecovery period.[47]

Treatment and Prevention

Treatment of severely affected individuals consists of: keeping the nostrils and eyes clear of discharges; oral or parenteral

Fig 5. This cat with acute herpesvirus type-1 infection has rhinitis and painful keratoconjunctivitis, but no oral or pharyngeal lesions. Though not evident in this photograph, each eye has a large, superficial corneal ulcer. Such ulcers must be differentiated from the more punctate indolent ulcers associated with herpesvirus keratitis. (From *Virus Infections of Carnivores,* courtesy of Elsevier Science Publishing)

antibiotics to treat secondary infections; fluid and electrolyte replacement in severe dehydration; oral alimentation when necessary by stomach, nasal or pharyngostomy tube; and specific topical antiherpetic eye medications to treat corneal ulcers. Systemic or topical corticosteroid use should be avoided. Treatment is usually least effective in very young kittens and cats debilitated by other diseases, such as FeLV and FIV infections. Recovery from primary infection usually takes a minimum of 2 weeks. Recurrent attacks are generally mild and last 3-10 days.

Cats can be vaccinated against FHV-1 infection with vaccines containing killed virus, relatively virulent virus given parenterally, or attenuated virus given parenterally or intranasally.[4,32,38,42,51] Parenteral vaccination with killed or live virus gives good systemic immunity but weak local immunity. Such immunity lessens, but does not abolish, clinical signs resulting from a vigorous challenge with virulent virus and does not prevent latent infection. Experimental intranasal vaccination with avirulent live virus has reportedly prevented establishment of the latent carrier state.[38] However, this does not appear to be the case in field situations.

Feline herpesvirus vaccines, regardless of type, should not be used as the sole means of disease prevention. In environments with unfavorable stress factors, exposure factors and husbandry practices, FHV-1 vaccines often do a poor job. Vaccination should only supplement good husbandry in such situations.

Live-virus-containing FHV-1 vaccines have been implicated as a cause of outbreaks of upper respiratory disease in catteries. This is more likely to occur in catteries that have been previously free of disease. Certain brands of vaccine are more likely to have this side effect than others.

Infection and Immunity

The exact nature of FHV immunity is not known; cell-mediated as well as humoral mechanisms are probably involved in cats as they are in other species.[43,49,51] Fargeaud and co-workers mentioned that cats naturally exposed to FHV had positive delayed hypersensitivity reactions to the virus.[19] This hypersensitivity could also be evoked by a viral subunit containing only the envelope glycoproteins. A delayed hypersensitivity reaction to viral antigen following experimental FHV-1 infection has also been observed by Tham and Studdert.[47] This reaction was most evident on intradermal injection of betapropiolactone-inactivated virus into the skin of the ears. Wardley and associates showed killing of FHV-1-infected cells by both lymphocytes and macrophages in conjunction with antibody.[49] They also demonstrated a more variable and less flamboyant antibody-independent cellular cytotoxicity.

Tham and Studdert demonstrated antibody-dependent and -independent cell-mediated killing of FHV-1-infected target cells by lymphocytes from immunized cats.[51] Target cell killing was both major histocompatibility complex restricted and unrestricted.

Similar to other herpesviruses, FHV-1 frequently persists in a nonreplicative or latent state. Latent infections develop in as many as 80% of infected cats. Infectious or latent virus is found mainly in tissues of the head. Gaskell and Povey studied virus distribution in 10 cats and found 1 active shedder, 7 cats that became active shedders after corticosteroid administration, and 2 cats treated with corticosteroids that did not actively shed virus. Feline herpesvirus, type 1, was isolated from homogenates of nasal turbinates (9 of 10), soft palates (3 of 10), tonsils (3 of 10), oral mucosa (3 of 10) and tongue (2 of 10).

It has been postulated that virus persists in the trigeminal nerve ganglia and other such structures. Gaskell and Povey recovered virus from the trigeminal ganglia of 2 active virus shedders.[22] Virus did not appear in the cultures for at least 2-8 weeks. Ellis, however, failed to activate FHV-1 shedding from nerve ganglia cultures of latent carriers.[18]

Latent carriers have been converted to active virus shedders by giving them corticosteroids for several days or by stressing them with activities as minor as movement from one animal quarter to another.[20,21] Virus activation also occurs in queens from stress of parturition and lactation, which may be an important source of infection for kittens.[23] When passive maternal immunity wanes, the kittens become infected.

There does not appear to be a good correlation between maternal virus-neutralizing antibody titers and duration of passive immunity in kittens.[23,41] Some kittens with high maternal titers to FHV-1 become infected, while others with low or undetectable titers resist. Maternal virus-neutralizing titers are usually 1:4 by 2-10 weeks. Kittens may become infected relatively early, while systemic maternal immunity is still present. This may allow the virus to establish itself in the body without clinical illness.[23]

Duration of immunity following experimental infection is variable.[48] Cats are solidly immune 21 days after infection, but most are again susceptible at 150 days. Recurrent disease is much milder and more transient than the primary disease. A similar situation occurs in nature. Recurrent bouts of transient rhinitis and conjunctivitis are common, especially in environments where primary disease is frequent and severe. Protection against recurrent disease is only partially mirrored by serum virus-neutralizing antibody levels.[48] Cats with higher antibody titers tend to be resistant, while previously exposed cats with lower or negative titers may or may not be resistant.

Animal and Public Health Considerations

Cats actively or latently infected with FHV-1 are only health hazards to susceptible domestic cats and closely related species. FHV-1 is not a human pathogen.

References

1. Bartholomew PT and Gillespie JH: Feline viruses I. Characterization of four isolates and their effect on young kittens. *Cornell Vet* 58:248-265, 1968.

2. Bittle JL and Peckham JC: Comments: Genital infection induced by feline rhinotracheitis virus and effects on newborn kittens. *JAVMA* 158:927-928, 1971.

3. Bittle JL et al: Serologic relationship of new feline cytopathogenic viruses. *Am J Vet Res* 21:547-550, 1960.

4. Bittle JL and Rubic WJ: Immunogenic and protective effects of the F-2 strain of feline viral rhinotracheitis virus. *Am J Vet Res* 36:89-91, 1975.

5. Brehaut L et al: Viruses associated with feline respiratory disease in Dunedin. *N Zeal Vet J* 17:82-86, 1969.

6. Burki F: Viren des Respirationsapparates bei Katzen. *Proc 17th Ann Mtg World Vet Congress* 1963, pp 559-564.

7. Burki F et al: Enzootischer, virusbedingter Katzenschnupfen in einem Tierheim. 2. Mitteilung: Virologischer und experimenteller Teil. *Zentralbl Vetmed* 11:110-118, 1964.

8. Crandell RA: Feline viral rhinotracheitis. *Adv Vet Sci Comp Med* 17:201-224, 1973.

9. Crandell RA and Despeaux EQ: Cytopathology of feline viral rhinotracheitis virus in tissue cultures of feline renal cells. *Proc Soc Ex Biol Med* 101:494-497, 1959.

10. Crandell RA et al: Comparative study of three isolates with the original feline viral rhinotracheitis virus. *Am J Vet Res* 21:504-506, 1960.

11. Crandell RA and Hershey DF: Cytochemical observations on intranuclear inclusion of feline viral rhinotracheitis virus. *Proc Soc Ex Biol Med* 114:187-190, 1963.

12. Crandell RA and Maurer FD: Isolation of a feline virus associated with intranuclear inclusion bodies. *Proc Soc Ex Biol Med* 97:487-490, 1958.

13. Crandell RA et al: Experimental feline viral rhinotracheitis in the cat. *JAVMA* 138:191-196, 1961.

14. Crandell RA and Weddington GR: Effects of nucleic acid analogues on the multiplication and cytopathogenicity of feline viral rhinotracheitis virus in vitro. *Cornell Vet* 57:38-42, 1967.

15. Ditchfield J and Grinyer I: Feline rhinotracheitis virus: A feline herpesvirus. *Virol* 26:504-506, 1965.

16. Ebner FF and Crandell RA: Growth of feline viral rhinotracheitis virus in cultures of feline renal cells. *Proc Soc Ex Biol Med* 105:153-156, 1960.

17. Ellis TM: Feline respiratory virus carriers in healthy cats. *Aust Vet J* 57:115-118, 1981.

18. Ellis TM: Feline viral rhinotracheitis virus: explant and cocultivation studies on tissues collected from persistently infected cats. *Res Vet Sci* 33:270-274, 1982.

19. Fargeaud D et al: Biochemical study of feline herpesvirus 1. *Arch Virol* 80:69-82, 1984.

20. Gaskell RM and Povey RC: Re-excretion of feline viral rhinotracheitis virus following corticosteroid treatment. *Vet Record* 93:204-205, 1973.

21. Gaskell RM and Povey RC: Experimental induction of feline viral rhinotracheitis virus re-excretion in FVR-recovered cats. *Vet Record* 100:128-133, 1977.

22. Gaskell RM and Povey RC: Feline viral rhinotracheitis: sites of replication and persistence in acutely and persistently infected cats. *Res Vet Sci* 27:167-174, 1979.

23. Gaskell RM and Povey RC: Transmission of feline viral rhinotracheitis. *Vet Record* 111:359-362, 1982.

24. Gillespie JH et al: Feline viruses. XII. Hemagglutination and hemadsorption tests for feline herpesvirus. *Cornell Vet* 61:159-171, 1971.

25. Hoover EA and Griesemer RA: Experimental feline herpesvirus infection in the pregnant cat. *Am J Pathol* 65:173-188, 1971a.

26. Hoover EA and Griesemer RA: Bone lesions produced by feline herpesvirus. *Lab Invest* 25:457-464, 1971b.

27. Hoover EA et al: Experimental feline viral rhinotracheitis in the germ free cat. *Am J Pathol* 58:269-282, 1970.

28. Horvath Z et al: On feline rhinotracheitis. *Acta Vet Sci Hung* 15:415-420, 1965.

29. Johnson RH: Feline panleucopenia virus. III. Some properties compared to a feline herpesvirus. *Res Vet Sci* 7:112-115, 1966.

30. Johnson RH and Sabine M: The isolation of herpesvirus from skin ulcers in domestic cats. *Vet Record* 89:360-362, 1971.

31. Johnson RH and Thomas RG: Feline viral rhinotracheitis in Britain. *Vet Record* 79:188-190, 1966.

32. Kahn DE and Hoover EA: Infectious respiratory diseases of cats. *Vet Clin No Am* 6:399-413, 1976.

33. Karpas A and Routledge JK: Feline herpes virus: Isolations and experimental studies. *Zentralbl Vetmed* 15:599-606, 1968.

34. Lee KM et al: Utilization of various cell culture systems for propagation of certain feline viruses and canine herpes virus. *Cornell Vet* 59:539-547, 1969.

35. Lindt S: Zur Morphologie und Atiologie der Erkrankungen des oberen Respiration-straktes bei Katzen. *Schweiz Arch Tierheilk* 197:196-203, 1965.

36. Miller GW and Crandell RA: Stability of the virus of feline viral rhinotracheitis. *Am J Vet Res* 23:351-353, 1962.

37. Natisse MP: A review of manifestations, diagnosis and treatment of ocular herpesvirus infection in a cat. *Comp Cont Ed Pract Vet* 4:962-970, 1982.

38. Orr CM et al: Interaction of an intranasal combined feline rhinotracheitis, feline calicivirus vaccine and the FVR carrier state. *Vet Record* 106:164-166, 1980.

39. Povey RC: Viral respiratory disease. *Vet Record* 84:335-338, 1969.

40. Povey RC: A review of feline viral rhinotracheitis (feline herpesvirus 1 infection). *Comp Immunol Microbiol Infect Dis* 2:378-387, 1979.

41. Povey RC and Johnson RH: Observations on the epidemiology and control of viral respiratory disease in cats. *J Small Anim Pract* 11:485-494, 1970.

42. Povey RC and Wilson MR: A comparison of inactivated feline viral rhinotracheitis and feline caliciviral disease vaccines with live-modified vaccines. *Feline Pract* 8(3):35-42, 1978.

43. Russell AS: Cell-mediated immunity to herpes simplex virus in man. *Am J Clin Pathol* 60:826-830, 1973.

44. Scott FW: Virucidal disinfectants and feline viruses. *Am J Vet Res* 41:410-414, 1980.

45. Spradbrow PB et al: The association of a herpesvirus with generalized disease in a kitten. *Vet Record* 89:542-544, 1971.

46. Tegtmeyer P and Enders JF: Feline herpesvirus infection in fused cultures of naturally resistant human cells. *J Virol* 3:469-476, 1969.

47. Tham KM and Studdert MJ: Clinical and immunological responses of cats to feline herpesvirus type-1 infection. *Vet Record* 120:321-326, 1987.

48. Walton TE and Gillespie JH: Feline viruses. VII. Immunity to the feline herpesvirus in kittens inoculated experimentally by the aerosol method. *Cornell Vet* 60:232-239, 1970.

49. Wardley RC et al: Observations on the recovery mechanism from feline viral rhinotracheitis. *Can J Comp Med* 40:257-264, 1976.

Additional References

50. Pelt CS and Crandell RA: Pancreatitis associated with feline herpesvirus infection. *Compan Anim Pract* 1(4):7-10, 1987.

51. Tham KM and Studdert MJ: Antibody and cell-mediated immune responses to feline herpesvirus 1 following inactivated vaccine and challenge. *Zbl Vet Med B* 34:585-597, 1987.

Chapter 4

Pseudorabies

Etiologic Agent

Pseudorabies, or Aujeszky's disease, was first described in eastern Europe.[2] A "mad itch" was described in the midwestern United States in the early 1800s.[14]

Pseudorabies virus belongs to the herpes group of DNA viruses. Pseudorabies virus is antigenically related to infectious bovine rhinotracheitis (IBR) virus of cattle. At least 9 different strains of the virus exist in nature, each differing in cytopathogenicity and virulence. It is readily propagated in chicken embryos and cell cultures from a variety of animal species. It causes intranuclear herpes-type inclusion bodies in infected cells.

Pseudorabies virus can survive in hay for 30 days in summer weather and 46 days during winter.[13] It is inactivated rapidly by temperatures above 60 C and by 0.5% sodium hydroxide, 5% phenol and 0.5% formaldehyde.

Pseudorabies occurs worldwide in cattle, sheep, rats, dogs and cats.[7] Many other species are susceptible to experimental infection. Pigs, however, are the natural hosts for pseudorabies virus. Disease in adult swine is mild and self limiting in 4-8 days; abortion is one complication. However, mortality is very high in piglets <15 days of age. Similar to herpesvirus infections in general, pseudorabies in pigs can be either latent or active.[1,3,11] The virus is shed from the oropharynx of some pigs and is present in saliva. Healthy boars may also transmit pseudorabies virus venereally in their semen.

Pathogenesis

Cats are infected by contact with infected swine or by eating inadequately or uncooked pork.[5,9,11] Cats may also be infected by eating infected rats. Rats are not permanent hosts for pseudorabies but apparently become infected by contact with infected swine.

The main route of infection for cats is oral, though the disease can be experimentally recreated by a number of different routes.[6,8] Initial virus replication occurs in the tonsils, followed by spread to local sensory nerves.[8,12] A viremic phase is uncommon in cats. The virus travels rapidly in the axoplasm of cranial nerves IX and X to the brainstem.[8] The earliest lesions are seen in the nucleus, tractus solitarius and area postrema of the medulla oblongata, as well as the ganglion of cranial nerve V. Subsequent spread is to the pons, thalamus, cerebellum, spinal cord and cerebral cortex. The course of the disease is extremely rapid and only minimal inflammatory changes are seen at the time of death. Clinical signs are related mainly to functional abnormalities in infected neurons.

Clinical Features

Clinical signs appear 2-9 days after natural exposure and 3-6 days following experimental infection. The subsequent course of the disease takes 2 forms. The peracute or "classic" form of disease develops in 60% of affected cats, while the remaining 40% develop a somewhat more prolonged and atypical type of infection.

Classic pseudorabies virus infection of cats usually lasts 24-36 hours and almost always terminates in death. Early signs of disease include anorexia, depression, lethargy, restlessness and resistance to being handled. Rectal temperatures are usually not elevated. These initial signs are rapidly accompanied by hypersalivation, exaggerated and repeated swallowing movements, retching, emesis and plaintive crying. Excessive salivation leads to wetting and matting of fur on the throat, neck and forelegs. Dyspnea and tachypnea are often seen. Affected cats resist attempts to have their mouths opened; putting pressure on the base of the tongue often elicits gagging and retching. Progressive hyperesthesia of areas of the skin is characteristic of classic pseudorabies. Cats scratch or rub the side of their faces with the ipsilateral foreleg. Areas of hyperesthesia may also be present on the neck or chest. Pruritic areas rapidly become self mutilated and bloody. Twitching of the facial musculature, penile erection, anisocoria and rhythmic tail movements are additional neurologic manifestations. Affected animals lose their swallowing reflexes several hours before death and become progressively more depressed.

In the 40% of cats with atypical disease, characteristic clinical signs are less noticeable and the disease course extends beyond 36 hours.[9] These cats are depressed and feeble, and make repeated attempts to swallow. Characteristic signs of classic disease, such as pruritus, restlessness, agitation and excessive vocalizations, are absent. Anisocoria, aimless pawing movements of the foreleg, and flagellar tail movements are seen in both forms of disease.

Pathologic Features

The most severe CNS lesions are found in the medulla oblongata and are characterized by nonsuppurative meningoencephalitis. Lesions tend to be focal and are characterized by proliferations of neuroglia, karyorrhexis of neurons, sparse perivascular neutrophil infiltrate and Cowdry type-A intranuclear inclusion bodies in glial and ganglion cells.[4,8,10] Similar but less severe lesions are seen in the pons, thalamus, cerebellum, cerebral cortex and spinal cord.[4,10] Pruritic lesions of the head, neck and trunk are usually associated with involvement of ganglia of related spinal or cranial nerves.[4]

Lesions in nonnervous tissue are uncommon in cats. Ulcerative tonsillar cryptitis has been described by Hagemoser and associates and Sabo and co-workers.[8,12]

Clinicopathologic Features

Antemortem diagnosis of pseudorabies in cats is based almost entirely on exposure history and clinical signs. The rapid disease course of 24-36 hours, absence of paralytic signs, overt aggressive behavior and intense pruritus tend to differentiate the disease from rabies or other neurologic conditions.

Though serologic examination is accurate in diagnosing pseudorabies in swine, cats usually die before a detectable immune response is mounted. Diagnosis is by identifying intranuclear Cowdry type-A inclusion bodies in neurons and glial cells, virus isolation on tissue culture, or animal inoculation studies. Inclusion bodies, however, are not always identifiable in feline tissue. To maximize chances of finding inclusion bodies, tissues should be selectively taken from the nucleus, tractus solitarius, and area postrema of the medulla oblongata, as well as the nerves and spinal cord regional to pruritic lesions. If inclusion bodies are not identified, suspensions of brain or tonsils can be inoculated into rabbits or susceptible cells in culture. Rabbits should be inoculated SC, after which localized pruritus occurs at the site. By pretreating the inoculum with specific pseudorabies virus-neutralizing serum, it is possible to block infection and definitively diagnose the infectious agent as pseudorabies virus.

Treatment and Prevention

Cats with clinical signs of pseudorabies invariably die despite supportive treatment. Survival has been alluded to on several occasions, but documentation has been absent.

Pseudorabies in cats can be prevented by keeping swine herds free of infection and by thoroughly cooking any pork fed to cats. Because cats can become infected by eating diseased rats, control of the rat population may also be required. Rats are not reservoir hosts for the virus, however, and disease control in swine also controls infection in rats.

Infection and Immunity

Pseudorabies virus infection of cats is a good example of a virus with wide host tropism that can cause subclinical infection in one species and highly fatal disease in others. The course of infection in cats (unnatural but highly susceptible hosts) is so peracute that the cats' defense mechanisms have insufficient time to react. By killing its host so rapidly, however, the virus precludes having cats as a reservoir. Moreover, the rapid disease course in cats and selective localization of virus in nervous tissue preclude viral shedding and cat-to-cat transmission.

Animal and Public Health Considerations

People appear to be resistant to pseudorabies virus infection. Therefore, infected cats do not pose a hazard to people. There are no reported accounts of transmission from cats to other cats or other animals.

References

1. Akkermans JPW: Aujeszky's disease and related problems. *Tijdschr Diergeneeskd* 106:332-336, 1981.

2. Aujeszky A: Ueber eine neue Infektionskrankheit bei Haustieren. *Zentralbl Bacteriol Abt I Orig* 32:353-357, 1902.

3. Baskerville A: Aujeszky's disease: recent advances and current problems. *New Zeal Vet J* 29:183-185, 1981.

4. Dow C and McFerran JB: Aujeszky's disease in the dog and cat. *Vet Record* 75:1099-1102, 1963.

5. Fankhauser R et al: Aujeszky's disease in dogs and cats in Switzerland. *Schweiz Arch Tierheilkd* 111:623-629, 1975.

6. Flir K: On the pathology of Aujeszky's disease in dogs. *Arch Exp Vet Med* 9:949-956, 1956.

7. Galloway IA: Aujeszky's disease. *Vet Record* 50:745-762, 1938.

8. Hagemoser WA et al: Studies on the pathogenesis of pseudorabies in domestic cats following oral inoculation. *Can J Comp Med* 44:192-202, 1980.

9. Horvath Z and Papp L: Clinical manifestations of Aujeszky's disease in the cat. *Acta Vet* 17:49-54, 1967.

10. Knösel H: On the histopathology of Aujeszky's disease in dogs and cats. *Zentralbl Veterinärmed B* 15:592-598, 1968.

11. Kretzschmar C: *Aujeszky's Disease*. Fischer Verlag, Jena, Germany, 1970.

12. Sabó AJ et al: Investigations on the pathogenesis of Aujeszky's disease of cats. *Arch Ges Virusforsch* 25:288-298, 1968.

13. Shope RE: An experimental study of "mad itch" with especial reference to its relationship to pseudorabies. *J Exp Med* 54:233-248, 1931.

14. Vandevelde M, in Greene CE: *Clinical Microbiology and Infectious Diseases of the Dog and Cat*. Saunders, Philadelphia, 1984. pp 381-385.

Chapter 5

Rabies

Etiologic Agent

Rabies virus belongs to the genus *Lyssavirus*, family Rhabdoviridae. Rhabdoviruses are bullet-shaped, enveloped and 75 by 180 nm in dimension (Fig 1). Their genome is made up of RNA. Rabies virus buds from the cell membrane and cytoplasmic profiles of endoplasmic reticulum. Aggregates of internally budding membrane-bound particles embedded in a proteinaceous matrix form characteristic inclusions (Negri bodies). Most rabies virus isolates belong to a common strain; various isolates differ slightly when tested by batteries of monoclonal antibodies to envelope and nucleocapsid proteins.[36] Characteristic monoclonal antibody-binding patterns can be used to differentiate certain isolates from others.[11]

The major envelope protein of rabies virus, glycoprotein G, is associated with surface spikes and thought to be involved in viral attachment to host cell surfaces. Antibodies to this protein are virus-neutralizing and are presumed to elicit protective immunity. The major core protein of rabies virus is associated with RNA and antigenically similar in all isolates. Antibodies to the core protein are associated with complement-fixation and immunofluorescent antibody reactivity.

As in most enveloped RNA viruses, virions are readily inactivated by disinfectant concentrations of phenols, chlorine, formalin and quaternary ammonium compounds. The virus is also very sensitive to sunlight and heat, and survival off the host animal is very brief. Virus in infected carcasses is inactivated in a day or less at ambient temperature, but can survive many days in refrigerated tissues. The virus can withstand freezing and can survive at -30 to -70 C for months or years. Repeated freezing and thawing, however, leads to rapid inactivation of the virus.

Pathogenesis

Rabies virus exists in many countries but has never been found in Antarctica, Australia, New Zealand and the Hawaiian Islands. It has been eradicated from England, Scandinavia, Iceland and Japan.[23] The principal reservoir for rabies virus is

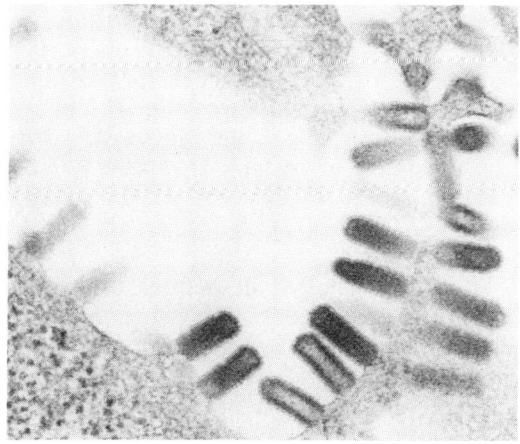

Fig 1. Rabies virus particles budding from the outer membrane of an infected cell. The bullet-shaped virions are about 75 x 180 nm. (Courtesy of Rhone-Merieux, Lyon, France)

wild animals. In far northern latitudes, the Arctic fox is the main reservoir; in more temperate zones, it is the gray and red fox. The most important reservoir host in North America is the striped skunk. The raccoon is an increasingly important reservoir for rabies in the mid- to lower-Atlantic region of the United States. Insectivorous bats spread rabies along their north-south migration paths in the western regions of North, Central and South America. Vampire bats are associated with over one-half million cases of cattle rabies in Mexico, Central and South America each year.[4] Wolves are reservoirs for rabies in some parts of the world where they still roam, as are the mongoose and jackal. Dogs and cats are important reservoirs for rabies in parts of the world where the infection is enzootic. They represent an important link to spread of the virus from wildlife reservoirs to people.

Relatively little is known about the natural course of rabies virus infection in wildlife. It is assumed that most infected animals eventually die. The incubation period between infection and clinical disease is not completely known. The common modes of transmission from one wild animal to another are also unclear. Bats apparently shed rabies virus in saliva and urine for prolonged periods before developing overt clinical signs.[4] The course of infection in bats may be slowed by hibernation, thus allowing the infection to overwinter.[29] Vampire bats usually develop furious rabies but can secrete virus in their saliva for some time before death. Vampire bats have also apparently recovered from clinical rabies and continued to shed virus in their saliva for prolonged periods.[4] Skunks are very sensitive to rabies virus infection, but the incubation period and clinical disease course can be very long. Once clinical signs appear in skunks, the disease course varies from 4 to 18 days, as compared to 1-8 days for cats.[26] Virus shedding occurs many days before and during clinical illness. The disease course in foxes is acute and similar to that in dogs and cats. The disease course in raccoons has not been well documented. From what is known about rabies in wildlife, it appears that some species, such as striped skunks and bats, are more likely to have chronic and atypical forms of the disease than domestic dogs and cats.

Though most infected animals eventually die from CNS disease, the importance of chronic, latent or asymptomatic active infections has become increasingly apparent. Recovery from clinical rabies has been described in dogs, cats, people and other species.[12,14,25,28] Some recovered dogs have shed rabies virus in their saliva for a prolonged period.[12] Such animals are classified as asymptomatic active virus carriers. Chronic, or atypical, rabies virus infections have been experimentally produced in cats and striped skunks.[25,28] The course of disease in some of these animals may exceed 2.5 years. The existence of latent rabies virus infections has been postulated but not yet demonstrated. Latent infections imply persistence of genomic virus in the tissues. Stress, changes in immunocompetence with pregnancy and with other infectious diseases, or other unknown factors may activate infections in such animals. Viral genome activation could then lead to clinical disease or an asymptomatic active carrier state.

The major sources of rabies for cats are bites of infected wild animals, live-virus rabies vaccines, and possibly ingestion of infected tissues. Cats are less susceptible to infection with street (virulent) strains of rabies virus than dogs, but are more susceptible to vaccine-induced rabies caused by "fixed" (attenuated) live strains of virus. The incidence of cat rabies has been fairly constant over the last several decades. Because of effective vaccination programs for dogs, however, cats have recently become of much greater relative importance as sources of human exposure. In fact, in areas of Europe, Asia and North America, the incidence of human exposures due to cats has frequently exceeded that due to dogs.

Infection usually follows bites. Infection resulting from virus deposited on mucous membranes is less efficient but has been reported in people.[6,37] Rabies is occasionally transmitted when animals eat infected carnivorous animals, such as cats.[5,7,13] Transplacental transmission has also been observed in skunks and cows.[16]

Rabies virus replicates for the first 24 hours in myocytes at the inoculation site. Virus then enters peripheral nerves via neuromuscular junctions and neurotendinal spindles. Virus can spread proximad up nerve axons at a maximum rate of 7 cm/day, but the actual rate depends on the age of the animal, site of inoculation, density of nerve endings, dose and strain of virus, and whether the initial site of inoculation is on the head or trunk. Virus travels proximad up peripheral nerves and enters the spinal cord or cranial nerve ganglia, where it replicates in the perikaryon of neurons and rapidly ascends to the forebrain. Virus then spreads rapidly through the nervous system. Involvement of lower-motor neurons leads ultimately to flaccid paralysis, while limbic involvement causes the characteristic behavioral signs. Neuronal dysfunction is associated with neuronal destruction and physiologic derangements associated with intraneuronal virus replication.

Virus infects the brain at about the same time it appears in other tissues, such as salivary and tear glands, adnexal glands of tactile hairs, mammary glands, kidneys and gravid uterus. Infection of these organs is believed to be caused by spread of virus via efferent motor and sensory nerves and not from recognizable viremia.

Clinical Features

Almost 90% of cats with naturally occurring rabies are <3 years of age, and males are more commonly afflicted than females.[22] The actual infection rate following natural exposure is unknown. Experimental infection with graded dilutions of various street rabies isolates caused rabies in 26 of 86 cats; the incubation period was 9-51 days, with a median of 18, and the period from first clinical signs to death was 1-8 days, with a median of 5.[35] Using larger and more standardized doses of rabies virus, Soulebot and co-workers induced rabies in 87.5% of cats.[30] The mean incubation period in this study was 15.9 days, and the mean time of death was 17.8 days postinfection. Cats inoculated IM with virus isolated from the salivary gland of a big brown bat showed disease after a median incubation period of 42 days.[32] The median clinical course was 5 days. Extrapolating from what is known about other species, the actual disease course in nature is probably similar. However, the incubation period is likely to be more variable and the infection rate lower.

Clinical rabies has been divided into 3 stages: prodromal; excitatory or furious; and paralytic or dumb. These stages are not always distinct in each animal and not every cat goes through each stage during the course of illness. For instance, about 70% of cats demonstrate the furious form of rabies.[33] The remaining 30% manifest mainly paralytic disease without ever showing excitatory or furious behavior.

Prodromal signs of rabies seldom last for more than a day in cats.[33] During this stage, there is a slight elevation of body temperature, and some pupillary dilation and impaired corneal reflexes. Some cats become restless, excessively alert and, at times, more attentive and affectionate to their owners. Others become irritable and withdrawn, and attempt to hide in dark places. Such animals may vigorously resist attempts to handle or restrain them.

The excitatory or furious stage of rabies in cats usually lasts 2-4 days. It often begins with variable signs of muscular twitching, generalized fine-muscle tremors, muscular weakness, increased accumulations of saliva and slight ascending incoordination beginning in the hind legs. These signs are often accompanied by aggression, vicious behavior and irritability. Difficulty in swallowing due to paralysis of pharyngeal muscles, extreme drooling, incoordination and occasionally convulsions become more noticeable toward the end of this stage.

The dumb or paralytic stage lasts 1-4 days. Cats showing no excitatory signs before this stage often survive longer than those that do. The paralytic stage is manifested by paralysis of pharyngeal muscles and progressive generalized paresis. Once the paralysis becomes generalized, death occurs within 24 hours or less. Paralysis of the jaw, a common sign of dogs with paralytic rabies, is uncommon in cats.

Atypical forms of rabies are occasionally observed in cats. One experimentally infected cat suddenly became comatose and died within 24 hours without other preceding clinical signs.[30] Chronic recrudescent forms of rabies have been described in 3 experimentally infected cats.[25,28] All 3 cats developed partial posterior paralysis 11-17 days after experimental or IM inoculation with virulent rabies virus. Paralysis was more severe in the leg in which the virus was injected. Clinical signs remained static, improved slightly or slowly worsened with time, but the cats remained alert, responsive and otherwise healthy for the next 2-2.5 years. Then, disease signs progressed rapidly and the cats were killed. The protracted disease course was accompanied by a progressive rise in CSF and serum rabies neutralizing-antibody titers. Viral antigen was difficult to demonstrate in the brain by immunofluorescent antibody tests. Virus was only reisolated by cultivating explants of brain tissue with susceptible cells from one-third of the cats. Histopathologic lesions in the brain were atypical of acute rabies and demonstrated considerably more mononuclear cell response.

Postvaccinal rabies is much more common in cats than in dogs. This disease is a relatively common sequela of vaccination with vaccine strains that have never been approved for cats, such as low-egg-passage Flury (LEP-Flury), or as an uncommon sequela of vaccination with such strains as Street-Alabama-Dufferin (SAD) that were originally approved for cats but later withdrawn from use in some countries.[1,9-11,34] Even the high-egg-passage Flury (HEP-Flury) strains, which are widely used in cats, are not free of disease-causing potential. Of 4 cats with vaccine-induced rabies that were tested for FeLV infection, 2 were positive.[10,11] This seems higher than can be accounted for by chance. Feline leukemia virus infection can be immunosuppressive to cats and greatly increases the incidence of infections with minimally pathogenic organisms. Clinical signs of postvaccinal rabies usually began at the injection site, most often the left hind leg. The incubation period is 11-17 days and the earliest clinical signs are localized to that leg. This is rapidly followed by extension of the disease process to the opposite hind leg. Affected cats often resent manipulation of the affected limb, tail or distal leg. Hind-limb involvement can be manifested by tonic rigidity or partial to complete flaccid paralysis. The disease can remain localized to the hind limbs or rapidly ascend to involve the forelegs and brain. Central nervous system involvement, when it occurs, is often manifested by unresponsive pupils, irritability, fever and depression. All the cats with postvaccinal rabies were killed when the disease was suspected. Therefore, the natural course of postvaccinal rabies in cats has not been determined. Dogs have recovered from postvaccinal rabies.[27] One cat appeared to be recovering before it was killed.[11]

Pathologic Features

Lesions of classic rabies are microscopic and limited to the CNS and mandibular salivary glands.[17,18] Lesions are concentrated in the brain between the pons and hypothalamus, especially in the hippocampus and gasserian ganglia. Cervical spinal cord involvement is also common. The disease causes nonsuppurative encephalitis, with neuronal degeneration that is often out of proportion to host reactive changes, including sparse lymphocytic cuffing of vessels, focal gliosis and neuronophagic nodules. Lapi and co-workers described specific lesions in the gasserian ganglia called Babes nodules, which are characterized by focal proliferation of glial cells and mild lymphoid-cell infiltration that encroach on surrounding neurons.[19] Glial nodules contain 6-100 cells.

Spherical intracytoplasmic inclusion bodies 2-8 μ in diameter may be seen within affected neurons in both experimentally and naturally infected animals. They are observed in about 20%-70% of cats infected with street isolates and in virtually none of the cats infected with so-called "fixed" or vaccine strains. These inclusions, called Negri bodies, are surrounded by a thin, clear halo and are best visualized with modified Van Gieson, Wilhite, Seller, Mann or Giemsa stain. Negri bodies are actually intracytoplasmic accumulations of budding virus particles embedded in a host- and virus-derived protein matrix. Some inclusions are composed only of matrix protein.

In addition to nervous system lesions, degenerative changes leading to necrosis may be observed in mucogenic acinar epithelial cells of the mandibular salivary glands. Virus can be readily detected in these cells by electron microscopy or immunofluorescent antibody staining. Cats with chronic recrudescent forms of rabies encephalitis have different microscopic lesions somewhat reminiscent of those of subacute sclerosing panencephalitis in people.[25,28] Microscopic changes include neuronal degeneration, neuronophagia and widespread moderate to dense inflammatory-cell infiltration into the parenchyma of the spinal cord, brain, and perineuronal and perivascular spaces. Cellular infiltrates are made up of lymphocytes, macrophages and many plasma cells. Negri bodies are not usually found in brain tissues, and viral antigens are difficult to detect by immunofluorescent antibody staining.

Clinicopathologic Features

Though rabies may be strongly suspected from clinical signs, the diagnosis is usually only confirmed at necropsy. The CSF in cats with chronic recrudescent or postvaccinal rabies usually contains significant levels of locally produced antibodies. Such antibodies are usually not present in CSF from cats with the more acute and classic form of rabies. Therefore, rabies is usually diagnosed by demonstration of the virus within brain tissue by microscopic identification of Negri bodies, immunofluorescent antibody (IFA) staining or mouse inoculation. Negri body staining is the least accurate of these 3 methods. Lobry identified Negri bodies in only 60% of rabid cats.[22] Mitchell and Monlux detected Negri bodies in only 1 of 5 proven cases of feline rabies.[24] Brain tissues of cats also frequently contain nonspecific "lyssa" or "cat bodies," which can be very difficult to differentiate from Negri bodies.[25] For these reasons, IFA staining has become the most accurate and widely used test for confirming rabies virus infection.

Mice are very susceptible to infection with street rabies isolates. Suspensions of brain tissue are inoculated intracerebrally into mice, and their brains and salivary glands are removed 5 days later. Impression smears from these tissues are examined by IFA techniques. If allowed to live, inoculated mice usually develop neurologic signs and die in 8-20 days.

Treatment and Prevention

Cats with clinical signs of rabies usually die within several days. Because of the potential for human exposure, treatment is discouraged. Cats with postvaccinal rabies may have self-limiting disease and might be given a chance (if FeLV-free) to recover naturally, provided the disease remains localized to the caudal spine. The decision to take such a course should rest with local public health authorities. It is often impossible to determine with absolute certainty that any given infection is due to street or fixed strains of virus.

Prevention of rabies in cats by vaccination is an increasingly urgent issue. With successful control of the disease in dogs, rabies in cats is often a more important human health hazard in many parts of the world. Large feral cat populations are a negative factor in instigating mandatory feline rabies immunization programs. However, for reasons of safety and peace of mind, many veterinarians recommend that household cats with outdoor access be routinely vaccinated.

Though several different types of vaccines are available for dogs, many of these have proven unsafe for use in cats due to their propensity to cause postvaccinal rabies. The LEP-Flury strains of virus produce a relatively high incidence of postvaccinal rabies in cats and have never been approved for use in this species. The SAD strain of rabies virus, adapted to growth in various cell cultures, was the mainstay for cat vaccination programs in the United States and many other countries. An unacceptably high incidence of postvaccinal rabies in cats associated with use of this strain, however, led to its withdrawal from the market in the United States. At present, the only modified-live-virus rabies vaccine licensed for use in cats in the United States is based on tissue culture-adapted HEP-Flury virus. Recently, several highly effective killed-virus rabies vaccines have appeared on the market.

The maximum duration of immunity associated with SAD-strain rabies vaccine has been 28 months.[21] This has been exceeded by several killed-virus products, which have shown good efficacy for as long as 3 years.[30] With availability of equally or more effective killed-virus vaccines, continued use of live-virus products for cats has been questioned.[10] The cost of killed-virus vaccine is still considerably more than for reasonably safe live-virus vaccines utilizing HEP-Flury strains of virus, and the cost: risk ratio must be considered. As killed-virus vaccines become cheaper to produce and sell, there is little doubt they will largely replace live-virus vaccines. Attenuted live-virus rabies vaccines should not be given to cats that have tested positive for FeLV or infections, or cats on immunosuppressive drugs. Such cats are apparently more susceptible to postvaccinal rabies.

Rabies vaccines should be given to cats 12 weeks or older, as younger animals can still have interfering maternal antibodies. The current recommendation is that cats be revaccinated at yearly intervals unless the vaccine is approved for longer periods. This regulation may change in different countries as more duration-of-immunity studies are done under conditions of near 100% seroconversion in vaccinates and 100% mortality in controls.[30]

Infection and Immunity

As in other animals, the immune system of cats seems unable to respond to rabies virus while the infection is still within the peripheral nerves. Once the infection breaks out into the brain and other tissues, there is inadequate time before death for a protective immune response. In cats with postvaccinal rabies or chronic recrudescent disease, considerable local and systemic production of virus-neutralizing antibodies occurs. The attenuated virulence of the vaccine virus and initial localization to the caudal spinal cord probably allow sufficient time for immunity to develop. Cats that develop chronic infections with street rabies isolates also appear to be more responsive to the infection than cats with the usual form of rabies. However, this immunity appears to be insufficient to completely eliminate the virus, and the disease can slowly progress for 2 years or more. As many as half of the cats with postvaccinal rabies appear to be concurrently infected with FeLV. This retrovirus infection causes acquired immunodeficiency syndrome in cats, which may explain the apparent virulence of vaccine strains in some animals.

Cats appear to have a moderate degree of natural resistance to rabies, manifested by the great variability in mortality reported by various investigators studying experimentally induced disease. Albelseth and Soulebot and co-workers obtained high mortality with large doses of virus.[2,30] Mortalities varying from 0 to 75% were reported by other researchers.[3,20,21,35] In spite of this variability, there appears to be a direct relationship between dose of the virus and mortality.[30] Cervical inoculation also appears to cause fatal infections more consistently than masseter muscle inoculation.[30]

Direct inoculation of cats with large doses of street virus does not always result in disease or even infection. Soulebot and associates observed 5 cats of 34 that failed to develop disease after experimental infection.[30] These cats failed to make antibodies after challenge-exposure, indicating infection had not taken hold in the body. Some cats may also develop active but abortive infections. These same researchers described a cat that resisted a massive challenge-exposure to rabies virus and became seropositive.

The great variability of responsiveness to virulent rabies virus infection also appears to extend to attenuated live-virus strains.[8,21] Dean and Guevin observed poorer protection (69-77%) with LEP- and HEP-Flury strains than with inactivated nerve tissue vaccine (96%).[8] The apparent superiority of some types of inactivated-virus vaccines in cats over attenuated live-virus vaccines was also alluded to by Soulebot and co-workers.[30] These observations seem paradoxical in light of the greater susceptibility of cats to fixed strains of rabies virus.

Animal and Public Health Considerations

Outbreaks of rabies among domestic cats usually coincide with epizootics in local wildlife populations; cat-to-cat transmission is extremely uncommon.[33] Rabid cats pose a health hazard to people. The public health importance of cat rabies varies greatly from one part of the world to another. Cat rabies is more of a human health hazard in affluent industrialized regions, such as Europe and North America, than in poorer rural areas, such as Africa and Central and South America. This probably reflects the closer association between cats and people in developed countries. Though the incidence of rabies in dogs has declined steadily since mandatory vaccination programs have been adopted, the relative incidence of rabies in cats has increased. In many areas of Europe and America, the yearly reported number of cases of cat rabies has equaled or exceeded that of dogs. In areas where cats are frequently treated as family members, cats are an important source of human exposure. Though human exposure to cats is great in some areas of the world, the number of human cases of rabies resulting from exposure to cats is surprisingly low. Only 9 of 236 human deaths from rabies were attributed to rabid cats in the United States between 1946 and 1967.[15] In East Germany, where cat rabies is an important cause of human exposure, only 3 of 23 human deaths from rabies between 1953 and 1961 could be traced to cats.[31]

Virus is present in the salivary glands and presumably saliva in 60-90% of rabid cats.[22,33] Cats with paralytic rabies are less likely to have virus in their salivary glands than cats with the furious form.[33] Virus shedding from the salivary glands occurs from 1 day before onset of signs to 3 days after and continues until death.[35] The level of virus shedding progressively increases during the disease course.

Unvaccinated cats that have bitten people should be confined in an approved isolation facility for 7-10 days. Any signs of illness suggestive of rabies during this time should be immediately reported to local health officials dealing with the exposure. Cats that have confirmed or probable contact with possibly rabid animals should be reported to local public health officials. The outcome in affected cats varies from immediate euthanasia to revaccination and quarantine, depending on vaccination status of the animal, probability of rabies infection in the suspect animal, nature of the exposure, local regulations, and feelings of the owners and health officials.

References

1. Anonymous: Follow-up on suspected vaccine-induced rabies in cats. *Morb Mort Weekly Rpt* 29(7):86-87, 1980.

2. Abelseth MK: Further studies on the use of ERA rabies vaccine in domestic animals. *Can Vet J* 8:221-227, 1967.

3. Abelseth MK: Rabies vaccinations of cats. *JAVMA* 158:1003-1006, 1971.

4. Acha PN: Epidemiology of paralytic bovine rabies and bat rabies. *Office Int Epizoot* 67:343-382, 1967.

5. Bell JF and Moore GJ: Susceptibility of carnivora to rabies virus administered orally. *Am J Epidemiol* 93:176-182, 1971.

6. Constantine DG: Rabies transmission by non-bite route. *Public Health Rpt* 77:287-289, 1962.

7. Correa-Giron EP et al: The infectivity and pathogenesis of rabies virus administered orally. *Am J Epidemiol* 91:203-215, 1970.

8. Dean DJ and Guevin VH: Rabies vaccination of cats. *JAVMA* 142:367-370, 1963.

9. Dean DJ et al: Isolation of rabies from the salivary gland of a cat dying from vaccination with modified live virus antirabies vaccine (LEP). *WHO Document on Rabies* 1959, p 132.

10. Erlewein DL: Post-vaccinal rabies in a cat. *Feline Pract* 11(2):16-17, 19-21, 1981.

11. Esh JB et al: Vaccine-induced rabies in four cats. *JAVMA* 180:1336-1339, 1982.

12. Fekadu M et al: Intermittent excretion of rabies virus in the saliva of a dog two and six months after it had recovered from experimental rabies. *Am J Trop Med Hyg* 30:1113-1115, 1981.

13. Fischman HR and Ward FE: Oral transmission of rabies virus in experimental animals. *Am J Epidemiol* 88:132-138, 1968.

14. Hattwick MA et al: Recovery from rabies. A case report. *Ann Intern Med* 76:931-942, 1972.

15. Held JR et al: Rabies in man and animals in the United States, 1946-65. *Publ Health Rpt* 82:1009-1018, 1967.

16. Howard DR: Transplacental transmission of rabies virus from a naturally infected skunk. *Am J Vet Res* 42:691-692, 1981.

17. Jones TC and Hunt RD: *Veterinary Pathology*. 5th ed. Lea & Febiger, Philadelphia, 1983.

18. Jubb KVF et al: *Pathology of Domestic Animals*. 3rd ed. Academic Press, New York, 1985.

19. Lapi A et al: The gasserian ganglion in animals dead of rabies. *JAVMA* 120:379-384, 1952.

20. Lawson KF and Crawley JF: The ERA strain of rabies vaccine. *Can J Comp Med* 36:339-344, 1972.

21. Lawson KF et al: ERA strain of rabies vaccine. Duration of immunity in cattle, dogs and cats. *VM/SAC* 62:1073-1074, 1967.

22. Lobry M: Survey on current knowledge of rabies in cats. *Bull Epiz Dis Afr* 13:17-22, 1965.

23. Martin ML and Sedmark PA: Rabies. Part I. Epidemiology, pathogenesis and diagnosis. *Comp Cont Ed Pract Vet* 5:521-528, 1983.

24. Mitchell FE and Monlux WS: Diagnosis and incidence of rabies in a selected group of domestic cats. *Am J Vet Res* 23:435-442, 1962.

25. Murphy FA et al: Experimental chronic rabies in the cat. *Lab Invest* 43:231-241, 1980.

26. Parker RL and Wilsnack RE: Pathogenesis of skunk rabies virus: quantitation in skunks and foxes. *Am J Vet Res* 27:33-38, 1966.

27. Pedersen NC et al: Rabies vaccine virus infection in 3 dogs. *JAVMA* 172:1092-1096, 1978.

28. Perl DP et al; Chronic recrudescent rabies in a cat. *Proc Soc Exp Biol Med* 155:540-548, 1977.

29. Sadler WW and Enright JB: Effect of metabolic level of the host upon the pathogenesis of rabies in the bat. *J Infect Dis* 105:267-273, 1959.

30. Soulebot JP et al: Experimental rabies in cats: Immune response and persistence of immunity. *Cornell Vet* 1:311-325, 1981.

31. Starke G et al: 10 Jahre Tollwutprophy-lave. *Monatsch Veterinaermed* 16:605-609, 1961.

32. Trimarchi CV et al: Experimentally induced rabies in four cats inoculated with a rabies virus isolated from a bat. *Am J Vet Res* 47:777-779, 1986.

33. Vaughn JB, in Baer GM: *The Natural History of Rabies*. Vol II. Academic Press, New York, 1975. pp 139-154.

34. Vaughn JB and Gerhardt P: Isolation of Flury rabies vaccine virus from the salivary gland of a cat. *JAVMA* 139:221-223, 1961.

35. Vaughn JB et al: Excretion of street rabies virus in saliva of cats. *JAVMA* 184: 705-708, 1963.

36. Wiktor TJ: Identification of rabies virus isolated from three cats vaccinated with a modified-live rabies vaccine. In: *Rabies Inform Exchange* 1:47-52, 1979.

37. Winkler WG: Airborne rabies virus isolation. *Bull Wildl Dis Assoc* 4:37-40, 1968.

Chapter 6

Feline Enteric Coronavirus Infection

Etiologic Agent

Feline enteric coronaviruses are pleomorphic and 75-250 nm or more in diameter (Fig 1).[10] Peplomers are typically petal-shaped, rather loosely spaced around the envelope and 15-30 nm long.[10,15]

Only 2 strains of feline enteric coronavirus (FECV) have been characterized. The first isolate, designated FECV-UCD, has not been propagated in tissue culture but has been maintained by fecal-oral passage in specific-pathogen-free (SPF) cats.[10] A second isolate, FECV-79-1683, was obtained from a cat with peracute and fatal hemorrhagic enteritis.[4] This strain replicates very well in tissue culture and produces a cytopathic effect similar to that of canine coronaviruses (CCV).[1,4,11]

Coronavirus particles, morphologically identical to those of FECV-UCD, were observed in stools of cats with diarrhea by Dea and co-workers.[2] This isolate shared some antigens with calf diarrhea coronavirus. Since calf diarrhea coronavirus is in a different antigenic group than FECV-UCD, FECV-79-1683, transmissible gastroenteritis virus (TGEV) of pigs and CCV, this coronavirus may be quite different from FECV-UCD and FECV-79-1683.[1,13,14] Hayashi and co-workers also observed coronavirus particles in the intestine of a cat with diarrhea.[3] In this cat, the virus appeared antigenically similar to FIPV, placing it in the same antigenic group as FECV-UCD and FECV-79-1683.

Feline enteric coronaviruses (FECV) are antigenically and morphologically similar to feline infectious peritonitis virus (FIPV).[1] The major difference between FECV and FIPV isolates has been the inability of the former to cause FIP. In truth, a spectrum of feline coronaviruses exists, ranging from purely enteritis-inducing agents to purely FIP-inducing agents.[11,12]

A great number of FECV strains exist in nature, and their close antigenic similarity

Fig 1. Negatively stained electron micrograph showing feline enteric coronavirus particles (125 nm) in the feces of a kitten. The petal-shaped envelope projections of coronaviruses produce a crown-like appearance; hence the name "corona."

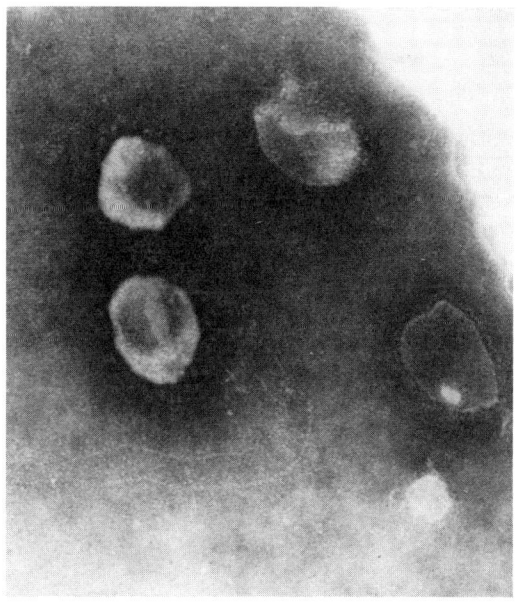

to FIPV strains precludes any accurate epizootiologic studies of either FIPV or FECV infections. Many so-called FIPV seropositive cats in earlier studies were probably infected with enteritis rather than FIP-inducing coronaviruses.[5,10]

The epizootiology of FECV infection has been studied in 2 relatively closed groups of cats. In the first group, FECV was found to be carried by many healthy seropositive cattery cats and shed in their feces.[10] Kittens in this cattery became seropositive at 5-16 weeks of age, usually without showing any illness. Specific-pathogen-free kittens placed in intimate contact with seropositive adult cats seroconverted in about 2 weeks.[10] The higher the immunofluorescent antibody (IFA) titer of the carrier cats, the faster seroconversion occurred in susceptible kittens, indicating that cats with higher titers shed more virus than cats with lower titers. Kittens in a second cattery also developed antibodies to FIPV after weaning.[15] Adult cats in this environment were seropositive and SPF kittens housed with these animals also became seropositive. Identity of the coronavirus shed by cats in this cattery was not determined. It was not observed in feces and was presumed to originate from sites other than the intestinal tract. If true, it means that non-enteritis-inducing coronaviruses may also exist in cats.

Pathogenesis

The major source of virus appears to be asymptomatic carrier cats that shed FECV in their feces.[10] Kittens become infected between 5 and 12 weeks of age. Systemic passive immunity as well as lactogenic immunity may play some role in delaying infection until kittens reach weaning age.

Virus replication, as determined by IFA staining, occurs predominantly in the small intestine.[10,11] The mature apical epithelium of the intestinal villi is the main target for the virus. Virus is also observed during the peak of infection in phagocytic cells in the mesenteric lymph nodes.[10,11] Using more sensitive isolation techniques, FECV-79-1683 was found at the highest concentration in the ileum, jejunum, duodenum and mesenteric lymph nodes, while intermediate amounts of virus were found in the cecum, tonsils and thymus.[11] Low levels of virus were present in the lungs; negligible amounts of virus were recovered from the spleen, kidney and liver. Virus shedding in the feces peaked about 7 days after oronasal infection and tapered off as immunity developed.[11] Virus could not be recovered by tissue culture after day 17. However, it was shed over a much longer period as evidenced by contact exposure studies between recovered and susceptible cats.

Infection occurs when carrier and susceptible cats are placed in contact with each other.[10,11] Infection can also spread when dirty litter pans are interchanged between rooms containing carrier and susceptible cats. There is evidence that animal caretakers can transmit the virus from room to room on their clothing.[10]

Clinical Features

Most experimentally infected cats do not develop clinical signs. If present, signs are usually mild and self-limiting, and appear 2-7 days postinfection. Transient vomiting sometimes precedes other signs by 12-24 hours.[10] Diarrhea follows and lasts about 48-96 hours. The stool may be soft and mucus-laden, or fetid and watery. Fatal hemorrhagic diarrhea has been described but is very uncommon.[4] Kittens with pronounced enteric signs are often depressed and sometimes anorectic. Transient low-grade fever and leukopenia occur in kittens with more severe disease.[10]

Pathologic Features

Gross lesions are uncommon. In severely affected cats, mesenteric lymphadenopathy and edema of the bowel may be visible. Histopathologic changes are also present to varying degrees, but are generally mild. Atrophy, fusion and sloughing of the apical portion of the villi are the most common abnormalities.[10] Lesions are more likely to be observed in the jejunum and ileum than the duodenum. Focal inflammatory infiltrates in the villi are uncommon. During recovery, there is pronounced epithelial hyperplasia and deepening of the crypt.

Clinicopathologic Features

Feline enteric coronavirus infection should be suspected in any young cat with acute diarrhea that may be preceded by vomiting. Serum antibodies, as detected by indirect IFA or enzyme-linked immunosorbent assay (ELISA) procedures, appear several days after onset of clinical signs and reach peak titers of 1:32-1:1024 over the next 2-4 weeks.[10] Transmissible gastroenteritis virus (TGEV) of swine, canine coronavirus (CCV), FIPV and FECV are equally suitable as antigen sources for IFA and ELISA procedures.[12] Diagnosis can be facilitated by examining diarrheic stools by electron microscopy for typical coronavirus particles (Fig 1). Isolation of FECV on tissue culture has been extremely difficult.

Treatment and Prevention

Kittens with severe vomiting and diarrhea may become dehydrated and depressed. Replacement of lost fluids and electrolytes with a balanced salt solution is important. If the animals are in shock, fluids should be given IV rather than SC. It is also wise to withhold all oral fluids and food when vomiting and diarrhea are the most severe. Signs usually disappear after 2 days or so, and mortality is low.

Elimination of feline coronaviruses (FIPV or FECV) from catteries is virtually impossible. Serologic tests do not accurately identify which cats are shedding the virus. Moreover, FECV infection is enzootic within virtually every cattery and 25% or more of household cats.[5] Fortunately, the disease caused by FECV is usually inapparent or mild and control is largely unnecessary.

Infection and Immunity

Antibodies detectable by IFA and virus-neutralization tests appear in the serum 10-14 days postinfection. Their appearance corresponds with disappearance of virus from the feces.[11] However, local rather than systemic immunity is more likely to be involved in recovery. Following recovery, serum IFA titers may remain persistently elevated or wax and wane at 2- to 12-month intervals.[10] It is tempting to postulate that antibody persistence indicates virus persistence, whereas waxing and waning of antibody levels correlate with loss and reacquisition of virus. This would explain why cats with high titers are apparently more infectious than cats with low titers.[10]

The close immunologic relationship between FECV and FIPV is reflected in a number of intriguing immunologic phenomena. First, because of the antigenic homology between these viruses, serologic tests used for diagnosis of FIP are often nonspecific because both viruses induce cross-reacting antibodies.[12] In any given coronavirus-seropositive cat, it is impossible to say which virus is responsible for the antibody being measured. Second, though FECV and FIPV strains induce cross-reacting humoral immunity, FECV infection does not confer protection against subsequent FIPV infection.[9,12] In fact, FECV immunity often decreases the time from infection to onset of clinical signs and enhances severity of the resulting FIP.[9,12] This phenomenon is both strain and host related. Preexisting FECV immunity enhances infection with FIPV strains, such as TN409, UCD1, UCD3 and UCD4.[11,12] It neither protects against nor enhances infection with FIPV strains, such as 79-1146.[11,12]

Failure of FECV strains to induce cross-reacting immunity to FIPV strains has been attributed to their inability to induce protective cell-mediated immunity.[12] It appears that only cellular immunity protects cats against FIP. Humoral immunity, whether induced by FIPV or FECV strains, is either disease-enhancing or disease-indifferent when passively transferred to kittens before FIPV challenge-exposure.[9] Failure of FECV strains to induce protective cell-mediated immunity may result from their lack of tropism to macrophages. Strains of FECV replicate almost selectively in mature intestinal epithelial cells. Any virus that escapes from the gut is taken up by macrophages in the regional lymph nodes.[10,11] There is no evidence, however, that virus replicates in these macrophages.[11] In FIPV strains, replication in macrophages is essential in pathogenesis of the disease.[13] Failure of FECV to persist in macrophages may also lead to a failure in induction of cellular immunity.

Animal and Public Health Considerations

The virus is readily transmitted by cat-to-cat-contact and through fomites carried by human caretakers.[10] Fomite transmission can be largely eliminated if care is taken not to transfer infected litter on clothes or hands.

There is no evidence that people can be infected with FECV. The extremely close relationship of FECV to TGEV and CCV has led some to postulate cat-to-pig or cat-to-dog transmission.[5,14,16] Whether or not this is an important problem in nature has yet to be determined.

References

1. Boyle JF et al: Plaque assay, polypeptide composition and immunochemistry of feline infectious peritonitis virus and feline enteric coronavirus. Adv Exp Med Biol 173:133-147, 1983.

2. Dea S et al: Coronavirus-like particles in the feces of a cat with diarrhea. Can Vet J 23:153-155, 1982.

3. Hayashi T et al: Enteritis due to feline infectious peritonitis virus. Jpn J Vet Sci 44:97-106, 1982.

4. McKeirnan AJ et al: Isolation of feline coronaviruses from two cats with diverse disease manifestations. Feline Pract 11(3):16-20, 1981.

5. Pedersen NC: Feline infectious peritonitis and feline enteric cornavirus infections. Part I. Feline enteric coronavirus. Feline Pract 13(4):13-19, 1983.

6. Pedersen NC and Black JW: Attempted immunization of cats against feline infectious peritonitis using either avirulent live virus or sublethal amounts of virulent virus. Am J Vet Res 44:229-234, 1983.

7. Pedersen NC et al: Pathogenic differences between various feline coronavirus isolates. Adv Exp Med Biol 173:365-380, 1983.

8. Pedersen NC and Boyle JF: Immunologic phenomena in the effusive form of feline infectious peritonitis. Am J Vet Res 41:808-876, 1980.

9. Pedersen NC et al: Infection studies in kittens utilizing feline infectious peritonitis virus propagated in cell culture. Am J Vet Res 42:363-367, 1981.

10. Pedersen NC et al: An enteric coronavirus infection of cats and its relationship to feline infectious peritonitis. Am J Vet Res 42:368-377, 1981.

11. Pedersen NC et al: Pathogenicity studies of feline coronavirus isolates 79-1146 and 79-1683. Am J Vet Res 45:2580-2585, 1984.

12. Pedersen NC and Floyd K: Experimental studies with three new strains of feline infectious peritonitis virus; FIPV-UCD2, FIPV-UCD3, and FIPV-UCD4. Comp Cont Ed Pract Vet 7:1001-1011, 1985.

13. Pedersen NC et al: Antigenic relationship of the feline infectious peritonitis virus to coronaviruses of other species. Arch Virol 58:45-53, 1978.

14. Siddell S et al: The biology of coronaviruses. J Gen Virol 64:761-776, 1983.

15. Stoddart CA et al: Experimental studies of a coronavirus and coronavirus-like agent in a barrier-maintained feline breeding colony. Arch Virol 79:85-94, 1984.

16. Woods RD et al: Lesions in the small intestine of newborn pigs inoculated with porcine, feline, and canine coronaviruses. Am J Vet Res 42:1163-1169, 1981.

Chapter 7

Feline Infectious Peritonitis

Feline infectious peritonitis (FIP) is a relatively new disease of cats. The first definitive reports of FIP were from the United States in the early 1960s.[27] It is doubtful the disease existed much before the early 1950s.[44] The reason for the sudden emergence of FIP is not known. It may be noteworthy that FIP appeared within a decade of the initial descriptions of transmissible gastroenteritis (TGE) of pigs in North America.[17] The causative agents for both diseases, though not identical, are closely related. The dramatic rise in incidence of FIP between 1950 and 1975 coincided with heightened interest in cats as primary pets, increased density of cats in urban areas and catteries, and emergence of cattery-associated diseases, such as FeLV infection.[44] Feline infectious peritonitis is now essentially worldwide in distribution.[1,29]

Etiologic Agent

Wolfe and Griesemer were the first to propose that FIP was caused by a virus.[74] Zook and co-workers observed virus particles in the tissues of experimentally infected cats, but were unable to characterize the agent.[78] Ward recognized the close similarity of FIP virus (FIPV) in tissues with members of the family Coronaviridae.[69]

Feline infectious peritonitis virus is a typical coronavirus. Virions are 90-120 nm in diameter and have numerous petal-shaped envelope projections called peplomers. Organization of the peplomers gives the particle a sun- or crown-like appearance; hence the prefix "corona." The viral genome consists of single-stranded RNA. The virion is comprised of 3 major proteins: a small envelope protein of around 25 kd (E1), a peplomer glycoprotein of 180 kd (E2), and a nucleocapsid protein of 55 kd (N).[3,28]

Feline infectious peritonitis virus is so closely related to TGE virus (TGEV) of swine and canine coronavirus (CCV) that they have all been described as strains of a single virus species.[28,57,64] However, there are distinct differences in the genetic structure of FIPV compared to other coronaviruses including TGEV.[10] Feline enteric coronavirus (FECV) is another closely related coronavirus included in this group.[53]

Feline infectious peritonitis virus was first cultivated in peritoneal macrophages and later in brains of suckling mice, rat and hamsters.[32,45] Many different isolates of FIPV have been recently grown in conventional tissue culture.[2,12,42,52,55]

Some strains, such as FIPV-Nor15 and FIPV-79-1146, are highly infectious when given orally or parenterally, and most infected cats develop FIP (Table 1).[12,55] Other strains, such as FIPV-Black (high passage) and FIPV-UCD2, rarely induce FIP by any exposure route and resemble FECV in almost all aspects.[49,55] Intermediate strains, such as FIPV-UCD3 and FIPV-UCD4, are probably the most representative of those occurring in nature. These strains are very infectious when given orally, yet do not cause FIP by this route.[55] However, both FIPV-UCD3 and

Table 1. Variations in infectivity and virulence of various feline coronavirus isolates.

Strain	Infectivity*	Ability to Cause FIP following:	
		oronasal or oral inoculation	intraperitoneal inoculation
FECV-UCD	high	none	none
FECV-79-1685	high	none	none
FIPV-UCD2	high	none	extremely low**
FIPV-TN406 (high passage)	moderate to low	none	extremely low
FIPV-UCD3	high	none	moderate
FIPV-UCD4	high	none	moderate to high
FIPV-UCD1	moderate to low	moderate	high
FIPV-TN406 (low passage)	moderate to low	moderate to high	high
FIPV-79-1146	high	high	high
FIPV-Nor15	high	high	high

* Infectivity is defined as the ability to cause seroconversion following oral or oronasal inoculation.

**Extremely low = less than 1 case in 20-40 inoculated cats.

FIPV-UCD4 cause FIP in 25% of specific-pathogen-free cats infected by the intraperitoneal route.

Fiscus and Teramoto serotyped various FIPV and FECV isolates with monoclonal antibodies to N, E1 and E2 proteins.[79] Using only 6 virus strains, they found as many as 8 different reactivities for anti-N, 4 for anti-E1, and 8 for anti-E2. As many as 7 unique E2 epitopes were found with 1 isolate (FIPV-UCD2) alone.

Pathogenesis

Feline infectious peritonitis is mainly a disease of domestic cats. It has also been recognized in the lion, mountain lion, leopard, cheetah, jaguar, lynx, caracal, sand cat and pallas cat.[6,8,14,48,60,61,66,68]

Feline infectious peritonitis is seen in cats of all ages, but incidence peaks in cats between 6 months and 5 years of age.[44,48] No significant sex predisposition exists. The disease is more frequent in purebred than domestic cats, and in catteries or multiple-cat households rather than single-cat homes. The incidence of FIP is highly variable. Usually the disease is sporadic and attacks isolated animals. Catteries may not suffer any deaths from FIP for years and then several cases might be seen in rapid succession. The disease may seem to disappear, only to reappear months or years later. Much higher infection rates have been seen in some groups of cats. A 3-49% yearly infection rate was observed in kittens raised in 1 cattery over a 4-year period and similar explosive outbreaks have been seen in several other catteries.[48,63] Feline infectious peritonitis often occurs in several kittens from the same litter, with deaths occurring over weeks to months.

Feline infectious peritonitis virus exists in populations as a latent or subclinical infection in apparently healthy cats.[55] The percentage of cats that act as reservoirs for the virus has not been determined, but it is only a fraction of those that have serum coronavirus antibodies.[48] Previous serologic studies have demonstrated coronavirus antibodies in 25% of outdoor cats and in 80% or more of cattery-reared animals in many parts of the world.[29,46] Because of the very high incidence of cross-reacting antibodies to FECV in cats, these studies probably grossly overestimated actual incidence of FIPV infection.[47,48] However, it is certain that FIPV-carrier cats are more frequent in catteries and multiple-cat households than in rural or free-roaming cat populations.

The mode of transmission of FIPV has not been determined. Queens that are asymptomatic carriers of FIPV inevitably infect most of their kittens before birth or during the first 5 weeks of life.[55] Almost all of these infected kittens remain healthy and a proportion of them become chronic latent or active virus carriers. Horizontal transmission between older cats has not been well documented under conditions of natural exposure. Because clinical disease is apparently uncommon following natural infection, the likelihood of detecting horizontal transmission is low. Feline infectious peritonitis has been experimentally transmitted in urine.[84] Fecal and oropharyngeal shedding, a common occurrence in closely related coronavirus infections of other species, is probably the major route of virus shedding.[24]

It has been postulated that FIPV may be a common spontaneous mutant of FECV.[48,55] If this is correct, then FECV-carrier cats (which are very common in nature) might serve as additional sources of FIPV.[53] Evidence suggesting that FIP and enteritis-inducing strains of feline coronaviruses are merely opposite extremes in a spectrum of morphologically and antigenically identical viruses has given credence to this theory.[3,50,55] Mutant viruses could be generated in rare individuals during the initial or carrier stages of FECV infection. These mutant viruses could infect the host from which they came or could be shed and infect other individuals.

The clinical outcome of FIPV infection depends on several complex and incompletely understood factors, including: age at time of infection; route of infection; immunologic responsiveness of host; and strain of virus. Among these variables, the strain of virus is the most important and is interrelated to all other factors. Highly pathogenic strains of FIPV, such as FIPV-Nor15 or FIP-79-1146, cause fatal FIP in almost all cats regardless of age, route of inoculation or immunologic responsiveness (Table 1). However, these strains may be largely laboratory artifacts and atypical of most field strains.[55] Outbreaks of FIP with extremely high morbidity and mortality are very uncommon in nature, which is the pattern of experimentally recreated disease produced by these strains. In contrast, strains of FIPV, such as FIPV-UCD2, FIPV-UCD3 and FIPV-UCD4, behave similarly in the laboratory. None of these 3 strains consistently induces FIP when given by the oral route, though they are infectious and evoke serum antibodies. When given intraperitoneally, FIPV-UCD3 and FIPV-UCD4 are more virulent, but still only cause FIP in 50% or so of infected cats.[55] FIPV-UCD2 seems to have lost alomst all ability to cause FIP regardless of route of infection; in this respect, it more closely resembles FECV.[55] Cats that fail to develop FIP after oral infection with FIPV-UCD2, FIPV-UCD3 and FIPV-UCD4 have very poor immunity to subsequent challenge-exposure with more virulent strains.[55] In some cats, the immune response may even cause more severe disease. Cats that fail to develop FIP after intraperitoneal infection with these 3 strains have either good or poor immunity to subsequent virulent challenge-exposure.[55] Moreover, cats that develop good immunity after initial infection with FIPV-UCD3 and FIPV-UCD4 do so mainly by premunition. Cats immunized with FIPV-UCD3 and FIPV-UCD4 frequently develop FIP and die after infection with FeLV, suggesting that FIPV had been maintained as a latent or subclinical infection.[55]

Though experimentally induced FIPV infections have provided much information about the pathogenesis of naturally occurring disease, this information may be misleading. Kittens infected by their mothers do not have the same disease course as experimentally infected kittens.[54] Kittens born to carrier queens develop a high degree of immunity to subsequent virulent FIPV challenge-exposure without signs of previous primary illness. In contrast, a large proportion of experimentally infected kittens dies of FIP and immunity in survivors is variable.[55] Possible explanations for differences in natural and experimental infections include age, route, presence of maternal immunity and immunologic responsiveness. Experimentally infected kittens were older, were given virus intraperitoneally (while the natural route of infection is unknown), had no maternal immunity and were more immunologically competent. Regardless of explanation, nature must somehow modulate conditions of natural infection to favor asymptomatic infections.

The initial site of FIPV replication in naturally occurring disease probably varies according to route of infection. In parenteral infection, virus probably replicates in macrophages within regional lymphoid organs. Following oral infection the initial site of replication is probably the intestinal mucosa. Hayashi and associates demonstrated FIPV in the intestinal epithelium of 2 of 4 cats with naturally occurring FIP and 12 of 14 cats with experimentally induced disease.[24] Orally administered FIPV replicates mainly in the mature apical epithelium of the intestinal villi in neonatal pigs and causes enteritis virtually indistinguishable from that of TGE.[76] Infection can also occur following experimental intratracheal inoculation of FIPV in cats, and virus replicates very well in intestinal epithelium in culture.[33,52]

Clinical disease is associated with dissemination of virus to target tissues via blood-borne phagocytes.[73] Dissemination is to tissue rich in phagocytic cells, in which FIPV replicates.[45] The ability of FIPV to replicate in phagocytic cells is a characteristic differentiating feature from FECV, which grows almost exclusively in mature epithelial cells.[53] Though FECVs can be found in macrophages within lymph nodes regional to sites of gut infection, apparently they do not replicate there.[53,54] Sites particularly rich in target cells include Kupffer cells of the liver, visceral peritoneum and pleura, uveal tract, and the meninges and ependyma of the brain and spinal cord.

Following dissemination, the ultimate course of the disease is dependent on the strain of FIPV and type and degree of immunity that develops. Low-virulence strains are rapidly contained by host immune responses, while high-virulence strains cause disease signs before protective levels of immunity are induced. Pathogenicity of low-virulence strains may be enhanced by factors adversely affecting host immune responses. Stress, poor nutrition, concurrent disease and genetic susceptibility factors all appear to be involved and may explain morbidity and mortality differences between groups of cats. Virus containment is a function of strong cell-mediated immunity; humoral immunity is not protective.

Many cats sequester FIPV for a prolonged time after initial infection. These subclinical or latent infections are usually caused by low-virulence strains of FIPV.[55] Maintenance of inactive infections is under immunologic control of the host. Situations interfering with established FIPV immunity can lead to disease recrudescence. Feline leukemia virus infections, pregnancy, surgical stress and rigors of cattery living are all frequent denominators in cats that develop clinical FIP.[44,48,55] Genetic factors and concurrent kittenhood illnesses also appear to interfere with establishment or maintenance of FIPV immunity.

Clinical Features

Feline infectious peritonitis refers to the principal clinical form of the disease, a transmissible inflammatory condition of the visceral serosa and omentum.[74] Montali and Strandberg described a second form of the disease, characterized by granulomatous involvement of such parenchymatous organs as the kidneys, mesenteric lymph nodes, bowel wall, liver, pancreas, CNS, and uveal tract of the eyes.[41,44] Granulomatous FIP is called "dry" or "noneffusive" because there is no inflammatory exudation into body cavities. Classic FIP, which comprises about 75% of cases, is termed "wet" or "effusive."

The incubation period of effusive FIP is 2-14 days under experimental conditions.[12,49,52,55] Noneffusive FIP has a longer incubation period. A transient and often inapparent bout of effusive FIP often develops weeks or months before onset of noneffusive FIP in affected cats. Feline infectious peritonitis in kittens 4-10 months old is often preceded by a long history of vague ill health and failure to grow at a normal rate. Chronic low-grade respiratory infection may precede onset of FIP in kittens. The respiratory disease is not due to FIPV, but rather to other agents. Failure to thrive and secondary infections indicate protracted low-grade illness that is suppressing both growth and immune competence.

The clinical course of naturally occurring effusive FIP is 1-6 weeks or longer. The onset of disease is heralded by appearance of a chronic fluctuating fever usually associated with a progressive decline in weight, activity and appetite. In terminal stages, cats go into shock and die. Peritonitis is seen in over 90% of cats with effusive FIP and in about 40% of those with pleuritis (Table 2).

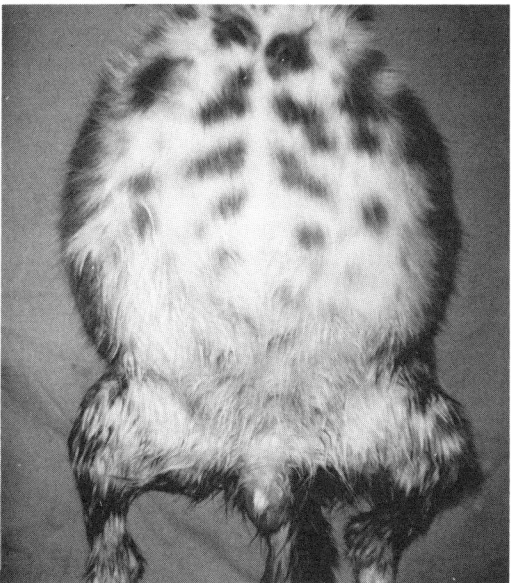

Fig 1A. Grossly distended abdomen of a kitten with effusive feline infectious peritonitis. Note the scrotal enlargement.

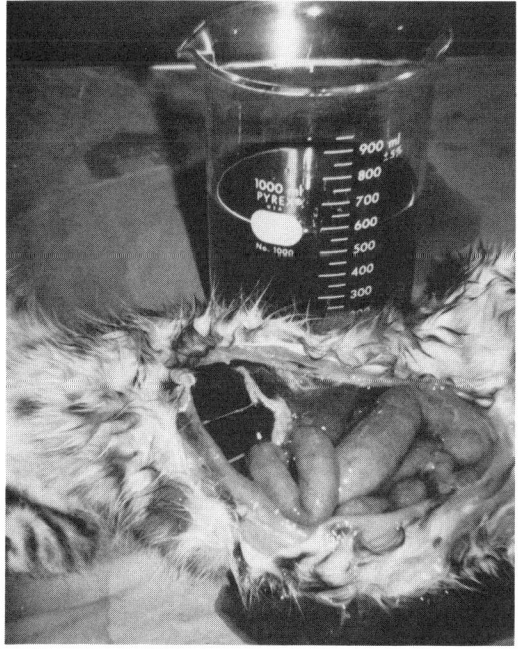

Fig 1B. Over 600 ml of a yellow, mucinous effusion was removed from the abdomen at necropsy.

Table 2. Variability in clinical signs of effusive FIP.

Clinical Signs Referable to Involvement of the:	Number of Cats
Peritoneal cavity	62
Peritoneal and pleural cavities	24
Pleural cavity	12
Peritoneal cavity and eyes	3
Peritoneal cavity and CNS	2
Peritoneal and pleural cavities, CNS	1
Peritoneal and pleural cavities, eyes	1
Peritoneal cavity and CNS	1
Peritoneal cavity, CNS, eyes	1
Total	107

Peritonitis is associated with abdominal distension due to ascites, while pleuritis usually causes hydrothorax and dyspnea (Fig 1). Fluid distension of the pericardial sac, and occasionally cardiac tamponade, may occur.[81] Intact males frequently develop scrotal enlargement due to extension of peritonitis to the tunics surrounding the testes (Fig 1). Peritoneal and pleural exudates are characteristic for the disease. Involvement of other organ systems, such as the eyes and CNS, is clinically apparent in only 10% of cats with effusive disease, though a somewhat higher proportion may have microscopic lesions in these and other nonserosal sites (Table 2).

Cats with noneffusive FIP are ill 1-12 weeks or more. As in the effusive form, a chronic fluctuating fever accompanies the disease, along with a progressive decline in

Table 3. Variability in clinical signs of noneffusive FIP.

Clinical Signs Referable to Involvement of the:	Number of Cats
Peritoneal cavity	30
CNS	22
Eyes	14
CNS and eyes	8
Peritoneal cavity and eyes	7
Peritoneal and pleural cavities	4
Peritoneal and pleural cavities, CNS	3
Peritoneal and pleural cavities, eyes	2
Peritoneal cavity, CNS, eyes	2
Pleural cavity	1
Pleural cavity, CNS, eyes	1
Total	94

general body condition and appetite. In addition, signs referable to specific organ systems are seen. Peritoneal cavity lesions are found in 50% of cats with noneffusive FIP and pleural cavity lesions in 10% (Table 3). Unlike cats wtih the effusive form, one-third of cats with noneffusive FIP demonstrate signs referable to the CNS and have clinically apparent ocular disease (Table 3).

Peritoneal cavity lesions in noneffusive FIP usually consist of irregular solitary or multiple masses within the kidneys, or hepatic or mesenteric lymph nodes (Fig 2). Granulomatous lesions in the liver, spleen, pancreas, omentum, serosal surfaces and intestinal walls are less frequent (Fig 2). Testicular enlargement is seen less frequently in cats with noneffusive FIP.

Thoracic cavity lesions of noneffusive FIP are usually clinically silent. When present, they are usually on the pleural surfaces or heart (Fig 3). Central nervous system involvement is varied in its clinical expression. Spinal signs, such as posterior paresis, incoordination, hyperesthesia, and palsy of the brachial, trigeminal, facial and sciatic nerves, have all been described.[25,36,38,44,65] Hydrocephalus, secondary to disease of the choroid and ependyma, has also been reported.[13,23,37] Cranial involvement can lead to dementia, personality changes (eg, rage, withdrawal) or convulsive disorders. Cerebellar-vestibular signs, such as nystagmus, head tilt or circling, have also been associated with FIP. Ocular lesions can occur by themselves or in association with lesions in the CNS or peritoneal cavity.[48] Uveitis and chorioretinitis are the predominant ocular manifestations of the disease (Fig 4).[4,5,11,15,65]

Miscellaneous sites for lesions in noneffusive FIP include the nasal passages, tongue, and distal small intestine. Granulomatous colitis due to FIPV has also been described.[82] In-utero infections with FIPV result in atypical disease. Pneumonia, pleuritis and hepatitis are the principal lesions in affected kittens.[40]

Pathologic Features

The pyogranuloma is the typical lesion of effusive FIP.[26,73,74] A pyogranuloma consists of necrotic debris and neutrophils, surrounded by a dense accumulation of phagocytic cells interspersed with a few lymphocytes and plasma cells. Considerable amounts of fibrin and protein-rich fluid are

Fig 2. Mesenteric and hepatic lymph nodes and liver from a cat with noneffusive feline infectious peritonitis. The lymph nodes are enlarged and involved with granulomatous adenitis. The liver capsule contains raised, whitish foci 0.5-1 cm in diameter, extending into the underlying parenchyma.

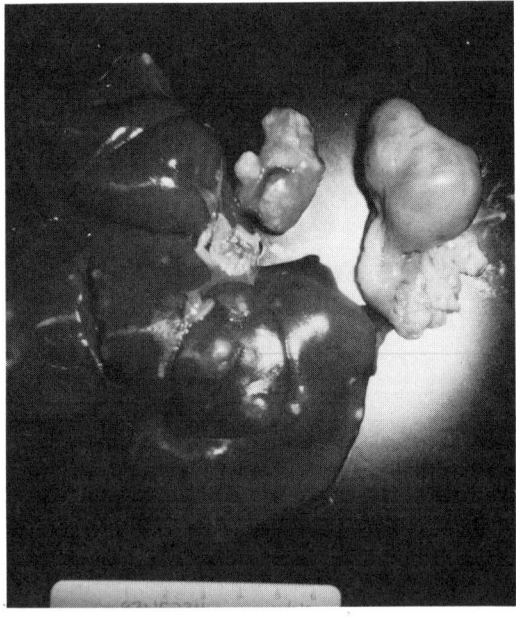

also deposited within and around the lesions.[73] Pyogranulomas appear as distinct or coalescing serosal plaques 0.5-2 mm or more in diameter (Fig 5). The visceral serosa of the thorax and abdomen is more likely to be involved. The omentum is often thickened, edematous and retracted into a compact mass. Though the pyogranulomatous process is usually surface oriented, a similar inflammatory reaction may extend into underlying tissues along penetrating veins. Focal lesions, often associated with phlebitis and a mixed inflammatory-cell infiltrate, may be seen deep in underlying muscle or organ parenchyma.

Lesions of noneffusive FIP are more typically granulomatous in nature, but nevertheless basically resemble the pyogranulamatous lesions of effusive disease. Granulomatous lesions vary in size, depending on the organ involved.[26,41,65] Ocular and CNS lesions more closely resemble the microscopic or small pyogranulomatous reactions seen in effusive FIP. Serosal, mesenteric and omental lesions also appear as small whitish plaques or nodules. Kidney, liver and mesenteric lymph node lesions are often very large, sometimes exceeding 5 cm in diameter. In contrast to the pyogranulomas of effusive FIP, lesions of noneffusive FIP are more typically granulomatous; the outer zone is characteristically more fibrous, and the number of plasma cells and lymphocytes much greater. Edema, hyperemia, and fibrin and protein exudation are also not as pronounced as in the pyogranulomatous lesions of effusive FIP.

Lymphoid lesions are common in both effusive and noneffusive FIP. Splenic enlargement may be due to histiocytic and plasmacytic infiltration of the red pulp, hyperplasia of lymphoid elements in the white pulp, necrotizing splenitis with fibrin deposition and polymorphonuclear cell infiltrates, or by more organized pyogranulomatous reactions. Gross lymph node enlargement is usually limited to thoracic and abdominal nodes and is due to lesions resembling those described for the spleen.

Fluorescent antibody staining of tissue sections from cats with both forms of the disease demonstrates FIPV in the lesions. In effusive FIP, a large amount of viral antigen is contained in phagocytic cells that

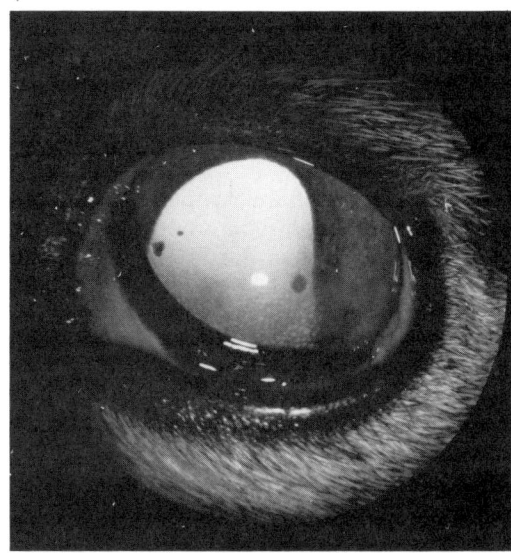

Fig 4. Keratic precipitates on the inner cornea of a cat with noneffusive feline infectious peritonitis. A granuloma on the right side of the iris caused iridal discoloration and an irregular D-shape of the pupil.

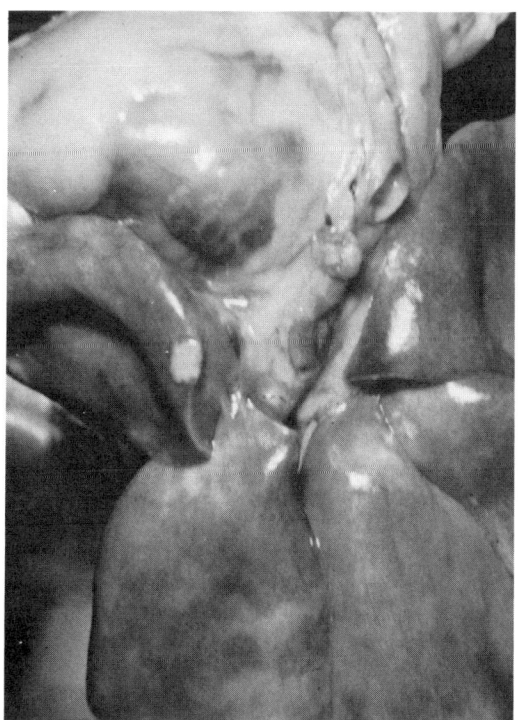

Fig 3. Lungs of a cat with noneffusive feline infectious peritonitis. A solitary, whitish granuloma is present on the edge of the left cranial lobe. Lymph node and liver lesions were also present in this cat (Fig 2).

make up the periphery of the pyogranulomas.[51,52,73] Less viral antigen is present in lesions of noneffusive FIP; it is usually found within a few macrophages adjacent to veins in the center of the lesions.

Clinicopathologic Features

Complete blood counts show similar changes regardless of the disease form. Leukocytosis with neutrophilia and lymphopenia is a common abnormality. In chronic disease, low-grade to moderately

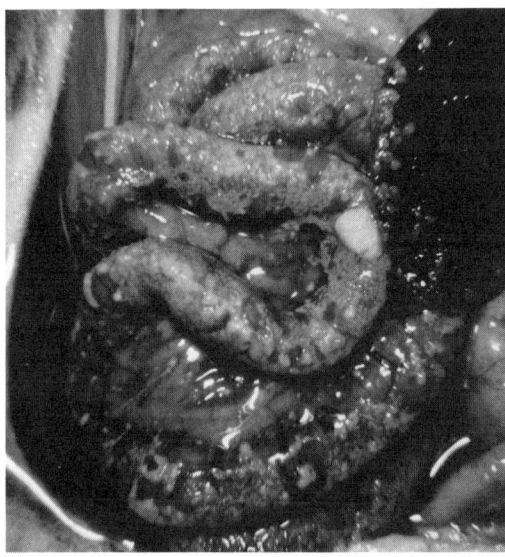

Fig 5. Abdominal viscera of a cat with noneffusive feline infectious peritonitis. The serosal surfaces of the intestines and spleen are covered with punctate, coalescing fibrinous plaques, the classic pyogranulomas of effusive FIP. Some peritoneal effusion remains, though most has been removed.

severe depression anemia is also seen. Total plasma protein levels are elevated in 50% of cats with effusive FIP and 75% of cats with noneffusive FIP. Plasma protein elevations are caused by variable increases in levels of alpha-2, beta and gamma globulins.[44] Serum haptoglobin elevations contribute to the increase in alpha-2 globulins.[21]

Disseminated intravascular coagulopathy (DIC) occurs in cats with effusive FIP.[71] It is usually clinically inapparent but may contribute to the production and character of pleural and abdominal effusions. The coagulopathy is associated with increased prothrombin and partial thromboplastin times, increased levels of fibrin degradation products, prolonged activated clotting time and decreased levels of intrinsic clotting factors.

Ascitic and pleural fluid from cats with effusive FIP is usually pale to dark yellow, and has a sticky viscous consistency, somewhat like synovial fluid or egg white. The exudate is very high in protein and contains 1600-25,000 or more leukocytes/μl. Neutrophils, lymphocytes, macrophages and mesothelial cells are the predominant cell types. Aqueous humor and CSF in cats with ocular or CNS disease also show similar increases in proteins and leukocytes. Synovial fluid from cats with effusive FIP is frequently inflammatory in character.

Following introduction of tests for detection of FeLV infection, 40-50% of cats with FIP were found to have concomitant FeLV infections.[9] With elimination of FeLV from many catteries, the proportion of cats with FIP and concurrent FeLV infections has greatly decreased.

Many serum antibody tests have been employed for diagnosis of FIP.[1,46] Unfortunately, they do not differentiate between cats infected with FECV and FIP, carrier cats and clinically ill animals, or FIPV shedders and nonshedders.[47,48] Antibody tests are only helpful if the clinician understands the serologic responses of cats experimentally infected with FIPV and related FECV.

When specific-pathogen-free, antibody-negative kittens are infected by oral or intratracheal instillation of FIPV, they react serologically in several ways, depending on the dose and strain of virus.[52,55] Some cats do not develop signs of infection after prolonged exposure and remain antibody negative. Infected cats that do not develop signs of illness demonstrate a flat antibody response, while cats that develop FIP show a progressive increase in antibody titer.

Virus-neutralizing antibodies tend to correlate with immunofluorescent antibody (IFA) titers in both groups of cats.[49] Some infected cats, however, only develop virus-neutralizing antibodies, and IFA titers are negligible.[47]

Serologic responses are much more difficult to interpret in the field because of the great amount of antigenic similarity between FIPV and FECV, and the ubiquitousness of FECV infection in nature. Boyle and co-workers were unable to show differences in antibody specificity of serum from cats infected with FECV or with various high- and low-pathogenicity FIPV isolates.[3] For this reason, serodiagnosis of FIP in the field is fraught with a great deal of inaccuracy. However, currently used serologic procedures still have some usefulness. Immunofluorescent antibody titers $\geq$1:3200 are usually associated with FIP, frequently of the noneffusive type. Titers this high are uncommon in cats infected with FECV but may occur in healthy cats with subclinical or latent FIPV infections. Titers of 1:100-1:3200 are common in cats with effusive FIP and in a portion of cats with noneffusive disease. Unfortunately, IFA titers of 1:25-1:1024 are also seen in many cats that have had previous FECV infections or inapparent FIPV infections. Cats with inapparent FIPV infections may be subclinical or latent carriers. Diagnosis of FIP in cats with titers in this range depends on the entire clinical and clinicopathologic picture. Positive coronavirus titers should alert clinicians to the possibility of FIP, while negative titers are often helpful in ruling it out. However, some cats with pathologically confirmed FIP have been seronegative by IFA, so a negative IFA titer is not always helpful. Seronegative cats are most likely to be younger and have fulminating effusive FIP.

Treatment and Prevention

No treatment has proven uniformly and consistently effective. Cats that develop FIP usually die in 1-16 weeks. Nevertheless, several cats have reportedly gone into remission after treatment with various drugs. Colgrove and Parker described cats that went into remission after treatment with tylosin and prednisolone.[7] They credited the antibiotic for the apparent cures, which sparked a decade of tylosin use for treatment of FIP. However, tylosin is now thought to have no value whatsoever in treatment of FIP, and the fortuitous response in the original cats was probably due to self cures or the prednisolone. Pedersen described some cats that went into remission after use of prednisolone and phenylalanine mustard or cyclophosphamide.[44] Madewell and co-workers also successfully treated a cat with effusive FIP with prednisolone and phenylalanine mustard.[39] However, such treatments have also proven to be of limited effectiveness.

In the author's experience, less than 10% of cats go into brief or sustained remission after treatment with immunosuppressive drugs. Successfully treated cats usually had milder illness, and were still eating and not overly debilitated when treated. In addition, owners were more apt to administer continuous supportive care in the form of fluid therapy, forced feeding and other such attentions. Debilitated animals inevitably die and drug therapy actually hastens their demise.

A number of dubious treatments are used for FIP. The FIPV is very sensitive to interferons *in vitro*,[83] but these are ineffective *in vivo*. Various immunostimulants and megadoses of vita-mins have also been advocated. These are equally ineffective.

Spontaneous remission is a complicating factor in evaluating treatment success. Not every cat with FIP dies. Necropsy of older cats without overt signs of FIP has occasionally demonstrated fibrous lesions on the spleen and liver that indicate past FIP infection. Cats with ocular signs and no other systemic manifestations of FIP have occasionally gone into remission with just topical treatment. Cats with chronic fever, enlarged mesenteric lymph nodes that were histologically compatible with FIP, and high coronavirus titers have spontaneously gone into remission without treatment. Finally, small quiescent lesions in the spleen and mesenteric lymph nodes have been discovered in some infected cats during routine ovariohysterectomies. Therefore, it is sometimes difficult to ascertain whether a treatment is successful or if remission was naturally induced.

Currently, no vaccines are available to prevent FIP. Though FIPV immunizes baby pigs against TGE, initial attempts to immunize cats with TGE virus of swine have been unsuccessful.[67,77] Immunization with killed FIPV has also proven uniformly unsuccessful.[34] Immunity derived from killed vaccines almost always renders cats more susceptible to challenge with the virulent live virus, and the resultant disease is usually more severe and fulminating.

Attenuated-live FIPV has also failed to immunize cats.[49] Kittens immunized oronasally with attenuated FIPV-TN406 developed both IFA and virus-neutralizing antibodies. Following challenge with virulent FIPV-TN406, however, the infection rate was enhanced in vaccinated kittens, as compared to nonvaccinates. Also, the incubation period was reduced and disease was more severe. Apparently, avirulent virus does not confer protective immunity but may elicit humoral immunity that is actually deleterious. Pedersen and Black postulated that avirulent virus failed to provide protective immunity because it did not persist in the body long enough.[49] This suggests that immunity to FIPV may involve establishment of a latent or asymptomatic carrier state.

Cats can be immunized against FIP using very small amounts of virulent virus.[49] However, this is not clinically relevant because the dose required to immunize some cats caused fatal FIP in others. Further, when 3 immunized cats were infected later with FeLV, 1 developed fatal effusive FIP. This also suggested that immunity in some of these cats was a result of persistent latent or asymptomatic FIPV infection. This same phenomenon of immunity by premunition was also described in a group of kittens infected with low-virulence strains of FIPV.[55]

Successful immunization of cats against FIPV infection has also been achieved in some cats by oral or intraperitoneal administration of virulent FIPV-UCD3 and FIPV-UCD4.[55] However, many of these cats may retain virus in their body, which could lead to FIP at a later date. This type of immunization is probably analogous to naturally occurring infection with FIPV and has very little clinical relevance.

The incidence of FIP within catteries can be decreased by proper management. Mortality tends to increase as the population of animals, especially kittens, increases. Losses from FIP are also proportional to the severity of other kittenhood diseases, including herpesvirus, calicivirus, chlamydial, mycoplasmal, dermatophytic, parasitic and enteric infections. Kittens kept in crowded catteries with a large number of other young animals suffer greatly from concurrent diseases. These diseases stress the kittens' immune system and are often associated with a temporary decrease in growth rate and an increase in susceptibility to disease in general. Feline leukemia virus infection, a bane of many catteries in the past, is the single most powerful potentiator of FIP in cats. Elimination of FeLV infection from many catteries has decreased the incidence of clinical FIP. Genetics also play an important role in FIP. Fragile strains of purebred cats are often more susceptible to FIP, probably because of decreased overall disease resistance. Death losses from FIP can sometimes be traced to certain breedings, and further breeding of pairs that produced affected kittens should be avoided. Breeding practices in catteries often result in an abundance of younger breeding animals. Younger animals are more apt to be carriers of disease agents than older animals; the carrier state is often only a protraction of acute illness. This is why catteries with breeding cats 4 years of age and older often have less disease than catteries with younger breeding stock.

Explosive epizootics of FIP with high mortality are occasionally seen in catteries. The enzootic form of infection differs greatly in that losses are sporadic. The reason for explosive outbreaks has not been determined, but they most likely result from introduction of carrier cats shedding a different strain of FIPV or introduction of carrier cats into catteries previously free of FIPV. Such virulent outbreaks seldom sustain themselves for more than 6-12 months. The infection apparently goes from epizootic to enzootic proportions as the remaining cats develop immunity to the virus and pass it on to subsequent litters of kittens.

Infection and Immunity

Immunity to FIPV appears to be largely cell mediated.[49,51,55] Humoral immunity either is not protective or, in some cases, enhances disease.[48,49,51,55,72] The type and strength of immunity also determine the disease form (effusive, noneffusive, recovery or asymptomatic carrier state).

Effusive FIP occurs in cats that mount a humoral immune response but fail to develop concurrent protective cell-mediated immunity.[55] In fact, even though coronavirus antibodies neutralize virus *in vitro*, they may actually play an important role in the immunopathogenesis of effusive FIP. The role of antibodies in effusive FIP was first demonstrated with passive serum-transfer experiments. Cornonavirus antibody-negative cats given antibody-positive serum from FIPV-immune or FIPV-susceptible cats actually developed a much more rapid and fulminating form of effusive FIP when challenge-exposed with virulent FIPV.[51,72] Humoral immunity that enhances disease can also be generated by infecting cats with closely related strains of FECV, attenuated strains of virulent FIPV, or autologous and homologous low-virulence strains of FIPV.[48,50,51,53,55] The effect of coronavirus cross-reacting antibodies on effusive FIP resembles the phenomenon described for dengue hemorrhagic shock syndrome in people.[18-20,58,59,62,72] Several closely related serotypes of dengue virus exist, and primary infection with any of these strains produces a self-limiting disease known as dengue fever. However, if a person with antibodies to 1 serotype is later infected with certain other serotypes, severe and frequently fatal disease (dengue hemorrhagic shock syndrome) occurs. This latter syndrome bears a striking resemblance to effusive FIP in both pathogenesis and clinical appearance. The occurrence of enhanced disease is somewhat strain dependent in both FIP and dengue hemorrhagic shock syndrome. Cross-reacting coronavirus antibodies sensitize cats to challenge-exposure with most strains of FIPV except for FIPV-79-1146.[54,55] Preexisting humoral immunity neither protects against nor enhances FIPV-79-1146 infection.

The antibody-mediated immunopathogenesis in effusive FIP appears similar to that described for dengue hemorrhagic shock syndrome.[18-20,58,59,62] Preexisting homologous or autologous antibodies appear to: enhance infectivity of FIPV inocula, perhaps by increasing viral opsonization by macrophages; enhance virus replication by facilitating infection of macrophages, a preferred virus replication site; enhance virus dissemination by facilitating infection and virus replication in migratory phagocytic cells; participate with complement and viral antigen in Arthus-type reactions around small veins; participate with complement and viral antigens in forming circulating immune complexes; and enhance release of specific macrophage factors that cause tissue damage by enhancing virus replication in macrophages.[34,35,45,47,51,55,72,73] The importance of enhancing coronavirus antibodies has been well established in laboratory situations but is unknown in the field.

Though humoral immunity is not protective, the role of cellular immunity has not been definitively established. However, circumstantial evidence in favor of protective cellular-type immunity is relatively strong and includes: resemblance of FIP to other infectious diseases in which cellular immunity is the main protective mechanism; inability to transfer FIPV immunity to susceptible hosts with specific immune sera; cats rendered immune to FIPV infection are in essence immune carriers of the virus, and the carrier state can be abrogated by FeLV infection, a potent suppressor of T-lymphocyte-mediated immunity; and about 50% of FIPV-immune cats demonstrate specific cellular immunity to FIPV as measured by lymphocyte blastogenesis or delayed-type hypersensitivity reactions.[49,51,55]

Noneffusive FIP is thought to occur in cats that produce partial cellular immunity sufficient to limit the spread and degree of virus replication but insufficient to completely contain the infection. Immunity is probably mediated mainly by macrophages that have been specifically activated by interactions with immune T-lymphocytes. In effusive FIP, macrophages are factories for virus replication and seem incapable of killing virus-infected cells. In contrast, macrophages of cats with good immunity can destroy virus and infected cells. However, elimination of virus is not complete. Some virus remains in a latent or sequential state in the body, probably in macrophages, for some time after recovery. Virus persistence in immune macrophages, though not yet demonstrated for FIP, is a consistent feature of similar diseases in which cellular immunity is important for protection.

The theory that cats with noneffusive FIP have only partial cellular immunity is based on several observations. Virus is present mainly within a few macrophages in the centers of granulomatous lesions, whereas in the effusive form, virus and virus-infected macrophages are abundant in the lesions.[44,51] Noneffusive FIP is also usually preceded by a transient bout of effusive disease, suggesting that noneffusive FIP represents a state of greater host immunity.[55] Furthermore, cats have gone through a noneffusive stage of disease during recovery, again indicating that noneffusive FIP results from partial protective immunity.

The duration of virus persistence in FIPV-recovered cats is not known. The disease can be reactivated in almost all cats within the first 2 months following infection.[55,56] We reactivated the disease in 6 of 7 cats 2-16 weeks postinfection and in none of 4 cats 7 months postinfection.[80] This situation resembles that seen in latent FeLV infections.[56] Latency in FeLV infection is merely an extension of the recovery process and usually resolves within 6 months of the disappearance of viremia. This appears to be characteristic of many infectious diseases in which cellular immunity is important for recovery; the longer the period after recovery, the more difficult it is to demonstrate persistence of the agent. Immunity to many infections, including FIP, must be a slow, ongoing process that takes weeks, months or years. In some individuals, the agent may persist for a lifetime. In fact, persistence of the organism in the host may be an essential requirement for perpetuation of immunity.[49,55] Indeed, when latently infected kittens eliminate the virus, they also lose their immunity.[80]

Animal and Public Health Considerations

Feline infectious peritonitis virus is a naturally occurring infection of domestic and wild Felidae. People are not hosts for the virus. Dogs and swine can be experimentally infected with FIPV; a mild to moderately severe TGE-like syndrome occurs in baby pigs.[76] However, it is doubtful that FIPV is a cause of naturally occurring enteritis in these species. The genome of TGEV, while very similar, is distinct from that of FIPV.[10]

Cats that carry FIPV or those with active disease should be considered infectious to other cats. Fortunately, only a very small percentage of cats naturally infected with FIPV ever develop disease. Further, by the time FIP is first diagnosed in a group of cats, the virus is usually well established. In practice, therefore, disease control by quarantine and isolation of individual animals seldom influences the natural course of disease in a group of cats.

References

1. Barlough JE et al: The worldwide occurrence of feline infectious peritonitis. *Feline Pract* 12(6):26-30, 1982.

2. Black JW: Recovery and *in vitro* cultivation of a coronavirus from laboratory-induced cases of feline infectious peritonitis (FIP). *VM/SAC* 75:811-814, 1980.

3. Boyle JF et al: Plaque assay, polypeptide composition and immunochemistry of feline infectious peritonitis virus and feline enteric coronavirus. *Adv Exp Med Biol* 173:133-147, 1984.

4. Campbell LH and Reed C: Ocular signs associated with feline infectious peritonitis in two cats. *Feline Pract* 5(3):32-35, 1975.

5. Campbell LH and Schiessl MM: Ocular manifestations of toxoplasmosis, infectious peritonitis and lymphosarcoma in cats. *Mod Vet Pract* 59:761-764, 1978.

6. Colby ED and Low RJ: Feline infectious peritonitis. *VM/SAC* 65:783-786, 1970.

7. Colgrove DJ and Parker AJ: Feline infectious peritonitis. *J Small Anim Pract* 12:225-232, 1971.

8. Colly LP: Feline infectious peritonitis. *Vet Clin No Am* 3:34, 1973.

9. Cotter SM et al: Multiple cases of feline leukemia and feline infectious peritonitis in a household. *JAVMA* 162:1054-1058, 1973.

10. De Groot RJ et al: Intracellular RNAs of the feline infectious peritonitis strain 79-1146. *J Gen Virol* 68:995-1002, 1987.

11. Doherty MJ: Ocular manifestations of feline infectious peritonitis. *JAVMA* 159:417-424, 1971.

12. Evermann JF et al: Characterization of a feline infectious peritonitis virus isolate. *Vet Pathol* 18:256-265, 1981.

13. Fankhauser R and Fatzer R: Meningitis und Chorioependymitis granuloma-tosa der Katze: mögliche Beziehungen zur felinen infectiösen Peritonitis (FIP). *Kleintierpraxis* 22:19-22, 1977.

14. Fowler ME: *Zoo and Wild Animal Medicine*. Saunders, Philadelphia, 1978. p 660.

15. Gelatt KM: Iridocyclitis-panophthalmitis associated with feline infectious peritonitis. *VM/SAC* 68:56-57, 1973.

16. Gillespie JH and Scott FW: Feline viral infections. *Adv Vet Sci* 17:163-200, 1973.

17. Haelterman EO: Epidemiological studies of transmissible gastroenteritis of swine. *US Livestock Sanit Assoc Proc* 66:305-315, 1962.

18. Halstead SB: *In vivo* enhancement of dengue infection with passively transferred antibody. *J Infect Dis* 140:527-533, 1979.

19. Halstead SB et al: Comparison of P388D1 mouse macrophage cell line and human monocytes for assay of dengue-2 infection-enhancing antibodies. *Am J Trop Med Hyg* 32:157-163, 1983.

20. Halstead SM et al: Original antigenic sin in dengue. *Am J Trop Med Hyg* 32:154-156, 1983.

21. Harvey JW and Gaskin JM: Feline haptoglobin. *Am J Vet Res* 39:549-553, 1978.

22. Hayashi T et al: Detection of corona-virus-like particles in a spontaneous case of feline infectious peritonitis. *Jpn J Vet Sci* 40:207-212, 1978.

23. Hayashi T et al: Pathology of noneffusive-type feline infectious peritonitis and experimental transmission. *Jpn J Vet Sci* 42:197-210, 1980.

24. Hayashi T et al: Enteritis due to feline infectious peritonitis virus. *Jpn J Vet Sci* 44:97-106, 1982.

25. Holliday TA: Clinical aspects of some encephalopathies of domestic cats. *Vet Clin No Am* 1:367-378, 1971.

26. Holmberg CA and Gribble DH: Feline infectious peritonitis: Diagnostic gross and microscopic lesions. *Feline Pract* 3(4):11-14, 1973.

27. Holzworth J: Some important disorders of cats. *Cornell Vet* 53:157-160, 1963.

28. Horzinek MC et al: Antigenic relationships among homologous structural polypeptides of porcine, feline and canine coronaviruses. *Infect Immun* 37:1148-1155, 1979.

29. Horzinek MC and Osterhaus ADME: Feline infectious peritonitis: A worldwide serosurvey. *Am J Vet Res* 40:1487-1492, 1979.

30. Horzinek MC and Osterhaus ADME: The virology and pathogenesis of feline infectious peritonitis. Brief Review. *Arch Virol* 59:1-15, 1979.

31. Horzinek MC et al: Feline infectious peritonitis virus. *Zentralbl Vetmed* (B) 24:398-405, 1977.

32. Horzinek MC et al: Feline infectious peritonitis (FIP) virus. III. Studies on the multiplication of FIP virus in the suckling mouse. *Zentralbl Vetmed* (B) 25:806-815, 1978.

33. Hoshino Y and Scott FW: Immuno-fluorescent and electron microscopic studies of feline small intestine organ cultures infected with feline infectious perito-nitis virus. *Am J Vet Res* 41:672-681, 1980.

34. Jacobse-Geels HEL et al: Isolation and characterization of feline C3 and evidence for the immune complex pathogenesis of feline infectious peritonitis. *J Immunol* 125:1606-1610, 1980.

35. Jacobse-Geels HEL et al: Antibody immune complexes and complement activity fluctuations in kittens with experimentally induced feline infectious peritonitis. *Am J Vet Res* 43:666-670, 1982.

36. Kornegay JN: Feline infectious peritonitis. *JAAHA* 14:580-584, 1978.

37. Krum S et al: Hydrocephalus associated with the noneffusive form of feline infectious peritonitis. *JAVMA* 167:746-748, 1975.

38. Legendre AM and Whitenack DL: Feline infectious peritonitis with spinal cord involvement in two cats. *JAVMA* 167:931-932, 1975.

39. Madewell BR et al: Infectious peritonitis in a cat that subsequently developed a myeloproliferative disorder. *JAVMA* 172:169-172, 1978.

40. McKeirnan AJ et al: Isolation of feline coronaviruses from two cats with diverse disease manifestations. *Feline Pract* 11(3):16-20, 1981.

41. Montali RJ and Strandberg JD: Extraperitoneal lesions in feline infectious peritonitis. *Vet Pathol* 9:109-121, 1972.

42. O'Reilly KJ et al: Feline infectious peritonitis: isolation of a coronavirus. *Vet Record* 104:348, 1979.

43. Osterhaus ADME et al: Feline infectious peritonitis (FIP) virus. IV. Propagation in suckling rat and hamster brain. *Zentralbl Vetmed:* 816-825, 1978.

44. Pedersen NC: Feline infectious peritonitis. Something old, something new. *Feline Pract* 6(3):42-51, 1976.

45. Pedersen NC: Morphologic and physical characteristics of feline infectious peritonitis virus and its growth in autochthonous peritoneal cell cultures. *Am J Vet Res* 37:567-572, 1976.

46. Pedersen NC: Serologic studies of naturally occurring feline infectious peritonitis. *Am J Vet Res* 37:1449-1453, 1976.

47. Pedersen NC: Feline infectious peritonitis and feline enteric coronavirus infections. Part I: Feline enteric coronavirus. *Feline Pract* 13(4):13-19, 1983.

48. Pedersen NC: Feline infectious peritonitis and feline enteric coronavirus infections. Part II: Feline infectious peritonitis. *Feline Pract* 13(5):5-19, 1983.

49. Pedersen NC and Black JW: Attempted immunization of cats against feline infectious peritonitis using either avirulent live virus or sublethal amounts of virulent virus. *Am J Vet Res* 44:229-234, 1983.

50. Pedersen NC et al: Pathogenic differences between various feline coronavirus isolates. Coronaviruses; molecular biology and pathogenesis. *Adv Exp Med Biol* 173:365-380, 1984.

51. Pedersen NC and Boyle JF: Immunologic phenomena in the effusive form of feline infectious peritonitis. *Am J Vet Res* 41:868-876, 1980.

52. Pedersen NC et al: Infection studies in kittens utilizing feline infectious peritonitis virus propagated in cell culture. *Am J Vet Res* 42:363-367, 1981.

53. Pedersen NC et al: An enteric coronavirus infection of cats and its relationship to feline infectious peritonitis. *Am J Vet Res* 42:368-377, 1981.

54. Pedersen NC et al: Pathogenicity studies of two new feline coronavirus isolates 79-1146 and 79-1683. *Am J Vet Res* 45:2580-2585, 1984.

55. Pedersen NC and Floyd K: Experimental studies with three new strains of feline infectious peritonitis virus FIPV-UCD2, FIPV-UCD3, and FIPV-UCD4. *Comp Cont Ed Pract Vet* 7:1001-1011, 1985.

56. Pedersen NC et al: The clinical significance of latent feline leukemia virus infection in cats. *Feline Pract* 14(2):32-48, 1984.

57. Pedersen NC et al: Antigenic relationship of the feline infectious peritonitis virus to coronaviruses of other species. *Arch Virol* 58:45-53, 1978.

58. Peiris JSM et al: Monoclonal anti-Fc receptor IgG blocks antibody enhancement of viral replication in macrophages. *Nature* 289:189-191, 1981.

59. Peiris JSM and Porterfield JS: Antibody-mediated enhancement of flavivirus replications in macrophage-like cell lines. *Nature* 28:507-511, 1979.

60. Pfeifer ML et al: Feline infectious peritonitis in a captive cheetah. *JAVMA* 183:1317-1319, 1983.

61. Poelma FG et al: Infectiöse Peritonitiss bei Karakal (*Felis caracal*) und Nordluchs (*Felis lynx lynx*). *Erkrankungen der Zootiere 13th Int Symp Helsinki*, 1974. pp 249-253.

62. Porterfield JS: Immunological enhancement and the pathogenesis of dengue hemorrhagic fever. *J Hyg* 89:355-364, 1982.

63. Potkay S et al: Feline infectious peritonitis in a closed breeding colony. *Lab Anim Sci* 24(2):279-289, 1974.

64. Siddell S et al: The biology of coronaviruses. *J Gen Virol* 64:761-776, 1983.

65. Slausen DO and Finn JP: Meningoencephalitis and panophthalmitis in feline infectious peritonitis. *JAVMA* 160:729-734, 1972.

66. Theobald J, in Fowler ME: *Zoo and Wild Animal Medicine*. Saunders, Philadelphia, 1978. pp 650-667.

67. Toma B et al: Echec de l'immunisation contre la pèritonite infectieuse fèline par injection de virus de la gastroentèrite transmissible du porc. *Recl Mèd Vèt* 155:799-803, 1979.

68. Tuch K et al: Feststellung der felinen infektiösen Peritonitis (FIP) bei Hauskatzen und Leoparden in Deutschland. *Zentralbl Vetmed* (B)21:426-441, 1974.

69. Ward JM: Morphogenesis of a virus in cats with experimental feline infectious peritonitis. *Virol* 41:191-194, 1970.

70. Ward JM: Inclusions in neutrophils of cats with feline infectious peritonitis. *JAVMA* 158:348, 1971.

71. Weiss RC et al: Disseminated intravascular coagulation in experimentally induced feline infectious peritonitis. *Am J Vet Res* 41:663-671, 1980.

72. Weiss RC and Scott FW: Antibody-mediated enhancement of disease in feline infectious peritonitis: Comparisons with dengue hemorrhagic fever. *Comp Immunol Microbiol Infect Dis* 4:175-189, 1981.

73. Weiss RC and Scott FW: Pathogenesis of feline infectious peritonitis: Pathologic changes and immunofluorescence. *Am J Vet Res* 42:2036-2048, 1981.

74. Wolfe LG and Griesemer RA: Feline infectious peritonitis. *Path Vet* 3:255-270, 1966.

75. Wolfe LG and Griesemer RA: Feline infectious peritonitis. Review of gross and histopathologic lesions. *JAVMA* 158:987-993, 1971.

76. Woods RD *et al*: Lesions in the small intestine of newborn pigs inoculated with porcine, feline and canine coronaviruses. *Am J Vet Res* 42:1163-1169, 1981.

77. Woods RD and Pedersen NC: Cross-protection studies between feline infectious peritonitis and porcine transmissible gastroenteritis viruses. *Vet Microbiol* 4:11-16, 1979.

78. Zook BC *et al*: Ultrastructural evidence for the viral etiology of feline infectious peritonitis. *Path Vet* 5:91-95, 1968.

Additional References

79. Fiscus SA and Teramoto YA: Antigenic comparison of feline coronavirus isolates: Evidence for markedly different peplomer glycoproteins. *J Virol* 6:2607-2613, 1987.

80. Pedersen NC: Virologic and immunologic aspects of feline infectious peritonitis virus infection. *Adv Exp Biol Med* 218:529-550, 1987.

81. deMadron E: Pericarditis with cardiac tamponade secondary to feline infectious peritonitis in a cat. *JAAHA* 22:65-69, 1986.

82. Van Kruiningen: The classification of feline colitis. *J Comp Path* 93:275-294, 1983.

83. Weiss RC and Toivio-Kinnucan M: Inhibition of feline infectious peritonitis virus replication by recombinant human leukocyte (α) interferon and feline fibroblastic (β) interferon. *Am J Vet Res* 47:1329-1335, 1988.

84. Hardy WD Jr and Hurvitz AI: Feline infectious peritonitis: Experimental studies. *JAVMA* 158:994-1002, 1971.

Chapter 8

Feline Calicivirus Infection

Etiologic Agent

Caliciviruses were first isolated from cats by Fastier in New Zealand and Bolin in the United States.[4,9] Both isolations were inadvertently made during attempts to grow panleukopenia virus from splenic extracts of kittens with fatal enteritis.[31] Feline calicivirus (FCV) was subsequently isolated from cats by researchers throughout the world.[3,5,7,15,18,21,27,28,32,34,39]

The FCV virion is about 32-40 nm in diameter and is an icosahedron with a surface covered by spherical spots about 10 nm in diameter in negative stains (Fig 1).[31] These spots are caused by stain accumulation in cup-shaped depressions. The prefix "calici-" is derived from the Greek word *kalyx* for cup or chalice.

About 22% of the virion is comprised of a 2600-kD, single-stranded RNA.[1] Feline calicivirus contains a single 60- to 65-kD structural protein, a feature that differentiates it from picornaviruses, which have 4 polypeptides. The amino acid composition of the single structural protein in FCV, San Miguel sea lion virus and vesicular stomatitis virus is similar.[30]

Feline calicivirus is not inactivated by lipid solvents, such as ether or chloroform. Infectivity is destroyed by heating to 50 C for 30 minutes. It is inactivated at a pH of 3 but becomes more stable as pH values increase. Infectivity is retained for at least 4 years at -65 C.[11]

Feline calicivirus replicates in cat, lion and dolphin cells, but not in sheep, cattle or hamster cells.[31] Some strains of FCV grow in vero (African green monkey) cells.[31,33] Feline calicivirus cannot be propagated in eggs or laboratory rodents.[2,20,34]

Feline calicivirus grows very rapidly in cat cells. Maximum levels of intracellular virus are produced within 6 hours; maximum levels of extracellular virus are detected 2 hours later.[31] Infected cells round up, become refractile and detach from the monolayer. Cytoplasmic blebbing

Fig 1. Electron micrograph of negatively stained calicivirus particles in a fecal culture from a cat with diarrhea. Note the stain-filled surface depressions. The virus's name is derived from these cup- or chalice-like indentations. The virions are 34 nm in diameter. The bar at the bottom of the photograph is 100 nm long. (Courtesy of Dr. Anthony E. Castro, University of California, Davis)

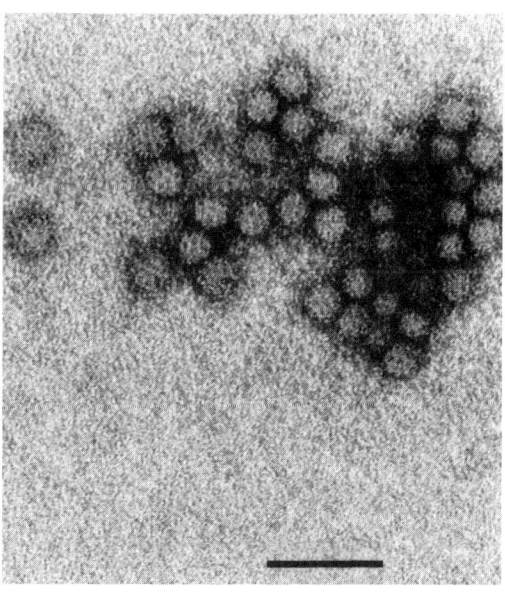

accompanies cell lysis and virus release. Virus replication occurs only in the cytoplasm. Single particles, irregular accumulations, paracrystalline arrays and linear arrays associated with microfibrils and membrane-bound cytoplasmic cisternae are all seen within infected cells.[31] These various structures are comprised of individual virus particles about 35 nm in diameter, with doughnut-shaped centers about 20 nm in diameter.

Feline calicivirus exists as a single species with several dozen or more strains.[11,32] Early literature dealing with a small number of isolates suggested very little serologic cross-reactivity among strains. As more strains were isolated, it became apparent that they formed an antigenic mosaic. One strain, FCV-F9, was neutralized by antisera generated to the majority of field isolates, and in turn, FCV-F9 antiserum neutralized most other strains. Accordingly, FCV-F9 was proposed as a reference strain.

Pathogenesis

Feline calicivirus causes disease mainly in domestic cats but has also been associated with illness in some wild Felidae.[28] Clinical illness is more common in catteries and multiple-cat households than in single-cat households. Clinical disease is most likely to occur in kittens and in situations in which other infectious diseases are also likely to be problems. Infections with different serotypes probably occur throughout life but are not likely to be of great clinical significance because of age resistance and lessening of concurrent kittenhood disease. It is unlikely that many cats escape infection.

Feline calicivirus persists as an active asymptomatic infection in many recovered cats. In some areas, up to one-third of the adult cats are silent oropharyngeal carriers. Virus can be isolated from the tonsillar tissues of recovered cats for at least 34 days.[15] Povey and Johnson and Walton described almost continuous shedding of virus from the oropharynx by FCV carriers.[25,35]

Maternal immunity protects kittens from infection for the first 3-9 weeks of life.[40] Kittens then become susceptible to infection by virus shed in saliva and ocular or nasal exudates of asymptomatic or clinically ill animals. Vaccination with live-virus vaccines is also a frequent cause of disease in kittens.

Probably the main route of infection is oral and the initial site of infection is the oropharynx. This localized primary infection is followed by transient viremia, with localization of virus in the epithelium of the nasal passages, conjunctiva, tongue, palate or other tissues. A diphasic temperature response follows experimental aerosol infection. The first temperature rise occurs about 24 hours after infection, and the second occurs between 96 and 168 hours. Recovery is rapid thereafter. Following experimental aerosol exposure, virus can be recovered from the conjunctival sac for 7 days, nasal passages and pharynx for at least 2 weeks, feces for 2 weeks, tonsils for 5 weeks and lungs for 10 days.

Clinical Features

The predominant clinical signs of naturally occurring FCV infection differ

Fig 2. Lingual ulcerations associated with acute calicivirus infection. (Courtesy of Dr. R.C. Povey, Langford, Inc., Guelph, Ontario)

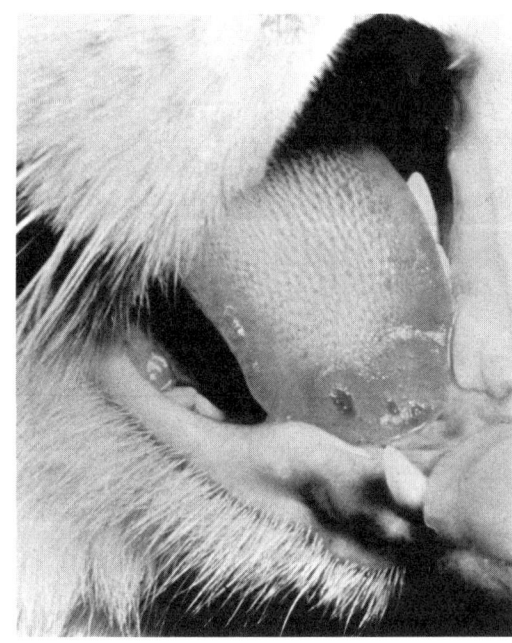

from one report to another. Upper respiratory disease is the principal form of infection described in the literature and has been only partially recreated by massive aerosol exposure to pneumotropic virus, usually FCV-255.[11] Conjunctivitis is neither a common nor pronounced feature of experimentally recreated disease and does not persist beyond 13 days. Rhinitis is also uncommon and is most severe by day 6 and disappears by day 10. Small vesicles occur in the palate and tongue of many experimentally infected cats. Vesicles rapidly rupture, leaving shallow erosions (Figs 2,3). Vesicles and erosions appear toward the end of the disease course and heal rapidly. Focal pneumonia is also a consistent lesion seen in kittens exposed to aerosols of FCV-255. The lungs are mottled with reddish areas of congestion and edema early in the course of infection. After several days, the pneumonic lesions consolidate to form elevated, firm areas in the lung that are pinkish-gray to pale red, have a patchy distribution and usually resolve by day 10.

The validity of experimental aerosol infection as a model for the naturally occurring disease has been questioned by Pedersen and co-workers.[19] They studied 2 strains of FCV that were associated with naturally occurring infections that manifested as transient fever, joint and muscle soreness (limping), and occasional oral and palatine ulcers. The entire disease course was 48-96 hours and recovery was rapid and complete. Upper respiratory tract signs were conspicuously absent even though the disease could be readily reproduced by oral or oronasal infection. A similar syndrome has been susequently observed in a number of catteries and commonly associated with use of live FCV vaccines. Such observations led to the conclusion that this is the predominant clinical form of disease in nature.

Caliciviruses have been isolated from feces of pound kittens undergoing epizootics of diarrhea. Though caliciviruses are associated with so-called outbreaks of winter dysentery in people, their role in epizootic diarrhea in kittens remains to be determined.

The role of other disease agents in potentiating FCV infection and *vice versa* should not be underestimated. Bittle and co-workers first reported synergism between FCV and feline panleukopenia virus infections.[2] They observed 82% mortality in kittens infected with FCV and panleukopenia virus at the same time. In contrast, mortality was only 10% in feline panleukopenia virus-infected cats and only 5% in cats infected with FCV alone. Feline rhinotracheitis virus, *Mycoplasma*, *Chlamydia* and bacteria are all involved in kittenhood infections. The resulting syndromes are often caused by combinations of these and other disease agents. This might explain how a somewhat atypical idea of naturally occurring FCV infection evolved. Naturally occurring FCV infection is not nearly as important as some of the literature suggests, and is not likely one of the most important illnesses of kittens.

Pathologic Features

Pneumotropic strains of FCV, such as FCV-255, cause upper and lower respira-

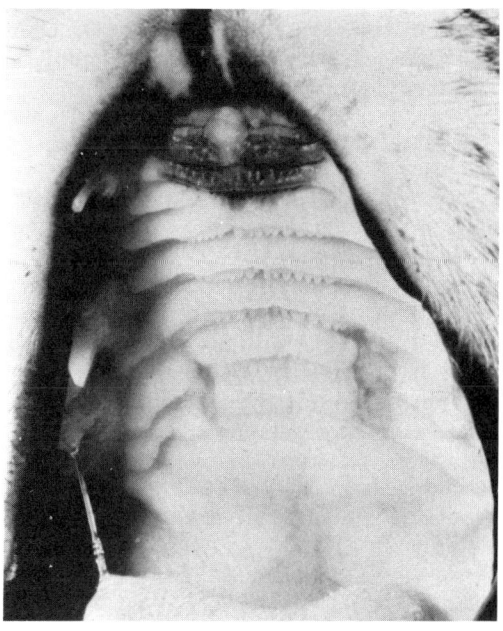

Fig 3. Ulcers at the junction of the hard and soft palates in a cat with acute calicivirus infection. These began as fluid-filled vesicles. They are more likely to be seen in kittens eating dry food. (Courtesy of Dr. Roger Johnson, University of Guelph, Ontario)

tory disease following aerosol administration. Pneumonia is the most consistent lesion seen in experimental disease; rhinitis and conjunctivitis are uncommon but mild when present.[15] Patchy focal areas of pneumonitis are initially associated with hypertrophy and hyperplasia of bronchial and bronchiolar epithelium and alveolar macrophages. Mononuclear cells rapidly aggregate in involved areas in the epithelial lining and air passages. Such changes are most noticeable between days 7 and 10 postinfection and resolve slowly thereafter. Neutrophils appear in the lesions early in the course but are replaced by lymphocytes and plasma cells in the resolution stage. Fatal pneumonia is almost always due to complicating secondary bacterial invasion.[11]

Glossal and palatine ulcers are common in both experimental and naturally occurring disease.[13,15] The ulcers are derived from fluid-filled vesicles (2-5 mm in diameter) in the epithelium. Oral lesions are more apt to be seen in kittens eating abrasive dried food than in kittens consuming soft canned food.[13]

Limping due to nerve, joint or muscle pain is a common feature of natural outbreaks. It is usually transient, seldom lasting more than 2-4 days, and accompanied by fever and variable oral ulcerations. The origin of the rheumatic signs has not been established and no histologic abnormalities are seen in joints, nerves or CNS.[19]

Clinicopathologic Features

Feline calicivirus can be readily isolated in tissue culture. Blood, feces and exudates from the oropharynx, nasal passages, conjunctival sacs or lungs produce a typical cytopathic effect within 12-72 hours, depending on the initial virus titer. Rapid growth of FCV in tissue culture may prevent isolation of concurrent reovirus, herpesvirus or panleukopenia virus. Therefore, it is important to alter the isolation procedure to identify as many participating agents as possible rather than the easiest one to isolate.

Treatment and Prevention

Fever, joint and muscle pain, and glossal and palatine ulcers disappear within 48-96 hours. Pneumonia, which is an uncommon sequela in nature, is usually due to secondary bacterial invasion of primary viral lesions. Likewise, purulent nasal and ocular discharges are almost always associated with complicating bacterial, chlamydial or mycoplasmal infections. Antibiotics are valuable to counteract secondary infections. Though early reports of FCV infection emphasized the seriousness of the disease, the mortality of uncomplicated FCV infection is very low.[19,40]

Because it is virtually impossible to eliminate carrier cats from the environment, control of FCV infection is largely by vaccination. However, it is important to note that FCV can exist in many cat populations without causing serious problems.[40] Concurrent disease, stress and other factors may combine to potentiate disease severity in certain outbreaks.

Before 1974, FCV vaccines generated very little enthusiasm. The great number of field strains and seeming lack of serologic cross-reactivity among them made vaccine development difficult.[5,6] On further study, however, the problem of antigenic diversity did not seem as formidable as it had previously. Certain strains, such as FCV-F9, were found to induce antibodies of extremely broad cross-reactivity.[17] Bittle and Rubic attenuated FCV-F9 by passage at low temperature and terminal cloning.[3] Two IM injections 4 weeks apart produced good protection against virulent FCV-255.[29] Subsequently, Davis and Beckenhauer used the naturally occurring avirulent FCV-M8 strain as a vaccine.[8] When administered intranasally and into the conjunctival sac, FCV-M8 produced good protection against FCV-255 with a single dose. Inactivated FCV vaccines have also recently appeared on the market.[26]

Though current vaccine strains produce various degrees of cross-protection, the protection they afford is not necessarily against all field isolates. Recently, 2 new strains of FCV, FCV-2280 and FCV-LLK, were isolated during outbreaks of fever and limping in vaccinated kittens.[19] The strain FCV-2280 was totally unaffected by vaccines containing FCV-F9, FCV-M8 and FCV-255. Infection with FCV-LLK was prevented by vaccines containing FCV-F9 and FCV-255 but not by vaccines containing FCV-M8. The ease with which vaccine-resistant strains can be isolated from catteries indicates that serologic differences are more important than recently believed and immunization less effective than reported.

Infection and Immunity

Feline calicivirus persists in the oropharynx of many cats and is actively shed in the saliva even with systemic immunity.[36-38] Carrier cats can be classified as low-, medium- or high-level virus shedders.[37] Susceptible cats can be infected in 2-3 days by high-level shedders, and in 11-13 days by low-level shedders. Unlike feline herpesvirus (rhinotracheitis), shedding is not influenced by natural or artificial stress.[37]

Various FCV isolates form an antigenic mosaic, and antibodies to one strain vary in degree of cross-reactivity with other strains. One isolate, FCV-F9, induces antibodies that cross-react with a majority of isolates. Another, FCV-M8, is neutralized by antibodies to most other isolates. Povey produced an antiserum that neutralized over 80 isolates by sequentially immunizing cats against 3 different isolates.[22]

After immunization of cats with such isolates as FCV-F9, antibodies that react most specifically with FCV-F9 are produced initially, but antibodies of much greater cross-reactivity begin to appear in higher titers after several weeks.[17,24] This phenomenon is helpful in immunization.

Maternal antibodies to FCV have a half-life of 15 days and persist in the serum of kittens for as long as 14 weeks.[14] Maternal immunity to FCV appears to be incomplete.[10,11,13] Kittens with maternal immunity can often be infected as young as 3-9 weeks of age.[13,36,40] Even though virus can be isolated from the oropharynx, clinical signs and an active humoral immune response do not occur until maternal immunity declines several weeks later.[13,40] At this point, clinical signs are either inapparent or relatively mild, and the resultant primary immune response develops slowly and reaches lower levels than in kittens free of maternal immunity at exposure. In contrast, kittens with very low maternal titers rapidly become ill after infection and the disease is more severe.[13] The immune response also comes on more quickly after infection and reaches higher levels.

Johnson postulated that maternal immunity may lessen severity of disease in situations with a high level of exposure that occurs earlier in life.[40] He followed the course of disease caused by the highly pathogenic FCV-255 strain in a small cattery where many of the cats were carriers. In this environment, the kittens showed few signs of illness due to FCV, even though they all became infected at an early age.

Tham and Studdert detected both humoral and cellular immunity in cats vaccinated and challenged with FCV.[41] Both antibody-dependent and -independent cell-mediated immunity to FCV infected cells appeared in immunized cats. The antibody-independent cytotoxicity was both major histocompatibility complex restricted and unrestricted.

Animal and Public Health Considerations

Feline calicivirus is only infectious to domestic and some wild Felidae. It is not a human pathogen.

References

1. Adlidinger HK et al: Extraction of infectious ribonucleic acid from a feline picornavirus. *Arch Ges Virusforsch* 28:245-247, 1969.

2. Bittle JL et al: Serologic relationship of new feline cytopathogenic viruses. *Am J Vet Res* 21:547-550, 1960.

3. Bittle JL and Rubic WJ: Immunization against feline calicivirus infection. *Am J Vet Res* 37:275-278, 1976.

4. Bolin VS: The cultivation of panleucopenia virus in tissue culture. *Virol* 4:389-390, 1957.

5. Bürki F: Picornaviruses of cats. *Arch Ges Virusforsch* 15:690-696, 1965.

6. Crandell RA: A description of eight feline picornaviruses and an attempt to classify them. *Proc Soc Exp Biol Med* (NY) 126:240-245, 1967.

7. Crandell RA and Madin SH: Experimental studies on a new feline virus. *Am J Vet Res* 21:551-556, 1960.

8. Davis EV and Beckenhauer WH: Studies on the safety and efficacy of an intranasal feline rhinotracheitis-calicivirus vaccine. *VM/SAC* 7:1405-1410, 1976.

9. Fastier LB: A new feline virus isolated in tissue culture. *Am J Vet Res* 18:382-389, 1957.

10. Gaskell RM and Wardley RC: Feline viral respiratory disease: a review with particular reference to the epizootiology and control. *J Small Anim Pract* 19:1-16, 1977.

11. Gillespie JH and Scott FW: Feline viral infections. *Adv Vet Sci* 17:163-200, 1973.

12. Hoover EA and Kahn DE: Lesions produced by feline picornaviruses of different virulence in pathogen-free cats. *Vet Path* 10:307-332, 1973.

13. Johnson RP: *Immunity to Feline Calicivirus in Kittens.* PhD Thesis, Univ of Guelph, Ontario, Canada, 1980.

14. Johnson RP and Povey RC: Transfer and decline of maternal antibody to feline calicivirus. *Can Vet J* 24:6-9, 1983.

15. Kahn DE and Gillespie JH: Feline viruses. X. Characterization of a newly isolated picornavirus causing interstitial pneumonia and ulcerative stomatitis in the domestic cat. *Cornell Vet* 60:669-683, 1970.

16. Kahn DE and Gillespie JH: Feline viruses: pathogenesis of picornavirus infection in the cat. *Am J Vet Res* 32:521-531, 1971.

17. Kahn DE et al: Induction of immunity to feline caliciviral disease. *Infect Immun* 11:1003-1009, 1975.

18. Kamizono M et al: Studies on cytopathogenic viruses isolated from cats with respiratory infections I. *Jpn J Vet Sci* 30:197-206, 1968.

19. Pedersen NC et al: A transient febrile limping syndrome of kittens caused by two different strains of feline calicivirus. *Feline Pract* 13(1):26-35, 1983.

20. Piercy SE and Prydie J: Feline influenza. *Vet Record* 75:86-89, 1963.

21. Povey RC: Viral respiratory disease. *Vet Record* 84:335-338, 1969.

22. Povey RC: Serological relationships among feline caliciviruses. *Infect Immun* 10:1307-1314, 1974.

23. Povey RC and Hale CJ: Experimental infections with feline calicivirus (picornaviruses) in specific-pathogen-free kittens. *J Comp Pathol* 84:245-256, 1974.

24. Povey RC and Ingersoll J: Cross-protection among feline caliciviruses. *Infect Immun* 11:877-885, 1975.

25. Povey RC and Johnson RH: Observations on the epidemiology and control of viral respiratory disease in cats. *J Small Anim Pract* 11:485-494, 1970.

26. Povey RC et al: Immunogenicity and safety of an inactivated vaccine for the prevention of rhinotracheitis, caliciviral disease, and panleukopenia in cats. *JAVMA* 177:347-350, 1980.

27. Prydie J: Viral disease of cats. *Vet Record* 79:729-738, 1986.

28. Sabine M and Hyne RHJ: Isolation of a feline picornavirus from cheetahs with conjunctivitis and glossitis. *Vet Record* 87:794-796, 1970.

29. Scott FW: Evaluation of a feline viral rhinotracheitis-feline calicivirus disease vaccine. *Am J Vet Res* 38:229-234, 1977.

30. Soergel ME et al: Amino acid composition of three immunological types of a calicivirus, San Miguel seal lion virus. *Virol* 72: 527-529, 1976.

31. Studdert MJ: Caliciviruses. Brief Review *Arch Virol* 58:157-191, 1978.

32. Studdert MJ et al: Viral diseases of the respiratory tract of cats: Isolation and properties of viruses tentatively classified as picornaviruses. *Am J Vet Res* 31:1723-1732, 1970.

33. Takahashi E et al: Studies on cytopathogenic viruses from cats with respiratory infections. II. Characterization of feline picornaviruses. *Jpn J Vet Sci* 33:81-87, 1971.

34. Torlone V: Agente citopatogeno isolato da una forma rinocongiuntivale del gatto. *Vet Ital* 11:915-928, 1980.

35. Walton TE: Comments on epizootiology of feline respiratory infections. *JAVMA* 158:960-963, 1971.

36. Walton TE and Gillespie JH: Feline viruses. VI. Survey of the incidence of feline pathogenic agents in normal and clinically ill cats. *Cornell Vet* 60:215-232, 1970.

37. Wardley RC: Feline calicivirus carrier state. A study of the host/virus relationship. *Arch Virol* 52:243-249, 1976.

38. Wardley RC and Povey RC: The pathology and sites of persistence associated with three different strains of feline calicivirus. *Res Vet Sci* 23:15-19, 1977.

39. Zwillenberg LO and Bürki F: On the capsid structure of some small feline and bovine RNA viruses. *Arch Ges Virusforsch* 19:373-384, 1966.

Additional References

40. Johnson RP: Feline calicivirus infection in kittens born by cats persistently infected with the virus. *Res Vet Sci* 37:114-119, 1984.

41. Tham KM and Studdert MJ: Antibody and cell-mediated immune responses to feline calicivirus following inactivated vaccine and challenge. *Zbl Vet Med B* 34:640-654, 1987.

Chapter 9

Feline Reovirus Infection

Etiologic Agent

Reoviruses were first isolated from a cat with suspected panleukopenia by Scott and co-workers.[6] The role of the reovirus in the disease was not determined, though panleukopenia virus was not present in the tissues. Subsequent isolates were made from cultures of cat tumors and kittens with panleukopenia virus-induced cerebellar hypoplasia.[1,3]

Feline reoviruses, like other mammalian reoviruses, contain double-stranded RNA. Virus particles are about 75 nm in diameter and made up of 92 prominent hollow-cored capsomeres.[6] Virus particles are seen mainly in the cytoplasm and always found in aggregates, either closely packed in well-organized paracrystalline arrays or in more diffuse reticular masses. Masses of virus particles are also seen within membrane-bound cytoplasmic vesicles.

All known mammalian reoviruses belong to 3 recognized serotypes: types 1, 2 and 3. Feline isolates belong to types 1 and 3.[6] Feline reovirus type 3 (FRV-3) has been isolated from the intestinal tract of a cat with severe enteritis and from the large intestines of 2 ataxic kittens.[1,6] Three isolates from feline tumor cell cultures were type 1 (FRV-1).[3]

Feline reovirus (FRV) grows well on cultured cat cells and produces a cytopathic effect characterized by slow cell death. Dying cells are ballooned, ragged and granular in appearance.[2] Complete destruction of the cell monolayer can take over a week and may take several passages to become readily apparent. Large, irregularly shaped intracytoplasmic inclusion bodies are stained blue by May-Grünwald-Giemsa stain.

Feline reoviruses are not highly species specific in cell culture, a characteristic of all known mammalian reovirus isolates. Feline reovirus type 3 replicates to titers of 1×10^5 TCID$_{50}$/0.1 ml in feline kidney cells, and to titers of one-tenth this in bovine kidney cells.[6] Feline reovirus type 1 grows in hamster, human, chimpanzee, cat and dog cells.[3,4]

Pathogenesis

Feline reoviruses have been isolated from cats as distant as New York and California. In a group of cats in Ithaca, New York, 50% had antibodies to FRV-3, while 71% had antibodies to FRV-1.[3,6] The source of virus in nature is unknown, but if feline reovirus infections resemble those of other mammals, many healthy cats probably harbor the virus in their respiratory and enteric passages. Fecal-oral transmission is the probable route for infection, given the ease with which FRV is isolated from rectal swabs and intestinal tissues.

Clinical Features

Very little information is known about the disease-causing potential of FRV in nature. Reoviruses of other animals typically inhabit both the respiratory and enteric tracts and may cause illness, contribute to disease or merely exist without inducing tissue damage. Two kittens inoculated with FRV-3 developed conjunctivitis and gingivitis, but were afebrile and had normal hemograms and appetite.[6] Of 28 kittens in contact with these 2 experimentally infected cats, 16 developed clinical illness 4-19 days after exposure. Of these 16 kittens, 14 had bilateral serous conjunctivitis and 5 developed mucopurulent conjunctivitis. The remaining 2 of these 16 kittens developed only mucopurulent conjunctivitis that persisted for 1-20 days. Hong inoculated 4 kittens soon after birth with FRV-1 and all died 2 days later after failing to nurse.[3] Cytoplasmic inclusion bodies were seen in the bronchiolar epithelium, but otherwise, no gross or microscopic lesions were present.

Pathologic Features

Except for conjunctivitis, no other diseases have been directly linked to FRV-1 or FRV-3. The presence of large, bluish intracytoplasmic inclusion bodies in hematoxylin and eosin- or May-Grünwald-Giemsa-stained tissue sections may be helpful in identifying lesions induced by FRV. A comparison of the viral inclusions of feline herpesvirus type 1, feline panleukopenia virus and FRV has been made by Scott and co-workers.[5]

Clinicopathologic Features

At present, the only reliable way to diagnose FRV infection is by virus isolation. Gillespie and Scott cautioned against discarding cultures too early.[2] The cytopathic effect is slow to develop and cultures may need 1-2 passages before being declared negative.

Treatment and Prevention

Similar to some other viral infections of cats, it is doubtful whether FRV is an important pathogen. For this reason, vaccines have not been developed and other control measures have been ignored.

Infection and Immunity

Neutralizing antibodies are produced in response to infection, but apparently do not prevent some cats from carrying the virus.[6] There is good evidence to suggest that FRV is either an innocent bystander or opportunist in feline diseases. It has been isolated from cats with chronic panleukopenia-like disease (FeLV or FIV infections?), cerebellar hypoplasia, and from cultures of primary feline leukemia virus-infected cells.[1,3,6]

Animal and Public Health Considerations

Though feline reoviruses are antigenically of the same serotypes as other mammalian isolates, there is no evidence they cause disease in people or other animals.

References

1. Csiza CK et al: Spontaneous feline ataxia. *Cornell Vet* 62:300-322, 1972.

2. Gillespie JH and Scott FW: Feline viral infections. *Adv Vet Sci Comp Med* 17:163-200, 1973.

3. Hong C: *Studies on a strain of reovirus Type 1 isolated from a feline leukemia cell culture.* MS Thesis, Cornell Univ, Ithaca, New York.

4. Scott FW: Feline reovirus. *JAVMA* 158:944-945, 1971.

5. Scott FW et al: Feline viruses. Isolation and characterization of feline panleukopenia virus in tissue culture and comparison of cytopathogenicity with feline picornavirus, herpesvirus, and reovirus. *Cornell Vet* 60:165-183, 1970.

6. Scott FW et al: Feline viruses: Isolation, characterization, and pathogenicity of a feline reovirus. *Am J Vet Res* 31:11-20, 1970.

Chapter 10

Feline Astrovirus Infection

Etiologic Agent

Astroviruses are small (30 nm in diameter) single-stranded RNA viruses.[4] They have been isolated from the feces of human infants, lambs, calves, dogs, poultry and cats with enteritis.[1,2,5,8-11] Astroviruses have also been associated with hepatitis in ducklings.[3] They most closely resemble picornaviruses and caliciviruses in genomic structure, but differ in polypeptide composition.[4] Astroviruses have been propagated in tissue culture, but require the addition of trypsin to the medium for optimum infectivity.[2,7]

Pathogenesis

Astroviruses of cats have been described in Europe and the United States.[2,5] Apparently healthy cats, or cats in the active or convalescent stages of infection, are probably the main reservoirs for the virus. The survival time of the virus in fomites or dried feces is unknown.

Astroviruses have been most frequently associated with transient gastroenteritis in young animals. The major route of infection is probably oral.[2] The mature epithelium of the small intestine is the main target for the virus.[9]

Astrovirus infection has been experimentally recreated in cats.[2] After 3 14-week-old kittens were fed a suspension of feces containing astrovirus from a naturally infected cat, an initial fever spike occurred on day 2 and a second around days 11 or 12. Each fever spike correlated with a mild episode of diarrhea. The kittens remained otherwise normal. Clinical signs probably result from transient disruption of the aborptive and secretory functions of the mature intestinal epithelium.

Clinical Features

Astrovirus was initially isolated from a 4-month-old kitten with transient diarrhea by Hoshino and co-workers.[5] A second isolation was made from a 1-year-old cat with more chronic diarrhea.[2] The main clinical sign in naturally infected cats has been loose, watery diarrhea lasting 2-8 weeks. Both of the naturally infected cats described in the literature were thin and partially anorectic, indicating that astrovirus infection may not have been their sole problem.[2,5] This assumption is supported by experimental transmission studies.[2] Experimentally infected cats had a very mild and transient diarrhea, and were not outwardly ill.

Pathologic Features

No descriptions are available of either naturally acquired or experimentally induced lesions. Lesions are likely to be very mild and probably resemble those of rotavirus and coronavirus infections.

Clinicopathologic Features

Astrovirus particles can be readily observed in diarrheic stools by electron microscopy using negatively stained grids.[2] The particles are found in clusters and have a characteristic 5- or 6-pointed star appearance to their surface (Fig 1).

Treatment and Prevention

Treatment of cats with astrovirus enteritis is purely symptomatic. If the diarrhea persists for more than 2 weeks, another cause of the diarrhea should be sought.

Infection and Immunity

Antibodies appear in the serum within a few days after infection and reach IFA titers of 1:80 to 1:160 by the fourth week.[11]

The mere presence of astrovirus particles in the feces of a cat with diarrhea should not be taken as positive proof for astrovirus-induced disease. Asymptomatic animals may shed the virus for prolonged periods.

Animal and Public Health Considerations

Feline astroviruses appear to be antigenically distinct from human astroviruses.[2] The relationship of feline astrovirus isolates to those of other animals and poultry is unknown, however.

References

1. Ashley CR et al: Astrovirus-associated gastroenteritis in children. J Clin Pathol 31:939-943, 1978.

2. Harbour DA et al: Natural and experimental astrovirus infection of cats. Vet Record 120:555-557, 1987.

3. Gough RE et al: Astrovirus-like particles associated with hepatitis in ducklings. Vet Record 114:279, 1984.

4. Herring AJ et al: Purification and characterization of ovine astrovirus. J Gen Virol 53:47-55, 1981.

5. Hoshino et al: Detection of astroviruses in feces of a cat with diarrhea. Arch Virol 70:373-376, 1981.

6. Kjeldsberg E and Hem A: Detection of astroviruses in gut contents of nude and normal mice. Arch Virol 84:135-140, 1985.

7. Lee TW and Kurtz JB: Serial propagation of astroviruses in tissue culture with the aid of trypsin. J Gen Virol 57:421-424, 1981.

8. McNaulty MS et al: Detection of astroviruses in turkey faeces by direct electron microscopy. Vet Record 106:561, 1980.

9. Snodgrass DR et al: Pathogenesis of diarrhoea caused by astrovirus infections. Arch Virol 60:217-226, 1979.

10. Williams FP: Astrovirus-like, coronavirus-like, and parvovirus-like particles detected in stools of beagle pups. Arch Virol 66:215-222, 1980.

11. Woode GN and Bridger JC: Isolation of small viruses resembling astroviruses and caliciviruses from acute enteritis of calves. J Med Microbiol 11:441-452, 1978.

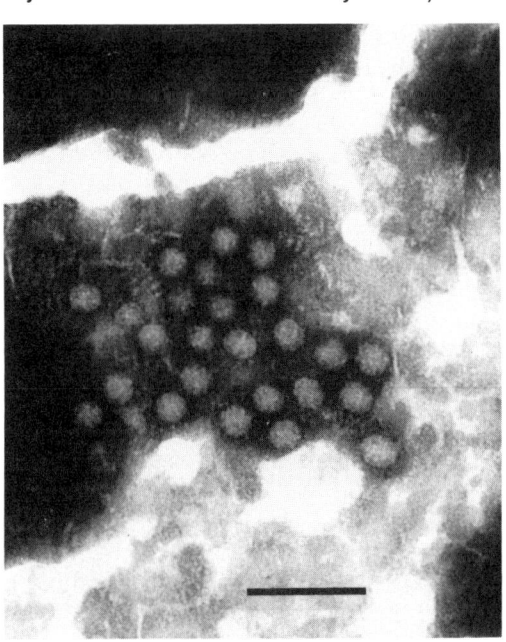

Fig 1. Electron micrograph of negatively stained astrovirus particles in the feces of a cat with diarrhea. Individual particles are about 30 nm in diameter. The bar at the bottom of the photograph is 100 nm long. (Courtesy of Dr. D.A. Harbour and Veterinary Record).

MISCELLANEOUS ENTERIC VIRUSES

Herbst and co-workers identified small 27-nm virus particles in the feces from one cat in a litter of 2-year-old cats with acute vomiting and diarrhea.[1] The particles had a thornapple appearance when negatively stained and examined by electron microscopy. The particles most closely resembled the Norwalk or Newbury (calici-like) agents isolated from similar disease syndromes in people and other animals. The Norwalk and Newbury agents are poorly defined viruses that are probably related to astroviruses and caliciviruses. The pathogenesis of the infection with these agents is virtually identical to that of astroviruses and rotaviruses.

Reference

1. Herbst W et al: 27-nm virus particles found in the faeces of a cat with vomiting and diarrhoea. *Zbl Vet Med B* 34:314-316, 1987.

Chapter 11

Feline Rotavirus Infection

Etiologic Agent

Snodgrass and co-workers observed typical rotavirus particles by electron microscopy in the feces of a 6-week-old kitten with diarrhea.[3] A similar case was subsequently described by Chrystie and associates.[1]

Rotaviruses are enveloped RNA viruses about 70 nm in diameter. The nucleocapsid has a spoke-like structure on negative stains and gives the virion the appearance of a wheel: hence the name rotavirus (rota = rotate) (Fig 1). Rotaviruses belong to the family Reoviridae. Rotaviruses have adapted themselves to almost all species, including people. Though some species crossover exists, isolates are most pathogenic for their species of origin.[5] Feline rotavirus isolates possess rotavirus group-specific antigens but differ from human isolates when tested with strain-specific antisera.[1]

Pathogenesis

Rotavirus infections are apparently worldwide and widespread in the cat population. Pearson and associates found that 23 of 50 cats in Louisiana were seropositive.[2] Similarly, Snodgrass and co-workers found 29 of 94 English cats with rotavirus antibodies in their serum.[3] Many normal cats presumably harbor and shed low levels of rotavirus in their feces. Virus may also be voided into the environment by sick animals and serve as a source of infection later. Bovine rotavirus can survive up to 9 months in dried feces at room temperature; it is reasonable to assume that rotaviruses from other species can do likewise.[4]

Kittens appear to be infected with rotaviruses early in life but disease signs usually are absent or minimal. Snodgrass and co-workers induced transient diarrhea in 2 3-day-old kittens with fecal extracts.[3] One of these neonatal kittens was colostrum deprived, while the other was not.

Fig 1. Electron micrograph of negatively stained rotavirus particles in the feces of a pig with acute diarrhea. The particles are identical to rotaviruses seen in other species, including cats. Note the spoke-like projections from the virion's periphery (arrow). The name "rota-" is derived from rotate or wheel. The bar at the bottom of the photograph is 100 nm long. (Courtesy of Dr. Anthony E. Castro, University of California, Davis)

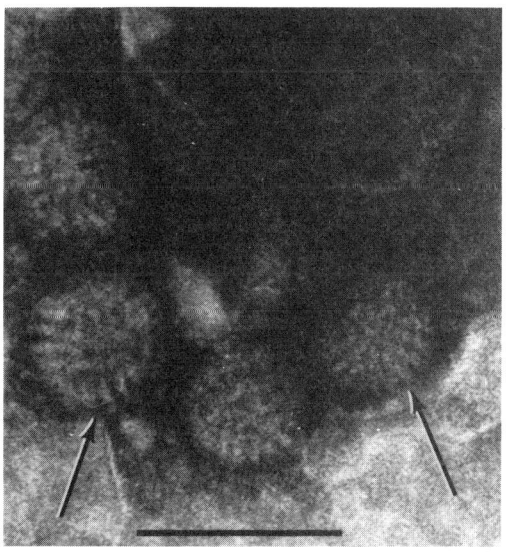

Though enteritis was more severe in the colostrum-deprived kitten, both sur-vived after a 1- or 2-day bout of relatively insignificant illness. In contrast, Woode found that calves with low maternal globulin levels developed pronounced enteritis, while calves with high globulin levels did not become ill.[4] Therefore, it seems that rotavirus infection is less severe in carnivores than in herbivores.

Clinical Features

Signs of rotavirus enteritis in cats are relatively mild and appear 2-6 days postinfection.[1,3] Diarrhea lasting for 1-2 days is the most common sign. Affected cats are not usually febrile, anorectic or dehydrated.

Pathologic Features

Usually no gross abnormalities are found in the intestinal tract. Virus can be found by indirect fluorescent antibody (IFA) staining and electron microscopy in epithelial cells of the jejunum and ileum. Histopathologic changes are mild and include swelling of intestinal villi with some infiltration of polymorphonuclear neutrophils and macrophages.[1]

Clinicopathologic Features

Rotavirus can be detected in cat stools by electron microscopy or enzyme-linked immunosorbent assays (ELISA) utilizing rotavirus group-specific antisera.

Treatment and Prevention

Cats seldom need treatment for rotavirus enteritis. If diarrhea is severe, oral food and water should be withheld for 24-48 hours and a balanced electrolyte solution given parenterally. Because of the mild nature of rotavirus infection in cats, there has been no impetus to develop vaccines or to devise husbandry procedures to limit viral spread.

Animal and Public Health Considerations

As far as is known, feline rotavirus is only pathogenic to cats. Some animal rotavirus species occasionally cause mild enteritis in people. However, Chrystie and associates found no relationship between the group-specific antigens of human and feline isolates.[1] This suggests that feline rotaviruses are probably not human pathogens.

References

1. Chrystie IL et al: Rotavirus infection in a domestic cat. Vet Record 105:404-405, 1979.

2. Pearson NJ et al: Prevalence of rotaviral antibodies in Louisiana cattle, dogs, and cats detected by an indirect fluorescent antibody test. Proc 23rd Ann Mtg Am Assn Vet Lab Diag, 1980. pp 129-133.

3. Snodgrass DR et al: A rotavirus from kittens. Vet Record 104:222-223, 1979.

4. Woode GN: Epizootiology of bovine rotavirus infection. Vet Record 103:44-56, 1978.

5. Woode GN et al: Studies on cross-protection induced in calves by rotavirus of calves, children and foals. Vet Record 103:32-34, 1978.

Chapter 12

Feline Syncytium-Forming Virus Infection

Etiologic Agent

Feline syncytium-forming virus (FeSFV) was first isolated from domestic cats in 1969.[14,23] These and subsequent isolates were obtained from various cat tumors.[10,13,16,28] The virus has also been isolated from a cat with feline infectious peritonitis, from cats with respiratory disease, and from both healthy and diseased cats in a study of experimentally induced cystitis.[6,15,19,27] Though FeSFV was recovered from tissues of many diseased cats, it was not thought to be involved in any of the disease processes. Feline syncytium-forming virus has also been isolated from many normal cats.[1,5,9,10,13,19,22,23]

The FeSFV is an enveloped, RNA-containing virus of the family Retroviridae, subfamily Spumavirinae.[7] The virus has also been called feline syncytial virus, feline foamy virus and feline syncytia-forming virus. It is included in an unnamed genus of serologically distinct bovine, hamster, simian and human syncytial viruses. In common with all retroviruses, FeSFV possesses the RNA-dependent DNA-polymerase (reverse transcriptase) enzyme, and infectious proviral DNA is found in infected cells.[2-4,20]

FeSFV is 100 nm in diameter, with a central core about 45 nm in diameter; its envelope has many short surface spikes (Fig 1). As in oncornaviruses, virus buds from the plasma membrane. Infected cells often fuse with each other, forming large, multinucleated syncytia (Fig 1).[4,11] Though FeSFV has been considered nononcogenic, it has reportedly caused malignant transformation of kidney cells *in vitro*.[16] Feline syncytium-forming virus has one major and several minor serotypes.[11]

Pathogenesis

Feline syncytium-forming virus can be isolated from virtually any tissue of an in-

Fig 1A. Mature feline syncytium-forming virus particles (arrows). Virions have a round nucleoid, and the envelope is studded with peplomer-like projections. (Courtesy of Dr. Robert Munn, University of California, Davis)

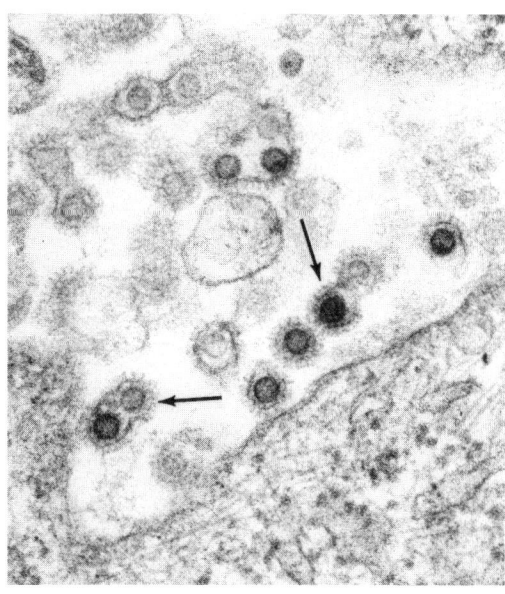

fected cat. The typical viral cytopathic effect is manifested only after 1-4 passages in tissue culture. This is a great nuisance to investigators who work with primary feline cell cultures. Within the body, virus is only found in a complete form in oropharyngeal secretions and cannot be identified by electron microscopy in other tissues or blood. Virus is not present in plasma or the red cell pack of whole blood. However, the buffy coat from peripheral blood is a rich source of infectious material.[21,26] The viral genome apparently exists in WBCs, even though virus replication is somehow suppressed *in vivo*. In this respect, FeSFV infection of cats resembles bovine leukemia virus infection.[17] Cultivation of blood cells with fetal cat cells *in vitro* appears to allow viral expression. Though the virus is latent in the blood and other tissues, cells within the oropharynx seem to actively produce intact virus, as evidenced by the ease of virus isolation from saliva.[5,13,26]

Any cat with serum antibodies to the virus, as detected by virus neutralization, immunodiffusion or immunofluorescence, is infected.[8,13,18,22] The incidence of FeSFV infection varies greatly with the geographic area and environment. The rate of infection in the general cat population in California rises dramatically after 1 year of age and reaches 50% or more by 3-4 years of age.[21] In New York City, however, the peak infection rate is nearer 25%. The incidence of FeSFV infection in apparently healthy cats is about 4% in Tokyo and 0-6% in Australia.[5,18,24] Unlike almost all other infectious diseases of cats, FeSFV infection does not occur at a higher rate among cats kept in close confinement (eg, in catteries). In a survey from California, 55 of 532 (9.4%) cattery cats of all ages were infected, as compared to 477 of 1398 (34.1%) in a random population of noncattery cats.[21]

Cats are infected by several routes. Recent studies suggest that 25-50% or more of kittens born to FeSFV-infected queens are infected *in utero*.[8,21] Why some fetuses within the same litter are spared is not understood. Infected and uninfected kittens can be distinguished at birth by culturing the buffy coat of their blood.[21] In addition, uninfected siblings lose their maternal precipitating antibodies at 2-4 weeks of age and their immunofluorescent antibody (IFA) titers by 6-8 weeks of age.[8,21] In contrast, maternal antibody titers in infected kittens drop during this same period, but rise after 8-10 weeks.[21] *In-utero* infection may occur by passage of maternal leukocytes into the fetus. Gillespie and Scott suggested that infection could occur postpartum by newborn kittens nursing an infected queen.[9] However, this route of exposure has not led to infection in experimental situations.[21]

Though *in-utero* exposure is one means of infection, it is apparently not the most important. Serologic studies in California demonstrate a progressive rise in infection rate from less than 10% at 1 year of age to over 60-70% at 8 years of age.[21] The reason for this dramatic rise in acquired infections has not been determined. Though virus is shed in high levels from the oropharynx, controlled cat-to-cat contact does not often lead to infection. In 1 experiment, infected and uninfected cats were deliberately

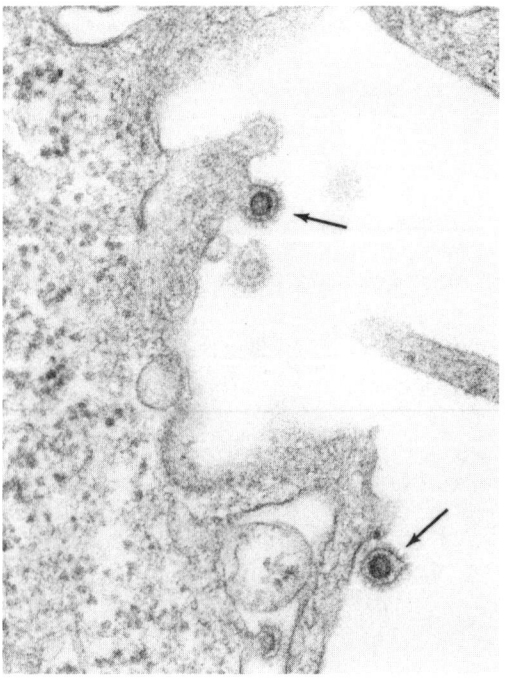

Fig 1B. Similar to other retroviruses, the virus buds from the cell's surface membrane, except that the nucleoid is fully formed before the bud is released (arrows). (Courtesy of Dr. Robert Munn, University of California, Davis)

housed together for 6 months to 3 years.[21] Only 1 of 5 susceptible cats became infected, and then only after being in contact with infected cats for 2 years. Infected cats also coexist with uninfected cats in catteries without any cat-to-cat spread of the virus.[21] Fleas are a problem in many catteries but do not seem to be vectors of the infection.

Clues to the natural mode of FeSFV transmission may be found in comparing confined cattery cats with free-roaming cats. The incidence of cat bites is much lower in cats kept in catteries. Because virus is present in oral secretions and is infectious mainly by parenteral inoculation, bites may be a means of transmission. Indeed, experimental bites from carrier to susceptible cats are about 50% successful in transferring the infection after a single exposure.[21] However, it does not seem likely this is the sole explanation for the rapid infection rate seen in free-roaming cats. Outdoor cats have a greater exposure to rodents and birds and are bitten by insects more frequently.

Feline syncytium-forming virus cannot be readily transmitted by the oral route. The disease is most easily reproduced by parenteral inoculation of cats with infectious tissue or tissue culture-propagated virus. Serum antibodies to FeSFV appear about 3 weeks after inoculation: virus can then be isolated by cultivating buffy-coat leukocytes and platelets with fetal cat cells, or by exposing cells to oropharyngeal secretions. Following parenteral inoculation, all cats become infected for life.

Clinical Features

Clinical signs of illness do not develop with experimental infection and hemograms have remained normal during a 3-year observation period.[8,10,14,16,21,22] In an attempt to statistically link latent FeSFV infection with specific diseases, the incidence of FeSFV infection in healthy and ill cats in general was compared with the incidence of infection in cats with specific disorders.[21] The incidence of FeSFV infection in over 200 randomly selected ill cats (without cancer) at the teaching hospital of the University of California was not significantly different from that in healthy age-matched cats in the same population. A study of about 100 cats from the New York City area also showed no relationship between illness in general and chronic FeSFV infection. Therefore, it can be concluded that FeSFV infection is not an important cause of noncancerous illnesses.

Limited studies have been done to see whether specific diseases were related to a higher incidence of FeSFV infection than could be accounted for by chance. Since FeSFV is a retrovirus and is present as a chronic infection, the incidence of cancer in FeSFV-infected cats was particularly interesting. In the California cat population, cats with myeloproliferative disease had a significantly higher ($P \leq .001$) incidence of FeSFV infection than age-matched healthy cats.[21] This increased incidence could not be accounted for by a relationship between feline leukemia virus (FeLV) and FeSFV infections. However, there was no significant relationship between FeSFV infection and incidence of lymphosarcoma. Further, no

Fig 2A. Cat in the initial stages of the periosteal proliferative (Reiter's) form of chronic progressive polyarthritis. The cat is febrile and has swelling, edema and erythema of tissues surrounding the carpal joints.

Fig 2B. The tarsal joints are grossly inflamed, to the extent that overlying skin is indurated. Affected joints are very painful on palpation.

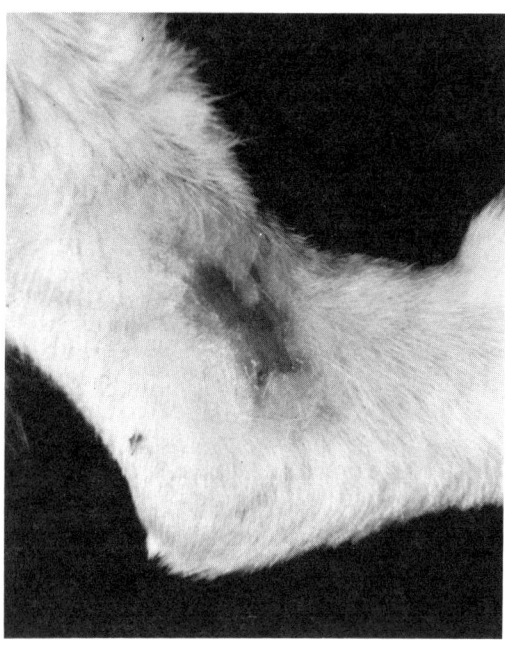

significant relationship was observed between FeSFV infection and a composite group of 73 nonFeLV-associated carcinomas and sarcomas.

There is a statistical link between FeSFV and feline immunodeficiency virus (FIV) infections of cats (see chapter 15).[29] Both viruses are spread in the same manner and involve identical risk groups. The recent discovery of FIV may invalidate some past studies of FeSFV, therefore. Feline immunodeficiency virus induces myeloproliferative disorders in a small proportion of experimentally and naturally infected cats. The apparent statistical relationship between FeSFV and myeloproliferative disease may have merely reflected a second, and at the time unknown, FIV infection.

In a recent report, FeSFV infection was statistically linked to chronic progressive polyarthritis of cats.[22] This condition occurs predominately in males 2.5-4.5 years of age, either as a periosteal proliferative polyarthritis similar to Reiter's arthritis of people or as a more insidious deforming condition resembling human and canine rheumatoid arthritis (Figs 2,3). In the initial series of cats with chronic progressive polyarthritis, all were infected with FeSFV and one-fifth were infected with FeLV. Both infections occur much more commonly with this arthritis than in age- and sex-matched normal cats from the same population. However, the disease has not been reproduced in male cats inoculated with either or both viruses. Chronic progressive polyarthritis possibly occurs only in certain genetically predisposed male cats infected with FeSFV. Feline leukemia virus may play a direct role in FeSFV infection pathogenesis or may potentiate FeSFV infection by altering normal immune reactions of the host.

A cat with chronic progressive polyarthritis was recently found to be infected with both FIV and FeSFV. As described above, these 2 infections frequently appear together in some animals. Lentiviruses, such as FIV, can cause arthritis in other species. This finding further complicates the interpretation of past studies on the

Fig 3. A cat with the Reiter's form of chronic progressive polyarthritis for over a year. The intense fever and joint swelling of the initial phase have subsided.

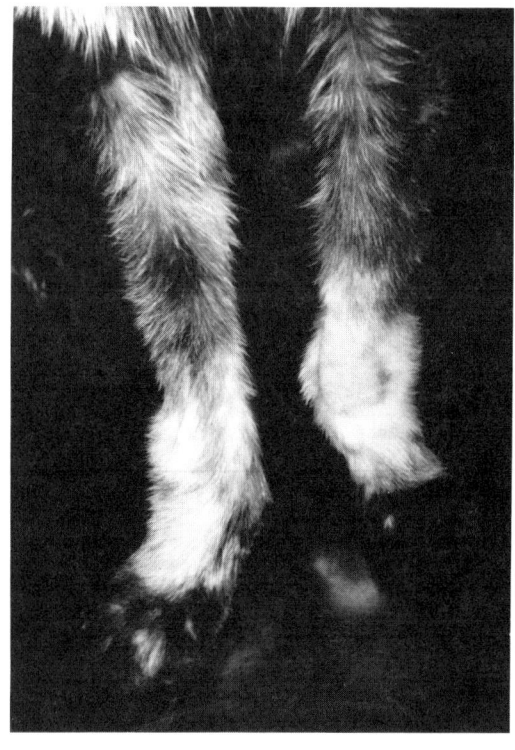

etiology of feline chronic progressive polyarthritis.

Clinicopathologic Features

The simplest method to detect FeSFV-infected cats is to measure serum antibodies. Infected cats have positive virus-neutralizing, immunoprecipitating and IFA assays.[8,9,21] Antibody testing will fail to pick up a small proportion of infected cats. These can only be detected by culturing blood or saliva.

Treatment and Prevention

Lack of a definitive correlation between infection and disease makes prophylaxis and control unnecessary.

Infection and Immunity

Both latent and active FeSFV infections are present in the body at the same time. Though large amounts are shed from the oropharynx, infectious virus cannot be directly recovered from other tissues. Latent virus is present in leukocytes of the blood and possibly other tissues as well. Virus in the leukocytes coexists with virus-neutralizing serum antibodies.

Coexistence of latent viral infection and high titers of virus-neutralizing antibody is a feature of certain viruses, including bovine leukemia virus, herpesvirus and cytomegalovirus infections. It is also consistent with syncytium-forming virus infections in other species. The ability of syncytial viruses to spread cell to cell in the presence of antibodies may result from failure of antibodies and complement to lyse infected cells, as well as a relative viral resistance to interferon.[12]

Animal and Public Health Considerations

There is no evidence that FeSFV is a hazard to people or animals other than cats.

References

1. Chappuis G and Tektoff J: Isolement et identification du virus syncytial félin. *Ann Microbiol* 125A:371-386, 1974.

2. Chiswell DJ and Pringle CR: Infectious DNA from cells infected with feline syncytium-forming virus (Spumavirinae). *J Gen Virol* 36:551-555, 1977.

3. Chiswell DJ and Pringle CR: Feline syncytium-forming virus proviral DNA: Time of synthesis and relationship to the host cell genome. *Virol* 90:344-350, 1978.

4. Chiswell DJ and Pringle CR: Feline syncytium-forming virus: Identification of a virion-associated reverse transcriptase and electron microscopical observations of infected cells. *J Gen Virol* 43:429-434, 1979.

5. Ellis TM et al: Isolation of feline syncytia-forming virus from oropharyngeal swabs of cats. *Aust Vet J* 55:202-203, 1979.

6. Fabricant CG et al: Feline viruses. XI. Isolation of a virus similar to myxovirus from cats in which urolithiasis was experimentally induced. *Cornell Vet* 59:667-672, 1969.

7. Fenner F: Classification and nomenclature of viruses. Second report of the International Committee of Taxonomy of Viruses. *Intervirol* 7:1-115, 1976.

8. Gaskin JM and Gillespie JH: Detection of feline syncytia-forming virus carrier state with a microimmunodiffusion test. *Am J Vet Res* 34:245-247, 1973.

9. Gillespie JH and Scott FW: Feline viral infections. *Adv Vet Sci Comp Med* 17:163-200, 1973.

10. Hackett AJ et al: Biological properties of a syncytia-forming agent isolated from domestic cats (feline syncytia-forming virus). *Proc Soc Exp Biol* 135:899-904, 1970.

11. Hackett AJ and Manning JS: Comments on feline syncytia-forming virus. *JAVMA* 158:748-754, 1971.

12. Hooks JJ et al: Viral spread in the presence of neutralizing antibody: Mechanisms of persistence in foamy virus infection. *Infect Immun* 14:1172-1178, 1976.

13. Jarrett O et al: Infection by feline syncytium forming virus in Britain. *Vet Record* 94:200-201, 1974.

14. Kasza L et al: Isolation of a virus from a cat sarcoma in an established canine melanoma cell line. *Res Vet Sci* 10.216-218, 1969.

15. Low RI et al: Report on the isolation of an agent from cell cultures of kidneys from domestic cats. *Vet Record* 88:557-559, 1971.

16. McKissick GE and Lamont PH: Characteristics of a virus isolated from a feline fibrosarcoma. *J Virol* 5:247-257, 1970.

17. Miller JM et al: Virus-like particles in phytohemagglutinin-stimulated lymphocyte cultures with reference to bovine lymphosarcoma. *J Natl Cancer Inst* 43:1297-1306, 1969.

18. Mochizuki M et al: Studies on cytopathogenic viruses from cats with respiratory infections. III. Isolation and certain properties of feline herpes viruses. *Jpn J Vet Sci* 39:27-37, 1977.

19. Mochizuki M and Konishi S: Feline syncytial virus spontaneously detected in feline cell cultures. *Jpn J Vet Sci* 41:351-362, 1979.

20. Parks WP and Todaro GJ: Biological properties of syncytium-forming ("foamy") viruses. *Virol* 47:673-683, 1972.

21. Pedersen NC, in Holzworth J: *Diseases of the Cat*. Saunders, Philadelphia, 1987. pp 268-272.

22. Pedersen NC et al: Feline chronic progressive polyarthritis. *Am J Vet Res* 41:522-535, 1980.

23. Riggs JL et al: Syncytium-forming agent isolated from domestic cats. *Nature* 222:1190-1191, 1969.

24. Sabine M and Love DN: Feline "foamy" viruses: Incidence in Australia. *Arch Ges Virusforsch* 43:397-400, 1973.

25. Scott FW: Feline syncytial virus. *JAVMA* 158:946-948, 1971.

26. Shroyer ER and Shalaby MR: Isolation of feline syncytia-forming virus from oropharyngeal swab samples and buffy coat cells. *Am J Vet Res* 39:555-560, 1978.

27. Takahaski E et al: Studies on cyto-pathogenic viruses isolated from cats with respiratory infections. II. Characterization of feline picornaviruses. *Jpn J Vet Sci* 33:81-87, 1971.

28. Whitman JE Jr et al: An unusual case of feline leukemia and an associated syncytium-forming virus. *Am J Vet Res* 36:873-880, 1975.

29. Yamamoto JK et al: Epidemiologic and clinical aspects of feline immunodeficiency virus (FIV) infection in cats from the continental United States and Canada and possible mode of transmission. *JAVMA*: In press, 1988.

Chapter 13

Feline Leukemia Virus Infection

Etiologic Agent

Jarrett and co-workers first identified retrovirus particles in a cat from a household that had lost several animals to lymphosarcoma.[54] The putative leukemia virus was first isolated from feline plasma by Kawakami and associates.[57] Transmission of lymphocytic leukemia with feline leukemia virus (FeLV) was first reported by Rickard and co-workers.[87] The similarities of feline retrovirus infections to murine and avian leukemia virus infections were initially apparent. During the next 5 years, the emphasis of FeLV research was on oncogenesis.[33] In 1973, an indirect fluorescent antibody (IFA) test was developed to accurately detect viremia in infected cats.[35] The test was rapidly applied to clinical use, mainly as a diagnostic procedure for lymphosarcoma. As a result of clinical testing, FeLV was determined to be: horizontally spread from cat to cat; associated with a great many diseases other than lymphosarcoma; and carried and shed by many apparently healthy cats for long periods before illness developed.[10,14,30,34,37]

Feline leukemia virus belongs to the family Retroviridae, genus *Oncornavirus* C and is thought to have evolved from murine leukemia virus several million years ago.[4,18] It is an enveloped virus about 110 nm in diameter and buds from the plasma membrane in a characteristic manner (Fig 1).[29] Feline leukemia virus has a buoyant density of about 1.16 g/ml in sucrose. The FeLV genome codes for 3 groups of proteins: group-specific antigens (gag); reverse transcriptase or RNA-dependent DNA polymerase (pol); and envelope (env) proteins.[2,9,29] The gag antigens make up the viral core and are composed of 10,000-, 12,000-, 15,000- and 27,000-dalton proteins (p10, p12, p15, p27).[5] Reverse transcriptase has a molecular weight about 70,000 daltons.[5] The virus envelope is made up of a 70,000-dalton major glycoprotein (gp70) that forms the surface projections and a 15,000-dalton transmembrane anchoring protein (p15E).[5] The envelope protein determines the subgroup specificity and *in vitro* host-cell range of the virus.[50]

Fig 1A. Mature FeLV particles in FeLV-infected cells (arrows). The FeLV virion has a rounded nucleoid and an envelope studded with short spikes. (Courtesy of Dr. Robert Munn, University of California, Davis)

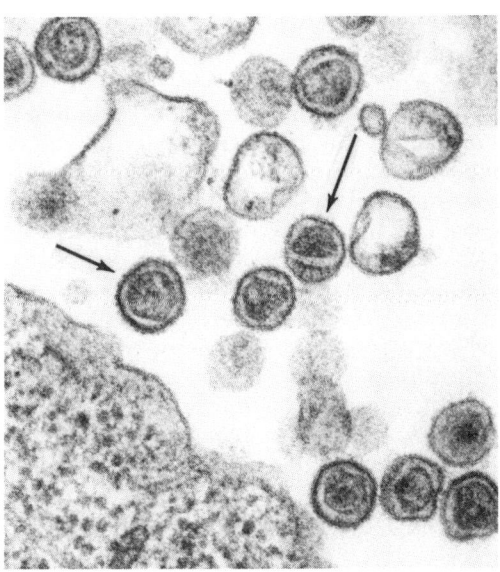

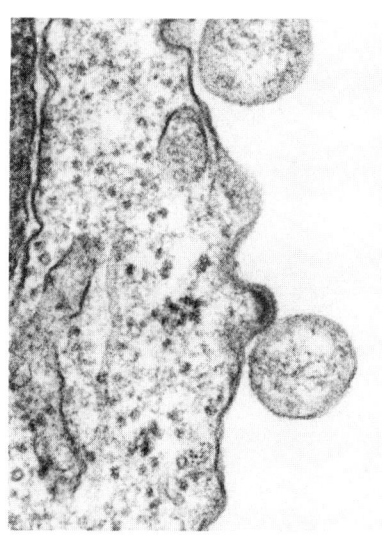

Fig 1B. The nucleoid is not completely developed by the time particles bud off the cell membrane. Uranyl acetate and lead citrate stain, 100,000X. (Courtesy of Dr. Robert Munn, University of California, Davis)

Feline leukemia virus is very labile outside the cat.[21] It loses its infectivity within minutes or hours at room temperature. Some strains even lose considerable infectivity when stored at -70 C. Feline leukemia virus is destroyed within minutes at 56 C and is sensitive to most disinfectants.

According to in-vitro host-range studies, FeLV isolates can be divided into 3 subgroups (A, B and C) or subgroup combinations.[29,95] Subgroup B occurs almost always with subgroup A in nature, while subgroup A can occur alone. Over 90% of FeLV isolates are subgroup A or AB; subgroup C is very uncommon.[49] Subgroup A FeLV does not grow in cells from other species; subgroup B grows in cat, dog, mink, hamster, pig, cattle, monkey and human cells, but not in mouse, rat or guinea pig cells; subgroup C grows in cat, dog, mink, guinea pig, cattle and human cells, but not in mouse, rat, hamster, pig or monkey cells.[96] Subgroup specificity can also be determined by an infectivity interference assay using purified stocks of known subgroup A, B, or C envelope pseudotypes of feline sarcoma virus.[95] Though FeLV infects a wide range of host cells in vitro, it is infectious only to domestic and some nondomestic (exotic) cats in vivo.

Subgroup differences cannot be clearly defined by serologic tests.[94] Immune sera from cats or goats infected with FeLV isolates of subgroups A, B and C were tested against various field isolates and the results compared to interference typing. Subgroup A isolates were serologically monotypic, but there was considerable antigenic variation in subgroup-B and -C isolates. Antiserum to subgroup A isolates cross-reacted weakly with a standard subgroup-C isolate. Four subgroup-B isolates were identical to each other, but were unrelated to subgroup-A or a fifth subgroup-B isolate. The 4 related subgroup-B strains cross-reacted with a standard subgroup-C isolate. Within subgroup C, 1 isolate was identical to the reference strain, but 2 other isolates were similar to subgroup-A strains. The extensive cross-reactivity to subgroup-A isolates has led to speculation that subgroup A is prototypic.[94]

The pathogenicity of various FeLV isolates appears to vary somewhat from one subgroup to another.[47] When equal amounts of various subgroups are given under identical conditions, viremia from subgroup A always appears sooner than viremia from subgroup B.[47,49] Subgroup-A isolates are also more efficiently transmitted under natural conditions. In fact, subgroup B is not readily transmitted by infected cats.[49] Infectivity of subgroups B and C seems enhanced by subgroup A in both natural and experimental infections. If kittens are infected with a mixture of subgroups A, B and C, subgroup-A viremia appears first, followed by viremia from subgroup C and much later by subgroup B. The subgroup type may also affect age resistance, which occurs most dramatically for subgroup C. Subgroup C virus produces persistent viremia in most neonatal cats, but infection is transient in most kittens inoculated after 2 weeks of age.[47,49]

Many FeLV strains exist in nature. In fact, most isolates have slight to pronounced genetic and structural differences.[93] Slight differences in strains usually do not make a large difference in pathogenicity.[47,49] There are exceptions, however. For instance, subgroup-C isolates have a greater tendency to induce aplastic anemia in experimentally infected cats.[43,47,49] The Rickard or F422 strain is a subgroup AB that has a strong tendency to induce thymic lymphosarcomas when injected into neonatal cats.[87] The Kawakami-Theilen strain of FeLV, a mixture of subgroups A, B and C, induces fatal anemia in newborn kittens but virtually no illness in older kittens.[44,80]

Pathogenesis

Feline leukemia virus infects domestic cats throughout the world. Wild cats do not harbor the infection but can be infected when exposed to domestic cats. The incidence of infection is directly related to population density; rural cats have the lowest infection rate and cattery or multiple-cat household cats have the highest.[16,88] Urban areas, where many cats live in apartments, condominiums and tenement houses, also may have a high incidence of infection.[13] Cats in most urban areas are still fairly free roaming, which leads to a high degree of contact between infected and susceptible animals. Cats that live their life entirely within high-rise apartments, as in New York City, have a very low incidence of infection.[34]

Feline leukemia virus is carried and shed by healthy, subclinically ill or chronically ill cats. In catteries with enzootic FeLV infection, about one-third of the cats are active carriers and shedders.[34,37] The incidence of active carriers in rural areas may be <1%, while in most urban areas the incidence is 2-6% or more.[47,88] Infected cats have very high levels of virus in their blood and shed almost equal amounts in their saliva.[22,41] Smaller amounts of virus are also found in urine and feces.[41] Tears contain levels of virus about equal to blood levels.[38]

There are 2 basic routes of infection: horizontal via excretions from infected to susceptible cats; and *in utero* from infected queens to their fetuses.[29,37] Though *in utero* infection results in fetal or neonatal death in 80% of affected cats, 20% of kittens born to FeLV-infected queens may carry this infection into later life.[75]

Queens that have recovered from FeLV infection usually provide their offspring with maternal antibodies that protect them against infection in the first 12 weeks or so of life.[51] Queens in the postviremic latent phase of infection occasionally infect 1 or more kittens *in utero*, probably by leukocytes that cross the placenta.[77] One FeLV-immune queen gave birth to 3 kittens. One kitten was infected and horizontally infected its littermates when they lost their maternal immunity.[77]

Cats are naturally exposed as they venture outdoors. In Glasgow, Scotland, for instance, the infection rate rises progressively with time, and by 3-8 years of age, most cats have been exposed to the virus.[88] Active FeLV infections are uncommon in cats 10 years or older. Cats usually contract the infection early in life and recover or die before they reach later life.

Horizontal spread of FeLV infection requires prolonged intimate contact between cats. The reasons for this are varied but involve the low stability of the virus in nature, relatively large dose of virus required to infect by the oronasal route, and age resistance. Prolonged intimate exposure allows virus spread by mutual grooming and sharing of litter pans. A simple wire partition between cats is often sufficient to prevent cross infections if there is no physical contact between cats or their excretions. Bite wounds are a much more efficient mode of transmission because a large amount of virus can be injected directly into the body. Infection can also be spread via blood transfusions and reuse of dirty instruments for sequential surgeries.

Neonatal kittens are most susceptible to infections, but resistance develops rapidly with age.[44] Following infection, 70-100% of neonates become persistently viremic for life. Kittens 8-12 weeks of age are much more resistant, and only 30-50% become persistently viremic following exposure.[79] Less than 10-20% of adolescent or adult cats become persistently viremic, and then only after exposure lasting as long as 1.5 years.[25] Age resistance can be virtually abolished by pretreating older cats with corticosteroids at the time of infection.[90]

Following oral or oronasal instillation, the virus first replicates in regional lymphoid tissue of the oropharynx.[89,91] Virus can be detected within several days in a few circulating mononuclear cells in the blood. These cells apparently carry virus to the target organs in other areas of the body, such as the spleen, lymph nodes, and epithelium of the intestine, bladder and salivary glands. About the same time that virus appears in secretion or excretions from these organs, it also reaches cells in the bone marrow and appears in peripheral blood leukocytes and platelets. Viremia in weanling kittens seldom occurs sooner than 2-4 weeks after infection.[48,79]

Viremia and virus shedding persists for less than 1-16 weeks in 70-90% or more of cats.[79] When viremia disappears, however, it usually does so in the first few days or weeks. Cats that remain viremic after 16 weeks usually remain persistently viremic for life, though on occasion viremia disappears after many months or years.

Virus shedding usually stops when viremia disappears.[48] In a few instances, virus continues to be shed in tears, urine, milk or saliva for several weeks or more following cessation of viremia.[48,74,122] Eventually, however, even this virus shedding ceases. Following recovery from viremia, virus persists as a latent infection in the bone marrow.[67,77,92] After 6 months, however, even latent infections become hard to demonstrate.[77] Therefore, latency appears to be merely an extension of the postviremia recovery process.

Latent infections can sometimes be converted to active infections by giving the cat glucocorticoids during the immediate postviremic period.[77,83,92] However, activation is very strain dependent, and latent infections with most field strains are activated only with difficulty.[77] Aviremic queens bred in the postrecovery period of FeLV-related disease sometimes give birth to kittens that are actively infected.[77] Reactivation of latent infections can occur spontaneously up to 6-8 months following recovery in ≤10% of recovered cats.[77]

Most of the mortality resulting from FeLV infection occurs in persistently viremic cats.[69] Disorders associated with the persistently viremic state can be divided into several categories: *in-utero* and neonatal deaths of kittens; lymphoid and myeloid neoplasms; aplastic or hypoplastic anemia; neuropathies; quasi-neoplastic syndromes; secondary or opportunistic infections due to acquired immunodeficiency; and immunologic disorders. About one-half to two-thirds of persistently viremic cats die of lymphoid or myeloid neoplasms and aplastic or hypoplastic anemia.

The pathogenesis of myeloid and lymphoid neoplasms in FeLV-infected cats is not fully understood. The virus does not contain oncogenes (cell-differentiation genes) and does not induce acute tumors *in vivo* or malignant cell transformation *in vitro* (see Chapter 14). The tumorigenic potential of FeLV appears to be related in some way to the repeated insertion and reinsertion of proviral DNA into random sites of the host's chromosomes. Infectious virus may contain new RNA due to rearrangements between viral and host DNA within the nucleus. When such viruses are reinserted back into host DNA of other cells through infection, the newly acquired genes are randomly distributed throughout the host's genome. This repositioning of host and viral genes somehow leads to tumorigenesis.

Though insertion of FeLV genes, and the rescue and repositioning of host genes, are thought to be a random process occurring throughout the host genome, the interaction does have some specificity. Many T-cell leukemias in FeLV-infected cats have a characteristic rearrangement of viral genes and the cellular *myc*-gene.[110,114,115,125,129] In some tumors, variant FeLV that is a recombinant of viral and cellular *myc*-genes can be isolated from the tumors.[110,129] Such variants are genomically truncated and replication defective, similar to FeSV (see Chapter 14). They require a replication-competent FeLV helper infection to obtain an infectious envelope. FeLV variants containing the *myc*-oncogene are not integrated into postnatal cat cells *in vitro* and do not cause acute malignancies *in vitro* or *in vivo*.[110] They may cause clonal T-cell tumors in a high percentage of kittens after a shorter-than-normal latent period, however.[129] Some isolates transform embryonic cat cells *in vitro*, suggesting that differentiation events occurring during embryogenesis in some way favor integration of the defective viral genome into host chromosomes.[110]

The neoplastic effect of FeLV appears to be a factor of the repeated and random integration and reintegration of viral genes into chromosomes, and the repositioning or activation of specific host genes. As such, all strains of FeLV should be equally efficient as carcinogens. This does not appear to be the case, however. The helper FeLVs of all FeSV strains belong to subgroup B. The Rickard strain of FeLV induces T-cell leukemias in a disproportionately high percentage of cats.[87] Slight differences in viral structure obviously have a great influence on the tumorigenicity of the isolate.

If virus-host gene interactions are related to oncogenesis, it stands to reason that all FeLV-infected cats, regardless of whether they have completely recovered or become persistently viremic, would have an increased incidence of cancer. Persistently viremic cats would be at greatest risk because they have the most virus-host gene interactions. This expectation has actually been observed; lymphomas occur 50 times more frequently in persistently viremic cats than in FeLV-recovered cats.[60] The fact that tumors can appear months or years after recovery from FeLV infection indicates that vestigial viral genes in the chromosomes may interact with host oncogenes at any time in the life of the animal. In this regard, FeLV infection resembles irradiation and carcinogenic drugs.

The mode by which FeLV causes non-neoplastic disorders is not fully understood.[30] The virus is not cytopathic to cells, and infected cells continue to function in a normal manner. Some FeLV-associated disorders appear to be related to the occurrence of mutant variant viruses during the course of infection.[126,133] Some variants involve viral gene deletions, while others are caused by rearrangement of host and viral genes. There is good evidence that anemia in FeLV-infected cats is related to subgroup-C FeLV.[133] Subgroup-C FeLV often arises *de novo* in cats infected with other subgroups.[49] A variant of FeLV has recently been linked to immunodeficiency.[126] Variants may cause disease because of differences in the way they replicate in the cells and changes in host-cell tropism.[126]

Immune complexes of viral antigens and host antibodies may also play a role in some FeLV-related diseases, such as glomerulonephritis, neuritis, polymyositis and uveitis.[11] Perturbations that occur in the host immune system as a result of the host's attempt to contain the virus may lead to autoimmune phenomena, such as hemolytic anemia.[99] Such perturbations may interfere with immunity to other latent or subclinical infections. The relationship between FeLV and feline infectious peritonitis virus may fall into such a category.[75] The means by which FeLV may cause generalized immunodeficiency is discussed in a subsequent section.

Clinical Features

Feline leukemia virus infection has 2 main clinical stages.[79] The initial stage occurs 2-6 weeks following infection and corresponds to the appearance of virus in the blood, saliva, urine and feces. This stage of the disease is manifested by varying degrees in severity of fever, malaise, generalized lymphadenopathy, leukopenia, thrombocytopenia and anemia. These signs usually persist for 1-16 weeks before all clinical abnormalities disappear. Death is uncommon during this stage of disease; when it occurs, it is usually a consequence of sepsis, hemorrhage and anemia. These disorders are usually a direct result of profound leukopenia, thrombocytopenia and anemia.

Cats that survive the initial stage of infection make either a real (true) or apparent (false) recovery.[79] True recovery is manifested by disappearance of both clinical signs and viremia. Cats that make an apparent or false recovery appear outwardly normal but

Fig 2A. Lateral thoracic radiograph of an FeLV-infected cat with thymic lymphosarcoma. Note the lack of lung detail cranial to the heart, characteristic of a thymic mass. (From *Virus Infections of Carnivores*, courtesy of Elsevier Science Publishing)

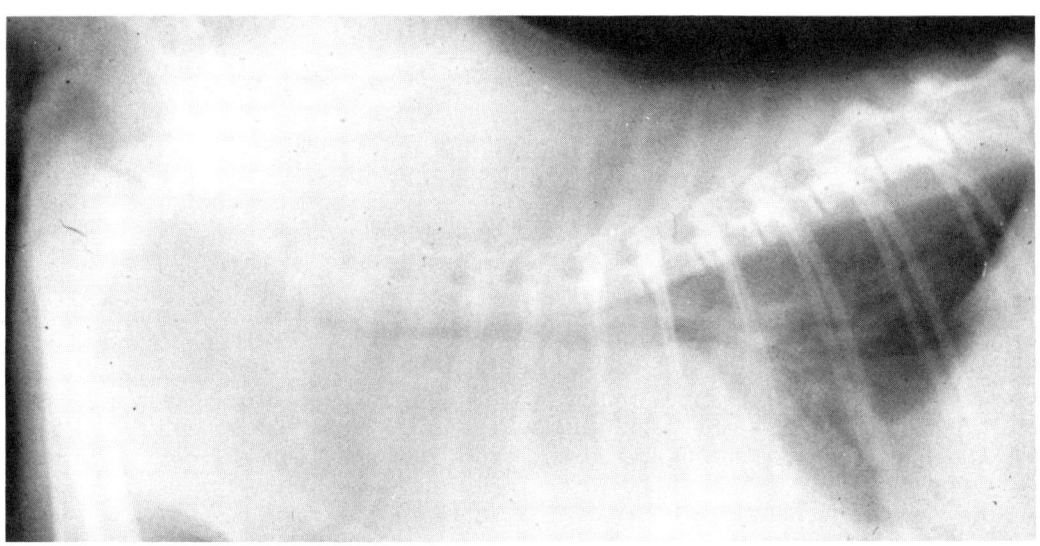

are persistently viremic for life. As a rule, cats that show either mild or inapparent signs during the initial stage of infection are usually among those that make a true recovery. The more severe the clinical signs are during the initial stage of infection, the more likely that the cat will become persistently infected.[79]

Cats that make a true recovery following initial infection usually suffer none of the long-term complications associated with FeLV infection. There is one exception, however. Completely recovered cats still suffer from a higher incidence of lymphoid tumors than cats that never were infected with the virus.[20] This increased incidence is much less than in persistently viremic animals.

The second stage of FeLV infection occurs following a period of apparent normalcy in persistently viremic cats. This may last months or years. The secondary stage of FeLV infection begins with the appearance of FeLV-related disease and is usually terminated by death. Mortality among persistently viremic cats is progressive and relentless, and averages about 50% each year that the cats remain infected. Most cats die within 3 years or so from some FeLV-related disease.[69] FeLV-related disease is either a direct consequence of infection (reproductive problems, lymphoid and myeloid neoplasms, aplastic or hypoplastic anemia, neuropathies or quasi-neoplastic syndromes) or an indirect consequence (immunodeficiency, immune-mediated diseases).

Reproductive problems in infected queens have been widely recognized but poorly documented.[29] Abortion, fetal resorption, stillbirths and neonatal deaths occur in over 80% of viremic queens. However, some kittens are born apparently healthy, but are viremic and carry this viremia into later life. The cause of fetal losses has not been well studied. Virus can be recovered from most fetal tissues and the placenta.[113] Lymphoid and thymic depletion can be seen in kittens, but the precise cause of death has not been ascertained.

Lymphoid neoplasms can be solid (lymphosarcoma) or more diffuse with involvement of the blood (lymphocytic leukemia). About 30% of FeLV-infected cats actually develop lymphoid tumors; the incubation period ranges from a few months to several years.[20] Hardy has classified lymphosarcoma as multicentric, thymic, alimentary or miscellaneous.[28] Multicentric lymphosarcomas tend to occur in cats around 4 years of age, and about 90% are associated with FeLV. Thymic lymphosarcomas occur in

Fig 2B. At necropsy, the thymic tumor filled the cranial thoracic cavity and had invaded the pericardium. (From *Virus Infections of Carnivores*, courtesy of Elsevier Science Publishing)

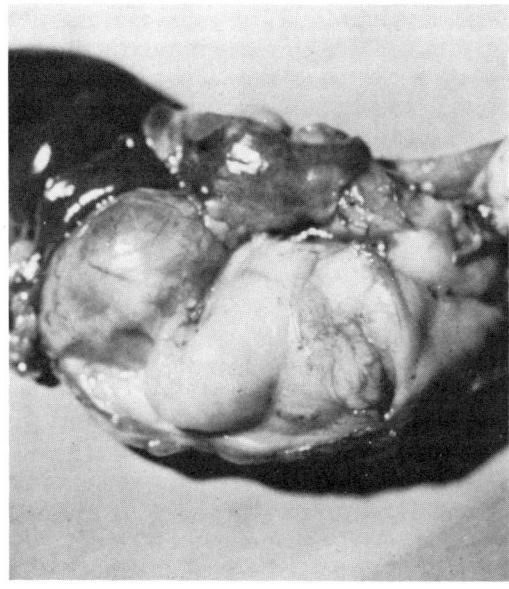

cats around 2.5 years of age and about 80% are associated with FeLV. Alimentary lymphosarcomas are common in older cats but only about 25% of these cats have active FeLV infections. Miscellaneous lymphosarcomas involve the skin, eyes, kidneys or nervous system. Ocular and neural lymphosarcomas are usually associated with FeLV infection, whereas renal and dermal lymphosarcomas occur more often in FeLV-negative cats. Less than one-third of cats with lymphosarcoma have leukemia (abnormal lymphoid cells in the blood). Leukemia can occur with any of the solid forms of lymphosarcoma but is most frequently associated with multicentric disease.[28] However, some cats may have only blood and marrow involvement.

Cats with thymic lymphosarcoma usually show acute dyspnea and pleural effusion. Abnormal lymphoid cells may be detected in the pleural fluid. Grossly, the thymus often fills the entire cranial thorax and can encircle the heart (Fig 2). Multicentric lymphosarcoma is often manifested by various combinations of generalized lymphadenopathy, anemia, hepatosplenomegaly and renal involvement; abnormal lymphocytes are often seen in the blood. Neural lymphosarcoma is most commonly manifested as acute posterior paresis or paralysis (Fig 3). Generalized CNS disease or more focal peripheral nerve palsies are less commonly observed. Ocular lymphosarcoma can occur by itself or in association with other forms of the disease. Ocular lymphosarcoma is the most frequent tumor in the eyes of cats and can involve the orbit, nictitating membrane, conjunctiva, cornea, fundus or iris and ciliary body (Fig 4).[106]

Myeloproliferative neoplasms arise from primitive stem cells, granulocytic precursors, erythroid precursors, or less commonly from megakaryocytes. Collectively these various myeloid cancers are called "myeloproliferative diseases."[28,40] Myeloproliferative disorders are only slightly less common than lymphoid tumors, occurring in about 20% of FeLV-infected cats.[20] They tend to be seen during the first 6 years of life, with a peak incidence around 4 years of age. Abnormal cells often appear late in the course of disease and the initial clinical signs are usually referable to anemia, hepatosplenomegaly and sometimes icterus.

Fig 3. Acute hindlimb paralysis in an FeLV-infected cat. Necropsy revealed focal lymphosarcoma of the spinal cord dura mater. (From *Virus Infections of Carnivores*, courtesy of Elsevier Science Publishing)

Fig 4. Iridal lymphosarcoma in an FeLV-infected cat. (Courtesy of Dr. Ned Buyukumihci, University of California, Davis)

About 70% of animals with myeloproliferative disease are persistently viremic.

Myeloproliferative diseases have been classified into the following types: reticuloendotheliosis; erythremic myelosis; erythroleukemia; myelogenous leukemia; megakaryocytic leukemia; and myelofibrosis.[28] Reticuloendotheliosis is characterized by primitive undifferentiated stem cells in the blood and bone marrow.[23] Erythremic myelosis is a disorder characterized by an increased number of nucleated RBCs without a corresponding increase in more differentiated reticulocytes. The granulocytic cell series is normal. Erythroleukemia is similar to erythremic myelosis except that both immature erythroid and myeloid cells are present in the blood. Myelogenous leukemias induced by FeLV usually arise from precursors of polymorphonuclear neutrophils or monocytes. Eosinophilic, basophilic and mast-cell leukemias are not FeLV-associated disorders. Megakaryocytic leukemia is an uncommon disease manifested by an increase in megakaryocyte and platelet numbers. Myelofibrosis is a terminal state of myeloproliferative disease manifested by marrow hypoplasia and fibrosis.

About 30% of cats with lymphosarcoma and myeloproliferative disease are not viremic for FeLV during clinical illness.[20,28,36] In at least a portion of these cats, however, FeLV is still present in the body as a latent bone marrow infection.[92] In other aviremic cats with lymphosarcomas and myeloproliferative diseases, FeLV is not even present as a latent infection.[67] These observations can be explained in 3 ways. First, FeLV-induced tumors are clonally derived, and once the malignant cell is generated, the resultant tumor is a distinct entity from the initiating FeLV infection. During the time this clone of cells expands, the host can mount an effective immune response to the FeLV infection. This immunity first leads to cessation of viremia and virus shedding and to eventual elimination of remaining foci of latently infected cells over the next 6 months.[77] If a tumor reaches clinical proportions during this latency period, the cat tests negative for viremia but positive for latent infection. Second, tumors may arise years after recovery from FeLV infection as a result of the insertion of viral genes into host chromosomes during the viremic phase of the infection. Such viral genes may recombine or interact with host genes at a later time. Gene interactions or recombinations might then lead to malignant transformation. The epizootiologic features of aviremic cats with lymphosarcomas and the possible role of prior FeLV infection have been described by Francis and associates.[20] Third, not all lymphoid and myeloid tumors are necessarily induced by FeLV infection. Other internal and external mutagenic factors are probably also involved in malignant transformation. Feline immunodeficiency virus may also be associated with myeloid and lymphoid neoplasms (see Chapter 15).

Aplastic and hypoplastic anemias are common in chronic FeLV carriers. Aplastic anemia is characterized by a progressive drop in the PCV and subsequent death. More commonly, the anemia is hypoplastic rather than aplastic and the PCV hovers at a low level for weeks or months. The PCV may also rise or fall in increments. Bone

Fig 5. Anisocoria in an FeLV-infected cat. The right pupil did not constrict upon exposure to light.

marrow aspirates or biopsies show hypoplasia of the RBC series or, in some cases, normal maturation with arrest at certain stages (dyshematopoiesis). If anemic cats live long enough, many develop myeloproliferative disease. In fact, anemia almost always precedes clinical expression of tumor cells by weeks or months.[78] Anemia is not always the sole abnormality in cats with hypoplastic or aplastic bone marrow. Thrombocytopenia and granulocytopenia are frequent accompanying features. Cats with hypoplastic or aplastic anemia do not usually show clinical signs until the PCV becomes lower than 15-20%. Listlessness, pallor of the mucous membranes and occasionally icterus are the signs most noticeable to the owner. Hepatomegaly and splenomegaly are usually detected on physical exam. These lesions are due to hepatic lipidosis, myeloid metaplasia or actual tumor infiltrates.

Neuropathies are infrequent but important features of chronic FeLV infection. Cats with neuropathies may have no histopathologic abnormalities or may have sparse focal lymphocytic infiltrates into peripheral nerves or the spinal cord. Persistent unilateral mydriasis (anisocoria) in the absence of blindness or intraocular disease is the most common neuropathy seen in FeLV-infected cats (Fig 5). The anisocoria is due to involvement of the short ciliary nerve innervating the muscles of the iris. Urinary incontinence may be another manifestation of neuropathy in infected cats. Barsanti and Downey found that 9 of 11 cats with urinary incontinence were FeLV infected.[3] The cats responded poorly to conventional therapy for urinary incontinence and no lesions were seen on histologic examination of 4 cats necropsied. Some cats with neuropathies show vague pain or hyperesthesia over the spine, or posterior paresis. Acute demyelinating myelopathies have also been seen in FeLV-infected cats.[30]

There are several miscellaneous quasineoplastic or neoplastic syndromes associated with the FeLV carrier state. Though uncommon, they are very flamboyant in clinical expression. Multiple cartilaginous exostoses are seen in younger FeLV-infected cats.[82] Multiple firm pea- to egg-sized growths occur on flat bones of the skull, ribs, scapula, spine and long bones of the limbs. The growths are basically chondromas. Chondrocytes within the tumors fluoresce strongly for FeLV, while chondrocytes in adjacent normal cartilage are not infected.[74] Affected cats slowly waste away and die. Benign cutaneous keratin horns on the footpads have also been associated with chronic FeLV infection.[7] They probably represent overgrowth of keratinocytes, similar to the hyperplasia of chondrocytes seen in multiple cartilaginous exostoses. Multicentric rapidly growing fibrosarcomas in cats years of age almost always occur in FeLV-infected cats (Chapter 14).[31]

The previous disorders are caused by direct effects of the virus. In contrast, the remaining disorders are indirectly related to FeLV infection. These disorders are either infectious disease potentiated by FeLV-induced immunosuppression or immune-mediated diseases.

Viral diseases potentiated by FeLV include feline infectious peritonitis (FIP) and upper respiratory infection (Fig 6). In the

Fig 6. Intractable herpesvirus type-1 infection in an FeLV-infected cat. Squinting is from painful keratoconjunctivitis. The nares are occluded by exudate from herpesvirus-induced rhinitis.

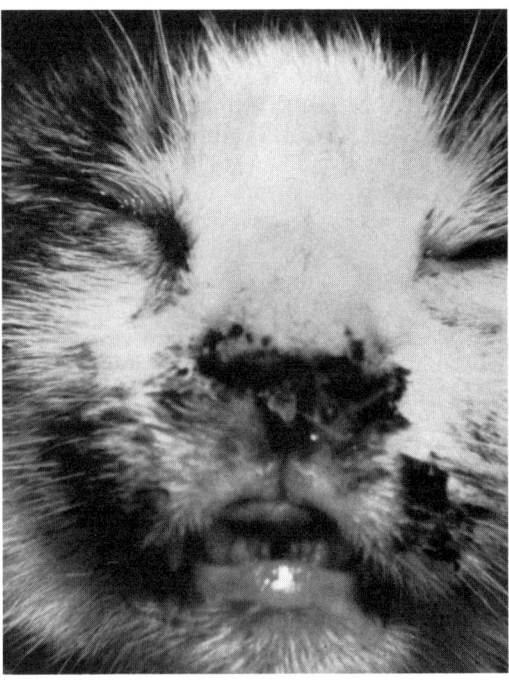

past, about 40% of cats suffering from FIP had concurrent FeLV viremia.[10] This relationship is not nearly as common as it used to be, due mainly to a great reduction in the incidence of FeLV infection in catteries. The precise mode of FeLV-induced enhancement of FIP virus infection is unknown. It does not appear to involve bone marrow suppression, depletion of phagocytic cells or suppression of humoral immunity. Concurrent FeLV infection somehow interferes with the established cellular immunity to latent or sequestered FIP virus infection, which often precedes FeLV infection by months or years. Feline infectious peritonitis in such cats usually appears within 2-16 weeks of establishment of chronic FeLV viremia.[75]

Severe and intractable rhinotracheitis virus infections have been seen in some FeLV-infected cats, especially debilitated or bone marrow-suppressed animals (Fig 6). FeLV-infected cats appear to have a higher incidence of viral upper respiratory disease than uninfected cats.[108]

Protozoal diseases enhanced by chronic FeLV infection include toxoplasmosis and hemobartonellosis. Toxoplasmosis is usually not associated with disease in healthy cats over 8-12 weeks of age.[12] About one-third of older cats with toxoplasmosis have concurrent FeLV infections. *Hemobartonella felis*, the causative agent of feline infectious anemia (FIA), exists as a subclinical infection in many normal cats. About 50-70% of cats clinically diagnosed with FIA are FeLV infected.[127] Many of these cats have preexisting hypoplastic anemia, or lymphoproliferative or myeloproliferative disorders,[132] so *Hemobartonella* treatment does not always correct the anemia.

Cryptococcosis, a disease caused by the yeast *Cryptococcus neoformans*, is also enhanced by FeLV infection. About one-fourth of cats with cryptococcosis are chronic FeLV carriers. The role of FeLV in the enhancement of both toxoplasmosis and cryptococcosis is unknown. Affected cats appear normal in other aspects.

FeLV-infected cats have an increased frequency of acute and chronic bacterial diseases.[32,86] Depending on the study, 30-50% of atypical bacterial infections of cats are FeLV associated. Most bacterial diseases occur in cats with subnormal peripheral WBC counts and, as such, a deficiency of phagocytes may be an important underlying cause. However, some FeLV-infected cats also have diminished antibody responses to bacterial antigens.[74] This may contribute to secondary infections. Low-grade proliferative periodontal gingivitis is seen in some FeLV-infected cats. Isolated tooth root abscesses and purulent otitis externa are also frequently related to FeLV infection (Fig 7). Peracute enterocolitis (panleukopenia-like syndrome) can be the ultimate cause of death in FeLV-infected cats with myeloproliferative diseases and low WBC counts, or in cats with suppressed cellular and humoral immunity.[85,86] Recurrent abscesses or abscesses that fail to heal normally are frequently associated with chronic FeLV infection. A peculiar necrotizing pneumonia caused by a saprophytic Gram-negative bacterium called EF4 occurs mainly in FeLV-infected cats.

Many immune-mediated diseases are associated with chronic FeLV viremia. Immune-mediated diseases in FeLV-infected cats have 2 major causes: high levels of antigen-antibody complexes circulating in the blood; interference with normal immunoregulation and autoantibody formation.

Immune-complex diseases in FeLV-infected cats are manifested in a number of ways. Glomerulonephritis is an almost inevitable histopathologic finding in cats chronically infected with FeLV, but it is usually of minor clinical importance. In fact, a negative correlation exists between FeLV infection and clinically apparent glomerulonephritis.[86] Many FeLV-infected cats have such vague signs as unthriftiness, episodic depression and minor neurologic problems associated with fine muscle tremors. These signs usually have no histopathologic basis but often subside with continuous use of small doses of corticosteroids. Severe polyneuropathy and myopathy are infrequently associated with FeLV infection. Affected cats develop severe muscle atrophy and myasthenia. This polyneuropathy/myopathy may be due to immune-complex disease.

About one-third to one-half of cats with autoimmune hemolytic anemia and thrombocytopenia are chronically infected with FeLV.[99] FeLV-related hemolytic anemia in cats is often a prelude to lymphosarcoma or myeloproliferative disease. Development of autoantibodies to platelets and RBCs has been attributed to some effect of FeLV infection on normal immunoregulatory mechanisms. Interference with normal immunoregulation leads to formation of antibodies to self-antigens.

Chronic progressive polyarthritis is another disorder that is potentiated by FeLV infection; about 20% of cats with this disease are FeLV carriers.[78] Chronic progressive polyarthritis is an acute, febrile polyarthritis resembling Reiter's disease in people or a low-grade destructive joint disease resembling human rheumatoid arthritis. The disease is partially responsive to immunosuppressive drug therapy. The precise role of FeLV in chronic progressive polyarthritis is unknown. The disease occurs only in male cats, and all of these cats tested were also infected with feline syncytium-forming virus (Chapter 12).

Pathologic Features

Pathologic and histopathologic changes in FeLV-infected cats are as numerous and diverse as FeLV-related diseases themselves. For this reason, only the salient features of FeLV-related diseases will be discussed, *ie*, bone marrow dyscrasias, lymphoid and myeloid neoplasms, lymphadenopathy and glomerulonephritis.

Bone marrow abnormalities are seen during the primary phase of the disease, when the host and virus interact for the first time, and in the secondary or terminal phase of the illness that occurs months or years later in chronically viremic cats.[79] Anemia, thrombocytopenia and leukopenia in the primary phase of the illness are associated with relative bone marrow hypoplasia rather than dysplasia or neoplasia. Anemia later in the course of the disease can have numerous causes, and a multiplicity of histopathologic changes are possible. Bone marrow hypoplasia, sometimes involving 1

Fig 7. Severe bacterial infection of the external ear canal and pinna in an FeLV-infected cat.

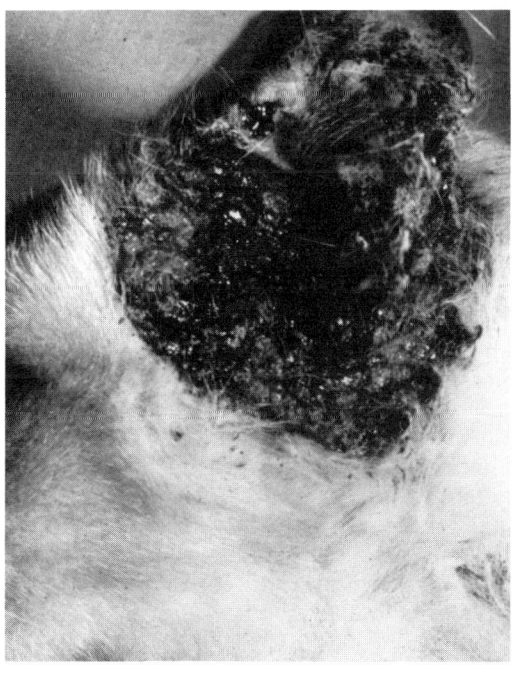

cell line more than another, is a frequent finding in chronically anemic cats. Bone marrow aplasia or hypoplasia can be infrequently associated with myelofibrosis.[40] In this condition, the marrow is replaced by fibrous tissue and histiocytes. In some anemic FeLV-infected cats, the marrow may appear hyperplastic. Hyperplasia may be caused by marrow infiltration with abnormal myeloid or erythroid cells, reactive changes associated with peripheral RBC destruction accompanying such disorders as autoimmune hemolytic anemia and hemobartonellosis, or hematopoietic dysplasia. Dysplasias are characterized by arrests in natural maturation sequences of RBC precursors. The condition mimics folate or vitamin B_{12} deficiency, for which it has been mistaken.[98] In actuality, it is probably a preleukemic state.

FeLV infection induces a peculiar macrocytosis in RBCs.[105] This is most apparent in FeLV-infected cats with nonregenerative anemia, but is also present to a lesser extent in FeLV-infected cats that are not anemic. In fact, the degree of RBC macrocytosis in FeLV-infected cats with nonregenerative anemia is almost as great as in uninfected cats with regenerative anemia. An increase in mean corpuscular volume was so consistent in FeLV-infected cats that is was considered highly indicative of FeLV infection by itself.[105] The only exception is uninfected cats with blood loss anemias, which are relatively infrequent in clinical populations compared to animals with FeLV infection. There is no good explanation for this phenomenon. Blood loss and intravascular hemolysis can complicate FeLV infection, but such events are usually associated with regenerative anemia. Macrocytosis does not respond to folic acid or vitamin B_{12} therapy, so vitamin deficiencies can be excluded. The most logical explanation is that FeLV infection of precursor cells has some intrinsic effect on erythropoiesis.[105] A similar phenomenon of thrombocytopenia and macrothrombocytosis has also been recognized in the primary phase of experimental FeLV infection.[6] It tends to last no longer than 6 weeks and is not seen in most chronically infected cats with normal platelet counts.

Cats with FeLV-induced bone marrow depression anemia often have an increased amount of intramedullary cancellous bone.[43] Though viral antigens are present in both osteoblasts and osteoclasts, it is not certain whether they cause the bone changes or if the bone changes are secondary to atrophy of the marrow elements.

Lymphoid neoplasms in cats are comprised of solid masses of cells ranging in maturity from immature lymphoblasts to mature lymphocytes. Holmberg and associates found that thymic lymphomas were comprised of T-lymphocytes, while alimentary lymphomas were derived from B-lymphocytes.[42] Multicentric lymphosarcomas were comprised of cells lacking both T- and B-lymphocyte cell-surface markers, and were presumably of a less-differentiated cell origin. Routine cytologic examination of various feline lymphosarcomas was not helpful in differentiating B-cell from T-cell tumors, but did demonstrate that lymphocytes within individual tumors were uniformly arrested at various stages in their normal differentiation from primitive to mature forms.[42]

Myeloid neoplasms usually originate in the bone marrow and invade the spleen, liver and other tissues to a lesser extent. Myeloid tumors are usually preceded by bone marrow dysplasia or hypoplasia.[79] This suggests that neoplasia is secondary to problems associated with bone marrow maturation. Malignant cells are usually present in the marrow for weeks or months before they appear in the blood. In terminal stages, abnormal cells are released into the marrow in large numbers. The terminal appearance of abnormal cells in the blood of cats with myeloproliferative disorders is reminiscent of the acute blast-cell crisis in leukemic people.

Generalized lymphadenopathy is common in FeLV-infected cats. It is particularly pronounced in the primary phase of infection in younger cats.[79] Lymph nodes may become 0.5-2 cm or so in diameter during this phase. Though cats in the primary phase of FeLV infection may appear to have lymphosarcoma, the lymph node enlargement is an immunoreactive and not neoplastic phenomenon. The peripheral lymphadenopathy seen in young cats with FeLV is histologically distinct.[70] The paracortical areas are often very enlarged and impinge on lymphoid follicles and sinuses. In some cases, B- and T-cell hyperplasia is present, with no change in node architecture.

Glomerulonephritis is a very common consequence of chonic FeLV infection. Jakowski and associates studied a household containing 100 cats, many of which were FeLV-infected.[46] Over a 4-year period, 29 of the cats necropsied had histologic evidence of glomerulonephritis. In 14 of these 29 cats, glomerulonephritis was the only histologic lesion. Even so, death due to FeLV-induced renal failure accounts for a small percentage of the total mortality from FeLV infection. Reinacher and Theilen found a negative relationship between most forms of clinically significant renal disease (including glomerulonephritis) in cats and FeLV infection.[86]

Feline leukemia virus-induced glomerulonephritis is characterized by hyaline thickening of the basement membranes of Bowman's capsule and the glomeruli.[46] In some cases, the deposits have the appearance of amyloid. Diffuse and focal glomerulosclerosis often accompanies the nephritis. A sparse interstitial mononuclear and plasma cell infiltrate is seen in the kidneys of many cats with FeLV-induced glomerulonephritis.

Clinicopathologic Features

Feline leukemia virus infection is diagnosed by assaying for viral antigens in the blood, or by more laborious tissue-culture isolation procedures from plasma or buffy coat. Viremic cats have high levels of viral proteins in their plasma and within the cytoplasm of peripheral blood leukocytes and platelets. The viral core protein p27 is particularly abundant and almost all tests are directed toward it.

The core protein p 27 can be detected in the blood of infected cats by either immunofluorescent antibody (IFA) staining or enzyme-linked immunosorbent assay (ELISA).[35,63,64] The IFA procedure uses goat or rabbit anti-p27 for the first antibody and an appropriate fluoresceinated antiglobulin as a second antibody. Viral antigens are detected in platelets and leukocytes on air-dried, acetone-fixed blood smears. If properly conducted, the IFA test has a high degree of accuracy. False positives are relatively infrequent. However, the IFA procedure is cumbersome to run. It also suffers from a low percentage of false negatives caused by blood smears with inadequate numbers of infected platelets and leukocytes, or by absence of virus in blood cells. Viral antigens are often present in the plasma but not in blood cells for a short period before and after true viremia.[64] A very low proportion of infected cats do not manifest virus in leukocytes yet have virus in their plasma and other secretions or excretions.[66]

The ELISA is currently the most widely used test for FeLV detection and usually employs polyclonal or monoclonal antibodies to p27.[56,63,64] The p27 ELISA is simple to run and requires < 100 μl of serum or plasma. It has been also adapted for use with tears and saliva.[38,122] Tear or saliva tests detect only 80-90% of serum-positive animals and should be used only for rapid or mass screening purposes. The p27 ELISA is very sensitive and specific if run properly. However, if the washing steps are not carefully and properly done, or if badly hemolyzed serum or whole blood is used, false positives can occur. This is probably the greatest single weakness of the procedure, but it can be virtually eliminated by proper wash techniques and avoidance of whole blood and hemolyzed serum.[64]

Latent FeLV infection cannot be detected by either ELISA or IFA staining.[77] To detect a latent infection, bone marrow cells must be cultured in vitro for up to 6 weeks.[67,77,92] Culture supernatants are then tested weekly for infectious virus or viral antigens.

Antibody tests are of some clinical relevance and are directed against viral structural proteins or against nonvirus-coded but infection-specific antigens.[26,29,65] Serum antibodies to all of the major virion proteins have been measured by ELISA or radioimmunoassay (RIA).[65,68] In general, both chronically viremic and recovered cats have serum antibodies to most structural proteins of FeLV. However, viremic cats have much lower levels of antibodies than recovered aviremic cats.[65] Recovered cats also demonstrate virus-neutralizing antibodies in their serum.[29,79,80] These antibodies are measured either by a focus inhibition assay, using appropriate indicator cells that transform when infected with FeLV, or by conventional infectivity-inhibition tests.[19,39,76] Virus-neutralizing antibodies appear shortly after cessation of active viremia and rise slowly over the next 1-3 months. Virus-neutralizing, RIA and ELISA antibodies tend to decrease with time.[74]

Antibodies to the so-called feline oncornavirus-associated cell-membrane antigen (FOCMA) are also produced as a consequence of FeLV infection.[15,17,29] These antibodies are detected by an IFA procedure using a living, FeLV-infected, transformed lymphoblastoid cell line.[15,17] The literature states that FOCMA is a nonvirion protein on the cell surface as a consequence of FeLV-induced transformation.[17] As such, its importance as a tumor-preventive antigen has been stressed.[15,16,26,29] Both viremic and recovered cats demonstrate FOCMA antibody, though recently recovered cats demonstrate the highest levels.[79] It has also been stated that high FOCMA antibody titers protect against development of lymphosarcoma in persistently viremic cats.[29] However, FOCMA antibody levels can be high and then decrease when tumors appear. Other cats fail to develop lymphosarcoma even though their FOCMA antibody levels are always low.[74] Moreover, the concept that FOCMA is a nonvirion antigen has recently been questioned by several groups. Mounting evidence supports the fact that FOCMA is probably the major envelope protein (gp70) of FeLV subgroup C.[103,104] Because the nature of FOCMA and the meaning of FOCMA antibodies remain so unclear, it seems unwise to use the test to make any clinical judgment beyond the fact that the cat is either infected or was infected in the past.

Treatment and Prevention

Treatment for FeLV infection is directed at the viral infection itself and the specific and varied FeLV-related diseases that occur as a result of infection. Treatment of the infection itself has been difficult. Ultimately, control of the infection is totally dependent on the host's ability to mount and sustain an effective immune response. Once the infection becomes persistent, however, the likelihood for eventual self cure is very low. Various immunostimulants,[138] megadoses of multivitamins or vitamin C, and a great number of strange concoctions and procedures have been claimed as cures for FeLV infection; none, however, has proven effective. Interferon preparations have reportedly alleviated or prevented some clinical manifestations of FeLV infection.

There have been reports of FeLV-infected cats that have been cured of viremia and/or clinical signs by extracorporeal absorption of their blood with *Staphylococcus* protein A columns.[111,118] Subsequent studies suggested that the therapeutic benefit of such procedures involves immunostimulation resulting from the leaching of small amounts of protein A from the columns.[120] A dosage of 20 µg/2.75 kg of body weight of highly purified *Staphylococcus* protein A given intraperitoneally twice weekly for 10-12 weeks has reportedly been effective in eliminating viremia and/or ameliorating clinical signs in a small proportion of persistently infected animals. This treatment appears to work by raising the blood levels of interferon and complement-dependent cytotoxic antibodies to FeLV-infected cells. Cats that failed to show increases in interferon and cytotoxic antibodies did not respond to the treatment. This treatment needs further evaluation.

The course of infection in healthy, persistently viremic cats can be influenced by a number of stressful situations. Infected cats living in high-stress, multiple-cat households are more apt to develop complicating disease than cats in single-animal households. Surgical procedures, such as ovariohysterectomy, castration or declawing, can sometimes precipitate crises in otherwise healthy carrier cats. Boarding, changes in homes and other such activities can also shorten the lives of infected animals. Therefore, it is important to maintain infected cats in environments as free from stress and disease exposure as possible.

Treatments for specific FeLV-related diseases are as varied as the diseases themselves. Lymphoid cancers can be treated with chemotherapy with a reasonable chance for remission but not cure. However, myeloid cancers respond poorly to treatment. Some secondary infectious diseases, such as hemobartonellosis, tooth infections, abscesses and ear infections, are treatable; others, such as FIP, are not. Immune-mediated disorders, such as autoimmune hemolytic anemia or thrombocytopenia, can be successfully treated with corticosteroids. Cats with aplastic anemia can be kept alive for weeks or months with blood transfusions.

Many FeLV-infected cats suffer from cycles of vague illness manifested by depression, anorexia, vague nervous twitches and weight loss. Such cats benefit greatly from intermittent small doses of glucocorticoids.

Prevention and control of FeLV have been based on routine testing and elimination of carriers.[29] These procedures have been extremely effective in eliminating infection within confined cat populations, such as in catteries. Though testing and elimination have controlled cattery infection, they have had less impact on the spread of disease in the general cat population. In relatively free-roaming cat populations, FeLV infection still remains an important disease. Testing and eradication consist of 7 steps: 1) test all cats for FeLV infection; 2) remove all FeLV-infected cats from the household; 3) clean all dishes, litter pans and bedding with hot water and soap, and wait 10 days before bringing a new cat into the home; 4) prevent any movement of cats in or out of the cattery; 5) retest all quarantined cats 12 weeks after the first test to detect any cats that might have been incubating the infection; 6) lift the quarantine when all cats in the cattery have tested FeLV negative in 2 tests done 12 weeks apart; and 7) test all new cats for FeLV before introduction into the household.[29] In addition, owners of free-roaming cats must be made aware that many cats in the surrounding environments may also be carriers. In this situation, decontamination of the home environment may be of minor importance as compared to limiting direct-contact exposures.

Using widespread test and removal, the Dutch have decreased their incidence of FeLV infection among the general cat population from 9.0% to 3.4% between 1974 and 1985.[134] The incidence in purebred catteries was decreased from 11.5% to 0% between 1974 and 1984.[134]

The first vaccine for FeLV infection was marketed in the United States by Norden Laboratories, Lincoln, Nebraska.[100] This vaccine is based on a prototype vaccine from Ohio State University and is reportedly highly immunogenic and about 80% effective in preventing persistent viremia, though far lower immunogenicity and efficacy have been observed by independent researchers.[76,130] It is hoped that much better vaccines will be forthcoming from the worldwide research on FeLV infection and immunity.

Cats have been successfully vaccinated with live-virus vaccines.[29,80] Relatively avirulent strains are available that produce a high degree of protection when given in small doses to older kittens.[80] However, these same strains induce fatal anemia in very young kittens.[44] Also, cats that have recovered from such live-virus vaccinations may be at a much greater risk of developing virus-negative lymphosarcoma later in life.[20,29,36] Doubts expressed by some people about the possible public health hazards of live FeLV have also made it unlikely that a live-virus vaccine will ever by employed for prevention of FeLV infections.[29]

The efficacy of killed whole-virus vaccines has been questioned.[97] However, some researchers have found them to be effective immunogens.[80,131] The main problem with killed whole-virus vaccines has been production cost. Very large amounts of virus are required; the cost to grow this amount of virus in culture and concentrate it into a single dose is high. Nevertheless, several killed whole-virus FeLV vaccines are now appearing on the market.

Vaccines against FeLV infection have also been made using live or inactivated FeLV-infected and transformed tumor cells.[52,55,72] These vaccines were effective immunogens in these studies. The efficacy of living-cell vaccines can probably be attributed to the living virus the cells contain. The efficacy of adequately inactivated whole-cell vaccines has been questioned by Pedersen and associates.[80] They found properly inactivated whole-cell vaccines to be ineffective.

Subunit vaccines for FeLV infection are a third possibility.[68] However, they are expensive to produce when virus is propagated and fractionated in a conventional manner. With the advent of genetic engineering and peptide synthesis, such vaccines have become economically feasible. The major envelope glycoprotein (gp70) of the virus has been targeted as the protective antigen. Bacteria or yeast can be genetically engineered to produce all or part of this protein in large fermented cultures. By knowing the amino acid sequence of the protein, small peptides can be produced that mimic certain regions of the virus envelope. Small peptides coupled to larger carrier proteins can then be used to immunize cats. Preliminary tests on such recombinant and peptide vaccines have been very discouraging, however.[74]

Initial tests on a native FeLV envelope subunit vaccine have been discouraging.[131] In fact, it rendered vaccinated cats more susceptible to infection. This finding may have been due to the way the vaccine was formulated. Virus incorporated into so-called "immune-stimulating complexes" (iscoms) has been much more immunogenic.[130]

Vaccinia virus, a very large pox virus, can also be genetically altered to incorporate the genes that code for the FeLV envelope proteins. The living genetically engineered virus can be injected intradermally into cats, in which it causes a short-lived dermal lesion. The altered vaccinia virus expresses gp70 protein within infected cells in the lesion. This natural type of stimulus will hopefully induce a protective immunity to FeLV. Initial tests on one such recombinant vaccinia vaccine have failed, however.[116]

Infection and Immunity

The ultimate outcome (recovery or persistent viremia) of FeLV infection is largely determined by events that occur within the host during the first 16 weks of infection.[79] Immunity during this critical period is greatly influenced by the age of the cat, dose and virulence of the virus and stress. Age resistance develops rapidly after 4-8 weeks of age. Cats exposed at very young ages usually become persistently viremic; older cats become aviremic.[44] Age-acquired resistance can be overcome to some extent by increasing the dose of challenge virus and using more virulent strains. It is most easily overcome, however, by subjecting the animal to artificial stress. A single injection of methylprednisolone given within the first 2 weeks after exposure dramatically increases the proportion of cats that become persistently infected.[90] This finding has been almost universally applied to FeLV vaccine evaluation.[80,100] Both age resistance and cortisone-augmented immuno-suppression have been linked to the activity of macrophages.[45] Macrophages apparently play a key role in the early stages of virus containment, virus spread and immunity.[45,91]

The termination of viremia appears to be associated with the appearance of virus-neutralizing antibodies in the blood.[47] The disappearance of viremia also corresponds with a cessation of virus production by infected cells. This cessation may be partly due to destruction of infected cells that express virus proteins on their surface by antibody-dependent or -independent T-lymphocyte and macrophage-mediated cytotoxicity, or by the effects of antibodies and complement.[24-27] In addition to destruction of infected cells, the genome of the virus actually appears to be suppressed, thus rendering the infected cell a nonvirus producer. This is not an effect of interferon, because interferon does not inhibit production of intact FeLV virions.[136] Infected cells apparently receive some sort of signal that causes the proviral DNA to become dormant. This signal is in some manner related to the associated immune response, but the mechanism of its action is not understood. The cessation of proviral DNA transcription correlates with the beginning of the latency phase of FeLV infection.

The latent phase of FeLV infection can be detected by culturing bone marrow cells *in vitro*, away from the inhibitory effects of the host's immune system.[77,92] Latency is a transient phase for most cats, and is terminated in most individuals within 1-6 months.[77] It is merely an extension, therefore, of the recovery process. Latency is followed by complete recovery, at which time the virus is no longer present in a form that can be activated in the body. Termination of latency may be related to the action of enzymes within the nucleus that gradually cut, bypass or delete the viral DNA that has incorporated itself into the host's chromosomes. Such reparative enzymes have been well documented in normal mammalian cells. Such a reparative process may explain why all cats have small pieces of FeLV DNA throughout their chromosomes at birth. These pieces of FeLV proviral DNA may represent remnants acquired from ancestors that were infected with the virus through eons of time.

The immunologic basis for the state of persistent viremia has not been determined. Antibodies continue to be detected in the serum, albeit at much lower levels than in recovered cats.[65] Many of these antibodies are complexed to viral antigens in the blood and tissues.[11] Though antibodies to viral proteins can be detected at various levels in the serum of persistently infected cats, none of these antibodies has virus-neutralizing activity. This mitigates against the possibility that persistence is due to the appearance of variant viruses that have altered envelope antigens.[128]

The persistently viremic state appears to involve some sort of immunologic tolerance. This tolerance develops rather abruptly. At one stage of the disease the cat is actively fighting the infection, as evidenced by the pronounced lymphadenopathy. At the other stage the lymph nodes become quiescent in the face of the same infection that previously evoked an intense immune response. As with any state of immunologic tolerance, it can sometimes be broken. A small proportion of FeLV-infected cats can terminate the persistent viremia after many months or even years. The tolerant state can sometimes be abrogated by immunologic manipulations.[111,118,120]

Feline leukemia virus infection has been likened to acquired immunodeficiency (AIDS) of people.[32,102] While human AIDS and FeLV infection have many dissimilarities, there is little doubt that some FeLV-infected cats are immunodeficient. Unlike the immunodeficiency of human AIDS, which involves specific components of the immune system, FeLV infection causes immunodeficiency in many different ways.[32,60] Immunodeficiency is not present in all FeLV-infected cats, and does not usually show up in *in-vitro* or *in-vivo* tests until clinical signs of illness appear. Reimann and associates found healthy FeLV-infected cats had normal peripheral leukocyte, lymphocyte, and B- and T-lymphocyte counts, and normal lymphocyte blastogenesis to concanavalin A and pokeweed mitogen as compared to uninfected housemates.[84] Clinical problems related to immunodeficiency often develop about the time abnormalities are seen in hemograms. Studies of several hundred experimentally infected cats showed that vague illness and secondary infections do not begin to appear until the WBC count, PCV and platelet count start to decrease.[74] However, development of FIP is an exception. Feline infectious peritonitis usually follows soon after FeLV infection and is not associated with pronounced bone marrow suppression.[75] Enhancement of FIP by FeLV infection appears to be very specific in nature and is somehow caused by interference between established FIPV immunity and developing FeLV immunity.[75]

Hardy has provided an excellent review of what is currently known about the immunopathogenesis of FeLV.[32] He described abnormalities in cellular and humoral immunity, phagocytosis and complement. Chronic FeLV infection can have a great effect on cell-mediated immunity. Almost one-fourth of FeLV-infected cats have lower than expected blood leukocyte counts, and two-thirds of these animals have depressed lymphocyte counts.[32] Essex and co-workers described similar reductions in lymphocyte counts.[14] Interestingly, FeLV-infected cats with secondary immunosuppressive diseases were much more likely to have leukopenia than healthy FeLV-infected cats, and two-thirds of these animals were anemic as well.[32] This again supports the role of bone-marrow suppression in development of immunodeficiency syndromes in FeLV-infected cats. The number of B-lymphocytes increases in the peripheral blood, lymph nodes and spleens of infected healthy cats but is greatly reduced in cats with secondary infections.[32] In contrast, relative numbers of T-lymphocytes increase in FeLV-infected cats with secondary diseases but not in healthy FeLV-infected animals. Cockerell and co-workers reported that blood lymphocytes from FeLV-infected cats had a greatly diminished response to phytomitogens.[8] The disease status of the cats was not well documented, however. Reimann and associates found phytomitogen responses the same in healthy FeLV-infected cats and in uninfected housemates.[84]

Thymic atrophy is a sequela of FeLV infection in neonatal kittens.[1] Growth is retarded and affected kittens suffer from intercurrent infections. They usually "fade away" and die by 8-12 weeks of age. However, this form of disease may largely be a laboratory artifact. Virtually all debilitating diseases in neonates are associated with some degree of thymic atrophy. Moreover, most naturally acquired FeLV infections in kittens occur after 8-12 weeks of age. Thymic atrophy and acute wasting syndromes are not common in this age group, probably because the thymus gland has completed much of its lymphoid tissue-seeding function by this time.

Though lymphoid cells are affected by FeLV infection, actual deficiencies of cellular immunity have not been consistently demonstrated. Perryman and associates found that neonatally infected kittens retained skin allografts longer than uninfected kittens.[81] These kittens were very cachectic, however, so prolonged graft survival could not be attributed just to thymic atrophy. Delayed hypersensitivity was studied in FeLV-infected cats sensitized with an intradermal injection of BCG.[74] The intensity of the localized response to BCG and the response of pinna skin to intradermal injections of old tuberculin were measured. Healthy FeLV-infected cats responded identically to healthy uninfected cats. However, FeLV-infected cats with low-grade illnesses and abnormal hemograms (anemia, leukopenia) had a much reduced local response to BCG and a greatly diminished intradermal tuberculin test.[74]

Humoral immunity is altered in FeLV-infected cats, but the degree of alteration varies with the antigen studied. Hardy found that FeLV-infected cats had significantly impaired humoral immunity to a small dose of sheep RBCs.[32] Similarly, Trainin and co-workers found FeLV-infected cats responded less than uninfected cats to synthetic antigens.[102] Healthy FeLV-infected cats had normal levels of IgG, IgM and IgA, as well as normal antibody titers to rhinotracheitis virus, coronavirus and calicivirus in the laboratory.[74] They had somewhat lower primary and secondary responses to sheep RBCs and to *Salmonella* lipopolysaccharide. Humoral-antibody suppression might be explained by increases in numbers of suppressor T-cells in the blood of FeLV-infected cats.[61]

Complement levels in healthy FeLV-infected cats were normal in 1 study but variably low in another.[27,74] However, cats with lymphosarcoma often have circulating immune complexes and reduced levels of complement.[11,59]

When FeLV-infected cats are injected with Newcastle disease virus, they produce normal amounts of viral interferons (alpha- and beta-interferons).[32] However, lymphocytes and spleen cells from healthy and ill FeLV-infected cats fail to produce normal levels of gamma-interferon *in vitro*.[107] A similar phenomenon has been described in human AIDS.[71] Spleen and lymph node cells from FeLV-infected cats produce normal amounts of alpha- and beta-interferons.

Deficiencies in phagocytic cells probably account for a portion of FeLV-induced immunosuppression. Bone-marrow suppression can lead to deficiencies in both neutrophils and monocytes. Kiehl and associates have shown that neutrophils from FeLV-infected cats, especially younger animals, have decreased chemotaxis in vitro.[58] The in-vitro bactericidal capacity of leukocytes from FeLV-infected cats is equal to that of leukocytes from uninfected animals.[74] As expected, leukocyte deficiencies are most often manifested by an increased incidence of bacterial infections of the upper and lower respiratory passages, skin and intestinal tract.

The mechanisms by which FeLV causes immunosuppression are varied. Bone marrow suppression can bring about deficiencies in granulocytes, monocytes and lymphocytes necessary to fight infection. Deficiencies that occur in the face of normal numbers of effector cells are more difficult to explain. One popular theory holds that the viral proteins themselves are immunosuppressive.[109] Living or ultraviolet-light-inactivated FeLV decreases the number of pokeweed mitogen-driven antibody-forming cells in vitro and depresses elaboration of acid-labile and gamma interferons.[112,137] Some whole-virus FeLV vaccines may also enhance the severity of FeSV or FeLV challenge-exposure in kittens.[109] The immuno-suppressive effects of whole FeLV have been linked to the transmembrane protein of the virus, p15E.[109] The p15E protein inhibits in-vitro mitogen-induced proliferation of lymphocytes, and its administration to cats has reportedly increased their susceptibility to FeLV infection.[109] It also interferes with the in-vitro helper effect of T-lymphocytes and blocks conversion of IgM to IgG synthesis of some FeLV-related antibodies.[109] Synthetic peptides corresponding to regions of p15E suppress polyclonal B-cell activation in vitro and IgG production by Staphylococcus protein A.[124] Though an attractive theory, it does not explain why persistently FeLV-infected cats remain healthy for months or years. The in-vitro activity of p15E also appears to be inordinately broad for a molecule that should produce very specific effects; in addition to lymphocytes, it also suppresses the in-vitro function of granulocytes and erythroid cell precursors.[119,135]

A second theory for FeLV-associated immunosuppression has recently been advanced. A defective variant of FeLV has been isolated along with its helper FeLV from a cat with lymphosarcoma.[126] The variant virus induced severe immunodeficiency in experimentally infected cats. The proviral DNA of the variant virus fails to integrate itself normally into the nucleus and is concentrated in the cytoplasm, providing one explanation for its biologic behavior. Similar variant viruses have not been isolated from other cats with naturally acquired immunodeficiency, however. The universality of the phenomenon is questionable, therefore.

Animal and Public Health Considerations

Feline leukemia virus infections appear to be limited to domestic cats and some wild Felidae. The potential health hazard of FeLV-infected cats to people is controversial.[101,121] This controversy has provided impetus for many past and current research studies. To date, these studies have not provided support for the role of FeLV in human disease.[101,121]

ENDOGENOUS FELINE C-TYPE RETROVIRUS

Endogenous C-type retroviruses exist in the somatic and germ cells of many different mammalian species. The intact proviral DNA is present in host-cell chromosomes but the genome is not expressed. Endogenous retroviruses have probably been acquired through natural infection by an exogenous (replicating) retrovirus from divergent species of animals. The genome, once it is inserted into the chromosomes, is then passed in the germ cells from one generation to the next.

The RD-114 virus is the principal endogenous retrovirus of cats. It was isolated by co-cultivating normal feline cells with a rhabdomycosarcoma cell line from a person. The virus was first thought to be human oncogenic virus but was later discovered within the DNA of many normal cat cell lines.[113] Apparently, proviral DNA was somehow transferred between the normal cat cells and the human tumor cells. Endogenous retroviruses, though not replicative in their host species, replicate as normal exogenous retroviruses within cells of other species.

The endogenous RD-114 virus can only be detected in cat cells by genetic probing or by co-cultivating cat cells with cells of other species. Since the genome is not activated in cat cells *in vitro* or *in vivo*, virions are not produced and the immune system of the host has no stimulus for antibody formation. Cats that carry endogenous RD-114 virus are serum antibody and antigen negative, therefore.[123] The presence of the RD-114 virus in the genome of cats causes no known disease. Cats that carry the RD-114 virus are not immune to infection by FeLV. FeLV and RD-114 virus are antigenically and genetically distinct.

References

1. Anderson LJ et al: Feline leukemia virus infection of kittens: mortality associated with atrophy of the thymus and lymphoid depletion. *J Natl Cancer Inst* 47:807-817, 1971.

2. Baltimore D: Viral RNA-dependent DNA polymerase in virions of RNA tumor viruses. *Nature* 226:1209-1211, 1970.

3. Barsanti JA and Downey R: Urinary incontinence in cats. *JAAHA* 20:979-982, 1984.

4. Benveniste RE et al: Evolution of type-C viral genes: origin of feline leukemia virus. *Science* 190:886-888, 1975.

5. Bolognesi DP et al: Assembly of type-C oncornaviruses: a model. *Science* 199:183-186, 1978.

6. Boyce JT et al: FeLV-induced thrombocytopenia and macrothrombocytopenia in cats. *Vet Pathol* 23:16-20, 1986.

7. Center SA et al: Multiple cutaneous horns on the foot pads of a cat. *Feline Pract* 12(4):26-30, 1982.

8. Cockerell GL et al: Lymphocyte mitogen reactivity and enumeration of circulating B- and T-cells during feline leukemia virus infection in the cat. *J Natl Cancer Inst* 57:1095-1099, 1976.

9. Coffin JM, in Stephenson JR: *Molecular Biology of RNA Tumor Viruses.* Academic Press, New York, 1980. pp 199-243.

10. Cotter SM et al: The association of feline leukemia virus with lymphosarcoma and other disorders in the cat. *JAVMA* 166:449-454, 1975.

11. Day NK et al: Circulating immune complexes associated with naturally occurring lymphosarcoma in pet cats. *J Immunol* 125:2363-2366, 1980.

12. Dubey JP et al: Effect of age and sex on the acquisition of immunity to toxoplasmosis in cats. *J Protozool* 24:184-186, 1977.

13. Essex M et al: Feline oncornavirus-associated cell membrane antigen. II. Antibody titers in healthy cats from household and laboratory colony environments. *J Natl Cancer Inst* 54:631-635, 1975.

14. Essex M et al: Naturally occurring persistent feline oncornavirus infections in the absence of disease. *Infect Immun* 11:470-475, 1975.

15. Essex M et al: Correlation between humoral antibody and regression of tumors induced by feline sarcoma virus. *Nature* 233:195-196, 1971.

16. Essex M et al: Immunosurveillance of naturally occurring feline leukemia. *Science* 190:790-792, 1975.

17. Essex M and Snyder SP: Feline oncornavirus-associated cell membrane antigens. I. Serological studies with kittens exposed to cell-free materials from various feline fibrosarcomas. *J Natl Cancer Inst* 51:1007-1012, 1973.

18. Fenner F: Classification and nomenclature of viruses. Second report of the International Committee of Taxonomy of Viruses. *Intervirol* 7:1-105, 1976.

19. Fischinger PJ et al: Simple quantitative assay for both xenotropic murine leukemia virus and ecotropic feline leukemia viruses. *J Virol* 14:177-179, 1974.

20. Francis DP et al: Feline leukemia and lymphoma: comparison of virus positive and virus negative cases. *Cancer Res* 39:3866-3870, 1979.

21. Francis DP et al: Feline leukemia virus: Survival under home and laboratory conditions. *J Clin Microbiol* 9:154-156, 1979.

22. Francis DP et al: Excretion of feline leukemia virus by naturally infected pet cats. *Nature* 269:252-254, 1977.

23. Gilmore CE et al: Reticuloendotheliosis, a myeloproliferative disorder of cats: a comparison with lymphocytic leukemia. *Path Vet* 1:161-183, 1964.

24. Grant CK et al: Antibodies from healthy cats exposed to feline leukemia virus lyse feline lymphoma cells slowly with cat complement. *J Immunol* 119:401, 1977.

25. Grant CK et al: Natural feline leukemia virus infection and the immune response of cats of different ages. *Cancer Res* 40:823-829, 1980.

26. Grant CK et al: Lysis of feline lymphoma cells by complement-dependent antibodies in feline leukemia virus contact cats. Correlation of lysis and antibodies to feline oncornavirus-associated cell membrane antigen. *J Natl Cancer Inst* 60:161, 1978.

27. Grant CK et al: Complement and tumor antibody levels in cats, and changes associated with natural feline leukemia virus infection and malignant disease. *Cancer Res* 39:75-81, 1979.

28. Hardy WD Jr: Hematopoietic tumors of cats. *JAAHA* 17:921-940, 1981.

29. Hardy WD Jr: The feline leukemia virus. *JAAHA* 17:951-980, 1981.

30. Hardy WD Jr: Feline leukemia virus nonneoplastic disease. *JAAHA* 17:941-949, 1981.

31. Hardy WD Jr: The feline sarcoma viruses. *JAAHA* 17:981-997, 1981.

32. Hardy WD Jr: Immunopathology induced by the feline leukemia virus. *Springer Seminars Immunopathol* 5:75-105, 1982.

33. Hardy WD Jr et al: Feline leukemia virus: occurrence of viral antigen in the tissues of cats with lymphosarcoma and other diseases. *Science* 166:1019-1021, 1969.

34. Hardy WD Jr et al, in Ito Y and Dutcher RM: *Comparative Leukemia Research 1973*. Univ Tokyo Press/Karger, Basel, Switzerland, 1975. pp 67-74.

35. Hardy WD Jr et al, in Dutcher RM and Chieco-Bianchi L: *Unifying Concepts of Leukemia*. S Karger, Basel, Switzerland, 1973. pp 778-799.

36. Hardy WD Jr et al, in Essex M et al: *Viruses in Naturally Occurring Cancers*. Cold Springs Harbor Laboratory, New York, 1980. pp 677-698.

37. Hardy WD Jr et al: Horizontal transmission of feline leukemia virus in cats. *Nature* 244:266-269, 1973.

38. Hawkins E et al: The use of tears for the diagnosis of feline leukemia virus infection. *JAVMA* 188:1031-1034, 1986.

39. Henderson IC et al: Mink cell line Mv1LU (CCL64). Focus formation and generation of nonproducer transformed cell lines with murine and feline sarcoma viruses. *Virol* 60:282-287, 1974.

40. Herz A et al: C-type viruses in bone marrow of cats with myeloproliferative disease. *J Natl Cancer Inst* 44:339-348, 1970.

41. Hinshaw VS and Blank HF: Isolation of feline leukemia virus from clinical specimens. *Am J Vet Res* 38:55-57, 1977.

42. Holmberg CA et al: Feline malignant lymphomas: comparison of morphologic and immunologic characteristics. *Am J Vet Res* 37:1455-1460, 1976.

43. Hoover EA and Kociba GJ: Bone lesions in cats with anemia induced by feline leukemia virus. *J Natl Cancer Inst* 53:1277-1284, 1974.

44. Hoover EA et al: Feline leukemia virus infection: Age-related variation in response of cats to experimental infection. *J Natl Cancer Inst* 57:365-369, 1976.

45. Hoover EA et al, in Hardy WD Jr et al: *Feline Leukemia Virus*. Elsevier/North Holland, New York, pp 195-202. 1980.

46. Jakowski RM et al, in Hardy WD Jr et al: *Feline Leukemia Virus*. Elsevier/North Holland, New York, pp 141-149. 1980.

47. Jarrett O, in Hardy WD Jr et al: *Feline Leukemia Virus*. Elsevier/North Holland, New York, pp 473-479. 1980.

48. Jarrett O et al: Detection of transient and persistent feline leukemia virus infections. *Vet Record* 110:225-228, 1982.

49. Jarrett O et al: The frequency of occurrence of feline leukemia virus subgroups in cats. *Intl J Cancer* 21:334-337, 1978.

50. Jarrett O et al: Determinants of the host range of feline leukemia viruses. *J Gen Virol* 20:169-175, 1973.

51. Jarrett O et al: Protection of kittens from feline leukemia virus infection by maternally-derived antibody. *Vet Record* 101:304-305, 1977.

52. Jarrett WFH et al: Vaccination against feline leukemia virus using a cell membrane antigen system. *Intl J Cancer* 167:134-141, 1975.

53. Jarrett WFH, in Clemmenson J and Yohn DS: *Comparative Leukemia Research*. S Karger, Basel, Switzerland, 1976. pp 209-211.

54. Jarrett WFH et al: Leukemia in the cat. A virus-like particle associated with leukemia (lymphosarcoma). *Nature* 202:567-569, 1964.

55. Jarrett O et al: Antibody response and virus survival in cats vaccinated against feline leukemia. *Nature* 248:230-232, 1974.

56. Kahn DE et al: Field evaluation of Leukassay F, an FeLV detection test kit. *Feline Pract* 10(2):41-45, 1980.

57. Kawakami TG et al: "C" type viral particles in plasma of cats with feline leukemia. *Science* 158:1049-1050, 1967.

58. Kiehl AR et al: Effects of feline leukemia virus infection on neutrophil chemotaxis *in vitro*. *Am J Vet Res* 48:76-80, 1987.

59. Kobilinsky L et al: Hypocomplementemia associated with naturally occurring lymphosarcoma in pet cats. *J Immunol* 122:2139-2142, 1979.

60. Lane HC and Fauci AS: Immunologic abnormalities in the acquired immuno-deficiency syndrome. *Ann Rev Immunol* 3:477-500, 1985.

61. Langweiler M et al: Role of suppressor cells in feline leukemia virus-associated immunosuppression. *Cancer Res* 43:1957-1960, 1983.

62. Lewis MG et al: Protection against feline leukemia by vaccination with a subunit vaccine. *Infect Immun* 34:888-894, 1981.

63. Lutz H et al: Monoclonal antibodies to three epitopic regions of feline leukemia virus p27 and their use in enzyme-linked immunosorbent assay of p27. *J Immunol Methods* 56:109-120, 1983.

64. Lutz H et al: Detection of feline leukemia virus infection. *Feline Pract* 10(4):13-23, 1980.

65. Lutz H et al, in Essex M et al: *Viruses in Naturally Occurring Cancer.* Cold Springs Harbor Laboratory, New York, 1980. pp 643-644.

66. Lutz H et al: Course of feline leukemia virus infection and its detection by enzyme-linked immunosorbent assay and monoclonal antibodies. *Am J Vet Res* 44:2054-2059, 1983.

67. Madewell BR and Jarrett O: Recovery of feline leukemia virus from nonviremic cats. *Vet Record* 112:339-342, 1983.

68. Mathes LE et al, in Hardy WD Jr et al: *Feline Leukemia Virus.* Elsevier/North Holland, New York, 1980. pp 211-216.

69. McClelland AJ et al, in Hardy WD Jr et al: *Feline Leukemia Virus.* Elsevier/North Holland, New York, 1980. pp 121-126.

70. Moore FM et al: Distinctive peripheral lymph node hyperplasia of young cats. *Vet Pathol* 23:386-391, 1986.

71. Murray HW et al: Impaired production of lymphokines and immune (gamma) interferon in the acquired immunodeficiency syn-drome. *New Engl J Med* 310:883-889, 1984.

72. Olsen RG et al: Immunization against feline oncornavirus disease using a killed tumor cell vaccine. *Cancer Res* 36:3642-3646, 1976.

73. Pedersen NC: Feline infectious peritonitis and feline enteric coronavirus infections. Part II: Feline infectious peritonitis. *Feline Pract* 13(5):5-14, 1983.

74. Pedersen NC, Univ California, Davis: Personal observation, 1984.

75. Pedersen NC: Virolgic and immunologic aspects of feline infectious peritonitic virus infection. *Adv Exp Biol Med* 218:529-550, 1987.

76. Pedersen NC et al: Evaluation of a commercial feline leukemia virus vaccine for immunogenicity and efficacy. *Feline Pract* 15(6):7-20, 1985.

77. Pedersen NC et al: The clinical significance of latent feline leukemia virus infection in cats. *Feline Pract* 14(2):32-48, 1984.

78. Pedersen NC et al: Feline chronic progressive polyarthritis. *Am J Vet Res* 41:522-535, 1980.

79. Pedersen NC et al: Studies of naturally transmitted feline leukemia virus infection. *Am J Vet Res* 38:1523-1531, 1977.

80. Pedersen NC et al: Safety and efficacy studies of live and killed feline leukemia virus vaccines. *Am J Vet Res* 40:1120-1126, 1979.

81. Perryman LE et al: Immunologic reactivity of the cat: immunosuppression in experimental feline leukemia. *J Natl Cancer Inst* 49:1357-1365, 1972.

82. Pool RR and Harris JM: Feline osteochondromatosis. *Feline Pract* 5(4):24-30, 1975.

83. Post JE and Warren L, in Hardy WD Jr et al: *Feline Leukemia Virus.* Elsevier/North Holland, New York, 1980. pp 151-155.

84. Reimann KA et al: Immunologic profiles of cats with persistent, naturally acquired feline leukemia virus infection. *Am J Vet Res* 47:1935-1939, 1986.

85. Reinacher M: Feline leukemia virus-associated enteritis. A condition with features of feline panleukopenia. *Vet Pathol* 24:1-4, 1987.

86. Reinacher M and Theilen G: Frequency and significance of feline leukemia virus infection in necropsied cats. *Am J Vet Res* 48:939-945, 1987.

87. Rickard CG et al: A transmissible virus-induced lymphocytic leukemia of the cat. *J Natl Cancer Inst* 42:987-1014, 1969.

88. Rogerson P et al: Epidemiological studies of feline leukemia virus infection. I. Serologic survey of urban cats. *Intl J Cancer* 15:781-785, 1975.

89. Rojko JL et al: Detection of feline leukemia virus in tissues of cats by a paraffin embedding immunofluorescence procedure. *J Natl Cancer Inst* 61:1315-1321, 1978.

90. Rojko JL et al: Influence of adrenal corticosteroids on the susceptibility of cats to feline leukemia virus infection. *Cancer Res* 39:3789-3791, 1979.

91. Rojko JL et al: Pathogenesis of experimental feline leukemia virus infections. *J Natl Cancer Inst* 63:759-768, 1979.

92. Rojko JL et al: Reactivation of latent feline leukemia virus infection. *Nature* 298: 385-388, 1982.

93. Rosenberg ZF et al: Comparative analysis of the genome of feline leukemia viruses. *J Virol* 35:542-546, 1980.

94. Russell PH and Jarrett O: The specificity of neutralizing antibodies to feline leukaemia virus. *Intl J Cancer* 21:768-788, 1978.

95. Sarma PS and Log T: Subgroup classification of feline leukemia and sarcoma viruses by viral interference and neutralization tests. *Virol* 54:160-169, 1973.

96. Sarma PS et al: Differential host range of viruses of feline leukemia-sarcoma complex. *Virol* 64:438-446, 1975.

97. Schaller JP et al: Active and passive immunization of cats with inactivated feline oncornaviruses. *J Natl Cancer Inst* 59: 1441-1450, 1977.

98. Schalm OW: Megaloblastic marrow cytology in the cat: Vitamin B12 and folic acid deficiencies and erythroleukemia. *Feline Pract* 4(5):16-19, 1974.

99. Scott DW et al: Autoimmune hemolytic anemia in the cat. *JAAHA* 9:530-539, 1973.

100. Sharpee RL et al: Feline leukemia virus vaccine: Evaluation of safety and efficacy against persistent viremia and tumor development. *Comp Cont Ed Pract Vet* 8:267-277, 1986.

101. Theilen GH and Madewell BR: *Veterinary Cancer Medicine*. 2nd ed. Lea & Febiger, Philadelphia, 1987. pp 374-381.

102. Trainin Z et al: Suppression of the humoral antibody response in natural retro-virus infection. *Science* 220:858-859, 1983.

103. Vedbrat SS et al, in Hardy WD Jr et al: *Feline Leukemia Virus*. Elsevier/North Holland, New York, 1980. pp 298-307.

104. Vedbrat SS et al: Feline oncornavirus-associated cell membrane antigen: A viral and not a cellularly coded transformation-specific antigen of cat lymphomas. *Virol* 124:445-461, 1983.

105. Weiser MG and Kociba GJ: Erythrocyte macrocytosis in feline leukemia virus associated anemia. *Vet Pathol* 20:687-697, 1983.

106. Williams LW et al: Ophthalmic neoplasms in the cat. *JAAHA* 17:999-1008, 1981.

107. Yamamoto J, Univ California, Davis: Unpublished observations, 1984.

Additional References

108. Bech-Nielsen S et al: Feline infectious peritonitis and viral respiratory diseases in feline leukemia virus-infected cats. *JAAHA* 17:759-765, 1981.

109. Blakeslee JR Jr and Rojko JL, in Olsen RG et al: *Comparative Pathology of Viral Diseases*, Vol II. CRC Press, Boca Raton, FL, 1985. pp 1-19.

110. Bonham L et al: Transforming potential of a myc-containing variant of feline leukemia virus *in vitro* in early passage feline cells. *J Virol* 61:3072-3081, 1987.

111. Day NK et al: Remission of lymphoma leukemia in cats following *ex vivo* immunosorption therapy using *Staphylococcus* protein A. *J Biol Response Modifiers* 3:278-285, 1984.

112. Engleman RW et al: Suppression of gamma interferon production by inactivated feline leukemia virus. *Science* 227:1368-1370, 1985.

113. Fischinger PJ et al: Isolation of an RD-114-like oncornavirus from cat cell line. *J Virol* 11:978-985, 1973.

114. Forrest D et al: Altered structure and expression of c-myc in feline T-cell tumours. *Virol* 158:194-205, 1987.

115. Fulton R et al: Retroviral transduction of T-cell antigen receptor beta-chain and myc genes. *Nature* 326:190-194, 1987.

116. Gilbert JH et al: Feline leukemia virus envelope protein expression encoded by a recombinant vaccinia virus: apparent lack of immunogenicity in vaccinated animals. *Virus Res* 7:49-67, 1987.

117. Hoover EA et al: Congenital feline leukemia virus infection. *Intl Symp Comp Leuk Res* 11:7-8 1983.

118. Jones FR et al: Treatment of feline leukemia and reversal of FeLV by *ex vivo* removal of IgG: A preliminary report. *Cancer* 46:675-684, 1980.

119. Lewis MG et al: Polymorphonuclear leukocyte dysfunction associated with feline leukaemia virus infection. *J Gen Virol* 67:2113-2118, 1986.

120. Liu WT et al: Remission of leukemia and loss of feline leukemia virus in cats injected with *Staphylococcus* protein A: Association with increased circulating complement-dependent cytotoxic antibody. *Proc Natl Acad Sci (USA)* 81:6471-6475, 1984.

121. Loar AS: The zoonotic potential of feline leukemia virus. *Vet Clin No Am (Sm Anim Pract)* 17:105-115, 1987.

122. Lutz H et al: Detection of feline leukemia virus in saliva. *J Clin Micro* 25:827-831, 1987.

123. Mandell MP et al: Endogenous RD-114 virus of cats: Absence of antibodies to RD-114 envelope antigens in cats naturally exposed to feline leukemia virus. *Infect Immun* 24:282-285, 1979.

124. Mitani M et al: Suppressive effect on polyclonal B-cell activation of a synthetic peptide homologous to a transmembrane component of oncogenic retroviruses. *Proc Natl Acad Sci (USA)* 84:237-240, 1987.

125. Miura T et al: Structural abnormality and over-expression of the myc-gene in feline leukemias. *Intl J Cancer* 40:564-569, 1987.

126. Mullins JI et al: Disease-specific and tissue-specific production of unintegrated feline leukemia virus variant in feline AIDS. *Nature* 319:333-336, 1986.

127. Nash AS and Bobade PA: *Haemobartonella felis* infection in cats from the Glasgow area. *Vet Record* 119:373-375, 1986.

128. Nicolaisen-Strouss K et al: Natural feline leukemia virus variant escapes neutralization by a monoclonal antibody via an amino acid change outside of the antibody-binding epitope. *J Virol* 61:3410-3415, 1987.

129. Onions D et al: Recombinant feline leukemia viruses containing the myc gene rapidly produce clonal tumours expressing T-cell antigen receptor gene transcripts. *Intl J Cancer* 40:40-45, 1987.

130. Osterhaus A et al: Comparison of serological reponses in cats vaccinated with two different FeLV vaccine preparations. *Vet Record* 121:260, 1987.

131. Pedersen NC et al: Possible immunoenhancement of persistent viremia by feline leukemia virus en-

velope glycoprotein vaccines in challenge-exposure situations where inactivated whole virus vaccines were protective. *Vet Immun Immunopath* 11:123-148, 1986.

132. Priester WA and Hayes HM: Feline leukemia after feline infectious anemia. *J Natl Cancer Inst* 51:289-291, 1973.

133. Testa NG et al: Haemopoietic colony formation (BFU-E, GM-CFC) during the development of pure red cell hypoplasia induced in the cat by feline leukemia virus. *Leukemia Res* 7:103-116, 1983.

134. Weijer K et al: Control of feline leukemia virus infection by a removal programme. *Vet Record* 119:555-556, 1986.

135. Wellman et al: Inhibition of erythroid colony-forming cells by an M_r 15,000 protein of feline leukemia virus. *Cancer Res* 44:1527-1529, 1984.

136. Yamamoto JK et al: A feline retrovirus induced T-lymphoblastoid cell-line that produces an atypical alpha type of interferon. *Vet Immun Immunopath* 11:1-19, 1986.

137. Yasuda M et al: Influence of inactivated feline leukemia retrovirus on feline alpha interferon and immunoglobulin production. *Clin Exp Immunol* 69:240-245, 1987.

138. Weiss RC: Immunotherapy for feline leukemia, using staphylococcal protein A or heterologous interferons: immunopharmacologic actions and potential use. *JAVMA* 192:681-684, 1988.

Chapter 14

Feline Sarcoma Virus Infection

Type-C oncornaviruses are classified into 3 major groups: chronic leukemia viruses; acute leukemia viruses; and sarcoma viruses. Sarcoma and acute leukemia viruses contain cancer-causing genes (oncogenes), which directly code for proteins that somehow cause virus-infected cells to behave in a malignant fashion. In contrast, chronic leukemia viruses, such as FeLV, cause cancer in a relatively small percentage of infected cats, and only after months or years. Chronic leukemia viruses do not cause direct transformation of cells *in vitro* or *in vivo*; their mode of causing tumors is more indirect and less understood.

Acute leukemia viruses cause tumors within days or weeks and have been recognized mainly in rodents and chickens. However, Toth and co-workers recently identified an acute leukemia virus that causes myelogenous leukemia in a high proportion of kittens after only a few weeks.[51] Retrovirus isolates containing the c-*myc* transforming gene have also been isolated from cats with T-cell leukemia.[23,28,30] In at least 1 case, FeLV-c-*myc* recombinant virus was infectious to cells in culture, but as of yet has not also infected and transformed cells *in vitro*.[22,23,28,30] Sarcoma viruses cause malignant transformation of fibroblasts *in vitro* and *in vivo* after several days.

Sarcomagenic retroviruses were first isolated from chickens by Rous, and Fujinami and Inamoto.[12,40] Sarcoma viruses were later isolated from rats, mice and primates.[18,21,27,48] The first feline isolate was by Snyder and Theilen.[45] A cell-free extract of a widely disseminated fibrosarcoma in a 2-year-old female domestic cat readily induced progressively growing fibrosarcomas in newborn kittens. Subsequently, the number of different sarcoma isolates obtained from spontaneously occurring multicentric fibrosarcomas of domestic cats has increased.

Etiologic Agent

Sarcoma viruses are mutants caused by *in-vivo* recombination of host and FeLV genes.[16] Therefore, feline sarcoma viruses (FeSV) arise spontaneously only in cats chronically infected with FeLV. Recombination usually involves transduction of cellular genes into the retrovirus genome.[6] Integration of host genes is usually accomplished at the expense of parent FeLV genes deleted from the new sarcoma virus. Following primary infection with FeLV, proviral DNA is inserted randomly throughout the host genome, providing ample opportunity for transduction. However, only a small percentage of FeLV-infected cats ever generate sarcoma viruses. Either the transducing event is exceedingly rare or only a small proportion of transductants result in tumors and sarcomagenic particles that can be rescued. The appearance of multicentric fibrosarcomas in FeLV-infected cats provides a visible way to recognize this event in natural infections.

Size of the virus-gene deletions and host-gene insertions varies among FeSV isolates (Table 1). The deleted FeLV parent genes usually code for parts of the FeLV *gag*

Table 1. Characteristics of currently known FeSV isolates.

FeSV Isolate	Designation of v-src	Size of gag-src Polyprotein (daltons)	Intact or Partial gag Proteins within gag-src	Tyrosine-Specific Protein-Kinase Activity
ST-FeSV	fes	85,000	p12,p15	yes
GA-FeSV	fes	110,000	p12,p15	yes
SM-FeSV	fms	170,000	p12,p15,p27	no
GR-FeSV	fgr	70,000	p15	yes
PI-FeSV	sis	76,000	?	yes
HZ1-FeSV	fes	96,000	p12,p15,p27	yes
HZ2-FeSV	abl	98,000	?	yes
HZ4-FeSV	kit	80,000	?	yes
HZ5-FeSV	fms	105,000	p15	no
NY-FeSV	rasK	?	?	binds guanosine triphosphate
FT-FeSV	sis	?	?	?
TP1-FeSV	fgr	83,000	p27	yes
TP2-FeSV	sis	?	?	yes
PT1-FeSV	sis	?	?	?

proteins, all of the FeLV *pol* gene, and all or part of the FeLV *env* gene. The amino terminus portion of the *gag* genes that code for FeLV p15 and p12 is usually present. Variable deletions exist in the remaining p10 and p27 genes.

As in almost all mammalian and avian sarcoma viruses, FeSV is replication defective. Because of gene deletions and truncations, the FeSV genome cannot code for all of the proteins necessary for assembly of an intact and infectious virus particle. However, this defect can be overcome if the FeSV genome replicates within FeLV-infected cells. The FeLV genome codes for all of the structural proteins necessary for virion assembly. Cells infected with both viruses utilizes a mixture of virus-coded proteins and RNA to produce virus particles. Some of the particles contain FeLV structural proteins, some particles contain both FeLV proteins and RNA, and some particles are structurally defective. In this manner, FeLV infection provides both exogenous genetic sequences that recombine with cellular genes and the means to "rescue" the replication-defective recombinant genome from the cell. Therefore, infectious stocks of FeSV are a mixture of FeLV and sarcoma viruses. In most cases, there is a 10-fold excess of FeLV to FeSV. Since FeLV "helps" the sarcoma virus to be infectious, it is often referred to as "helper virus." Because sarcomagenic RNA is encapsulated and enveloped by FeLV proteins, FeSV possesses the structural and physical properties of FeLV (see Chapter 13).

Currently, 14 different FeSV isolates have been obtained from spontaneously occurring multicentric fibrosarcomas in pet cats. Of these isolates, 11 have been well characterized and the rest only partially studied (Table 1). According to convention, FeSV isolates are designated by the initials of their discoverers. The Snyder-Theilen FeSV (ST-FeSV) was isolated in 1969, followed by the Gardner-Arnstein FeSV (GA-FeSV), Susan McDonough FeSV (SM-FeSV), Parodi Irgens FeSV (PI-FeSV), Noronha-Youngren FeSV (NY-FeSV), Gardner-Rasheed FeSV (GR-FeSV), Hardy-Zuckerman (HZ1,2,4 and 5-FeSV), Friis-Theilen FeSV (FT-FeSV), Theilen-Pedersen (TP1 and 2-FeSV) and Pedersen-Theilen FeSV (PT1-FeSV).[4,5,10,14,16,17,19,26,33,36,43,58,59] Oncogene characteristics and gene products of these various isolates are listed in Table 1.

The sarcomagenic genes of various sarcoma viruses have been designated *src*.[6] They are also referred to as v-*src*, a term that denotes their viral origin. The v-*src* genes of various FeSV isolates are derived from corresponding host-cell genes. The cellular genes that give origin to v-*src* are referred to as c-*src*.[6,11,15] The nature of the v-*src* varies among FeSV isolates. Many of the feline v-*src* genes are closely related to v-*src* genes of various avian and murine sarcoma viruses, as well as other FeSV isolates (Table 1). This indicates a finite number of cellular genes associated with malignant transformation *in vitro* or *in vivo*. These genes are preserved in a similar form in virtually every animal species. Each different FeSV v-*src* gene is also designated by initials. By convention, closely related v-*src* genes are given the same designation regardless of their species of origin. For instance, the v-*src* of ST-FeSV is designated *fes*. The *fes* gene is also present in the Fujinami avian sarcoma virus, GA-FeSV and HZ1-FeSV. The v-*src* gene of SM-FeSV is unrelated to all other sarcoma genes and has been designated *fms*.

The various v-*src* genes displace normal viral genes, usually in the distal portion of the *gag* genes, the entire *pol* gene, and all or part of the *env* gene. Therefore, the basic genomic map of most FeSV isolates is *gag* (partial)-*src*-env (partial). The normal complete configuration of the parent leukemia virus is *gag-pol-env*. Because the viral genetic material has been replaced by a smaller amount of cellular genetic material, the FeSV genome is usually smaller than the intact FeLV genome. During viral protein synthesis by host cells, v-*src* gene products are usually linked to a portion of the remaining FeLV *gag* and *env* proteins. This large polyprotein is referred to as *gag-X* or *gag-src*. The precise amount of *gag* protein in the *gag-src* complex varies from isolate to isolate (Table 1). The specific *gag-src* polyproteins are designated by their chemical composition (protein or glycoprotein), molecular weight in kilodaltons and specific *src*-gene product. For instance the *gag-src* protein of ST-FeSV has been designated p85 $^{gag-fes}$. Therefore, the ST-FeSV gene product is an 85,000-dalton protein containing both *fes*- and *gag*-related moieties.

Cell-transvection experiments indicate the entire *gag-src* gene product is necessary for cell transformation.[2] Cleavage within either the *gag* or *src* regions abolishes its transforming activity. Preservation of the long terminal repeat region flanking the remnant of the *env* gene is also essential for transformation.

The specific *gag-src* gene products of various FeSV strains have several common features: elaboration of these proteins by the cell is somehow responsible for malignant transformation, and all but 2 of the isolates tested (eg, p170 $^{gag-fms}$ and p 80 $^{gag-kit}$) are potent kinases for phosphorylation of tyrosine residues. The exact role of tyrosine phosphorylation *in vivo* and *in vitro* is still a matter of conjecture.[6] Reynolds and coworkers demonstrated that ST-FeSV- and GA-FeSV-induced cell transformation was associated with increases in intracellular protein kinase activity.[38] In contrast, SM-FeSV transformation was not associated with a rise in protein kinase activity within the cells. This was somewhat expected, as the p170 $^{gag-fms}$ protein either does not function as a tyrosine kinase or, at best, is a poor tyrosine phosphokinase.[3,54] In addition, some *gag-src* proteins of sarcoma viruses from other species do not act as protein kinases. Therefore, cell transformation cannot be explained solely on phosphokinase activity. The c-*sis* gene product is very similar to human platelet-derived growth factor (PDGF).[56] The c-*erb*-B gene product is similar to the receptor for epidermal growth factor (EGF) and the c-*fms* gene product is related to the receptor for macrophage colony-stimulating factor (CSF-1).[9,41] Thus, a role for these proteins in reactions other than phosphorylation is established. The *fgr* gene products of GR-FeSV and TP1-FeSV contain a portion of actin, a cytoskeletal protein.[29] The various transforming proteins also have somewhat different cellular sites of action. Many *gag-src* proteins are elaborated on the cell membranes, while others are intracytoplasmic or nuclear.[6]

Pathogenesis

Virus-induced fibrosarcomas in domestic cats occur worldwide in the same environments as FeLV and must be differentiated from nonvirus-induced fibrosarcomas. Though both are morphologically similar and usually arise in the skin, there are important differentiating features.[48] Virus-induced fibrosarcomas tend to be multicentric and are usually found in FeLV-infected cats less than 7 years of age. Nonvirus-induced fibrosarcomas are usually solitary and locally invasive. They also tend to occur in cats over 7 years of age and are not associated with active FeLV infection. Solitary nonviral fibrosarcomas in older FeLV-negative cats are about 40 times more common than virus-induced fibrosarcomas.[16]

Virus-induced fibrosarcomas occur spontaneously in FeLV-infected cats, but there is no evidence of horizontal spread from cat to cat. Cats with virus-induced fibrosarcomas appear to shed only FeLV and, except within the tumors themselves, very little infectious sarcomagenic virus is detected in the rest of the body.[8,34] Therefore, the defective FeSV genome does not seem to be as efficiently packaged by FeLV proteins as the intact FeLV genome.

Pathogenesis of virus-induced fibrosarcomas in cats has largely been determined by experimental studies. However, natural disease occurs spontaneously, endogenously and secondary to long-standing FeLV infection. In contrast, experimental tumors are induced with exogenous agents; sarcomagenic and leukemogenic viruses are given at the same time. Further, most older kittens and adult cats reject experimentally induced fibrosarcomas. Naturally occurring virus-induced fibrosarcomas are always progressive and fatal, though it is possible that many are rejected before they become clinically apparent.

Fibrosarcomas can be induced with subcutaneous injections of cell-free tumor extracts, living FeSV-transformed syngeneic, allogeneic or xenogeneic cells, or purified virus. Various strains of FeSV differ greatly in virulence. Some isolates, such as ST-FeSV, SM-FeSV and PI-FeSV, induce rapidly growing tumors after a short incubation period.[19,26,45] Other isolates, such as TP1-FeSV, TP2-FeSV and PT1- FeSV, produce slowly growing tumors that persist for months before regressing or metastasizing.[33] Newborn or fetal kittens are very susceptible to tumor induction, but age resistance is rapidly acquired and peaks by 12-16 weeks or more.[44]

Following inoculation with tumorigenic FeSV stocks, systemic spread of the "helper" FeLV infection and local transformation of susceptible target cells at the inoculation site occur.[8,34] Target cells appear to be mainly fibroblasts. Certain strains of FeSV may induce melanosarcomas when injected into such sites as the eye.[1] Tumors resembling hemangiosarcomas or rhabdomyosarcomas are also occasionally seen. The FeSV can even cause transformation of B-lymphocytes *in vitro*.[35] However, such lymphoid tumors are never seen *in vivo*.

Clinical Features

Tumors begin to appear at the inoculation site within 5-14 days or more. Within 7-14 days, retrovirus can also be detected in the blood. With the exception of a small proportion of cats in the terminal stage of progressive tumor growth, the retrovirus in the blood is almost exclusively feline leukemia "helper" virus.[8,34] Infectious sarcomagenic particles are found in the highest concentration within the tumors and not in

Fig 1. Experimentally induced viral fibrosarcoma in a young cat. The cat was inoculated SC between the scapulae with a cell-free tumor extract containing the Snyder-Theilen strain of FeSV. The tumor weighed over 200 g within 30 days.

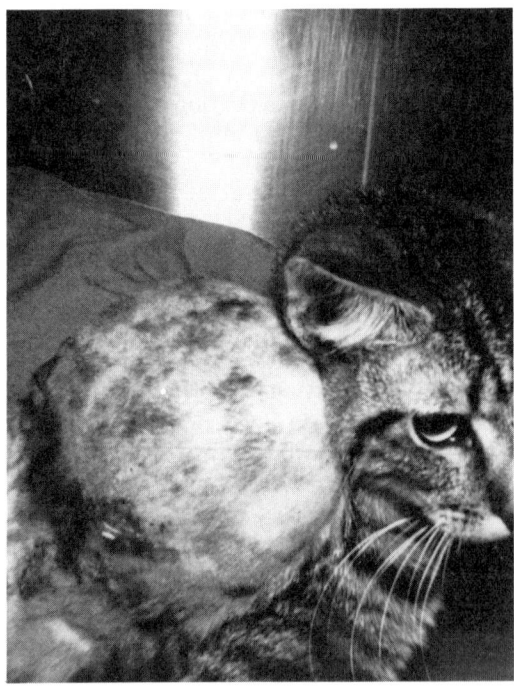

the circulation. This indicates the FeSV genome is less efficiently packaged than the FeLV genome. Tumors can grow slowly or rapidly and reach 25% or more of the cat's body weight (Fig 1). Metastases are more common in cats with slower-growing tumors. Metastatic lesions are most frequently seen in the eyes, liver, kidneys, lungs, subcutis, mouth and CNS. Metastatic tumors frequently appear at sites of trauma, such as multiple needle punctures, tooth eruptions, and ear tag placements. Irritation caused by these various events probably leads to localized inflammation and fibroplasia. Rapidly dividing fibroblasts within these sites are probably ideal targets for virus transformation.

Cats with progressive, slow-growing tumors can survive 14-180 days or more. However, kittens with fast-growing tumors rarely live longer than 2-3 weeks. When tumor regression occurs, it begins around day 14 and can be complete by days 21-28. Tumor regression is an immunologic event associated with lymphoid-cell, macrophage and plasma-cell infiltration and necrosis.[46] The reaction is best described as an acute or subacute granulomatous inflammation. Tumor regression also corresponds to the appearance of cytotoxic lymphocytes and antibody in the peripheral blood.[20,24,25]

Naturally occurring virus-induced sarcomas are usually seen in cats 1-7 years of age. Tumors appear as small, nonhealing ulcerative nodules in the skin over the trunk and limbs. Nodular growths often extend into adjacent skin, subcutis and underlying muscles. Tumors frequently recur at the site of excision, which often fails to heal and leaves an open, draining sore. Within a few weeks, additional nodules appear in surrounding skin and muscle, and in sites distant from the primary lesion. Secondary tumors may result from metastasis of primary lesions or from new tumors induced by the virus. Metastasis to internal organs, such as the liver, spleen, lungs and serosal surfaces, does not usually occur until relatively late in the course of illness. In rare circumstances, the tumor metastasizes diffusely along cuticular planes and exudes fluid into the subcuticular space.

Some cats survive with slowly spreading cutaneous tumors for many weeks or months before becoming cachectic.

Pathologic Features

Almost all naturally occurring FeSV-induced tumors are histologically classified as fibrosarcomas. Melanosarcomas, rhabdomyosarcomas and hemangioma-type tumors are less common in naturally occurring infections.[1] Fibrosarcomas are characterized histologically by whorls and interwoven bundles of plump, immature fibroblasts interspersed with connective tissue.[50] Individual tumor cells are often spindle shaped or polygonal. Some tumors, especially those that are experimentally induced, contain numerous mucin- or blood-filled sinuses lined by cords of tumor cells.[46] Such tumors are difficult to distinguish from hemangiosarcomas. In some cases, the tumor cells have the appearance of neoplastic muscle cells or pigmented melanocytes.

Naturally occurring FeSV-induced tumors are virtually devoid of host inflammatory-cell infiltrates. Progressively growing tumors in experimentally inoculated kittens also lack significant inflammatory-cell infiltrates. Regressing tumors are markedly infiltrated by host inflammatory cells and are common in experimentally inoculated cats but are not recognized in naturally occurring infections.[43] Necrosis is prominent in the central regions of regressing tumors. The rim of surviving tumor is densely infiltrated with macrophages, giant cells, neutrophils, mast cells, plasma cells and lymphocytes. Eventually the tumor is replaced by scar tissue.

Clinicopathologic Features

Histologically confirmed fibrosarcomas that occur in FeLV-infected cats are almost always virus-induced and transmissible.

Treatment and Prevention

No known treatment exists for naturally occurring FeSV-induced tumors. Excision is often incomplete. Further, the multicentric nature of the tumors usually makes this approach ineffective. FeSV-induced tumors can be prevented by eliminating exposure to FeLV.

Infection and Immunity

Naturally occurring virus-induced fibrosarcomas seem to grow unimpeded by host immunity. In contrast, experimentally induced tumors frequently grow for a short period and then regress. Tumor regression is intimately associated with the appearance of both cytotoxic antibodies and lymphocytes in the blood.[20,24,25] Therefore, immunity to FeSV-induced tumors in cats resembles the immunity demonstrated for sarcoma virus-induced tumors in other species. It is unknown why naturally occurring tumors evoke such a poor immune response, whereas experimentally induced tumors are highly immunogenic. One possibility is that naturally occurring tumors represent only the proportion that occurs in unresponsive hosts. Most naturally occurring virus-induced tumors are presumably rejected before ever becoming clinically apparent. The second possibility is that concurrent FeLV infection leads to an acquired immunodeficiency syndrome that negates the normal host immune response. Indeed, cats with experimentally induced, progressively growing tumors always have a persistent feline leukemia "helper" virus viremia, while retroviremia usually disappears in cats with regressing tumors.[8,34]

The target antigen for host immunity has not been precisely determined. However, it appears that recognition antigens are present on the surface of the tumor cell membrane. These antigens can be of several possible types: virus associated (*gag* or *env*); virus specific nonvirion associated; transformation specific; or embryonic. Viral antigens are elaborated on the surface of productively transformed tumor cells, but there is circumstantial evidence that virus-specific antibody and cytotoxic lymphocytes are not solely responsible for rejection. In a small percentage of experimentally inoculated cats, tumors are rejected in the face of persistent retrovirus infection.[8,34] This suggests that nonvirus-associated antigens on the surface of FeSV-induced tumor cells may also be involved.

Animal and Public Health Considerations

Feline sarcoma virus induces fibrosarcomas following experimental inoculation in a number of different animal species, including cats, rabbits, dogs, sheep, rats, pigs and several species of nonhuman primates.[13,14,48,50,57] However, tumor induction is facilitated in nonfeline species by first adapting the virus to cells of the intended host species *in vitro* or by inoculating the virus into fetuses. Tumors induced in heterospecies are generally regressive.[32,49,50,57] Tumors induced in fetal puppies have grown progressively, but those induced in sheep usually regress *in utero*.[49,50] Regressive tumors induced in marmosets and neonatal puppies do not produce virus, while progressively growing tumors in fetal puppies do.[50] However, virus expression occurs in tumors that do not produce virus when the tumor cells are cultured *in vivo* away from the inhibitory effects of the host immune system. Though FeSV can induce tumors in many species, it has only been naturally isolated from cats.

There is no evidence that FeSV-induced tumors are naturally contagious from cat to cat. Feline sarcoma virus is not infectious to people.

References

1. Albert DM et al: Feline uveal melanoma model induced with feline sarcoma virus. *Invest Ophthalmol* 20:606-624, 1981.

2. Barbacid M: Cellular transformation by subgenomic feline sarcoma virus DNA. *J Virol* 37:518-523, 1981.

3. Barbacid M and Lauver AV: Gene products of McDonough feline sarcoma virus have an *in vitro*-associated protein kinase that phosphorylates tyrosine resi-dues: lack of detection of this enzymatic activity *in vivo*. *J Virol* 40:812-821, 1981.

4. Besmer P et al: The Hardy-Zuckerman 2-FeSV, a new feline retrovirus with oncogene homology to Abelson-MuLV. *Nature* 303:825-828, 1983.

5. Besmer P et al: The Parodi-Irgens feline sarcoma virus and simian sarcoma virus have homologous oncogenes, but in different contexts of the virus genomes. *J Virol* 46:606-616, 1983.

6. Bishop JM: Cellular oncogenes and retroviruses. *Ann Rev Biochem* 52:301-354, 1983.

7. Chen AP et al: Feline sarcoma virus-specific transformation related proteins and protein kinase activity in tumor cells. *Virol* 124:274-285, 1983.

8. deNoronha F et al: Circulating levels of feline leukemia and sarcoma viruses and fibrosarcoma regression in persistently viremic cats. *Cancer Res* 43:1663-1668, 1983.

9. Downard J et al: Close similarity of epidermal growth factor receptor and V-*erb*-B oncogene protein sequences. *Nature* 307:521-527, 1984.

10. Ferdinand F-J et al: New FeSV isolates from spontaneous fibrosarcomas in cat. *Zbl Bakt Hyg I Abl Orig A* 253:13, 1982.

11. Franchini G et al: "Onc" sequences (v-*fes*) of Snyder-Theilen feline sarcoma virus are derived from noncontinuous regions of a cat cellular gene (c-*fes*). *Nature* 290:154-157, 1981.

12. Fujinami A and Inamoto K: Ueber Geschwülste bei Japanischer Haushühnern ins-besondere über einen transplantablen Tumor. *Zeitschr Krebsforsch* 14:94-119, 1914.

13. Gardner MB et al: Feline sarcoma virus induction in dogs and cats. *JAVMA* 158:1046-1054, 1971.

14. Gardner MB et al: Experimental transmission of feline fibrosarcoma to cats and dogs. *Nature* 226:807-809, 1970.

15. Groffen J et al: Transforming genes of avian (v-*fps*) and mammalian (v-*fes*) retroviruses correspond to a common cellular locus. *Virol* 125:480-486, 1983.

16. Hardy WD Jr, in Holzworth J: *Diseases of the Cat*. Saunders, Philadelphia, 1987. pp 246-268.

17. Hardy WD Jr et al, in Yohn DS and Blakeslee JR: *Advances in Comparative Leukemia Research*. Elsevier Biomedical, New York, 1982. pp 205-206.

18. Harvey JJ: An unidentified virus which causes the rapid production of tumors in mice. *Nature* 204:1104-1105, 1964.

19. Irgens K et al: Isolement d'un virus sarcomatogène feline à partir d'un fibrosarcome spontanè du chat: etude du pouvoir sarcomatogène in vivo. *CR Acad Sci*, Paris 276:1783-1786, 1973.

20. Johnson L et al: The nature of immunity to Snyder-Theilen fibrosarcoma virus induced tumors in cats. *Vet Immunol Immunopathol* 9:283-300, 1985.

21. Kirsten WH and Mayer LA: Morphologic responses to a murine erythroblastosis virus. *J Natl Cancer Inst* 39:311-335, 1967.

22. Lees G et al in: *Proc 4th Int FeLV Meeting*. St Thomas, US Virgin Islands, 1983. p 32.

23. Levy LS et al: Isolation of a feline leukemia provirus containing the oncogene *myc* from a feline lymphosarcoma. *Nature* 308:853-856, 1984.

24. McCarty JM and Grant CK: Feline cytotoxic immune mechanisms against virus-associated leukemia and fibrosarcoma. *Cell Immun* 81:157-168, 1983.

25. McCarty JM and Grant CK: Cellular immune response in the blood of cats is restricted to autochthonous feline sarcoma virus transformed cells. *Intl J Cancer* 31:627-631, 1983.

26. McDonough SK et al: A transmissible feline fibrosarcoma of viral origin. *Cancer Res* 31:953-956, 1971.

27. Moloney JB: A virus-induced rhabdomyosarcoma of mice. *Natl Cancer Inst Monographs* 22:137-142, 1966.

28. Mullins JI et al: Viral transduction of c-*myc* gene in naturally occurring feline leukaemias. *Nature* 308:856-858, 1984.

29. Naharro G et al: Gene product of v-*fgr* onc: hybrid protein containing a portion of actin and a tyrosine-specific kinase. *Science* 223:63-66, 1984.

30. Neil JC et al: Transduction and rearrangement of the *myc* gene by feline leukaemia virus in natural occurring T-cell leukaemias. *Nature* 308:814-820, 1984.

31. Onions D et al in: *Proc 4th Int FeLV Meeting*. St Thomas, US Virgin Islands, 1983. p 70.

32. Pearson LD et al: Oncogenic activity of feline fibrosarcoma virus in newborn pigs. *Am J Vet Res* 34:405-409, 1973.

33. Pedersen NC, Univ California: Unpublished observations, 1983.

34. Pedersen NC et al: Biological behavior of tumors and associated retroviremia in cats inoculated with Snyder-Theilen fibrosarcoma virus and the phenomenon of tumor recurrence after primary regression. *Infect Immun* 43:631-636, 1984.

35. Pierce JH and Aaronson SA: In vitro transformation of murine pre-B lymphoid cells by Snyder-Theilen feline sarcoma virus. *J Virol* 46:993-1002, 1983.

36. Rasheed S et al: Origin and biological properties of a new feline sarcoma virus. *Virol* 117:238-244, 1982.

37. Reynolds FH Jr et al: Involvement of a high molecular-weight polyprotein translational product of Snyder-Theilen sarcoma virus in malignant transformation. *J Virol* 37:643-653, 1981.

38. Reynolds FH Jr et al: Differences in mechanisms of transformation by independent feline sarcoma virus isolates. *J Virol* 38:1084-1089, 1981.

39. Reynolds FH Jr et al: Feline sarcoma virus p115-associated protein kinase phosphorylates tyrosine. *J Biol Chem* 255:11040-11047, 1980.

40. Rous PA: A sarcoma of the fowl transmissible by an agent separable from the tumor cells. *J Exp Med* 13:397-411, 1911.

41. Sherr CJ et al: The c-*fms* proto-oncogene product is related to the receptor for the mononuclear phagocyte growth factor, CSF-1. *Cell* 41:665-676, 1985.

42. Shibuya M et al: Homology exists among the transforming sequences of avian and feline sarcoma viruses. *Proc Natl Acad Sci USA* 77:6536-6540, 1980.

43. Snyder HW Jr et al: Isolation of a new fibrosarcoma virus (HZ1-FeSV): Biochemical and immunological characterization of its translation product. *Virol* 132:205-210, 1984.

44. Snyder SP and Dungworth DL: Pathogenesis of feline viral fibrosarcomas: dose and age effects. *J Natl Cancer Inst* 51:793-798, 1973.

45. Snyder SP and Theilen GH: Transmissible feline fibrosarcoma. *Nature* 221:1074-1075, 1969.

46. Snyder SP et al: Morphological studies on transmissible feline fibrosarcomas. *Cancer Res* 30:1658-1667, 1970.

47. Stewart MA et al: Conservation of the c-*myc* coding sequence in transduced feline v-*myc* genes. *Virol* 154:121-134, 1986.

48. Theilen GH et al: C-type virus in tumor tissue of a woolly monkey (*Lagothrix* spp) with fibrosarcoma. *J Natl Cancer Inst* 47:881-889, 1971.

49. Theilen GH and Madewell BR: *Veterinary Cancer Medicine*. 2nd ed. Lea & Febiger, Philadelphia, 1987.

50. Theilen GH et al, in Dutcher RM: *Comparative Leukemia Research*. S Karger, Basel, Switzerland, 1970. pp 393-400.

51. Toth SR et al: Histopathological and hematological findings in myeloid leukemia induced by new feline leukemia virus isolate. *Vet Pathol* 23:462-470, 1986.

52. Twardzik DR et al: Similar transforming growth factors (TGFs) produced by cells transformed by different isolates of feline sarcoma virus. *Virol* 124:201-207, 1983.

53. Van de Ven WJM et al: Characterization of a 170,000-dalton polyprotein encoded by the McDonough strain of feline sarcoma virus. *J Virol* 35:165-175, 1980.

54. Van de Ven WJM et al, in Hardy WD Jr et al: *Feline Leukemia Virus*. Elsevier/North Holland, New York, 1981. pp 321-334.

55. Veronese F et al: Monoclonal antibodies specific to transforming polyprotein encoded by independent isolates of feline sarcoma virus. *J Virol* 43:896-904, 1982.

56. Waterfield MD et al: Platelet-derived growth factor is structurally related to putative transforming protein p28^{sis} of simian sarcoma virus. *Nature* 304:35-39, 1983.

57. Wolfe LG et al: Oncogenicity of feline fibrosarcoma viruses in marmoset monkeys: pathologic, virologic, and immunologic finding. *J Natl Cancer Inst* 49:419-537, 1972.

58. Youngren SD and de Noronha F, in Hardy WD Jr: *Proc 4th Int FeLV Meeting*. St Thomas, US Virgin Islands, 1983. p 16.

59. Ziemiecki A et al: Biological and biochemical characterization of a new isolate of feline sarcoma virus: Theilen-Pedersen (TP1-FeSV). *Virol* 138:324-331, 1984.

Chapter 15

Feline Immunodeficiency Virus Infection

Etiologic Agent

Feline immunodeficiency virus (FIV), formerly feline T-lymphotropic lentivirus (FTLV), is one of the most recently discovered infectious agents of cats. The virus belongs to the subfamily Lentiviridae of the family Retroviridae.[21] Feline immunodeficiency virus is enveloped, has short membrane spikes, is about 100-110 nm in diameter and contains a cone-shaped nucleoid (Fig 1).[12,21] Like other retroviruses, it buds from the outer membrane of infected cells and has the reverse transcriptase enzyme.[12,21] Maximum reverse transcriptase activity of FIV requires the cation magnesium; feline leukemia virus (FeLV) requires manganese.[12,21] It possesses the basic *gag-pol-env* gene structure of all retroviruses. Like lentiviruses, the genome is large, with over 9,000 base pairs, and contains a number of genes that regulate the transcription of viral proteins. The envelope protein is around 130 kD in size, and is heavily glycosylated.[11] The transmembrane protein is around 40 kD in size, and with core proteins of 28, 17, and 10 kD.[11,21] Feline immunodeficiency virus is antigenically related to equine infectious anemia virus, but unrelated to human and simian immunodeficiency viruses.[11] It is genetically related to all of these viruses, however. Like all species-specific lentiviruses, no 2 of them have much more than 30% cross species genetic homology.[18]

Feline immunodeficiency virus has several biologic features in common with human and simian immunodeficiency viruses (HIV and SIV), which are the causative agents of acquired immunodeficiency syndrome (AIDS) in people and rhesus macaques.[2,3,5,19] Unlike the animal lentiviruses that cause equine infectious anemia, caprine arthritis-encephalitis and ovine Visna-Maedi, but similar to HIV and SIV, FIV has a high degree of tropism for T-lymphocytes.[12,21]

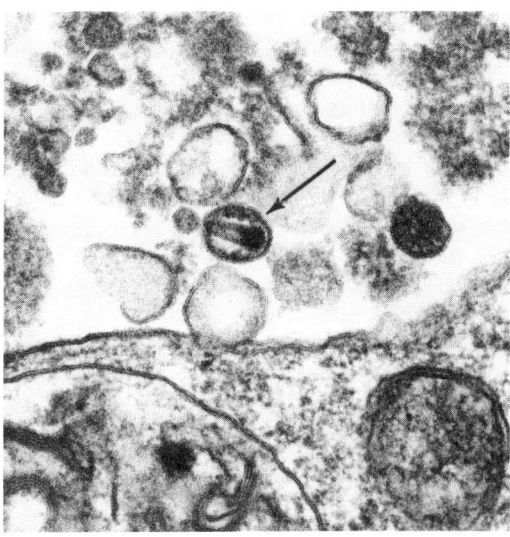

Fig 1A. Mature FIV particle (arrow) in a culture of feline T-lymphocytes. The virion has a cone-shaped nucleoid, with nucleic acid concentrated at one end.

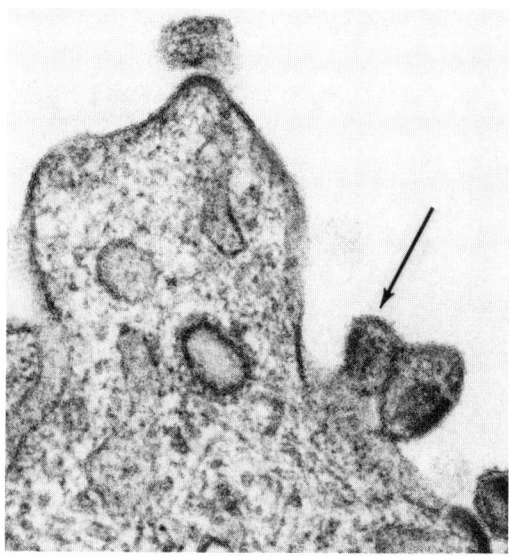

Fig 1B. FIV particles (arrow) bud from the surface of infected cells, similar to FeLV, except that there is no space between the condensing nucleic acid and the cell membrane.

Pathogenesis

Feline immunodeficiency virus was first recognized in cats in Northern California.[12] The infection has been subsequently recognized throughout the United States and Canada, Europe and Japan.[4,6,7,20]

The infection rate varies greatly, depending on environmental factors. Depending on the area, the incidence of FIV among the general cat population ranges from less than 1% to as high as 8%, similar to that of FeLV. From 14% to 29% of cats with clinical signs suggestive of immunodeficiency test positive for the virus.[7,20] The highest rates of infection are in areas where there is a high density of freely roaming cats. Japan, where there are many freely roaming animals, has a higher incidence than countries where the cat population is less dense and a greater proportion of cats are kept strictly indoors.[6,7,20] The infection rate seems to be lower in cities than in suburban areas or smaller towns. Purebred catteries have the lowest rate of infection.[7,20] In every study, male cats have been infected over twice as frequently as females.[7,20] Most clinically ill cats have been over 5-6 years of age, though infected kittens as young as 6 months have been identified.[7,20] It is not uncommon to find diseased animals that are over 10-15 years of age.[7,20] This age incidence contrasts with that for FeLV, which is more common in cats less than 5-6 years of age and rare in aged animals. About one-sixth of clinically ill FIV-infected cats are also infected with FeLV.[7,20]

Feline immunodeficiency virus appears to be transmitted predominantly by bites.[20,21] The virus is shed in the saliva, and puncture of the skin by a canine tooth of an infected cat is highly efficient in transmitting the infection.[20] Clinically ill cats shed much more virus in their saliva than apparently normal individuals.[20,21] The presence of mouth lesions may also increase the infectivity of an infected animal. Transmission by intimate contact in indoor situations, where biting does not usually occur, is highly inefficient;[21] this is different than in FeLV infection.[14] In-utero transmission is either nonexistent or uncommon, again different from FeLV infection.[21] Neonatal transmission from infected queens to their kittens, via milk or maternal grooming, also does not occur to any extent.[21] Infected queens, therefore, usually give birth to healthy kittens that remain uninfected. The transmissibility of the virus by blood-sucking insects, such as fleas, remains to be determined.

Infection occurs in 2 stages. The initial stage of the infection has been experimentally studied in specific-pathogen-free kittens.[21] Experimentally infected kittens develop transient leukopenia and fever beginning about 4 weeks after infection. These signs last from several days to 4 weeks. The leukopenia is mainly due to an absolute, and sometimes profound, neutropenia.[21] Platelet and RBC counts remain normal. Generalized lymphodenopathy appears at about the same time and lasts 2-9 months.[12,21] The initial stage of fever, leukopenia and lymphadenopathy is reminiscent of the initial stage of FeLV infection.[14] The leukopenia seen in the primary phase of FeLV infection involves other cell types in addition to neutrophils, and is usually accompanied by thrombocytopenia and varying degrees of anemia. The lymphadenopathy of FeLV infection is usually of shorter duration, rarely lasting more than 12-16 weeks.[14] Most FIV-infected cats recover from the initial stage of the disease

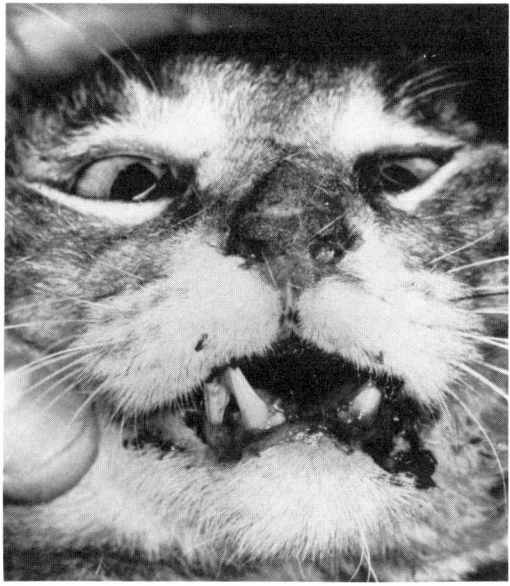

Fig 2. Chronic rhinitis and periodontitis in a cat with chronic FIV infection. (Courtesy of Dr. Takuo Ishida, Nippon Veterinary and Zootechnical College, Tokyo, Japan)

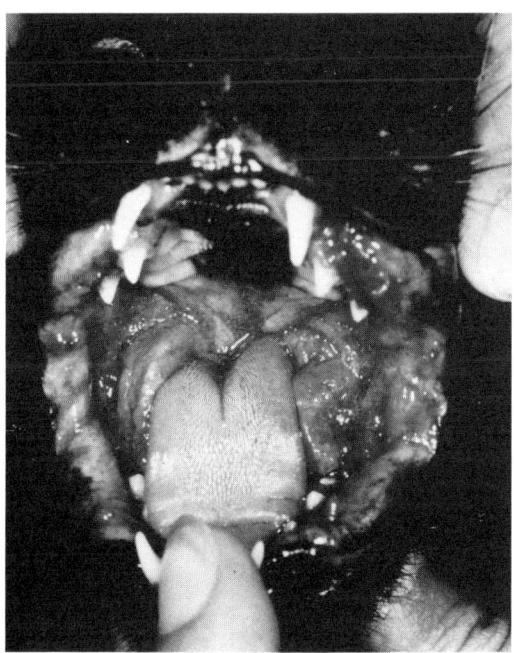

Fig 3. Severe stomatitis, periodontitis and tooth loss in a cat with chronic FIV infection. (Courtesy of Dr. Takuo Ishida, Nippon Veterinary and Zootechnical College, Tokyo, Japan)

after a brief period of malaise; some kittens, however, may succumb to local or generalized sepsis during this period.[12,21] Sepsis is probably due to the profound neutropenia and not to a more specific immunodeficiency. The initial stage of FIV infection is not dissimilar to the initial stage of HIV infection in people. People infected with HIV develop a transient mononucleosis-like illness several weeks after infection. They then return to a state of normal or near normal health that lasts until the secondary, or AIDS stage, of illness appears.

Most FIV-infected cats are seen in the so-called AIDS-like phase of the illness, when secondary and opportunistic infections, neurologic signs and myeloid or lymphoid tumors are seen. This second stage of disease has not yet been recreated in experimentally infected cats, so it is not certain how long after the initial stage of infection that immunodeficiency and other clinical manifestations of disease appear. It is apparently months or years later, however, as judged by experience with the naturally occurring disease.[7,20] This feature of FIV infection is identical to that of HIV infection of people and human AIDS. The AIDS phase of HIV infection of people occurs on the average of 6 years after initial infection.[15] As in infected people, FIV-infected cats entering the AIDS-stage of illness become progressively more immunocompromised with time.

Clinical Features

Most FIV-infected cats go through the initial stage of disease unnoticed by the owners. If lymphadenopathy is recognized, or if sepsis occurs, the cat may be seen by the veterinarian. More often, however, owners do not detect any problems until the immune system begins to weaken and secondary or opportunistic infections occur. Chronic infections of the oral cavity are seen in about 50% of FIV-infected cats in both North America and Japan.[7,20] Thirty percent of infected cats have infections of the upper respiratory tract (rhinitis, conjunctivitis), and 20% have chronic enteritis.[7,12,20] A smaller proportion of cats has infections of the skin, external ear canal, urinary tract and other organs.[7,20]

Oral cavity infections are usually associated with resident aerobic and anaerobic bacteria. They are manifested as gingivitis at its earliest stage, but this usually evolves into periodontal disease, cheilitis and stomatitis with time (Figs 2,3). Many teeth may be lost naturally or by extraction as a result of oral involvement. Cats have been known to live with progressively worsening signs for many years before succumbing. Upper respiratory tract disease (conjunctivitis, rhinitis) is often associated with chronic herpesvirus infection and infection by other resident bacteria, such as *Pasteurella*, *Bordetella*, streptococci and staphylococci (Fig 4).

Intestinal tract disease is particularly severe in many FIV-infected cats. This aspect of the feline disease is most similar to the "African" or "slim" form of human HIV infection.[16] Bowel disease is manifested by persistent or intermittent diarrhea, progressive thickening of the intestinal walls, weight loss, and terminal emaciation. Because of the fastidious toilet habits of cats, signs of bowel disease may go unnoticed and the cats are presented for weight loss or infections at other sites in the body. The cause of the intestinal disease is unknown but probably involves overgrowth of either normal resident flora or minimally pathogenic opportunistic microorganisms. *Yersinia pseudotuberculosis* has been isolated from the bowels of some affected cats. Others might have overgrowths of intestinal viruses (coronavirus, astrovirus) and protozoa (*Giardia*, *Cryptosporidium*, *Coccidia*).

Skin lesions are seen in a smaller proportion of cats, often associated with involvement of other organs. Chronic pustular dermatosis, usually associated with staphylococci, and generalized parasitic infections (demodectic mange, notoedric mange) have been recognized in FIV-infected cats. Abscesses that heal poorly or fistulate have also been observed in affected individuals. Such lesions should be cultured or biopsied for fungi or mycobacteria. Purulent infections of the external ear canals have been seen more frequently in FIV-infected cats than in normal animals. Ear infections are usually chronic and may be associated with aural hematomas and deformation of the pinnae.

Neurologic signs may be the sole or accompanying manifestation of FIV infection in 1-5% or more of affected cats. Neurologic disease is usually a direct result of the virus and not from other opportunistic organisms. Toxoplasmosis and cryptococcosis may attack the nervous system in a small proportion of FIV-infected cats. Neurologic signs are almost always of a cerebral nature and involve behavioral abnormalities, rather than locomotor signs. Dementia, compulsive roaming, hiding, rage, loss of toilet training, and excessive movements of the mouth and tongue are the most frequent neurologic complaints. Convulsions are less common signs. Ocular disease, particularly anterior uveitis, has been observed in a very small proportion of FIV-infected cats. It is not certain whether ocular disease is primary to the viral infection or secondary to infection by opportunistic organisms, such as *Toxoplasma*.

Fig 4. Chronic staphylococcal furunculosis, with numerous pustules, on the inner aspect of the pinna of a cat with FIV infection. (Courtesy of Dr. Linda Lowenstine, University of California, Davis)

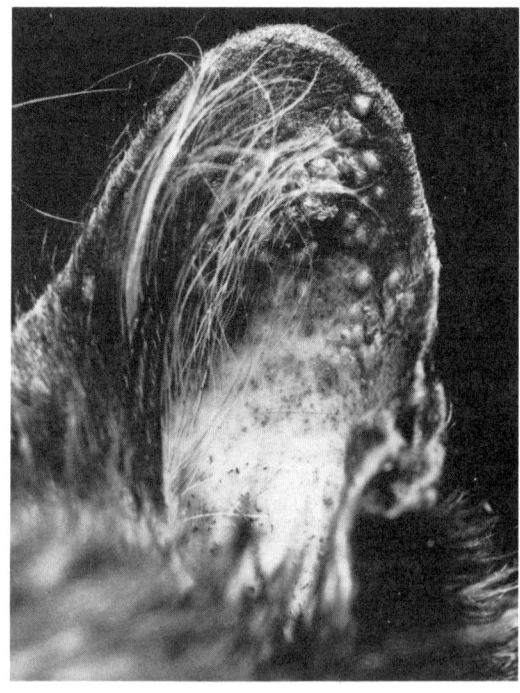

About one-third of FIV-infected cats in the AIDS phase of illness are grossly anemic.[20] Anemia can sometimes be profound. As in FeLV infection, the causes of the anemia are varied. It can be an anemia of chronic disease, a hemolytic-type anemia (immune mediated or hemobartonellosis), or be due to myeloproliferative-type disorders (myeloid dysplasia, preleukemia, or frank leukemia).[7,20,21]

The nature and range of opportunistic infections associated with FIV infection have not been fully elucidated. Hemobartonellosis, generalized demodectic and notoedric mange, cryptococcosis, aspergillosis of the bowel, atypical mycotic and mycobacterial infections, chronic herpesvirus infection of the upper respiratory tract, chronic bowel parasitism (cryptosporidiosis, giardiasis, coccidiosis), and toxoplasmosis are a few diseases that warrant FIV testing.[7] Feline infectious peritonitis does not appear to be FIV related.[20]

There is a possible relationship between naturally occurring FIV infection and the "panleukopenia-like" syndrome that has been described in older cats that have been properly vaccinated for feline panleukopenia virus infection.[5,17] The syndrome is manifested by severe, acute enterocolitis with leukopenia. Mortality can be high in some cases. In a study of 218 cats with such a syndrome, Reinacher found that 62 of 218 cats (mainly postweanling kittens) had feline panleukopenia virus infection, and 16 of 218 cats (mainly cats around 2 years of age) were probably FeLV infected.[17] Neither of these agents could be identified in 45 of 218 cats. Many cats in this latter group may have been FIV infected.

Lymphosarcomas have been seen in a number of FIV-infected cats that were FeLV negative.[7,20] These tumors often develop in sites of chronic infection in the nasal passages, oropharynx and intestines. Myeloproliferative disorders, often accompanied by severe anemia and pancytopenia, have also been seen in FIV-infected cats in the absence of FeLV.[20] A specific-pathogen-free cat experimentally infected with FIV also developed a fatal myeloproliferative disorder.[21]

Pathologic Features

The principal lesions seen in the terminal stages of FIV infection are concentrated in the alimentary tract. Mild to severe gingivitis, periodontitis and stomatitis, usually accompanied by a diffuse lymphocytic-plasmacytic infiltrate, are the most common features of FIV infection. Respiratory tract lesions are usually suppurative, with underlying necrosis and lymphocytic-plasmacytic-cell infiltration. Herpesvirus inclusion bodies may be widespread in epithelial cells in individuals with this complicating infection.

Diffuse enterocolitis is common and characterized by enterocyte necrosis in the glands, and villus atrophy and fusion. Dilated crypts in the small intestine and colon are variably lined by greatly hypertrophied or attenuated enterocytes. Multiple foci of subacute ulceration and pyogranulomatous transmural inflammation may be seen in the proximal colon and distal small intestine.

Lymphoid lesions vary greatly, depending on the stage of the disease. In the initial stages of infection, lymphadenopathy is prominent and lymph nodes exhibit exuberant follicular hyperplasia in the cortex and medullary cords.[21] Large, variably shaped follicles with disrupted mantle zones and small lymphocyte intrusion into germinal centers are common. Interfollicular (paracortical) areas are often compressed by the enlarged follicles. Dysplastic follicles are composed of small lymphocytes, sometimes mixed with large histiocytic cells. The red pulp of the spleen is hypercellular and shows changes similar to those in the lymph nodes. The secondary or AIDS stage of the disease is characterized by a wider spectrum of lymphoid changes. Some lymphoid tissues may be hyperplastic, especially in the B-cell series, while others are depleted or atrophic. Exhaustion and hyalinization of the follicles may be prominent in depleted lymphoid tissues. Thymic lesions are difficult to evaluate in older cats that normally have atrophic thymuses. However, thymic atrophy is profound in younger animals that would normally have considerable amounts of thymic tissue.

Lymphoid tumors in FIV-infected cats often arise out of surrounding areas of lymphocytic-plasmacytic inflammation. They appear to be mainly of the B-cell type. Myeloproliferative disorders are characterized by infiltration of large homogeneous-appearing myeloid cells in the spleen and bone marrow. Myeloid dysplasia, with maturation arrests at various stages of differentiation has also been observed in some animals.

Clinicopathologic Features

Any cat with chronic, poorly responsive or refractory infections should be tested for FIV infection. Cats with infectious diseases that are of an opportunistic nature should also be tested. Since FeLV and FIV infections often coexist, it is important to test such animals for both viruses. At the present time, most tests for FIV infection involve antibody detection. Since the presence of serum antibodies is directly related to persistent infection, antibody tests accurately detect almost all infected individuals.

Three basic procedures are used to test for FIV antibodies: enzyme-linked immunosorbent assay (ELISA); indirect immunofluorescent antibody assay (IFA); and Western blotting. Currently available ELISA procedures are highly sensitive in detecting antibodies and are probably over 98% specific when used to test high-risk populations, ie, cats with signs of the disease or cats in contact with known infected individuals. A greater proportion of nonspecific (false) positive test results may occur in low-risk groups, ie, cats kept strictly indoors, cats with no known exposure, or purebred cattery cats. False positives are generally associated with antibodies that react with minor cell culture contaminants in the ELISA antigen. False-positive reactions are generally weak; some true positives may also be weak, however.

The ELISA is the assay of choice for high-risk animals. When used on such populations, further confirmatory testing is probably not necessary. Confirmatory testing, either by IFA or Western blotting, should be considered for weakly positive samples from cats in low-risk categories. The IFA procedure is slightly less sensitive than ELISA and may give a low percentage of false negatives. If properly conducted, however, it rarely gives a false-positive reaction. The same can be said for Western blotting.

A proportion of FIV-infected cats may have too little antibody to be detected.[21,22] Such cats may be an early stage of infection or in the AIDS phase of illness in which there is a state of antigen excess with suppression of antibody production. Hopefully, tests will be devised to detect such animals.

Hematologic abnormalities are common in both the initial stage of the infection and in the secondary or AIDS stage of illness. Varying degrees of leukopenia, seldom lower than 3000 cells/μl, are seen transiently in the initial stage of infection.[21] This is usually associated with mild to profound neutropenia. The RBC and platelet counts are usually normal.[21] Anemia and leukopenia are seen in about one-third of cats in the terminal AIDS stage of illness. The leukopenia is usually associated with neutropenia and/or lymphopenia.[20] The anemia is usually mild and of the depression type. In some cats with myeloproliferative disorders, the anemia is often profound and may be associated with varying degrees of leukopenia and anemia. Bone marrow in anemic cats may be hypocellular, normocellular or hypercellular, depending on the type of anemia present. Abnormal myeloid cells may be seen in abundance in some marrow aspirates. Myeloid dysplasia, with evidence of maturation arrest, may be evident in some animals.

Cats coinfected with both FIV and FeLV tend to be younger than cats infected only with FIV, have more severe disease signs, and die earlier.[7] Feline immunodeficiency virus infection is also strongly linked to feline syncytium-forming virus (FeSFV) infection.[20] Three-fourths of a group of FeSFV-infected cats in one study were coinfected with FIV. This high rate of coinfection of cats with FeSFV and FIV probably results from the common modes of transmission of these 2 agents. FeSFV is also spread by bites and the same animals at risk for FIV infection are at risk for FeSFV infection (see Chapter 12).

Treatment and Prevention

Only cats in the AIDS stage of disease should be treated. Treatment is largely supportive and symptomatic, and directed primarily at the secondary or opportunistic infections. Cats in the earlier phases of AIDS-like illness often respond favorably to such treatment. As the disease progresses, however, the response becomes less favorable. The usefulness of human anti-HIV drugs, such as azathymidine, lymphokines, interferons and immunostimulants has not yet been adequately explored in cats.

The most successful way to prevent the infection is by not allowing cats to run free. Even if a susceptible cat is housed indoors with an infected individual, the likelihood of transmission is small. Strictly indoor cats rarely resort to biting, and biting is the principal mode of infection. Casual transmission, though uncommon, has been described in at least one closed cattery that took in homeless outdoor cats.[12] Contact transmission is much less efficient than with FeLV, and infected and uninfected cats can live together indoors with a lower risk for disease spread than with FeLV.

Infection and Immunity

Whether or not FIV infection of cats is analogous in all aspects to HIV infection in people remains to be determined. However, there are great similarities in progression of disease in HIV-infected people and FIV-infected cats. Both diseases start with a brief, self limiting illness. Following this initial bout of disease, infected people and cats return to a state of normalcy or near normalcy. With time, usually many months or years, the immune system deteriorates and secondary or opportunistic infections began to appear.[15] These respond initially to symptomatic treatment, but as the immune system becomes progressively more crippled, treatment becomes less and less effective.

The AIDS stage of HIV infection in people is heralded by a progressive decrease in T-cell immunity.[9,15] Events leading to the highly selective depression of cellular immunity in people have been partially elucidated.[9] Development of this deficiency is preceded by a gradual reversal in the T4:T8 lymphocyte ratio. This is caused mainly by an absolute decrease in the T4 lymphocyte class. The T4 cells are thymic-derived lymphocytes bearing the T4 surface antigen and function as helper/inducer cells in cellular immunity. The B-cell system in AIDS patients appears intact and even hyperactive.[9] Total immunoglobulin levels show an absolute increase. Antibody titers to cytomegalovirus, Epstein-Barr virus and hepatitis B virus also increase.[1,15] However, total levels of antibody to whole HIV and HIV-core protein decrease.[1] Virus-neutralizing antibodies tend to stay constant in the blood or decrease slightly as AIDS develops. The selective decrease in T-cell-mediated immunity in HIV-infected people with AIDS is reflected by the types of opportunistic infections that develop. Opportunistic infections seen in human AIDS patients are usually associated with organisms that tend to be intracellular, thus requiring cellular immunity for elimination. Mycobacteria, *Toxoplasma*, *Cryptococcus*, *Pneumocystis carinii*, cytomegalovirus, Epstein-Barr virus, and hepatitis B virus are just a few. Identical or related types of organisms have been associated with disease in FIV-infected cats.[7]

Cats experimentally infected with FIV begin to make antibodies 2 weeks after infection.[21] The titer of these antibodies rises rapidly and then plateaus. Cats with naturally acquired FIV infection and in the AIDS stage of illness tend to have lower antibody levels than experimentally infected cats in the asymptomatic stage of infection. This observation suggests that FIV antibodies in cats behave similarly to HIV antibodies in people over the course of the respective infections. It is not yet known whether any of the antibodies produced in FIV-infected cats are virus neutralizing. The presence or absence of neutralizing antibodies is a relatively moot point, however, because no infected cat ever recovers from the infection.

Similar to HIV-infected people, FIV-infected cats appear to be infected for life. This is typical of all lentivirus infections; the chance of recovery, even in the face of immunity, is virtually nil. This feature of lentivirus infections makes them resistant to known vaccine strategies. It is seemingly impossible to develop a vaccine for an infection against which the host cannot immunize itself, even in a small percentage of cases.

Very little is known about the immunologic abnormalities that occur in FIV infection. Mitogen studies on peripheral blood lymphocytes during the initial stage of infection show a 3- to 4-fold increase in responses to phytohemagglutinin (PHA), concanavalin A (conA) and *Staphylococcus* enterotoxin A (SEA).[22] Pokeweed mitogen (PWM) responses are normal to slightly increased, and lipopolysaccharide (LPS) responses are somewhat depressed. Mitogen responses return to normal in the asymptomatic phase of the disease that follows the initial stage of infection. Cats in the AIDS stage of FIV infection usually have normal or near-normal responses to PHA and LPS, and mildly to greatly decreased responses to conA, SEA and PWM.

Animal and Public Health Considerations

Feline immunodeficiency virus has a distant genetic relationship to HIV of people. It is one member of a large group of lentiviruses that appear to have adapted themselves species by species over eons of time. The adaptation of HIV to people is a very recent event in lentivirus evolution. The current theory is that HIV is a mutant of SIV. Though lentiviruses have apparently adapted themselves to a number of species of animals by mutation, once that adaptation occurs, they become very species specific. Lentiviruses of one species of animals do not readily infect a divergent species of animals. This high degree of species specificity obviates FIV's being a public health concern. Preliminary studies have failed to identify FIV antibodies in the blood of people in intimate contact with infected cats, inadvertently bitten by infected cats, or accidently injected with infectious materials.[21]

References

1. Birx DL et al: Defective regulation of Epstein-Barr virus infection in patients with acquired immunodeficiency syndrome (AIDS) or AIDS-related disorders. *New Engl J Med* 314:874-879, 1986.

2. Chalifoux LV et al: Lymphoproliferative syndrome in an immunodeficient rhesus monkey naturally infected with an HTLV-III-like virus (STLV-III). *Lab Invest* 55:43-40, 1986.

3. Fultz PN et al: Isolation of a T-lymphotropic retrovirus from naturally infected sooty mangabey monkeys (*Cercocebus atys*). *Proc Natl Acad Sci* 83:5286-5290, 1986.

4. Harbour DA et al: Isolation of a T-lymphotropic lentivirus from a persistently leucopenic domestic cat. *Vet Record* 122:84-86, 1988.

5. Hardy WD Jr: Feline leukemia virus nonneoplastic disease. *JAAHA* 17:941-949, 1981.

6. Ishida T et al: Detection of feline T-lymphotropic lentivirus (FTLV) infection in Japanese domestic cats. *Jpn J Vet Sci* 50:39-44, 1988.

7. Ishida T et al: Feline immunodeficiency virus (FIV) in Japan. *JAVMA: In press*, 1988.

8. Kanki PJ et al: Isolation of a T-lymphotropic retrovirus related to HTLV-III/LAV from wild-caught African green monkeys. *Science* 230:951-954, 1985.

9. Lane HC and Fauci AS: Immunologic abnormalities in the acquired immunodeficiency syndrome. *Ann Rev Immunol* 3:477-500, 1985.

10. Moore FM et al: Distinctive peripheral lymph node hyperplasia of young cats. *Vet Pathol* 23:386-391, 1986.

11. O'Connor T et al: Biochemical and immunological characterization of the major structured proteins of feline T-lymphotropic lentivirus. *J Virol, In press*, 1988.

12. Pedersen NC et al: Isolation of T-lymphotropic lentivirus from cats with an acquired immunodeficiency. *Science* 235:290-293, 1987.

13. Pedersen NC et al: The clinical significance of latent feline leukemia virus infection in cats. *Feline Pract* 14(2):32-48, 1984.

14. Pedersen NC et al: Studies of naturally transmitted feline leukemia virus infection. *Am J Vet Res* 38:1523-1531, 1977.

15. Polk BF et al: Predictors of the acquired immunodeficiency syndrome developing in a cohort of seropositive homosexual men. *New Engl J Med* 316:61-66, 1987.

16. Quinn TC et al: AIDS in Africa: an epidemiologic paradigm. Science 234:955-963, 1986.

17. Reinacher M: Feline leukemia virus-associated enteritis. A condition with features of panleukopenia. Vet Pathol 24:1-4, 1987.

18. Stephens RM et al: Equine infectious anemia virus gag and pol genes: relatedness to Visna and AIDS virus. Science 231:589-594, 1986.

19. Wong-Staal F and Gallo RC: Human T-lymphotropic retroviruses. Nature 317: 395-403, 1985.

20. Yamamoto JK et al: Epidemiologic and clinical aspects of feline immunodeficiency virus (FIV) infection in cats from the continental United States and Canada and possible mode of transmission. JAVMA:In press, 1988.

21. Yamamoto JK et al: The pathogenesis of experimentally induced feline immunodeficiency virus (FIV) infection in cats. Am J Vet Res 49:1246-1258. 1988.

22. Yamamoto JK, Univ California, Davis: Unpublished observations, 1988.

Section II

Bacterial Diseases

Bacteria are single-celled microorganisms that possess a rigid cell wall. They lack a distinct nucleus and contain a single strand of DNA. Bacteria divide by binary fission.

Unlike viruses, rickettsiae, chlamydiae and mycoplasmas, bacteria are not obligate cellular parasites. Many live a free existence and obtain simple nutrients from their environment. Other bacteria live as commensal parasites of higher life-forms. Commensal bacteria require special nutrients found only within certain environments; many live on normal body secretions in the orifices of the GI, respiratory and urogenital tracts, as well as on the skin and its appendages.

Bacteria are usually not pathogenic to animals. Under certain circumstances, however, bacteria or their toxins invade living tissues and cause disease. Factors favoring disease include environmental alterations that favor sudden increases in bacterial numbers or inadequacies in host defense mechanisms.

Bacteria causing disease in cats are often identical to those infecting people and other animals. Bacterial diseases in cats are also amazingly similar to their counterparts in other species. The following classification has been used for pathogenic bacteria of cats.[1]

Class Schizomyces
  Order Pseudomonadales
    Family Pseudomonadae
      Genus *Pseudomonas*
    Family Spirillaceae
      Genus *Campylobacter*
  Order Eubacteriales
    Family Lactobacillaceae
      Genus *Streptococcus*
    Family Micrococcaceae
      Genus *Staphylococcus*
    Family Corynebacteriaceae
      Genus *Corynebacterium*
      Genus *Listeria*
    Family Clostridiaceae
      Genus *Clostridium*
    Family Bacillaceae
      Genus *Bacillus*
    Family Brucellaceae
      Genus *Bordetella*
      Genus *Pasteurella*
    Family Bacteriodaceae
      Genus *Fusobacterium*
    Family Enterobacteriaceae
      Genus *Salmonella*
      Genus *Yersinia*
      Genus *Escherichia*
  Order Spirochaetales
    Family Leptospiraceae
      Genus *Leptospira*
Class Actinomycetes
  Order Actinomycetales
    Family Nocardiaceae
      Genus *Nocardia*
    Family Dermatophilaceae
      Genus *Dermatophilus*
    Family Mycobacteriaceae
      Genus *Mycobacterium*
    Family Actinomyecetaceae
      Genus *Actinomyces*

Reference

1. Greene CE: *Clinical Microbiology and Infectious Diseases of the Dog and Cat.* Saunders, Philadelphia, 1984. p 17.

Chapter 16

Pseudomonas Infection

Etiologic Agent

Pseudomonas spp are motile, aerobic, Gram-negative rods, 0.4 by 2.5μ in size. Warm-blooded animals, such as cats, are infected by 2 species: *P aeruginosa* and *P pseudomallei*. These organisms are often found in moist or unsanitary environments. *Pseudomonas* spp are particularly troublesome as hospital contaminants, where they grow in large numbers in nooks and crannies of cages, drains, sinks, rubber hoses of anesthetic machines, unclean or poorly cleaned endotracheal tubes and various solutions (antiseptics, liquid fluorescein drops, nitrofurazone ointments and solutions).

Pathogenesis

Pseudomonas spp infections in cats are generally superficial and become septicemic very rarely. *Pseudomonas* spp are usually opportunistic rather than primary pathogens. They are also much less common in cats than in other species, such as dogs. *Pseudomonas* spp, especially *P aeruginosa*, have been associated with purulent ear infections, corneal ulcers, bladder infections, superficial pyodermas and chronic rhinitis.

Clinical Features

Purulent otitis externa associated with *P aeruginosa* is relatively common in dogs but uncommon in cats. It is often secondary to underlying ear problems. Situations that predispose to otitis externa include primary pruritic ear mite infestations, fibrous polyps arising from the Eustachian tubes that perforate the ear drums or immunodeficiencies associated with FeLV or FIV infections.

Rapidly enlarging corneal ulcers that frequently perforate have been associated with *Pseudomonas* spp infection. Herpetic ulcers, corneal abrasions or conjunctival diseases (*Mycoplasma, Chlamydia*) may be secondarily contaminated with *Pseudomonas* spp by injudicious use of corticosteroids, antibiotics or contaminated eye solutions.

Pseudomonas spp are frequent secondary contaminants of superficial skin lesions, especially those caused by trauma and kept bandaged or dressed. The warm moist environment under dressings can actually favor growth of *Pseudomonas* spp. Purulent exudate from such wounds is often slimy and greenish, with a characteristic sweet odor similar to that emitted by cultures of the organism.

Pure cultures of *Pseudomonas* are commonly obtained form the nasal exudate of cats with chronic rhinitis. Such organisms are often highly resistant, due to the chronic antibiotic treatment that many of these cats undergo.

Treatment and Prevention

Pseudomonas spp infections can be very resistant to antibiotics, especially if the organisms are of hospital origin. Cultures and antibiotic sensitivity tests are important. *Pseudomonas* spp are most sensitive to such aminoglycosides as gentamicin and amikacin, or cephalosporins.

Pseudomonas spp ulcers of the eyes should be treated vigorously and promptly to avoid perforation and loss of the globe. A third eyelid flap should be created and the eye treated with topical gentamicin pending bacterial cultures and antibiotic sensitivities. Corticosteroids should not be used topically or systemically.

Pseudomonas spp infections of the skin are usually associated with bandaged wounds. Whenever possible, wounds should be left open to the air. Ointments and antiseptic solutions should be used sparingly, as they can actually delay healing and, in some cases, favor growth of *Pseudomonas* spp.

Pseudomonas spp infections of the external ears should be treated with appropriate topical antibiotics. However, it is important to check for underlying problems.

Chronic rhinitis due to *Pseudomonas* spp should be treated systemically with antibiotics for at least 2 weeks. This often resolves signs, but recurrence is common. The recurrent nature of nasal infections suggests the presence of other underlying causes.

Chapter 17

Campylobacteriosis

Etiologic Agent

Campylobacter spp are Gram-negative curved rods 1.5-3.5 μ in length and 0.2-0.4 μ in width.[2] *Campylobacter jejuni* is the main pathogen in this genus. Unlike other *Campylobacter* spp, *C jejuni* is catalase-positive, produces H_2S and is susceptible to nalidixic acid. *Campylobacter jejuni* is also the only pathogenic *Campylobacter* sp that grows well at 42 C. It can be selectively grown on blood agar (Skirrow's medium) at 42 C in an atmosphere containing 85% N_2, 10% CO_2, and 5% O_2.[16] This medium contains vancomycin, novobiocin, polymyxin B and trimethoprim lactate to inhibit growth of other fecal bacteria. Organisms remain viable at 4 C for 3 weeks in feces and 5 weeks in urine, and for less time at 25 C.[1] Viable organisms were still present in bile kept at 37 C for 2 months.

Pathogenesis

Campylobacter jejuni is found worldwide and carried by many different species of animals, including poultry, wild and caged birds, sheep, goats, dogs, cats, swine, hamsters, primates and people. Infected animals shed the organism in their feces. Canine and feline isolates are identical to human isolates.[13]

The incidence of *C jejuni* infection in dogs and cats is difficult to determine due to variations in isolation rates. These variations are due to differences in the sensitivity of isolation techniques, sources of animals (kennels, pounds, animal shelters, veterinary practices) and age of the animals. The highest recovery rates are from animals that are young or in high-density environments. Isolation rates vary from 0.5% to 45% or more in dogs and from 2% to 45% in cats.[7] However, isolation rates in cats in most studies are usually only a fraction of those in dogs.

The relatively high incidence of *C jejuni* infections in kittens from high-density environments is compatible with what is known about infectious diseases in general. Young animals are the most susceptible to infection and continue to shed organisms until good immunity develops, a process that sometimes takes many weeks. Hamsters and ferrets experimentally infected with *C jejuni* shed organisms for several months.[6] Puppies have shed organisms for at least 40 days.[5] Environmental factors favoring serious infection include: overcrowding with increased contact between animals; poor sanitation and increased fecal contamination of the environment; large numbers of kittens and a proportionate increase in carrier individuals; concurrent diseases and lowered resistance; and increased stresses in the population.[6,12]

The role of *C jejuni* in disease has only recently been demonstrated. It causes vibrionic hepatitis in poultry and transient enterocolitis in animals and people.[16] However, epidemiologic studies have had variable success in linking *C jejuni* to disease. Some studies show the same incidence of infection in dogs or cats with diarrhea and asymptomatic animals.[8,9] In other studies, however, the infection rate is considerably higher in animals with diarrhea than in asymptomatic animals.[7]

Cats with acute diarrhea, cats in the postinfection convalescent stage of disease, and chronic asymptomatic carriers are sources of the bacteria. Outbreaks usually occur when susceptible and infected cats commingle.[12]

Infection with *C jejuni* is by the fecal-oral route. The infection is generally limited to the cecum and colon, though bacteremias are sometimes associated with severe primary bowel disease. The incubation period is 3-7 days.

Clinical Features

Clinical signs of *C jejuni* infection are seen mainly in 6- to 12-week-old kittens during the postweaning period. However, whether the infection is clinically apparent is related to a variety of poorly understood factors. The level of infecting organisms, nutritional status, presence of concurrent diseases and status of passive and active immunities all play some role in the disease outcome. It is not unusual that the disease strikes weanling kittens that have stopped nursing. The kittens suddenly lose the passive local (lactogenic) immunity provided by their mother's milk. Their passive systemic immunity also wanes, their diet is markedly changed, they are exposed to other young animals, and the stress level is high.

Diarrhea, which is sometimes profuse and watery but more often soft and mucoid, is the predominant sign of *C jejuni* infection in kittens.[12] Fever is generally absent and anorexia mild. Vomiting and colic are sometimes observed in the acute stages of illness. Dehydration can be rapid and severe in young kittens with profuse watery diarrhea. Death has been occasionally reported in severely affected kittens.[14] The diarrhea usually subsides within 3-7 days, but the stool may remain somewhat soft for 2-4 weeks. Bloody diarrhea is not a common sign of *C jejuni* enterocolitis in kittens.

Pathologic Features

Lesions in cats have not been described, but changes are identical in most species that have been studied. Gross changes are limited to the distal intestinal tract, particularly the colon, and include mild redness of the mucosa. Histopathologic findings include epithelial flattening, loss of brush borders, congestion, edema, mixed inflammatory cell infiltrates of the lamina propria, epithelial-gland hyperplasia, goblet-cell depletion, diffuse infiltration of crypt walls with polymorphonuclear neutrophils, focal accumulations of neutrophils, and microabscess formation in mucosal crypts.[2,15]

Clinicopathologic Features

Highly motile spiral or S-shaped organisms can be seen in fresh fecal suspensions viewed by phase or subdued-light (contrast) microscopy. This can be of some value in tentatively diagnosing *C jejuni* enterocolitis. The organism can be readily isolated on selective *Campylobacter* media. Small, flat, grayish, mucoid colonies appear within 24-48 hours. Typical Gram-negative spiral or S-shaped organisms are seen in stained smears. The sensitivity of isolation can be enhanced by preculturing fresh feces in special enrichment broth and then subculturing onto agar plates 12-24 hours later.[4,5] Samples that cannot be immediately cultured or requiring transport can be placed on enriched semisolid *Brucella* medium and stored for 3 weeks or longer at 25 C.[20]

Overinterpretation of culture results should be avoided. Many healthy kittens in the same environment also shed organisms, and a number of other enteric pathogens can cause similar disease signs. These other diseases also tend to occur in the postweaning period. A rapid response to specific antibiotic therapy can be helpful in confirming *C jejuni* as the responsible organism.

Treatment and Prevention

Campylobacter jejuni is resistant to penicillin, cephalosporins and trimethoprim.[2,12] Sensitivity to ampicillin, trimethoprim-sulfonamides and metronidazole is intermediate. Almost all *C jejuni* isolates are sensitive to erythromycin, which is considered the drug of choice.[12] Erythromycin is administered PO at 20-40 mg/kg divided TID for 5 days. Tetracycline, aminoglycosides, clindamycin, chloramphenicol and furazolidone are also effective.

Kittens with severe and profuse diarrhea should not be given food or water PO for 24-72 hours. Fluids and electrolytes should be given parenterally. *Campylobacter jejuni* enterocolitis usually responds well to treatment, and clinical signs resolve within 2-5 days. Cats with milder signs do not necessarily require treatment; signs usually resolve after a few days to a week.

Prevention of *C jejuni* infection in catteries usually requires drastic changes in environment and husbandry. The disease is most severe in situations in which many breeding cats and kittens are crowded into inadequate quarters.

Infection and Immunity

Most *C jejuni* isolates are obtained from animals <6 months of age.[7] Bacterial shedding continues for up to 2 months or more after infection, indicating that development of complete immunity is a slow process. This is true of many enteric infections of dogs and cats. Shedding of *Salmonella* also continues for weeks or months after initial infection. Interference with the natural course of salmonellosis with antibiotics can actually prolong the carrier state by removing the stimulation necessary to evoke protective immunity. Animals that have not established immunity immediately become reinfected with *Salmonella* following cessation of antibiotic treatment. Work with human campylobacteriosis suggests that antibiotic therapy does not have a similar effect. Cultures done several weeks to months after treatment are usually negative.[11]

Animal and Public Health Considerations

Campylobacter jejuni is a cause of severe acute enterocolitis in people, especially in children. In underdeveloped areas of the world, person-to-person transmission by the fecal-oral route is common. Human infection in more developed countries is usually associated with ingestion of contaminated lamb, beef, pork, poultry or unpasteurized milk. Contaminated water is another common source of human infection. Exposure to infected dogs and cats has been estimated to account for no more than 5% of human infections.[17] Dogs are generally more infectious to people than cats, largely due to their higher incidence of infection.[18] Puppies and kittens are more infectious than older animals and diarrheic individuals are more of a health hazard than asymptomatic individuals.[3,10,18,19] Young kittens and puppies are more apt to harbor the infection. Animals with diarrhea shed more organisms and are more likely to contaminate the environment. People, especially children, who develop acute enterocolitis after contact with a diarrheic kitten should be checked by their physicians for *C jejuni*. If positive cultures are obtained from the patient, fecal cultures from the pets might be warranted. Pets shedding *C jejuni* should not be destroyed without good reason. The infection is self limiting in both people and animals, and the number of people infected by pets is relatively small. Infected animals can be isolated from people for 40 days or so and then samples obtained for culture. Alternatively, animals shedding *C jejuni* can be treated with erythromycin for 5 days.

References

1. Blaser MJ *et al*: Survival of *Camplobacter fetus* subsp *jejuni* in biological milieus. *J Clin Microbiol* 11:309-313, 1980.

2. Blaser MJ and Reller LB: *Campylobacter* enteritis. *New Engl J Med* 305:1444-1452, 1981.

3. Blaser MJ et al: *Campylobacter* enteritis associated with a healthy cat. *JAMA* 247:816, 1982.

4. Bruce D and Ferguson JR: *Campylobacter jejuni* in cats. *Lancet* 2:595-596, 1980.

5. Druce D et al: *Campylobacter* infections in cats and dogs. *Vet Record* 107:200-201, 1980.

6. Fox JG: Campylobacteriosis - a "new" disease in laboratory animals. *Lab Anim Sci* 32:625-637, 1982.

7. Fox JG et al: Canine and feline campylobacteriosis: epizootiology and clinical and public health features. *JAVMA* 183:1420-1424, 1983.

8. Holt PE: Incidence of *Campylobacter*, *Salmonella* and *Shigella* infections in dogs in an industrial town. *Vet Record* 107:254, 1980.

9. Holt PE: The role of dogs and cats in the epidemiology of human *Campylobacter* enterocolitis. *J Small Anim Pract* 22:681-685, 1981.

10. Hosie BD et al: *Campylobacter* infections in normal and diarrhoeic dogs. *Vet Record* 105:80, 1979.

11. Karmali MA and Fleming PC: *Campylobacter* enteritis in children. *J Pediatr* 94:527-533, 1979.

12. Junttila J et al: *Campylobacter*-associated epidemic in cats. *Compan Anim Pract* 1(7):16-18, 1987.

13. McOrist S and Browning JW: Carriage of *Campylobacter jejuni* in healthy and diarrhoeic dogs and cats. *Aust Vet J* 58:33-34, 1982.

14. Murtaugh RJ and Lawrence AE: *Campylobacter jejuni*-associated enteritis. *Feline Pract* 14(6):37-40, 42, 1984.

15. Prescott JF and Munroe DL: *Campylobacter jejuni* enteritis in man and domestic animals. *JAVMA* 181:1524-1530, 1982.

16. Skirrow MB: *Campylobacter* enteritis: a "new" disease. *Brit Med J* 2:9-11, 1977.

17. Skirrow MB: *Campylobacter* enteritis in dogs and cats: A new zoonosis. *Vet Res Commun* 5:13-19, 1981.

18. Skirrow MB et al: *Campylobacter jejuni* enteritis transmitted from cat to man. *Lancet* 1:1188, 1980.

19. Svedham A and Norkrans G: *Campylobacter jejuni* enteritis transmitted from cat to man. *Lancet* 1:713-714, 1980.

20. Wang WL et al: Enriched *Brucella* medium for storage and transport of cultures of *Campylobacter fetus* subsp *jejuni*. *J Clin Microbiol* 12:479-480, 1980.

Chapter 18

Streptococcus Infection

Etiologic Agent

Streptococci are Gram-positive cocci about 1 μ in diameter that form long chains under optimum growth conditions. Streptococci are commensal organisms that live on mucous membranes of the nasal passages, oropharynx, colon and distal genitourinary tract (urethra, vagina, prepuce). Both pathogenic and nonpathogenic species of streptococci coexist in healthy animals and people. The most common isolate from cats is *S canis*.[1]

Streptococci produce a number of different exotoxins, including streptolysins (hemolysins), streptokinases, deoxyribonucleases and hyaluronidases. Such toxins are particularly important in group-A streptococci. Group-G streptococci, which commonly infect cats, are less toxigenic.

Streptococci are classified by the type of hemolysins they produce or by specific antigenic differences in their capsular-polysaccharide proteins. Three groups of streptococci are identifiable by hemolytic reactions: beta (clear zone of hemolysis), alpha (zone of partial hemolysis) and gamma (nonhemolytic). Beta-hemolytic strains are usually more pathogenic than alpha-hemolytic strains, which in turn are more pathogenic than nonhemolytic strains. Based on capsular-polysaccharide antigen, Lancefield groups A-H and K-T have been recognized. Certain Lancefield groups are more apt to be associated with disease than others depending on the species of animal. Lancefield group-G beta-hemolytic streptococci, such as *S canis*, are most frequently associated with disease in cats. Group-B streptococci (*eg, S agalactiae*) have also been isolated from 2 cats, 1 with septic peritonitis secondary to renal dialysis and another with postpartum metritis.[2] *Streptococcus pneumoniae* has been isolated from the blood and synovial fluid of an aged cat with acute fever, joint swelling and lameness.[9]

Healthy cats are the primary source of streptococci. The level of bacterial growth in mucous membranes of the mouth, nasal passages and distal genitourinary tissues varies greatly, depending on the age of the animals. Blanchard found that 50% of female cats <2 years of age in the Davis, California, area carried *S canis* in their vaginal tract.[1] The carrier rate in older cats was lower.

Pathogenesis

Three main forms of streptococcal infections have been recognized in cats: epizootic, neonatal and localized. Each form of the disease will be discussed as a distinct clinical entity, though the various forms often occur together in the same environment. Streptococcal infections are enhanced by a number of unfavorable environmental factors that are most likely to occur in catteries, multiple-cat households and animal facilities (pounds, humane shelters, laboratory animal facilities).

Clinical Features

The epizootic form of streptococcosis has been seen mainly in large experimental cat colonies.[1,3-6] This form occurs less frequently in catteries and is virtually nonexistent in normal outdoor/indoor pet cat populations. Outbreaks usually occur among cats kept in close confinement and in free-housed group of 4 or more animals, rather than in individually caged cats. Animals affected with epizootic streptococcosis were usually fed from common bulk feeders. Infection rates vary from 2.3% to 28% over several months. The highest incidence of disease is in the postweaning period from 8 to 10 weeks of age or in new animals introduced into an enzootic environment.

The most common clinical signs associated with this form of infection are acute fever, submandibular edema and lymphadenopathy. The mandibular lymph nodes often spontaneously rupture and drain, or require lancing. Conjunctivitis, sinusitis and abscesses on the feet and legs develop in some animals. Dyspnea, due to a severe suppurative pleuritis and hydrothorax, occurs in a small proportion of affected cats.

The epizootic form of the disease has been experimentally recreated.[4] Adolescent and adult cats fed about 1×10^9 organisms became febrile on day 2, with anorexia, listlessness, and swelling and edema of the mandibular lymph nodes. Draining abscesses often occurred in the area of the enlarged nodes over the following 24 hours. Conjunctivitis, laryngitis and tracheitis were associated signs. The course of experimental disease was further elucidated by Swindle and co-workers.[4] Streptococci ingested with food rapidly colonized the tonsils and disseminated via the lymphatics to regional lymph nodes in the head and neck. Purulent inflammation of the lymph nodes was followed by toxemia and fever.

The neonatal form of streptococcal infection occurs more frequently in large breeding catteries.[1] Sporadic cases of epizootic disease in weanling and adolescent kittens are often seen in the same environment. The disease has a predilection for kittens born to primiparous queens.[1] Kittens are usually infected during birth from vaginal secretions or when the queen severs the umbilicus. Umbilical vein infections are more frequent when the umbilical vein is chewed off at the level of the abdominal wall. If the umbilical cord is left long, infection is limited to the dried-up portion and cannot travel up the cord and reach the patent part of the vein. Kittens infected at or shortly after birth often develop a small abscess of the umbilical vein in the inner abdominal wall. Infection at this site is seldom apparent on gross examination. The infection then showers organisms directly into the bloodstream. Infected kittens usually become listless within the first week of life and "fade away" and die over the next few days. It is not uncommon for entire litters to be affected. Subsequent litters are less likely to succumb from the infection.

Streptococci can be isolated from a number of localized pyogenic processes, in pure form or as mixed bacterial infections. Abscesses of the skin and subcutis, conjunctivitis, mastitis and uterine, vaginal, oral, ear and wound infections are just a few processes associated with streptococci.[2]

Pathologic Features

Pathologic findings in epizootic streptococcosis are relatively stereotyped. Many affected cats have tonsillitis, with acute inflammation and microabscess formation in the lymph nodes of the head and neck. Acute rhinitis, unilateral or bilateral otitis media, acute splenitis, and reactive hyperplasia and histiocytosis of lymphoid tissue throughout the body are associated findings.[5,6]

Pathologic features of neonatal streptococcosis include omphalophlebitis and thrombosing bacteremia.[1] Gross or microscopic abscessation of the abdominal portion of the umbilical vein is common, and bacterial thrombi are observed within vessels in the liver, spleen, lungs and kidneys. Gross and microscopic abscesses are seen in the liver; suppurative meningoencephalitis is common.

Clinicopathologic Features

Epizootic streptococcal lymphadenitis is easily diagnosed on the basis of clinical history (environment, feeding practices) and signs of acute fever and adenitis of the lymph nodes of the head and neck. Pure cultures of beta-hemolytic streptococci are obtained from lymph node exudates.

Neonatal streptococcosis must be differentiated from the myriad diseases that cause mortality in kittens during the first 2 weeks of life. Careful necropsy, histopathologic examination of tissues and bacterial cultures usually pinpoint the problem. Special attention should be given to examination and culture of the umbilical cord remnant within and outside of the abdomen.

Treatment and Prevention

Streptococci are sensitive to a number of antibiotics, but penicillin is the drug of choice. Antibiotic therapy should be combined with drainage of abscessed lymph nodes and evacuation of pleural exudate in cats that also have streptococcal pleuritis.

If neonatal streptococcal infections are a problem, prophylactic treatment of all kittens born to primiparous queens is indicated. A single SC injection of benzathine penicilliin at 35,000 IU/kg at birth often prevents systemic disease and decreases mortality.

An outbreak of streptococcal lymphadenitis in a cat colony was successfully halted by treating all animals in the group with 150,000 IU procaine penicillin and 150,000 IU benzathine penicillin SC.[6] However, such treatment will not eliminate the organism from the premises. Prevention of infection involves changes in husbandry practices to prevent overcrowding and maintain clean feeders. Infected cats should be segregated from uninfected cats. Elimination of communal bulk feeders and use of individual caging also help prevent spread of disease during an outbreak.

Infection and Immunity

Pathogenic strains of streptococci cause similar syndromes in people and many species of animals. Streptococcal diseases of animals are usually related to certain husbandry practices. Overcrowding of animals, infrequently cleaned communal feeders, and premises with a high proportion of younger animals are common predisposing factors. Such conditions favor an increasing level of streptococci in the environment and a higher primary infection rate. The larger the exposure dose of pathogenic streptococci, the higher the incidence and severity of primary infections. An increased incidence of primary infection leads to a higher proportion of cats that carry and shed the organism during the primary phase of illness and in the postconvalescent period. The severity of pathogenic streptococcal infections in a group of cats is proportional to the percentage of asymptomatic cats that carry the organism in the oropharynx, prepuce and vagina.

The reason for higher incidence of streptococcal infections in neonatal kittens born to primiparous queens is not completely understood. Blanchard found that queens <2 years of age harbored significant levels of *S canis* in their vaginal canals throughout pregnancy and at parturition.[1] In contrast, queens >2 years of age had progressively decreasing levels of vaginal streptococci beginning at midgestation. Cultures from older queens at parturition were often negative. The basis of the effect of pregnancy on vaginal populations of streptococci is unknown. Pregnancy, at least in relation to herpesvirus and *Toxocara* infections of cats, is usually immunosuppressive. The immunosuppressive effect of pregnancy is also well recognized in people. Therefore, it is unlikely the pregnancy-associated decrease in streptococcal vaginal populations in older cats is due solely to immunologic mechanisms. Hormonal effects of pregnancy may alter the nature of the membranes and secretions of the vaginal tract and make the local environment less favorable for bacterial growth.

Animal and Public Health Considerations

Pathogenic streptococci vary among animal species. Streptococcal disease are associated with different groups of streptococci in people more so than in cats. Streptococci isolated from people are usually of human and not animal origin. Occasionally, however, group-G beta-hemolytic streptococci are isolated from infants with neonatal septicemia and from local purulent processes of adult people.

Cats have been implicated as asymptomatic reservoirs for group-A streptococci of people.[7,8] Group-A streptococci are the main cause of pharyngitis in children. It is possible, however, that the cats were infected by the children. Greene found that cats shed group-A streptococci for 1, 2 or 3 weeks after being removed from homes where human outbreaks were occurring.[8] Stallings and co-workers isolated *Streptococcus pneumoniae* from an aged cat with acute fever, septicemia and septic arthritis.[9] An infant in the household had a cold for 3 weeks and was also culture positive. This was almost certainly an incident of human-to-cat transmission.

References

1. Blanchard PC: *Group G streptococcal infections in kittens: Pathogenesis, immune response and maternal carrier state.* PhD dissertation. Univ of California, Davis, 1987.

2. Dow SW et al: Group B streptococcal infection in cats. *JAVMA* 190:71-72, 1987.

3. Goldman PM and Moore T: Spontaneous Lancefield group G streptococcal infection in a random source cat colony. *Lab Anim Sci* 23:565-566, 1973.

4. Swindle MM et al: Contagious streptococcal lymphadenitis in cats. *JAVMA* 177: 829-830, 1980.

5. Swindle MM et al: Pathogenesis of contagious streptococcal lymphadenitis in cats. *JAVMA* 179: 1208-1210, 1981.

6. Tillman PC et al: Group G streptococcal epizootic in a closed cat colony. *J Clin Microbiol* 16:1057-1060, 1982.

Additional References

7. Cooperman SM: Cherchez le chien: household pets as reservoirs of persistent or recurrent streptococcal sore throats in children. *NY State J Med* 82:1685-2687, 1982.

8. Greene CE: Zoonotic aspects of group A streptococcal infection in dogs and cats. *JAAHA* 24:218-222, 1988.

9. Stallings B et al: Septicemia and septic arthritis caused by *Streptococcus pneumoniae* in a cat: possible transmission from a child. *JAVMA* 191:703-704, 1987.

Chapter 19

Staphylococcus Infection

Etiologic Agent

Staphylococci are Gram-positive cocci about 1 μ in diameter that grow in grape-like bunches. They grow best under conditions of reduced oxygen tension and tend to be resistant to many environmental insults and common disinfectants. Staphylococci live both free in the environment and as commensal parasites of the skin and upper respiratory tract of people and animals.

Both pathogenic and nonpathogenic strains of staphylococci exist in nature. Pathogenic strains tend to possess extracellular toxins, such as coagulase, staphylokinase, hemolysin and epidermolysins. Some strains also produce enterotoxins associated with food poisoning. Coagulase has been commonly used to differentiate pathogenic from nonpathogenic strains, resulting in some confusion in the older literature on staphylococci nomenclature. Coagulase-positive isolates were generally referred to as *S aureus*, and coagulase-negative isolates as *S epidermidis*. Hajek proposed the name *S intermedius* for coagulase-positive staphylococci that differed from *S aureus* in cell-wall composition and biochemical reactions.[3] *Staphylococcus intermedius* was much more prevalent than *S aureus* as an isolate from animals.[6] It is now apparent that over 16 different species of staphylococci exist in nature.[7] Twelve species seem to be commonly found on cats.[2] *Staphylococcus aureus* and *S intermedius* are the main coagulase-positive species, while *S epidermidis*, *S xylosus*, *S hemolyticus*, *S hominis*, *S hyicus*, *S capitis*, *S warnerii*, *S saprophyticus*, *S sciuri* and *S simulans* are the principal coagulase-negative species. Cox and co-workers isolated staphylococci from all 113 normal cats they tested.[2] All of the tested cats had staphylococci in 1 or more sites, which included 4 sites on the coat, superficial nares, mouth, pharynx, ears, eyes, anus, prepuce and vagina. Over 60% of the total isolates were from the haircoat and 2-9% of the isolates were from each of the other sites. The most common coagulase-positive *Staphylococcus* from normal cats was *S intermedius*, while *S simulans* was the most common coagulase-negative species. Cox and associates also found that household cats carried a much broader range of species than cattery cats.[2]

Staphylococci have a great propensity to develop antibiotic resistance due to production of beta-lactamase. This enzyme inactivates penicillin antibiotics.

Pathogenesis

Staphylococci, in particular *S aureus*, are mainly opportunistic pathogens. Their almost ubiquitous presence in the environment and on skin and mucous membranes allows them easy access to deeper host tissues.

Clinical Features

Coagulase-positive staphylococci are associated with a number of infections in cats and other animals. Staphylococcal dermatitis is especially common in dogs but uncommon in cats. Staphylococcal dermatitis in puppies is probably associated with their relative lack of acquired immunity to the organism. However, primary staphylococcal dermatitis is surprisingly uncommon in kittens. When present, it is usually manifested by crusty, erythematous dermatitis around the nail beds and margins of the eyelids and lips. Staphylococci are common secondary invaders in other dermatopathies, including allergic dermatitis, flea-bite dermatitis, seborrhea oleosa and sicca, autoimmune skin diseases, and dermal wounds, burns and abrasions. Staphylococci have also been associated with abscesses, oral infections, external ear infections, conjunctivitis, metritis, mastitis, gall bladder and biliary tract infections, and bacteremia. Cutaneous granuloma with fistulation (botryomycosis) caused by a *Staphylococcus* has been reported in a cat.[8] Chronic staphylococcal dermatitis has been seen in some FIV-infected cats.

Pathologic Features

Staphylococci are generally associated with superficial or deep acute inflammatory processes indistinguishable from those caused by other bacteria. Deeper and more low-grade infections may be more pyogranulomatous in nature.[8]

Clinicopathologic Features

Staphylococci can be readily isolated from diseased tissues. However, care must be taken to avoid overinterpretation of a positive isolation. Coagulase-positive staphylococci are readily isolated from most normal cats.[4] Organisms often invade diseased tissues and contribute in varying degrees to the disease process. Therefore, specific antibiotic treatment for the staphylococcal component of the infection might result in some improvement of the condition but will not be curative.

Treatment and Prevention

Antibiotic sensitivity tests should be done on most isolates of coagulase-positive staphylococci. Resistance to antibiotics is increasingly common. Of 621 animal isolates of coagulase-positive staphylococci, about two-thirds were resistant to at least 1 of 11 tested antimicrobials. Resistance to penicillin was most common (60%), followed by streptomycin (34.7%) and tetracycline (33%). Only 10% of isolates were resistant to erythromycin, neomycin, lincomycin, methicillin, chloramphenicol, nitrofurantoin, cephalothin or gentamicin. The study also demonstrated a strong correlation between prior treatment with antimicrobials and the resistance pattern of the isolates. Therefore, staphylococcal infections acquired during hospitalization are more likely to demonstrate beta-lactamase-induced antibiotic resistance.

Infection and Immunity

Most staphylococcal infections occur as a result of breeches in the normal integrity of the skin or mucous membranes caused by other diseases or by diminished host immune function. Conditions that favor massive increases in the numbers of pathogenic staphylococci, such as seborrhea, also favor disease. Very young animals are more prone to staphylococcal infections because of their incomplete but developing immunity to the organism. Old, debilitated animals are also prone to staphylococcal infections because of impaired host defenses.

Animal and Public Health Considerations

Pathogenic staphylococci of phage types known to cause disease in people have been isolated from normal cats.[5] Realistically, most people and animals carry their own pathogenic staphylococcal flora, and disease is virtually never a function of mere exposure. Therefore, infected cats should not be considered hazards to other cats or people.

References

1. Biberstein EL *et al*: Antimicrobial sensitivity patterns in *Staphylococcus aureus* from animals. *JAVMA* 164:1183-1186, 1974.

2. Cox HU *et al*: Distribution of staphylococcal species on clinically healthy cats. *Am J Vet Res* 46:1824-1828, 1985.

3. Hàjek V and Marsalek E, in Jeljaszewicz J: *Proc 3rd Intl Symp Staphylococci and Staphylococcal Infections*. Gustav Fischer Verlag, Stuttgart, 1976. pp 11-23.

4. Hearst BR: Low incidence of staphylococcal dermatitides in animals with high incidence of *Staphylococcus aureus*. Part 1: Preliminary study of cats. *VM/SAC* 62:475-477, 1967.

5. Mann PH: Antibiotic sensitivity testing and bacteriophage typing of staphylococci found in the nostrils of dogs and cats. *JAVMA* 134:469-470, 1959.

6. Raus J and Love DN: Characterization of coagulase-positive *Staphylococcus intermedius* and *Staphylococcus aureus* isolated from veterinary clinical specimens. *J Clin Microbiol* 18:789-792, 1983.

7. Skerman VBD *et al*: Approved lists of bacterial names. *Intl J Syst Bacteriol* 30:225-420, 1980.

8. Walton, DK *et al*: Cutaneous bacterial granuloma (botryomycosis) in a dog and cat. *JAAHA* 19:537-541, 1983.

Chapter 20

Listeriosis

Etiologic Agent

Listeria monocytogenes is the main pathogenic organism in the *Listeria* genus. It is a small, weakly Gram-positive, motile coccobacillus that prefers to grow in aerobic or microaerobic conditions. The organism is commonly isolated from water, soil and sewage, and can survive in moist environments for months. Silage is a common source of infection for large animals and farmers.

Listeria monocytogenes is worldwide in distribution and has been isolated from virtually every type of animal.[10,11] It sporadically colonizes healthy animals and has been isolated from the feces of about 1% of normal people and an even higher percentage of people in contact with affected individuals. *Listeria monocytogenes* has also been isolated from about 0.1% of wild-trapped rodents in the Soviet Union, 0.2% of free-living mammals and birds in Czechoslovakia, and >1% of wild and domestic animals in Denmark.[10,12-14] The infection rate is much higher in animals with suspected CNS disease. Of 20 red fox brains submitted for rabies examination in Georgia, 5 were infected with the organism.[15] Of 155 brain specimens from domestic and wild animals submitted for rabies examination in North Dakota, 38 also yielded *L monocytogenes*.[10] The isolation rate in cats in this same study was 1 of 15 (6.7%).

Listeria monocytogenes exists in 11 serotypes. Serotype 1b and less commonly serotype 4 are most often associated with disease in the United States.[1]

Pathogenesis

Listeria monocytogenes has been associated with 3 distinct syndromes in animals: uterine infections and abortion; septicemia with visceral abscessation; and encephalitis.[8] Animals apparently contract the infection by ingesting infected prey or contaminated feed and water. In 1 cat, the infection seemed to be introduced in a grass awn that penetrated the bowel and entered the peritoneal cavity.[16] Initial replication is thought to occur in the intestinal epithelium, with spread to regional lymph nodes and then hematogenous spread to other organs.

Clinical Features

Listeriosis is relatively uncommon in cats. This may largely be due to cats' high degree of natural resistance.[4] The septicemic form is the major type of disease described in the literature.[3,11,16] However, the relatively high incidence of listeriosis lesions in cat brains submitted for rabies examination indicates the encephalitic form is also relatively common in cats.[10]

The septicemic form of feline listeriosis is usually manifested by colic, abdominal pain on palpation, vomiting, diarrhea, fever and depression. The condition has invariably been fatal within a few days in cases described in the literature.

Clinical signs associated with the encephalitic form of listeriosis in cats have not been described. Isolation of the organism from cats with rabies-like signs suggests that the signs may be similar to those in any other form of encephalitis.

Pathologic Features

Gross changes in cats with septicemic listeriosis include mesenteric lymph node enlargement, hyperemia of the distal small bowel mucosa, and microabscessation of the liver and sometimes spleen. One cat had associated exudative peritonitis. However, the disease in this cat appeared to be introduced into the abdomen by a grass awn that had migrated through the bowel wall.[16]

Clinicopathologic Features

Listeriosis is seldom diagnosed before necropsy and culture isolation.

Treatment and Prevention

Ampicillin and penicillin G are the antibiotics of choice for treatment of listeriosis.[1] The organism is also susceptible to trimethoprim-sulfonamides, chloramphenicol, clindamycin, erythromycin, gentamicin and tetracyline.[1] Cephalosporins generally have poor activity against *Listeria*. Unfortunately, the disease in cats is seldom diagnosed before death.

Infection and Immunity

The disease in people has a predilection for relatively immunocompromised individuals, such as pregnant women, infants and older people with debilitating diseases.[1] Cats seem very resistant to experimentally induced disease, and the number of affected cats is relatively small.[4] There is no indication that the few reported feline cases were associated with any predisposing immunosuppressive condition.

Immunity to *L monocytogenes* in people and animals is assumed to be largely cell mediated.[2] The organism maintains itself in an intracellular environment, and humoral immunity has little effect on the disease course.

Animal and Public Health Considerations

Listeriosis is considered a zoonotic disease because both people and animals can be infected by the same organism.[6] However, there is no evidence that people are infected by contact with diseased animals. In fact, the source of infection in people is usually not determined, and many infected individuals have no history of contact with any of the usual reservoirs.[1]

References

1. Barza M, in Wyngaarden JB and Smith LH Jr: *Cecil's Textbook of Medicine*. Saunders, Philadelphia, 1985. pp 1609-1611.

2. Bottone EJ and Sierra MF: *Listeria monocytogenes*: Another look at the "Cinderella among pathogenic bacteria." *Mt Sinai J Med* 44:42, 1977.

3. Decker RA *et al*: Listeriosis in a young cat. *JAVMA* 168:1025, 1976.

4. Graham R *et al*: Listeriosis in domestic animals. *Univ Ill Expt Station Bltn* 499:3-94, 1943.

5. Gray ML: *2nd Symp on Listeric Infection*. Montana State College, Bozeman, 1963. p 398.

6. Hamilton HB and Greene CE, in Greene CE: *Clinical Microbiology and Infectious Diseases of the Dog and Cat*. Saunders, Philadelphia, 1985. pp 874-896.

7. Held R: Listeriose bei einer Katze. *Zentralblatt Bakteriol* 173:485-486, 1958.

8. Jubb KVF and Kennedy PC: *Pathology of Domestic Animals*. 3rd ed. Academic Press, New York, 1985.

9. Larsen HE: Listeric infection among animals in Denmark. *2nd Symp on Listeric Infection*. Montana State College, Bozeman, 1963. pp 27-29.

10. McIlwain PK *et al*: Occurrence of *Listeria monocytogenes* in the brains of wild and domestic animals. *Am J Vet Res* 27:1497-1499, 1966.

11. Nilsson A and Karlsson KA: *Listeria monocytogenes* isolations from animals in Sweden from 1948 to 1957. *Nord Vet Med* 11:305-315, 1959.

12. Ogneva NS: Study on the incidence of listeriosis among rodents in Moscow. *Material Sci Conf Tomsk*. 1962. pp 107-109.

13. Olsufèv NG and Emelyanova OS: Discovery of *Listeria monocytogenes* infection from wild rodents, insectivores, bats and *Ixodes* ticks. *Zhur Mikjrobiol Epidemiol Immunobiol* 22:67-71, 1951.

14. Seeman J: *Listeria monocytogenes* in rodents. *Cesk Epidemiol Mikrobiol Immunol* 6:140-145, 1957.

15. Sholtens RG and Brim A: Isolations of *Listeria monocytogenes* from foxes suspected of having rabies. *JAVMA* 145:466-469, 1964.

16. Turner T: A case of *Escherichia monocytogenes* (*Listeria monocytogenes*) in the cat. *Vet Record* 74:778, 1962.

Chapter 21

Clostridial Infections

TETANUS

Etiologic Agent

Tetanus is caused by a heat-stable toxin (tetanospasmin) produced by *Clostridium tetani*, a motile, Gram-positive, spore-forming, anaerobic bacillus. The vegetative stage of the organism produces spore-like structures that are highly resistant to environmental factors. Spores are ubiquitous in soil. They have been isolated from the feces of many farm animals and are particularly prevalent where farm animals are kept.

Pathogenesis

Tetanus occurs when spores are introduced into wounds or damaged tissues. Spores form vegetative bacilli only under anaerobic conditions. Putrefying infections and avascular wounds are most frequently associated with tetanus; therefore, tetanus in cats usually associated with large traumatic wounds on the distal extremities (wildlife traps), surgical incisions (castration, ovariohysterectomy, declaw), and postparturient metritis. Penetrating foreign bodies are infrequent vehicles for infection.

The vegetative form of *Cl tetani* is responsible for toxin production. On a dry-weight basis, tetanospasmin is second only to botulism toxin in toxicity to people and animals. Horses are the most sensitive to tetanospasmin, followed closely by people. Cats are 2400-7200 times less sensitive to the effects of tetanus toxin than horses.[4,19] Therefore, tetanus is a far more serious problem in horses than in cats. This may also explain why cats with tetanus usually have large wounds; only such wounds generate sufficient toxin to cause clinical signs.

Tetanospasmin enters nerve axons at the neuromuscular end-plates and is carried to the cell body of the associated neurons in the spinal cord. Tetanospasmin accumulates in regions of the cell body that receive afferent synaptic terminals from inhibitory neurons.[6,18] Some toxin is also carried via the bloodstream and enters the nerve bodies directly. Tetanus toxin spreads from spinal neurons to the brain. The toxin affects the spinal cord, brain and sympathetic nervous system. However, spinal signs predominate in cats and are caused by alterations in the normal myotactic reflexes.[20] Inhibitory neuron interference increases alpha-motor neuron activity and stimulation of motor end-plates without interstimulatory relaxation.

Clinical Features

Clinical signs appear 2-14 days after the initial wound. Signs begin in the limb regional to the source of toxin and become generalized within 24 hours. Even during the generalized phase of the disease, however, signs remain most severe in the limb regional to the wound.

Signs of tetanus begin with spastic extension of 1 or more limbs, usually a hind limb. Muscular stiffness becomes more generalized, and as extensor rigidity becomes severe, the animal becomes laterally recumbent. The tail is usually erect and held over the back, the head and neck are thrown back, and the limbs are extended (Fig 1). Prolapse of the nictitating membranes and trismus of the facial muscles are variable (Fig 2). Urinary retention is common. The slightest stimulation often provokes convulsive episodes of muscular spasms. Death is caused by exhaustion, cachexia, dehydration and breathing difficulties.

Pathologic Features

Other than the entry wounds, no gross or histopathologic features are associated with tetanus.

Clinicopathologic Features

Tetanus is diagnosed exlusively by the classic clinical signs and history of recent wounds, parturition or surgical procedures.

Treatment and Prevention

Many cats reported in the literature have been euthanized or have died within a few days.[2,4,5,8,10-12] Others, usually with better

Fig 1. Contracture of facial muscles in a cat with tetanus. The ears are pulled together and erect, and the palpebral fissures are narrowed. (Courtesy of Dr. A. deLahunta, New York College of Veterinary Medicine, and *JAAHA*)

Fig 2. A cat with tetanus exhibiting extreme rigidity of the limbs, arched back and dorsally curved tail. (Courtesy of Dr. A. deLahunta, New York College of Veterinary Medicine, and *JAAHA*)

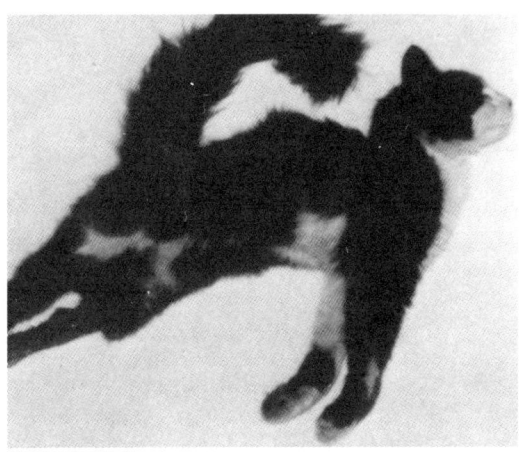

supportive care, recovered over several weeks.[7,9,13-15,21] Cats with tetanus should be treated similarly to other affected species. The primary wounds should be opened, cleaned and debrided if necessary. Penicillin antibiotics should be given for at least 7 days. Animals should be kept in a quiet, dark cage and handled as little as possible. The urinary bladder should be manually expressed several times daily if necessary or an indwelling urinary catheter placed until normal bladder tone returns. Use of antitoxin is debatable; it can cause anaphylactic reactions in some animals, is expensive, and is of much less value in the advanced stage of disease when animals are often presented. Promazine tranquilizers should be used if muscle spasms are not overly intense and unrelenting. A continuous IV drip with 10% glyceryl guaiacolate in water can effectively relax muscle spasms in severely affected individuals. The induction dosage is 50-100 mg/kg. The drug should be given at a level just sufficient to relax muscle spasms and allow unimpaired breathing and eating. Fluids and nutrients can usually be provided in liquid form with a syringe and short feeding tube or eyedropper. Parenteral fluids and nutrition are usually not necessary unless oral feeding becomes impossible. The nadir of clinical signs is often reached within a few days of presentation, and recovery begins after 6-14 days.

However, complete recovery can take as long as 4-6 weeks.

Infection and Immunity

Tetanus can be prevented by immunization with tetanus toxoid. The amount of tetanus toxin associated with disease is usually considerably below the amount required for immunization. Therefore, animals that recover from tetanus are not necessarily immune to the disease. The extremely low incidence of tetanus in cats makes tetanus immunization unwarranted. This is not the case in such species as people and horses, in which the disease is relatively common and potentially fatal.

Animal and Public Health Considerations

Tetanus is not communicable among animals or from animals to people.

MISCELLANEOUS CLOSTRIDIAL DISEASES

Clostridium novyi has been isolated from disseminated osteomyelitis in a cat.[3] Bone infection was associated with periosteal reaction involving the femur, humerus and tibia bilaterally. A primary focus of infection was not identified and blood cultures were negative. The organism was cultured from bone marrow and bone biopsies. The cat was treated successfully with procaine penicillin G, potassium penicillin and metronidazole. A feline leukemia virus test was negative.

Severe gangrenous myositis due to *Cl chauvoei* and *Cl septicum* was seen in a 6-month-old cat 24 hours after ovariohysterectomy.[16] Gross examination showed a crepitant swelling over the ventrolateral aspects of the chest and abdominal wall, and severe, diffuse, serosanguineous subcutaneous edema. The cat died within 12 hours. At necropsy, the pectoral and intercostal muscles and muscular part of the diaphragm were black, dry and spongy. A pronounced butyric acid (butter-like) odor was detected. The involved muscles were filled with gas. The cat was a barn animal and the presumed mode of entry was from spores that multiplied in response to anaerobic conditions in the tissues around the ovariohysterectomy incision.

Botulism, caused by the potent neurotoxins of *Cl botulinum*, has not been recognized as a naturally occurring disease of cats.[1] Cats are sensitive to the effects of the toxin, however.[17] The disease does occur in other carnivores, such as dogs. Dogs usually contract botulism by eating carrion, a practice that cats usually avoid.[1] The lack of disease in cats has been attributed to their more selective feeding habits.

Clostridium spp, in particular *Cl villosum*, have been isolated from some suppurative mixed-bacterial infections of cats (Chapter 26).

References

1. Barsanti JA, in Greene CA: *Clinical Microbiology and Infectious Diseases of the Dog and Cat.* Saunders, Philadelphia, 1984. pp 599-607.

2. Bateman JK: Tetanus in a kitten. *Vet Record* 11:805, 1931.

3. Dunn JK et al: Disseminated osteomyelitis caused by *Clostridium novyi* in a cat. *Can Vet J* 24:312-315, 1983.

4. Fildes P et al: A case of tetanus in a cat. *Vet Record* 43:731, 1931.

5. Goetz EF: Tetanus in a cat. *JAVMA* 169:174, 1976.

6. Green J et al: Is there retrograde axonal transport of tetanus toxin in both alpha and gamma fibers? *Nature* 265:370, 1977.

7. Groulade M: Un cas de tétanos chez le chat. *Bltn Acad Vèt* 20:254-255, 1947.

8. Hopson CG and Green G: Tetanus in a cat. *Vet Record* 12:302, 1932.

9. Killingsworth C et al: Feline tetanus. *JAAHA* 13:209-215, 1977.

10. Kodituwakku GE and Wijewanta EA: Tetanus in a cat. *Brit Vet J* 114:48-50, 1958.

11. Lettow E: Tetanus bei einer Katze. *Berl Munch Tier Wochenschrift* 68:197-198, 1955.

12. Loeffler K et al: Tetanus bei Hund und Katze *Dtsch Tierärztl Wochenschrift* 69:476-479, 1962.

13. Miller ER: Tetanus in the cat. *Vet Record* 61:40, 1949.

14. Miller ER: The use of promazine hydrochloride in a case of tetanus in the cat. *Vet Record* 75:135-136, 1963.

15. Nam CC: Clinical communication: Tetanus in a cat. *Malayan Vet Med Assn J* 1:56, 1956.

16. Poonacha KB et al: Clostridial myositis in a cat. *Vet Pathol* 19:217-219, 1982.

17. Prèvot AR and Sillioc R: Une ènigme biologique: chat et botulisme. *Ann Pasteur Inst* 89:354-357, 1955.

18. Schwab MB and Thoenen H: Electron microscopic evidence for a trans-synaptic migration of tetanus toxin in spinal cord motor neurons: an autoradiographic and morphometric study. *Brain Res* 105:213-227, 1976.

19. Topley and Wilson: *Principles of Bacteriology and Immunity*. 7th ed. Williams & Wilkins, Baltimore, 1984.

20. Weinstein L: Tetanus. *New Engl J Med* 289:1293-1296, 1973.

Additional Reference

21. Baker JL et al: Tetanus in two cats. *JAAHA* 24:159-164, 1988.

Chapter 22

Bacillary Infections

ANTHRAX

Etiologic Agent

Anthrax is caused by *Bacillus anthracis*, a large, nonmotile, saprophytic Gram-positive rod. *Bacillus anthracis* is a facultative anaerobe in the vegetative state but forms highly resistant spores under anaerobic conditions. It is primarily a pathogen of sheep and cattle, in which it causes peracute and massive septicemia. Spores from decomposing carcasses contaminate the soil for many years.

Pathogenesis

Carnivorous animals, such as dogs and cats, are susceptible to anthrax, though the disease is very uncommon in these species. Cats are usually infected when fed meat that contains anthrax spores.[2] Spores can also be introduced into the body through wounds or by inhalation. Spores are carried to regional lymphoid tissue, where the vegetative form grows rapidly. Organisms replicate within the blood and other organs, and bacteremia develops within hours.

Clinical Features

Clinical signs are minimal. Animals may appear normal but die a few hours later.[2] Hemorrhage from external orifices is common in cattle and sheep but is not seen in cats.

Pathologic Features

Gross pathologic changes are minimal in cats with anthrax.[2] Lung congestion and dark, unclotted blood in large vessels and the heart are the main findings at necropsy.

Clinicopathologic Features

Diagnosis is by microscopic examination of postmortem blood smears, which teem with bacilli.

Treatment and Prevention

Fortunately, anthrax in cats is very uncommon. The condition is invariably and rapidly fatal once the infection becomes blood borne. Cats should not be fed raw meat from animals with suspected anthrax.

Infection and Immunity

The capsular proteins of *B anthracis* inhibit phagocytosis of the organism. This allows the organism to gain access to the blood and grow almost unimpeded.

Animal and Public Health Considerations

Anthrax is transmissible among many different species of animals. Infected carcasses should be incinerated or chemically decomposed to prevent environmental contamination with spores. *Bacillus anthracis* infects people but usually enters the body through skin abrasions or wounds and causes mainly localized abscesses. Infection can spread systemically if the local infection is untreated. Fulminating and frequently fatal inhalation (pulmonary) and GI forms of anthrax have been recognized in people.

TYZZER'S DISEASE

Etiologic Agent

Tyzzer's disease is caused by *B piliformis*, a Gram-negative, spore-bearing rod. This organism is an obligatory intracellular parasite of the intestinal epithelium. *Bacillus piliformis* has not been grown in artificial media but has been propagated in embryonating chicken eggs and intracerebrally in mice.

Pathogenesis

Tyzzer's disease occurs in a number of animal species, including laboratory rodents, primates, horses, dogs and cats. The major source of the organism is probably rodents. The disease is relatively stereotyped in most species in which it occurs. Initial replication appears to occur in the intestinal tract, especially the colon, with hematogenous spread to the liver.

Clinical Features

The disease in cats has been seen mainly in laboratory-housed kittens as a naturally occurring infection or following inadvertent inoculation with contaminated tissue.[1,3,4] The infection has been described on occasion in household cats.[7]

Cats with Tyzzer's disease are usually anorectic and depressed, and die within 1-3 days. Diarrhea is variably present but is not severe.

Pathologic Features

Gross and microscopic changes are concentrated in the liver and distal intestinal tract.[1,4,5] Mild hyperemia and mucosal reddening are present in the terminal ileum and colon, mesenteric lymph nodes are often enlarged and hyperemic, and the liver contains numerous small hemorrhagic lesions up to 1 mm in diameter. Hepatic lesions often have an irregular border and pale red or yellow centers. Microscopic changes consist of random focal areas of hepatic necrosis and hemorrhage, with macrophage and polymorphonuclear neutrophil infiltration. Hepatocyte vacuolation is prominent in areas of normal parenchyma bordering on lesions. Long, filamentous organisms are found in bundles and tangled masses within the cytoplasm of hepatocytes in the periphery of the lesions. Free organisms can sometimes be seen within areas of hepatic necrosis in sinusoids or among cell debris. The mucosa of the terminal ileum and proximal colon is often desquamated and hypertrophied, with neutrophil and lymphocyte infiltration. Organisms are present within affected mucosal cells. Foci of necrosis are seen sometimes in the spleen, gastric mucosa, mesenteric lymph nodes and adrenal glands.

Clinicopathologic Features

Diagnosis of Tyzzer's disease is based on identification of typical masses or bundles of intracytoplasmic bacilli on stained sections of affected tissues.

Treatment and Prevention

The disease is usually recognized only at necropsy and after histopathologic examination of tissues. No affected cats have been treated at an earlier stage.

Infection and Immunity

Tyzzer's disease in animals is often associated with environmental overcrowding or immunosuppression. The disease in cats has occurred predominantly in laboratory-maintained animals.[1,3-5] In the studies of Bennett and co-workers, affected cats had been experimentally infected with feline leukemia virus (FeLV) as neonates.[1] A naturally occurring case in a 10-year-old household cat has been described by Schneck.[7] The cat had a chronic history of weight loss and diarrhea but unfortunately was not tested for FeLV infection. The clinical signs of this cat also resembled those of feline immunodeficiency virus (FIV) infection. Tyzzer's disease also occurred as an outbreak in kittens with familial hyperlipoproteinemia.[3]

Animal and Public Health Considerations

The infection is apparently transmissible among animal species. Kubokawa and co-workers observed 2 cases of Tyzzer's disease in golden hamsters housed in the same room with infected cats.[5] Disease was first observed in cats and appeared to spread to the hamsters over the next several weeks. It was not certain whether the organism spread from the hamsters to the cats or *vice versa*. Enzootic Tyzzer's disease is more common in rodents, and the hamsters were the more probable source of infection in this outbreak. Tyzzer's disease has not been observed in people but it occurs in nonhuman primates.

MISCELLANEOUS BACILLI

Rapid death associated with enteritis has been seen in a cat with *B cereus* septicemia.[6]

References

1. Bennett AM *et al*: Tyzzer's disease in cats experimentally infected with feline leukemia virus. *Vet Microbiol* 2:49-65, 1977.

2. Cripps JHH and Young RC: A case of anthrax in a cat and in a monkey. *Vet Record* 72:1054, 1960.

3. Jones BR *et al*: Tyzzer's disease in kittens with familial hyperlipoproteinemia. *J Small Anim Pract* 26:411-419, 1985.

4. Kovatch RM and Zebarth G: Naturally occurring Tyzzer's disease in a cat. *JAVMA* 162:136-138, 1973.

5. Kubokawa K *et al*: Two cases of feline Tyzzer's disease. *Jpn J Exp Med* 43:413-421, 1973.

6. Nilèhn PO: Infectioner med antrax-liknande mikrober. *Nord Vet Med* 10:325-330, 1958.

7. Schneck G: Tyzzer's disease in an adult cat. *VM/SAC* 70:155-156, 1975.

Chapter 23

Bordetellosis

Etiologic Agent

Bordetella bronchiseptica is a small, aerobic Gram-negative coccobacillus. It is a normal inhabitant of the upper respiratory tract of many species of animals and people.

Pathogenesis

Bordetella bronchiseptica is associated with "kennel cough" in dogs, a condition manifested by tracheobronchitis and a chronic dry cough. In cats, however, it is more often isolated from animals with clinical or subclinical pneumonia.[1,5] The organism can be routinely isolated from oropharyngeal swabs in 3-10% of normal cats.[5,6] Disease appears to be triggered by crowding and stress, and is usually recognized in laboratory cat colonies and catteries.[1,5] Snyder and co-workers observed that the carrier rate increased rapidly from 10% to 48% in a group of randomly obtained cats kept in close confinement for 3 weeks.[5] Disease appears to be caused by increased colonization in the upper respiratory tract, coupled with other stresses that may lower resistance. The predisposing role of respiratory viruses, such as feline herpesvirus or calicivirus, has not been elucidated. Viral infections can set the stage for *B bronchiseptica*-induced tracheobronchitis in dogs.[7] Snyder and co-workers reported 3 of 7 cats with *B bronchiseptica* pneumonia and concurrent rhinotracheitis.[5]

Clinical Features

Pneumonia induced in cats by *B bronchiseptica* can be generalized or focal in nature. Therefore, clinical signs are variable. Manifestation of clinical signs is further obscured by feline behavior. Cats with pneumonia often do not show typical pneumonic signs even when severely infected. Of 10 cats with fatal *B bronchiseptica* pneumonia described by Snyder and associates, only 7 were noticeably ill before death.[5] Of those 7 cats, 3 had signs of rhinotracheitis, 1 had a cough, and 1 behaved as if it had chronic pneumonia. Of the 7 remaining cats, 2 showed nonspecific signs of listlessness, anorexia, dehydration and emaciation before death. All 10 animals had gross lesions in their lungs.

Pathologic Features

Primary lesions of *B bronchiseptica* infection in cats are limited mainly to the lungs. Gross lesions consist of reddish areas of consolidation involving 1 or more lung lobes. Large, firm, grayish nodules 2-5 mm in diameter are occasionally seen in the lungs of some cats. Purulent exudate can be seen on the cut surface of affected lungs in about one-third of the cats.

Histopathologic findings are compatible with bronchopneumonia. Interstitial disease is less common. The pulmonary parenchyma is congested and edematous, with focal necrotic areas surrounding bronchioli. Inflammatory exudate in the bronchioli and alveoli consists of polymorphonuclear neutrophils, macrophages and lymphocytes.

Clinicopathologic Features

Recognition of existing pneumonia is the first and most difficult step in diagnosing bordetellosis in cats. In certain catteries where disease is common, the pattern of bordetellosis in younger cats is stereotyped. The bronchopneumonia usually is diagnosed by thoracic radiography. Tracheal aspiration and culture can confirm the role of *B bronchiseptica* in the disease. Isolation of *B bronchiseptica* from oropharyngeal swabs should be interpreted with caution; many cats, especially those living in enzootic areas, are asymptomatic carriers.

Treatment and Prevention

Bordetella bronchiseptica pneumonia can be readily treated with antibiotics, such as chloramphenicol, gentamicin, kanamycin and tetracycline.[2] Therapy should be continued for about 14 days.

Problems with *B bronchiseptica* in groups of cats can be minimized with proper husbandry. Overcrowding of animals, stress on the population and the presence of numerous younger animals kept in poorly ventilated quarters are factors that predispose to disease. Bordetellosis can be a complication of feline herpesvirus and calicivirus infections; these diseases are also likely to be more severe under poor husbandry conditions.

Avirulent live and inactivated *B bronchiseptica* vaccines are available for "kennel cough" in dogs.[3,4] The former is given intranasally and the latter parenterally. They have been used in cats by some breeders but their safety and efficacy have not been determined.

Infection and Immunity

Bordetellosis is largely an environmentally potentiated disease. A percentage of normal animals carry small numbers of the organisms in their oropharynx for months and years. In highly stressful and overcrowded conditions, levels of organisms can increase dramatically, and exposure of young susceptible animals is much greater. Exposure to a low level of organisms favors asymptomatic colonization of the upper respiratory passages, while high-level exposure favors colonization and tissue invasion, especially if coupled with stress. Viral infections, which temporarily damage mucociliary-clearance mechanisms and induce microscopic areas of interstitial pneumonia, may allow *Bordetella* to move from the oropharynx into the lower airways. The organism can then invade tissues at sites of viral damage.

Animal and Public Health Considerations

Bordetella bronchiseptica infection is relatively common in many species but clinical disease is uncommon. For this reason, infected cats should not be considered human or animal health hazards.

References

1. Fisk SK and Soave OA: *Bordetella bronchiseptica* in laboratory cats from central California. *Lab Anim Sci* 23:33-35, 1973.

2. Roudebush P and Fales WH: Antibacterial susceptibility of *Bordetella bronchiseptica* isolates from small companion animals with respiratory disease. *JAAHA* 17:793-797, 1987.

3. Shade FJ and Goodnow RA: Intranasal immunization of dogs against *Bordetella bronchiseptica*-induced tracheobronchitis (kennel cough) with modified-live *Bordetella bronchiseptica* vaccine. *Am J Vet Res* 40:1241-1243, 1979.

4. Shade FJ and Rapp VJ: Studies of vaccine incorporating an extracted *Bordetella bronchiseptica* antigen for controlling canine bordetellosis. *VM/SAC* 77:1635-1639, 1982.

5. Snyder SB *et al*: Respiratory tract disease associated with *Bordetella bronchiseptica* infection in cats. *JAVMA* 163:293-294, 1973.

6. Switzer WP *et al*: Incidence of *Bordetella bronchiseptica* in wildlife and man in Iowa. *Am J Vet Res* 27:1134-1136, 1966.

7. Thayer, GW, in Greene CE: *Clinical Microbiology and Infectious Diseases of the Dog and Cat.* Saunders, Philadelphia, 1984. pp 430-436.

Chapter 24

Pasteurellosis

Etiologic Agent

Pasteurella multocida is a small, nonmotile, Gram-negative, ovoid bipolar rod. The organism is a commensal parasite of the oral cavity of many species of animals, including cats.[10] *Pasteurella multocida* has been isolated from 80% of swabs taken from the canine teeth and adjacent gingiva of normal cats. Schenk and Oudar and associates isolated *Pasteurella* spp from the oral cavity and respiratory tract of 60-75% of normal cats.[5,6] The rate of isolation is higher from animals with dental tartar and gingival disease than from animals with clean teeth.[1]

Pathogenesis

Pasteurella spp exist in a number of different serotypes that differ greatly in virulence in mouse-inoculation tests. Soltys found that 8 of 8 mouth isolates from healthy cats were nonpathogenic, while 4 of 10 isolates from wounds and abscesses were pathogenic.[9] Curtis and Ollerhead found that 3 of 6 oropharyngeal isolates from normal cats were nonpathogenic to mice, 1 was weakly pathogenic and 2 were highly pathogenic.[3]

Clinical Features

Pasteurella is most frequently isolated as a facultative anaerobe along with other anaerobic bacteria from infected wounds and abscesses in cats (Chapter 26). It has also been isolated from purulent infections of the external ear canals, conjunctiva, nasal passages and sinuses, tooth root abscesses, periodontal infections and surgical wounds. Omphalophlebitis in kittens can be caused by *Pasteurella* spp. Similar to *Bordetella* spp, *Pasteurella* spp are commonly associated with pneumonia in colony- or laboratory-reared cats.[8] *Pasteurella* spp are frequent secondary invaders in cats with primary viral pneumonia and are commonly isolated from thoracic exudates in cats with empyema.

Pasteurella spp enter tissues through bites or licking of wounds. Organisms are frequently isolated from the claws of cats, but cat scratches are less apt to be associated with infections than bites.[1] Soltys isolated *P multocida* from 24 of 46 infected cat-fight wounds and abscesses.[9] It has also been isolated from the spinal cord of a cat that developed ascending meningomyelitis after being bitten in the caudal back by another cat.[2]

Pathologic Features

Lesions caused by *P multocida* often exude a great deal of grayish pus. *Pasteurella* spp infections in cats tend to remain localized. Local tissue necrosis is usually minimal; when necrosis does occur, it is generally localized to the skin overlying the abscess.

There are no specific pathologic features of *Pasteurella* spp infections in cats. Disease processes associated with these organisms are generally of a purulent nature.

Clinicopathologic Features

Pasteurella spp infections are easily diagnosed by routine cultures of purulent exudates.

Treatment and Prevention

Fresh wounds should be cleansed. Purulent infections should be opened to allow drainage of the exudate and then cleansed periodically until exudation ceases and the wounds begin to heal. Systemic antibiotics are an important part of treatment and should be given for 5-10 days. Feline isolates of *P multocida* are most sensitive to tetracycline and chloramphenicol, only moderately or relatively sensitive to penicillin, and more or less resistant to sulfas.[1] Trimethoprim-sulfonamides are effective for treatment of *Pasteurella* spp respiratory infections.[4]

Infection and Immunity

Pasteurella spp infections in cats are interesting in 2 respects. First, cats seem resistant to the septicemic forms (hemorrhagic fever) of pasteurellosis that are common in other species. Second, though cats are notorious carriers of pathogenic strains of *Pasteurella* spp, they seem fairly susceptible to wound infections with the organism.

Animal and Public Health Considerations

Pasteurella spp are transmitted from cat to cat almost exclusively by bites. Therefore, affected cats are not a hazard to other cats.

Pasteurellosis is probably the most common zoonotic disease passed from cat to people, a topic extensively reviewed by Weber and associates.[10] Pasteurellosis exists in people in 2 clinical forms: localized infection caused by animal bites, usually from cats; and a systemic form manifested variably as sinusitis, pneumonia, empyema, puerperal sepsis, bacteremia or brain abscess. The origin of *P multocida* in the systemic form is usually unknown, though many affected people have a history of animal exposure.

Cat bites preceded 301 of 1234 (24.3%) human *Pasteurella* spp infections reported in the British Isles from 1975 to 1979.[3] Oudar and co-workers noticed a high proportion of veterinary students developing *Pasteurella* spp infections following cat bites.[5] Weber and co-workers noted that 60-80% of human *Pasteurella* spp infections caused by animal scratches or bites were associated with cats.[10]

Localized pasteurellosis in people occurs at the site of the bite, usually in soft tissues of the hand. Joint infections can be a serious consequence of bites that penetrate into the synovial spaces. The wound becomes painful and inflamed within a few hours.[10] The infection spreads rapidly to surrounding tissues and along lymphatics to the regional lymph nodes. The most common local complications are abscess formation and tenosynovitis.[10] The condition is most severe after the first bite; subsequent bites are less likely to become infected. Cat-bite wounds should be cleansed as soon as possible. If pain, redness and swelling begin to develop at the site after a few hours, medical attention should be sought as soon as possible.

The role of healthy cats in the spread of *Pasteurella* spp to turkeys has been studied by Curtis and Ollerhead.[3] They found that *P multocida* was readily recovered from the throats of cats on poultry farms, but that only some isolates could cause pasteurellosis in chicks. Feline strains were invariably more closely related to the strains isolated from rats on the farms than from those associated with outbreaks of pasteurellosis among turkeys.

Cat bites can also have a devastating effect on small birds. It has been estimated that 60% of wild birds rescued from the jaws of cats die from pasteurellosis.[7] This suggests that prophylactic antibiotic therapy for birds undergoing such trauma is almost mandatory.

References

1. Arnbjerg J: *Pasteurella multocida* from canine and feline teeth, with a case report of glossitis calcinosa in a dog caused by *P multocida*. *Nord Vet Med* 30:324-332, 1978.

2. Balk MW et al: Ascending meningomyelitis resulting from a bite wound in a cat. *JAVMA* 164:1126, 1974.

3. Curtis PE and Ollerhead GE: *Pasteurella multocida* infection of cats on poultry farms. *Vet Record* 110:13-14, 1982.

4. Greene CE: *Clinical Microbiology and Infectious Diseases of the Dog and Cat*. Saunders, Philadelphia, 1984.

5. Oudar J et al: *Bltn Soc Vèt Mèd Comp Lyon* 74:353-357, 1972.

6. Schenk H: *Staatlichen Bakteriologischen unter Suchungsan-Staft*. Munchen, Germany, 1938.

7. Smit TH et al: *Pasteurella multocida* infecties bij vogels na een kattebeet. *Tijdsch Diergeneesk* 105:327, 1980.

8. Snyder SB et al: Respiratory tract disease associated with *Bordetella bronchiseptica* infection in cats. *JAVMA* 163:293-294, 1973.

9. Soltys MA: *Pasteurella septica* in cats and the action of aureomycin and chloromycetin on experimental pasteurellosis. *Vet Record* 63:689-691, 1951.

10. Weber DJ et al: *Pasteurella multocida* infections. Report of 35 cases and review of the literature. *Medicine* 63:133-154, 1984.

Chapter 25

Tularemia

Etiologic Agent

Francisella tularensis is a Gram-negative pleomorphic bacillus. Two strains of the organism have been differentiated by biochemical and animal virulence studies, referred to as Jellison A and B. Strain A is found only in North America, is highly lethal for domestic rabbits and causes severe disease in people. Strain B is not lethal for cottontail rabbits and causes mild disease in people. It is usually isolated from water or rodents, and is widespread in Europe, Asia and North America. The more virulent A strain ferments glycerol and contains citrulline urease, a differentiating feature from the less virulent B strain.

Francisella tularensis is the cause of an enzootic disease of wild rabbits, muskrats, beavers and contaminated small rodents. Cats are usually infected by feeding on infected wild rabbits, though drinking water or being bitten by rabbit ticks and fleas are other possible routes of exposure.[2,5]

Pathogenesis

Very little is known about the natural course of infection in domestic cats. Presumably, the bacteria enter the body by the oral route, with primary sites of infection in lymphoid tissues of the oropharynx and intestinal tract. Thereafter, the course of the disease closely resembles that of *Yersinia pseudotuberculosis* infection, with hematogenous dissemination of bacteria to the liver and spleen.

Clinical Features

The incidence of disease following ingestion of the organism is not precisely known. Clinical signs can occur as soon as 5 days following exposure and consist of fever, depression and anorexia.[1] Death or recovery occurs in 5-10 days in older cats. A more acute course, often ending in death, is seen in kittens.[5] Icterus is frequently seen toward the end of the disease course.

Pathologic Features

Cats dying of tularemia usually have small, multifocal, whitish abscesses throughout the liver and spleen.[1,3]

Clinicopathologic Features

The organism can be grown from fresh lesions or identified in tissues by IFA staining.[1,3] Cats that recover from tularemia develop high tube-agglutinating-antibody titers to the organism.[2-4]

Treatment and Prevention

The antibiotics of choice are streptomycin, gentamicin, tetracycline and chloramphenicol. However, only limited information is available on treating diseased cats. Packer and co-workers described 3 cats unsuccessfully treated with penicillin and streptomycin.[3]

Infection and Immunity

Tularemia in cats resembles pseudotuberculosis in many respects. A significant proportion of infected cats become ill. Mortality seems high in kittens, but some older cats may spontaneously recover after 5-10 days of illness.[3,5] Quenzer and associates described a 4-month-old kitten that recovered after inapparent illness.[4]

Animal and Public Health Considerations

There is no evidence for transmission of tularemia from cat to cat or to other animals. However, there are several cases of cat-to-person transmission. Human infection has usually followed bites from cats that were ill or that had recently ingested wild rabbits.[2-5] Human infection from infected cats is not always associated with a demonstrable portal of entry.[3]

Human tularemia is usually ulceroglandular, with recurrent skin lesions at the site of entry and enlarged regional lymph nodes. A pneumonic form is less common.

References

1. Ditchfield J et al: Tularemia of muskrats in eastern Ontario. *Can J Publ Hlth* 51:474-478, 1960.

2. Miller LD and Montgomery EL: Human tularemia transmitted by bite of cat. *JAVMA* 130:314, 1957.

3. Packer RM III et al: Tularemia associated with domestic cats. Georgia, New Mexico. *Morb Mort Weekly Rpt* 31:39-41, 1981.

4. Quenzer RW et al: Cat-bite tularemia. *JAMA* 238:1845, 1977.

5. Rudesill CL: Tularemia from the bite of a nursing kitten. *JAMA* 108:2118, 1937.

Chapter 26

Anaerobic Bacterial Infections

Etiologic Agent

Anaerobic bacteria play a major role in many suppurative infections of people and animals. Most of the genera and species involved are normal inhabitants of the mouth and distal intestinal and genitourinary tracts. The most commonly isolated anaerobic bacteria belong to the genera *Bacteroides* and *Fusobacterium*. *Bacteroides* spp are straight or curved rod-shaped bacteria. *Fusobacterium* spp are highly pleomorphic, existing in rod and filamentous forms. *Bacteroides* spp involved in suppurative processes of cats include *B fragilis, B asaccharolyticus, B disiens, B bivius, B melaninogenicus/ intermedius, B zoogleoformans, B distasonis, B vulgatus, B gingivalis* and so-called corroding strains.[2,3,6,7,10,12,13] *Fusobacterium* spp include *F russii, F necrophorum, F naviforme* and *F symbiosum*.[2,7,11-13] Another common anaerobe isolated from suppurative processes in cats is *Peptostreptococcus anaerobius*.[1,6,8,11,13] Motile *Borrelia*-like organisms have also been occasionally isolated.[4] *Clostridium villosum* is another anaerobe frequently recovered from pyogenic processes in cats.[6,11]

Pathogenesis

Anaerobic organisms are frequently isolated as mixed cultures from pyogenic processes in cats, often in association with facultative anaerobes. Common facultative anaerobes isolated in combination with anaerobic bacteria include *Pasteurella multocida*, *Corynebacterium pyogenes*, *Actinomyces meyeri, A viscosus* and *A odontolyticus*.[1,2,4,5,8,11] *Actinomyces*-like organisms are sometimes seen on stained smears of pus but have not been isolated.[8] Streptococci, lactobacilli and *E coli* are facultative anaerobes less frequently isolated from feline pus.[8]

Love and co-workers isolated 87 bacterial strains from 19 cats with empyema (pyothorax).[11] Among the isolates, 80.5% were anaerobes and 19.5% were facultative anaerobes. *Bacteroides* spp comprised 42.5% of anaerobic isolates, followed by *Clostridium villosum* at 16.1% and *Peptostreptococcus anaerobius* at 12.6%. *Clostridium villosum* was the most commonly isolated species of anaerobic bacterium. *Pasteurella multocida* was the most common facultative anaerobe, comprising 64.7% of the isolates. Berg and associates isolated 314 anaerobic bacteria from suppurative material collected from various sites on 30 cats and 227 dogs.[1] The genera were similar to those recognized by Love and co-workers but contained several different species.[11] Since isolates were not broken down according to host species, it was not possible to determine which were from cats and which from dogs.

Love and co-workers cultured 36 cat abscesses; 32 contained from 1 to 8 species of anaerobes per culture.[8] Species of *Bacteroides, Fusobacterium, Peptostreptococcus, Clostridium* and *Propionibacterium* comprised 95.8% of anaerobic isolates. *Bifidobacterium, Lactobacillus* and *Eubacterium* comprised the remainder. Facultative anaerobes were isolated from about 28% of the samples. *Pasteurella multocida*, *Actinomyces* spp and streptococci made up the bulk of facultative anaerobic isolates. Lactobacilli and *E coli* were uncommon isolates.

Infections caused by anaerobic and facultative anaerobic bacteria are almost always highly suppurative. They usually involve the nasal passages (chronic rhinitis and sinusitis), oral cavity (chronic gingivitis, periodontitis), subcutaneous tissues (abscesses, cellulitis) or bone (osteomyelitis). They are usually opportunistic and either secondarily invade tissue damaged by other pathologic processes, or are inoculated directly into tissues in which they are not normally found. For instance, accumulation of dental tartar often leads to gingivitis and eventual periodontitis. When the periodontitis becomes severe, tooth root abscessation is common. Herpesvirus infection can damage the nasal passages and sinuses and predispose to chronic bacterial invasion. Cat bites can directly inoculate oral bacteria into the subcutaneous tissues and bone. Immunosuppressive diseases, especially feline leukemia virus (FeLV) and feline immunodeficiency virus (FIV) infections, can predispose the nasal, oral, skin and intestinal tissues to infection by resident flora. Foreign bodies, such as pieces of plant material or bone, can also transport infection by normal bacterial flora into deeper sites. Pyothorax in cats occurs by 3 possible routes: cat bites that penetrate the chest cavity; opportunistic bacterial infections of primary pneumonic processes, with spread to the pleura and chest cavity; and migrating foreign bodies.

Clinical Features

Infections caused by various anaerobic and facultative anaerobic organisms are either acute or chronic. Cat-bite abscesses and pyothorax are usually acute, while nasal and oral cavity diseases are usually chronic. Suppurative peritonitis associated with normal oral flora has been described in 2 cats.[13] In 1 of these cats, the disease was insidious and may have been present for almost 2 years. The second cat had more acute bacterial peritonitis that occurred several weeks after a suppurative cat-bite abscess on the flank was treated. Chronic osteomyelitis of the radius (after a cat bite) and mandible (after a tooth root infection) in 2 cats has also been associated with anaerobic organisms.[5]

The clinical presentation of animals with pyogenic anaerobic bacterial infections depends on the site of involvement. Cats with pyothorax usually show acute dyspnea and fever. Cats with bacterial peritonitis may have a much more chronic course of fever, depression, weight loss and abdominal distension. Cat-bite abscesses or cellulitis usually cause acute depression, fever, focal swelling (edema, hemorrhage, exudation), redness and pain. The most common sites for cat-bite abscesses or cellulitis are the distal limbs, tail and tailhead, and around the face and neck.

Pathologic Features

Pyogenic processes caused by anaerobic and facultative anaerobic bacteria range from highly suppurative and necrotizing to pyogranulomatous in nature, depending on chronicity.

Clinicopathologic Features

Purulent exudates range from yellow to yellow-green or reddish. They are often malodorous and may contain sulfur-like granules if actinomycetes are present. The characteristic putrid odor of anaerobic bacterial infections is due to production of volatile fatty acids. These can be readily detected in small amounts by gas chromatography.[14] The exudate contains large numbers (>100,000 cells/μl) of polymorphonuclear neutrophils and smaller numbers of macrophage/monocyte-type cells. The neutrophils are often toxic, hypersegmented and degenerating. Bacteria are usually seen within and outside of cells on stained smears. Most *Bacteroides* spp and *Fusobacterium* spp are Gram negative, while *Clostridium* spp, *Actinomyces* spp and *Peptostreptococcus* spp are Gram positive.

Anaerobic bacteria, such as *Bacteroides* spp, *Fusobacterium* spp and *Clostridium* spp, require special culture conditions and are often slow to grow. Isolation of anaerobic and facultative anaerobic organisms may be of doubtful significance, depending of the site of isolation. For instance, isolation of anaerobic bacteria from swabs of the mouth or superficial wounds (which cats often lick) may be meaningless. However, isolation of anaerobic organisms from abscesses, peritoneal and pleural exudates, or curetted bone are much more meaningful.

Prevention and Treatment

Most anaerobic organisms are susceptible to penicillin, ampicillin, chloramphenicol, cephalosporins, clindamycin and metronidazole. They tend to be resistant to aminoglycosides, such as gentamicin and amikacin. The response is not always good if underlying reasons for the infection are not also treated. Severe periodontal disease cannot be cured in the face of chronic tooth-root abscesses. If infections are secondary to immunosuppressive disease, therapy is only palliative. In chronic bone infections with sequestrum formation, therapy should include curettage of devitalized bone.[6]

Infection and Immunity

Infections with anaerobic and facultative anaerobic organisms are usually opportunistic. Infection depends on the breakdown of normal local or systemic defense barriers (as in chronic oral and nasal cavity disease) or inoculation of organisms into tissues where they do not normally exist (as in pyothorax, osteomyelitis, peritonitis, subcutaneous abscesses).

The additive or synergistic role of individual bacterial species in mixed anaerobic infections (the rule rather than the exception) needs further study. Dickie isolated a *Borrelia*-like organism and *Corynebacterium pyogenes* from the thoracic exudate of a cat with pyothorax.[4] Isolates were not particularly pathogenic by themselves but were very pathogenic when inoculated into cats in combination. Facultative anaerobes are hardly ever the sole isolate from pyogenic processes of this type and are always accompanied by some type of anaerobic bacteria. It may be possible that most aerobic organisms obtain some sort of nutritional supplementation from the coinfecting anaerobes or *vice versa*. Indeed, *B melaninogenicus* growth is greatly facilitated by vitamin K, a substance produced by some strains of bacteria. One strain of organism might also elaborate toxins that cause necrosis and local tissue hypoxia, thus favoring anaerobic conditions. Other anaerobic bacteria may produce penicillinase that lessens the effectiveness of antibiotic therapy. There is also evidence that anaerobic bacteria may consume alternate complement pathway components, thus limiting bacterial opsonization.

Animal and Public Health Considerations

Anaerobic infections, being largely opportunistic in nature, are a minimal animal and public health hazard. Anaerobic strains of bacteria may also be fairly species specific. For instance, Love and associates compared strains of *B zoogleoformans* isolated from soft-tissue infections of rats and periodontal diseases of people.[7] Though feline and human isolates were phenotypically identical, their genetic (DNA) homology was only 70%. This was lower than the intergroup genetic homology seen in the same phenotypic strains isolated only from cats or people.

References

1. Berg JN et al: Occurrence of anaerobic bacteria in diseases of the dog and cat. Am J Vet Res 40:876-881, 1979.

2. Berkhoff GA: Recovery and identification of anaerobes in veterinary medicine: A 2-year experience. Vet Microbiol 2:237-252, 1978.

3. Biberstein EL et al: Bacteroides melaninogenicus in disease of domestic animals. JAVMA 153:1045-1049, 1968.

4. Dickie CW: Feline pyothorax caused by Borrelia-like organism and Corynebacterium pyogenes. JAVMA 174:516-517, 1979.

5. Hirsh DC et al: Obligate anaerobes in clinical veterinary practice. J Clin Microbiol 10:188-191, 1979.

6. Johnson KA et al: Osteomyelitis in dogs and cats caused by anaerobic bacteria. Aust Vet J 61:57-61, 1984.

7. Love DN *et al*: Comparison of *Bacteroides zoogleoformans* strains isolated from soft tissue infections in cats with strains from periodontal disease in humans. *Infect Immun* 47:166-168, 1985.

8. Love DN *et al*: Isolation and characterization of bacteria from abscesses in the subcutis of cats. *J Med Microbiol* 12:207- 212, 1979.

9. Love DN *et al*: Characterization of *Fusobacterium* species isolated from soft tissue infections in cats. *J Appl Bacteriol* 48:325-331, 1980.

10. Love DN *et al*: Characterization of *Bacteroides* species isolated from soft tissue infections in cats. *J Appl Bacteriol* 50:567-575, 1981.

11. Love DN *et al*: Isolation and characterization of bacteria from pyothorax (empyaema) in cats. *Vet Microbiol* 7:455-461, 1982.

12. Russ VR, in Buchanan RE and Gibbons NE: *Bergey's Manual of Determinative Bacteriology*. 8th ed. Williams & Wilkins, Baltimore, 1905.

13. Scott PC *et al*: Suppurative peritonitis in cats associated with anaerobic bacteria. *Aust Vet J* 61:367-368, 1984.

14. Van den Bogaard AEJM Jr: Presumptive diagnosis of anaerobic infections in veterinary medicine by gas chromatography. *Abstracts World Vet Congress XIII*. Montreal, Canada, 1987. p 173.

Chapter 27

Salmonellosis

Etiologic Agent

Salmonella spp are motile, Gram-negative bacilli that inhabit the intestinal tracts of a wide range of mammals, birds, amphibians and reptiles. The organism exists in numerous biochemical and antigenic types. *Salmonella choleraesuis, S arizonae, S typhimurium* and *S enteritidis* are the most important species in veterinary medicine. *Salmonella enteritidis* occurs in hundreds of different serotypes that are often named after localities in which they were identified, such as Dublin, Khartoum, Minnesota, Chester, Manhattan and Newport. *Salmonella typhimurium* is the most important pathogen of the genus.

Many *Salmonella* spp and serotypes have been isolated from the feces of normal cats. However, isolation rates have varied from virtually zero to 44%, depending on the source of animals and locality. Isolation rates from normal free-roaming cats is generally 5% or less.[1,2,9,13,17] Shimi and Barin isolated *Salmonella* spp from over 18% of pet cats in Iran.[12] Isolation rates are even higher among random-source cats purchased for experimental use. Fox and Beaucage found that one-third of the shipments of cats sent to research institutions contained infected cats and that, overall, 10.6% of such cats were carrying *Salmonella* spp.[4]

Pathogenesis

Salmonella spp are passed from animal to animal by the fecal-oral route. *Salmonella* spp can also grow in pet foods; this can be another source of infection. Organisms can survive for some time in fomites in the environment. Environmental and fecal contamination are considered synonymous. An outbreak of *Salmonella* infection in cats has been linked to an epidemic of salmonellosis in migratory song birds in the northeastern United States.[18] Cats apparently contracted the infection by preying on diseased birds. *Salmonella* spp replicate initially in the GI tract. However, GI tract colonization following ingestion requires quite large doses of organisms, about 1×10^6 to 1×10^9 viable bacteria.[14] This is probably why salmonellosis is more apt to be seen in dense populations of cats and in conditions of close confinement and poor sanitation. If enough organisms escape the acidic environment of the stomach, they attach to the ileal villi. They then invade and multiply within the villi and reach the mesenteric lymph nodes. Bacteremia is infrequent.

Clinical Features

Infection with *Salmonella* spp is usually inapparent. In high-stress situations and environments that favor massive exposure, infection can be clinically apparent. Kittens are also more likely to be clinically affected than adult cats.[3] Therefore, clinical outbreaks of salmonellosis have largely been limited to hospitalized populations of cats or cats in high-density colony-type environments.[4,16] Spontaneous outbreaks of salmonellosis in individual pet animals are uncommon but have been described.[5-7,10,11]

The most common clinical form of salmonellosis in cats is acute gastroenteritis, resembling feline panleukopenia, usually manifested by sudden onset of vomiting, diarrhea, fever and depression 2-5 days after exposure.[18] The clinical course ranges from 2-7 days.[18] In severely affected cats, the disease is rapidly terminated by bacteremia and endotoxic shock.[10,15] Neurologic signs have been associated with intestinal signs in at least 1 kitten.[10] The author observed a kitten with intestinal signs and hemolytic anemia. Recovery following milder disease occurs in 3-5 days.[11,18]

Miscellaneous forms of salmonellosis have been also observed in cats. Purulent conjunctivitis associated with salmonellosis has been seen in a cat and experimentally recreated in kittens.[4,5] Acute peritonitis associated with S typhimurium has been observed in a kitten.[7] Salmonella choleraesuis has been associated with abortion in a queen.[6]

Pathologic Features

Cats with Salmonella spp gastroenteritis demonstrate reddening of the intestinal mucosa, as well as congestion and reddening of the mesenteric lymph nodes. In septicemic cats, petechial and ecchymotic hemorrhages and focal necrosis are seen in the liver, spleen, heart, lungs and brain.[10,15]

Clinicopathologic Features

Cats with acute salmonellosis are often leukopenic.[15,18] The clinical signs, coupled with leukopenia, resemble those of panleukopenia virus infection. The organism is readily isolated from affected organs and rectal swabs.

Treatment and Prevention

Outbreaks of salmonellosis in hospitals and similar settings are often associated with antibiotic-resistant strains. Chloramphenicol and trimethoprim-sulfonamides are the drugs of choice. However, there is some controversy about use of antibiotics to treat uncomplicated cases of Salmonella gastroenteritis. Antibiotics can actually favor the growth of antibiotic-resistant Salmonella spp and depress the normal inhibitory flora. Antibiotic therapy also delays establishment of immunity and prolongs fecal shedding in many cats. Such cats should be treated supportively by withholding food or water during the period of vomiting and diarrhea, administering parenteral fluids and enforcing rest. Unfortunately, clinical salmonellosis in cats is often acute and severe, and a decision to treat is often made before a diagnosis is confirmed by culture. Timoney observed 61% mortality among affected cats in one outbreak.[16] Therefore, acute salmonellosis in cats should not be viewed lightly.

Infection and Immunity

Clinical salmonellosis is difficult to recreate experimentally. Cats can be experimentally infected by oral inoculation with virulent Salmonella spp, but they shed the organisms without becoming ill.[16] This suggests that factors in addition to the dose of organisms are important in causing disease. Cats experimentally infected with Salmonella spp shed organisms for only about 10 days, though an occasional cat sheds for 4 weeks or more.[15]

Immunity to Salmonella spp infection appears to be mainly cell mediated. Organisms often persist following establishment of immunity in intestinal epithelial cells and mononuclear cells within mesenteric lymph nodes. Stress factors can delay development of cellular immunity, thus increasing the duration and severity of infection and likelihood of bacteremia. Severe stress or use of corticosteroids can also transiently depress immunity and allow recrudescence of bacterial shedding in latent carriers. Persistent feline leukemia virus (FeLV) infection can also lower resistance in some cats and predispose to fatal salmonellosis.

Animal and Public Health Considerations

There is little doubt that cats can carry and shed Salmonella in their stool. Serotypes found in cats are often identical to those that are pathogenic to people and other animals.[8,9,11,12] Considering the number of cats that are carriers of Salmonella spp, however, there are relatively few reports of people infected by exposure to cats. People are more often infected by other types of animals, and cats and people in the same household may both become infected at the same time from a common source.[8,11]

References

1. Borland, ED: *Salmonella* infection in dogs, cats, tortoises and terrapins. *Vet Record* 96:401-402, 1975.

2. Bruner DW: *Salmonella* cultures typed during the years 1950-1971 for the service laboratories of the New York State Veterinary College at Cornell University. *Cornell Vet* 63:138-143, 1973.

3. Buxton, A: *Salmonellosis in animals—a review*. Commonwealth Agri Bureaux, Farnham Royal, Bucks, England, 1957. pp 48-49, 101.

4. Fox JG and Beaucage CM: The incidence of *Salmonella* in random-source cats purchased for use in research. *J Infect Dis* 139:362-365, 1979.

5. Fox JG et al: Experimental *Salmonella*-associated conjunctivitis in cats. *Can J Med* 48:87-91, 1984.

6. Hemsley LA: Abortion in two cats, with the isolation of *Salmonella choleraesuis* from one case. *Vet Record* 68:152, 1956.

7. Ingham B and Brentnall DW: Acute peritonitis in a kitten associated with *Salmonella typhimurium* infection. *J Small Anim Pract* 13:71-74, 1972.

8. Kauffmann AF: Pets and *Salmonella* infection. *JAVMA* 149:1655-1661, 1966.

9. Khan AQ: *Salmonella* infections in dogs and cats in the Sudan. *Brit Vet J* 126:607-612, 1970.

10. Krum SH et al: *Salmonella arizonae* bacteremia in a cat. *JAVMA* 170:42-44, 1977.

11. Madewell BR and McChesney AE: Salmonellosis in a human infant, a cat, and two parakeets in the same household. *JAVMA* 167:1089-1090, 1975.

12. Shimi A and Barin A: *Salmonella* in cats. *J Comp Path* 87:315-318, 1977.

13. Tacal JV and Menez CF: *Salmonella* studies in the Philippines. *Philippine J Vet Med* 2:46-57, 1974.

14. Tanaka Y et al: Experimental carrier in dogs produced by oral administration of *Salmonella typhimurium*. *Jpn J Vet Sci* 38:569-578, 1976.

15. Timoney JF: Feline salmonellosis. *Vet Clin No Am* 6:395-398, 1976.

16. Timoney JF et al: Feline salmonellosis. *Cornell Vet* 68:211-219, 1978.

17. Van der Gulden WJI and Janssen FCI: *Salmonella* in dogs and cats bought for experimental purposes. *Tijdsch voor Diergeneesk* 95:495-497, 1970.

Additional Reference

18. Scott FW: *Salmonella* implicated as cause of song bird fever. *Feline Hlth Topics* 3(3):5-6, 1988.

Chapter 28

Yersinia Infections

PLAGUE

Etiologic Agent

Yersinia pestis is a small, Gram-negative, bipolar aerobic bacillus. The plague bacillus possesses a large number of antigens and toxins important in virulence and pathogenicity. One component (fraction 1) of the capsule activates complement and inhibits phagocytosis. The cell wall contains a typical Gram-negative endotoxin. The organism also possesses a potent cardiotoxic exotoxin, a coagulase and a second antiphagocytic factor (VW antigen).

Yersinia pestis inhabits the proximal digestive tract of rodent fleas. Fleas are a source of infection for rodents, which in turn are reservoirs for infection of other animals and people. Rodent populations infected with plague have been identified in most areas of the world. In the United States, pockets of plague are common in mountainous regions of California, Colorado, Utah, Arizona and New Mexico. Domestic and urban rats (*Rattus rattus* and *R norvegicus*) are important reservoirs for plague in populous areas. Wild rodents, such as mice, chipmunks, ground squirrels, rock squirrels, prairie dogs, gerbils and possibly rabbits, are important reservoirs in the wild. Birds, such as pigeons, ducks, turkeys and chickens, are very resistant to plague, as are pigs and cattle.[1] Rabbits and guinea pigs appear to be highly susceptible, while ferrets are relatively susceptible. Dogs were found to be resistant by DeSouza and co-workers but relatively susceptible (they became ill but recovered) by Rust and associates.[1,10]

Pathogenesis

Plague is primarily an enzootic infection transmitted among rodents by flea bites. Infection rates in local rodent populations wax and wane, depending on flea and rodent numbers. Warmer climates favor flea growth; therefore, warmer areas of the world suffer more from plague. Warm, humid weather favors rapid growth of fleas, and when flea populations reach levels of 1 or more per rodent, conditions become ideal for an enzootic infection to become epizootic in the rodent population. Warm, humid conditions also allow infected fleas to live longer off the rodent host, and increase the chances for fleas to feed on animals other than rodents. However, hot and dry or cold weather is unfavorable for flea survival, and outbreaks of plague are uncommon in such conditions.

Epizootics of *Y pestis* infection among wild-rodent populations are referred to as sylvatic plague. Outbreaks can be quite localized and limited to a single village, city block or campground. The limited range of an outbreak is caused by the propensity of rodents to cluster around a single food and water source. Outbreaks of sylvatic plague can decimate a local population of rodents in a very short time. Weniger and co-workers observed numerous empty rodent burrows surrounding a home in which plague had occurred in a person and a cat.[13] Infected rodent fleas were recovered from empty burrows less than 300 m from the house where the infected person lived. Infected rodents and rodent fleas were also isolated from university grounds where both a child and a cat developed plague.

Rodents become infected with plague through the feeding of rodent fleas. Infectivity of fleas is enhanced by the action of the *Y pestis* coagulase on ingested blood. Coagulase causes ingested blood to clot in the proventriculus of the flea, which impedes passage of the blood meal into the stomach. Fleas often regurgitate this clot during feeding, thus ensuring that viable bacteria are deposited into the bite wound.

Cats are infected with *Y pestis* by ingesting infected rodents or by being bitten by infected rodent fleas. Ingestion appears to be the more important route of transmission.[7] The incubation period in cats following oral or parenteral infection can be as short as 1-2 days.[9] Bacteria replicate initially in the oral cavity and then spread rapidly to the tonsils and regional lymph nodes of the head and neck. Bacteremia ensues, with localization in the lungs, liver and spleen. Hematogenous spread to distant skin and subcutaneous tissue is occasionally seen.[10]

Clinical Features

Plague in cats often runs an acute course of 4-6 days and terminates in death. A more chronic form lasting 20 days or so is also seen in cats. Mortality is extremely high in untreated cats.[10] As in the disease in people, plague occurs in 2 forms in cats. The most common form is bubonic plague, a disease characterized by marked lymphadenitis regional to the site of bacterial entry. Pneumonic plague, the second form of the disease, is seen in about 20% of feline cases. It is manifested by fulminating suppurative pneumonia and bacteremia. Bubonic and pneumonic plague often coexist in the same animal. Therefore, pneumonic plague can result from breathing in aerosolized bacteria or from localization of blood-borne bacteria.

The bubonic form of feline plague is characterized by pronounced swelling of the mandibular and cervical lymph nodes, perinodal edema and swelling, conjunctivitis, purulent to hemorrhagic nasal discharge, tonsillitis and pharyngitis.[6,8,11-13,15] Death occurs within a few days. Lymph node abscessation and fistulation in the groin and hind limb have also been described.[8,9]

Pneumonic plague is characterized by wheezing, coughing, dyspnea, frothing or drooling, hemoptysis, ocular and nasal discharge, and rapid death.[6,9,13,14] Enlargement of lymph nodes of the head and neck may occur in some animals.

Pathologic Features

The most detailed discussion of pathologic changes in cats with plague has been provided by Rust and co-workers.[10] Lymphadenitis is typically suppurative, with a tendency toward hemorrhage, necrosis and abscessation. Adenitis is sometimes severe enough to cause inflammation, hemorrhage and edema in surrounding tissues. The pneumonia is typically of hematogenous origin and widespread throughout the lungs, which may appear reddened and congested. A small amount of purulent exudate can be expressed from cut surfaces of the lungs. Lung lesions resemble those in the lymph nodes, with focal areas of necrosis surrounded by more normal tissue infiltrated with neutrophils and lymphocytes. Numerous bacterial colonies and hemorrhage are seen within necrotic foci. Discrete areas of necrosis are sometimes seen in the spleen and liver. Pleuritis was seen in conjunction with pneumonia in a cat with pneumonic plague.[6]

Clinicopathologic Features

Plague should be suspected in any cat with lymphadenitis and/or abscessation in the area of the head, neck or groin, especially if the animal has been in areas known to harbor the disease or has been in contact with rodents several days before illness. The organism can be identified in purulent exudates by IFA staining and can be readily cultured from blood and involved tissues. Cats recovering from plague have elevated *Yersinia* antibody titers.[12]

Treatment and Prevention

Treating cats with plague can be hazardous to handlers, and precautions should be taken to prevent exposure. Lancing, draining and flushing of abscessed lymph nodes can be especially hazardous. If therapy is to be effective, it should be started as soon as possible. Streptomycin, tetracycline and chloramphenicol are the antibiotics of choice. Four cats with bubonic plague were successfully treated with tetracycline.[2,8,15] Another cat recovered after a submandibular abscess was drained and flushed with neomycin; the cat was given penicillin IM.[3] A cat that recovered after similar treatment was described by Rollag and associates.[9]

Plague can be prevented by keeping cats away from potentially infected rodents. Most foci of plague are in rural areas. The presence of plague in the region is often known by local physicians, veterinarians and public health authorities. Problems arise when pet animals are brought into plague areas and then return to their homes before signs appear. In these situations, neither the owner nor the attending veterinarian may be aware of the potential for plague. Fortunately, plague in cats is relatively uncommon. One veterinarian who resided in a small rural town where plague had been previously reported diagnosed plague in 3 cats in a 2-year period.[2]

Infection and Immunity

Yersinia pestis possesses antiphagocytic substances that prevent phagocytosis and host containment. This might explain the high incidence of bacteremia in both people and cats with localized forms of plague. However, this is not the only explanation for virulence. Dogs can also be infected, but recovery is common.[10] Mortality in untreated cats and people is very high. However, cats have recovered from natural infection without treatment. Of 5 cats exposed to plague, 2 survived; 1 of the survivors that was tested had antibodies to *Y pestis*.[13] A queen that had nursed 4 kittens that succumbed to plague became ill but spontaneously recovered.[12] The course of experimental plague in cats has been studied by Rust and co-workers.[11] Death or recovery occurs within 7 days of the onset of signs. The disease is sometimes chronic, with emaciation and death occurring after 2-3 weeks.[10] Therefore, cats appear to have some ability to respond to the infection under favorable circumstances.

Cats develop high levels of antibodies to the fraction-I antigen of *Y pestis*. Titers may be as high as 1:2048 by day 12.[8,10] After this time, antibody titers plateau and persist for 300 days or more.[10] It is important to measure *Y pestis* antibodies in cats by hemagglutination rather than complement fixation (CF). Unlike dogs, cats do not produce CF antibodies to fraction-I antigen.[10] Serologic tests can be used to confirm plague in cats that have recovered from suspicious illness.[5,8,11]

Animal and Public Health Considerations

Cats with plague are definite hazards to other cats and people. Multiple cases of plague among groups of cats are not uncommon.[2,9,12,13] It is not clear in these situations whether the cats cross-infected each other or were all infected from a common wild-rodent reservoir.

The role of cats in human plague has only recently been appreciated. It has been estimated that about 3% of the cases of human plague in the western United States between 1970 and 1979 were caused by exposure to infected cats. The exact route of exposure is sometimes unknown but usually involves bites, scratches and exposure to infectious exudates (saliva, pus, nasal and conjunctival secretions).[2-6,12-14] Human exposure to cats is usually direct. Cats do not appear to act as vehicles for infected fleas. At least 2 cases of plague in veterinarians have been traced to cats.[3,6] Both veterinarians had lanced and drained infected lymph nodes, though 1 of the veterinarians had also been bitten.[3]

Plague in cats and people should be immediately reported to public health officials. Prophylactic antibiotic treatment is often given to individuals that have been exposed to infected animals or people.[4] People in charge of treating infected cats should take special precautions.[15] Those include isolation, gloves, masks, surgical gowns and disinfection.

References

1. DeSouza A Jr et al: Report on experiments undertaken to discover whether the common domesticated animals of Terceira Island are affected by plague. *J Hyg* 10:196-208, 1910.

2. Fitch R et al: Feline plague, California. *Morb Mort Weekly Rpt* 26:362, 1977.

3. Goethals RM et al: Human plague associated with domestic cats, California, Colorado. *Morb Mort Weekly Rpt* 30:265-266, 1981.

4. Green W et al: Plague, Arizona, Colorado, New Mexico. *Morb Mort Weekly Rpt* 26:215-216, 1977.

5. Isaäcson M et al: Unusual cases of human plague in southern Africa. *So Afr Med J* 47:2109-2113, 1973.

6. Kaufmann AF et al: Public health implications of plague in domestic cats. *JAVMA* 179:875-878, 1981.

7. Poland J and Barnes A, in Steele J: *CRC Handbook Series in Zoonoses*. Vol I. CRC Press, Cleveland, 1979. pp 515-597.

8. Raflo NL: Bubonic plague in a cat. *JAVMA* 188:534-535, 1986.

9. Rollag OJ et al: Feline plague in New Mexico: Report of five cases. *JAVMA* 179:1381-1383, 1981.

10. Rosser WW: Bubonic plague. *JAVMA* 191:406-408, 1987.

11. Rust JH Jr et al: The role of domestic animals in the epidemiology of plague. I. Experimental infection of dogs and cats. *J Infect Dis* 124:522-526, 1971.

12. Rust JH Jr et al: The role of domestic animals in the epidemiology of plague. II. Antibody to *Yersinia pestis* in sera of dogs and cats. *J Infect Dis* 124:527-531, 1971.

13. Thornton DJ et al: Cat bite transmission of *Yersinia pestis* infection to man. *J So Afr Vet Assoc* 46:165-169, 1975.

14. Weniger BG et al: Human bubonic plague transmitted by a domestic cat scratch. *JAVMA* 251:927-928, 1984.

15. Werner SB et al: Primary plague pneumonia contracted from a domestic cat at South Lake Tahoe, California. *JAVMA* 251:929-931, 1984.

PSEUDOTUBERCULOSIS

Etiologic Agent

Yersinia pseudotuberculosis is a Gram-negative, bipolar-staining bacillus. The organism exists in a number of serovars; types IA and IIA are most commonly associated with disease in cats.[1] Yanagawa and co-workers found the predominant serovars in the intestinal tracts of healthy cats in Japan to be I, III and IV.[15]

Yersinia pseudotuberculosis has been associated with a similar syndrome in numerous species of domestic and wild mammals and birds.[5] It has also been isolated from small reptiles and amphibians. Yanagawa and co-workers recovered *Y pseudotuberculosis* from the intestinal contents and mesenteric lymph nodes in 11 of 373 (2.9%) apparently normal cats.[15]

Pathogenesis

Disease associated with *Y pseudotuberculosis* tends to be seen most often in older rural and free-roaming cats.[7] Cats are presumably infected by eating rodents and birds. Though numerous cases of feline pseudotuberculosis have been described in the literature, the disease is relatively uncommon. In a European study, bacterial infections accounted for only 6% of the deaths in cats, and only a fraction of these deaths were caused by pseudotuberculosis.

The disease has not been extensively studied in the laboratory, so the precise route of infection and pathogenesis are unknown. Many normal cats carry the bacteria in their intestinal tracts, which indicates that factors other than exposure are related to clinical disease. Experiments in cats and canaries indicate that systemic infection is aided by conditions that impair bowel integrity.[3,4] Organisms appear to spread from the bowel via the portal circulation to the liver, which is the target organ for the disease in most species of animals.[9]

Clinical Features

Clinical signs of naturally occurring pseudotuberculosis in a large number of cats have been reviewed by Mollaret and Mair and associates.[7,8] Additional cases have been subsequently reported.[1,5,10,12-14]

The period between infection and clinical signs varies from a few days to several months, with an average of 3 weeks. Acute pseudotuberculosis in cats is usually manifested by sudden onset of anorexia, vomiting or diarrhea, variable fever and signs of abdominal discomfort (restlessness, crying, pain on palpation, labored breathing). Jaundice is evident in some animals. These early signs may go unnoticed in cats with the chronic form of disease. Chronic pseudotuberculosis is manifested initially by slow progression of anorexia, depression and weight loss. Intestinal signs tend to become pronounced in the later stages of illness and are manifested by intermittent fetid diarrhea and constipation, jaundice and, in some animals, anemia. Hepatomegaly and splenomegaly are variable features of acute and chronic disease; nodules can sometimes be palpated on the hepatic surface (Fig 1). One cat had a swollen mandibular lymph node, having the clinical appearance of bubonic plague.[1]

Fig 1. Spleen of a cat with chronic intestinal pseudotuberculosis. Numerous focal or coalescing necrotic or inflammatory lesions are scattered throughout the splenic surface. (Courtesy of Dr. Linda Lowenstine, University of California, Davis)

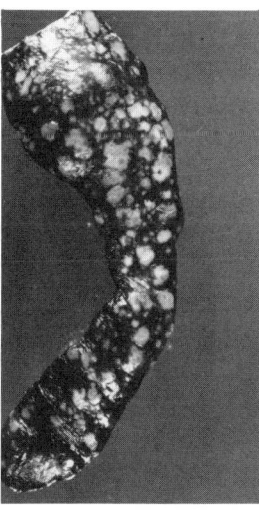

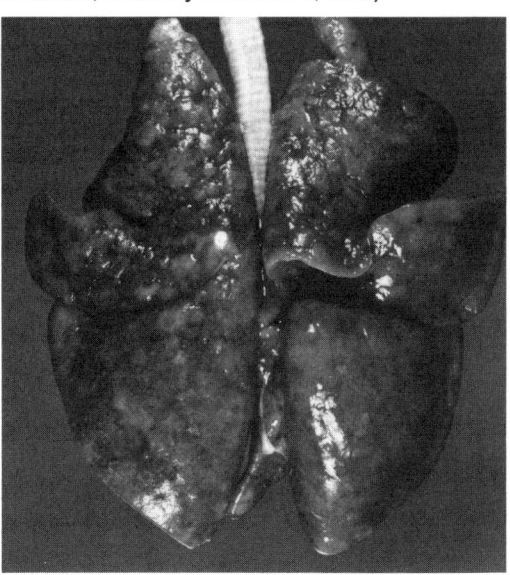

Fig 2. Lungs of a cat with severe *Yersinia pseudotuberculosis* pneumonia. This form of tuberculosis is relatively uncommon, as lesions are usually centered around the intestines, liver and spleen. (Courtesy of Dr. Ernst Biberstein, University of California, Davis)

Pathologic Features

The most detailed description of lesions of feline pseudotuberculosis has been provided by Mollaret.[8] A serosanguineous peritoneal exudate is often present. Numerous grayish-white to yellow nodules 0.5-5.0 mm in diameter are found throughout the liver. The spleen is occasionally enlarged and indurated (Fig 1). The mesenteric lymph nodes are frequently enlarged and hemorrhagic. The inflammatory process in the liver sometimes extends to the surface of the diaphragm. The gastric and especially the intestinal mucosae are often hyperemic and edematous. Involvement of the lungs, kidneys and other organs is relatively uncommon (Fig 2).

Hepatic lesions consist of foci of severe necrosis surrounded by a zone of polymorphonuclear cells containing numerous Gram-negative bacilli. Hepatic parenchyma peripheral to this zone is infiltrated with many lymphocytes and plasma cells.

Clinicopathologic Features

Pseudotuberculosis in cats is seldom diagnosed before exploratory surgery or necropsy. Elevations in liver enzyme activity and total bilirubin levels are common but not specific. Ultrasound examination of the liver and ultrasound-guided biopsies can help establish a diagnosis without laparotomy.

Serum antibodies to *Y pseudotuberculosis* are often present during clinical illness and are usually measured by agglutination procedures.[1]

Yersinia pseudotuberculosis can usually be readily isolated from involved tissues. Bacteremia is usually not present and blood cultures are often unrewarding.

Treatment and Prevention

Most cats with pseudotuberculosis described in the literature were destroyed because of the severity of the disease. However, when therapy was attempted, it was usually successful. Spearman and coworkers treated a cat with the typical disease with hetacillin, fluids and a special diet for 20 days.[14] The response was favorable, but complete recovery took 3 months. Allard successfully treated a cat with more localized disease with tetracycline for 10 days.[1] Tetracycline, chloramphenicol, penicillin and streptomycin are the drugs of choice for pseudotuberculosis.

Infection and Immunity

Yersinia spp have been isolated from the intestinal tract of cats suffering from chronic enteritis and primary feline immunodeficiency virus (FIV) infection. Feline immunodeficiency virus infection causes an acquired immunodeficiency syndrome in cats. Therefore, it is possible that some cases of *Y pseudotuberculosis* infection have been secondary to immunosuppressive disorders.

Animal and Public Health Considerations

Cats with pseudotuberculosis are not health hazards to other cats. However, several reports document cat-to-person infection.[7,8] In some cases, the human contact was with apparently healthy cats. However, Paul and Weltmann described a man who died of *Y pseudotuberculosis* bacteremia after having worked in a garden contaminated with feces of a cat suffering from chronic diarrhea.[11] The causative organism was isolated from the cat at necropsy. *Yersinia pseudotuberculosis* has been most frequently associated with appendicitis and mesenteric lymphadenitis in people.[2,8]

References

1. Allard AW: *Yersinia pseudotuberculosis* in a cat. *JAVMA* 174:91-92, 1979.

2. Butler T, in Wyngaarden JB and Smith LH: *Cecil's Textbook of Medicine.* Saunders, Philadelphia, 1985. p 1603.

3. Gorel P et al: Diagnostic expérimental et pathogénie de la pseudotuberculose du chat. *Bltn Soc Sci Vét Lyon* 57:205-227, 1955.

4. Hofstad MS: *Diseases of Poultry.* 6th ed. Iowa State Univ Press, Ames, 1972. pp 241-246.

5. Hubbert WT: Yersiniosis in mammals and birds in the United States. *Am J Trop Med Hyg* 21:458-463, 1972.

6. Isler D and Lott-Stolz G: Die wichtigsten Krankheitsund Todesursachen der Katze Sektionsfälle 1965-1976. *Kleintier Praxis* 23:333-334, 1978.

7. Mair NS et al: *Pasteurella pseudotuberculosis* infection in the cat: two cases. *Vet Record* 81:461-462, 1967.

8. Mollaret HH: L'infection à bacille de Malassez et Vignal chez le Chat I: La maladie naturelle. *Recl Méd Vét* 141:1079-1094, 1965.

9. Obwolo MJ: A review of yersiniosis (*Yersinia pseudotuberculosis* infection). *Vet Bltn* 46:167-171, 1976.

10. O'Sullivan BM et al: Concurrent infection with *Yersinia pseudotuberculosis* and *Platynosomum fastosum* in a cat. *Aust Vet J* 52:232-233, 1976.

11. Paul F and Weltmann O: Pseudotuberkulose beim Menschen. *Wien Klin Wschr* 47:603-604, 1934.

12. Rahko T and Saloniemi H: Beobachtungen uber die Pathologie der natürlichen *Yersinia pseudotuberculosis*-Infektion bei der Catze. *Dtsch Tierärztl Wschr* 76:611-613, 1969.

13. Robinson W: *Pasteurella pseudotuberculosis* infection in the cat. *Vet Record* 91:676-677, 1972.

14. Spearman JG et al: *Yersinia pseudotuberculosis* infection in a cat. *Can Vet J* 20:361-364, 1979.

15. Yanagawa Y et al: Isolation of *Yersinia enterocolitica* and *Yersinia pseudotuberculosis* from apparently healthy dogs and cats. *Microbiol Immunol* 22:643-646, 1978.

Chapter 29

Escherichia coli Infection

Etiologic Agent

Escherichia coli is the only important member of the genus. It is a variably motile, Gram-negative bacillus that inhabits the distal digestive tract. Similar to *Salmonella* spp, *E coli* resists environmental destruction and can survive outside the animal for long periods. Also similar to *Salmonella* spp, *E coli* has a great many different somatic (O), capsular (K) and flagellar (H) antigens.

Escherichia coli produces a typical Gram-negative endotoxin associated with the lipopolysaccharide cell wall. Certain serotypes also produce a potent enterotoxin that causes transient gastroenteritis in many species of animals. A Shiga-like toxin has also been recognized in *E coli* strains from cats with diarrhea than normal cats.[1] Some pathogenic strains of *E coli*, including the majority of those isolated from disease conditions in cats, produce a hemolysin. Hemolytic strains of *E coli* are believed to be more pathogenic than nonhemolytic strains.

Pathogenesis

Escherichia coli spp, being natural inhabitants of the distal intestinal tracts of all animals, are pathogenic only under certain conditions. Massive initial colonization of the gut with enterotoxigenic strains, especially in young animals, can lead to severe and acute gastroenteritis. *Escherichia coli* can secondarily complicate other diseases (wounds, colonization of damaged heart valves, etc). Septicemic *E coli* infections also occur in immunocompromised hosts or following severe damage to the bowel mucosa.

The pathogenesis of neonatal *E coli* infections is unknown. The high frequency of bacterial pyelonephritis in kittens with *E coli* septicemia suggests that the infection ascends the urinary tract and then enters the blood. Alternatively, the pyelonephritis may be secondary to a blood-borne infection. Pneumonia results from inhalation of infectious birth fluids at parturition or as a hema-togenous infection. The latter route is possibly associated with umbilical vein infection. Neonatal kittens that succumb from bacterial septicemia may be immunodeficient due to insufficient ingestion of colostrum at birth.

Abaas and Franklin studied 48 *E coli* strains isolated from normal cats and cats with diarrhea.[1] Shiga-like toxin production was a common feature of strains isolated from the cats with diarrhea. In a group of 112 cats examined during an outbreak of diarrhea, 93% yielded hemolytic *E coli* with recognized pathogenic O groups. In a control group of 55 normal cats, 22% carried pathogenic strains.[9] The pathogenic *E coli*, usually serotype 06, persisted in the cats for at least 10 months following recovery. Such carrier cats serve as a ready source of infection for susceptible cats brought into the cattery. Conversely, newly introduced cats may also carry different pathogenic strains of *E coli* that infect resident animals.

Clinical Features

Escherichia coli infections of cats are generally of 4 types: pyelonephritis and bacteremia in neonatal kittens; transient gastroenteritis; bacteremia in older immunocompromised hosts; and localized infection.

Neonatal colibacillosis is common in kittens. Scott and co-workers found that hemolytic strains of *E coli* were the most consistent bacterial isolates from kittens that died during the first weeks of life.[11] This form of disease usually affects single kittens in litters, although entire litters can be involved. Langman described a queen that had a history of entire litters of fading kittens, and 1 kitten had *E coli* septicemia.[4] Hara and associates described pyelonephritis in very young kittens associated with hemolytic strains of *E coli*.[4] Affected kittens often had swollen kidneys at necropsy.

Transient gastroenteritis associated with pathogenic strains of *E coli* has been infrequently described in cats.[6,9] Following ingestion, *E coli* attach by their pili to intestinal mucosal cells and secrete enterotoxins or Shiga-like toxins. The toxin interferes with fluid and electrolyte transport of the crypt epithelial cells and causes transient osmotic diarrhea. Infection is terminated when local immunity is established and bacteria-coated intestinal epithelial cells slough, usually after 4-7 days. Very young animals, which are more sensitive to acute fluid and electrolyte imbalances, are more apt to be clinically affected than older animals. Prerequisites for clinical disease include exposure to very large numbers of toxin-producing *E coli* and exposure to strains against which the animal has little or no previous immunity. Therefore, disease is more likely in high-density populations where sanitation is poor and fecal contamination is high, and in environments with a frequent influx of susceptible or carrier animals. Cattery environments are much more apt to have transient outbreaks of *E coli* gastroenteritis than households.

Fulminating bacterial septicemia, often due to *E coli*, is common in older immunocompromised cats. Predisposing conditions include feline panleukopenia and various forms of feline leukemia virus (FeLV) infection. Feline panleukopenia is associated with profound depletion of WBCs and severe intestinal damage. Both situations favor rapid movement of bacteria from the intestine to the bloodstream. Cats with myeloproliferative disease, aplastic anemia and various preleukemic disorders often have profound leukopenia and diminished immunoresponsiveness. Such animals may develop severe enterocolitis and bacteremia.

Escherichia coli have been associated with a number of localized infectious processes in cats. Acute and chronic pyelonephritis in mature cats, though uncommon, is usually associated with *E coli*. *Escherichia coli* has also been isolated from cat-bite abscesses and wound infections. Septic endometritis associated with *E coli* was described by Mansson and Lindblad, and Scott and co-workers.[6,11] *Escherichia coli* has also been commonly associated with pyometra in cats.[2,12] Though *E coli* is frequently associated with cystitis in dogs, it is rarely associated with cystitis in cats.[10] *Escherichia coli* has occasionally been isolated from cats with gallbladder infections. Several weanling kittens with *E coli* pneumonia and septicemia have been observed. Fulminating necrotic colitis has been attributed to *E coli*, though definitive proof is lacking.[3]

Pathologic Features

Lesions caused by *E coli* infection are highly variable, consistent with the numerous clinical forms. Kittens with pyelonephritis have pronounced kidney enlargement and suppurative parenchymal disease. Septicemic forms are often associated with thrombotic phenomena and necrosis. Intestinal disease associated with enterotoxigenic strains usually causes mild or inapparent tissue changes.

Clinicopathologic Features

Escherichia coli is readily isolated from affected tissues, and blood if bacteremia is present.

Treatment and Prevention

Moss and Frost studied the pattern of antibiotic resistance of *E coli* isolated from rectal swabs taken from 93 cats in the Brisbane area.[8] *Escherichia coli* strains that were resistant to common antibacterials (tetracycline, streptomycin, ampicillin and sulfanilamides) were obtained from 26% of the cats sampled. Cephalosporins, aminoglycosides and chloramphenicol were usually effective against most isolates.

Infection and Immunity

Similar to the pattern of infection caused by normal commensal bacteria, *E coli* is only pathogenic under conditions that increase the degree of exposure, or damage local and systemic immune defenses.

Animal and Public Health Considerations

Escherichia coli is ubiquitous and pathogenic strains are widespread. Affected or healthy cats carrying potentially pathogenic serotypes are not considered a public or animal health hazard.

References

1. Abaas S and Franklin A: Shiga-like toxin production from *Escherichia coli* associated with cat diarrhea. *Abstracts World Vet Congress XIII*. Montreal, Canada, 1987. p 167.

2. Choi W and Kawata K: O group of *Escherichia coli* from canine and feline pyometra. *Jpn J Vet Res* 23:141-143, 1975.

3. Erbeck DH and Hagee JH: A successful course of therapy for necrotic colitis. A newly recognized disease entity of cats. *VM/SAC* 69:603-605, 1974.

4. Hara M *et al*: Characterization of *Escherichia coli* isolated from bacterial pyelonephritis of kittens. *Bltn Azabu Vet Coll* 1:81-97, 1976.

5. Langman BA: Bacterial gastro-enteritis in cats. *Vet Record* 76:190, 1964.

6. Mackel DC *et al*: Observations on occurrence in cats of *Escherichia coli* pathogenic for man. *Am J Hyg* 71:176-178, 1960.

7. Mansson I and Lindblad G: Observations of haemolytic *Escherichia coli* in dogs and cats. *Proc Nordic Vet Congress* 14:67, 1962.

8. Moss S and Frost AJ: The resistance to chemotherapeutic agents of *Escherichia coli* from domestic dogs and cats. *Aust Vet J* 61:82-84, 1984.

9. Rhoades HE *et al*: Serological identification of *Escherichia coli* isolated from cats and dogs. *Can J Comp Med* 35:218-223, 1971.

10. Schechter RD: The significance of bacteria in feline cystitis and urolithiasis. *JAVMA* 156:1567-1573, 1970.

11. Scott FW *et al*: Kitten mortality complex (neonatal FIP?). *Feline Pract* 9(2):44-56, 1979.

12. Kenney KJ *et al*: Pyometra in cats: 183 cases (1978-1984). *JAVMA* 191:1130-1132, 1987.

Chapter 30

Leptospirosis

Etiologic Agent

Leptospira spp are spirochete-like bacteria. The body of the organism (protoplasmic cylinder) is wound around a central axial filament. They move by flexing and rotating around their long axis. Two species, *L biflexa* and *L interrogans*, have been recognized. Most pathogenic *Leptospira* are serotypes of *L interrogans*. Serotypes of *L interrogans* are listed in most of the older literature as species. The older nomenclature will be used in this discussion.

Leptospira interrogans exists in a great number of serologic types defined by agglutination-adsorption procedures using monovalent immune rabbit serum. Many serotypes cause infection in cats, including *L bataviae, L javanica, L icterohaemorrhagiae, L canicola, L grippotyphosa, L pomona, L ballum, L djasiman, L sentot, L autumnalis, L mini mini, L bratislava, L sejroe* and *L australis*.

Leptospira spp are commensal parasites of mammals. They inhabit the renal tubules of carrier animals and are shed in urine. *Leptospira* spp are relatively sensitive to the outside environment but can persist for hours under moist, warm conditions. Infection is more common in environments with a high density of carrier and susceptible animals, in warmer climates and in rainy, humid areas.

The incidence of leptospiral infection in cats is variable. Esseveld and Collier found 25-45% of cats were seropositive for *L bataviae* or *L javanica*.[3] They isolated *L bataviae* and *L javanica* from the kidneys of 13 of these seropositive animals. Murphy and associates found 17 of 350 cats from the Pennsylvania area were seropositive for *L pomona, L djasiman, L sentot, L autumnalis* or *L grippotyphosa*. However, no organisms were isolated from urine, aqueous humor or kidneys. Hemsley found 15 of 180 cats in the Croydon, England, area seropositive for *L icterohaemorrhagiae* or *L canicola*.[7] Otten and associates found 8 of 86 cats in the Hamburg port area seropositive, while Lucke and Crowther found 8 of 118 sick and healthy cats in the Bristol, England, area seropositive for *L canicola, L icterohaemorrhagiae, L mini mini, L javanica, L pomona, L sejroe* or *L australis*.[9,13]

Pathogenesis

Leptospira usually enters the body through the mouth and penetrate the intact mucosa. Leptospiremia reaches peak intensity between days 4 and 7. The organism rapidly localizes in the kidneys and liver, and leptospiruria occurs. Leptospiremia in cats is generally terminated by day 7 postinfection, while leptospiruria persists for 14-55 days.[4] *Leptospira* can persist in the kidney for days or weeks in the absence of detectable urine shedding. However, chronic renal carriage is much less frequent in cats than in dogs.

Clinical Features

Cats experimentally infected with various serotypes of *Leptospira* do not usually show clinical signs of illness.[4,8,11,13] However, mild to moderately severe nephritis is histologically evident in many experimentally inoculated cats.

The importance of *Leptospira* in naturally occurring disease in cats has not been determined. Hemsley found 3 of 4 tested cats with nephritis seropositive.[6] However, no *Leptospira* spp were seen in the kidneys, and all 3 seropositive animals were over 9 years of age. Chronic kidney disease is common in aged cats and is not usually due to *Leptospira*. A similar occurrence of chronic nephritis in an aged seropositive cat was documented by Rees.[14] Again, no *Leptospira* spp were seen at necropsy. When Lucke and Crowther examined 8 sick cats seropositive for *Leptospira* spp, only 1 had nephritis, and no *Leptospira* spp were seen in tissues or isolated from the kidneys.[9]

More convincing evidence of clinical disease following naturally occurring infection has been provided by several investigators. Carlos and co-workers examined 8 cats that were febrile and icteric.[2] Only 1 of these cats was seropositive; *L grippotyphosa* was isolated from its urine. Bryson and Ellis isolated *Leptospira* from the thoracic fluid, aqueous humor and kidney of a cat that had widespread hemorrhages in internal organs and excessive straw-colored fluid in the chest and abdomen.[1] Mason and associates described a jaundiced, depressed cat that was seropositive for *L pomona*.[10] The cat had focal nephritis and *Leptospira* in kidney lesions. Harkness and co-workers described a healthy cat with subclinical interstitial nephritis.[6] *Leptospira pomona* was recovered from both urine and kidney tissue, and organisms were seen in the spleen and kidney. Therefore, it appears likely that cats occasionally develop a classic type of leptospirosis following both experimental and natural infection.

Pathologic Features

Experimentally induced leptospirosis in cats is usually asymptomatic, though mild histopathologic lesions are frequently observed in the kidneys and liver. Of 6 animals experimentally infected with *L pomona*, 5 had macroscopic enlargement of the liver with prominent yellowish interlobular markings.[4] Capsular scarring and cortical irregularity were seen in 1 of 6 of these cats. Microscopic lesions ranged from slight centrilobular congestion to marked perilobular degeneration. Hepatocytes in the periportal area were swollen and vacuolated. The renal cortices of cats infected with *L pomona* contained numerous foci of lymphocytes subcapsularly, perivascularly and between tubules. Minimal tubular-cell degeneration was seen. Similar histologic lesions were described by Modric in the lungs, liver and kidneys of cats experimentally infected with *L australis*, *L pomona* and *L icterohaemorrhagiae*.[11] Van der Hoeden described severe nephritis in a 4-week-old kitten experimentally inoculated with *L grippotyphosa*.[15] Widespread perivascular hemorrhages, which are common in dogs, have only been described in 1 cat.[1]

Clinicopathologic Features

Antibodies to *Leptospira* spp are measured by agglutination assays using live or formalin-fixed reference strains. Cats experimentally and naturally infected with *Leptospira* appear to produce strain-specific agglutinating antibodies. However, attempts to use complement-fixation tests for diagnosis of leptospiral infection in cats have been unrewarding.[13] Only a small percentage of seropositive cats yield *Leptospira* by culture or animal inoculation.[3,10,11]

Leptospiral organisms can be identified in kidney sections by silver stains but are sometimes hard to differentiate from normal tissue structures. Organisms can be isolated from some cats with special *Leptospira* culture media. Cultures are maintained for a month or more and periodically examined for characteristically motile spirochetes by dark-field microscopy. Cell-free preparations of tissues or urine can also be inoculated into species that are very sensitive to leptospirosis, such as guinea pigs or hamsters.

Treatment and Prevention

There is very little information on treatment of feline leptospirosis. Most infected cats do not show clinical signs and, therefore, go untreated. Two cats with advanced disease were treated but died several days later.[1,10] Penicillin is the treatment of choice in dogs to clear leptospiremia, followed by dihydrostreptomycin to terminate the carrier state.

Vaccines are routinely used to prevent leptospirosis in dogs. Canine vaccines have not been evaluated in cats. However, because of the mild and self-limiting course of the disease in cats, vaccination is unwarranted.

Infection and Immunity

Cats appear highly immunoresponsive to leptospiral infection. Leptospiremia is usually terminated a week after infection, and urine shedding generally disappears several days to a month later. Cats eliminate the renal carrier state following recovery from acute disease much more readily than dogs. Therefore, chronic interstitial nephritis is an unlikely complication of leptospirosis in cats.

Animal and Public Health Considerations

Cats can be infected with many of the same strains of *Leptospira* as other animals. Some of these strains are potentially pathogenic to people. The infrequency and self-limiting nature of leptospirosis in cats make cats of minor importance in human exposure. Nevertheless, care should be taken when handling infected cats.

References

1. Bryson DG and Ellis WA: Leptospirosis in a British domestic cat. *J Small Anim Pract* 17:459-465, 1976.

2. Carlos ER *et al*: Leptospirosis in the Philippines: Feline studies. *Am J Vet Res* 32:1455-1456, 1971.

3. Esseveld H and Collier WA: Leptospirose bei Katzen auf Java. *Z Immunforsch Exp Ther* 93:512-528, 1938.

4. Fessler JF and Morter RL: Experimental feline leptospirosis. *Cornell Vet* 54:176-190, 1964.

5. Hamilton JM: Nephritis in the cat. *J Small Anim Pract* 7:445-449, 1966.

6. Harkness AC *et al*: An isolation of *Leptospira* serotype *pomona* from a domestic cat. *New Zeal Vet J* 18:175-176, 1970.

7. Hemsley LA: *Leptospira canicola* and chronic nephritis in cats. *Vet Record* 68: 300-301, 1956.

8. Klaarenbeek A and Winsser J: De leptospirosen bij de kleine huisdieren. Een statistisch en experimenteel onderzoek. *Tijdsch voor Diergeneesk* 65:666-670, 1938.

9. Lucke VM and Crowther ST: The incidence of leptospiral agglutination titers in the domestic cat. *Vet Record* 77:647-648, 1965.

10. Mason RW *et al*: Suspected leptospirosis in two cats. *Aust Vet J* 48:622-623, 1972.

11. Modric Z: Prirodna i eksperimentalna leptospiroza u macke. *Vetinarski Archiv* 48:147-156, 1978.

12. Murphy LC *et al*: The prevalence of leptospiral agglutinins in the sera of the domestic cat. *Cornell Vet* 48:3-9, 1958.

13. Otten E *et al*: Leptospiren-Infektionen bei der Hauskatze. *Z Trop Parasitol* 5:187-204, 1954.

14. Rees HG: Leptospirosis in a cat. *New Zeal Vet J* 12:64, 1964.

15. Van der Hoeden J: Epizootiology of leptospirosis. *Adv Vet Sci* 4:277-339, 1958.

Chapter 31

Nocardiosis

Etiologic Agent

Nocardia spp appear as aerobic, filamentous, branching actinomycetes during rapid growth. In older cultures, they are often seen in coccobacillary forms as well. All *Nocardia* spp contain mycolic acid, a feature they share with mycobacteria. The principal species in the genus is *N asteroides*, which is common in many parts of the world. *Nocardia brasiliensis* is found in more tropical climates, including the southern United States, Mexico, Central and South America, and southern Africa. However, cases have been recognized in areas as far north as Virginia and northern California.[1] Various *Proactinomyces* spp are related to *Nocardia* spp and can cause similar types of disease.

Pathogenesis

Various nocardial organisms exist as saprophytes in soil, straw, grasses and decaying vegetation. Infection occurs by inhalation or wound contamination.

Clinical Features

Two forms of nocardiosis have been recognized in cats: thoracic and cutaneous. Cutaneous nocardiosis has been described in 4 cats, 2 of which were infected with *N asteroides*, 1 with *N brasiliensis* and 1 with a *Nocardia* sp similar to *Proactinomyces mesenteriucus*.[1,4,8,11] The cutaneous form of nocardiosis is characterized by a slowly spreading subcutaneous infection. Lesions are most common on the distal limbs and occasionally involve underlying bone. The history may include predisposing trauma. Lesions begin with swelling and discoloration of the skin, which eventually breaks open and exudes a grayish, mucinous exudate. Lesions slowly spread to involve nearby areas of skin and regional and more distant lymph nodes. Skin overlying infected subcutaneous tissues sometimes sloughs and exposes underlying tissues. The infection usually responds poorly or temporarily to antibiotics and local treatment. Affected cats become cachectic over time. Internal organ involvement is common but not extensive in the terminal stages of disease.

The thoracic form of nocardiosis in cats has been described by a number of investigators.[2,3,5,7,8,10] This form of disease is essentially an exudative pleuritis and pneumonia, indistinguishable from more common forms of mixed bacterial pyothorax. Signs generally go unnoticed until the disease is quite advanced. Affected cats are dyspneic, have soft coughs, and exhibit varying degrees of weight loss, fever and depression. The chest cavity is usually filled with a grayish to blood-tinged purulent exudate that may or may not contain "sulfur granules."

Pathologic Features

Nocardiosis in people is characterized by suppuration and abscess formation. Necrosis, fibrosis, contiguous spread, sinus formation and granules, which are common features of *Actinomyces* spp infection in

Fig 1. Smear of pleural exudate from a cat with nocardial pleuritis contains filamentous nocardial organisms, seen within a clump of inflammatory cells. Kinyoun stain, 1000X. (Courtesy of Dr. Ernst Biberstein, University of California, Davis)

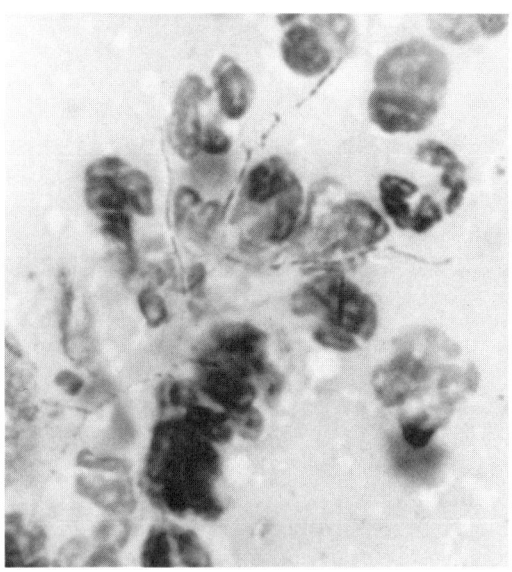

cats, are usually absent in the human disease. Nevertheless, suppuration can also be a prominent feature of feline nocardiosis.

Lesions in cats with thoracic nocardiosis are confined mainly to the lungs and pleural membranes. Lesions in cats with cutaneous disease are concentrated in subcutaneous tissues, underlying muscle and regional lymph nodes. Distant lesions in lung, kidney, spleen and liver are frequently seen in advanced cases. Tissues generally show a multifocal pyogranulomatous process.[1,8] The centers of microabscesses are usually necrotic and contain randomly or radially organized mycelia. Leukocytes, predominantly polymorphonuclear neutrophils and macrophages, tend to concentrate around the periphery of such masses. Stainable organisms are more apt to be seen in cutaneous lesions than in internal organs. Lesions within the lung, lymph nodes and liver consist of focal necrosis and granulomatous inflammation.

Clinicopathologic Features

Nocardial organisms are often identified in stained smears of cutaneous or pleural exudates. However, identification of organisms in tissue is more difficult. *Nocardia asteroides* in tissue does not stain with conventional hematoxylin and eosin preparations. Organisms in tissues and exudate are filamentous and stain positively by Gram and Kinyoun procedures (Fig 1). They are only weakly positive with classic Ziehl-Neelsen acid-fast stains.

Nocardial organisms can be grown with some difficulty from exudates and infected tissues. Colonies appear within 6 days or more on Sabouraud's dextrose agar incubated aerobically at 22 C and 37 F. Various *Nocardia* spp are differentiated from each other on the basis of colony morphology, ability to grow at various temperatures, biochemical reactions with various media, and pathogenicity to guinea pigs.

Fluorescent-antibody staining with specific antisera can help identify organisms within tissue sections or smears of exudate.

Treatment and Prevention

Nocardial infections can be extremely difficult to treat. Though the organisms are sensitive to many different antibiotics, the response is usually transient at best. One possible explanation for the resistance of nocardial infections is the propensity of these organisms to form nonenveloped "L-forms." Another is the difficulty in achieving adequate antibiotic concentrations in areas of suppuration and necrosis. A third possibility is that nocardiosis in cats, as in human and canine disease, has a propensity to occur in immunocompromised hosts. Such animals understandably have a much poorer response to antibiotic therapy.

Antibiotic sensitivities should be conducted whenever possible. The antimicrobial of choice for treating nocardiosis is usually trimethoprim-sulfonamide. Alternative drugs include amikacin, minocycline and chloramphenicol. Treatment may have to be continued for as long as 5 months. If thoracic disease is present, chest drains should be placed and exudates removed. Therapy should continue for several weeks after clinical signs resolve.

Infection and Immunity

Nocardiosis in people frequently occurs in immunocompromised hosts, such as individuals with systemic lupus erythematosus, sarcoidosis, silicosis, alveolar proteinosis, chronic granulomatous disease, dysglobulinemias or malignancies or those undergoing corticosteroid therapy.[6] This is also true to some extent in dogs; nocardiosis has often been associated with canine distemper virus infection. It would be prudent, in light of the nature of disease in these species, to search for underlying immunosuppressive disorders, such as feline leukemia virus and feline immunodeficiency virus in cats as well. Indeed, we have observed both cutaneous and thoracic nocardiosis in 2 cats with the latter virus infection. A third cat with cutaneous nocardiosis was FeLV and FIV negative.

Immunity to nocardial infection is largely cell mediated, similar to immunity against related mycobacteria. The role of humoral immunity has not been defined.

Animal and Public Health Considerations

People can develop severe and potentially fatal nocardial infections. However, human infection almost always occurs from contact with environmental reservoirs. Further, many people and animals are exposed to *Nocardia* spp but few develop disease. For these reasons, infected cats are not considered health hazards to people or other animals.

References

1. Ajello L *et al*: Isolation of *Nocardia brasiliensis* from a cat. *JAVMA* 138:370-376, 1961.

2. Akün RS: Nokardiosi bei zwei Katzen in der Türkei. *Deut Tierärztl Wchnschr* 59:202-204, 1952.

3. Armstrong PJ: Nocardial pleuritis in a cat. *Can Vet J* 21:189-191, 1980.

4. Bakerspiegel A: An unusual strain of *Nocardia* isolated from an infected cat. *Can J Microbiol* 19:1361-1365, 1973.

5. Campbell B and Scott DW: Successful management of nocardial empyema in a dog and cat. *JAAHA* 11:769-773, 1975.

6. Drutz DJ, in Wyngaarden JB and Smith LH Jr: *Cecil's Textbook of Medicine*. Saunders, Philadelphia, 1985. pp 1613-1614.

7. Langham RF *et al*: Nocardiosis in the dog and cat. *Mich State Univ Vet* 19:102-107, 119, 1959.

8. Marder MW *et al*: Clinical pathological conference (Systemic mycosis in a cat; *Nocardia asteroides*). *Feline Pract* 3(5):20-31, 1973.

9. Marlow C: Nocardiosis in the cat. *Bltn Feline Advisory Bureau*. 17(3):3-5, 1979.

10. Osborne AD: Some conditions of importance in cat practice. *Vet Record* 75:1206, 1963.

11. Wilkinson GT: Cutaneous *Nocardia* infection in a cat. *Feline Pract* 13(4):32-34, 1983.

Chapter 32

Dermatophilosis

Etiologic Agent

Dermatophilus congolensis is the most pathogenic species in the genus. It is the major cause of cutaneous streptothricosis in cattle. In sheep, *Dermatophilus dermatonomus* and *D pedis* cause mycotic dermatitis (lumpy wool) and strawberry foot rot, respectively.

The main causative agent of dermatophilosis of cats is probably *D congolensis*. However, identification of this organism has usually been based on its microscopic appearance in tissue sections or impression smears and not by culture. A positive isolation of *D congolensis* from a cat was reported by Jones.[3]

Dermatophilus congolensis is a slender, Gram-positive, filamentous actinomycete with characteristic transverse and longitudinal divisions. Free coccal forms and coccal forms with tubular filamentous extensions are also seen in culture and tissues.

Dermatophilus spp are normal inhabitants of the skin of horses, cattle, sheep and other mammals. A saprophytic soil phase has not been identified. Infection with these organisms is more common in warm, humid climates.

Pathogenesis

Dermatophilosis is a superficial disease of the integument of sheep, cattle, horses and dogs. In cats, however, it is almost always a subcutaneous infection and the integument is involved by extension. Cats are probably infected through minor abrasions and penetrating wounds to the mucous membranes of the mouth, epithelium of the tongue, and the skin. Many infected cats are from farm environments and have had contact with host animals. Others have no known exposure to cows, sheep or horses.

Dermatophilus congolensis infection can readily be induced by rubbing cultures of the organism into scarified skin of sheep, guinea pigs, mice and cats.[3] Following infection of the skin of a kitten, scabs appeared at the site by day 3 and were prominent by day 7. An adult cat inoculated subcutaneously developed an abscess at the injection site.[3]

Clinical Features

Dermatophilus lesions of cats occur mainly in 4 forms: lingual and tonsillar crypt granulomas; granulomatous lymphadenitis with fistulation, usually involving popliteal lymph nodes; cutaneous dermatophilosis; and miscellaneous lesions.

Proliferative masses on the dorsum of the tongue and extending into the tonsillar crypts have been described in 2 cats.[1,5] A piece of feather was found imbedded in the center of the lesion in 1 cat.[5] Both cats had swallowing difficulties and some degree of respiratory embarrassment. Their tongues protruded and they drooled. The lingual masses in these cats were as large as 3 cm in diameter.

Localized lymphadenitis and fistulation have been described in 3 cats.[3,4] Firm subcutaneous swellings 1.5-10 cm in diameter were present near the popliteal lymph node. Fistulous tracts extended from the masses to the overlying skin. The masses involved the popliteal lymph nodes in each case.

Cutaneous dermatophilosis has been described in 1 cat.[2] The primary lesion was in subcutaneous tissue of a hind paw. A secondary subcutaneous lesion was observed proximal to the popliteal lymph node in the same leg.

Dermatophilus spp lesions have also been observed in sites other than subcutaneous tissue and the oral cavity. A large solitary granuloma has been identified in the serosal layer of the bladder.[5]

Pathologic Features

Dermatophilus spp lesions are either pyogranulomatous or granulomatous in nature. Central necrosis is common in most larger lesions. Areas of necrosis are surrounded by a band of degenerating neutrophils, which in turn are surrounded by a band of lymphocytes, plasma cells and epithelioid cells. The outermost layer is often composed of dense, concentrically arranged layers of fibrous tissue. Characteristic organisms are usually visualized in the central necrotic zone and in the opposing layer of degenerating neutrophils.

Fig 1. *Dermatophilus congolensis* organisms in a smear from a cow with exudative dermatitis. Note the organisms' segmented appearance. Gram stain, 1250X. (Courtesy of Dr. Andrew Lackner, University of California, Davis)

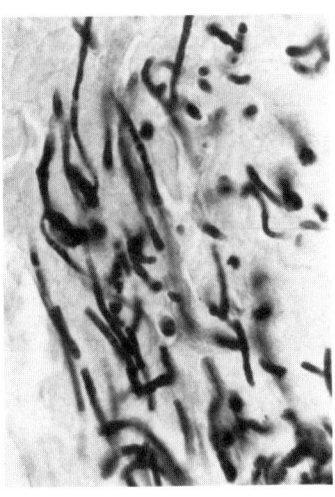

Clinicopathologic Features

Dermatophilosis is usually diagnosed by microscopic examination of tissue sections or impression smears. The organism is stained by many different histologic stains, including Gram's, hematoxylin and eosin, and methylene blue. Filamentous branching structures composed of numerous individual coccoid bodies are characteristic. The filaments are divided longitudinally and horizontally, appearing like a stack of coins (Fig 1). The organism has been cultured from lesions of cats. It grows aerobically on blood-agar plates at room temperature and both anaerobically and aerobically at 37 C.[3]

Treatment and Prevention

Lesions should be excised and the animals treated for several weeks with penicillin or a similar antibiotic. The prognosis after such treatment appears to be good.[1,3,4]

Infection and Immunity

There is no evidence that dermatophilosis occurs in cats with impaired resistance. Affected cats have appeared normal before and after the infection.

Animal and Public Health Considerations

Infected cats are not health hazards to people or other animals.

References

1. Baker GJ *et al*: Oral dermatophilosis in a cat: a case report. *J Small Anim Pract* 13:649-654, 1972.

2. Carakostas MC *et al*: Subcutaneous dermatophilosis in a cat. *JAVMA* 185:675-676, 1984.

3. Jones RT: Subcutaneous infection with *Dermatophilus congolensis* in a cat. *J Comp Pathol* 86:415-421, 1976.

4. Miller RI et al: Probable dermatophilosis in 2 cats. *Aust Vet J* 60:155-156, 1983.

5. O'Hara PJ and Cordes DO: Granulomata caused by *Dermatophilus* in two cats. *New Zeal Vet J* 11:151-154, 1963.

Chapter 33

Mycobacteriosis

Mycobacterium spp cause 3 syndromes in domestic cats: systemic mycobacteriosis (classic tuberculosis), feline leprosy and atypical mycobacteriosis. Systemic mycobacteriosis is caused by *M bovis*, *M tuberculosis*, *M avium* or *M microti* (vole bacillus). Feline leprosy is caused by an organism identical or closely related to *M lepraemurium*, and atypical mycobacteriosis is caused by several species of Runyan Type-IV mycobacteria.

Various species of mycobacteria survive in soil and water, or in amphibians, rodents, birds and mammals. They possess an elaborate cell wall that is rich in mycolic acid. This lipid retains carbol-fuchsin stains even when heated and acid and alcohol decolored. This "acid-fastness" is a property somewhat unique to mycobacteria and is useful for identifying these organisms in tissues and exudates.

SYSTEMIC MYCOBACTERIOSIS

Etiologic Agent

Systemic mycobacteriosis in domestic cats is associated mainly with *M bovis*. About 96% of the cases in the literature were caused by this organism, while *M tuberculosis*, *M avium* and *M microti* comprised the remainder, in that respective order of frequency.[5,16,31,38,41,46]

The major reservoir for *M bovis* is dairy cattle. Cats are infected when fed contaminated milk, milk products or meat.[8,22,31] They may also be exposed to *M bovis* through infected people. Feline *M tuberculosis* infections are usually traced to infected people in the same environment. The means by which cats are exposed to *M avium* and *M microti* are not precisely known but probably involve natural predation of small birds and rodents by cats.

The relatively high incidence of *M bovis* in cats with systemic mycobacteriosis is not due just to a higher rate of exposure. Cats are highly sensitive to *M bovis* infection and relatively resistant to *M tuberculosis* infection. They are highly resistant to *M avium* and *M microti* infections. Few *M avium* and *M microti* infections in cats have been described in the literature.[3,10,17,18,42-44]

The incidence of bovine-type tuberculosis in cats has dropped dramatically since bovine tuberculosis-eradication programs have been instituted in many parts of the world and pasteurization of milk has become mandatory. Before control of infection in dairy cattle, 7-13% of the cats necropsied in Europe were infected with *M bovis*.[19] Infection rates approaching 50% were observed in cat populations on some dairies.[19,39] Incidence of bovine tuberculosis in cats in central Europe now is probably 0.2% or less.[19] With control of bovine tuberculosis, a higher proportion of cats are infected by other species.[31] Nevertheless, as long as isolated cases of tuberculosis in cattle exist, sporadic cases of bovine tuberculosis will almost inevitably be seen in cats. Infections in cats will also remain a problem in undeveloped countries that have no bovine tuberculosis-control programs.

Pathogenesis

There are 3 principal routes of mycobacterial infection: oral; localized exposure through skin or mucous membranes; and primary pulmonary exposure.[19,22,38,41] The most prevalent route is oral, occurring in 70% or more of affected cats. Primary infection through the skin or mucous membranes is probably caused by bites, scratches or licks from animals feeding on infected material.[1,38] Primary pulmonary infection following inhalation of the organism is uncommon.[38]

The incubation period of experimentally induced *M bovis* infection in cats may be as short as 3 weeks.[2,43] The incubation period of the natural disease is probably from 2 months to a year or more, probably reflecting exposure to far fewer organisms. Initial lesions most commonly begin in the wall of the alimentary tract and are considered "incomplete" because they are neither well encapsulated nor grossly apparent at necropsy.[22,38] However, indistinct macroscopic or poorly circumscribed microscopic lesions are often seen in the intestinal walls after close inspection of the tissues.[41] Primary pulmonary lesions are equally difficult to identify and are often associated with the hilar lymph nodes.[38] Infection spreads from the primary disease complex in the parenchyma of the intestine or lungs by lymphatic and hematogenous routes.[19,38] Hematogenous or lymphatic dissemination from the skin to distant sites is less common than dissemination from internal organs.

Clinical signs are not seen until secondary lesions in tissues adjacent to the portal of entry become quite large, or until disseminated lesions appear in other organs. Common sites of secondary infection include the tonsils, retropharyngeal, cervical and mesenteric lymph nodes, cecum, Peyer's patches, and nasal turbinates. Serosal, mucosal and dermal surfaces or bone overlying such areas often become involved by extension late in the disease, leading to facial deformities, draining tracts and rapidly spreading peritonitis or pleuritis.[19,38] Disseminated lesions occur in parenchymatous organs such as the lungs, kidneys, pancreas, uterus, adrenal glands, testes, myocardium, parotid salivary glands, liver, spleen, bones and joints, meninges, cerebellum, cerebrum and eyes.[1,2,4,6,7,9,11,13-15,21,24,25-28,30,32-36,40,43,44,47-49]

Clinical Features

Cats with systemic mycobacteriosis are usually 5 years of age or less. Progressive weight loss and cachexia are the most consistent outward signs of disease in cats. Once cachexia and emaciation begin, the disease course usually accelerates and death rapidly ensues in days or weeks. Some cats may have a more intermittent disease course lasting for weeks or months.

Intestinal tract involvement occurs in 80% or more of affected cats. Clinical signs include vomiting, inappetence, diarrhea and palpable masses in the mesenteric lymph nodes, small intestine, cecum, pancreas, uterus, kidney, liver, spleen or omentum. Ascites, associated with an exudative peritonitis, occurs in some cats with intestinal tract disease.

Pulmonary involvement is observed in 40% of cats with systemic mycobacteriosis. In many of these animals, lung lesions are metastatic from enteric foci rather than primary in origin.[19] Lung lesions appear radiographically as discrete or multiple nodular densities up to several centimeters in diameter. Pulmonary parenchymal disease often extends to the regional lymph nodes, the visceral and parietal pleura and the pleural cavity. Pleural effusions are common in such situations. Clinical signs associated with thoracic disease usually go unnoticed until parenchymal disease or fluid effusions become quite extensive. Therefore, dyspnea is a sign of advanced disease. Coughing is uncommon.

Enlargement of a single mandibular or cranial cervical lymph node is often the only lesion in the head or neck area. A chronic nasal discharge is seen in cats with nasal pasage involvement. Swellings and deformities over the bridge of the nose may be associated with nasal disease.

Skin lesions are seen in about 10% of cats with systemic mycobacteriosis. They are often secondary extensions from underlying diseased lymph nodes of the head and neck. Lesions are more common on the face and neck but can occur almost anywhere on the trunk and limbs. Primary skin infections are uncommon and often spread to regional lymph nodes and surrounding tissues. Skin lesions are plaque-like, ulcerated, soft and fluctuant.

Tuberculosis in females may be manifested as metritis. Infection enters the uterus hematogenously or from serosal lesions.

Eye involvement is an uncommon manifestation of systemic mycobacteriosis in cats. The disease usually attacks the choroid and is often bilateral. Ocular disease can be the predominant clinical manifestation or only a part of the total syndrome. Central nervous system, bone and joint involvement are infrequent and may be manifested by neurologic abnormalities, lameness and draining bone fistulas.

Pathologic Features

The tubercle is the basic lesion of systemic mycobacterial infection.[19,22,38,41] Individual tubercles vary in size from microscopic to 2-5 cm or more in diameter. The typical tubercle in cats is less necrotic, with more cellular proliferation than those occurring in people. Larger tubercles may caseate in the center or liquefy and form cavitary lesions. Smaller lesions tend to coalesce, especially in the lungs, lymph nodes, and on pleural and serosal surfaces. Tubercles in organs, such as the liver and kidneys, tend to be more solitary.

Tubercles in cats are comprised of collections of large, pale, eosinophilic epithelioid cells surrounded by a narrow rim of fibrous tissue. Sparse to moderately intense accumulations of plasma cells and lymphocytes are found within and surrounding this outer capsule. Neutrophils are occasionally seen in the center of tubercles, but multinucleated giant cells are uncommon. Organisms are found in small numbers within epithelioid cells and free in exudates in the caseated cores of lesions.

Clinicopathologic Features

Systemic mycobacteriosis should be considered in any cat with a chronic wasting syndrome associated with localized or widespread granulomatous inflammation. This type of disease may be reflected by a chronic infection-type anemia, leukocytosis, neutrophilia, lymphopenia, monocytosis, hypergammaglobulinemia and hyperfibrinogenemia. Antemortem diagnosis is based on identification of typical Ziehl-Neelsen acid-fast organisms in exudates, impression smears of lesions, or histologic sections of biopsy specimens. Organisms are slow and difficult to grow in special culture media. Serologic and skin testing are considered unreliable in cats.

Tuberculous cats respond erratically to intradermal skin and ophthalmic testing with extracts of *Mycobacterium*, such as with old tuberculin, standard tuberculin and second-strength tuberculin. Snider and associates found no reactors among 24 cats infected with bovine tuberculosis.[39] Griffith reported that 6 of 11 cats responded positively when tested by the subcutaneous rather than intradermal route.[13] Hawthorne and Lauder reported that tuberculous cats developed a more rapid and flamboyant skin reaction than uninfected cats when inoculated intradermally with BCG.[16]

Francis found the serum complement-fixation test for *Mycobacterium* spp was accurate in cats.[12] However, serum complement-fixation tests were positive in only 57% of cats experimentally infected with *M bovis*.[29] Nowacki found hemagglutination and hemolysis tests more accurate in experimentally infected cats.[29] These latter tests have never been applied to cats with naturally occurring disease and are not readily available.

Treatment and Prevention

Mycobacterium bovis and *M tuberculosis* respond to a number of antituberculosis drugs, such as isoniazid, streptomycin, rifampin and ethambutol. Isoniazid, ethambutol and rifampin in combination are particularly effective for treating human tuberculosis and have been used successfully in dogs. However, very little information is available on combination drug therapy for systemic mycobacteriosis of domestic cats. Moreover, the wisdom of treating a cat with systemic mycobacteriosis should be questioned. Most of these drugs are merely suppressive and long-term or indefinite therapy is necessary. It is also highly unusual to make the diagnosis in cats before death or early enough for therapy to be effective.

Infection and Immunity

Though cats appear quite sensitive to *M bovis* infection, they have a natural resistance to infection by other *Mycobacterium* spp. The nature of this resistance is not known. The resistance of cats to certain species, such as *M avium*, *M tuberculosis* and *M microti*, and the rarity of disease lead one to question the immunologic status of the few cats that are clinically infected. The possible relationship of systemic mycobacteriosis caused by strains other than *M bovis* and acquired immunodeficiency, such as from feline leukemia virus or feline immunodeficiency virus infections, has not been explored.

Immunity to mycobacterial organisms is largely cell-mediated in all species of animals studied. Antibodies are produced but appear to be markers rather than mediators of infection and immunity. The more widespread and pyogranulomatous nature of lesions in cats with systemic tuberculosis, compared to the more typical granulomatous lesions in people, suggests that cats respond much more poorly than people. The less granulomatous nature of lesions in cats is reminiscent of the lepromatous and tuberculoid forms of leprosy in people. The lepromatous form of leprosy in people and cats is characterized by diffuse pyogranulomatous inflammation with large numbers of organisms within macrophages. In this situation, macrophages apparently have not been activated by cellular immune phenomena. In the tuberculoid form, however, organisms are hard to identify in exudates and phagocytic cells, and the host response is more organized and flamboyant.

Though cats have less of a granulomatous response to mycobacteria than other species, they are not necessarily immunodeficient. Obviously, very few cats exposed to these organisms ever become clinically ill, suggesting that most cats are extremely efficient at containing the organisms. This is especially true for immunity to *Mycobacterium* spp that cats are likely to contact while hunting. It is probably no accident that cats have evolved a high degree of resistance to *M avium* and *M microti*, species with which they have been in contact through predation over eons of time.

Animal and Public Health Considerations

Mycobacterium bovis and *M tuberculosis* are highly pathogenic to people, while *M avium* is considered a poor human pathogen. Infected cats occasionally shed organisms in the sputum, especially when lung disease is present, and in the feces when the intestinal tract is involved.[38] Organisms can also be shed from draining skin lesions and nasal exudates of cats with rhinitis. Surgeons or pathologists may also come in contact with the organisms during routine exploratory surgeries, biopsy procedures or necropsies. Nevertheless, documented cases of cat-to-person infection have not been reported.[45]

Cat-to-cat transmission of *Mycobacterium* spp has not been documented. However, there is some evidence that *M bovis* infected cats might serve as a reservoir for infection in cattle.[28]

References

1. Bethelon M: Observations sur la tuberculose ûtérine de la chatte. *Recl Med Vet* 119:5-7, 1943.

2. Blähser S: Uber nicht alltägliche Todesursachen und einige plötzliche Todesfälle bei der Katze. *Kleintierpraxis* 7:192-201, 1962.

3. Buergelt CS et al: Disseminated avian tuberculosis in a cat. *Calif Vet* 36:13-15, 1982.

4. Cella F: Di un caso di carpite tubercolare primitiva in un gatto. *Clin Vet* 65:412-423, 1942.

5. Cobbett L: The type of tubercle bacillus found in tuberculosis of the cat. *J Comp Pathol Ther* 39:142-148, 1926.

6. Collet P: Les localisations osseuses de la tuberculose chez le chat. *Bltn Soc Sci Vet Lyon* 43:112-117, 1942.

7. Collet P and Lucam F: Tuberculose du cervelet chez un chat. *Bltn Soc Sci Vet Lyon* 42:52-60, 1941.

8. Diehl KE: An epizootic of bovine tuberculosis traced from slaughter. *JAVMA* 155:1888-1889, 1971.

9. Dobson N: Tuberculosis of the cat. *J Comp Pathol Ther* 43:310-316, 1930.

10. Dorssen van CA: Infectie met *Mycobacterium microti* bij een Kat. *Tijdschr Diergeneeskd* 85:404-412, 1960.

11. Douville M: Sur le diagnostic et la nature des lésions cutanées ulcéreuses chez le chat (Tuberculose cutanée et arthrite tuberculeuse. Erythème papulo-érosif. Sarcome et épithéliome) *Rev Vet* 74:209-217, 1922.

12. Francis J: Tuberculosis in small animals. *Mod Vet Pract* 42:39-42, 1961.

13. Griffith AS: Tuberculosis of the cat. *J Comp Pathol Ther* 39:71-82, 1926.

14. Grossman A: Mycobacterial hepatitis associated with long-term steroid therapy. *Feline Pract* 13(6):37-41, 1983.

15. Hancock WI and Coats G: Tubercle of the choroid in the cat. *Vet Record* 23:433-436, 1911.

16. Hawthorne VM and Lauder IM: Tuberculosis in man, dog, and cat. *Am Rev Resp Dis* 85:858-869, 1962.

17. Hix JW et al: Avian tubercle bacillus infection in the cat. *JAVMA* 138:641-647, 1961.

18. Huitema H and van Vloten J: Murine tuberculosis in a cat. *Anton van Leeuwenhoek* 26:235-240, 1960.

19. Innes JRM: The pathology and pathogenesis of tuberculosis in domesticated animals compared with man. *Brit Vet J* 96:96-105, 1940.

20. Isaac J et al: An outbreak of *Mycobacterium bovis* in cats in an animal house. *Aust Vet J* 60:243-245, 1983.

21. Isler D and Lott-Stolz G: Die wichtigsten Krankheits-und Todesursachen der Katze. Sektionsfälle 1965-1976. *Kleintierpraxis* 23:333-334, 336-337, 1978.

22. Jennings AR: The distribution of tuberculosis lesions in the dog and cat, with reference to the pathogenesis. *Vet Record* 61:380-385, 1949.

23. Kuwabara T: Susceptibility of cats to tubercle bacilli. *Kit Arch Exp Med* 15:318-329, 1938.

24. Lawford JB and Neame H: Binocular choroidal tuberculosis with detachment of the retina in two kittens. *Brit J Ophthalmol* 7:305-313, 1923.

25. Mason JH: Tuberculosis in a cat. *Brit Vet J* 80:370-371, 1924.

26. Matthias D and Niemand HG: Augentuberkulose bei einer Katze. *Z Infektionskr Haustiere* 59:203-210, 1943.

27. Methner U: Beitrag zur Tuberkulose des Hundes und der Katze. *Tierarztl Umschau* 12:85-89, 1957.

28. Milbradt N and Roemmele O: Tuberkulöse Katze infiziert Rinderbestand. *Deutsch Tierärztle Wschr* 67:17, 1960.

29. Nowacki J: Haemagglutination, haemolysis and complement fixation tests in the diagnosis of experimental tuberculosis in cats. *Abstract Vet Bltn* 38:1766, 1968.

30. Orr CM et al: Tuberculosis in cats. A report of two cases. *J Small Anim Pract* 21:247-253, 1980.

31. Parodi A et al: Mycobacteriosis in the domestic carnivora-present-day epidemiology of tuberculosis in the cat and dog. *J Small Anim Pract* 6:309-326, 1965.

32. Pezzoli G: La tuberculosi del testicolo nel gatto. *Zooprofilassi* 9:289-298, 1954.

33. Reif JS: Solitary pulmonary lesions in small animals. *JAVMA* 155:717-722, 1969.

34. Robin V and Fontaine M: Tuberculose génitale du chat. *Recl Méd Vet* 130:213-216, 1954.

35. Robin V and Lesbouyries G: Les ostéoarthrites tuberculenses des carnivores domestiques. *Rev Gén Méd Vét* 35:177-183, 1926.

36. Seren E: Contributo clinico, radiografico, anatomistopatologico e batteriologico allo studio della tubercolosi renale del gatto. *Nuova Vet* 14:177-189, 1936.

37. Smith JE: Symposium on disease of cats III. Some pathogenic bacteria of cats with special reference to their public health significance. *J Small Anim Pract* 5:517-523, 1964.

38. Snider WR: Tuberculosis in canine and feline populations. *Am Rev Resp Dis* 104:877-887, 1971.

39. Snider WR et al: Tuberculosis in canine and feline populations. Study of high risk populations in Pennsylvania, 1966-1968. *Am Rev Resp Dis* 104:866-876, 1971.

40. Stableforth AW: A bacteriological investigation of cases of tuberculosis in five cats, sixteen dogs, a parrot, and a wallaby. *J Comp Pathol Ther* 42:163-188, 1929.

41. Stünzi H: Zur Pathologie der Katzentuberkulose. *Schweiz Arch Tierheilk* 96:604-612, 1954.

42. Suter MM von et al: Atypisches mykobakterielles hautgranulom bei einer Katze in der Schweiz. *Zentralbl Veterinarmed A* 31:712-718, 1984.

43. Teuscher E: Hirntuberkulose bei hund und Katze. *Schweiz Z Allg Path Bakt* 17:776-779, 1954.

44. Teuscher E: Hirntuberkulose bei hund und Katze. *Schweiz Med Wschr* 85:18, 1955.

45. Toma B et al: Law tuberculose feline et son danger pout l'hjomme. *Comp Immunol Microbiol Infect Dis* 1:185-192, 1979.

46. Verge J and Senthille F: Recherches sur la fréquence des différents types de bacilles tuberculeux dans l'infection spontanée du chat. *Ann de l'Institu Pasteur* 68:114-117, 1942.

47. Walzl H: Zur tuberkulose des Zentralnervensystems bei der Katze. *Monatsh Tierheilk die Rindertuberkulose* 5:199-205, 1956.

48. Willemse A and Beijer EGM: Bovine Tuberculose bij een kat (Bovine tuberculosis in a cat). *Tijdschr Diergeneesk* 104:717-721, 1979.

49. Wolff A: Tuberculosis in a domestic cat. *VM/SAC* 61:553, 1966.

FELINE LEPROSY

Etiologic Agent

Feline leprosy is caused either by *Mycobacterium lepraemurium* or a very closely related species. Evidence favoring *M lepraemurium* as the causative agent is compelling. *Mycobacterium lepraemurium* and mycobacterial isolates from feline leprosy lesions are both notoriously difficult to grow in artificial media.[3,13,14,18] *Mycobacterium lepraemurium* and the feline leprosy bacillus have similarities when grown on Ogawa egg yolk medium under rigid temperature and CO_2 conditions.[10,13] Murine and feline leprosy isolates have identical cytochrome b_1 and react the same in various biochemical tests.[10] Both produce caproporphyrin III pigment in Ogawa egg yolk medium. Guinea pigs infected with *M lepraemurium* or feline leprosy bacillus react interchangeably and to the same degree with lepromin made from either organism. Both the feline and murine leprosy bacilli infect mice, rats and guinea pigs, thus differentiating them from *M leprae*, the causative agent of human leprosy.[7] However, they are erratic in causing disease in experimentally inoculated cats. Some cats are susceptible and others resistant.[10] The feline leprosy bacillus appears to lose infectivity for cats when passed several times through rats, though 1 isolate passed for years through mice was still infective to cats.[6,10]

Pathogenesis

Cats with feline leprosy have been identified in many parts of the world, including England, western Canada, the United States, Netherlands, Australia and New Zealand.[3-6,14,17-22] The infection is more common in coastal areas and port cities than inland. Infection is probably acquired when cats come into contact with rodents. The incubation period following experimental inoculation is from 2 months to 1 year or more.[16,18] This potentially long incubation period makes it difficult to reconstruct events that might have occurred at the time of initial exposure.

The initial lesions in feline leprosy is a focal granuloma of the skin and subcutaneous tissues.[17] Infection spreads to adjacent areas of skin and subcutis over months or years. Dissemination beyond regional lymph nodes is uncommon.

Clinical Features

Cats with leprosy are usually 2-5 years of age and of random breed and sex. Owners become aware of solitary or multiple raised, painless, plaque-like lesions, 1-3.5 cm in diameter in the skin and underlying subcutis. The surfaces of the lesions are often ulcerated but usually not fistulated and exudative (Fig 1). Lesions can occur anywhere on the body but tend to be concentrated on the head and limbs.[14,15] Small lesions are occasionally found on the tongue and lips.[9] Lesions, even if multiple, are usually concentrated in 1 area and seldom extend beyond regional lymph nodes. Lesions frequently recur following excision. Dissemination to adjacent muscles, spleen, bone marrow, liver, kidney and lungs has rarely been observed.[3,8,9,14,22] Cats with disseminated disease are much more likely to suffer from wasting and depression than cats with localized lesions. Cats with localized disease remain surprisingly healthy otherwise.

Feline leprosy must be differentiated from atypical mycobacteriosis, which also involves the skin and subcutis. Skin lesions caused by atypical mycobacteria tend to be more ulcerated, fistulated and exudative. They are also less firm and plaque-like on palpation. Most important, atypical mycobacteria are much easier to culture than *M lepraemurium*.

Pathologic Features

Feline leprosy can be subdivided by histopathologic features into tuberculoid or lepromatous forms.[9] The tuberculoid form of feline leprosy is associated with poorly capsulated accumulations of epithelioid histiocytic cells interspersed with a few neutrophils and surrounded by an outer zone of loose fibrous tissue containing moderate numbers of perivascular lymphocytes and plasma cells.[3,4,9,14,17] Lesions vary from <1 mm to ≥3 cm in size. Caseation is common in the centers of larger lesions. Acid-fast bacilli are rarely seen in histiocytic cells but may be common in caseous exudates. The lepromatous form makes up about one-third of the cases seen in cats.[9] In this form, granulomas are composed of large sheets of foamy macrophages that contain large numbers of organisms. Bacilli are usually arranged within histiocytes as dense parallel accumulations referred to as globi. Caseation necrosis is less common in the lepromatous than the tuberculoid form.

Lymph nodes regional to the primary lesions in the skin and subcutaneous tissues are frequently enlarged. In addition to lymphoid hyperplasia, lymph nodes are often infiltrated with epithelioid cells and macrophages to such an extent that normal nodal architecture is obscured. However, acid-fast bacilli are difficult to find within the lymph nodes.[6,9,13]

Invasion of local nerves is a prominent feature of human leprosy but is observed in only one-third of cats with feline leprosy.[9] Moreover, adjacent nerves appear to be surrounded by the disease process rather than invaded by it.

Clinicopathologic Features

Diagnosis is by biopsy and histologic examination of the lesions. Samples from granulomatous lesions should be stained with acid-fast stains. The feline leprosy bacillus stains equally well with both Ziehl-Neelsen and Fite stains. Skin inoculation with tissue extracts from infected cats and rats (lepromin) have produced delayed hypersensitivity reactions in cats but have not been diagnostically evaluated.[7]

Treatment and Prevention

Excision has been the treatment of choice.[11] Lesions should be excised as widely as possible to minimize recurrence at the incision site. Recurrence can be expected in a substantial proportion of animals and necessitates additional surgery. If primary or recurrent lesions remain small and show little tendency to spread, they can be left un-

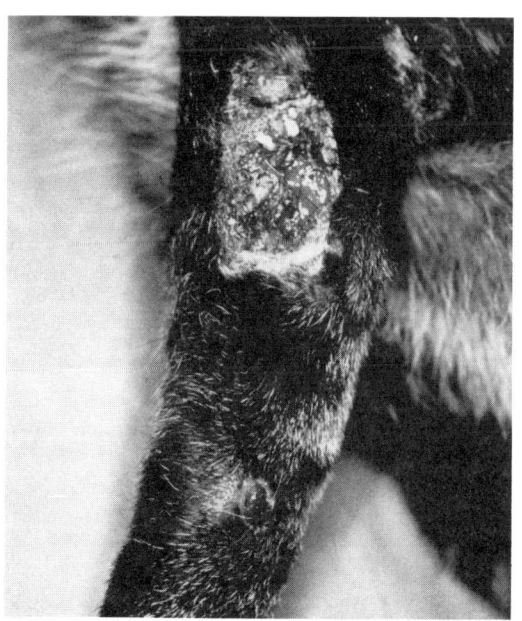

Fig 1. Large nonhealing ulcer and small carpal ulcer on the foreleg of a cat with feline leprosy. Note the scarcity of exudate and the erosive appearance of the lesions. (Courtesy of Dr. Peter Ihrke, University of California, Davis)

treated. Spontaneous regression over a period of months has been described in such situations.

Dapsone has been used with limited success in some cats, but the response is variable and the drug is often toxic.[1,2,11] Signs of toxicity in cats include hemolytic anemia and liver disease.[1] Recommended dosages of dapsone have varied from 50 mg PO BID for several weeks to 1 mg/kg PO BID-TID for 2-4 weeks. Scott recommends no more than 1 mg/kg TID.[16]

The most promising treatment for feline leprosy involves surgical removal of the lesion, coupled with oral clofazimine.[11] Clofazimine is a bright red substituted-iminophenazine dye that has been used to treat people with dapsone-resistant leprosy.[23] Cats should be given the drug once daily 2-8 mg/kg for 6 weeks, then twice weekly for 1-2 more months. Lesions usually begin to regress after 1 week and are no longer palpable by the sixth week of treatment. Side effects seen after 6 weeks of treatment include a pinkish-orange discoloration of the skin, an orangish-yellow discoloration of the subcutaneous fat and possible weight loss. Elevated serum alkaline phosphatase activity is observed after 12 weeks of therapy. Side effects disappear with a few weeks to 3 months after use of the drug is discontinued. They are less evident at lower drug dosages.

Infection and Immunity

Human leprosy is thought to involve a specific immunologic deficiency to *M leprae*. Such a relationship has not been shown in cats, though only some experimentally inoculated cats develop lesions.[10] Newborn kittens are more susceptible than older cats. Preliminary evidence suggests that FeLV is not involved in feline leprosy. The relationship of the disease to feline immunodeficiency virus (FIV) infection remains to be determined, although two cats that were recently tested for the virus were negative.

Cats show a pronounced gradation in immune responsiveness to *M lepraemurium*. Cats with lesions that contain a small number of organisms probably develop strong cell-mediated immunity and never manifest clinically apparent disease. Other cats develop a somewhat incomplete form of immunity that effectively destroys most, but not all, of the organisms within tissue macrophages. These animals develop the tuberculoid form of the disease. Lepromatous disease probably occurs in cats that develop very poor cellular immunity. This is indicated by the large numbers of mycobacteria-laden macrophages in the lesions and the apparent inability of the macrophages to effectively destroy intracellular bacilli.

Animal and Public Health Considerations

There is no evidence that *M lepraemurium*, or the feline form of this organism, is infectious to people. There are also no reports of cat-to-cat spread of infection.

References

1. Allan GS and Wickham N: Mycobacterial granulomas in a cat diagnosed as leprosy. *Feline Pract* 6(5):33-36, 1976.

2. Austin VH: Clinical forum-Cutaneous lesions of feline leprosy. *Feline Pract* 16(4):30, 1986.

3. Brown LR *et al*: A non-tuberculous granuloma in cats. *New Zeal Vet J* 10:7-9, 1962.

4. Frye FL *et al*: Feline lepromatous leprosy. *VM/SAC* 69:1272-1273, 1974.

5. Gee BR *et al*: Disease resembling feline leprosy. *Can Vet J* 16:30, 1975.

6. Lawrence WE and Wickham N: Cat leprosy: infection by a bacillus resembling *Mycobacterium lepraemurium*. *Aust Vet J* 39:390-393, 1963.

7. Leiker DL and Poelma FG: On the etiology of cat leprosy. *Intl J Lepr* 42:312-315, 1974.

8. Matthews JA and Liggitt HD: Disseminated mycobacteriosis in a cat. *JAVMA* 183:701-702, 1983.

9. McIntosh DW: Feline leprosy: A review of forty-four cases from western Canada. *Can Vet J* 23:291-295, 1982.

10. Mori T and Kohsaka K: Identification of cat leprosy bacillus grown in mice. *Intl J Lepr* 54:584-595, 1986.

11. Mundell, AC: The effectiveness of clofazimine in the treatment of feline leprosy. *Abst Am Acad Vet Dermatol*, Washington, DC, April 1988.

12. Muller GH: Clinical Forum Cutaneous lesions of feline leprosy. *Feline Pract* 16(4):30, 1986.

13. Pattyn SR and Portaels F: *In vitro* cultivation and characterization of *Mycobacterium lepraemurium*. *Intl J Lepr* 48:7-14, 1980.

14. Poelma FG and Leiker DL: Cat leprosy in the Netherlands. *Intl J Lepr* 42: 307-311, 1974.

15. Robinson M: Skin granuloma of cats associated with acid-fast bacilli. *J Small Anim Pract* 16:563-567, 1975.

16. Scott DW: Feline Dermatology 1900-1978: A monograph. *JAAHA* 11:261-270, 1980.

17. Schiefer HB, in Latapi F: *Proc 11th Intl Leprosy Congress*, 1978. p 58.

18. Schiefer HB *et al*: A disease resembling feline leprosy in western Canada. *JAVMA* 165:1085-1087, 1974.

19. Schiefer HB and Middleton DM: Experimental transmission of a feline mycobacterial skin disease (feline leprosy). *Vet Pathol* 20:460-471, 1983.

20. Thompson EJ *et al*: Observations of cat leprosy. *New Zeal Vet J* 27:233-235, 1979.

21. Wilkinson GT: A non-tuberculous granuloma of the cat associated with an acid-fast bacillus. *Vet Record* 76:777-778, 833-834, 1964.

22. Wilkinson GT, in Kirk RW: *Current Veterinary Therapy VI*. Saunders, Philadelphia, 1977. pp 569-571.

23. Yawalker, SJ and Vischer, W: Lamprene (clofazimine) in leprosy. *Lepr Rev* 50:135-144, 1979.

ATYPICAL MYCOBACTERIOSIS

Etiologic Agent

Atypical mycobacteriosis is a term given to infections caused by mycobacteria belonging to the Runyan type-IV group. The most important feline pathogens in this group include *M fortuitum*, *M cheloni*, *M smegmatus*, *M phlei*, *M thermoresistible*, *M xenopi* and an occasional mycobacterium of unknown type.[1,2,4,6-10] *Mycobacterium avium* has also been associated with a localized skin nodule on the foot of a young cat.[3] Most atypical mycobacteria grow rapidly in culture, a feature that differentiates them from agents that cause systemic mycobacteriosis and feline leprosy. Atypical mycobacteria are found throughout the world but tend to be more prevalent in warmer and more humid (tropical or semi-tropical) climates.

Pathogenesis

Atypical mycobacteria tend to contaminate the environment and are found in both soil and water.[2,10] Rodents, amphibians or other animals that cats feed upon may also be infected.[3,6] The organisms appear to gain entrance through the skin and subcutaneous tissues. Cat bites and scratches, abrasions caused by thorns, branches and automobile accidents, non-sterile injections, and surgical incisions have all been directly incriminated as portals of entry in cats and people.[1,2,7,10] Organisms do not necessarily enter the tissue when the wound is created; cats can contaminate preexisting wounds during grooming, and organisms within the mouth or on the fur can be transferred from site to site.

Infection with *M fortuitum*, *M cheloni*, *M phlei*, *M thermoresistible* and *M xenopi* usually involves both the dermis and subcutis during the initial phase of the disease.[1,2,4,5,7-9] However, infection with *M smegmatus* appears to begin in the subcutaneous fat and either remains localized or breaks out onto the overlying skin at a later date. The incubation period from the time of infection to appearance of lesions is not known but is probably several weeks to months. Dissemination from localized cutaneous and subcutaneous sites of infection is uncommon. Kunkle and co-workers described a secondary serosal nodule adherent to the stomach and spleen in a cat.[2]

Clinical Features

Lesions of atypical mycobacteriosis can be found anywhere on the body but appear more frequently in the inguinal area, lumbosacral region, ventral abdomen, flank and chest wall (Figs 2,3). Infected cats usually have draining, fistulated wounds several centimeters or more in diameter. Regional lymph nodes are often enlarged. In some cats, deeper subcutaneous swellings either spontaneously progress to a fistulous lesion or are aided in this course by surgical exploration. *Mycobacterium cheloni* infections are somewhat different because of their tendency to form abscesses rather than fistulating wounds.[4,7] Initial attempts

Fig 2. Attempted excision of a *Mycobacterium smegmatus* lesion in the groin of a cat resulted in a large, nonhealing wound. Smaller subcutaneous nodules, some of them ulcerating, are evident around the lesion's periphery. (Courtesy of Spencer Jang, University of California, Davis)

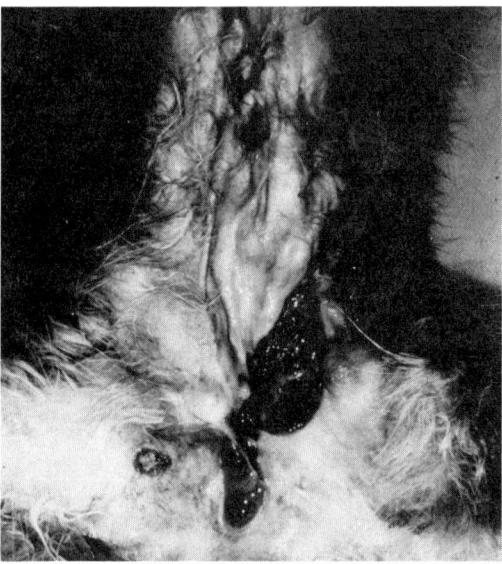

at antibiotic treatment are usually unsuccessful, as is excision. Incomplete excision often leads to dehiscence of the incision and a large open wound. When this occurs, atypical mycobacteriosis should be suspected. Throughout the course of the disease, cats often remain surprisingly healthy, though severely affected cats may lose some condition.

If left untreated, lesions may: remain active but nonexpanding; appear to heal and then recur at intervals of weeks or months; spread slowly to involve more and more tissue; or reach a peak size and slowly disappear over weeks or months. Cats that are otherwise healthy and active may have lesions for many months and even years. Systemic spread is uncommon.

Lesions caused by *M smegmatus*, and less commonly *M fortuitum*, are different from lesions caused by other atypical mycobacteria. Infection with *M smegmatus* usually begins in the underlying fat and causes granulomatous panniculitis. Skin lesions that emanate from the subcutaneous fat appear as multiple, punctate, reddened depressions about 1-5 mm in diameter.[10] Serosanguineous fluid exudes from the central portions of the lesions. These multiple punctate sinuses resemble a salt-shaker top. Skin surrounding the fistulating lesions is thickened, often devoid of hair, and covered with a clear to grayish mucinous exudate.

Pathologic Features

Lesions of atypical mycobacteriosis are characterized by clusters of neutrophils and macrophages surrounded by lymphocytes and plasma cells. This type of pyogranulomatous inflammation is typical of both mycotic and mycobacterial infections in

Fig 3. *Mycobacterium fortuitum* infection in the dorsal flank area of a cat. The infection has dissected beneath the skin and broken out at numerous sites. (Courtesy of Dr. Peter Ihrke, University of California, Davis)

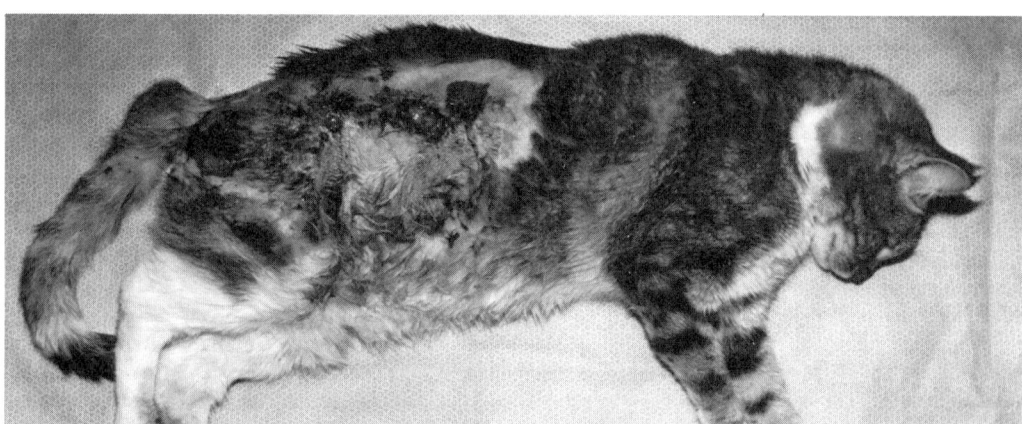

cats. Organisms are found, often with some difficulty, within histiocytes using acid-fast stain.[2,7] Organisms in *M smegmatus* infections are often limited to fat vacuoles and the surrounding cellular response is almost devoid of organisms.[10]

Clinicopathologic Features

The disease is diagnosed by demonstration of acid-fast organisms on biopsies or culture of mycobacteria from the lesions. Care must be taken in selecting biopsy and culture sites. Wound surfaces and the exudate are often contaminated with such resident flora as staphylococci, streptococci, *Pasteurella* spp and *E coli*. Therefore, it is important to culture material from deep within the lesion. Likewise, biopsies should be deep enough to include a full thickness of skin and some subcutaneous tissue. Biopsies should not be taken of the edges of fistulating wounds because they are likely to show only chronic inflammatory changes.

Most atypical mycobacteria grow rapidly at 37 C on a number of nonmycobacterial media, such as blood-agar plates. However, *M xenopi* grows optimally at 44 C. Though *M thermoresistible* grows optimally at 37 C, it also grows at temperatures as high as 52 C.[8] Cultures should be performed even if smears of exudate or tissue do not show acid-fast organisms.

Infection and Immunity

Apparently, some cats have great difficulty in mounting an effective immune response to atypical mycobacteria. However, there is no evidence of any acquired or congenital immune deficiency in affected individuals. Underlying feline leukemia virus (FeLV) infections have been absent.[27] Several cats with atypical mycobacteriosis have had underlying FIV infections.

Mycobacterium smegmatus evokes a different host response than other atypical mycobacteria. The organism is found almost exclusively in fat vacuoles in the center of the pyogranulomatous lesions in subcutaneous fat. Surrounding histiocytes are virtually devoid of organisms. Wilkinson suggested that the surrounding mononuclear-cell reaction might be in response to infected fat vacuoles (and not to organisms *per se*), and that as long as the organisms persisted in fat, they were protected against host immunity.[10]

Treatment and Prevention

In-vitro antibiotic susceptibilities should be determined for all isolates whenever possible. Once sensitivities are available, a combination of several drugs is usually recommended. *Mycobacterium xenopi* is often sensitive to a combination of isoniazid, rifampin and streptomycin. *Mycobacterium fortuitum-cheloni* is usually susceptible to high dosages of amikacin combined with doxycycline, erythromycin, cefoxitin, or a sulfonamide. Despite appropriate susceptibilit, test indications, antibiotic treatment may still be ineffective.[2,7] In such cases, resection is the only option, even if it must be repeated several times. Antibiotic treatment, even coupled with surgery, is apt to fail in *M smegmatus* infections.

Norfloxacin, a newly marketed fluorinated 4-quinolone, has activity against a wide range of bacteria, including some atypical mycobacteria. The therapeutic dosage in dogs is 10-20 mg/kg PO q12h. A similar dosage should be used for cats.

Conservative treatment may be preferable to repeated excision.[2,7] Even though lesions persist in some cases, the disease is of little other consequence and cats sometimes live for many years with only minimal discomfort.[2]

Animal and Public Health Considerations

There is no evidence for cat-to-cat or cat-to-person transmission of atypical mycobacteriosis.

References

1. Dewevre PJ *et al*: *Mycobacterium fortuitum* infection in a cat. *JAAHA* 13:68-70, 1977.

2. Kunkle G *et al*: Rapidly growing mycobacteria as a cause of cutaneous granulomas: report of five cases. *JAAHA* 19:513-521, 1983.

3. Suter MM et al: Atypisches mykobakterielles Hautgranulom bei einer Katze in der Schweiz. *Zentralbl Veterinärmed A* 31:712-718, 1984.

4. Thorel MF and Boisvert H: Abcès du chat à *Mycobacterium cheloni*. *Bltn Acad Vét* 47:415-422, 1974.

5. Toma B et al: La tuberculose féline et son danger pour l'homme. *Comp Immunol Microbiol Infect Dis* 1:185-192, 1979.

6. Tomasovic AA et al: *Mycobacterium xenopi* in a skin lesion of a cat. *Aust Vet J* 52:103, 1976.

7. White SD et al: Cutaneous atypical mycobacteriosis in cats. *JAVMA* 182:1218-1222, 1983.

8. Willemse T et al: *Mycobacterium thermoresistible* extrapulmonary infection in a cat. *J Clin Microbiol* 21:854-856, 1985.

9. Wilkinson GT et al: Cutaneous granulomas associated with *Mycobacterium fortuitum* infection in a cat. *J Small Anim Pract* 19:357-362, 1978.

10. Wilkinson GT et al: Pyogranulomatous panniculitis in cats due to *Mycobacterium smegmatus*. *Aust Vet J* 58:77-78, 1982.

Chapter 34

Actinomycosis

Etiologic Agent

Actinomyces spp are Gram-positive, aerobic to microaerophilic, coccobacillary bacteria.[5] They often form filamentous structures in tissues. The exudate from infected foci frequently contains "sulfur granules," concretions of organisms and host proteinaceous material. Various species of *Actinomyces* live in the oral cavities and alimentary tracts of animals including cats.[5] Actinomycosis occurs worldwide.

Though there are numerous descriptions of actinomycosis in cats, the exact species of organism involved has seldom been determined. Species that have been identified in cats include *A viscosus*, *A cati*, *Streptothrix canis* and *Streptomyces griseus*.[1,3,11,13]

Pathogenesis

Actinomycosis of cats occurs in 2 basic forms: pyogenic processes (subcutaneous abscesses, pyothorax) and pyogranulomatous processes.[5] Mycetomas are occasionally associated with *Actinomyces* spp. Lesions of *Actinomyces* spp characteristically occur in 1 of 5 areas: cutaneous and subcutaneous; pleural and/or pulmonary; peritoneal and/or serosal; CNS; and bone.[10] Central nervous system involvement is rare in cats.

Prévot and associates identified *Actinomyces* spp in only about 5% of suppurative processes in cats.[12] This is somewhat different than the pattern in dogs, in which isolations of *Actinomyces* spp are common.

Suppurative processes in cats are more likely to be associated with *Pasteurella multocida*, *Bacteroides* spp, *Fusobacterium* spp, streptococci, staphylococci, *E coli*, spirochetes, *Klebsiella* spp, *Proteus* spp, *Enterobacter* spp or *Corynebacterium* spp.[15] The main reservoir for *Actinomyces* spp in cats is the mouth. Subcutaneous abscesses almost always can be traced to a bite from another cat. Disease in the oral cavity, lungs or pleural cavity is usually caused by invasion of tissues by organisms that normally inhabit the oral cavity.

Clinical Features

Suppurative processes of cats generally involve the subcutaneous tissues (abscesses) or the pleural cavity (pyothorax). Actinomycotic granulomas, sometimes associated with peritonitis, are occasionally seen in the abdominal cavity.[9] The pus from such processes is fetid and grayish-green to blood-tinged, and contains numerous sulfur-like granules. Subcutaneous abscesses are usually found on the head, distal limbs or tail, and are almost always associated with cat bites. Though pyothorax in cats may occasionally be associated with bites, it is usually due to pleural extension of underlying pneumonia.

Pyogranulomatous lesions associated with *Actinomyces* spp have been described in a number of cats. Unlike abscesses, these lesions are more encapsulated and may contain some pus or pus-like material in the center. Granulomatous involvement of the lungs, bone, peritoneal cavity and subcutaneous tissue has been described.[2,6,7,11] Pyogranulomatous periodontitis with periorbital involvement has been reported by Chastain and associates.[4] An actinomycotic abscess has also been seen in the mandible.[7] A nodular actinomycotic lesion has been recognized in the oropharynx near the tonsillar crypt in a cat.[8] An interesting spinal syndrome due to *Actinomyces* spp has been described in 2 cats.[1,14] The disease in both cats started with a bite-induced abscess over the tailhead. The initial abscess in 1 cat appeared to heal; in the other cat, a slowly evolving fistulous infection persisted at the site. The infection penetrated into the epidural space and caused caudal paresis several weeks later.

Pathologic Features

Actinomyces spp are associated with lesions that are frankly purulent (abscesses), pyogranulomatous or granulomatous (mycetomas). "Sulfur granules," 0.2-0.5 mm in diameter, are a characteristic feature of actinomycotic exudates.[5] The central portions of the granules stain eosinophilic with hematoxylin and eosin stain, while the peripheral portions stain basophilic. Gram-positive, interwoven, branching filaments occupy the central portion. In the peripheral portion, individual filaments radiate outward toward the periphery of the granule.

Clinicopathologic Features

Actinomycosis is usually diagnosed by examination of exudates or biopsy material. Organisms are found mainly in the diphtheroid form in exudates and in the filamentous form in granules. Various *Actinomyces* spp can be isolated with some difficulty on blood agar under aerobic conditions at 37 C. Incubation in 5% CO_2 usually promotes growth.

Treatment and Prevention

Actinomyces spp are susceptible to a number of antibiotics. However, the drug of choice is usually penicillin.[5] Alternative antibiotics include tetracycline, erythromycin, cephalosporins, lincomycin and clindamycin. However, infections often recur if treated with antibiotics alone because adequate antibiotic penetration is difficult to achieve. When possible, antibiotic treatment should be maintained for 4-5 weeks or more and combined with excision and/or drainage.

Animal and Public Health Considerations

Cats with actinomycosis are not a health hazard to other animals or people.

References

1. Bestetti G et al: Paraplegia due to *Actinomyces viscosus* infection in a cat. *Acta Neuropathol* 39:231-235, 1977.

2. Brion A: L'actinomycose du chien et du chat. *Rev Méd Vét* 91:121-158, 1939.

3. Cedervall Von A: Uber steptothrikose bei karnivoren. *Nord Vet Med* 6:159-172, 1954.

4. Chastain CB et al: Actinomycotic periodontitis in a cat. *JAAHA* 13:65-67, 1977.

5. Hardie EM, in Greene CE: *Clinical Microbiology and Infectious Diseases of the Dog and Cat*. Saunders, Philadelphia, 1984. pp 663-674.

6. Hutyra F et al, in Greig JR: *Special Pathology and Therapeutics of the Diseases of Domestic Animals*. 4th Engl ed. Vol I. Baillière, Tindall and Cox, London, 1938. pp 703-704.

7. Libke KG and Walton AM: Actinomycosis-like infection in the mandible of a cat. *Mod Vet Pract* 55:201-202, 1974.

8. Lotspeich M: Actinomycosis in a cat. *VM/SAC* 69:571, 1974.

9. Martin HM: Actinomycosis in the dog and cat. *Univ Penn Bltn Vet Ext* 87:15-19, 1942.

10. McGaughey CA: Actinomycosis in carnivores: a review of the literature. *Brit Vet J* 108:89-92, 1952.

11. Poenaru ID: Les mycetomes actinomycosiques chez le chat. *Archiva Vet* 29:1-4, 1937.

12. Prévot AR et al: Le syndrome "actinomycose" des carnivores. *Inst Pasteur Ann* 101:771-792, 1961.

13. Reinke SI et al: Actinomycotic mycetoma in a cat. *JAVMA* 189:446-448, 1986.

14. Stowater JL et al: Actinomycosis in the spinal canal of a cat. *Feline Pract* 8(1):26-27, 1978.

15. Suter PF and Zinkl JG, in Ettinger SJ: *Textbook of Veterinary Internal Medicine*. Saunders, Philadelphia, 1983. pp 840-883.

Chapter 35

Miscellaneous Bacterial Infections

SERRATIA INFECTION

Serratia marcescens is a Gram-negative rod considered largely nonpathogenic. It exists in a number of serotypes based on differences in O and H antigens. Though generally considered nonpathogenic, it can cause septicemic disease under certain circumstances. Most infections with this organism in people and animals are nosocomial (hospital acquired).[6,8]

Two incidences of *S marcescens* infection have been reported in cats. The first case was a 1-year-old castrated cat that developed suppurative peritonitis and hepatitis following extensive automobile-induced trauma and hospitalization.[1] In the second case, *S marcescens* was isolated from 50% of all contaminated intravenous catheters from dogs and cats in a large veterinary hospital.[2] The source of the bacteria was contaminated benzalkonium chloride-impregnated swabs used to prepare the catheter sites. Most of the animals were hospitalized due to trauma, usually from automobiles. The most common site of isolation was from the point of catheter insertion, though the organism was also recovered from the respiratory tract, skin, genitourinary tract, wounds, abscesses, CSF and abdominal drains of 81 clinically ill dogs and cats. One cat had an infected intravenous catheter and *S marcescens* was isolated from the liver at death. The numerous sites from which the organism was recovered in this large outbreak among dogs and cats indicates that *S marcescens* has a great tendency to become systemic in compromised hosts.

Serratia marcescens can become quite resistant to antibiotics, a characteristic common to many nosocomial organisms. Hospital isolates were consistently susceptible only to kanamycin and gentamicin.[6] Chloramphenicol and nalidixic acid were also frequently effective.

RHODOCOCCUS INFECTION

Rhodococcus equi, formerly *Corynebacterium equi*, is a major cause of pneumonia in foals. The organism exists in nature in a number of different serotypes. It is a Gram-positive pleomorphic rod that grows both aerobically (under conditions of 5% CO_2) and anaerobically. It is considered an opportunist in animals other than horses, which are its probable host. It has been isolated from several people with acquired immunodeficiency syndrome (AIDS).

Two reports of *R equi* infection in cats have been published. A 4-year-old male Siamese cat had a subcutaneous abscess on the foreleg and regional lymphadenopathy.[3] The abscess contained a caseous exudate, typical of abscesses caused by this organism in horses. The cat responded well to surgical drainage of the abscess and erythromycin therapy for 15 days. The isolate was resistant to penicillin and tetracycline and had a type-6 capsular antigen. The second animal was a 5-month-old female domestic cat that had a history of slow growth and unthriftiness.[4] A 4-cm mass was palpable in the abdomen, the prescapular lymph nodes were slightly enlarged, and harsh lung sounds and an intermittent cough were present. A cranial mediastinal mass and pleural fluid were seen on thoracic radiographs. Thoracentesis yielded a cellular exudate containing many mature and immature lymphocytes. The cat was feline leukemia virus (FeLV) negative. A tentative diagnosis of lymphosarcoma was made and the cat was euthanized. The mesenteric and mediastinal masses were granulomatous rather than neoplastic in nature and originated from lymph nodes. *Rhodococcus equi* was isolated from the mediastinal mass and small, coccoid, Gram-positive rods were visualized in tissue sections.

MORAXELLA INFECTION

Moraxella lacunata is a cause of conjunctivitis in people. It is related to *M bovis*, the causative agent of pinkeye in cattle. This group of organisms appears to have a predilection for the conjunctival sac. They are Gram-negative coccobacilli.

Moraxella lacunata was responsible for an outbreak of conjunctivitis in a cattery containing 23 adults and 30 kittens.[7] The infection ran its course in about 9 weeks. Individual animals were sick for 10-30 days. Isolates from this outbreak were sensitive to tetracycline but not penicillin. The source of the infection was not determined, though a worker in the cattery had suffered from conjunctivitis 2 weeks earlier.

FLAVOBACTERIUM INFECTION

Flavobacterium meningosepticum is a rare cause of neonatal septicemia and meningitis in children. A similar organism was isolated from the CSF of a 9-month-old castrated cat that had a sudden onset of fever, hyperesthesia, incoordination, partial blindness, and depressed photomotor and righting reflexes.[5] The CSF contained many polymorphonuclear neutrophils and small Gram-negative bacilli singly and in pairs. The cat recovered after chloramphenicol treatment.

References

1. Armstrong PJ: Systemic *Serratia marcescens* infections in a dog and cat. *JAVMA* 184:1154-1157, 1984.

2. Fox JG et al: Nosocomial transmission of *Serratia marcescens* in a veterinary hospital due to contamination of benzalkonium chloride. *J Clin Microbiol* 14:157-160, 1981.

3. Higgins R and Paradis M: Abscess caused by *Corynebacterium equi* in a cat. *Vet Record* 21:63-64, 1980.

4. Jang SS et al: A cat with *Corynebacterium equi* lymphadenitis clinically simulating lymphosarcoma. *Cornell Vet* 65:232-239, 1975.

5. Sims MA: *Flavobacterium meningosepticum*: A probable cause of meningitis in a cat. *Vet Record* 95:567-569, 1974.

6. Wilkowske CJ et al: *Serratia marcescens*. Biochemical characteristics, antibiotic susceptibility patterns, and clinical significance. *JAVMA* 214:2157-2162, 1970.

7. Withers AR and Davies ME: An outbreak of conjunctivitis in a cattery caused by *Moraxella lacunatus*. *Vet Record* 73:856-867, 1961.

8. Yu VL: *Serratia marcescens*: Historical perspectives and clinical review. *New Engl J Med* 300:887-893, 1979.

Chapter 36

Unclassified Bacterial Infections

EF-4 INFECTION

Etiologic Agent

Eugonic fermenter-4 (EF-4) is a Gram-negative pleomorphic bacillus occurring singly, in pairs and in short chains.[3] Group EF-4 bacteria are similar to *Pasteurella multocida* in ecologic distribution and pathogenic potential. The group is composed of 2 biovars differing in their ability to produce a dihydrolase for arginine. The 2 biovars may represent 2 species, though polyacrylamide gel electrophoresis of cell proteins indicates they are very closely related.[6]

EF-4 bacteria are apparently normal saprophytes in the oral cavity of dogs and cats.[1] They are worldwide in distribution and have been isolated in the United States.[1-7]

Pathogenesis

EF-4 bacteria are associated with infected dog- or cat-bite wounds in people, and a peculiar necrotizing pneumonia of domestic and wild cats.[1-6] The mode of entry for the infection in cats is unknown. The presence of the organism as a normal inhabitant of the oral cavity indicates that pulmonary disease occurs as an opportunistic infection.

Clinical Features

Cats with EF-4 pneumonia have generally been mature animals 1-9 years of age.[3,5] The 1 young affected animal reported in the literature was a 5-month-old tiger cub.[4] Affected cats generally have acute depression, dehydration, dyspnea and fever. Auscultation of the chest frequently reveals harsh, dry rales. Thoracic radiographs demonstrate characteristic discrete focal densities

Fig 1. Typical appearance of pulmonary lesions caused by EF-4 infection. The whitish nodules are subpleural and associated with necrosis, edema, hemorrhage and inflammation. (Courtesy of Spencer Jang, University of California, Davis)

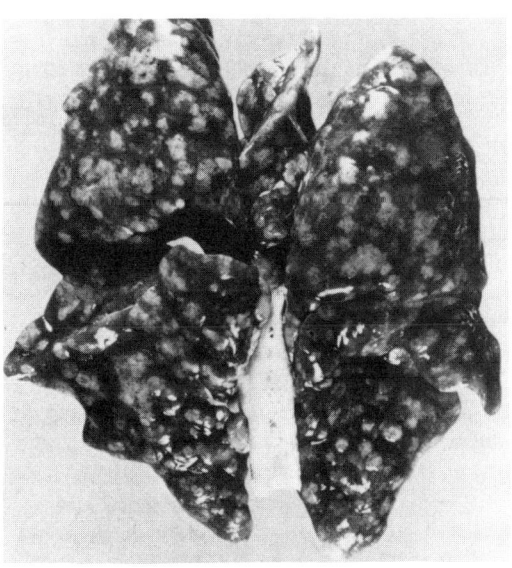

throughout the lungs. The disease course is very rapid and mortality is extremely high.

Pathologic Features

Gross lesions are usually limited to the respiratory tract. The trachea often contains a small amount of frothy, blood-tinged exudate and numerous firm, white to tan nodules 0.3-1.0 cm in diameter scattered throughout the lung parenchyma (Fig 1).[3] The nodules are pink, fleshy and moist on cross-section. Fibrinous pleural adhesions can be seen between lung lobes. Petechial hemorrhages are often seen on the pleural surfaces and the bronchial lymph nodes are usually enlarged and reddened.

Histopathologic lesions consist of numerous pulmonary nodules concentrated in subpleural locations. Discrete nodules are 0.2-0.4 mm in diameter, but often coalesce to form larger lesions up to 1.0 cm in diameter. Pulmonary nodules involve several lobules; alveoli within involved lobules contain mononuclear and polymorphonuclear inflammatory cells. Numerous bacterial colonies can be observed within the lesions. Inflammatory lesions are associated with fibrin deposition in alveoli, necrosis of alveolar walls, edema, congestion and hemorrhage. Reticuloendothelial hyperplasia is usually prominent in the spleen.

Clinicopathologic Features

Leukopenia has been a feature of the disease and is usually associated with a toxic or degenerative left shift. In at least 1 cat, a rare bacterium was present within granulocytes in the blood.[3]

Tests for feline leukemia virus (FeLV) were not conducted on cats reported in the literature. Two cats with EF-4 pneumonia seen since the original report of the disease by Jang and co-workers have both been FeLV positive. Hemograms were reported from 2 cats by Jang and co-workers.[3] In 1 of these hemograms, 2% of cells observed could not be classified. The other cat was anemic and had almost a total lack of WBCs. These changes suggest that these 2 animals may also have been FeLV-infected. The presence of feline immunodeficiency virus (FIV) infection should also be determined.

EF-4 necrotizing pneumonia is usually diagnosed by culture of lung tissue or tracheal exudate. The organism grows readily on blood agar plates and Brewer's thioglycollate broth incubated at 37 C with 5% CO_2. Growth also occurs under anaerobic conditions. Unlike most classified Gram-negative bacteria, EF-4 bacteria fail to use a large number of different sugars, except for glucose.[3] EF-4 isolates also fail to yield a positive Voges-Proskauer test.[7]

Treatment and Prevention

To date, no cat has survived more than a few days after diagnosis in spite of vigorous antibiotic therapy. Failure of treatment is due in part to the acute, widespread and severe nature of the pulmonary disease. Cats are also at an advanced stage of disease when clinical signs are seen. The role of underlying immunosuppression and its possible effect on treatment remains to be determined.

Infection and Immunity

Available evidence suggests that EF-4 infections in cats are opportunistic. Feline leukemia virus infection appears to play an important role in some cases. Whether or not all cases have underlying and predisposing causes remains to be determined.

Animal and Public Health Considerations

The organism is ubiquitous in the mouths of healthy cats and dogs. Disease in cats is very uncommon and appears to involve factors that lower natural host resistance.

EF-4 bacteria have been implicated in suppurative infections in people as a result of dog or cat bites.[1,2,7] However, such infections are uncommon as compared to those caused by *Pasteurella multocida*. Infected cats are probably not much more contagious than healthy animals. Nevertheless, every bite wound should receive prompt attention.

References

1. Bailie WE et al: Aerobic bacteria flora of oral and nasal fluids of canines with reference to bacteria associated with bites. *J Clin Microbiol* 7:223-231, 1978.

2. Goldstein EJC et al: Bacteriology of human and animal bite wounds. *J Clin Microbiol* 8:677-672, 1978.

3. Jang SS et al: Focal necrotizing pneumonia in cats associated with a Gram-negative eugonic fermenting bacterium. *Cornell Vet* 63:446-454, 1973.

4. Lloyd J and Allen JG: The isolation of group EF-4 bacteria from a case of granulomatous pneumonia in a tiger cub. *Aust Vet J* 56:399-400, 1980.

5. McFarland PJ et al: Pathological changes associated with group EF-4 bacteria in the lungs of a dog and cat. *Vet Record* 111:336-338, 1982.

6. Peel MM and Holmes B: Isolation of Group EF-4 bacteria in Australia. *Aust New Zeal J Med* 10:435-437, 1980.

7. Tatum HW et al, in Lennette EH et al: *Manual of Clinical Microbiology*. 2nd ed. Am Soc Microbiol, Washington DC, 1974. p 270.

Chapter 37

Cat Scratch Disease

Etiologic Agent

Cat scratch disease is a condition of people rather than of cats. Cats are implicated in most cases of the disease, and veterinarians are often called upon to advise clients on the disorder. The causative agent of cat scratch disease is an unculturable small Gram-negative bacillus.[8] The organism is identifiable in tissues by the Warthin-Starry silver or immunoperoxidase stains.[6] It is often observed within capillary walls in involved regional lymph nodes and, on occasion, in tissues at the primary inoculation site.[5,8]

About 90% of human infections result from a scratch, lick or bite from a cat, usually a kitten.[6,7] The disease has been observed less commonly following dog bites, or from puncture wounds associated with thorns, wood splinters or fish bones. Epidemiologic studies indicate that cats may be mechanical vectors and not hosts of the organism for the following reasons: cats implicated as the source of human infection fail to react to cat scratch antigen when skin-tested; involved cats appear to only transmit the causative agent for a brief period, usually 2-3 weeks; and attempts to isolate the causative agent from cat saliva or claws have been unsuccessful.[6]

Pathogenesis

Cat scratch disease occurs throughout the world, more commonly in children than adults, and more frequently in males than females.[6,7] Most cases occur in fall and winter in cooler climates, while seasonal variation is minimal in the tropics. About 2000 cases are reported annually in the United States but the true incidence is unknown. Positive skin tests for the infection are seen in 12-29% of veterinarians and <5% of healthy people in other occupations, indicating that subclinical or mild infections are common.

The organism can apparently enter the body through broken skin or by mucous membrane contact. About 90% of patients have primary skin infections, 7% have primary conjunctival infections, and 2% have primary infections of other mucous membranes.[6,7]

The disease begins at the site of initial contact.[6,7] The earliest skin lesion is a single small papule or pustule, or a number of erythematous macules. Conjunctivitis is common in individuals exposed by the conjunctival route, while small mucosal granulomas are associated with primary infection of the mucous membranes. Infection spreads via lymphatics to the regional lymph nodes. However, lymphangitis is not a feature of the disease. Regional lymphadenitis occurs 3-50 days after exposure.[6,7]

Cat scratch disease is usually limited to the site of infection and the regional lymph node(s). Systemic spread has been observed in <5% of individuals.[6,7] Systemic manifestations occur from involvement of the CNS, lungs and bone.[2,6]

Clinical Features

Most patients are not seen until regional lymphadenopathy becomes prominent. An erythematous papular or pustular lesion at the site of infection is detectable in 54-96% of affected people after careful examination.[6,7] Fever, malaise and influenza-like symptoms lasting 1-3 weeks are seen at onset of lymphodenopathy in <50% of affected individuals. More widespread skin disorders, characterized by maculopapules, petechiae, erythema nodosum or erythema multiforme exanthema, are associated with the disease in <5% of patients. Splenomegaly is detected in about 16% of affected people.[6]

The involved lymph nodes are usually in the axilla, neck or groin, variably tender on palpation and 1-8 cm in diameter. Lymph node enlargement usually persists for 2-4 months and rarely for up to 2 years. Suppuration, detected by needle aspiration, occurs later in the course of the disease in 13% of patients.[6] Spontaneous rupture and drainage of a suppurative node occurs in <6% of patients.

In people with primary conjunctival lesions, infection often spreads to the lymph nodes of the head and neck and results in a condition called the oculoglandular syndrome of Parinaud. The parotid area is often swollen due to periauricular lymph node enlargement.[1]

When CNS involvement occurs, it appears within 1-6 weeks of the adenopathy. The encephalitic form of the disease may be manifested (in order of frequency) by coma, convulsions, encephalopathy, meningitis, radiculitis, polyneuritis, myelitis with paraplegia, and lethargy and/or confusion.[6] Neurologic manifestations progress over 1-2 weeks and then gradually resolve over the next 1-6 months. Atypical pneumonia and localized osteomyelitis are uncommon systemic manifestations of the disease.[2,6] Osteomyelitis can result from hematogenous spread or extension from adjacent affected lymph nodes.[2]

Pathologic Features

Characteristic lesions of cat scratch disease are seen mainly in affected lymph nodes. The earliest lesion is characterized by reticular-cell hyperplasia, followed by necrotizing granulomatous changes sometimes associated with giant cells. Multiple microabscesses appear in the nodes later in the course of disease, only to be replaced by frank abscess formation. Differential diagnoses in the latter stages include tularemia, brucellosis, tuberculosis or sarcoidosis.[6] Hodgkins' disease is the main differential diagnosis in the earlier stages of infection.[3] Cat scratch disease has also mimicked malignant lymphoma in some individuals.[4]

Clinicopathologic Features

Cat scratch disease should be strongly considered in any child or adolescent with persistent localized lymphadenopathy lasting longer than 3 weeks.[6,7] The diagnosis is strengthened by the presence of dermal or conjunctival lesions and history of exposure to a cat within the previous 2 weeks. The diagnosis is less readily made in patients with atypical forms of the disease.

Diagnosis of cat scratch disease is usually confirmed when 3 of the following 4 findings are present: history of contact with an animal, usually a cat, and presence of a primary dermal or eye lesion; aspiration of sterile pus from an involved lymph node or laboratory tests that exclude other causes of adenopathy; a positive delayed-hypersensitivity reaction in the skin to cat scratch antigen; and a node biopsy revealing characteristic histopathologic changes, especially if organisms can be identified with Warthin-Starry silver stain.[6]

The cat scratch skin test is positive in about 90% of affected individuals, providing that the duration of illness has been at least 3-4 weeks. The antigen for the test is made from pus collected from patients. A positive reaction consists of a wheal or papule occurring 48-72 hours after intradermal inoculation.

There is no known way to identify whether a cat is harboring the causative agent. Cats invariably react negatively to cat scratch antigen, and the causative agent has not been identified in saliva or on the claws of potentially infectious cats.

Treatment and Prevention

The course of cat scratch disease is usually benign and the disease spontaneously resolves within 2-3 months. The disease does not usually respond to antibiotic therapy. Aspiration of pus from suppurated nodes may be necessary to relieve pain and discomfort.

Infection and Immunity

Cat scratch disease is typical of a number of bacterial and fungal infections that enter the body through skin abrasions or mucous membranes and spread slowly to regional lymph nodes. Immunity appears to be largely cell mediated, as evidenced by the strong delayed-hypersensitivity reactions evoked in affected individuals. This immunologic responsiveness remains strong for many years following recovery.[6]

Animal and Public Health Considerations

Though cat scratch disease can be reproduced with pus in people, monkeys, baboons and the Hartley strain of guinea pigs, there is no evidence of natural person-to-person transmission. There is also no evidence that cats are clinically infected with a similar organism.

Veterinarians are often called upon to pass judgment on cats associated with human exposure. This is probably best left to people who are considered experts in the disease. Margileth reports that cats only appear to transmit the organism for 2- to 3-week periods or less.[6] If this is the case, implicated cats can be loosely quarantined from children and adolescents for 2-3 weeks and then allowed to live a normal life. The disease is also very sporadic, and only an infinitesimally small portion of cat bites, scratches or licks lead to the disease. It has also been noted that 12-29% of veterinarians test positive with the cat scratch antigen, as compared to <5% of other healthy people and family contacts.[6] Therefore, many veterinarians have been unknowingly infected with the organism at some stage in their careers. Given this information, it is wise not to overreact to the disease or condemn the cat.

References

1. Carithers HA: Oculoglandular disease of Parinaud. A manifestation of cat scratch disease. *Am J Dis Child* 132:1195-1200, 1978.

2. Carithers HA: Cat scratch disease associated with an osteolytic lesion. *Am J Dis Child* 137:968-970, 1983.

3. Knight PJ *et al*: When is lymph node biopsy indicated in children with enlarged nodes? *Pediatrics* 69:391-396, 1982.

4. Luddy RE *et al*: Cat scratch disease simulating malignant lymphoma. *Cancer* 50:584-586, 1982.

5. Margileth AM *et al*: Cat scratch disease: Bacteria in skin at the primary inoculation site. *JAMA* 242:928-931, 1984.

6. Margileth AM, in Wyngaarden JB and Smith LJ Jr: *Cecil's Textbook of Medicine*. Saunders, Philadelphia, 1985. pp 1618-1620.

7. Margileth AM: Cat scratch disease - a therapeutic dilemma. *Vet Clin No Am* 17: 71-103, 1987.

8. Wear DJ *et al*: Cat scratch disease: A bacterial infection. *Science* 221:1403-1405, 1983.

Section III

Mycoplasmal, Rickettsial, Chlamydial and L-Form Diseases

Mycoplasmal, rickettsial and chlamydial organisms are more similar to bacteria than to viruses. *Rickettsia* spp and *Chlamydia* spp possess both ribonucleic acid (RNA) and deoxyribonucleic acid (DNA), while *Mycoplasma* spp and bacterial L-forms contain circularized double-stranded DNA. Rickettsial and chlamydial organisms possess many of the enzyme systems needed for a free-living existence but lack essential metabolic processes necessary for energy production. Therefore, they are obligate parasites of living host cells, which provide the energy and metabolites they cannot produce.

Mycoplasma spp belong to the class Mollicutes, family Mycoplasmataceae. They are about 250 nm long, making them intermediate in size between most viruses and bacteria. They lack a rigid cell wall and move with some difficulty using intracytoplasmic appendages. They stain Gram-negative and divide by binary fission. *Mycoplasma* spp live within phagocytic and epithelial cells and in surrounding extracellular spaces.

Rickettsia spp belong to the class Microtatobiotes, families Rickettsiaceae and Anaplasmataceae. Rickettsiaceae contains the genera *Rickettsia, Coxiella, Ehrlichia* and *Neorickettsia*; only *Coxiella* is an important pathogen for cats. Anaplasmataceae contains the genus *Hemobartonella*, the most important pathogen to cats among this group. *Rickettsia* spp vary from 300 to 2000 nm in size and divide by binary fission. They tend to invade and grow within phagocytic mononuclear cells in the blood, spleen, bone marrow and other organs. *Hemobartonella* spp are 100-500 nm in diameter, attach to the surfaces of RBCs and have no intracellular stage of replication.

Chlamydia spp belong to the order Chlamydiales, class Microtatobiotes. The infectious form of the organism, the elementary body, is about 300 nm in diameter and possesses a rigid cell wall. *Chlamydia* spp divide by binary fission and parts of their life cycle occur both within and outside of the host cell. They are generally found as parasites of epithelial cells of the mucous membranes of the conjunctiva, upper respiratory passages and genital tract.

L-forms are cell wall-deficient forms of common bacteria. When cultured under special conditions, L-forms may revert to their parental cell-walled state. In most other aspects, L-forms resemble *Mycoplasma* spp.

Chapter 38

Mycoplasmosis

Etiologic Agent

Mycoplasma and mycoplasma-like organisms belong to 3 groups: *Mycoplasma* spp; *Ureaplasma (T-mycoplasma)* spp; and *Acholeplasma* spp. *Mycoplasma felis* and *M gatea* are the most prevalent mycoplasms in cats.[1,2,11,28] These 2 organisms differ in their ability to cleave egg-yolk lipids, produce ammonia from arginine, reduce methylene blue, and lyse avian and sheep RBCs. They also differ in their sensitivity to neomycin and novobiocin. *Mycoplasma felis* is antigenically distinct from other mammalian *Mycoplasma* spp, while *M gatea* is related to *M arthritidis*, *M salivarium*, *M hominis* (type 1) and *M orale* (types 1 and 2).[8] Minor strains of *Mycoplasma* spp that have been isolated from cats include *M arginini*, *M feliminutum*, *M pulmonis*, *M arthritidis*, and *M gallisepticum*.[8,28,30,32] *Mycoplasma feliminutum* has only been isolated from cats on 1 occasion and probably lives naturally on other species of animals.[11,28] *Mycoplasma arginini* is also a common isolate from wild Felidae and other species of animals.[1,13,29,30] *Mycoplasma pulmonis*, *M arthritidis* and *M gallisepticum* are likewise normal inhabitants of animals other than cats.

Ureaplasma spp can be differentiated from *Mycoplasma* spp by their ability to metabolize urea to produce ammonia. They can be isolated from the oral and genital tracts of many normal cats.[10,27,30] Feline *Ureaplasma* spp are unrelated to human strains.[10]

The major strain of *Acholeplasma* isolated from cats is *A laidlawii*. It is found in many species of animals, including poultry, cattle and swine.[27]

Mycoplasma spp, *Ureaplasma* spp (*T-mycoplasma* spp) and *Acholeplasma* spp are all commonly isolated from domestic cats. Tan and Miles isolated *M felis*, *M gatea* and *M arginini* from 4.2%, 62.2% and 6.7% of normal cats, respectively.[29] Among 149 isolations of *Mycoplasma* spp from 90 healthy cats by Heyward and associates, 29 were *M felis*, 118 *M gatea* and 1 *M feliminutum*.[11] Likewise, cultures from the conjunctival sacs of 120 normal cats by Campbell and associates yielded 12 isolates of *Mycoplasma* spp, 7 of which were *M felis*.[3] *Ureaplasma* spp have been isolated from the oral cavity, vagina and prepuce in 25 of 36 normal cats.[10] *Acholeplasma* spp isolations from normal domestic cats vary greatly with the environment. Rural cats have a higher incidence than urban cats because of their more frequent contact with other domestic animal species that carry the organism. Tan and Miles isolated *A laidlawii* from 22.2% of normal cats.[29] In an earlier study, these researchers made 45 isolates of *Mycoplasma* spp from 32 normal cats, 10 of which were *A laidlawii*.[27]

Pathogenesis

The pathogenicity of mycoplasmal strains varies greatly in the cat. *M felis* has been isolated 7-8 times more frequently from cats with respiratory disorders than from normal animals. *Mycoplasma arginini* was isolated at about the same rate in sick and normal animals.[29] The lack of pathogenicity of *M arginini* for cats was reconfirmed by subsequent studies of Tan and co-workers.[25] Likewise, *A laidlawii* appears to be nonpathogenic for cats and probably exists as a saprophyte in many species of animals.[29] Tan and co-workers isolated *M gatea* more often from normal than sick cats and assumed it was nonpathogenic.[25] However, *M gatea* has been isolated from an older animal with widespread arthritis and tenosynovitis. This appeared to have been an opportunistic infection in an immunocompromised animal.[18]

Mycoplasmal infections are probably acquired at a relatively young age. Many older animals harbor the organisms in the mucous linings of the conjunctival sac, oropharynx and genital tracts (prepuce and vagina). Infection of kittens may occur at birth or shortly thereafter through exposure to vaginal or oropharyngeal secretions from the queen. If kittens are not infected at birth or within the first few weeks of life, they will almost certainly be exposed to the organisms as they contact carrier animals after weaning.

Following infection, the subsequent course of disease is probably influenced by the animal's immunologic status. Animals most susceptible to disease include fetuses that are not immunologically competent, neonates that have immature immune systems and low levels of specific maternal systemic and local (lactogenic) antibodies, and postweaning kittens that are partially immunologically competent but have lost their maternal immunity. Older cats that have become immunocompromised through some other primary illness may also be at risk.

Clinical Features

Mycoplasma spp and mycoplasma-like organisms are important pathogens in lambs, kids, calves, foals and poults. Infections in these species are initially localized but frequently disseminate hematogenously to the lungs and joints. The disease-causing potential of mycoplasmal organisms in cats appears to be much less. Initial infections remain localized and disseminated disease is uncommon in immunocompetent individuals. Conjunctivitis is the most common clinical manifestation of mycoplasmosis in cats.

Cello was the first to associate *Mycoplasma* spp with conjunctivitis in cats.[3] He showed that *Mycoplasma* spp isolated from naturally diseased animals would not cause conjunctivitis in normal cats but would readily do so in animals that had first received an intrapalpebral inoculation of corticosteroids. Subsequent studies linked *Mycoplasma* spp to conjunctivitis merely because it was isolated more frequently from inflamed eyes than normal eyes.[9,16,26,31] However, those studies did not consider primary infection and co-infection with other agents, such as herpesvirus or *Chlamydia* spp.[2,19] It was not until 1974 that conclusive evidence was obtained for the role of *Mycoplasma* spp in conjunctivitis.[23] These latter experiments involved kittens, which are more sensitive to infection than adults.

Fig 1. Mycoplasmal conjunctivitis in a cat. The conjunctiva is swollen and glistening, and the hair around the lower eyelid is wet from the serous discharge.

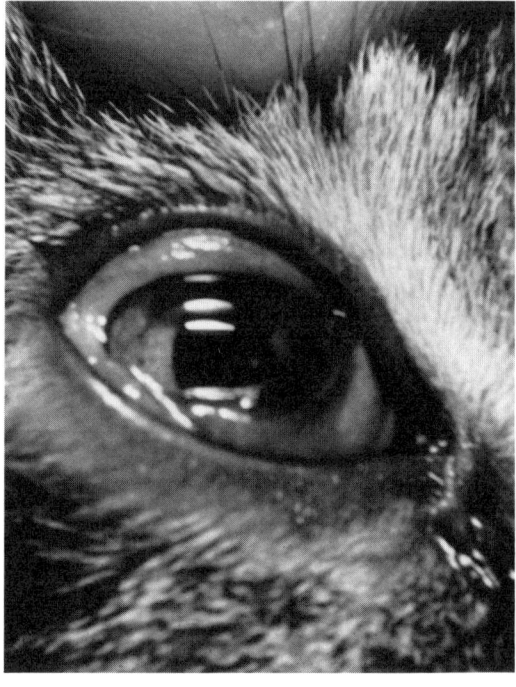

Mycoplasmal conjunctivitis is most frequently caused by *M felis*.[28] It is predominantly a cattery disease and is seldom seen in kittens from single-cat homes. It usually develops shortly after kittens are weaned, around 8-12 weeks of age. The earliest signs are acute swelling and reddening of the conjunctiva in 1 or both eyes (Fig 1). Conjunctivitis may be associated with some squinting and photophobia. Inflammation of the conjunctiva varies greatly; conjunctival membranes may be only slightly reddened or may be so swollen that the globe is barely visible. Early in the disease, the exudate is usually serous but it may become somewhat purulent with time. A diphtheritic or fibrinous coating may sometimes be seen on the inflamed conjunctiva and is highly conducive to formation of conjunctival-corneal adhesions. Sneezing is either mild or not seen and, if present, is more apt to be due to excessive nasolacrimal drainage from the inflamed conjunctiva than from rhinitis. Severe concurrent sneezing and nasal discharge in kittens with unilateral conjunctivitis usually indicate a complicating herpesvirus infection. *Mycoplasma* spp tend to disappear from the conjunctival sac upon recovery but may persist in the oropharynx. Conjunctivitis may recur in older cats, especially following stress or major disease outbreaks among younger animals. Recurrent disease resembles the primary infection but is usually milder and seldom lasts longer than 7-10 days.

Corneal-conjunctival adhesions may be important sequelae in cats with diphtheritic-type inflammation. Secondary infections of the conjunctiva with staphylococci or *Pseudomonas* spp can sometimes occur and, if improperly treated, can lead to corneal ulceration and even perforation.

Mycoplasmal conjunctivitis in cats is often associated with chlamydial conjunctivitis.[6,7] Chlamydial conjunctivitis has virtually the same pathogenesis as mycoplasmal conjunctivitis. Therefore, it is not surprising that *Mycoplasma* spp and *Chlamydia* spp infections often occur together.

Pneumonia is an important systemic complication of localized mycoplasmosis in many species of animals but is surprisingly uncommon in cats. Switzer isolated *Mycoplasma* spp from the lung of a kitten with pneumonia.[22] Tan induced mild pneumonia in only 1 kitten that was experimentally infected with *M felis*.[23] It has been postulated that *Mycoplasma* spp may play a synergistic role with viruses in causing respiratory disease in cats.[20] This was not borne out in studies by Spradbrow and co-workers.[21] They isolated *Mycoplasma* spp commonly from the upper respiratory passages (conjunctival sac, nasal cavity, tonsils) of cats with respiratory disease, but not from lung suspensions. The author observed an outbreak of mycoplasmal pneumonia and conjunctivitis in 6 adult cats that had received an injection of methylprednisolone 2 weeks earlier and in a litter of 4-week-old kittens.

Arthritis and tenosynovitis, though common in other domestic species, are uncommon manifestations of mycoplasmosis in cats. This again indicates the marked resistance that cats have to systemic spread of *Mycoplasma* spp. Moise and co-workers isolated *M gatea* from the synovium of an 8-year-old cat with chronic fibrinopurulent tenosynovitis.[18] This infection appeared to be opportunistic because the cat also had a chronic nasal infection and hypogammaglobulinemia. Though the cat was feline leukemia virus (FeLV) negative, the possibility of some other concurrent virus-induced immunosuppression (feline immunodeficiency virus infection) or nonviral immuno-compromising disease was not established. Mycoplasmal polyarthritis has been observed in a severely immunocompromised cat by Hooper and co-workers.[14] Mycoplasmal polyarthritis has also been observed in 2 aged cats seen at the Veterinary Medical Teaching Hospital, University of California, Davis. Both cats had advanced cancer and were undergoing extensive therapy when arthritis occurred.

Urethritis and cystitis have been associated with *Mycoplasma* spp and *Ureaplasma* spp in people. They have also been isolated infrequently from dogs with cystitis. Though they have been frequently isolated from the distal genital tracts of male and female cats, they have not been associated with disease. They have not been isolated from cats with feline urologic syndrome, a disease that is probably of dietary origin.

Mycoplasma spp have caused fetal death and abortions in people, cattle and sheep. Tan and Miles inoculated 3 pregnant queens intranasally and intravaginally with the T-385 strain of *Ureaplasma*; 1 queen aborted 9 days later and the same organism was isolated from the inflamed uterus.[30] The remaining queens developed a transient fever 12-36 days postinoculation. One of these queens gave birth to normal-sized kittens that died 10 days later and the other queen gave birth to small kittens that died by 17 days of age. The T-385 strain of *Ureaplasma* was isolated from the cardiac blood of the only kitten sampled. Uninfected pregnant control queens did not abort, and produced healthy surviving kittens. Moise and associates caused 1 queen to abort 3 days after experimental infection with *M gatea*.[18] Lindley observed abortion in a queen that succumbed 2 months later from what appeared to be mycoplasmal peritonitis and pleuritis.[17] Given the high incidence of mycoplasmal infection in catteries and the established role of the organism in fetal disease in other species (and possibly cats), further studies of the role of these organisms in feline abortions are needed.

Mycoplasma-like spp was isolated from subcutaneous abscesses in 3 cats.[15] The infections responded to tetracycline. This organism was probably a bacterial L-form and not a true *Mycoplasma*. A definite *Mycoplasma* spp was isolated from a chronic pulmonary abscess in a cat.[33]

Pathologic Features

Mycoplasmal organisms cause purulent and fibrinopurulent inflammatory reactions early in the course of primary or systemic infection. The inflammatory reaction observed in conjunctival membranes of cats with primary conjunctivitis is predominantly neutrophilic with epithelial-cell hyperplasia.[7] The tenosynovitis observed by Moise and associates in immunosuppressed cats with naturally or experimentally induced *M gatea* infection was also fibrinopurulent in nature.[18] Chronic mycoplasmal pneumonia and arthritis in affected species are characterized by chronic fibrinous exudation, fibrosis and a mixed inflammatory infiltrate predominated by lymphocytes and plasma cells.

Clinicopathologic Features

Organisms can be identified in conjunctival scrapings stained with Giemsa or Macchiavello stains. They appear as small coccoid rods within epithelial cells and free in surrounding fluids (Fig 2). Chlamydial inclusion bodies, which are often present in the same smears, appear intracytoplasmically in epithelial cells and are not often found free in surrounding media. Mycoplasmal organisms can be cultured using specific types of agar and broth enriched with equine serum. Identification of *Mycoplasma* spp, *Ureaplasma* spp or *Acholeplasma* spp is by colony size and morphology on agar, susceptibility to various antibiotics, serologic reactions or responses in selective biochemical media.[8,12]

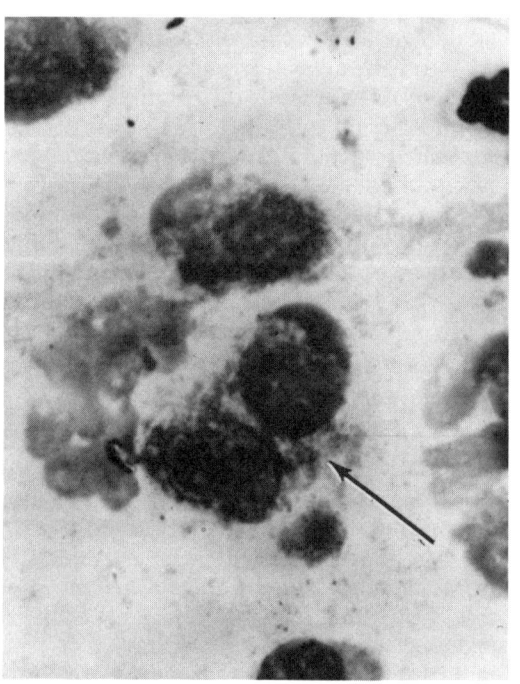

Fig 2. Conjunctival scraping from a kitten with conjunctivitis shows polymorphonuclear neutrophils and predominantly epithelial cells. Numerous small coccoid bodies can be seen within the cytoplasm of an epithelial cell (arrow). Wright's-Giemsa stain, 1400X.

Treatment and Prevention

Mycoplasmal conjunctivitis is treated topically with appropriate nonsteroidal ophthalmic ointments. For best results, medication should be applied QID or more frequently. Tetracycline-type antibiotics are preferred for initial treatment. They are also active against *Chlamydia* spp, which often complicate mycoplasmal conjunctivitis in cats.

Some mycoplasmal isolates are resistant to tetracycline. Erythromycin or spectinomycin should be used in such cases. *Mycoplasma* spp are resistant to penicillins, cephalosporins and aminoglycosides. Systemic antibiotic treatment is not warranted in kittens with localized disease. It only adds to the stress of the condition and may induce intestinal upset. Therapy should be continued for at least 3-5 days after conjunctivitis has completely resolved. Conjunctivitis, especially in kittens, may recur after therapy is discontinued. Therapy must be reinstituted in such cases. If systemic infections are suspected, oral or parenteral tetracyclines are the drugs of choice. However, they can permanently discolor the permanent teeth when given to kittens.

Mycoplasmosis in catteries can be controlled to a great extent with proper design and management. This includes limiting stress and numbers of kittens, and isolating kittens by litters from other young cats.

Infection and Immunity

Cats appear to have a great deal of natural resistance to systemic spread of mycoplasmal infections from primary disease sites in the upper respiratory tract. Therefore, cats are spared from the most serious manifestations of the disease. The reason for this species resistance is not known but it also extends to chlamydial immunity. *Chlamydia* spp and *Mycoplasma* spp are responsible for virtually the same type of localized and systemic diseases in cats and other animals. Therefore, it is not surprising that cats show a similar type of resistance to both organisms. Cello was the first to show the importance of artificially induced stress and local immunity in recreating conjunctivitis in older cats in his classic studies of feline mycoplasmosis.[3] An intrapalpebral inoculation of methylprednisolone rendered the eye susceptible to infection and disease.

Opportunistic mycoplasmal infections have been seen in older immunocompromised cats. They most likely mimic systemic forms of infection, *eg*, arthritis and serosal disease, seen in susceptible species of animals. The author has observed severe mycoplasmal pneumonia and conjunctivitis in 6 adult cats that had received an injection of methylprednisolone 2 weeks earlier.

Animal and Public Health Considerations

Cats with mycoplasmal infections are not considered public health hazards. The main pathogenic *Mycoplasma* species is *M felis*, an inhabitant of cats that has not been identified in other species. Therefore, cats are the principal reservoir for their own infections. Though cats apparently spread the infection to each other, the myriad environmental and host-resistance factors that influence disease are probably more important than actual exposure in determining the clinical outcome of mycoplasmosis.

References

1. Blackmore DK and Hill A: The experimental transmissions of various mycoplasma of feline origin to domestic cats. (*Felis catus*). *J Small Anim Pract* 14:7-13, 1973.

2. Blackmore DK *et al*: The incidence of mycoplasma in pet and colony-maintained cats. *J Small Anim Pract* 12:207-217, 1971.

3. Campbell LH *et al*: *Mycoplasma felis*-associated conjunctivitis in cats. *JAVMA* 163:991-995, 1973.

4. Campbell LH *et al*: Ocular bacteria and mycoplasma of the clinically normal cat. *Feline Pract* 3(6):10-12, 1973.

5. Cello RM: Association of pleuro-pneumonia-like organisms with conjunctivitis of cats. *Am J Ophthalmol* 43:296-297, 1957.

6. Cello RM: Ocular infections in animals with PLT (Bedsonia) group agents. *Am J Ophthalmol* 63 Suppl:1270-1274, 1967.

7. Cello RM: Clues to differential diagnosis of feline respiratory infections. *JAVMA* 158:968-973, 1971.

8. Cole BC et al: Characterization of mycoplasma strains from cats. J Bacteriol 94:1451-1458, 1967.

9. Colegrave AJ et al: Chronic rhinitis in cats. Vet Record 76:67-68, 1964.

10. Harasawa R et al: Isolation of T-mycoplasmas from cats in Japan. Microbiol Immunol 21:179-181, 1971.

11. Heyward JT et al: Characterization of mycoplasma species of feline origin. Am J Vet Res 30:615-622, 1969.

12. Hill A: Further studies on the morphology and isolation of feline mycoplasmas. J Small Anim Pract 12:219-223, 1971.

13. Hill A: Comparison of mycoplasmas isolated from captive wild felines. Res Vet Sci 18:139-143, 1975.

14. Hooper PT et al: Mycoplasma polyarthritis in a cat with probable severe immune deficiency. Aust Vet J 62:352, 1985.

15. Keane DP: Chronic abscesses in cats associated with an organism resembling mycoplasma. Can Vet J 24:289-291, 1983.

16. Laborde G: *Mycoplasmas of the cat: Isolation, identification and discussion of their role in feline respiratory diseases*. Doctoral Thesis, Univ Lyon, 1971.

17. Lindley JW: A case of *Mycoplasma* sp found in cats. Southwest Vet 19:320-321, 1966.

18. Moise NS et al: *Mycoplasma gatea* arthritis and tenosynovitis in cats: Case report and experimental reproduction of the disease. Am J Vet Res 44:16-21, 1983.

19. Povey RC and Wardley RC: *Mycoplasma* species in a cat colony. Vet Record 92:27-28, 1973.

20. Schneck GW: *Mycoplasma* species in association with feline viruses. Vet Res 91:594-595, 1972.

21. Spradbrow PB et al: The isolation of mycoplasmas from cats with respiratory disease. Aust Vet J 46:109-110, 1970.

22. Switzer WP, in Merchant and Packer: *Veterinary Bacteriology and Virology*. 7th ed. Iowa State Univ Press, Ames, 1967. pp 531-548.

23. Tan RJS: Susceptibility of kittens to *Mycoplasma felis* infection. Jpn J Exp Med 44:235-240, 1974.

24. Tan RJS et al: Ecology of mycoplasmas in clinically healthy cats. Aust Vet J 53:515-518, 1977.

25. Tan RJS et al: Significance and pathogenic role of *Mycoplasma arginini* in cat diseases. Can J Comp Med 41:349-354, 1977.

26. Tan RJS and Markham J: Isolation of *Mycoplasma* from cats with conjunctivitis. New Zeal Vet J 19:28, 1973.

27. Tan RJS and Miles JAR: *Mycoplasma* isolations from clinically normal cats. Brit Vet J 128:87-90, 1972.

28. Tan RJS and Miles JAR: Characterizations of mycoplasmas isolated from cats with conjunctivitis. New Zeal Vet J 21:27-32, 1973.

29. Tan RJS and Miles JAR: Incidence and significance of mycoplasmas in sick cats. Res Vet Sci 16:27-34, 1974.

30. Tan RJS and Miles JAR: Possible role of feline T-strain mycoplasmas in cat abortion. Aust Vet J 50:142-145, 1974.

31. Wilkinson GT: *Diseases of the Cat*. Pergamon Press, Oxford, 1966. pp 273-274.

32. Wilkinson GT: Mycoplasmas of the cat. Vet Ann 20:145-150, 1980.

Additional Reference

33. Crisp MS et al. Pulmonary abscess caused by *Mycoplasma* spp in a cat. JAVMA 191:340-342, 1987.

Chapter 39

Q Fever

Etiologic Agent

Q fever is caused by *Coxiella burnetii*, a rickettsial organism of worldwide distribution.[1] Unlike other rickettsiae, it resists desiccation and survives in the environment for long periods.[1] It can be propagated in mice, hamsters, guinea pigs and embryonated chicken eggs.

Coxiella burnetii has 2 different life cycles in nature.[1,2] The first cycle involves domestic livestock, in particular, sheep, goats, cattle, swine, camels and buffalos.[1] It is spread from infected to susceptible livestock in a horizontal fashion. The second cycle involves 39 or more species of Ixodid and Argasid ticks, avian mites, and a number of species of wild mammals and birds.[1] Bandicoots are an important wildlife reservoir in Australia.[1] Wild rodents and birds may act as reservoirs in other regions of the world.[1] In this cycle, the organism is maintained as a vertical infection within arthropods, a horizontal infection from arthropods to wild animals, or as a horizontal infection among the wild animals themselves. The infection in wildlife is usually asymptomatic. Cats are participants in this second life cycle.

Coxiella burnetii has a particular affinity for the placenta. Up to 1×10^{12} organisms may be present in a gram of ovine placental tissues, with lesser numbers in amniotic fluid, milk and feces.[2] The organism contaminates soil, dust, wool, hides, bedding and other similar materials. Infection in the first cycle is associated with inhalation of aerosols containing desiccated organisms. Infection in the second cycle involves tick bites, as well as aerosols.

Cats were shown to be susceptible to experimentally induced *C burnetii* infection by Gillespie and Baker in 1952.[3] The existence of Q fever as a natural infection of cats has only been appreciated in the last few years.[4-7] The clinical importance of the infection to cats appears to be minimal. Rather, cats are an important urban reservoir for the agent in some regions of the world. Marrie and co-workers found that 24.1% of cats from Nova Scotia had antibodies to phase-II and 6% to phase-I antigens.[6] None of the dogs in this area was seropositive, suggesting that cats were exposed to the organism in Nova Scotia in a very specific manner. Randhawa and associates found that 19.8% of pound cats in southern California had antibodies by the capillary agglutination and microhemagglutination tests to *C burnetii*.[8] Wileburg's group found that 9% of the cats in central and northern California had microhemagglutinating antibodies to the organism.[10]

Pathogenesis

Rickettsial infections generally go through 2 basic clinical phases.[9] The early phase follows entrance of the organism into the body and lasts 1-2 weeks or so. The organism replicates briefly at the point of entry and then becomes blood-borne. The organisms then rapidly replicate within endothelial cells of small blood vessels, leading to endothelial cell necrosis, hypertrophy and proliferation. Disease in the early phase is associated with the direct effects of the organism on blood vessels.

The late phase of the infection follows the early phase and lasts for weeks, months or years. A carrier state develops during this phase and clinical signs are usually mild or inapparent. Tissue damage in the late phase is associated with direct damage by the organisms, as well as immunopathologic mechanisms.

Cats inoculated subcutaneously with the organism develop fever, lethargy and anorexia within 48 hours of inoculation.[3] These signs disappear within 3 days without any apparent complications. Cats infected orally or by contact with other infected animals do not develop any clinical signs of disease. The organism can be reisolated from the blood of some cats for up to 1 month following infection and for 2 months or more from the urine. *Coxiella burnetii* has been isolated from the uterus of an asymptomatic cat 8 weeks postpartum, indicating that some cats carry and shed the organism for long periods.[5]

The source of the organism for cats in nature is unknown. Cats may be infected when bitten by rodent ticks or avian mites or from the ingestion of infected small wild mammals and birds.[6] Cat-to-cat transmission has been observed on a single occasion under experimental conditions.[3] Serologic evidence for natural transmission between an infected queen and her kittens has also been reported.[5]

Clinical Features

Most naturally acquired infections in cats are apparently asymptomatic or mild enough to go unnoticed. Gillespie and Baker described a mild self-limiting early-phase disease in cats that were infected subcutaneously but not orally.[3] Fever, depression and anorexia appeared 2 days after infection and persisted for only 3 days. No other clinical signs were observed. Late-phase disease either does not exist in cats or is rare and nondescript. Cats, like many other species of domestic and wild animals, can apparently carry the organisms for prolonged periods while in a state of normal health.

A queen that was naturally infected with *C burnetii* gave birth to 3 kittens, 1 of which died shortly after birth.[5] This indicates that fetal infection can occur, and that it can lead to mortality. Circumstantial evidence supporting the linkage between stillbirths in cats and Q fever also comes from epidemiologic studies of the human disease. People in Nova Scotia that are exposed to parturient cats are at a significantly greater risk of acquiring Q fever than people not exposed to parturient cats; people exposed to stillborn kittens are at still greater risk.[7]

Pathologic Features

Lesions of Q fever have not been described in cats. Pneumonitis, of the viral or psittacosis type, occurs in the early phase of infection in one-half or more of human patients.[2,4,5] This is often accompanied by focal, noncaseating granulomatous hepatitis. Vegetative valvular endocarditis is a major lesion in the late phase of Q fever in people.[2]

Clinicopathologic Features

The organism can be readily isolated by mouse, hamster or guinea pig inoculation with contaminated tissues, urine or blood. *Coxiella burnetii* can be also identified in tissues by direct immunofluorescent antibody (IFA) staining.[5]

Tests for serum antibodies have been widely used in people and animals. About two-thirds of infected people develop complement-fixing antibodies to the phase-II antigen of the organism by the second week of illness, and over 90% by the fourth week.[2] Complement-fixing antibodies to the phase-I antigen usually appear only in individuals that develop late-phase disease. The presence of antibodies to the phase-I antigen indicates persistence of the organism in the body. An indirect IFA test is also widely used for detection of antibodies to phase-I and -II antigens in people.[5]

Complement-fixing antibodies to *C burnetii* can be detected at relatively low titers in cats, starting around 4 weeks postinfection.[3] Antibodies have also been measured in cats by capillary tube agglutination and microhemagglutination tests.[1,10] Phase-I and -II antibodies have been measured in cats by IFA.[5]

Treatment and Prevention

The early phase of Q fever in people is treated with tetracycline for 1-2 weeks.[2] Chloramphenicol is also effective. Relapses are retreated the same as initial attacks. People with late-phase disease are treated for a much longer period. The infection in cats is mild and self-limiting, and would normally not be detected or treated. There is no experience with treatment of chronically infected cats to eliminate the carrier state. One cat with a chronic asymptomatic uterine infection was spayed.[5] This step alone would negate much of the infectivity of the cat for people.

Infection and Immunity

About one-fourth of naturally and experimentally infected cats become chronic carriers of the organism.[3,6] The infection apparently persists in a low-grade and asymptomatic form in the urogenital tract. During pregnancy, the organism localizes in the placenta and multiplies to amazingly high levels. The fetal fluids are rich in organisms; therefore, parturition is the most common factor in human exposure. The predilection of C burnetii for the gravid uterus is reminiscent of Brucella canis infection of dogs and B abortus infection of cattle.

The measurement of antibodies to phase-I and -II antigens is a good indicator of the disease status in people and cats.[2,5] Antibodies to phase-II antigens are a product of the early-phase infection, while antibody production to phase-I antigens requires more chronic stimulation.

Animal and Public Health Considerations

There is good evidence supporting cat-to-cat transmission. One cat in contact with experimentally infected animals became infected over a period of 8 weeks, and an infected queen may have passed the infection to her kittens.[3,5] It is unlikely that this is the sole source of infection in nature, however. Cats are involved with the second, or wildlife, cycle of transmission. This cycle involves ingestion of infected prey species, such as small rodents, as well as bites from arthropod vectors.

Q fever is an important disease of people. It is manifested in the early phase by 1-2 weeks of fever, malaise, muscle soreness, rigors and headache. Pneumonitis may be evident clinically and radiographically. Hepatomegaly and abdominal tenderness are frequent accompanying signs. Myocarditis, pericarditis and abdominal tenderness are rare manifestations of early-phase disease. Late-phase disease occurs in a small proportion of individuals and is usually manifested by vegetative valvular endocarditis and vague constitutional signs.

The principal reservoir of human Q fever has been sheep, goats and cattle. Most human infections are associated, therefore, with environments where farm animals are kept or with products derived from them. For this reason, Q fever has been considered a rural or occupational illness. The cat has emerged as an important urban reservoir for Q fever in Nova Scotia.[4-7] It is doubtful, however, that the organism is only of public health importance in urban centers in maritime Canada. The infection has been also detected in cats in urban areas of the United States.[8,10]

The discovery of cats as a reservoir for human infection in Nova Scotia is of particular interest. Kosatsky and associates were the first to suggest that cats may be a reservoir for human disease in urban Nova Scotia.[4] This was followed by a description of an outbreak of Q fever in a group of people that met frequently to play poker.[5] Twelve of the poker players came down with Q fever 19-30 days following the time of parturition of a household cat that was later found to be a carrier of the organism. Subsequent studies have confirmed the importance of cats as a reservoir for urban Q fever in this area of Canada. Marrie and co-workers found that 20 of 51 people with Q fever had exposure to parturient cats (compared to 6 of 102 matched controls).[7] The risk of people acquiring Q fever was even higher among people exposed to stillborn kittens (11 of 51, vs 0 of 102 matched controls).

References

1. Babudieri B: Q fever: a zoonosis. *Adv Vet Sci* 5:81-181, 1959.

2. Eickhoff TC: Q fever. In: *Textbook of Medicine*. Saunders, Philadelphia, 1985. pp 1686-1687.

3. Gillespie JH and Baker JA: Experimental Q fever in cats. *JAVMA* 13:91-94, 1952.

4. Kosatsky T et al: Household outbreaks of atypical pneumonia attributed to Q fever in Nova Scotia. *Can Dis Weekly Report* 8:169-170, 1982.

5. Langley JM et al: Poker players' pneumonia. An urban outbreak of Q fever following exposure to a parturient cat. *New Engl J Med* 319:354-356, 1988.

6. Marrie TJ et al: Seroepidemiology of Q fever among domestic animals in Nova Scotia. *Am J Publ Health* 75:763-766, 1985.

7. Marrie TJ et al: Exposure to parturient cats is a risk factor for acquisition of Q fever in Maritime Canada. *J Infect Dis* (in press), 1988.

8. Randhawa AS et al: Coxiellosis in pound cats. *Feline Pract* 4(6):37-38, 1974.

9. Weissman CL Jr: Rickettsial diseases. In: *Textbook of Medicine*. Saunders, Philadelphia, 1985. pp 1672-1677.

10. Wileburg P et al: Environmental exposure to *Coxiella burnetii*. Seroepidemiologic survey among domestic animals. *Am J Epidemiol* 111:437-443.

Chapter 40

Hemobartonellosis

Etiologic Agent

Hemobartonella felis is the causative agent of feline infectious anemia. The organism is a Gram-negative rod, coccus or discoid obligate RBC parasite belonging to the family Anaplasmataceae, order Rickettsiales. *Hemobartonella* spp are more closely related to bacteria than to viruses. They contain both ribonucleic acid (RNA) and deoxyribonucleic acid (DNA) and replicate by binary fission.[16,18,25] In some earlier reports, *H felis* was called *Eperythrozoon felis*. However, *Hemobartonella* spp are more tightly attached to the RBC membrane and are less commonly observed in ring forms than *Eperythrozoon* spp.[16]

Hemobartonella felis has never been cultivated in artificial media; its entire existence is intimately associated with RBC surfaces. Organisms are about 0.5 µ in diameter and found partially embedded in the RBC membrane (Fig 1). Discoid organisms with a central depression predominate on scanning electron micrographs.[15,19]

The mode of transmission of *H felis* is poorly understood. Certain cats in any given population appear to be chronic carriers of the organism.[20] Infectivity resides in the cellular component of blood and not in serum or urine.[26] Cat-to-cat transmission can occur by oral or parenteral administration of whole blood.[6,12,26] The natural route of transmission is largely unknown. Transmission via blood-sucking arthropods, such as fleas and ticks, has been postulated but never experimentally proven. However, arthropod transmission is important in related infections of other species.[16] Nash and Bobade observed a significantly higher rate of flea infestation in cats with hemobartonellosis than in uninfected cats.[20] Infection at a very early stage of life has been recognized and suggests *in-utero* or lactogenic transmission.[4,9,10,12] Iatrogenic transmission with transfused blood from healthy donors has been recognized.[8,26]

Pathogenesis

Knowledge of the pathogenesis of hemobartonellosis comes mainly from experi-

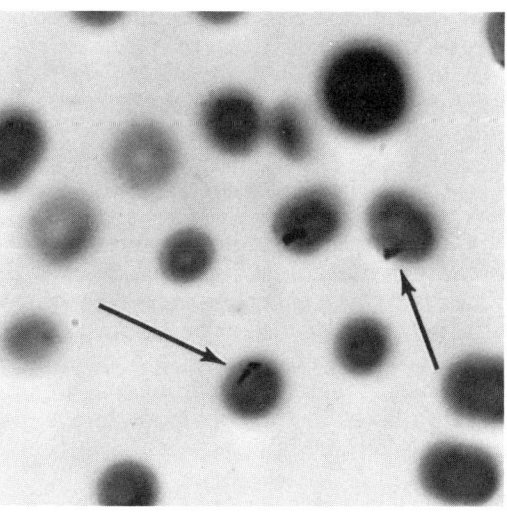

Fig 1. *Hemobartonella felis* bodies (arrows) on the surface of RBC of a cat with hemobartonellosis. They are 0.5-1 µ long and coccoid to rod-shaped, and stained darkly with Wright's-Giemsa stain. The organisms are in focus while the RBC are out of focus because the organisms lie on the RBC surface and indent into it or protrude from it. Wright's-Giemsa stain.

mental studies. *Hemobartonella* bodies appear on peripheral RBCs 2-21 days after parenteral inoculation.[6,8,12,26] Longer prepatent periods of 22-51 days have been observed following oral inoculation.[8] The appearance of organisms on RBCs signals the beginning of the acute phase of disease which often lasts longer than 1 month.[12] This phase is characterized by cyclic waves of RBC parasitism that last 1-4 days, interspersed with brief periods when parasites are absent or sparse. The number of parasitemic episodes in the acute state is 3-9 per animal, with 3-11 days between peaks of parasitemia.[12] Waves of parasitemia are associated with rapid drops in the RBC numbers; relatively parasite-free interludes are associated with equally rapid, but less dramatic rises in the RBC mass. The acute stage is terminated either by death or onset of a more chronic recovery phase.

The chronic recovery phase of the disease is characterized by small numbers of organisms and a slow increase in RBC numbers. From the time of inoculation, 2-4 months are often required for RBC numbers to return to normal.[12] There is very little correlation between waves of parasitism, numbers of parasites, duration in infection, and rate of increase in RBC numbers in the chronic recovery phase.

After RBC numbers return to normal, most infected cats apparently remain chronic carriers for the rest of their lives. Parasites are often difficult to find, though periods of minor parasitism are sometimes observed.[12] The reservoir within the body for this organism in carrier cats in unknown. However, organisms have been observed within splenic and pulmonary macrophages.[17]

Clinical Features

Clinical hemobartonellosis increases in incidence with age and peaks at 4-8 years.[14,20] Male cats were more frequently affected than females in one study and at about the same frequency in another.[7,20] Hemobartonellosis is much more common in cats allowed to roam outdoors than in individuals kept mainly in doors.

Hemobartonellosis occurs in 2 clinical forms: primary (uncomplicated) and secondary. Primary hemobartonellosis occurs in cats with no other diseases and can be clinically inapparent or apparent. Inapparent primary infections are usually detected when healthy cats are blood tested for other reasons.[31] Such cats usually are not anemic, even though as many as 10% of their RBC may be parasitized.[31]

Clinically apparent primary hemobartonellosis accounts for less than half of the total cases. Affected cats show fever, anorexia, depression, weight loss and anemia of several days or weeks duration. Hepatosplenomegaly and generalized lymphadenopathy may or may not be noticeable; jaundice is absent or mild. Parasites usually are evident in RBCs, a careful search of the smear or mutiple blood sampling may be required in some cases. If untreated, more than a third of them will die.[25] Recovered animals become chronic carriers. Chronic carriers may have recurrent bouts of disease over periods of months or years. Organisms may become more difficult to detech at each subsequent attack. Because the anemia of hemobartonellosis is Coombs' positive, initial or recurrent attacks with small numbers of parasites may be mistaken for autoimmune hemolytic anemia.

Secondary hemobartonellosis accounts for most clinical cases. Secondar disease occurs in carriers that have developed unrelated diseases that interfere that interfere with established *Hemobartonella* immunity. Diseases that act as immunodepressants are of 2 types: retroviral infections and miscellaneous nonviral diseases. Feline leukemia virus (FeLV) is the best defined retroviral potentiator of hemobartonellosis. Nash and Bobade detected FeLV in half of cats with hemobartonellosis.[20] Feline immunodeficiency virus (FIV), a more recently discovered retrovirus, may be nearly as important as FeLV in the disease. In addition to retroviruses, various miscellaneous disorders have been associated with hemobartonellosis. Flint and Moss observed a high incidence of chronic and poorly healing abscesses in cats with hemobartonellosis.[6] Bobade and associates diagnosed hemobartonellosis in FeLV-negative cats with a wide range of disease, such as chronic diarrhea, colonic impaction, pancreatitis and hepatitis, oral infections, membranous glomerulopathies, polyarthritis and non-FeLV-associated cancers.[31] A number of these predisposing disorders are themselves FeLV- or FIV-related diseases, so studies reported before these viruses were recognized should not be overinterpreted.

Cats with secondary hemobartonellosis usually are much sicker than cats with the primary disease.[31] In addition to signs related to the overlying disease, these cats usually are moderately to severely anemic. Their anemia is also much more refractory to treatment and the mortality higher.[31]

Pathologic Features

Cats with underlying FeLV-related diseases develop a mixture of pathologic changes, most of which are typical for myeloproliferative disease, aplastic anemia or various dyshematopoietic disorders. The gross pathologic findings in cats with primary hemobartonellosis are minimal and usually referable to anemia.[5] The spleen is often enlarged due to reticuloendothelial and lymphoid hyperplasia. Hepatomegaly is also prominent in many affected cats and is due to increased reticuloendothelial activity and hypoxic changes assoiacted with profound and chronic anemia. Cats with severe and rapidly progressive anemia often have enlarged hearts and small amounts of pericardial fluid. Erythrophagocytosis by mononuclear cells is commonly seen in the spleen, liver and bone marrow, and occasionally in the peripheral blood. Gretillat described lung changes in some cats with chronic hemobartonellosis consisting of patchy atelectasis, thickening of alveolar walls, and accumulations of macrophages in and around the alveoli.[9] Schwartzman and Besch also observed focal areas of chronic pneumonia in a cat.[24]

Clinicopathologic Features

The anemia of hemobartonellosis varies greatly, depending on the nature of the infection. Cats with concurrent hemobartonellosis and FeLV infection usually have macrocytic hypochromic anemia.[31] The anemia in cats with overlying non-FeLV-related disease is generally milder than that associated with FeLV infection, and is often normocytic normochromic.[31] Nucleated RBC in the blood, in the abscence of reticulocytes, indicate underlying myeloproliferative disease. Some cats with hemobartonellosis may be frankly leukemic with abnormal cells in the blood. The relationship between occult overt or preleukemias has been well recognized.[22] The relationship between hemobartonellosis and myeloproliferative disorders is not direct; both FeLV and FIV infections often underlie both hemobartonellosis and myeloproliferative disease, and are the probable cause of the malignancies.

The PCV usually falls below 20% before clinical signs become apparent.[23] By this time, about 50% of the animals have large numbers of parasitized RBCs in the circulation.[12] By repeated daily observations over a 5-day period, oragnisms can often be identified in most affected individuals. The rise and fall in parasite numbers in the blood can be very abrupt. Harvey and Gaskin observed heavy parasitemia at 1 sampling and no organisms a few hours later.[12]

Hemobartonella spp bodies are easily visualized with Romanowky or new methylene blue stains.[25] Living organisms can be stained with brilliant cresyl blue. Immunofluorescent antibody and acridine orange stains have also been used to identify the organism in blood smears.[25] Such stains require use of a fluorescent microscope and are unsuitable for general use in practice. The organisms are less than one-tenth the diameter of RBCs and appear as cocci on thick blood smears or dis- to rod-shaped organisms on thin blood smears (Fig 1).[12] They must be differentiated from normal RBC inclusions or chromatin remnants in reticulocytes.[21] ELISA for *Hemobartonella felis* have recently been developed.[27]

The relative accuracy of various staining procedures in detecting *Hemobartonella* has been reported.[27] Of 57 cats tested, 15 were identified as positive by acridine orange staining; only 5 of those 15 were positive on Giemsa staining. However, Giemsa staining detected 1 positive not identified by acridine orange staining. Therefore, it may be important to use several stains on a blood sample.[20]

In addition to being parasitized, RBCs from cats with active hemobartonellosis often have positive Coombs's tests. Experimental studies show that positive Coombs' tests occur about 15 days after parasites appear on the cell surface.[18] The appearance of immunoglobulin on RBC membranes was found to coincide with RBC phagocytosis by blood mononuclear cells. Peripheral RBCs became more sensitive to osmotic lysis at the same time. This increased osmotic fragility persisted through the course of experimental disease whether or not parasites were present on RBC surfaces. Positive Coombs' tests and increased fragility of RBCs in cats with active hemobartonellosis are reminiscent of the same reactions seen in cats with autoimmune hemolytic anemia (AIHA). Indeed, differentiation between recurrent bouts of hemobartonellosis and AIHA is sometimes very difficult, especially if organisms are present in very small numbers.[11]

Treatment and Prevention

Tetracycline at 25 mg/kg PO TID for 3 weeks is the accepted treatment for the disease. Prednisolone at 1-2 mg/kg PO daily for the first 7-14 days is often used as adjunct therapy for cats with severe anemia. The rationale for corticosteroid treatment is the same as in AIHA: to decrease erythrophagocytosis of antibody-coated RBCs and diminish autoantibody production. Combination tetracycline-corticosteroid treatment is often used empirically because of uncertainties about the autoimmune or infectious basis of the anemia.

Tetracycline is rickettsiostatic but not rickettsicidal. Similar to anaplasmosis of cattle, a disease caused by related organism, drug therapy works by damping the primary clinical phase of the infection while allowing development of premunitional immunity. Cats continue to carry the organism following treatment; though the animal may appear normal, organisms may appear at times in the blood.[30] Drug therapy is likely to fail in anemic cats with predisposing immunosuppressive conditions. It is important, therefore, to determine at the onset whether the *Hemobartonella* infection is primary or secondary.

The usefulness of chloramphenicol and arsenicals for treatment of hemobartonellosis remains unresolved. Such arsenicals as neoarsphenamine and oxophenarsine are toxic to many cats and are either difficult to obtain or no longer marketed.[7] Though they are effective in experimental and natural disease, they do not appear to be as effective as tetracycline.[7,8] Thiacetarsamide (Caparsolate:CEVA), given IV at 0.05-0.1 ml/lb on days 1 and 3, has been used by many practitioners to treat "tetracycline-refractory" infections. This type of arsenical is less toxic, but its efficacy has never been determined in a controlled manner. Chloramphenicol PO at 25 mg/kg BID for 21 days is an effective treatment. However, it appears to be somewhat less effective than tetracycline. For these reasons, arsenicals and chloramphenicol should be used mainly to treat cats that appear refractory to tetracycline.

Some French and Nigerian strains of *Hemobartonella felis* have reportedly been resistant to oxytetracycline.[9] Among various antibacterials tested, only a combination of spiramycin, metronidazole and chloramphenicol proved effective. Chlorpromazine, at 4-7 mg/kg IM on day 1 and 2-3 mg/kg PO daily for days 2-9, has also been effective in treating antibiotic-resistant strains. The mechanism of action of chlorpromazine for antibiotic-resistant strains is unknown, but possible modes of action have been discussed.[9,30] Blood transfusions are necessary in cats with rapid decreases in the PCV $\leq 15\%$. Iron-deficiency anemia has been observed in kittens with hemobartonellosis. Whether this was a cause or effect of the illness was not determined.[4] These kittens seemed to benefit by iron therapy; a possible therapeutic benefit of iron was also described by Wilkinson.[29]

Infection and Immunity

Immunity to *Hemobartonella felis* is relatively primitive. After initial infection, the spleen becomes more active in entrapping parasitized RBCs, cleansing organisms from cell surfaces and returning cells to the circulation. This explains why RBCs are sequestered during periods of heavy parasitism subsides.[12,19] The increased osmotic fragility of RBCs after infection is also explained by this splenic cleansing action. The process of removing parasites from the RBC surfaces, and the parasitism itself, appear to damage RBC membranes enough to alter fragility.[19] Antibody binding to RBC membranes may also contribute to increased fragility.

Immunity to hemobartonellosis evolves slowly, taking 3-4 weeks or more to develop. The period of developing immunity corresponds to the acute phase of the illness described by Harvey and Gaskin.[12] With development of effective "red cell-cleansing immunity," parasitism becomes less intimately associated with RBC destruction and the PCV slowly returns to normal. This stage of immunity corresponds to the chronic phase of the disease, which lasts 1-3 months.[12] By the time RBC numbers return to normal, immunity is strong enough to contain the infection but not eliminate it. Recovered animals are immune by premunition as long as they remain chronic carriers of the organism.

Though the spleen appears intimately associated with immunity to hemobartonellosis, the role of splenectomy on disease severity has been uncertain. Flint and coworkers reported that splenectomy did not alter the course of experimentally induced hemobartonellosis in adult cats.[8] This is not surprising, considering what is known about a related infection, anaplasmosis of cattle. Calfhood resistance to anaplasmosis of can be abolished by splenectomy, while splenectomy in adult animals has little effect. As in anaplasmosis, hemobartonellosis is more severe in older cats than kittens.[14,20] If anaplasmosis and hemobartonellosis are similar in other aspects, then splenectomy in mature cats would not greatly alter severity of *Hemobartonella* infection. Maede found that *Hemobartonella* organisms were less effectively removed by adult splenectomized cats; parasitemia lasted twice as long as in nonsplenectomized animals.[17] Splenectomy performed after cats had recovered from the disease caused transient reappearance of organisms in the blood but no significant decrease in RBC numbers.[8,13,26]

The relationship between FeLV infection and hemobartonellosis is also unclear. Most FeLV-infected cats with visible RBC parasitism appear to have anemia more related to FeLV infection than to *Hemobartonella* infection. Other studies indicate that the anemias of FeLV and *Hemobartonella* infections are synergistic.[31,32]

Studies on drug-induced immunosuppression related to *Hemobartonella* infections have been conducted. Recrudescence of parasitemia in healthy carrier cats can not be induced by treatment with cyclophosphamide or 6-mercaptopurine, or with experimentally induced abscesses. However, corticosteroid treatment rapidly activates the infection.[13]

Animal and Public Health Considerations

The infectivity of carrier animals for other cats has not been studied by controlled contact exposure. However, available evidence suggests that infection cannot be readily transferred by casual contact. *Hemobartonella felis* does not appear to be infectious to other species of animals or people.[8]

References

1. Balazs T *et al*: Feline haemobartonellosis - a case report. *Can J Comp Med* 25:220-222, 1961.

2. Clark R: *Eperythrozoon felis* in a cat. *J So Afr Vet Assn* 13:15, 1942.

3. Cotter SM *et al*: Association of feline leukemia virus with lymphosarcoma and other disorders in the cat. *JAVMA* 166:449-454, 1975.

4. Fisher EW *et al*: Anaemia in a litter of Siamese kittens. *J Small Anim Pract* 24:215-219, 1983.

5. Flint JC and McKelvie DH: Feline infectious anemia-diagnosis and treatment. *Proc Ann Mtg Am Vet Med Assn* 92:240-242, 1955.

6. Flint JC and Moss JC: Infectious anemia in cats. *JAVMA* 122:45-48, 1953.

7. Flint JC et al: Feline infectious anemia. I. Clinical aspects. *Am J Vet Res* 19:164-168, 1958.

8. Flint JC et al: Feline infectious anemia. II. Experimental cases. *Am J Vet Res* 20:33-40, 1959.

9. Cretillat S: Feline haemobartonellosis. *Feline Pract* 14(6):22-27, 1984.

10. Harbutt PR: A clinical appraisal of feline infectious anemia and its transmission under natural conditions. *Aust Vet J* 39:402-404, 1963.

11. Harvey JW, in Greene CE: *Clinical Microbiology and Infectious Diseases of the Dog and Cat.* Saunders, Philadelphia, 1984. pp 576-587.

12. Harvey JW and Gaskin JM: Experimental feline haemobartonellosis. *JAAHA* 13:28-38, 1977.

13. Harvey JW and Gaskin JM: Feline haemobartonellosis: attempts to induce relapses of clinical disease in chronically infected cats. *JAAHA* 14:453-456, 1978.

14. Hayes HM and Priester WA: Feline infectious anemia: risk by age, sex, and breed, prior disease, seasonal occurrence, mortality. *J Samll Anim Pract* 14:797-804, 1973.

15. Jain NC and Keeton KS: Scanning electron microscopic features of *Haemobartonella felis*. *Am J Vet Res* 34:697-700, 1973.

16. Kreier JP and Ristic M: The biology of hemotrophic bacteria. *Ann Rev Microbiol* 35:325-338, 1981.

17. Maede Y: Sequestration and phagocytosis of *Haemobartonella felis* in the spleen. *Am J Vet Res* 40:691-695, 1979.

18. Maede Y and Hata R: Studies on feline haemobartonellosis. II. The mechanism of anemia produced by infection with *Haemobartonella felis*. *Jpn J Vet Sci* 37:49-54, 1975.

19. Maede Y and Sonoda M: Studies on feline haemobartonellosis. III. Scanning electron microscopy of *Haemobartonella felis*. *Jpn J Vet Sci* 37:209-211, 1975.

20. Nash AS and Bobade PA: *Haemobartonella felis* infection in cats from the Glasgow area. *Vet Record* 119:373-375, 1986.

21. Norsworthy GD: Diagnosis of feline infectious anemia. *Feline Pract* 6(2):26-32, 1976.

22. Priester WA and Hayes HM: Feline leukemia after feline infectious anemia. *J Natl Cancer Inst* 51:289-291, 1973.

23. Schalm OW et al: *Veterinary Hematology.* Lea & Febiger, Philadelphia, 1975.

24. Schwartzman RM and Besch ED: Feline infectious anemia. *Vet Med* 53:494-500, 1958.

25. Small E and Ristic M: Haemobartonellosis. *Vet Clin No Am* 1:225-230, 1971.

26. Splitter EJ et al: Feline infectious anemia. *Vet Med* 51:17-22, 1956.

27. Turner CMR et al: Unreliable diagnosis of *Haemobartonella felis*. *Vet Record* 119:534-535, 1986.

28. Wilkinson GT: Feline infectious anaemia: A case in a cat and its successful treatment. *Vet Record* 75:324-325, 1963.

29. Wilkinson GT: Two further clinical cases of feline infectious anaemia. *Vet Record* 77:453-454, 1965.

Additional References

30. Blum JJ: Effect of chlorpromazine on active transport of amino acids of tetrahymena. *J Protozool* 27:498-502, 1980.

31. Bobade PA et al: Feline hemobartonellosis: clinical, haemotological and pathological studies in natural infections and the relationship to infection with feline leukaemia virus. *Vet Record* 122:32-36, 1988.

32. Kociba GJ et al: Enhanced susceptibility to feline leukemia virus in cats with *Hemobartonella felis* infection. *Leukaemia Rev Intl* 1:88-89, 1983.

Chapter 41

Chlamydiosis

Etiologic Agent

Chlamydia psittaci is an obligate intracellular organism more closely related to bacteria than to viruses. *Chlamydia* spp contain deoxyribonucleic acid (DNA) and ribonucleic acid (RNA), divide by binary fission, and possess bacterial-type ribosomes and cell walls. Similar to bacteria, they are inhibited by antibiotics. Unlike bacteria, however, they lack the enzymes necessary to generate adenosine triphosphate and must depend on the host cell for energy.

All strains of *C psittaci* possess a genus-specific cell-wall lipopolysaccharide antigen. Fukushi and associates identified at least 4 different avian and mammalian serovars of *C psittaci* based on their reaction ro 11 monoclonal antibodies.[22] Therefore, *C psittaci* of cats is not identical to *C psittaci* of psittacine birds, which also causes ornithosis in people. Some descriptions of the feline agent use the nomenclature *C psittaci* var *felis* to make this distinction. Feline strains of *C psittaci* may also differ from nonfeline strains in amino acid requirements.[1,9]

Chlamydia psittaci of cats is primarily an inhabitant of mucosal cells of the conjunctiva and genital tract. It mainly causes conjunctivitis. Yet, unclassified *Chlamydia* spp inhabit the gastric mucosa of many normal cats.[7] Though the gastric organism causes mild upper respiratory disease and gastritis in highly immunocompromised cats, its role in feline chlamydiosis has not been determined.[6] In all likelihood, organisms in the stomach are the same as those in the conjunctiva and genital tract.

Chlamydia psittaci has been associated with disease in cats in Canada, Australia, England, Iran and the United States.[3,9,13,16,17,21] It is enzootic in most cattery populations and is widespread among groups of free-roaming domestic and feral cats.[3,16,18,21]

Some asymptomatic cats carry *Chlamydia* spp in epithelial cells in the conjunctiva, gastrointestinal tract and distal genital tract. Carrier cats shed low levels of organisms in secretions and feces, but shedding may increase in situations of heavy stress.[21] Transmission is horizontal from clinical or subclinical carriers to susceptible animals and occurs at birth or in the postweaning period when maternal immunity has waned.

Pathogenesis

Chlamydia spp attach to cell membranes of target mucosal cells and move into these cells by endocytosis. When the organism enters the cell, it is called an elementary body. Elementary bodies are about 300 nm in diameter but transform in the cellular phagosome to larger reticulate bodies that are 800-1000 nm in diameter. The reticulate body divides rapidly by binary fission and forms a large inclusion body that can occupy most of the cytoplasmic space. Reticulate bodies within the inclusion body rapidly condense to form elementary bodies that are released by the cell into the extracellular fluids. The elementary bodies infect adjacent mucosal cells and the cycle continues until suppressed by host immunity.

Clinical Features

There has been a tremendous amount of confusion on the types of disease syndromes caused by *C psittaci* in cats. The organism was first isolated by Baker from cats with so-called "pneumonitis," a moderate to severe respiratory tract disease.[2] This was done before the role of viruses in respiratory tract infections of cats was appreciated. After this, all upper respiratory diseases of cats were assumed to be caused by *Chlamydia*. With the discovery of respiratory viruses in cats and the recognition that *C psittaci* caused mainly conjunctivitis under experimental conditions, chlamydial infections in cats were considered far less important.[4] This is unfortunate because chlamydiosis is still a troublesome, though not highly fatal, infection of cats kept in high-density, high-stress cattery environments.

Chlamydia psittaci has been associated with 2 major and several minor syndromes of cats. The 2 major syndromes include ophthalmitis neonatorum (neonatal conjuncti-

Fig 2. Typical chlamydial conjunctivitis in an 8-week-old kitten. The conjunctivitis is usually unilateral in the early stages, with pronounced epiphora and conjunctival swelling.

vitis) in newborn kittens and conjunctivitis of 6- to 12-week-old postweaning kittens. Minor syndromes include fatal neonatal pneumonia, abortion, stillbirths and possibly infertility. All of these syndromes have similarities to human chlamydial disease.

Neonatal conjunctivitis tends to affect entire litters of kittens, and may be particularly troublesome and recurrent in certain queens. Infection is thought to be caused by retrograde passage of vaginally carried organisms up the nasolacrimal ducts during parturition. Conjunctivitis initially occurs behind the closed eyelids and is generally exudative in nature. The first noticeable sign is a delay in the opening of the eyelids at the normal age of 7-10 days (Fig 1). Bulging of the eyelids is sometimes associated with accumulation of honey-colored crusty exudate along the closed lid margins. When the eyelids are forced open, a copious amount of whitish to grayish mucoid material exudes. The underlying conjunctivitis is noticeable when the exudate is carefully cleaned away. Failure to open the eyelids and drain the exudate can result in corneal ulcers, some of which perforate. Aside from the ocular problems, kit-

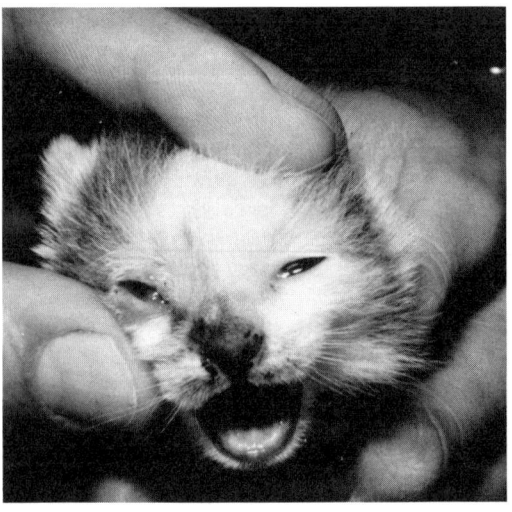

Fig 1. Kitten with ophthalmitis neonatorum. The first signs are failure of the eyes to open at the normal time, bulging of the closed eyelids, and a honey-colored exudate along the lid margins. If the eyelids are forced open, a typical mucinous, cloudy exudate is evident behind the eyelids. The underlying conjunctivitis is apparent when the exudate is wiped away.

tens appear normal and grow at a normal rate. Conjunctivitis persists for as long as 2-4 weeks in untreated animals.

Conjunctivitis in 6- to 12-week-old kittens is the most common clinical manifestation of chlamydial infection in cats.[3,8] This form of the disease has been experimentally recreated on several occasions.[4,8,14] Conjunctivitis appears 5-10 days after aerosol exposure.[8] A low-grade fever appears between days 11 and 15 and lasts for 3-8 days. Fever is less likely to be observed in animals with naturally occurring disease and kittens continue to eat and grow at a normal or near normal rate. Conjunctivitis in both natural and experimentally induced cases is often unilateral in the initial stages (Fig 2). Conjunctivitis can involve both eyes, though it tends to remain more severe in 1 eye. Rhinitis is mild or inapparent, and sneezing is infrequent. The course of the primary disease is 2-6 weeks in kittens and 2 weeks or less in older cats.

Chronic chlamydial conjunctivitis sometimes occurs in cats with abnormal ocular conformation. One adult Persian with severe facial foreshortening, exophthalmia, lagophthalmos and chronic epiphora from poor nasolacrimal duct drainage had associated bacterial and chlamydial infections (Fig 3).

Recurrent bouts of conjunctivitis, often precipitated by apparent or inapparent stresses, can be seen in older cats. Recurrent disease is due to reactivation of subclinical infections or reinfection of cats with waning immunity. Recurrent attacks of conjunctivitis are similar to the primary episode but are seldom as severe or long lasting (5-15 days).

Chlamydia spp are frequently associated with severe and sometimes fatal pneumonia in young livestock species, and systemic spread from the respiratory tract to joints is common. Systemic disorders, such as pneumonia or polyarthritis, are infrequent in cats. Disease in cats tends to remain localized and probably reflects kittens' ability to mount a better immune response to the organism. Occasionally, however, systemic forms of chlamydiosis are seen. Shewen and co-workers isolated *Chlamydia* spp from the lungs of 3 kittens from a litter of 6 that died in the first few days of life.[13] The lungs appeared grossly consolidated. This condition would be analogous to chlamydial neonatal pneumonitis of human infants. These authors also commented on the high incidence of abortion associated with outbreaks of chlamydial infection in a cattery. Abortion is a sequela of chlamydial infection in people and several livestock species. However, the role of *Chlamydia* in abortions in cats is not known. Infertility presumably associated with chlamydial infection was reported by Johnson.[9] Again, the role of chlamydial infection in infertility of queens is unknown. *Chlamydia* spp are a major cause of Fallopian tube inflammation and infertility in women.

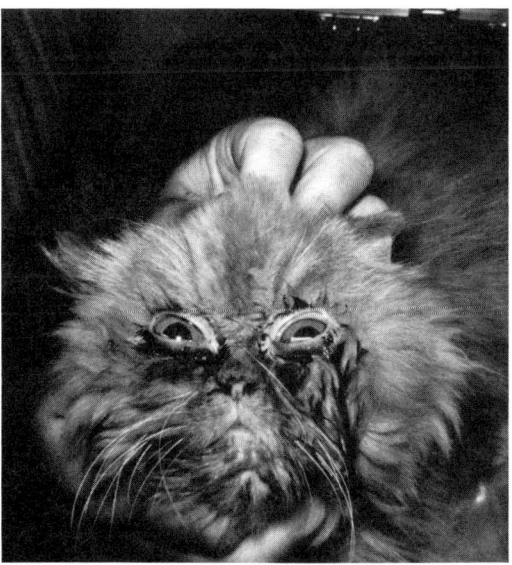

Fig 3. Adult Persian cat with long-standing bilateral conjunctivitis. *Chlamydia psittaci* was seen in conjunctival scrapings. The conjunctivitis cleared with use of tetracycline ophthalmic ointment. However, reinfection is common after therapy is discontinued. Cats with compressed faces may be predisposed to chronic bacterial, mycoplasmal and chlamydial infections because of the relative dryness of their central cornea (lagophthalmos) and excessive tear spillage from abnormal lacrimal apparatus anatomy.

Pathologic Features

Conjunctival lesions consist of epithelial degeneration, desquamation and reactive hyperplasia with subepithelial neutrophilic inflammation. Subsequently, however, the inflammatory reaction contains progressively more macrophages, lymphocytes and plasma cells. Reactive hyperplasia of conjunctival epithelium becomes even more pronounced. Prominent lymphoid nodules are apparent late in the disease, before recovery.

Lung lesions following experimental aerosol exposure consist mainly of mild and diffuse increases in free alveolar macrophages.[8] In some cats, small foci of pneumonia are also grossly apparent. Lesions involve distal peribronchiolar tissues and are characterized by thickening of the interstitium with macrophages, neutrophils, lymphocytes and plasma cells. Hyperplasia of type-II pneumocytes and intraalveolar infiltration of macrophages and neutrophils with inflammation of overlying pleura are also seen in areas of gross involvement. Nasal lesions are microscopic and characterized by intramucosal neutrophil infiltration, with no involvement of overlying mucociliary epithelium.[8]

Clinicopathologic Features

Conjunctivitis that usually starts in 1 eye is presumptive evidence for chlamydial infection, especially if it occurs in weanling or older cats. The main differential diagnosis is mycoplasmal conjunctivitis, which may be almost identical. In fact, chlamydial and mycoplasmal diseases are often concurrent.[4] Older cats with acute unilateral conjunctivitis should be examined closely for conjunctival foreign bodies, which may cause similar signs.

Definitive diagnosis of chlamydial infections is by identification of the organism in epithelial cells or by isolation. Conjunctival scrapings can be stained by conventional or immunofluorescence techniques, the latter being more sensitive. The organism is easily identifiable with Giemsa or Macchiavello stain (Fig 4).[4] Elementary bodies or larger inclusion bodies are prevalent in conjunctival epithelial cells early in the course of disease but become more difficult to identify with time. Direct or indirect fluorescent-antibody staining using *C psittaci* antibody is more sensitive in these later stages, though sometimes even this test can be negative. *Chlamydia psittaci* can also be

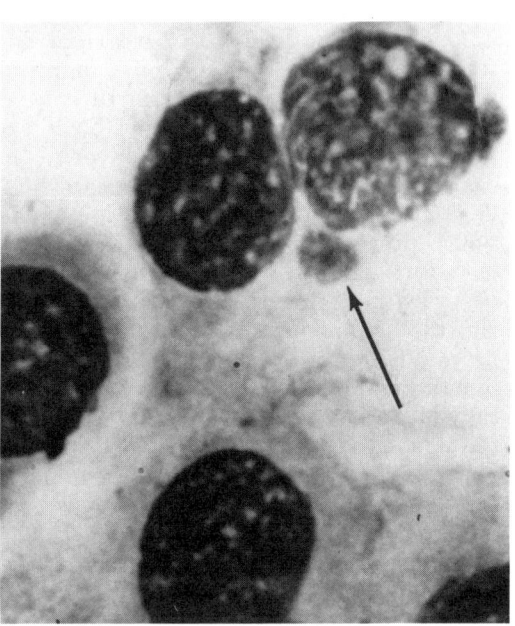

Fig 4. Conjunctival scraping from a kitten with conjunctivitis shows typical chlamydial inclusion bodies in an epithelial cell (arrow). Wright's-Giemsa stain, 1500X.

isolated and cultivated *in vitro*. This procedure previously required yolk-sac inoculation of embryonated chicken eggs, which is expensive and time consuming. The organism can now be isolated in tissue culture using McCoy cells, though attention must be paid to the special amino acid requirements of feline strains.[1,9,18] Wills and coworkers compared antigen-capture ELISA to cell-culture isolation.[19] Antigen detection by ELISA of conjunctival swabs was as accurate as cell-culture isolation for up to 41 days after exposure. However, ELISA was less sensitive than cell culture at 47-76 days postexposure.

Treatment and Prevention

Tetracycline is the drug of choice for treatment of cats with *C psittaci* infection. Cats with chlamydial conjunctivitis should be treated with topical tetracycline ophthalmic ointment TID or more frequently for 2 or more weeks. Response is prompt but recurrences are frequent when medication is prematurely withdrawn. Tetracycline and related bacteriostatic antibiotics inhibit growth of the organism, but ultimate recovery depends on development of host immunity, a process that can take as long as 6 weeks. Withdrawal of medication before immunity is established allows for regrowth of the organism and disease recrudescence. Drug hypersensitivity to a number of ophthalmic preparations is common in cats and is indicated by a worsening of the condition while on drug treatment, especially if it follows an initial response. Use of corticosteroid ophthalmic preparations should be avoided because they can actually delay recovery and predispose the eye to secondary bacterial infection, corneal ulceration and, occasionally, loss of the globe.

Systemic therapy is questionable in cats with localized disease. Systemic tetracycline can cause discoloration of erupting permanent teeth in kittens. Systemic therapy with such drugs can also predispose to drug fevers, inappetence and GI upsets. Such potential side effects are not compensated for by therapeutic benefit. Infection is very superficial; higher drug levels are achieved at infected cells with topical treatment rather than systemic treatment. However, systemic treatment might be beneficial in cases of infertility associated with persistent genital infections.[9]

Several vaccines are available for prevention of *C psittaci* infection in cats. Chlamydial vaccines usually contain attenuated living organisms and are generally given parenterally in combination with other feline vaccines.[10,11] Chlamydial vaccines should be considered poor at best.[5,14,20] Natural infection evokes weak and often transient immunity. A chronic carrier state in the face of immunity is the rule rather than the exception. Therefore, it is doubtful that artificially induced immunity would be more effective. Chlamydial vaccines in cats decrease the severity of the acute phase of laboratory-induced infection but do not prevent colonization of the conjunctiva, gastrointestinal or genital tracts with virulent organisms or the chronic carrier state.[14,20] Vaccines appear to perform much better in environments and under conditions in which the disease is generally not severe anyway. They perform poorly in high-density situations in which disease is most severe. This is supported by experimental evidence; cats vaccinated with live chlamydial vaccines developed incomplete resistance to challenge-exposure.[14,20] Though clinical signs of primary infection were diminished, two-thirds of vaccinated cats shed virulent organisms for 21-35 days after challenge and one-third for 61 days or more.[14]

Infection and Immunity

Chlamydial infection stimulates both humoral and cellular immunity.[15] Local and systemic antibodies appear following infection and serum IgG neutralizes elementary bodies. In spite of such immunity, recovery from clinical infection is slow, and persistence of the organism in epithelial cells is common. Once immunity develops, it is generally weak and of relatively short duration. Protective immunity is easily overcome by severe challenge-exposure and is rapidly depressed by stress. Therefore, recurrent disease is common in environments where primary infection is frequent and severe. Recurrent disease results either from reinfection in the face of weak immunity and high exposure, or from reactivation of subclinical infections following stress. Recurrent infections are more apt to be seen within the first 1-2 years of life. Cellular immunity is often slow to develop and takes many months or even years to become solid enough to overcome severe exposure or stress-induced suppression.

The role of stress in chlamydial infections of cats cannot be underestimated. Stress can be mimicked by corticosteroid administration. Corticosteroids given 40-44 days after infection increased the severity of chlamydial conjunctivitis in cats, an effect that lasted for 4 5 days. Corticosteroids also increase shedding of *Chlamydia* by carrier cats.[14] These findings have 2 major implications: disease can be increased in severity and prolonged in duration by stressful situations or corticosteroid administration; and the overall level of chlamydial shedding within a group of cats can be greatly increased by stress or corticosteroids. Stressful environments are not only more conducive for spread of the organism but are also more apt to produce clinically apparent disease (primary and recurrent infections). Management of chlamydiosis in catteries, where the disease is most rampant, should be directed more to husbandry practices than routine vaccination.

Animal and Public Health Considerations

Feline strains of *C psittaci* cause disease in both cats and people. However, their role in disease of other species has not been determined.[21] Experimentall evidence suggests that *C psittaci* infections in livestock and domesticated wild birds are due to strains that are species adapted, though not entirely species specific.[22]

Cats showing clinical signs are considerably more infectious to other cats than asymptomatic carriers. Infection requires intimate exposure; fleeting contacts or aerosol exposure over a distance are not usually of great consequence. Spread via fomites is also unlikely.

People exposed to cats with active *C psittaci* conjunctivitis have developed conjunctivitis themselves.[9] Human cases of conjunctivitis due to feline strains of *C psittaci* resemble the feline disease in most aspects, except they are usually of shorter duration. It often involves only 1 eye, the conjunctiva is reddened and edematous, and there is a considerable amount of epiphora and irritation. Untreated, the disease lasts for about 1-2 weeks. It is doubtful whether *C psittaci* of feline origin is associated with other chlamydial diseases is people, *eg*, trachoma, neonatal chlamydial infections, ornithosis or genital infections. These diseases are caused by different strains or species of *Chlamydia*.

References

1. Allan I and Pearce JH: Amino acid requirements of strains of *Chlamydia trachomatis* and *C psittaci* in McCoy cells. Relationships with clinical syndrome and host origin. *J Gen Microbiol* 129:2001-2007, 1983.

2. Baker JA: A virus-causing pneumonia in cats and producing elementary bodies. *J Exp Med* 79:159-172, 1944.

3. Cello RM: Ocular infections of animals with PLT (Bedsonia) group agents. *Am J Ophthalmol* 63:1270-1273, 1967.

4. Cello RM: Clue to differential diagnosis of feline respiratory infections. *JAVMA* 158:968-973, 1971.

5. Cello RM: Microbiological and immunologic aspects of feline pneumonitis. *JAVMA* 158:932-938, 1971.

6. Gaillard ET *et al*: Pathogenesis of feline gastric chlamydial infection. *Am J Vet Res* 45:2314-2321, 1984.

7. Hargis AM *et al*: Chlamydial infection of the gastric mucosa in twelve cats. *Vet Pathol* 20:170-178, 1983.

8. Hoover EA *et al*: Experimentally induced feline chlamydial infection (feline pneumonitis). *Am J Vet Res* 39:541-547, 1978.

9. Johnson FWA: Isolation of *Chlamydia psittaci* from nasal and conjunctival exudate of a domestic cat. *Vet Record* 114:343-344, 1984.

10. Kolar JR and Rude TA: Clinical evaluation of a commercial feline pneumonitis vaccine. *Feline Pract* 7(2):47-50, 1977.

11. Mitzel JR and Strating A: Vaccination against feline pneumonitis. *Am J Vet Res* 38:1361-1363, 1977.

12. Schachter J *et al*: Human infection with the agent of feline pneumonitis. *Lancet* 1:1063-1065, 1969.

13. Shewen PE *et al*: Feline chlamydial infection. *Can Vet J* 19:289-292, 1978.

14. Shewen PE *et al*: A comparison of the efficacy of a live and four inactivated vaccine preparations for the protection of cats against experimental challenge with *Chlamydia psittaci*. *Can J Comp Med* 44:244-251, 1980.

15. Stamm WE, in Wyngaarden JB and Smith LH: *Cecil's Textbook of Medicine*. 17th ed. Saunders, Philadelphia, 1985. pp 1668-1669.

16. Studdert MJ *et al*: Isolation of *Chlamydia psittaci* from cats with conjunctivitis. *Aust Vet J* 57:515-517, 1981.

17. Tabatabayi AH and Rad MA: First isolation of *Chlamydia psittaci* from a cat in Iran. *Feline Pract* 11(6):35-38, 1981.

18. Wills J *et al*: Isolation of *Chlamydia psittaci* from cases of conjunctivitis in a colony of cats. *Vet Record* 114:344-346, 1984.

19. Wills J *et al*: Evaluation of a monoclonal antibody-based ELISA for detection of *Chlamydia psittaci*. *Vet Record* 119:418-420, 1986.

20. Wills J *et al*: Effect of vaccination on feline *Chlamydia psittaci* infection. *Infect Immun* 55:2563-2567, 1987.

Additional References

21. Gethings PM *et al*: Prevalence of *Chlamydia*, *Toxoplasma*, *Toxocara* and ringworm in farm cats in south-west England. *Vet Record* 121:213-216, 1987.

22. Fukuski H *et al*: Monoclonal antibody typing of *Chlamydia psittaci* strains derived from avian and mammalian species. *J Clin Micro* 25:1978-1981, 1987.

Chapter 42

Cell Wall-Deficient Organism (L-Form) Infection

Etiologic Agents

Cell wall-deficient organisms are variants of common bacteria. The alternative name, "L-forms," comes from the Lister Institute, where they were first recognized by Klieneberger-Nobel.[4] The first L-form isolate was found to coexist in culture with *Streptobacillus moniliformis*, in what was thought to be a symbiotic relationship.[4] Dienes and Van Rooyen recognized that the L-forms originally described by Klieneberger-Nobel were actually cell wall-deficient forms of *Streptobacillus moniliformis*, thus establishing the relationship between cell wall-deficient organisms and their parent bacteria.[2,8,10] L-forms can be induced from many different types of Gram-positive and Gram-negative bacteria by treating normal cultures with lysozyme or antibiotics that affect cell wall synthesis. Using such techniques, L-forms have been induced from *Clostridium*, *Mycobacterium*, *Nocardia*, *Staphylococcus*, *Streptococcus*, *Streptobacillus*, *Escherichia coli*, *Hemophilus*, *Salmonella*, *Proteus* and *Neisseria*. Cell wall-deficient organisms also can be isolated from tissues and exudates of people that have not been treated with antibiotics.[3] In such cases, the cell wall-deficient state is apparently induced by other factors, possibly host immunity and genetic selection.

Cell wall-deficient organisms are difficult to distinguish from *Mycoplasma* by light microscopy. Under phase microscopy, however, *Mycoplasma* spp possess a definite shape, while L-forms are highly variable in size and are 1-4 μ in diameter. Pleomorphism of cell wall-deficient organisms is most apparent under electron microscopy (Fig 1).[4] *Mycoplasma* can also be differentiated from L-forms by measuring penicillin-binding proteins.[5]

Fig 1. Budding bacterial L-forms (arrows) in the tissues of a cat experimentally infected with a field isolate. The L-form on the left has a partial cell wall. The organism on the right is diphasic; the right-hand bud has a cell wall, but the left-hand bud does not. Note the variable size and chromatin content of parent and daughter cells. Uranyl acetate and lead citrate stain, 45,000X.

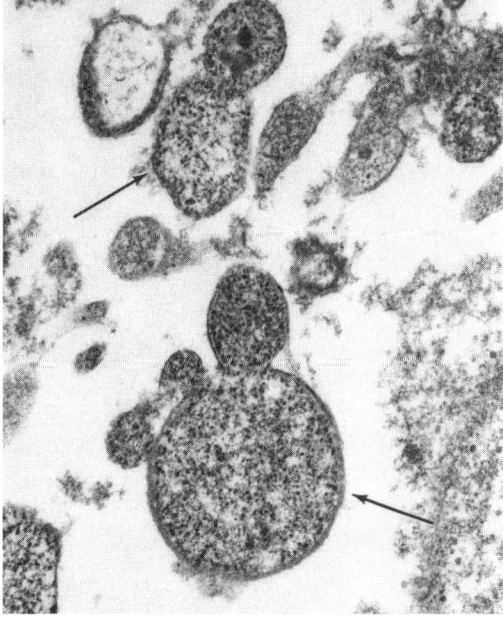

Normal bacteria replicate by coordinated cytoplasmic and nuclear binary fission, yielding daughter cells of equal size. Reproduction of L-forms is uncoordinated and daughter organisms contain variable amounts of cytoplasm and nucleic acid (Fig 1).[6] Therefore, L-forms differ greatly in size and nucleus:cytoplasm ratio. In some cases, reproduction appears bud-like. Elementary-like bodies within larger parent cells have also been observed.[4]

Cell wall-deficient organisms have recently been implicated in a specific syndrome of domestic cats.[1,7,11] The uniform appearance of the disease and pattern of antibiotic resistance and susceptibility suggest that identical or closely related L-forms are involved. The organisms could not be cultured on standard aerobic and anaerobic bacterial media or on a number of highly specialized mycoplasmal substrates. One isolate has been experimentally passed from naturally infected to specific-pathogen-free cats with a crude inoculum made from infected tissues and exudates.[1] Cell wall-deficient organisms were seen in electron micrographs of tissues from experimental-

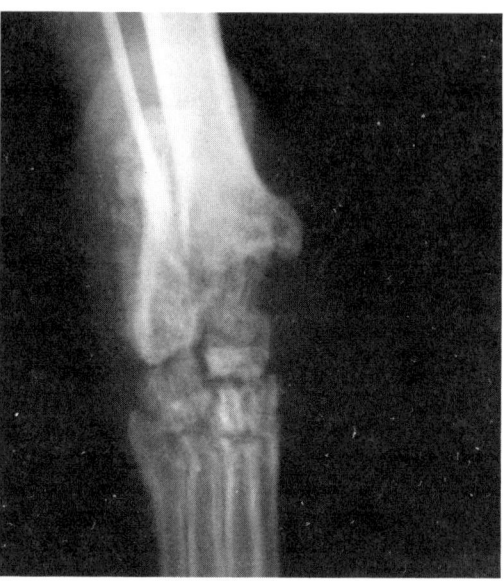

Fig 3. Radiograph of the right tarsus of a cat with bacterial L-form arthritis for 9 weeks shows periarticular soft tissue swelling, osteoporosis of the bones forming the joint, collapse of joint spaces, destruction of articular cartilage and subchondral bone, and periosteal new bone formation. (Courtesy of Dr. Terry Carro, University of Florida, Gainesville)

ly recreated lesions. Organisms were most prevalent in phagocytic cells and highly pleomorphic in nature, typical of other L-forms (Fig 1). The organism has not yet been cultured *in vitro* and its parental origin has not been determined.

Pathogenesis

Infections with cell wall-deficient organisms are seen sporadically in cats of all ages. Most affected cats have been free roaming.[1,7] Initial infection usually occurs at the site of a penetrating wound, most often a cat bite. Contamination of an ovariohysterectomy incision has been observed in 1 animal.[7] A large outbreak of bacterial L-form abscesses in a private practice was caused by the use of a contaminated antiseptic solution that was used to clean cat fight wounds.[11] Cat-to-cat transmission, probably from ingestion of purulent discharges, has been observed in 1 household.[1]

Following experimental subcutaneous inoculation, cellulitis appears at the site within 4-5 days and rapidly spreads.[7] The infection often breaks through the overly-

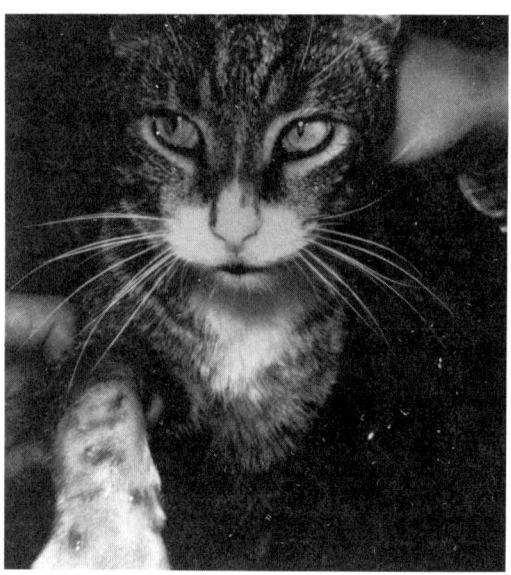

Fig 2. Cat with bacterial L-form cellulitis and carpal arthritis. The paw and carpus are badly swollen. Numerous tracts have broken through the skin, draining a mucinous, slightly cloudy exudate. The infection did not respond to several broad-spectrum antibiotics used over 2 weeks, but resolved after several days of tetracycline therapy.

ing skin and forms multiple, draining fistulous tracts.

Clinical Features

Most affected cats have fever and rapidly progressing cellulitis, usually on the forelegs.[1,7] The overlying skin is often reddened, edematous and depilated. The initial cellulitis usually breaks through the overlying skin at mulitple sites (Fig 2). The exudate from fistulous tracts is cloudy, grayish and mucinous, and contains many neutrophils. Joints, especially the carpus and tarsus, are involved in 50% or more of affected cats (Fig 3). Joint involvement occurs from hematogenous spread or extension of nearby cellulitis. If spread is hematogenous, the involved joint(s) may be distant from the original site of infection.

In some cats, the initial cellulitis is deeper and does not fistulate. Such lesions are often surgically probed and incised. These procedures inevitably cause dehiscence and a large, open, suppurating wound.

Pathologic Features

Biopsies from early lesions show mainly suppurative inflammation and tissue necrosis.[1,7] Necrosis tends to involve mainly the subcutaneous fat. As the infection becomes more chronic, pyogranulomatous inflammation is more apparent. Synovitis often extends along adjacent tendon sheaths. Lesions are not usually seen in internal organs. Organisms have not been observed with conventional or specialized (Gram, acid-fast, silver or PAS) stains.

Clinicopathologic Features

The first indication that infection is due to cell wall-deficient organisms is failure to culture organisms and visualize microbes in smears of exudates. A poor response to antibiotics other than tetracycline is also seen. Infection with cell wall-deficient organisms must be differentiated from similar suppurative dermal infections caused by mycobacteria or fungi. These infections tend to be more chronic and slowly developing than those caused by cell wall-deficient organisms. Also, mycobacterial and fungal organisms are usually seen.

Treatment and Prevention

Cell wall-deficient organisms are not sensitive to beta-lactam antibiotics, which inhibit cell wall synthesis. The antibiotic sensitivity pattern of human cell wall-deficient organisms is quite variable.[8] This is understandable, given the variability in antibiotic sensitivities possessed by their cell wall-intact parent bacteria. Cell wall-deficient organisms of cats appear to be uniformly resistant to almost all modern antibiotics. However, they are remarkably susceptible to tetracycline. Since tetracycline is not a commonly used antibiotic, veterinarians often try a series of more modern broad-spectrum antibiotics, to no avail. The recommended dosage of tetracycline or its derivatives is 25 mg/kg PO TID. The fever usually breaks within 24-28 hours; discharges diminish and become less purulent shortly thereafter. Antibiotic therapy should be continued for at least 1 week after all signs of infection have disappeared. Open wounds should be allowed to heal by secondary intention.

Infection and Immunity

Cats are either uniformly susceptible or uniformly resistant to experimental infection.[2] Resistant cats do not develop any lesions at the site of inoculation. In contrast, susceptible cats do not mount an effective immune response and the infection spreads slowly for weeks or months. The nature of resistance and susceptibility patterns seen among experimentally infected cats has not been elucidated. Cats with naturally acquired infections do not have any evidence of underlying immunodeficiency.

The cell wall-deficient state robs the host immune response of its most important target, the complex glycoproteins of the cell wall. There is evidence indicating that once cell wall-deficient organisms are phagocytized, they are less susceptible to death than their parent organisms.[9] This allows them to survive for long periods within phagocytes and may explain the apparent ease with which cell wall-deficient organisms are recovered from tissues, blood and urine of people with a variety of disease syndromes that seem unrelated.[3] The fact that they can survive so long in tissues does not necessarily mean that they contribute to any lesions in the area. In fact, the ubiquitous nature of L-forms in people has led some researchers to question the organisms' role in many of the disease processes from which they have been isolated.

Animal and Public Health Considerations

Cat-to-cat transmission of cell wall-deficient organisms has been observed only once.[1] In this situation, a cat with a suppurative fistulating skin wound and arthritis (that appeared to occur after a cat bite) infected 2 of its housemates by contact. There was no evidence that the transmission occurred from bites. It appeared most likely the cats were infected from wound exudates on the first animal. Both contact-infected cats developed suppurative infections of several joints; 1 animal also had a fistulous tract in the paralumbar musculature.

Cell wall-deficient organisms have been implicated in a number of human diseases, but a distinct cause-effect relationship remains to be established for most of these conditions. For instance, cell wall-deficient forms of *Mycobacterium pseudotuberculosis* have been implicated in some cases of human Crohn's disease. L-forms may also play a role in nocardiosis, tuberculosis, leprosy, dermatologic diseases, aphthous stomatitis, uveitis, rheumatic fever, gonorrhea and septicemia.[3] There is no evidence that cats are a reservoir for cell wall-deficient organisms that may serve as human pathogens. Until the feline cell wall-deficient organisms are better characterized, however, nothing can be said about their public health significance.

References

1. Caro T et al: A specific disease entity of cats caused by a probable bacterial L-form. *JAVMA*. In press, 1988.

2. Dienes L: Alterations of the L-forms of a spore-bearing bacillus. *J Bacteriol* 104: 1378-1385, 1970.

3. Dominigue GJ: *Cell Wall-Deficient Bacteria*. Addison-Wesley, Reading, MA, 1982.

4. Klieneberger-Nobel E: The natural occurrence of pleuropneumonia-like organisms in apparent symbiosis with *Streptobacillus moniliformis* and other bacteria. *J Pathol Bacteriol* 40:93-105, 1935.

5. Martin HH et al: Differentiation of Mycoplasmatales from bacterial protoplast L-forms by assay for penicillin-binding proteins. *Arch Microbiol* 127:297-299, 1980.

6. Patterson SK and Gilpin RW, in Dominigue GJ: *Cell Wall-Deficient Bacteria*. Addison-Wesley, Reading, MA, 1982. pp 1-58.

7. Pedersen NC, Univ California: Unpublished observations, 1987.

8. Schmitt-Slomska J, in Dominigue GJ: *Cell Wall-Deficient Bacteria*. Addison-Wesley, Reading, MA, 1982. pp 489-523.

9. Schmitt-Slomska J et al: Incidence of cellular and humoral factors on group A streptococcal L-forms. I. Microscopic study of the association of L-forms with polymorphonuclear leukocytes and mouse peritoneal macrophages. *Ann Microbiol (Inst Pasteur)* 124B:329-350, 1973.

10. Van Rooyen CE: The biology, pathogenesis and classification of *Streptobacillus moniliformis*. *J Pathol Bacteriol* 43:455-472, 1936.

Additional Reference

11. Keane DP: Chronic abscesses in cats associated with an organism resembling *Mycoplasma*. *Can Vet J* 24:287-291, 1983.

Section IV

Fungal Diseases
(Mycoses)

Fungi are classified as eukaryotes (true cells) that contain a membrane-bound nucleus with several chromosomes. Pathogenic fungi can be diphasic; they can exist in 1 form in nature and in another form within tissues of infected animals. The "perfect" form or sexual phase in the fungal life cycle involves mating. Spores formed from mating are a major determinant of taxonomic classification. The usual state in which the organism survives in tissues or the environment may have a different name from the individual organism that has achieved a state of perfection. For instance, *Cryptococcus neoformans* is the name given to the common environmental and tissue form of 4 different serotypes of pathogenic *Cryptococcus* spp. However, the perfect forms are *Filobasidiella neoformans* (serotypes A and D) or *Filobasidiella bacillispora* (serotypes B and C). The perfect form of *Blastomyces dermatitidis* has been given the name *Ajellomyces dermatitidis*. However, the diseases these agents cause are named after the tissue form of the organisms, ie, cryptococcosis and blastomycosis.

Fungal diseases, or mycoses, are enzootic or opportunistic. Enzootic mycoses occur in well-defined geographic areas where particular species of fungi are found. *Coccidioides immitis*, the causative agent of coccidioidomycosis, is only found in a climatic area known as the lower Sonoran life zone. People and animals are exposed only when they enter this region. Opportunistic mycoses are caused by organisms that are usually worldwide and more or less ubiquitous in the environment. Examples of opportunistic mycoses include sporotrichosis, candidiasis, aspergillosis and mucormycosis.

Mycoses have also been classified as superficial or deep. Superficial mycoses usually involve the skin and subcutis and arise from direct inoculation. Deep mycoses are also known as "systemic mycoses." They enter the body through the respiratory tract and spread to many organs and tissues.

Mycotic infections of people have been divided into the following groups: coccidioidomycosis, paracoccidioidomycosis, histoplasmosis, blastomycosis, cryptococcosis, dermatomycosis, sporotrichosis, candidiasis, aspergillosis, mucormycosis, mycetoma (maduromycosis) and chromomycosis. With the exception of paracoccidioidomycosis, which is very uncommon in cats, this classification scheme also covers mycotic diseases in cats.

Chapter 43

Coccidioidomycosis

Etiologic Agent

Coccidioidomycosis is caused by the soil fungus *Coccidioides immitis*.[2,3] This is a biphasic fungus with its mycelial phase found 20 cm deep in soil, particularly in and around rodent burrows. The mycelial form of the organism produces box-like arthroconidia (arthrospores) that are 2-5 μ in diameter, an easily aerosolized size. Once in host tissues, arthroconidia transform into large (10-80 μ) structures called spherules. The cytoplasm of spherules is segmented into numerous smaller endospores that are 2-5 μ in diameter. Rupture of spherules causes release of myriad endospores that mature into spherules when taken up by phagocytic cells.

Coccidioides immitis is found mainly in the arid lower Sonoran life zone, a climatic region characterized by high year-round temperatures, sparse rainfall that occurs partly in summer, and low humidity. This region comprises vast areas of the southwestern United States and neighboring portions of Mexico. This same life zone is present in areas of Central and South America.[3] The creosote bush is considered an indicator plant of the lower Sonoran life zone. The fungus is dormant in the summer but can be activated by summer rains; mycelia grow rapidly and reach the surface where they sporulate and are then readily disseminated by hot winds. The fungus is destroyed by freezing temperatures. Though widespread in the American Southwest, its range has been somewhat curtailed by irrigation in such areas as the San Joaquin Valley of California.

Pathogenesis

People and dogs are most susceptible to infection.[2,4] Cats have a surprisingly high resistance to *C immitis* infection and only sporadic cases have been recognized.[1,5-7] The primary routes of infection are through contamination of wounds and by inhalation of arthroconidia. Once in the skin or air passages, arthroconidia are taken up by phagocytic cells and transform into spherules. The spherules eventually destroy the engulfing phagocytic cells, rupture and release numerous smaller endospores. These endospores are rapidly engulfed by surrounding macrophages and the cycle continues. The host's attempt to immunologically contain the localized infection causes a cutaneous granuloma (skin entry) or peribronchiolar granuloma (respiratory entry). If sufficient cellular immunity is not established within several weeks, infection spreads to the regional lymph nodes via lymphatic vessels. The regional lymph nodes are a formidable barrier to hematogenous spread in cats. If the organism does gain access to the bloodstream, it usually ends up in areas rich in reticuloendothelial tissue, such as marrow cavities of flat and long bones, lung, skin, meninges of the brain and spinal cord, uveal tract of the eyes, spleen, liver and intestine.

Clinical Signs

Clinical signs of coccidioidomycosis in 4 cats have been referable to granulomatous pneumonia; granulomatous disease of the pleura, hilar lymph nodes, muscle, skin, and subcutaneous tissue over the back; and fistulating wounds of the hind limb with regional lymphangitis and lymphadenitis.[5,7] Unilateral coccidioidomycotic uveitis in a 12-year-old cat has also been described.[1] Though few cats have been affected, the pattern of disease is essentially the same as in dogs and people.

Pathologic Features

Granulomas are the basic lesion of coccidioidomycosis. Granulomas are comprised of dense aggregates of histiocytes interspersed with neutrophils. Lesions are surrounded by a loose capsule of fibrous tissue containing lymphocytes and plasma cells. Coccidioides immitis spherules varying from 50 to 100 μ in diameter are present in very small numbers within the lesions.

Clinicopathologic Features

Diagnosis of coccidioidomycosis is usually by microscopic identification of the organisms in tissue sections and, occasionally, in exudates from draining skin lesions. Organisms can be cultured on conventional media, but culture isolation from tissue or exudate is not always rewarding, even when spherules are present.

Diagnosis of coccidioidomycosis is often confirmed in people and dogs by serologic assays. Precipitating antibodies (IgM) often appear in the blood of people and dogs very soon after infection. If the infection is particularly severe and persistent, or if dissemination occurs, complement-fixing antibodies (IgG) appear in the serum and progressively increase. Therefore, complement-fixing antibodies are used in dogs and people as indicators of severe or disseminated disease. Among cats that have been tested, none demonstrated complement-fixing antibodies even in the face of extensive disease.[1,5,7] Of 2 cats tested for precipitating antibodies, 1 was positive and 1 negative.[5,7] Elicitation of a delayed hypersensitivity reaction with extracts of the organism (coccidioidin) has been used in people to detect previous exposure to the organism. Such tests have not been very useful in dogs; 1 cat tested had a negative or questionable reaction.[5]

Treatment and Prevention

Many cats in enzootic areas are probably infected with Coccidioides immitis, but fortunately few have progressive disease. Therefore, spontaneous recovery does occur and can complicate evaluation of chemotherapy. Localized cutaneous coccidioidomycosis in cats and dogs usually resolves spontaneously after 2 months or more.[7] However, spontaneous resolution in animals with disease that has spread beyond the hilar lymph nodes is not common. There are no reports in the literature describing treatment of cats with coccidioidomycosis. However, the drugs of choice are ketoconazole and amphotericin B. Such treatment has been successful in cats with histoplasmosis. However, histoplasmosis in people and dogs is much more amenable to such therapy than coccidioidomycosis.[2,3] Details of amphotericin B and ketoconazole therapy are given in the discussion of cryptococcosis (Chapter 46).

Infection and Immunity

Immunity to C immitis is thought to be exclusively cell mediated. Humoral antibodies are produced during the course of infection in people and dogs, but they result merely from antigenic stimulation and have no beneficial effect on the disease. Antibody titers in tested cats with coccidioidomycosis were either weak or nonexistent.[1,5,7] This suggested these animals were anergic or in a state of immune incompetence seen in some dogs and people with the disease. When anergy occurs, it can lead to a more fulminating type of infection. Immune incompetence to C immitis can be specific or nonspecific, and acquired or congenital. None of the cats with coccidioidomycosis had a history that suggested a generalized state of immune incompetence or of prior therapy with immunosuppressive drugs. Feline leukemia virus (FeLV) infection potentiates disease in some cats with cryptococcosis. However, there is no evidence that FeLV is involved in cats with coccidioidomycosis. One cat with ocular disease that was tested for FeLV was negative.[1] The relationship of feline immunodeficiency virus (FIV) infection and coccidioidomycosis in cats remains to be studied.

Animal and Public Health Considerations

There have been no reports of cat-to-cat or cat-to-person transmission of coccidioidomycosis. Infected people and dogs are not considered public health risks.

References

1. Angell JA et al: Ocular coccidioidomycosis in a cat. *JAVMA* 187:167-169, 1985.

2. Barsanti JA and Jeffery KL, in Greene CE: *Clinical Microbiology and Infectious Diseases of the Dog and Cat.* Saunders, Philadelphia, 1984. pp 710-721.

3. Drutz DJ, in Wyngaarden JB and Smith LH Jr: *Cecil's Textbook of Medicine.* Saunders, Philadelphia, 1985. pp 1761-1762.

4. Maddy KT: Coccidioidomycosis in animals. *Vet Med* 54:233-242, 1959.

5. Reed RE et al: Coccidioidomycosis in two cats. *JAVMA* 143:953-956, 1963.

6. Schwartz W: *Coccidioides immitis* infection in a cat. *Southwestern Vet* 34:94, 1981.

7. Wolf AM: Primary cutaneous coccidioidomycosis in a dog and a cat. *JAVMA* 174:504-506, 1979.

Chapter 44

Histoplasmosis

Etiologic Agent

Histoplasma capsulatum is a diphasic fungus with a mycelial phase that occurs in the environment.[1,4] The fungus grows as a yeast in culture at 37 C and in tissues. The mycelial phase produces macroconidia (8-16 μ) and microconidia (2-5 μ). The smaller microconidia are easily aerosolized and inhaled. The yeast form in tissues and cultures is about 3 μ in diameter and does not have a noticeable capsule. The yeast form replicates by budding. Buds are single and connected by a narrow neck.

Histoplasma capsulatum is found in major river valleys throughout the temperate and tropical regions of the world.[1,4] In the United States, it is most commonly found in lands drained by the Mississippi, Missouri and Ohio Rivers and their tributaries. The enzootic area runs diagonally from as far north as the St Lawrence Waterway to the Rio Grande River of Texas. States with the highest incidence of disease include Arkansas, Mississippi, Missouri, Texas, Oklahoma, Tennessee, Kansas, Kentucky, Iowa, Illinois and Indiana. However, sporadic cases have been recognized in virtually every state.

The organism is a soil saprophyte that preferentially grows in moist, moderate temperature environments. It is found mainly in the upper layers of soil enriched by bird and bat feces. Microconidia are frequently found in small numbers as air pollutants in enzootic areas. This leads to extremely high subclinical infection rates in the human and animal populations, but only a sporadic incidence of clinical disease. Certain microenvironments are particularly dangerous because of the high likelihood for massive exposure and, therefore, clinical illness.[1,4] These environments include old bat- or bird-roosting areas that are being demolished or disturbed.

Pathogenesis

Infection occurs almost exclusively from inhaling infectious microconidia and macroconidia.[1,4,14] The organism transforms to a yeast in tissues and divides by binary fission. Yeasts attract macrophages to the area, resulting in a localized inflammatory reaction. The yeast spreads from the peribronchiolar lesions to regional lymph nodes in the mediastinum. If immunity develops rapidly, the infection is halted at the regional nodes. Any dissemination is to areas rich in reticuloendothelial tissues, such as the lungs, bone marrow, lymph nodes, spleen, liver, intestinal wall, skin, CNS and uveal tract of the eyes.

Clinical Signs

Cats with histoplasmosis are usually <5 years of age and of random breed and sex.[2,3,6-11,13,14] Most animals have a history of living in or visiting enzootic areas and some have specific histories of contact with highly infectious microenvironments.

Many cats in enzootic areas are subclinically infected. Organisms can be recovered from tissues (particularly the peribronchial lymph nodes) of 20-40% of healthy pound cats in enzootic areas. This pattern of infection is consistent with histoplasmosis in people. Clinical disease in cats is rare but usually begins in the lungs and disseminates widely.

Clinical signs evolve over 1-3 months before the terminal phase of illness. Early signs include progressive weight loss leading to cachexia, fluctuating fever and anorexia.[14] More specific signs depend on localization of the disease. About 70% of cats have diffuse pulmonary involvement but only half of these animals show any signs of respiratory disease, such as cough or dyspnea.[14] Hepatomegaly and generalized lymphadenopathy are seen in about 25% of the cats, grossly apparent eye disease in 10%, lameness in 10%, ulcerated skin lesions or cutaneous masses in 5-10% and GI signs in 10%. Though gross eye involvement is not common, funduscopic examination reveals choroidal granulomas with or without retinal detachment in a much larger proportion of animals.[14] Lameness is generally associated with active osteomyelitis that most commonly involves the appendicular skeleton, in particular the carpal and tarsal joints.[7,14]

Pathologic Features

Gross and histopathologic features of feline histoplasmosis have been well documented.[2,3,6-9,11,13] Pulmonary granulomas are usually diffuse throughout the lungs and several millimeters to several centimeters in diameter. Hilar and mediastinal lymph nodes are frequently enlarged, even in the absence of extensive pulmonary disease. Cutaneous lesions are often thickened and ulcerated on the surface; a mucinous, grayish exudate may be present. Ocular lesions are concentrated in the choroid. Lymphoid and bone marrow involvement is often diffuse in nature rather than distinctly granulomatous. In fact, organisms are commonly identified in aspirates of bone marrow, lymph nodes, spleen and liver. Likewise, the lungs might contain a diffuse inflammatory infiltrate rich in organisms. Like other deep mycotic infections of cats, granulomatous or pyogranulomatous lesions are the hallmark of the disease. However, histoplasmosis tends to be much more diffuse throughout the reticuloendothelial system than coccidioidomycosis. Organisms are also much more prevalent and can be visualized in areas other than those involved with granulomatous disease.

Clinicopathologic Features

Diagnosis is almost always made by identifying the yeast phase of the organism in exudates, needle aspirates of liver, spleen and bone marrow, or tissue biopsies. Yeasts in exudates can be readily differentiated from *Cryptococcus* spp by the absence of a protective capsule. In tissue sections, aspirates and exudates, the organisms are free and within macrophages.

Serologic diagnosis of histoplasmosis in cats suffers from many of the same problems associated with serologic diagnosis of coccidioidomycosis and blastomycosis. Complement-fixation tests are usually negative, even in severely affected animals.[12] Agglutination and immunodiffusion tests are also usually negative.[12,14] Skin testing is not reliable in cats and is usually negative, even in cats from which organisms can be cultured.[12]

Treatment and Prevention

Histoplasmosis is potentially treatable with amphotericin B or ketoconazole.[10,14] However, of 4 cats treated with amphotericin B, 3 failed to respond.[14] Ketoconazole has proven effective in two-thirds of treated cats (see Chapter 46).[10,14]

Infection and Immunity

Cats appear relatively resistant to histoplasmosis. This is inferred from the observation that up to 40% of cats in enzootic areas have organisms that can be cultured from their bronchial lymph nodes.[5,12] However, these organisms are seldom associated with lesions and cannot usually be observed, even with special stains. Though the infection rate seems high, only a small percentage of cats develop clinical illness. The widespread nature of the disease in these cats suggests that some animals have problems immunologically responding to the infection. As in coccidioidomycosis, however, cats that develop histoplasmosis usually have no prior history of acquired or congenital immunosuppressive disorders. Wolf found that 2 of 18 cats with histoplasmosis had underlying FeLV infection, a rate about 2-5 times the expected frequency.[14]

Immunity to histoplasmosis is probably cell mediated. Humoral antibodies, when present, are produced in response to antigens of the organism but are of no protective value.

Animal and Public Health Considerations

Infected animals are not considered hazards to other animals or people.

References

1. Barsanti JA, in Greene CE: *Clinical Microbiology and Infectious Diseases of the Dog and Cat.* Saunders, Philadelphia, 1984. pp 687-699.

2. Blass CE: Histoplasmosis in a cat. *JAAHA* 18:468-470, 1982.

3. Breitschwerdt EB *et al*: Feline histoplasmosis. *JAAHA* 13:216-222, 1977.

4. Drutz DJ, in Wyngaarden JB and Smith LH Jr: *Cecil's Textbook of Medicine.* Saunders, Philadelphia, 1985. pp 1759-1761.

5. Emmons CW *et al*: Histoplasmosis. Proved occurrence of inapparent infection in dogs, cats and other animals. *Am J Hyg* 61:40-44, 1955.

6. Gabbert NH *et al*: Pancytopenia associated with disseminated histoplasmosis in a cat. *JAAHA* 20:119-122, 1984.

7. Goad MEP and Roenick WJ: Osseous histoplasmosis in a cat. *Feline Pract* 13(2):32-36, 1983.

8. Gwin RM *et al*: Multifocal ocular histoplasmosis in a dog and cat. *JAVMA* 176:638-642, 1980.

9. Mahaffey E *et al*: Disseminated histoplasmosis in three cats. *JAAHA* 13:46-51, 1977.

10. Noxon JO *et al*: Disseminated histoplasmosis in a cat: Successful treatment with ketoconazole. *JAVMA* 181:817-820, 1982.

11. Percy DH: Feline histoplasmosis with ocular involvement. *Vet Pathol* 18:163-169, 1981.

12. Rowley DA *et al*: Histoplasmosis: pathologic studies of fifty cats and fifty dogs from Loudoun County, Virginia. *J Infect Dis* 95:98-108, 1954.

13. Stark DR: Primary gastrointestinal histoplasmosis in a cat. *JAAHA* 18:154-156, 1982.

14. Wolf AM and Belden MN: Feline histoplasmosis: A literature review and retrospective study of 20 new cases. *JAAHA* 20:995-998, 1984.

Chapter 45

Blastomycosis

Etiologic Agent

Blastomycosis is caused by a dimorphic fungus.[8] The yeast form, which is found in tissues and grows on blood agar at 37 C, is called *Blastomyces dermatitidis*. The perfect form (sexual phase) of the organism (*Ajellomyces dermatitidis*) is a soil saprophyte. The mycelial form is seen on Sabouraud's agar cultured at 20 C. Young cultures are woolly and white but turn tan to brown over time. Initial cultures produce small (3-5 μ) conidia; larger (7-18 μ) chlamydospores are produced as the colonies age.

Blastomyces dermatitidis is enzootic to the continental United States, and to a lesser extent, Canada, Mexico, Central America and Africa.[8] The enzootic area in the United States is similar to that of *Histoplasma capsulatum*, except that it is more confined to lands east of the Mississippi River and extends farther north into the southeast portions of Quebec and Saskatchewan in Canada. Areas of highest disease incidence include Arkansas, Mississippi, Tennessee, North Carolina, Kentucky, Ohio, Indiana and Illinois.[14,19]

Unlike *Histoplasma capsulatum* and *Coccidioides immitis*, which are easily isolated from soil throughout their enzootic areas, *B dermatitidis* grows profusely only in select microenvironments. Even in these microenvironments, the organism rarely persists and repeat isolations after a few weeks or months are unusual.[8,14] Environmental factors that encourage transient growth of the organism have not been well defined. *Blastomyces dermatitidis* has been isolated from barn soil where infected dogs had been housed and from pigeon manure at a site of human exposure.[12] Foggy, wooded lake areas are also more likely to harbor these organisms.[16]

The incidence of infection within enzootic areas has not been well defined. Dogs, horses and people seem most susceptible to infection. Dogs, which are reportedly 10 times more sensitive than people to blastomycosis, have mortality as high as 87% following artificial exposure.[12,13,20,22] Thus, dogs develop clinical disease at a much higher rate after infection with *Blastomyces* than with *Histoplasma* or *Coccidioides*. This is thought to be the pattern of blastomycosis in people and other animals, *ie*, fewer individuals within enzootic areas are infected, but a relatively greater proportion develop clinical disease than with histoplasmosis or coccidioidomycosis.

Pathogenesis

Infection occurs when spores are inhaled into the lungs or introduced into skin wounds.[14] Cutaneous blastomycosis is a self-limiting disease localized to the site of entry, draining afferent lymphatic vessels and regional lymph nodes. The initial lesion is a localized granuloma in the skin.

Respiratory infections usually begin with inhalation of spores. Cats appear relatively sensitive to this route of infection; 100% of cats infected with conidia by inhalation had pulmonary infections 3 weeks later.[6] Spores are taken up by phagocytic cells in the airways and transported to peribronchiolar tissues. The spore forms (conidia and chlamydospores) transform into yeasts in the tissue. Primary infection is characterized by rapid proliferation of yeast and infiltration of macrophages and polymorphonuclear neutrophils. After several days, lymphocytes and plasma cells appear in the loose fibrous tissues surrounding the foci of infection. Organisms spread to the hilar lymph nodes during the early stages of infection, causing both lymphadenitis and immune hyperplasia. Effective cellular immunity begins to appear by the second week of infection. This is associated with more efficient killing of organisms by macrophages and eventual elimination or containment of the infection. Hematogenous spread from regional lymph nodes to distant sites is associated with failure to mount an effective cell-mediated immune response.

Clinical Features

The disease affects cats of all ages and both sexes. There appears to be a preponderance of Siamese cats with the illness, but whether this is real or a statistical aberration is not known.[10,14-16] Blastomycosis occurs in localized and disseminated forms in cats.

Localized cutaneous blastomycosis has been described in 2 cats. The first case involved an isolated ulcerated lesion around the nail of a forepaw.[10] Except for this lesion, which was painful on palpation and caused nonweight-bearing lameness, the cat was normal. Radiographs of the leg showed that the disease did not involve underlying bone. Campbell and co-workers described a cat that developed severe edema and cutaneous ulceration of the distal foreleg several weeks after treatment for a puncture wound at the same site.[5] No other lesions were noted on physical examination or thoracic radiographs.

Disseminated blastomycosis is the most common form seen in cats. In almost all cases, the lungs are the primary site of infection.[1,3,10,13,16,21,23] Clinical signs of illness are generally seen only during the last 1-3 weeks and initially consist of depression, weight loss and fever. Dyspnea and a soft productive cough were noticed in only about one-third of cats with respiratory involvement. Pleural effusions, either purulent or serosanguineous, are seen in some cats with pulmonary disease. Lesions in disseminated blastomycosis are usually not limited to the lungs. Involvement of the spleen, serosa and omentum has been reported in a cat with liver disease.[15] Ocular involvement has also been reported in cats with blastomycosis.[1,15,18] Similar to histoplasmosis, intraocular disease is not always grossly apparent and ophthalmoscopic examination is important. Gross changes in the eye resemble those described for histoplasmosis. Central nervous system disease probably occurs in 10-20% or more of cats with disseminated disease.[17,18] Granulomatous lesions of varying sizes are also sometimes found in the frontal sinus, nasal passages and mouth. Skin lesions are seen in 10-20% of cats with disseminated disease. Cutaneous lesions can be of hematogenous origin and involve only the skin and subcutis, or can be extensions of deeper processes. Bone and joint involvement is relatively uncommon in feline blastomycosis.

In a very small percentage of cats, focal lesions are present in the eye or brain. Such lesions are probably residual to early disseminated infections. A cat with an isolated cerebral abscess and no other lesions has been reported.[17] This cat had a history of depression for 1 week, apparent blindness at the time of hospitalization, and head pressing 1 day before death.

Pathologic Features

The pathologic features of feline blastomycosis have been reported in some detail.[14,15,17,18,21] Gross findings are usually centered around the chest and abdomen. The thoracic and abdominal cavities often contain ≥ 50 ml of yellowish to serosanguineous fluid. The lungs usually have a meaty appearance and the visceral and parietal pleurae are covered with fibrin strands. A few or many whitish to yellowish nodules are seen in the lungs and may be hemorrhagic. Lesions are 0.5 mm to several centimeters in diameter. Generally, however, the more numerous the lesions, the smaller they are. When serosal surfaces are involved, they are often edematous and gelatinous or covered with a thick, grayish fibrinous exudate. Granulomatous lesions similar to those in the lungs, but usually less numerous, can sometimes be seen in the liver. The liver and spleen are often enlarged. The principal lesion is a necrotizing granulomatous reaction centered around blood vessels and masses of organisms. Plasma cells, lymphocytes, large macrophages and neutrophils predominate in the lesions. Organisms appear as thick-walled budding yeasts 6-20 μ in diameter. Similar lesions, though more diffuse and smaller, can sometimes be seen in other tissue, such as the spleen, kidney, pancreas, serosal surfaces, omentum, adrenal glands, brain, and choroid and retina of the eyes. Skin lesions are typical of those seen in internal organs.

Clinicopathologic Features

Cats with disseminated disease often have low-grade depression anemia, normal or slightly lower than normal leukocyte counts, and lymphopenia. Diagnosis is usually by identification of the yeast in biopsied tissues, fine-needle aspirates, impression smears of skin lesions, or exudates of draining cutaneous lesions.[13] Yeasts stain well with most tissue and blood stains. Typically, they are double-walled, with a single broad-based bud. In contrast, *H capsulatum* has a single bud connected to the parent organism by a narrow neck.

Cultures are a less effective diagnostic method.[13] Typical yeast forms of the organism grow well at 35 C on blood agar. Mycelial growth is seen on Sabouraud's agar at 20 C. For optimum diagnosis, cultures should be observed for at least 1 month. Organisms are most easily identified in the yeast stage.

Agar-gel immunodiffusion, complement fixation (CF), counterimmunoelectrophoresis and agar-gel precipitin tests have been developed for diagnosis of blastomycosis in people. However, there is considerable cross-reactivity with *Histoplasma* spp, especially in the CF test. Agar-gel immunodiffusion and counterimmunoelectrophoresis tests are considered the most accurate serologic predictors of clinical infection in dogs.[13] However, neither test is as accurate in dogs as microscopic examination of tissue preparations. Serologic diagnosis of blastomycosis in cats has not been extensively studied. Hatkins and associates studied the immunodiffusion test in 12 cats with suspected disease; all animals tested negative.[14] Therefore, it appears that serologic diagnosis of blastomycosis in cats is fraught with the same problems that occur with diagnosis of feline coccidioidomycosis and histoplasmosis.

Treatment and Prevention

If the disease is localized to the skin or eyes, excision can be curative or signs may spontaneously resolve over time. A cat with paronychial disease spontaneously recovered over a 6-week period.[10] Amputation of the foreleg also appeared to cure 1 cat with localized forelimb cellulitis.[5] This pattern of recovery following cutaneous infection is also typical of cutaneous coccidioidomycosis and atypical mycobacteriosis, which are similar types of diseases.

Disseminated disease is almost always progressive and rapidly fatal in cats. Amphotericin B has been the drug of choice for treatment of blastomycosis in people and dogs, but there is less experience with use of this drug in cats.[2,5,9,15] A suggested dosage for cats is 0.1-0.5 mg/kg IV on alternate days for a total cumulative dosage of 4 mg/kg. Toxicity should be monitored by periodic blood tests. Ketoconazole has proven less effective in treatment of blastomycosis in people.[7] However, preliminary reports indicate that ketoconazole is much more effective in canine blastomycosis than in human disease.[14] The responsiveness of cats is not known (see Chapter 46).

Infection and Immunity

Immunity to *B dermatitidis* is largely cell mediated. Protective immunity, which halts the disease at the site of primary infection or in the regional lymph nodes, is probably very common. Therefore, clinical signs would only be seen in cats with primary cutaneous lesions or disseminated disease. The reason that some cats develop disseminated disease is not known. None of the reported cats had predisposing problems or corticosteroid treatment, and none tested for feline leukemia virus infection was positive. The relationship of blastomycosis and feline immunodeficiency virus infection remains to be determined.

Animal and Public Health Considerations

No instances of cat-to-cat or cat-to-person transmission of blastomycosis have been recorded. Dogs with blastomycosis are not considered public health hazards to people or other animals, though cutaneous blastomycosis in people has resulted from bites of infected dogs. Therefore, reasonable care should be taken in handling infected tissues or exudates.

References

1. Alden CL and Mohan R: Ocular blastomycosis in a cat. *JAVMA* 164:527-528, 1974.

2. Barsanti JA, in Greene CE: *Clinical Microbiology and Infectious Diseases of the Dog and Cat.* Saunders, Philadelphia, 1984. pp 675-686.

3. Breshears DE: What is your diagnosis? *JAVMA* 152:1555-1556, 1968.

4. Brooks C: What is your diagnosis? *JAVMA* 187:183-184, 1985.

5. Campbell KL et al: Cutaneous blastomycosis. *Feline Pract* 10(3):28,30,32, 1980.

6. Denton JF and DiSalvo AF: Respiratory infection in lab animals with conidia of *Blastomyces dermatitidis*. *Mycopathol Mycol Appl* 36:129-136, 1968.

7. Dismukes WE et al: Treatment of systemic mycoses with ketoconazole: Emphasis on toxicity and clinical response in 52 patients. *Ann Intern Med* 98:13-19, 1983.

8. Drutz DJ, in Wyngaarden JB and Smith LH Jr: *Cecil's Textbook of Medicine.* Saunders, Philadelphia, 1985. pp 1762-1764.

9. Dunbar M et al: Treatment of canine blastomycosis with ketoconazole. *JAVMA* 182(2):156-157, 1983.

10. Easton KL: Cutaneous North American blastomycosis in a Siamese cat. *Can Vet J* 2:350-351, 1961.

11. Foster RC and Dunn TJ: Blastomycosis: A practical therapeutic approach. *VM/SAC* 76:200-204, 1981.

12. Furcolow ML et al: Prevalence and incidence studies of human and canine blastomycosis. *Am Rev Resp Dis* 102:60-67, 1970.

13. Furcolow ML and Smith CD: A new hypothesis on the epidemiology of blastomycosis and the ecology of *Blastomyces dermatitidis*. *Trans NY Acad Sci* 35:421-430, 1973.

14. Hatkin JM et al: Two cases of feline blastomycosis. *JAAHA* 15:217-220, 1979.

15. Jasmin AM et al: Systemic blastomycosis in Siamese cats. *VM/SAC* 64:33-37, 1969.

16. McDonough ES and Kuzma JF: Epidemiological studies on blastomycosis in the state of Wisconsin. *Sabouraudia* 18: 173-183, 1980.

17. McEwen SA and Hulland TJ: Cerebral blastomycosis in a cat. *Can Vet J* 25:411-413, 1984.

18. Nasisse MP et al: Ocular changes in a cat with disseminated blastomycosis. *JAVMA* 187:629-631, 1985.

19. Neunzig RJ: Epidemiology, diagnosis, and treatment of canine and feline blastomycosis. *VM/SAC* 78:1081-1088, 1983.

20. Sarosi GA et al: Canine blastomycosis as a harbinger of human disease. *Ann Intern Med* 91:733-735, 1979.

21. Sheldon WG: Pulmonary blastomycosis in a cat. *Lab Anim Care* 16:280-285, 1966.

22. Smith CD et al: Distribution of *Blastomyces dermatitidis* in dogs with skin tests and serologic results following airborne infections. *Sabouraudia* 13:192-199, 1975.

23. Welsh RD: Feline blastomycosis. *Southwestern Vet* 35:13, 1982.

Chapter 46

Cryptococcosis

Etiologic Agent

Cryptococcus neoformans is a pathogen that exists in tissues as a heavily encapsulated yeast. It has 4 serotypes.[8] Serotypes A and D show mating compatibility, as do serotypes B and C. The perfect form (sexual phase) of serotypes A and D is called *Filobasidiella neoformans*, while the perfect form of serotypes B and C is called *Filobasidiella bacillispora*. The sexual phase of pathogenic cryptococcal organisms is only seen under very select growing conditions; for this reason, it often exists in nature as an unencapsulated yeast. Basidiospores are produced by the sexual phase.

Most infections in the United States are associated with serotype A.[8] Serotypes B and C are further restricted to southern California. Serotype D is more prevalent in Europe. Serotypes A and D are found in highest concentration in pigeon droppings, while serotypes B and C occupy yet undefined microenvironmental niches.[8] Though *C neoformans* can be isolated from external parts and in the crop of birds, pigeons are not infected. The organism merely lives a saprophytic existence in voided pigeon feces.

Pathogenesis

The precise route of infection is not known. Inhalation of unencapsulated yeast or basidiospores from the mycelial phase into the lungs and hematogenous spread is thought to be involved in infection of people.[8] However, the high incidence of nasal lesions in cats has led to the suggestion that infection in cats begins locally in the nasal passages. This may not be accurate because intravenously injected organisms preferentially localize in the nasal passages, uveal tract of the eyes, and meninges of cats.[2] Localized infections of the skin of cats have also been recognized, indicating that some infections might result from wound contamination.

Once organisms enter the tissue, they transform into heavily encapsulated yeasts that replicate by budding. Except after

Fig 1. Cat with nasal cryptococcosis has an exudate from the right naris and a deformed nose. (From *Virus Infections of Carnivores*, courtesy of Elsevier Science Publishing)

cutaneous infection, dissemination occurs very rapidly. Tissues most involved in disseminated lesions are the nasal passages, skin, optic nerve and uveal tract, meninges of the brain and spinal cord, regional and distant lymph nodes, lungs, joints, bones and internal organs.

Clinical Features

Cats with cryptococcosis have been of many breeds, both sexes and all ages. The clinical course is often long, especially if the CNS is not involved. Cats with localized nasal or skin disease have lived in fairly good health for many months. Anorexia, wasting and fever are more apt to be seen in cats with widely disseminated disease. Additional clinical signs of cryptococcosis depend largely on the site of disease localization and severity of the disease (Table 1).

Almost 50% of cats with cryptococcosis have nasal cavity involvement.[1,4,11,14-16, 18,22,23,25,28,31-33,37,41,42,44,45] Sneezing, snuffling and a serous to mucoid grayish nasal exudate are the most common clinical signs (Fig 1). Such signs are sometimes present for many weeks or months before the animals are examined. Over time, nasal disease breaks through surrounding bone and invades the bridge of the nose, side of the nose, or orbit. Nasal disease often involves overlying skin and may distort facial features.[11,16,18,25,36] Extension into the hard and soft palates and temporal bones is less common.[5,14,22] Extension of the infection through the cribriform plate or optic nerves to the brain and into the osseous bulla and external ear canals has been reported.[15,28] Fleshy masses may protrude from the nares.

Skin disease is an important clinical feature of infection in about 25% of affected cats.[3,13,17,25,32,34,40,43,45] However, skin lesions are infrequently the sole manifestation of disease at necropsy (Table 1). Infection is often carried to the skin from distant sites via the blood or by extension from underlying disease in the nasal passages, mandibular and retropharyngeal lymph nodes, bones or joints. Skin lesions grow rapidly, are usually multiple and firm on palpation, and frequently ulcerate. They often exude a scant serosanguineous to mucopurulent

Table 1. Sites of disease (gross or microscopic) in cats with cryptococcosis. Data were collected from necropsied cats described in the literature.

Site	Number of Cats Affected
nasal	2
nasal, CNS	2
nasal, eyes	1
nasal, skin	4
nasal, CNS, skin	1
nasal, internal organs	3
eyes	2
skin*	3
internal organs**	2
CNS, internal organs	2
CNS, eyes	1
skin, internal organs	3
eyes, internal organs	1
CNS, skin	1
CNS, eyes, internal organs	3
skin, nasal, internal organs	3
skin, CNS, internal organs	1
skin, CNS, nasal, internal organs	1
	36

*Skin—Disease limited to epidermis and/or subcutis that does not occur as an extension of underlying nasal bone, joint or lymph node infection.

**Internal organs—In order of frequency, the following organs were involved: lungs (11), kidney (9), internal lymph nodes (5), liver (4), spleen (3), lining of mouth (2), myocardium (2), tongue (2), palate (1), bone other than nasal (1), adrenal gland (1).

discharge. When the overlying scab is removed, the underlying lesion has a ground-glass type of appearance. Skin lesions vary from several millimeters to several centimeters in diameter and tend to concentrate on the head, nose, orbits, lips, pinnae and neck. More diffuse subcutaneous swellings involving the neck have been seen in several cats.[7,21,29,36] Such swellings often involve the adjacent cervical and retropharyngeal lymph nodes. Masses in the area of the mandibular lymph nodes have also been reported.[26,38]

Central nervous system involvement is seen clinically in about 1 of 7 cats with cryptococcosis. Clinical signs of CNS disease can be the predominant manifestation or only a part of a more widespread problem that often includes ocular lesions.[6,10,18-20,35,43]

Though CNS involvement is often not clinically apparent, one-third or more of affected cats have CNS lesions at necropsy (Table 1). Central nervous system disease almost always occurs as part of a more disseminated infection (Table 1). Central nervous system signs result mainly from diffuse, hematogenously acquired meningoencephalomyelitis. However, CNS signs in 1 cat were due to brain compression from an inward-growing nasal and orbital process.[14] Dementia, head pressing, posterior paresis, generalized ataxia, cerebellar-vestibular signs (head tilt, circling, loss of balance), paralysis of a single limb and seizures have all been associated with CNS disease.

Ocular disease as the sole clinical manifestation of cryptococcosis is uncommon.[11,18] Subclinical ocular infections are far more common. Ocular disease often occurs in cats with concurrent CNS involvement or with lesions in other parts of the body (Table 1). Subclinical lesions usually consist of raised, grayish foci in the center of the retina. Such lesions are fairly characteristic of cryptococcosis (Fig 2). Clinical disease can be classified as a mild to severe exudative chorioretinitis that is usually bilateral. Retinal detachment, hyphema, dilated pupils and blindness are common sequelae of intraocular disease.

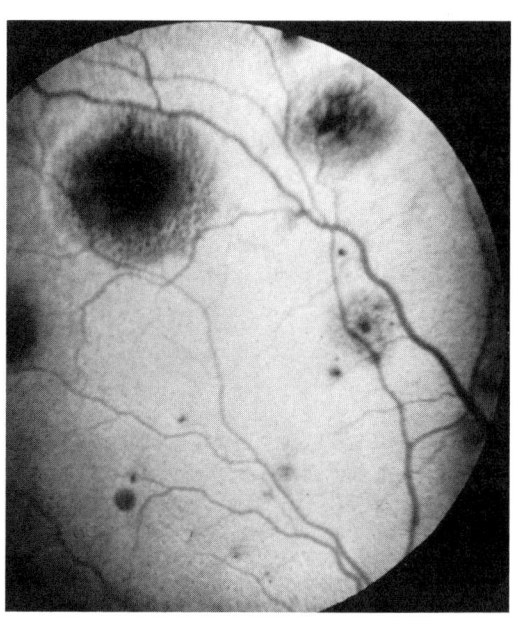

Fig 2. In a cat with ocular cryptococcosis, retinal lesions represent focal accumulations of organisms in the choroid, elevating the retina. This type of lesion is highly characteristic of cryptococcal chorioretinitis.

Lung disease is recognized at necropsy in slightly less than one-third of affected cats, usually as a feature of more widely disseminated disease (Table 1). However, several cats with primary lung disease have been reported.[27,41,46] Patchy inflammatory lesions throughout the lungs are the most common radiographic and necropsy finding. Cryptococcosis is a differential diagnosis for solitary anterior mediastinal masses.

Lymph node enlargement regional to skin lesions is common.[17,19,26,38,39] Hilar lymph nodes can be enlarged in cats with lung disease. Lymphadenitis sometimes extends to tissues around the nodes and to the skin.

Involvement of the kidney, spleen, tongue, skeletal muscles, heart muscle, intestinal tract, osseous bulla, gingiva, bones and joints has also been seen in cats with cryptococcosis.[17,19,28]

Pathologic Features

Cryptococcosis causes a more diffuse inflammatory reaction than other systemic

Fig 3. Impression smear of nasal exudate from a cat with nasal cryptococcosis shows numerous yeast bodies 2-12 μ in size. New methylene blue stain, 500X.

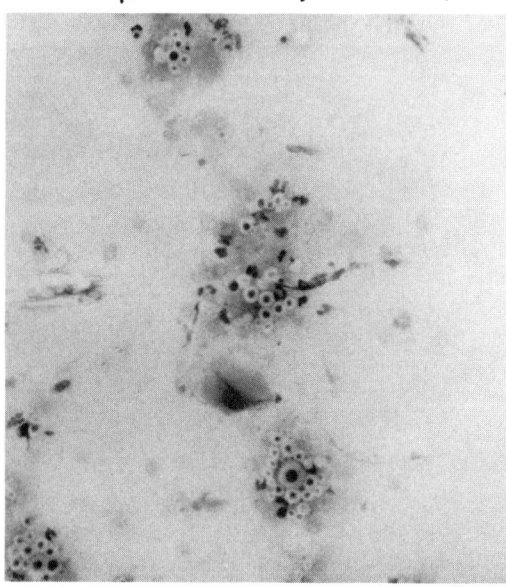

mycoses. However, as with other systemic mycotic infections in cats, the reaction is typically pyogranulomatous. Therefore, lesions consist of a mixture of macrophages, neutrophils, plasma cells and lymphocytes. These lesions are usually not well encapsulated and yeasts are present in large numbers within and without phagocytic cells. The inflammatory reaction to yeasts can be very sparse, especially in the brain and eyes; lesions may consist almost entirely of aggregates of budding yeasts.

Clinicopathologic Features

Cryptococcosis can usually be diagnosed by microscopic examination of nasal or cutaneous exudates, CSF, aqueous humor, or biopsies of nasal and dermal lesions. Yeast forms can be found in surprisingly large numbers in such specimens. They can be visualized with routine Giemsa, new methylene blue or conventional tissue stains (Fig 3). Stained smears show a central nuclear structure surrounded by a clear halo. The halo is formed by the thick capsule, which does not take up stain. Wet mounts of exudates, tissue aspirates or impression smears can also be stained with common India ink. Encapsulated yeasts appear as round, clear areas in a sea of black.

Cryptococcal infection of cats can also be readily diagnosed by serologic tests.[8,28,32] The capsule is composed of a polysaccharide that is usually present in large concentrations in serum or plasma. A latex agglutination test, using particles coated with anticryptococcal-polysaccharide antibodies, provides a simple and accurate means to detect this antigen in blood. Cats with widely disseminated disease usually have antigen titers from 1:16 to over 1:1024. Cats with mild localized disease generally have very low or negative antigen titers.

Treatment and Prevention

The published successes with these various treatments can probably be attributed as much to the form and severity of infection as to the particular drugs involved. Several types of treatments have been tried with varying degrees of success. Amphotericin B used alone has been successful in treating several cats.[1,31,43,51] The recommended dosage is about 0.3 mg/kg IV every other day. The drug is diluted 10-fold or more in saline or dextrose before injection so as to prevent thromophlebitis. The blood urea nitrogen (BUN) level usually rises after 9-11 treatments. When this occurs, treatment should be stopped and reinstituted when the BUN falls. The BUN level usually rises again after 7-9 treatments in the second cycle, and again drug use must be temporarily discontinued. By giving the drug in cycles and monitoring the BUN level for toxicity, a cumulative dose as high as 16.25 mg has been given to a cat over a 4-month period. Amphotericin B incorporated into liposomes is being experimentally studied. Such preparations appear to be less nephrotoxic and more effective than the free form.

Flucytosine, at a dosage of 100-150 mg/kg divided QID, has been successful in a small number of cats. However, success is usually predicated on giving the drug at least QID to maintain effective blood levels and prevent drug resistance. Pretreatment tests to determine if the isolate is sensitive to flucytosine should be done whenever possible. Treatment should be continued for at least 1 month after signs have disappeared and cryptococcal antigenemia is no longer detectable. Even when these precautions are taken, drug resistance and disease recurrence following discontinuation of treatment appear to be high. Side effects of flucytosine include thrombocytopenia and increased serum liver enzyme levels.

Amphotericin B and flucytosine are synergistic when given together, and this has become the treatment of choice for cryptococcal meningitis in people.[8] Combination therapy should probably be considered the treatment of choice in cats with cryptococcosis of the brain and eyes. This treatment protocol has had a much better success rate than amphotericin B alone but is by no means completely effective.[33,42] Recurrence of disease following discontinuation is one problem; inability to maintain high intraocular and intrathecal drug levels is another. There is some indication in people that the success rate increases after each treatment cycle. However, this has not been studied in feline disease.

Ketoconazole has emerged as a popular treatment for cryptococcosis in cats that do not have CNS or ocular signs. The recommended dosage is 10-20 mg/kg PO daily or divided BID. Dosages above this, though more effective, may cause nausea and anorexia. Hansen described a cat with severe cryptococcosis that failed to respond to ketoconazole at recommended dosages but went into disease remission when treated at 72 mg/kg daily for 10 months.[13] Toxicity was not observed during the treatment period. Because of great variations in toxicity and efficacy from cat to cat, the actual dosage of ketoconazole should be titrated to provide maximum blood levels without toxicity. In addition to anorexia, long-term ketoconazole therapy can suppress adrenal gland function. If cats seem excessively weak or lethargic while receiving the drug, they should be supplemented with small doses of glucocorticoids.

A new generation of systemic imidazole compounds are in the test stages. Some of them have much greater and broader-spectrum antifungal activity than ketaconazole. Their side effects, in particular adrenal suppression, are also much less. They will undoubtedly replace ketaconazole in the near future.

Autogenous bacterins have reportedly been helpful in treating cats with cryptococcosis.[44,45] Considering the high antigen levels already present in the blood of infected cats, the rationale of such therapy is questionable.

Progress of drug therapy should be evaluated by following antigen levels in the blood.[13,28,32,33] Antigen levels should fall to levels of 1:16 or lower over several months. A continued decline to undetectable levels is evidence of complete cure; drug therapy should be continued for another 1-2 months to minimize the chance of recurrence. Frequently, however, antigen levels fall to low levels and no further, even though the cat might be much improved clinically. Under such circumstances it is unwise to withdraw therapy. In a few cases, disease is localized to the skin, subcutis or nasal passages. In such cases, antigen levels in the blood are generally low. Excision of the lesion or excision coupled with drug treatment has been curative in several such cases.[23,24,26,38]

Though many drugs and combinations of drugs are available to treat cryptococcosis and successes have been reported, the prognosis is still considered poor. For every successfully treated cat, several animals are treated unsuccessfully. Treatment failure is most likely in cats with high antigen levels in their blood and CNS, ocular or widely disseminated disease. Treatment successes are more likely in cats with localized disease, no CNS signs and low antigen levels. Because of relapses, successful treatment cannot be judged until 3 months or more have passed following cessation of therapy.

Infection and Immunity

Cryptococcosis in people is surprisingly uncommon, considering the ubiquitous nature of the organism in the environment. Therefore, most exposures in people and animals apparently are not severe enough to allow infection and clinical disease. A substantial proportion of people that develop disseminated cryptococcosis have underlying immunosuppressive conditions, such as clinical or subclinical lymphoreticular neoplasms, diabetes mellitus or acquired immunodeficiency syndrome (AIDS) caused by human immunodeficiency virus infection or use of immunosuppressive drugs. Therefore, it is not surprising that 20-30% of cats with cryptococcosis also have underlying feline leukemia virus (FeLV) infections.[2] Cats with cryptococcosis also have a greater than expected incidence of feline immunodeficiency virus (FIV) infection.

The extremely high levels of capsular antigen seen in cats with disseminated diseases appear to depress the humoral immune response. A latex-agglutination test, using particles coated with capsular antigen, is also available to measure serum antibodies. Antibody titers are essentially zero when free antigen is present. With successful treatment, levels of antigen fall and eventually antibody titers begin to rise. The disappearance of antigen and appearance of antibody is considered a very good prognostic sign in people.

Animal and Public Health Considerations

Cats with cryptococcosis, even though they may shed very large numbers of organisms, are not considered health hazards to people or other animals. Yeast forms from tissues are not nearly as infectious as the organisms from pigeon feces. Moreover, infection is very uncommon among people and animals that come into contact with the organism in nature.

References

1. Barrett RE and Scott DW: Treatment of feline cryptococcosis: Literature review and case report. *JAAHA* 11:511-518, 1975.

2. Blouin P and Cello RM: Experimental ocular cryptococcosis: Preliminary studies in cats and mice. *Invest Ophthalmol Vis Sci* 19:21-30, 1980.

3. Brown RJ et al: Dermal cryptococcosis in a cat. *Mod Vet Pract* 59:447, 1978.

4. Buchanan CA: Feline cryptococcosis: A case report and review. *Southwestern Vet* 35:41-44, 1982.

5. Campbell CK et al: Cryptococcosis in a cat. *Vet Record* 87:406-409, 1970.

6. Clark L and Roubin GS: Cryptococcosis in a cat. *Aust Vet J* 46:544-548, 1970.

7. Cordes DO and Royal WA: Cryptococcosis in a cat. *New Zeal Vet J* 15:117-121, 1967.

8. Drutz DJ, in Wyngaarden JB and Smith LH Jr: *Cecil's Textbook of Medicine.* Saunders, Philadelphia, 1985. pp 1265-1267.

9. Duckworth RH et al: *Cryptococcus neoformans* infection in a cat. *Vet Record* 96:48, 1975.

10. Fischer CA: Intraocular cryptococcosis in two cats. *JAVMA* 158:191-198, 1971.

11. Fowler NG et al: Cryptococcosis in a cat. *Vet Record* 77:292-293, 1965.

12. Gwin RM et al: Ocular cryptococcosis in a cat. *JAAHA* 13:680-684, 1977.

13. Hansen BL: Successful treatment of severe feline cryptococcosis with long-term high-dose ketoconazole. *JAAHA* 23:193-196, 1987.

14. Holzworth J: Cryptococcosis in a cat. *Cornell Vet* 42:12-15, 1952.

15. Holzworth J and Coffin DL: Cryptococcosis in the cat: A second case. *Cornell Vet* 43:546-550, 1953.

16. Howell J and Allan D: A case of cryptococcosis in the cat. *J Comp Pathol* 74:415-418, 1964.

17. Howlett CR et al: Systemic cryptococcosis in a cat. *Aust Vet J* 49:535-538, 1973.

18. Humphrey JD et al: Cryptococcosis in a cat in Papua New Guinea. *Aust Vet J* 53:197, 1977.

19. Ivoghli B et al: Disseminated cryptococcosis in a cat. *VM/SAC* 69:423-426, 1974.

20. Johnston LAY and Lavers DW: Cryptococcal meningitis in a cat in North Queensland. *Aust Vet J* 39:306-307, 1963.

21. Kaplan W et al: The discovery of *Histoplasma capsulatum* in Connecticut soil incidental to the investigation of a case of feline cryptococcosis. *Mycopathol Mycol Appl* 14:1-8, 1960.

22. Lau RE et al: Cryptococcosis in a cat. *VM/SAC* 66:777-780, 1971.

23. Legendre AM et al: Treatment of feline cryptococcosis with ketoconazole. *JAVMA* 181:1541-1542, 1982.

24. Madewell BR and Holmberg CA: Lymphosarcoma and cryptococcosis in a cat. *JAVMA* 175:65-68, 1979.

25. Medleau L et al: Cutaneous cryptococcosis in three cats. *JAVMA* 187:169-170, 1985.

26. Moore R: Treatment of feline nasal cryptococcosis with 5-flucytosine. *JAVMA* 181:816-817, 1982.

27. Moore DR and Bullmore CC: Pulmonary cryptococcosis in a cat. *Feline Pract* 14(1):14-18, 1984.

28. Noxon JO et al: Ketoconazole therapy in canine and feline cryptococcosis. *JAAHA* 22:179-183, 1986.

29. Okoshi S and Hasegawa A: Cryptococcosis in a cat. *Jpn J Vet Sci* 30:39-42, 1968.

30. Olander HJ et al: Feline cryptococcosis. *JAVMA* 142:138-143, 1963.

31. Palumbo NE and Perri S: Amphotericin B therapy in two cases of feline cryptococcosis. *VM/SAC* 70:553-557, 1975.

32. Pentlarge VW and Martin RA: Treatment of cryptococcosis in three cats, using ketoconazole. *JAVMA* 188:536-538, 1986.

33. Prevost E et al: Successful medical management of severe feline cryptococcosis. *JAAHA* 18:111-114, 1982.

34. Roberts ED et al: Feline cryptococcosis. *Iowa State Univ Vet* 26:30-33, 1963-64.

35. Rosenthal JJ et al: Ocular and systemic cryptococcosis in a cat. *JAAHA* 17: 307-310, 1981.

36. Rutman MA et al: Feline cryptococcosis. *Feline Pract* 5(3):36-43, 1975.

37. Ryer K and Ryer J: A case of feline mycotic rhinitis caused by *Cryptococcus neoformans*. *VM/SAC* 76:1150-1151, 1981.

38. Schulman J: Ketoconazole for successful treatment of cryptococcosis in a cat. *JAVMA* 187:508-509, 1985.

39. Sisk DB and Chandler FW: Phaeohyphomycosis and cryptococcosis in a cat. *Vet Pathol* 19:554-556, 1982.

40. Thrall MA et al: Feline cryptococcosis treatment with amphotericin B. *Feline Pract* 6(3):17-28, 1976.

41. Trautwein G and Nielsen SW: Cryptococcosis in 2 cats, a dog, and a mink. *JAVMA* 140:437-442, 1962.

42. Weir EC et al: Short-term combination chemotherapy for treatment of feline cryptococcosis. *JAVMA* 174:507-510, 1979.

43. Wilkinson GT: Feline cryptococcosis: A review and seven case reports. *J Small Anim Pract* 20:749-768, 1979.

44. Wilkinson GT: Feline cryptococcosis. *Aust Vet Practit* 14(2):64, 1984.

45. Wilkinson GT et al: Successful treatment of four cases of feline cryptococcosis. *J Small Anim Pract* 24:507-514, 1983.

46. Yamamoto S et al: Isolation of *Cryptococcus neoformans* from pulmonary granuloma of a cat and from pigeon droppings. *Jpn J Vet Sci* 19:179-189, 1957.

Chapter 47

Dermatomycosis

Etiologic Agents

Dermatomycosis (dermatophytosis, ringworm or tinea) is a skin condition caused by a group of fungi known as dermatophytes. Dermatophytes penetrate and parasitize keratinous body tissue, such as skin, hair, feathers, horns or nails.

Dermatophytes have previously been classified in the subdivision Deutermycotinia (fungi imperfecti) because they appeared to lack a distinct sexual form. Recently, however, the perfect form (sexual phase) of several dermatophytes has been recognized, thus changing their classification to the subdivision Ascomycotinia (true fungi), family Gymnoascaceae. There are presently over 35 species of dermatophytes belonging to 3 genera: *Epidermophyton* spp, *Microsporum* spp and *Trichophyton* spp. Some species of dermatophytes are zoophilic (animal parasites), some are anthropophilic (human parasites), and others are geophilic (soil parasites) (Table 1).[12]

Among the 35 or so species of dermatophytes, 6 are of particular interest in cats. *Microsporum canis* accounts for 75-98% of ringworm seen in cats in most parts of the world.[1,4,14,16,32] *Microsporum distortum* is a major cause of feline ringworm in southern New Zealand but is uncommon in other areas. *Microsporum gypseum* accounts for 0.5-30% of the cases of feline ringworm.[4,14-16,28] *Trichophyton mentagrophytes*, though a common dermatophyte of dogs, is seen in only 1% or so of cats with ringworm.[4,11,14,16,25,32] *Trichophyton verrucosum* and *T rubrum*, the causes of

Table 1. Principal environmental reservoirs of common and uncommon dermatophytes of people and animals.

Genus	Animals	People	Soil
Trichophyton	T equinum T mentagrophytes (several varieties)	T rubrum	T terrestre
Microsporum	M canis M distortum M equinum T gallinae	M audouinii	M gypsum-complex M nanum M cookei

bovine and human dermatomycosis, are also involved in <1% of cats with ringworm.[35]

Microsporum cookei and *M gallinae* have been rarely implicated to dermatophytosis in cats.[43] *Trichophyton terrestre* has been associated with ringworm in a cat from the United States.[48] Usually it is present on the cat's fur as a contaminant or inapparent infection.[41]

Microsporum canis grows rapidly on Sabouraud's dextrose agar and forms a white, fluffy colony that becomes silky and yellow around the periphery over time.[31] The mycelial phase produces both microconidia and macroconidia. After several weeks in culture, the aerial mycelia become tan in the center of the colony and yellowish on the periphery. Colonies are orangish-brown on the underside. A perfect form of the organism, *Nannizzia otae*, has been recognized. Infected hairs fluoresce a bright yellow-green under a Wood's lamp. This form causes infection in a large number of animals and in people, and cats are a principal host.

Microsporum distortum grows at a moderate rate on Sabouraud's dextrose agar and forms velvety or fluffy colonies that submerge themselves in the medium.[31] Colonies are radially grooved or flat, light to dark-buff on the top, and pale-buff on the reverse side. The culture produces many long, single-celled, pyriform microconidia. A perfect form of this organism has not yet been identified. The natural reservoir for this fungus has not been determined but it could be dogs, cats and monkeys. Infected hairs fluoresce under a Wood's lamp.

Microsporum gypseum grows rapidly on Sabouraud's dextrose agar and forms a flat, granular, buff to rose colony.[15,31] The reverse side is rose to cinnamon. Mycelia produce numerous cylindric, ellipsoid or fusiform macroconidia borne on short stalks.[15] Based on examination of sexual spores, *M gypseum* is in fact composed of 3 perfect species: *Nannizzia incurvata*, *N gypsea* and *N fulva*. The fungus is geophilic, worldwide in distribution and ubiquitous in the environment. Hairs infected with *M gypseum* do not fluoresce under a Wood's lamp.

Trichophyton mentagrophytes occurs in at least 3 varieties: var *mentagrophytes*, var *erinacei* and var *quinckeanum*.[31] It forms fine to coarse granular colonies on Sabouraud's dextrose agar. Young colonies are slightly folded and either remain that way over time (var *mentagrophytes*) or become very folded (var *quinckeanum*). The reverse sides are red to ochre (var *mentagrophytes*), yellow (var *erinacei*) or non-pigmented (var *quinckeanum*). Cultures produce macroconidia. The perfect states of these 3 varieties of *Trichophyton* have been called *Arthroderma benhamiae* and *A vanbreuseghemir*. The var *mentagrophytes* is found on small and large wild and domestic animals, var *erinacei* on hedgehogs, rats and mice, and var *quinckeanum* on mice, cats, cattle, dogs, fowl, horses, people, rabbits and sheep. Infected hairs do not fluoresce under the Wood's lamp.

Trichophyton verrucosum produces smooth, rarely downy, white to ochre colonies on Sabouraud's dextrose agar.[31] Chlamydospores are produced in large numbers in culture. Microconidia are most apt to be seen if the medium is supplemented with thiamin. Growth is slow at 25 C but more rapid at 37 C. A perfect form for this organism has not yet been identified. Cattle are its most important host. Infected hairs do not fluoresce under a Wood's lamp.

Trichophyton terrestre produces either creamy-white downy or red-pigmented granular colonies on Sabouraud's dextrose agar.[41] Large numbers of one-celled cylindric to cigar-shaped microcondidia are borne singly. Some isolates also produce 2- to 4-cell cylindric to cigar-shaped macrocondidia. The perfect states of this fungi are called *Arthroderma insingulare*, *A lenticularum* and *A quadrifidum*.[41] Infected hairs do not fluoresce under a Wood's lamp.

Pathogenesis

Cats are exposed to dermatophytes from other animals or spores in the environment. Spores of *M canis* have survived in the environment as long as 13 months.[18] Severity of environmental contamination is somewhat proportional to the numbers of kittens raised in the area, density of cats in the quarters, degree of sanitation (removal of hairs, keratinous debris), and level and type of disinfection. The type of cats housed in the environment might also be important. There is clinical and experimental evidence that domestic longhaired cats have milder disease than domestic shorthaired cats but are much more likely to be carriers and shedders of the organisms. Among purebreds, however, American Persians seem to have more severe and chronic infections than other breeds.

Animal-to-animal passage is also important, especially with *M canis*, which accounts for most cases of ringworm in cats. Though cats with clinical lesions are more apt to shed large numbers of spores, up to 40% of apparently normal cats in an enzootic environment can also be infected.[2,9,33,40] Quaife and Womar isolated *M canis* spores from 4-35% of apparently asymptomatic cats at 4 different cat shows.[33] Baxter isolated *M canis* from 78 of 200 (39%) and *T mentagrophytes* from 6 of 200 (3%) normal cats in New Zealand.[2] Aho and associates recovered *T terrestre* from 7.2% of normal cats in 7 catteries in Finland.[41] *Microsporum gypseum* has also been isolated from the hairs of normal cats.[8] In a survey of *M canis* infection among 1059 cats seen for various reasons, 5.9% were infected.[19] The infection rate among domestic shorthaired cats was 3.8%, while among purebred cats it was 16.9% in Persians and 38.8% in Siamese. The greater incidence in cattery-bred cats indicates the importance of environment on infection rate. In this same study, the highest isolation rate was from kittens <3 months of age (12.6%).[19] The infection rate remained fairly consistent at 3-5% through age 4, and was <1% after 4 years of age. Isolations were much more apt to be negative in cats over 4 years of age. This marked decrease in the carrier state after 4 years of age is also reflected in a marked drop in incidence of active lesions.[27]

Much more information is available about *M canis* infection in cats than for other *Microsporum* spp or *Trichophyton* spp. The pathogenesis of infection with these other organisms is probably the same, except for differences in reservoir hosts.

Rebell and co-workers studied experimentally induced *M canis* and *T mentagrophytes* infections in young kittens.[34] A small erythematous lesion was first noticed at the inoculation site 4 days after infection. Lesions grew in size until day 28 and then regressed. Viable organisms could be isolated for a week or more after lesion regression in *M canis* infections and 3 weeks or more in *T mentagrophytes* infections. O'Sullivan detected palpable thickening at the inoculation site between days 18 and 20 after infection of kittens with *M canis*.[30] Lesions persisted for a mean duration of 33 days. Fluorescence of hairs was demonstrated by day 12 postinoculation and persisted until around day 52. Viable organisms, as identified by culture, persisted for 106-127 days.

Infection with dermatophytes usually involves dermal contact with spores in the environment or on carrier animals. *Microsporum canis* spores remain viable on hairs for 315-422 days at room temperature.[18] In *M canis* infections in catteries, kittens may be infected very shortly after birth. Kittens born into households free of dermatophytes usually do not become infected until they go into new homes and come into contact with infected animals and contaminated environments.

The severity of clinical disease depends on many factors. Kittens that are malnourished, sickly, concurrently infected with viral, bacterial and parasitic agents, in highly stressful surroundings, and born into environments with a high level of animal and environmental contamination develop much more severe disease than normal kittens. Genetics may also play a role. Persian cats have a much higher incidence of clinical infections, and the disease course is more severe and chronic than in other breeds.

Shortly after contacting the skin, spores transform into mycelia, which grow on and into the keratinized layer of the hair. Hyphae eventually grow down proximad into hair follicles along hair shafts. Hyphal branches invade the cortex and medulla of the intrafollicular hair by penetrating between the overlapping scales of the cuticle.[22] Eventually the entire intrafollicular portion of the hair, except for the keratin-free bulb, is invaded by fungal elements. Invasion of the bulb is only seen in dead aborted hairs or in hairs that have become separated from the papilla in the shedding process. During their proximal growth, mycelia on the surface of the intrafollicular portion of the hair shaft form arthrospore-like structures that are spherical to polyhedral and 2-3 μ in diameter. As more and more spores develop, they tend to form a sheath around the intrafollicular portion of the hair.[22] This spore sheath forms continuously and grows out with the hair, eventually becoming very long.

Ringworm lesions slowly expand by centrifugal growth within the interfollicular keratin layer and vertical growth along the intrafollicular hair shaft. The actual ringworm "lesion" only comprises a portion of the infected area; fluorescent hairs often extend many millimeters around the lesion. Typical ringworm lesions occur because of loss of diseased hairs by early breakage, increased desquamation of keratinized skin, host inflammatory responses and, sometimes, secondary bacterial infection.

Fig 2. Litter of kittens with severe acute dermatomycosis caused by *Microsporum canis*. Note the concentration of lesions around the head, loss of whiskers and eyelashes, and low-grade conjunctivitis. (Courtesy of Dr. Peter Ihrke, University of California, Davis)

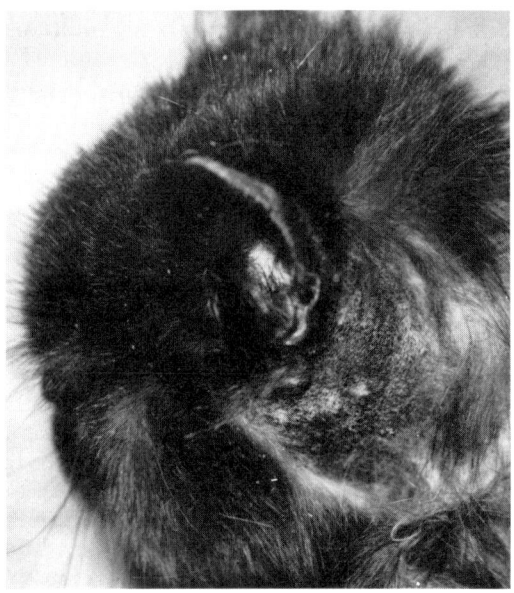

Fig 1. Persian kitten with a chronic ringworm lesion behind the ear. The lesion is scaly and pigmented. Hair has been lost from the center of the lesion, while peripheral hairs are thinned and apparently dead. (Courtesy of Dr. Peter Ihrke, University of California, Davis)

Spread of ringworm infection appears to be halted by immunologic means around day 30 after clinical lesions appear. However, this event can be greatly delayed in sickly, malnourished or heavily stressed kittens with an impaired immune response. Large numbers of infectious spores remain on the hairs after recovery, and these are only lost when the hairs grow out and are eventually shed. This process can take another month or more. Even though recovery is widespread and very dramatic, it is not always complete. Small numbers of chronically infected hair follicles can remain for many more months or years.

Clinical Features

Ringworm is a much more common disease among purebred than domestic cats, probably because the cattery environment favors infection.[27] Lesions begin to appear in some kittens during the second or third week of life. More often, however, the first lesions appear around weaning age. Over

70% of affected animals are young cats rather than adults.[2,13,19,27] The earliest lesions tend to concentrate on the face and paws, but any area of the body can be affected.[3-5,13,27] Initial lesions consist mainly of small plaques that are somewhat erythematous. Eventually hairs in the central part of the lesion are lost, while hairs around the periphery appear discolored and otherwise dead (Fig 1). Lesions slowly expand and coalesce with each other to form large, scaly, grayish-brown areas of hyperkeratosis and alopecia (Fig 1). Over time, hairs in the central part of the lesions begin to regenerate. This central area of hair regrowth, surrounded by a zone of alopecia, which in turn is surrounded by areas of dead hair, gives lesions a ring-like appearance.

Involvement of the vibrissae and eyelashes is especially severe (Fig 2).[3] Intrafollicular mycelial growth in these larger hairs is so great that the hairs are weakened and fall out very early in the disease course. Sometimes the earliest clinical sign noted by the owner is loss of whiskers. Extensive hair involvement around the eyelids can also lead to pronounced depilation and a mild conjunctivitis-like syndrome (Fig 2).

Lesions are frequently found in the skin around the toes and nails. The keratin layer of the nail may be involved and this may cause nail deformities.[23] The number of lesions on the body is highly variable. Lesions often remain relatively small and localized; they may not be clinically apparent unless inspected closely. In severe cases, a large proportion of the body can be involved. Such severe cases are least likely to respond to therapy and often persist for weeks or months before resolving. Cats with smaller lesions and more localized disease usually recover spontaneously within a month or so.

Deeper nodular skin lesions (mycetomas) have been associated with *M canis* infection in cats.[38,42,46] Persian cats are especially prone to this condition. The lesions were poorly circumscribed, solid or cystic in nature, and granulomatous in appearance on histologic examination. The mycetomas can be particularly extensive and severe in some animals.[46]

Pathologic Features

Dermatophytes are essentially parasites of keratin.[22] Early hair loss is caused by massive invasion and weakening of the hair cuticle. Infection spares the nonkeratinized bulb from which the new hair grows, thus providing a continued substrate for fungal growth.[22] Involvement of the skin's keratin layer leads to an increased rate of keratin sloughing and formation (hyperkeratosis). Inflammatory reactions in tissues surrounding infected hairs are mild in *M canis* infections. However, *Trichophyton mentagrophytes* infections elicit a more severe inflammatory response.[34]

Clinicopathologic Features

Lesions of many different skin disorders can be mistaken for ringworm. Biopsies are essential when the clinical history, age of the animal, appearance and progression of lesions, and fluorescence studies do not clearly indicate a diagnosis of ringworm. When the disease appears typical, very little diagnostic testing is needed. A minimum workup should consist of Wood's lamp fluorescence and examination of hairs for mycelia and spores.

Fungal elements of *M canis* and *M distortum* fluoresce a whitish- to bluish-green when examined closely under a Wood's lamp. Hairs at the periphery of the lesions are most likely to fluoresce. Fluorescence is usually concentrated on the proximal end of the hair but can extend the entire length. Hairs infected with *M gypseum*, *T mentagrophytes* and *T verrucosum* do not fluoresce.

Skin scrapings containing hairs or hairs pulled from the periphery of lesions can be examined microscopically for fungi. Visualization of fungi can be aided by dissolving the hairs to be examined in 10% KOH. Heating the mixture briefly under a flame hastens the process. Branching hyphae that sometimes invade the hair structure, as well as spores, can be readily identified with some experience.

Treatment and Prevention

Treatment is directed at individual infected animals, potential carriers and the environment. In household pets, treatment is directed mainly at the affected animal. With enzootic disease in catteries, all 3 points need consideration.

Treatment of individual cats with ringworm has consisted of systemic antifungal medications, topical treatment, and/or combined topical and systemic therapy. All 3 modes of treatment have been successful. However, the efficacy of any particular treatment must be evaluated in context of natural immunity and "self cure." Many articles on drug therapy describe complete cures in a 30-day period, the same length of time in which most animals become disease free if untreated. Also, most treatments fail in particularly severe cases, while most treatments succeed in mild cases.

Griseofulvin, a metabolic product of several species of *Penicillium* molds, has been commonly used for treatment of feline dermatomycosis.[7,13,30] It is usually given orally and is carried systemically to keratinized cells, where it is deposited. An oral dosage of 25 mg/kg divided BID, preferably given with a fatty meal, for as long as 8 weeks has been recommended for cats. Kaplan and Ajello treated 18 cats with visible lesions with griseofulvin; 10 of 18 were clinically normal after 3 weeks, 16 of 18 after 4 weeks and 18 of 18 after 5 weeks.[13] However, only 8 of 22 cats were rendered culture negative through use of griseofulvin alone during this period. The efficacy of systemic griseofulvin therapy has reportedly been increased by shaving the animal to remove dead hair and including topical antifungal therapy.[30] Resistance to griseofulvin has been seen occasionally. Griseofulvin given at newer recommended dosages has limited toxicity for cats. Toxicity appears to be idiosynchratic and not close related.[45] It has caused pruritic drug reactions in the skin, angioneurotic edema of the skin, mucous membranes or viscera, pyrexia, lethargy, diarrhea, vomiting, developmental anomalies in kittens born to queens treated while pregnant, anemia, leukopenia, neurologic problems, and partial weight loss and anorexia.[37,44,45]

Ketoconazole is the newest systemic drug used to treat dermatomycosis in cats.[6,39] Ketoconazole is an imidazole compound that alters permeability of fungal cell walls by specifically interfering with the alpha-demethylation of lanosterol. The suggested dosage is 10 mg/kg PO daily for up to 8 weeks. In a double-blind study in people, the cure rate against *T mentagrophytes* for ketoconazole was 83%, vs 32% for griseofulvin. De Keyser and Van den Brande treated 60 cats with ketoconazole at 10 mg/kg daily for 10-20 days.[6] Treatment was more successful after 20 days of therapy, with a reported cure rate of 95% among cats with active ringworm lesions. Pintori and coworkers found that ketoconazole gave much quicker regression of ringworm lesions than griseofulvin. The drug irritates the GI tract and suppresses the adrenal glands. Toxic signs include anorexia, fever, depression and diarrhea. Newer, safer and more effective systemic imidazole compounds will probably replace ketoconazole in the next few years.

Topical treatment is commonly used for localized ringworm, or in combination with systemic drugs in severe generalized disease. In 1 study, the time for resolution of lesions was reduced by more than half in cats that received both topical and systemic treatments, vs that in cats that received only systemic treatment.[5] Many substances have activity against dermatophytes, including undecylenic acid, mercaptan, tolnaftate, iodophor, iodochlorhydroxyquin, chlorhexidine, nystatin, thiabendazole, clotrimazole, miconazole and numerous other new topical imidazoles, dilute chlorine solutions, and organic and inorganic iodides. Hyperthermia, using high-energy radio waves, has also been used effectively for topical treatment of local ringworm lesions in cats.[26] If lesions are extensive or widespread, total body clipping of hair facilitates treatment and eliminates a great amount of infectious hairs. As in systemic therapy, topical treatment is usually more successful in cats with milder, more recent infections than in cats with chronic disease.

Mycetomas due to *M canis* are very difficult to treat medically and they frequently recur following surgical removal. Ketoconazole and amphotericin plus griseofulvin have proven unsuccessful in 2 cats, and 3 of 4 cats treated surgically have had recurrences.[38,42,46]

Identification and elimination or isolation of carrier cats has been an elusive goal of many veterinarians and cat breeders. Carriers can often be identified by using the "brush technique," in which large areas of the body can be sampled.[2,5] Carrier cats are more likely to be <4 years of age. In many cattery environments, even those without much clinically apparent ringworm, 5-40% of cats in the lower age range are carriers. Many veterinarians and cattery owners recognize the difficulty and expense of mass culturing, and have attempted to eliminate carrier cats by chronic treatment of all cats in the environment with a systemic antidermatophyte (griseofulvin in particular).[5] Such attempts are usually doomed to failure and can be deleterious to the health of cats being treated and their unborn young. It is difficult to clear all inapparent infections with systemic therapy; infections cleared in this manner readily recur when therapy is discontinued. Topical treatment of all cats in the environment is also ineffective for the same reasons.

In addition to carrier cats, the environment must be considered. Spores of most dermatophytes survive for a year or more in the environment and are very difficult to kill with disinfectants and heat treatment. This is especially true if they are protected by porous surfaces, dust, dirt and other debris. Therefore, decreasing the number of spores in the environment can be difficult. When possible, cages should be constructed of impervious materials that can be easily washed with soap and hot water. This loosens material in which spores are imbedded and allows spores to be washed away. Litter should be swept up as often as possible between washings. The most important step to reduce environmental contamination is to decrease contamination from infected animals. This is most effectively accomplished by proper husbandry practices.

Ultimately, cattery owners must realize that ringworm, in particular *M canis*, is enzootic in most environments where cats are kept. However, whether or not the organisms cause a significant number of clinically apparent infections is related more to husbandry practices than to inherent characteristics of the organism. Cattery owners are quick to blame outside animals for introducing infection to their animals; in truth, many infections are generated from within. Catteries with relatively few breeding animals, and especially with older breeding cats, have far fewer problems with clinical ringworm than catteries with many younger breeders. Kittens are most susceptible to infection. Adolescent and young cats (<4 years of age) are most likely to be carriers.[19] The more kittens that are produced in a cattery, the more susceptible hosts there are for the organism to attack. Litters of older kittens in such catteries are often in intimate contact with litters of younger kittens. Older kittens are more likely to have subclinical lesions or be postinfection carriers. If the incidence of clinical disease in kittens is high, the amount of environmental contamination is great. Many infected kittens, in addition to a high degree of environmental contamination, ensure that each generation of kittens will receive a great deal of exposure. Segregating litters, maintaining the best sanitation possible to reduce environmental contamination, and limiting the number of breeding animals all contribute to a lower incidence of clinical infections.

The severity of ringworm in a cattery or multiple-cat household is often related to the magnitude of upper respiratory infections, ear mite and flea infestations, congenital defects (indicating weak or inbred bloodlines) and the state of nutrition. Stress levels in the cattery also contribute to an overall increase in many diseases, including ringworm. Factors that contribute to the level of cattery stress include overcrowding, frequent movement of cats in and out of the cattery, poor ventilation, severe or frequent changes in temperature and humidity, lack of privacy, and caging. Ultimately, it is not often possible to rid an environment of dermatophytes. However, it is possible to create an environment in which disease is inapparent or mild and self limiting.

Fig 3. This 8-month-old cat had dermatomycosis (*Microsporum canis*) at 3-4 months of age. The cat was apparently fully recovered until it received an IM injection of methylprednisolone at 10 mg/kg. Dermatomycosis reappeared on the face within 2 weeks, and spread rapidly to the remainder of the body. Note the poor haircoat, extensive hair loss on the head, and low-grade conjunctivitis.

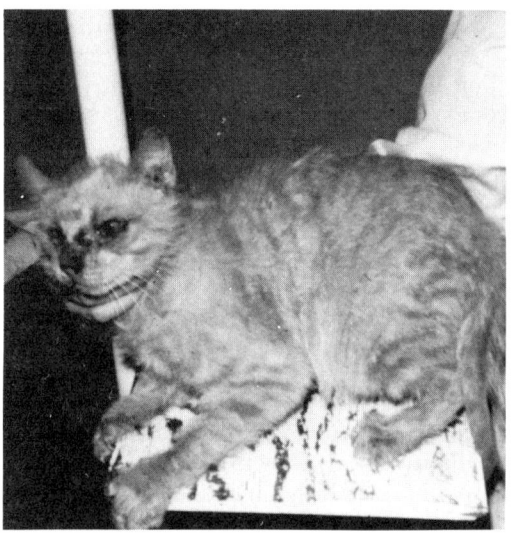

Infection and Immunity

Dermatophytes are superficial parasites of the keratin layer of skin and hair. They do not invade deeply and are slow to elicit host immunity. Moreover, their location away from living tissues makes it difficult for the host to bring serum and cellular factors into contact with the organisms. Nevertheless, some type of immunity develops. The nature of this immunity is not precisely known, but in people and guinea pigs, it seems to involve cellular mechanisms. Guinea pigs and people that have recovered from dermatophyte infections develop delayed hypersensitivity reactions to extracts of the organisms injected intradermally. However, such responses have not been elicited in cats. Failure to evoke such reactions in recovered cats does not indicate that cats are defective in cellular immunity or that some other type of protective mechanism is involved. Delayed hypersensitivity reactions in the skin are notoriously hard to elicit in cats when cellular immunity is obviously present.

Immunity to dermatophyte infection is not complete when clinical lesions disappear. Infected hair follicles remain for many months, and perhaps years, albeit few in number as compared to their numbers during the active stage of disease. The decrease in recognizable lesions and asymptomatic fungal carriage in cats >4 years of age suggests that absolute immunity can take many months or years to develop in some individuals.[19]

Corticosteroid treatment in the first 1-4 months following recovery from active infection can sometimes cause severe recurrence of clinical disease (Fig 3). Corticosteroid therapy after this time is much less apt to cause clinical exacerbations of ringworm. Reactivation of disease is particularly severe when long-acting corticosteroids, such as methylprednisolone, are used. Just as long-acting corticosteroid can activate disease, chronic stress (which causes continuous corticosteroids release from the adrenals) can greatly delay natural recovery and is associated with severe and generalized disease that seems refractory to all types of therapy. Any cat with severe ringworm that is refractory to treatment should be examined closely for underlying congenital or acquired diseases.

Individual Persian cats are especially prone to clinical disease. Lesions tend to be more widespread and heal slower. Persians are also prone to more deeply situated lesions (mycetomas).[38,42,48] This predisposition extends to dermatophytes other than *M canis*.[41] The nature of this increased susceptability is unknown.

Recurrent infections are seen in both human and feline dermatomycosis. Recurrent disease, unless associated with some immunosuppressive condition, is generally much milder, more localized and more transient. Only 1 in 7 recovered kittens was totally resistant to reinfection when exposed

3 months later. Lesions in reinfected kittens were relatively small, did not tend to spread to secondary sites, and did not last as long.[17] This indicates that immunity is slow to develop and is tenuous at best, especially in the months preceding recovery from primary infection.

Animal and Public Health Considerations

Cats are the main source of *M canis* dermatophyte infection in people, while *T mentagrophytes* is more commonly spread by cattle.[9,10] Kittens with or without clinical lesions are the most infectious, and children are the most susceptible.[20,24] The highest infection rate is among children ≤10 years old. The incidence of disease declines rapidly in children >11 years. Most adults are resistant to infections or, if infected, lesions are apt to be small and self limiting. Infected children are not very infectious to other children. The disease course in people, though not as severe, is identical to that in cats. Lesions tend to concentrate on the scalp, forearm, trunk and neck. Recurrent infections in some people are common. Secondary infections are almost always more localized, mild and transient than primary infections.

To limit spread of infection from a cat with clinical disease to people, infected animals should be clipped as close as possible to remove infected hairs and dipped periodically in mercaptan, chlorhexidine or organic iodide solutions to destroy as many remaining surface spores as possible. Infected cats should be handled mainly by adults or older children, who are usually immune. The level of infectivity decreases greatly as lesions disappear, but infected cats can still shed some organisms for months or longer afterwards.

References

1. Al-Doory Y et al: A survey of ringworm in dogs and cats. *JAVMA* 153:429-432, 1968.

2. Baxter M: Ringworm due to *Microsporum canis* in cats and dogs in New Zealand. *New Zeal Vet J* 21:33-37, 1973.

3. Collins GD and Smith OG: Ringworm in a Siamese cattery. *Can Vet J* 1:412-415, 1960.

4. Conroy JD: *Microsporum* infections in cats. *JAVMA* 145:115-121, 1964.

5. Dawson CO and Noddle BM: Treatment of *Microsporum canis* ringworm in a cat colony. *J Small Anim Pract* 9:613-620, 1968.

6. De Keyser H and Van den Brande M: Ketoconazole in the treatment of dermatomycosis in cats and dogs. *Vet Quarterly* 5:142-144, 1983.

7. Donovan EF and Bohl EH: Use of griseofulvin in the treatment of ringworm. *Vet Med* 55:49-55, 1960.

8. Fuentes CA et al: Occurrence of *Trichophyton mentagrophytes* and *Microsporum gypseum* on hairs of healthy cats. *J Invest Dermatol* 23:311-313, 1954.

9. Gentles JC et al: Correlation of human and animal ringworm in west of Scotland. *Brit Med J* 2:678-682, 1957.

10. Georg LK: The diagnosis of ringworm in animals. *VM/SAC* 49:157-166, 1954.

11. Georg LK et al: *Trichophyton mentagrophytes* infections in dogs and cats. *JAVMA* 130:427-432, 1957.

12. Kaplan W: Epidemiology and public health significance of ringworm in animals. *Arch Derm* 96:404-408, 1967.

13. Kaplan W and Ajello L: Oral treatment of spontaneous ringworm in cats with griseofulvin. *JAVMA* 135:253-261, 1959.

14. Kaplan W et al: Recent developments in animal ringworm and their public health implications. *Ann NY Acad Sci* 70:636-649, 1958.

15. Kaplan W et al: Ringworm in cats caused by *Microsporum gypseum*. *Vet Med* 52:347-348, 1957.

16. Kaplan W and Ivens MS: Observations on the seasonal variations in incidence of ringworm in dogs and cats in the United States. *Sabouraudia* 1:91-102, 1961.

17. Keep JM: The epidemiology and control of *Microsporum canis* Bodin in a cat community. *Aust Vet J* 35:374-378, 1959.

18. Keep JM: The viability of *Microsporum canis* on isolated cat hair. *Aust Vet J* 36:277-278, 1960.

19. Keep JM: A survey of *Microsporum canis* infection of cats in Sydney. *Aust Vet J* 39:330-332, 1963.

20. Kristensen S and Krogh HV: A study of skin diseases in dogs and cats. VII. Ringworm infection. *Nord Vet-Med* 33:134-140, 1981.

21. La Touche CJ: Microsporosis due to *M canis* in schoolchildren and domestic animals. *Brit Med J* 2:1081, 1952.

22. La Touche CJ: Some clinical and microscopic features of *Microsporum canis* Bodin infection of the skin and its appendages as it occurs in the cat. *Vet Record* 65:680-681, 1953.

23. La Touche CJ: Onychomycosis in cats infected by *Microsporum canis* Bodin. *Vet Record* 67:578-579, 1955.

24. La Touche CJ: The importance of the animal reservoir of infection in the epidemiology of animal-type ringworm in man. *Vet Record* 67:666-669, 1955.

25. La Touche CJ and Forster RA: Chronic infection in a cat due to *Trichophyton mentagrophytes* (Robin) Blanchard. *Sabouraudia* 3:11-13, 1963.

26. Lueker DC and Kainer RA: Hyperthermia for the treatment of dermatomycosis in dogs and cats. *VM/SAC* 76:658-659, 1981.

27. Menges RW and Georg LK: Observations on feline ringworm caused by *Microsporum canis* and its public health significance. *Proc Ann Mtg AVMA*, 1955. pp 471-474.

28. Okoshi S and Hasegawa A: *Microsporum gypseum* isolated from feline ringworm. *Jpn J Vet Sci* 29:195-199, 1967.

29. Olsen CD and Quist KD: A ringworm epidemic caused by *Microsporum canis* in a rural community. *JAVMA* 137:291-292, 1960.

30. O'Sullivan JG: Griseofulvin treatment in experimental *Microsporum canis* infection in the cat. *Sabouraudia* 1:103-107, 1961.

31. Padhye AA, in Steele JH: *CRC Handbook Series in Zoonoses*. CRC Press, 1980. pp 441-458.

32. Pepin GA and Austwick PKC: Skin diseases, mycological origin. *Vet Record* 82:208-213, 1968.

33. Quaife RA and Womar SM: *Microsporum canis* isolation from show cats. *Vet Record* 110:333-334, 1982.

34. Rebell G et al: Experimental *Microsporum canis* infections in kittens. *Am J Vet Res* 17:74-78, 1956.

35. Refai M and Miligy M: *Trichophyton rubrum* infection in a family transmitted from a cat. *Mykosen* 11:191-194, 1968.

36. Schwäblein-Sprafke U and Tuchen M: *Microsporum canis*-Endemic durch Rassekatzen in Raum Karl Marx Stadt. *Dermatol Monatsschr* 168:105-110, 1982.

37. Scott FW et al: Teratogenesis in cats associated with griseofulvin therapy. *Teratology* 11:79-86, 1975.

38. Tuttle PA and Chandler FW: Deep dermatophytosis in a cat. *JAVMA* 183:1106-1108, 1983.

39. Woodard DC: Ketoconazole therapy for *Microsporum* spp dermatophytes in cats. *Feline Pract* 13(5):28-29, 1983.

40. Woodgyer AJ: Asymptomatic carriage of dermatophytes by cats. *N Zeal Vet J* 25:67-69, 1977.

Additional References

41. Aho R et al: Mycological and epidemiological studies in *Trichophyton terrestre* in cats. *Mykosen* 30:157-165, 1987.

42. Bourdin M et al: Premiere observation d'un mycetoma a *Microsporum canis* chez un chat. *Rec Med Vet* 151: 475-479, 1975.

43. Dvořák J and Otcenásek M: natural relationship of dermatophytes to the millieu of their existence. A review. *Mykosen* 25:197-209, 1982.

44. Helton KA et al: Griseofulvin toxicity in cats: Literature review and report of seven cases. *JAAHA* 22:453-458, 1986.

45. Kunkle GA and Meyer DJ: Toxicity of high doses of griseofulvin in cats. *JAVMA* 191:322-323, 1987.

46. Miller WH Jr and Goldschmidt MH: Mycetoma in the cat caused by a dermatophyte. *JAAHA* 22:255-260, 1986.

47. Pintori G et al: La dermatomicosi del cane e del gatto. *Boll Assoc Ital Vet Piccoli Anim* 25:307-312, 1986.

48. Scott DW et al: Dermatophytosis due to *Trichophyton terrestre*. Infection in a dog and cat. *JAAHA* 16:53-59, 1980.

Chapter 48

Sporotrichosis

Etiologic Agent

Sporothrix schenckii is a dimorphic fungus. The organism is found mainly on vegetation or in soil, where it exists as hyphae that produce conidia 2-3 μ in diameter. *Sporothrix schenckii* forms round to cigar-shaped, yeast-like structures in tissue and in agar at 37 C. It reverts to the mycelial form when grown in agar at 25 C.[3,7]

Human sporotrichosis is most common in Mexico, Central America and Brazil, and is more prevalent in the United States than Europe.[7,8] The geographic incidence is probably similar in cats. In Brazil, 8 cases of feline sporotrichosis occurred over an 18-month period.[9]

People that frequently contact abrasive vegetation, such as sphagnum moss, timber, hay or thorn bushes, are at highest risk. Hence the name "rose gardener's disease." Some cases may also involve transmission by insect or animal bites.[7] Cats may also be exposed through contact with contaminated vegetation. Pulmonary infection from inhalation of the small conidia is uncommon in people.

Pathogenesis

Infection with *S schenckii* usually occurs through gross or inapparent abrasions of the skin.[3,7] The organism can occasionally penetrate intact skin.[8] Once the organism enters the skin, it reverts to the yeast phase. Strains that grow optimally at 37 C reproduce more rapidly and, in people, have a greater tendency to invade lymphatics and occasionally spread systemically.[7] However, strains that grow optimally at 35 C grow much more slowly in tissues and rarely spread beyond the cutaneous site of inoculation.

Sporotrichosis was first experimentally recreated in cats in 1909.[5,6] These studies suggested that kittens were much more susceptible than adult cats. These results differed from those of a more recent study in which 18 of 20 adult cats inoculated in the paw developed localized lesions within 5 weeks.[2] Infection in the latter cats spread proximad up the afferent lymphatics, and secondary lesions sometimes occurred in overlying skin. Gross visceral involvement occurred in only 1 cat, but organisms were recovered on culture from the viscera of 9 other animals. This pattern seems to also occur in naturally occurring infections; only 1 naturally infected cat with disseminated lesions has been described. Interestingly, organisms cultured from this animal also caused a fulminating local and disseminated infection in an experimentally inoculated cat.[10]

Clinical Features

Sporotrichosis has mainly been described in mature cats.[1,4,6-12] Initial lesions are usually on the distal limbs, particularly the pads or digits. Secondary lesions are often seen proximal to primary foci and in distant sites of the body. Secondary lesions are usually on the head, tail and caudal back. Lesions probably result from oral cutaneous spread that occurs during grooming rather than by hematogenous or lymphatic dissemination.

Lesions usually are several millimeters to a centimeter or more in diameter and are present for several weeks before the animals are examined. Lesions often ulcerate and exude a slight to moderate amount of clear to serosanguineous fluid (Fig 1). Weight loss is usually minor to moderate when the animal is initially examined but can become more severe over time.

Disseminated lesions are usually granulomatous. When observed, they have been in the regional lymph nodes and lungs.[10] Lesions in other viscera are usually minimal on gross inspection and consist mainly of organisms with very little host reaction.[2,10] Weight loss is more apt to be seen in cats with disseminated or lymphatic and cutaneous lesions than in cats with cutaneous lesions alone.

Pathologic Features

Lesions are both suppurative and granulomatous in nature. Evolution of sporotrichosis lesions in cats has been followed experimentally by Barbee and co-workers.[2] Primary lesions are usually wart-like but rapidly break through the overlying epidermis and ulcerate. Surrounding and underlying tissues become thickened. Primary lesions usually grow slowly by extension centrifugally and deep. Afferent lymphatics draining primary lesions often become thickened and marked at intervals with small, hard nodules. Secondary skin lesions can break out from involved draining afferent lymphatics. Lymph nodes regional to primary foci are often enlarged, but are not always involved directly with the disease process. Organisms are easily cultured from regional lymph nodes even though lesions may be limited to reactive hyperplasia.

Histologic examination of cutaneous lesions shows epidermal ulceration and surrounding areas of hyperplasia that may extend deeply into the dermis.[1,2,4,8,10,12] Chronic localized lesions in people may also have a pronounced epithelial hyperplastic nature and are sometimes confused with neoplasia. The surrounding dermis is often

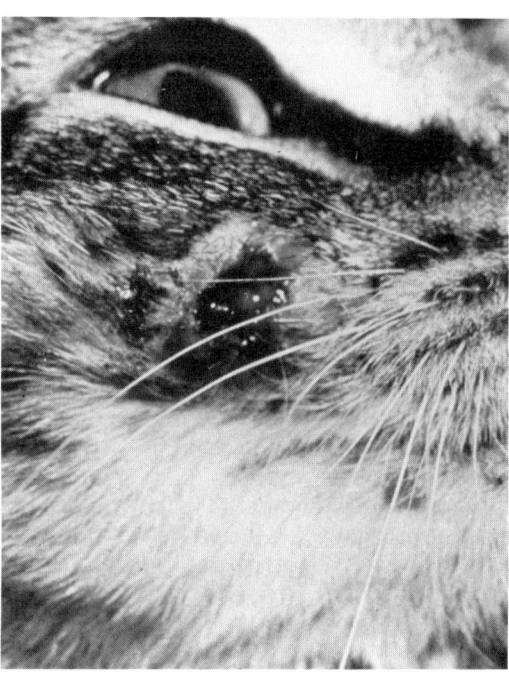

Fig 1. Cutaneous sporotrichosis lesion on the upper lip of a cat. The chronic lesion is slowly spreading and has a fleshy, mucinous appearance. (Courtesy of Dr. Ernst Biberstein, University of California, Davis)

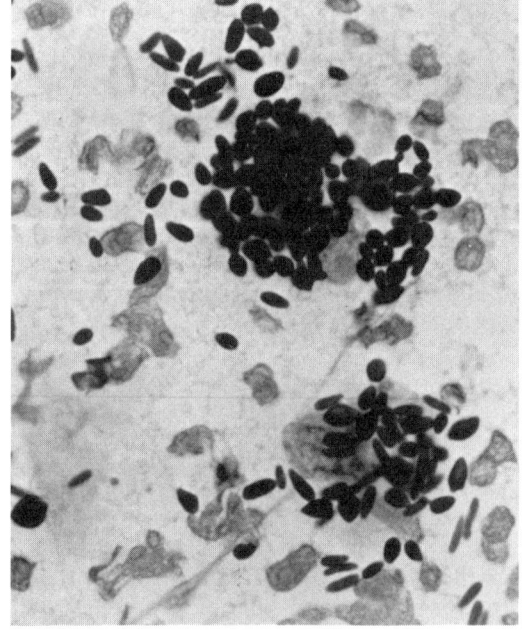

Fig 2. Impression smear from a cutaneous sporotrichosis lesion shows several clusters of Sporothrix schenckii organisms, 3 x 8 μ in size. PAS stain, 1200X. (Courtesy of Dr. Ernst Biberstein, University of California, Davis)

involved in a pyogranulomatous reaction with neutrophils, macrophages and occasional giant cells. Large numbers of yeast bodies are seen within macrophages and free in the tissues. Yeast capsules do not stain well with hematoxylin and eosin; the bodies appear as 1- to 3-μ circular structures surrounded by a clear zone. Periodic acid-Schiff stain, which penetrates the capsule, shows the organisms to be 3-8 μ in diameter, with readily discernible cigar-shaped buds (Fig 2). The extremely large numbers of organisms seen in feline sporotrichosis lesions are atypical for lesions of people and other animals.[8]

Visceral lesions, when observed, are more typically granulomatous in nature, with suppurative or caseated centers.

Clinicopathologic Features

Yeasts are not easily observed in exudates but can be readily cultured from exudates or biopsied tissues.[3,7] A low, brownish mycelial growth is seen on Sabouraud's agar at 25 C, while cream-colored yeast colonies are seen at 37 C. The mycelial phase is characterized by fine, branching septate hyphae, with conidia on the tips of conidiophores in grape-like clusters.

Diagnosis is usually by histopathologic examination of biopsied skin lesions or impression smears (Fig 2). Yeast structures can sometimes be mistaken for *Histoplasma* in routine hematoxylin and eosin-stained sections but are fairly characteristic on PAS or Gomori's methenamine silver stains. Fluorescent-antibody staining of tissue sections is considered highly accurate in people and has been successfully applied to at least 1 cat.[7,12]

Serologic tests are available for diagnosis of sporotrichosis in people but they have not yet been applied to cats. Latex- or yeast-agglutination procedures are the most sensitive and accurate tests for diagnosis of sporotrichosis in people.[7]

Treatment and Prevention

Though many sporotrichosis lesions probably regress naturally, lesions large enough to concern owners usually continue to spread if untreated. Well-circumscribed lesions in easily accessible sites can be removed by wide excision. Medical treatment is used only if lesions recur at the surgical site. However, cats with multiple skin lesions should be treated medically from the onset. The treatment of choice is potassium or sodium iodide, given PO in drop form. The recommended dosage of NaI for cats is 20 mg/kg BID for 4 weeks.[4] Higher dosages are frequently associated with acute toxicity (depression, anorexia, vomiting, heart failure).[4,12] The mode of action of iodide is unknown; it does not inhibit growth of the organism *in vitro*.[3]

Ketoconazole, miconazole and flucytosine have not proven particularly effective for treatment of sporotrichosis in people.[7] Burke and co-workers slowed the progressive course of the disease in 1 cat with ketoconazole.[4] However, complete remission did not occur until iodide treatment was started. Amphotericin B is superior to KI in treatment of disseminated disease.[7] Newer systemic imidazoles such as itraconazole may be more effective than ketoconazole.

Infection and Immunity

Immunity to the organism is largely cellular in nature.[7] Antibodies produced during the course of infection do not appear to alter the course of disease.

Immunosuppressed people seem more likely to develop disseminated disease.[7] The only cat with disseminated sporotrichosis and tested for feline leukemia virus was positive.[4] Whether this will be true for other cats with disseminated disease remains to be determined.

Animal and Public Health Considerations

Because of the apparent ease with which infection can spread from 1 site of the skin to another by grooming and scratching, the public and animal health significance of sporotrichosis in cats is important to consider. There is a report of 3 people in a household that contracted cutaneous sporotrichosis from an infected cat.[11] Dunstan has also reported on 7 incidents in Michigan over a 3-year period in which sporotrichosis was passed from infected cats to people.[8] In 5 of these cases, the infected individuals were veterinarians or veterinary assistants. In 4 of the 7 human cases, infection involved merely contact; there were no bites, scratches or abrasions of the human skin to allow entrance of the organism. After reviewing all possible zoonotic cases of sporotrichosis in people, Dunstan concluded that virtually all of them involved cat-to-person transmission.[8] The much larger number of organisms in cat lesions as compared to those in lesions in other species may account for the high zoonotic potential of feline sporotrichosis.

Sporotrichosis in people is similar to the disease in cats.[7] It is a noncontagious, subacute to chronic infection of the skin and regional lymphatics. Pulmonary disease can result from inhalation of spores. Rarely, disseminated lesions occur in joints, bones and skin.

References

1. Anderson NV et al: Cutaneous sporotrichosis in a cat: A case report. *JAAHA* 9:526-529, 1973.

2. Barbee WC et al: Animal model: Sporotrichosis in the domestic cat. *Am J Pathol* 86:281-284, 1977.

3. Barsanti JA, in Greene CE: *Clinical Microbiology and Infectious Diseases of the Dog and Cat.* Saunders, Philadelphia, 1984. pp 722-727.

4. Burke MJ et al: Successful treatment of cutaneolymphatic sporotrichosis in a cat with ketoconazole and sodium iodide. *JAAHA* 19:542-547, 1983.

5. DeBeurmann L et al: Sporotrichose experimentale du chat. *C R Soc Biol* 66:338-340, 1909.

6. DeBeurmann L et al: Sporotrichose cutanee du chat. *C R Soc Biol* 66:370-372, 1909.

7. Drutz DJ, in Wyngaarden JB and Smith LH Jr: *Cecil's Textbook of Medicine.* Saunders, Philadelphia, 1985. pp 1767-1768.

8. Dunstan RW et al: Feline sporotrichosis. *JAVMA* 189:880-883, 1986.

9. Freitas DC et al: Esporotricose em caes e gatos (sporotrichosis in dogs and cats). *Rev Sao Paulo U Fac Med Vet* 7:381-387, 1965.

10. Kier AB et al: Disseminated sporotrichosis in a cat. *JAVMA* 175:202-204, 1979.

11. Read SI and Sperling LC: Feline sporotrichosis. Transmission to man. *Arch Derm* 118:429-431, 1982.

12. Werner RE Jr et al: Sporotrichosis in a cat. *JAVMA* 159:407-411, 1971.

Chapter 49

Chromomycosis

Etiologic Agents

Chromomycosis is a term broadly applied to infections caused by dematiacious or brown-pigmented fungi.[7] The term phaeohyphomycosis is also used for infections caused by this group of organisms.[1] Phaeohyphomycosis is differentiated from chromomycosis by the absence of granules in the lesions. However, this discussion considers them together. These fungi are genetically related soil saprophytes that form morphologically identical structures in tissues. They include a number of different species of the genera *Phialophora* (*Exophiala*), *Drechslera, Fonsecaea, Brachycladium* and *Cladosporium*. The most commonly involved species in cats have been *Cladosporium trichoides* (syn. *C bantianum*), *Phialophora verrucosa, P gougerotti, Drechslera specifera, Brachycladium spiciferum* and *Exophiala jeanselmei*.

In nature, each species has its own char-acteristic appearance and exists as hyphaeated fungi. In tissue, they appear as irregularly shaped hyphae and as pleomorphic, thick-walled, dark, yeast-like forms 4-12 μ in diameter.

Pathogenesis

Three forms of chromomycosis occur in people: cutaneous, cystic and cerebral.[7] Cutaneous and cerebral forms of the disease have also been described in cats. The cystic form in people is associated with deep encapsulated lesions in muscle or subcutaneous tissues, and has not been recognized in cats. Keratitis is an additional manifestation of the feline infection.

Cutaneous chromomycosis in cats occurs as a result of traumatic inoculation of the skin or deeper tissues. The initial lesion is a small, reddened papule that can enlarge to form a warty plaque. Lesions can remain plaque-like, ulcerate, or form fistulating lesions or atypical deep abscesses.[3,4,9,10,14,19]

Cerebral chromomycosis caused by *Cladosporium trichoides* is a distinct syndrome in both people and cats.[2,7,11] Like its human counterpart, the disease in cats is characterized by small to large, single or multiple cerebral abscesses (Fig 1).[5,11,16]

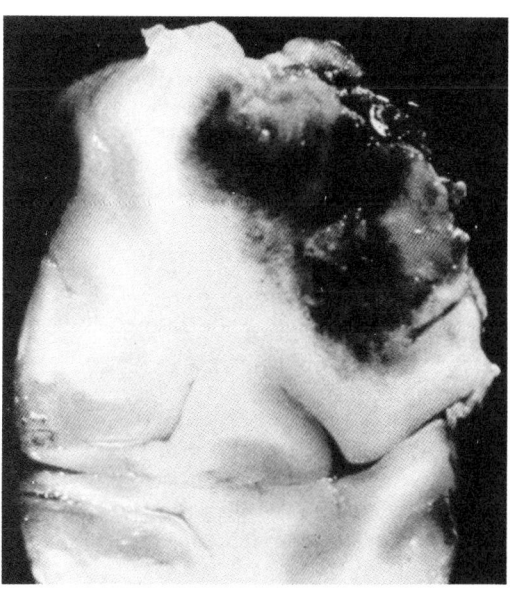

Fig 1. *Cladosporium trichoides* abscess in the brain of a cat. (Courtesy of Spencer Jang and *Sabouraudia*)

The condition has been experimentally recreated; 1 of 2 cats inoculated IV with 9 x 10^5 organisms developed a cerebral abscess.[18] The organism appears to have predilection for cerebral tissues.

The mode of entry for the organism in cerebral chromomycosis has not been determined. One cat had conjunctivitis due to a foxtail barley awn before the onset of CNS signs.[11] However, other cats have had no predisposing lesions.[5,11,16] *Cladosporium* spp have been recovered from the conjunctival sac of many healthy animals, including cats.[17] A cat with *Cladosporium* keratitis died several months later with neurologic signs.[13] Though the initial portal of entry appears to be the conjunctiva, experimental evidence supports that the organism reaches the brain in the bloodstream.[16]

Clinical Signs

The cutaneous form of chromomycosis is usually manifested as intact or ulcerated plaque-like lesions in the skin and subcutaneous tissues of the face or distal limbs.[3,4,6,10,19] Fistulating wounds, either primary or following unsuccessful excision, have also been described.[9,14] Unlike sporotrichosis, lesions in chromomycosis tend to remain solitary and do not invade the lymphatics. Lesions are usually not painful, tend to grow slowly and do not commonly regress spontaneously.

Though most lesions are seen in the skin or subcutaneous tissues, 1 cat had corneal involvement that may have preceded CNS spread. A second cat with *Cladosporium* keratitis did not respond to keratectomy and topical antifungals, and had the globe removed.[5] This cat died 6 months later with neurologic signs. Unfortunately, a necropsy was not done.

Similar to cutaneous chromomycosis, cerebral chromomycosis is uncommon. However, it is rather stereotyped in its presenting features. Clinical signs in 4 naturally occurring cases and 1 experimentally induced case included: weakness and lethargy,[16] ataxia, impaired righting reflexes and locomotion that progressed to total recumbency;[16] hemiparesis and compulsive circling;[5] dementia and depression that progressed to respiratory arrest;[11] and seizures, dementia and head pressing.[11] The clinical signs develop rapidly and the entire course ranges from a few days to a week or so. The depression and dementia, are due mainly to rapidly increasing intracranial pressure. The entire clinical course is 7-14 days.

Pathologic Features

Cutaneous lesions are typically granulomatous. Occasionally they have suppurative centers. Yellow-brown hyphae are found free and within phagocytic cells, and are best visualized with PAS or methenamine silver stain (Fig 2). They are scattered singly and in groups throughout the lesions. Hyphal elements are extremely variable in size and shape. In addition to hyphal elements, pleomorphic yellow- to brown-staining, thick-walled spores can be seen free and within phagocytic cells.

Cerebral lesions vary from true abscesses with fibrous capsules to less discrete coalescing foci of pyogranulomatous inflammation.[5] Weakly branching hyphae 3-6 μ in

Fig 2. Hyphae of *Cladosporium trichoides* in brain tissue of a cat with a cerebral abscess. (Courtesy of Spencer Jang, University of California, Davis)

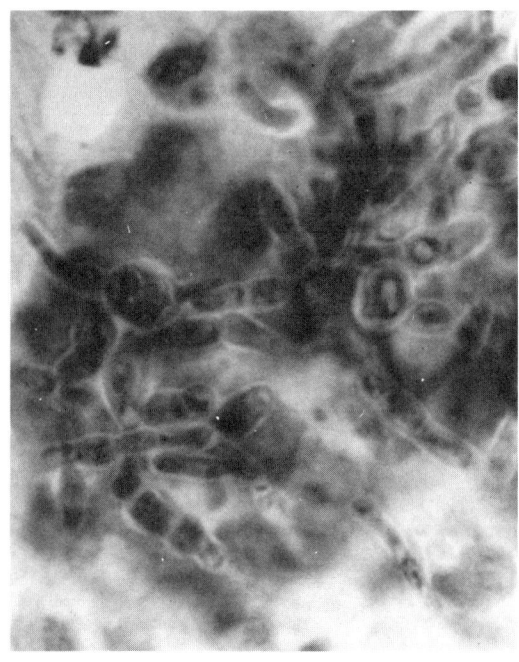

width are seen within epithelioid and multinucleated giant cells and extracellularly. Hyphal elements stain light brown to basophilic with H&E stain. Hyphae can sometimes be seen within thrombosed and nonthrombosed blood vessels.

Clinicopathologic Features

Cutaneous chromomycosis is usually diagnosed on examination of biopsy tissues. Pleomorphic yellow- to brown-staining hyphae and spores are characteristic for this group of organisms. They are readily cultured on Sabouraud's agar. Colonies appear within 1 week but identifying features may take longer to develop.

Cerebral chromomycosis is almost always diagnosed at necropsy. The CSF reflects the inflammatory nature of the disease with elevations of protein content, cell numbers and pressure. It is usually not helpful for visualizing or culturing organisms. Cerebral chromomycosis should be strongly considered in any mature cat with a rapid onset of neurologic signs referable to increased intracranial pressure and cerebral involvement.

Treatment and Prevention

Cutaneous or corneal chromomycosis should be treated surgically before lesions become too large. However, recurrence is seen in ≥50% of cases within 6 months.[12,15] Topical antifungal medications are of no benefit. Intralesional amphotericin B has been tried in people with variable success, but the drug is very irritating and painful when given in this manner. Flucytosine used in the same way as for cryptococcosis has been successfully used in people, but drug resistance is a problem. However, flucytosine used in combination with ketoconazole was unsuccessful in treatment of 2 cats with cutaneous chromomycosis.[15] Amphotericin B in combination with flucytosine was successfully used to treat a recurrent skin lesion in a cat.[13] Ketoconazole alone or in combination with other drugs has not been effective.[15]

The course of the superficial disease in cats is often very long. Some cats have been followed for over 1.5 years.[15] If treatment fails, periodic excision as the disease recurs can provide satisfactory control for prolonged periods. This procedure has been used successfully, with eventual cure, in at least 1 cat.[14]

Cerebral chromomycosis is considered untreatable in cats. Most cases are diagnosed at necropsy. Therapeutic experience with this disease in people has been discouraging and very limited.

Infection and Immunity

Similar to other mycotic infections, cellular immunity is probably most important. Several cats with chromomycosis have had concurrent diseases that might have affected the course of disease. The single report of disseminated chromomycosis occurred in a cat with leukemia.[16] Another cat had a nasal squamous-cell carcinoma and cutaneous chromomycosis.[9] A third cat with widely disseminated visceral and CNS disease was also feline leukemia virus positive.[1] In 2 additional cats, chromomycosis was associated with either *Cryptococcus neoformans* or *Stemphylium* infections, again suggesting problems with host immune incompetence.[18,19]

Animal and Public Health Considerations

There is no evidence that cats with either cutaneous or cerebral chromomycosis are infectious to people or other animals.

References

1. Ader PL: Phycomycosis in fifteen dogs and two cats. *JAVMA* 174:1216-1223, 1979.

2. Barsanti JA, in Greene CE: *Clinical Microbiology and Infectious Diseases of the Dog and Cat.* Saunders, Philadelphia, 1984. pp 738-746.

3. Bostock DE and Coloe PJ: Phaeohyphomycosis caused by *Exophiala jeanselmei* in a domestic cat. *J Comp Pathol* 92:479-482, 1982.

4. Bridges CH and Beasley JA: Maduromycotic mycetomas in animals. *JAVMA* 137:192-201, 1960.

5. Dillehay DL *et al*: Cerebral phaeohyphomycosis in two dogs and a cat. *Vet Pathol* 24:192-194, 1987.

6. Dion WM et al: Feline cutaneous phaeohyphomycosis caused by *Phialophora verrucosa*. Can Vet J 23:48-49, 1982.

7. Drutz DJ, in Wyngaarden JB and Smith LH Jr: *Cecil's Textbook of Medicine*. Saunders, Philadelphia, 1985. pp 1773-1774.

8. Elliott GS et al: Antemortem diagnosis of paecilomycosis in a cat. JAVMA 184:93-94, 1984.

9. Haschek WM and Kasali OB: A case of cutaneous feline phaeohyphomycosis caused by *Phialophora gougerotti*. Cornell Vet 67:467-471, 1977.

10. Hill JR et al: Phaeomycotic granuloma in a cat. Vet Pathol 15:559-561, 1978.

11. Jang SS et al: Feline brain abscesses due to *Cladosporium trichoides*. Sabouraudia 15:115-123, 1977.

12. McKeever PJ et al: Chromomycosis in a cat: successful medical therapy. JAAHA 19:533-536, 1983.

13. Miller DM et al: Keratomycosis caused by *Cladosporium* sp in a cat. JAVMA 182:1121-1122, 1983.

14. Muller GH et al: Phaeohyphomycosis caused by *Drechslera spicifera* in a cat. JAVMA 166:150-154, 1975.

15. Pukay BP and Dion WM: Feline phaeohyphomycosis: Treatment with ketoconazole and 5-fluorocytosine. Can Vet J 25:130-134, 1984.

16. Reed C et al: Leukemia in a cat with concurrent *Cladosporium* infection. J Small Anim Pract 15:55-62, 1974.

17. Samuelson DA et al: Conjunctival fungal flora in horses, cattle, dogs, and cats. JAVMA 184:1240-1242, 1984.

18. Sisk DB and Chandler FW: Phaeohyphomycosis and cryptococcosis in a cat. Vet Pathol 19:554-556, 1982.

19. Sousa CA et al: Subcutaneous phaeohyphomycosis (*Stemphylium* sp and *Cladosporium* sp infections) in a cat. JAVMA 185:673-675, 1984.

Chapter 50

Aspergillosis, Mucormycosis, Candidiasis and Penicilliosis

Cats suffer from a stereotyped disease syndrome caused by fungi of the genera *Aspergillus, Mucor, Rhizopus, Absidia, Penicillium* and *Candida*. For purposes of this discussion, the syndrome caused by each of these fungi will be considered to be identical in all aspects.

Etiologic Agents

The genus *Aspergillus* belongs to the phylum Ascomycetes, class Plectomyces. *Penicillium* spp belong to a closely related genus. Over 300 species of *Aspergillus* exist in nature, but only a few cause disease in people and animals.[4] The most important species include *Aspergillus fumigatus, A clavatus, A glaucus, A nidulans, A niger, A flavus* and *A terreus*. *Aspergillus* spp are ubiquitous in almost every environment. They have been isolated from objects as different as grasses and construction material, and from environments as distinct as barns and refrigerators.[4] *Aspergillus* spp are prodigious spore formers. Spores develop from bottle-shaped sterigmata that radiate like petals from globular dilatations on the ends of stalk-like conidiophores. Spores of these organisms are present in the air and are almost continuously inhaled and ingested. Once in tissues, *Aspergillus* forms septate hyphae in tissues.

The order Mucorales, which contains the genera *Mucor, Rhizopus* and *Absidia*, belongs to the phylum Phycomycetes (Zygomycetes). Like *Aspergillus*, they exist in nature in many environments. Speciation is rarely attempted in veterinary medicine. For this reason, the term mucormycosis (zygomycosis) applies to the disease caused by any of the genera of the order Mucorales. Mucorales form nonseptate hyphae in tissues.

The genus *Candida* is made up of several species, *C albicans* being the most important. They belong to the phylum Ascomycetes, class Hemiascomycetes. *Candida* spp inhabit the mucous membranes of the alimentary and genital tracts of most mammals. They usually exist as a yeast in such environments, but form pseudohyphae in tissues and reproductive hyphae on special media.

Pathogenesis

Aspergillosis, mucormycosis, penicilliosis and candidiasis are considered opportunistic infections that occur in immunocompromised hosts. More than one-half of infected cats have had identifiable predisposing diseases.[12] Most were also treated with corticosteroids and/or antibiotics at the time of diagnosis.[12] Predisposing diseases have been either of an immunosuppressive nature or traumatic. From 20% to 50% of affected cats had what was diagnosed as feline panleukopenia (parvovirus enteritis). About one-fifth of the cats were FeLV infected, or had some disease that was FeLV-associated, such as FIP or hemobartonellosis. Upper respiratory disease occurring as a sequela of live-virus vaccination (herpesvirus?) was a predisposing disease in

281

one cat.[12] Surgical trauma and dystocia were predisposing factors in several cats, and another animal had diabetes mellitus.[10] Cats with FIV infection and candidiasis have also been recognized.

Underlying immunosuppressive disorders lower host resistance and allow inhaled or ingested spores (*Aspergillus*, *Penicillium* and Mucorales) to invade tissues, or allow resident populations of fungi (*Candida*) to overgrow and become invasive. High levels of broad-spectrum antibiotics suppress normal bacterial flora and allow for fungal overgrowth in people. Corticosteroids have an immunosuppressive effect of their own. When used with antibiotics, they favor fungal growth and invasion.

Among 52 cases reported in the literature, 23 cats have been infected with *Aspergillus* spp, 21 with Mucorales, 5 with *Candida*, 2 with both *Aspergillus* spp and Mucorales, and 1 with *Penicillium* sp.[12] About three-fourths of affected cats were seen during winter months.[12] The syndrome appears to be more common in Europe than in other areas of the world, and occurs more often in colder climates than in warmer regions. The incidence in one veterinary center in Europe was about 3 in 1000 necropsies and appeared to be increasing over the last 2 decades.[12]

Clinical Features

Systemic aspergillosis, penicilliosis, mucormycosis or candidiasis has affected males and females in equal numbers. One-third are under 1 year of age, and three-fourths 3 years old or less. The duration of clinical signs ranged from 3 to 14 days. A few cats were ill for several weeks or months before death.[12] Cats that were sick for some time before death were more apt to be adults. Mortality has been extremely high.

Systemic aspergillosis, penicilliosis, mucormycosis or candidiasis is almost always diagnosed at necropsy, indicating the nondescript nature of the clinical signs. Listlessness, anorexia, wasting and fever are common to most affected cats. Additional signs are often present and depend on the predisposing condition, if any, and the tissue localization of the organisms. The infection is localized to the intestinal tract in somewhat less than one-half of the cases,[1,2,5,8,9,11,12,16,19,21,22] the intestinal tract and lungs in about one-fifth of cases,[5,12,20] and in the lung in about one-third of cases.[5,7,10,11,12,13,15] Additional sites of involvement, often in combination with lung and intestinal disease, include the nasal sinuses, orbits, liver, kidneys, spleen, myocardium, uterus, lymph nodes and brain. One cat had lesions only in the urinary bladder,[6] and another had necrotizing lesions of the ear, jaw muscle, pharynx and lungs.[12] Orbital cellulitis was a prominent feature in 2 cats; the infection appeared to enter the orbits from the nasal sinuses.[14,23]

Three-fourths of the cats with either lung or lung and intestinal involvement were infected with *Aspergillus* spp. A similar proportion of cats with Mucorales infection had involvement of only the intestines or nonpulmonary tissues. All of the cats with *Candida* infections had intestinal involvement.[11,17,21] The cat with *Penicillium* sp infection had lesions in the lungs, nasal sinuses and orbits.[14] The differences in localization of these various fungi suggested that *Aspergillus* and *Penicillium* enter the body via the respiratory tract, while Mucorales and *Candida* enter through the intestines. Cats with lung involvement were often dyspneic, but coughing was not reported. Cats with intestinal disease often had vomiting and diarrhea. One-half of the cats were icteric at the time of presentation. Icterus was usually due to extensive tissue hemorrhaging and the extravascular destruction of red blood cells and not to actual liver disease.

Pathologic Features

Fungal lesions in the lungs and nonintestinal tissues are usually poorly demarcated and characterized by extensive hemorrhage, necrosis and edema. Intestinal lesions are usually concentrated in the jejunum and colon. The duodenum, ileum, and cecum are less frequently involved. Intestinal lesions are usually well demarcated, segmental, and acute to subacute in duration. Hyphal elements are usually found in tissues surrounding blood vessels. Vasculitis and thrombosis are characteristic lesions. Vascular thrombosis and hemorrhage are not always seen in areas where hyphae are found. Inflammatory infiltrates are amazingly sparse; granulomatous and purulent inflammations are prominent in only a few cases. Lymphoid tissues are surprisingly inactive, or in some cases, atrophic. Lymphoid changes probably reflect the underlying immunosuppression that is often associated with the syndrome.

The appearance of hyphae in the tissues can be used to differentiate aspergillosis from mucormycosis and candidiasis. *Aspergillus* spp have uniform 2- to 7-μ septate dichotomously branched hyphae. The hyphae often branch at a 45° angle. The hyphae of Mucorales are broad, wavy, nonseptate and thick-walled. The hyphae branch at right angles at irregular intervals. *Candida* forms pseudohyphae in tissues. These are essentially chains of elongated yeast separated by constrictions (resembling chains of sausages).

In addition to these pathologic findings, affected cats may have lesions referable to underlying or overlying conditions, such as FIP or feline panleukopenia.

Clinicopathologic Features

Various species of *Aspergillus, Candida, Penicillium* and Mucorales can be cultured from lesions. Speciation is based on the appearance of the spores. Though vasculitis is a characteristic feature of these systemic fungal infections, organisms are rarely present in the blood, and blood cultures are likely to be unrewarding. Isolation of fungi from tissues, especially if they had been dead for some time, is not proof of fungal infection. Fungal elements should also be observed invading into the tissues.

A leukopenia is a characteristic finding in most cats with this syndrome. The leukopenia is either associated with an absolute neutropenia, or with both neutropenia and lymphopenia.

Treatment and Prevention

Treatment of cats with systemic aspergillosis, penicilliosis, mucormycosis or candidiasis is usually ineffective. The diagnosis is seldom made before death, and the diseases are uncommon enough to have a relatively low index of suspicion. Moreover, even if the diagnosis is made before death, the immunodeficiency that underlies most cases usually negates the efficacy of treatment.

Candida is sensitive to ketoconazole therapy, while *Aspergillus* and Mucorales are usually unresponsive. Amphotericin B is the drug of choice for the treatment of these latter organisms in people. A more thorough discussion of antifungal therapy is given in Chapter 46.

Infection and Immunity

It is generally believed that macrophages are important in destroying spores, while neutrophils are important for killing mycelia. Therefore, both limbs of the immune response must be subverted for disease to occur, *ie*, cellular immunity must be suppressed and the numbers (or function) of neutrophils decreased.

Though feline panleukopenia virus infection is thought to have an important role in systemic aspergillosis, penicilliosis, mucormycosis and candidiasis, the evidence is purely circumstantial. Evidence favoring a role of feline panleukopenia virus is based on several observations. First, systemic fungal diseases and feline panleukopenia virus infection tend to occur in young cats. Second, many cats with these systemic fungal infections are profoundly panleukopenic. Third, many cats with panleukopenia virus infection are treated vigorously with broad-spectrum antibiotics, and often with corticosteroids as well (thus predisposing to both sporulation and invasion). Fourth, bowel lesions in areas away from the involved intestine resemble those associated with panleukopenia virus infection. Fifth, feline panleukopenia virus is known to induce a transient immunodeficiency state above and beyond its ability to depress the

WBC count.[18] Sixth, similar opportunistic fungal infections have been seen as a sequel to confirmed canine parvovirus infection. In spite of circumstantial evidence, none of the reported studies of the syndrome appears to have utilized virus isolation, immunofluorescent antibody staining, or fecal electron microscopy to confirm the presence or absence of feline panleukopenia virus in affected cats.

Both FeLV and FIV infections can induce profound leukopenia in their own right. Indeed, FeLV has been associated with a so-called panleukopenia-like syndrome.[3] FeLV and FIV have also been identified in cats with systemic aspergillosis, mucormycosis and candidiasis. Like feline panleukopenia virus infection, FeLV and FIV can induce both neutropenia and depressed cellular immunity.

Animal and Public Health Considerations

Cats infected with these various fungal agents are not public health hazards to cats, other animals or people. The organisms are ubiquitous in the environment and only cause disease in certain predisposed individuals.

References

1. Ader PL: Phycomycosis in fifteen dogs and two cats. *JAVMA* 174:1216-1223, 1979.

2. Bolton GR and Brown TT: Mycotic colitis in a cat. *VM/SAC* 67:978-980, 1972.

3. Cotter SM, in Greene CE: *Clinical Microbiology and Infectious Diseases of the Dog and Cat*. Saunders, Philadelphia, 1984. pp 490-513.

4. Drutz DJ, in Wyngaarden JB and Smith LH Jr: *Cecil's Textbook of Medicine*. Saunders, Philadelphia, 1985. pp 1770-1771.

5. Fox JG et al: Systemic fungal infections in cats. *JAVMA* 173:1191-1195, 1978.

6. Kirkpatrick RM: Mycotic cystitis in a male cat. *VM/SAC* 77:1365-1371, 1982.

7. Köhler H et al: Einige Beobachtungen über das Auftreten von System-Mykosen bei Tieren in Österreich. *Zbl Vet Med B* 25:785-799, 1978.

8. König H et al: Einige Mucomykosen bei Rind, Schwein, Katze, Reh und Flamingo. *Schweiz Arch Tierheilkunde* 109:260-268, 1967.

9. Langheinrich DA and Nielsen SW: Histopathology of feline panleukopenia: A report of 65 cases. *JAVMA* 158:863-871, 1971.

10. Loupal G: Hämorragischer Lungeninfarkt infolge Mucormykose bei einer Katze mit Diabetes mellitus. *Dtsch Tierärztl Wschr* 89:104-107, 1982.

11. McCausland IP: Systemic mycoses of two cats. *N Zeal Vet J* 20:10-12, 1972.

12. Ossent P: Systemic aspergillosis and mucormycosis in 23 cats. *Vet Record* 120:330-333, 1987.

13. Pakes SP et al: Pulmonary aspergillosis in a cat. *JAVMA* 151:950-953, 1967.

14. Peiffer RL et al: Orbital cellulitis, sinusitis, and pneumonitis caused by *Penicillium* sp in a cat. *JAVMA* 176:449-451, 1980.

15. Sautter JH et al: Aspergillosis in a cat. *JAVMA* 127:518-519, 1955.

16. Schiefer B and Weir E: Soormykose des Darmes bei Katzen. *Dtsch Tierärztl Wschr* 66:275-277, 1959.

17. Schiefer B: Zur Histopathologie der durch *Candida*-, *Aspergillus*-, und *Mucor*-arten verursachten Darmmykosen bei Katzen mit Panleukopenie. *Dtsch Tierärztl Wschr* 72:73-76, 1965.

18. Schultz RD et al: Effect of feline panleukopenia virus infection: a development of cellular and humoral immunity. *Cornell Vet* 66:324-332, 1976.

19. Stokes R: Intestinal mycosis in a cat. *Aust Vet J* 49:499-500, 1973.

20. Vogler GA and Wagner JE: What's your diagnosis? *Lab Anim* 5:14-16, 1976.

21. Van Kruiningen HJ et al: The classification of feline colitis. *J Comp Pathol* 93:275-294, 1983.

22. Weiland F: Darmmykose bei einer Katze. *Dtsch Tierärztl Wschr* 77:232-233, 1970.

23. Wilkinson GT et al: *Aspergillus* spp infection associated with orbital cellulitis and sinusitis in a cat. *J Small Anim Pract* 23:127-131, 1982.

Chapter 51

Mycetomas

Etiologic Agents

Mycetomas are localized lesions caused by either invasion or inoculation of certain fungi or actinomycetes directly into exposed areas of skin. They are characterized by swelling, sinus formation, exudation and granular material in the linings of fistulous tracts or in the exudate. The granular material varies somewhat in size and color, depending on the causative agent. Granules are composed of colonies of organisms embedded in host-derived proteinaceous debris.

Mycetomas are caused by either true fungi (eumycetomas) or actinomycetes (actinomycetomas). The various agents that cause mycetomas live as saprophytes in soil and plant debris. About half of the mycetomas in people are caused by fungi and half by actinomycetes. This pattern also seems to apply to cats and certain other animals. Three feline cases have been caused by *Streptomyces* (actinomycetes).[3,6,7] The most common fungi associated with this disease in people and non-felids are *Petriellidium boydii*, *Aceromonium* spp, *Trichophyton* spp, *Microsporum* spp, *Neotestudina rosattii*, *Madurella mycetomi*, *M grisea*, *Exophiala jeanselmei*, *Leptosphaeria senegalensis* and *L thompkinsii*. Mycetomas caused by many of these fungi have also been reported in cats. In addition, a granulomatous lesion under the tongue caused by *Cephalosporium potranii* has been described in a cat.[9] *Madurella grisea* has been cultured from a subcutaneous granuloma over the bridge of the nose of a cat.[2] *Microsporum canis* has also caused subcutaneous mycetomas in a number of cats.[1,2,4,8]

Pathogenesis

Mycetomas often begin at the site of previous trauma. Of 2 feline actinomycetic mycetomas, 1 was associated with bird shot and the other began on the foot, a common site for traumatic implantation in people (Madura foot).[3,6,7] Trauma has also been

Fig 1A. Chronic *Streptomyces griseus* infection on the groin of a cat. The lesion first appeared on the back paw and over 6 months spread to the stifle and inner aspect of the thigh. (Courtesy of Dr. Peter Ihrke, University of California, Davis)

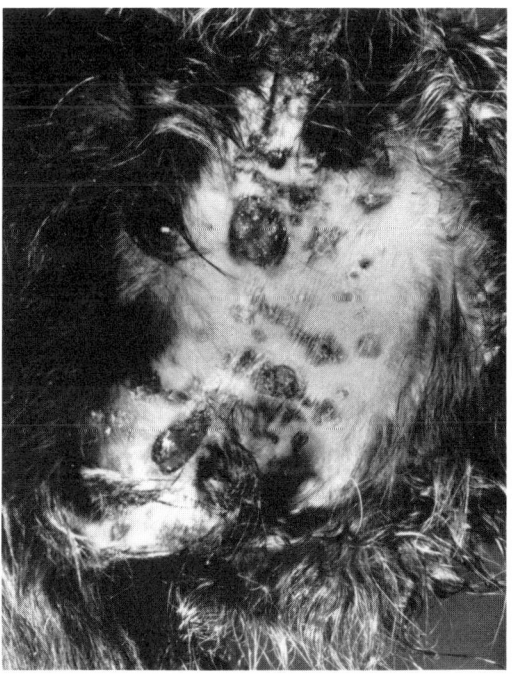

implicated as a source of entry for fungal mycetomas.[1,2] Mycetomas in people usually remain localized, though secondary nodules can appear in the same area. The general health of most people is not affected. However, the infection often spreads beyond the primary site in cats.[1-3,7]

Clinical Features

Mycetomas due to *Streptomyces* spp have been described in 3 cats.[3,6,7] One of the cats had a 4-cm, ovoid subcutaneous mass over the scapula that developed over a 1-month period.[3] Lesions in a second cat first appeared on a hind paw and spread to the stifle and inner thigh over the next 6 months (Fig 1).[7] Areas of the skin on the distal limb were alopecic, swollen and hyperpigmented, and contained multiple draining tracts. Fistulous tracts exuded serosanguineous fluid. The largest thigh lesion was 7 x 5 x 3 cm and firm on palpation. The masses in the first cat were composed of connective tissue and had multiple communicating fistulae and small pockets of brownish-yellow granular material. The masses in the second cat were gray and gelatinous, and contained numerous black, minute grains.

Mycetomas due to fungi appear to concentrate in subcutaneous areas on the nose, distal limbs, ears, trunk and tail base, and under the tongue.[1-4,8,9]

Pathologic Features

Mycetomas are slow-growing subcutaneous masses that reach 5-10 cm or more in diameter. They are composed of numerous interconnecting fistulous tracts and pockets lined by a slippery, glistening pseudomembrane. The surrounding host reaction is basically pyogranulomatous, with extensive fibrosis.

In the case of mycetomas due to dermatophytes, the wall of such lesions may consist of masses of interwining hyphae.[1,2,4,8] Rice- to sand-sized granules are loosely associated with pockets and fistulous tracts and are sometimes seen in exudates. They are basically colonies of organisms embedded in proteinaceous debris. Considerable emphasis has been placed on

Fig 1B. The infection had dissected subcutaneously. Removal of the skin revealed a gelatinous mass. The black grains throughout the lesion are *Streptomyces* colonies and proteinaceous material. (Courtesy of Dr. Peter Ihrke, University of California, Davis)

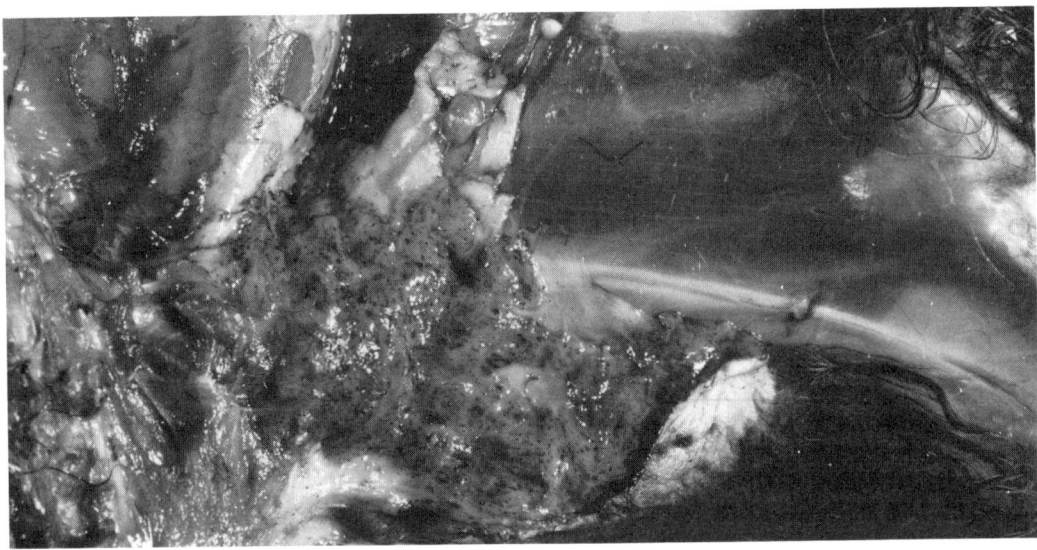

the color and size of these granules as predictors of the types of organisms involved. Certain agents produce somewhat characteristic granules but this can vary with species and individual animals. Both cases of actinomycetic mycetomas in cats were due to *Streptomyces griseus*; the granules were described as yellow-brown in 1 and black in the other.[3,5,6] Granular material of unstated size and color has also been associated with discharges from mycetomas induced by *Microsporum* spp.[1,2] Holzworth described bluish granules in a mycetoma of the ear canal caused by an unidentified fungus.[2]

Clinicopathologic Features

Diagnosis is usually by examination of biopsied tissues, microscopic examination of crushed or sectioned granules, or culture. Tissues and granules of actinomycetomas are composed of fine, beaded, branching filaments ≤ 1 μ in diameter. Tissue organisms and granules from eumycetomas contain larger branching hyphae and spores. Cultures should be of the appropriate type to isolate actinomycetes or fungi. Microscopic examination of the granules before culture can assist in selecting the most appropriate isolation procedures.

Treatment and Prevention

Cats with mycetomas are usually treated initially with excision. This may be accompanied by ancillary treatment with an appropriate antibiotic. Recurrences are common at the surgery site or in adjacent and more distant subcutaneous and muscular tissues.

Treatment of both actinomycetomas and eumycetomas is difficult in people and animals. Organisms persist in granules within fistulous tracts and tissue pockets, making therapeutic concentrations of antibiotics in the site of growth difficult to achieve. Excision also has limitations, mainly because the infections are usually more widespread than they appear. Therefore, it is important to widely excise the lesions as early as possible. Even with seemingly appropriate treatment, the mortality can be high.

Infection and Immunity

Organisms are sheltered from the immune system of the host by their presence in granules. These granules have no blood supply and are loose in fistulous tracts and pockets. Therefore, the immune system has a difficult time gaining access to the organisms. In 1 cat, chronic and widespread mycetoma caused by *Microsporum* appeared to result from chronic use of corticosteroids.[2] There appears to be a genetic predisposition to dermatophyte-caused mycetomas in Persian cats.[1,4,8] This breed appears to be more sensitive to both superficial and deep infections with dermatophytes.

Animal and Public Health Considerations

Mycetomas are not contagious to animals or people.

References

1. Bourdin M et al: Première observation d'un mycétome à *Microsporum canis* chez un chat. *Recl Méd Vét* 151:475-480, 1975.

2. Holzworth J et al, in Holzworth J: *Diseases of the Cat*. Saunders, Philadelphia, 1987. pp 320-358.

3. Lewis GE et al: Mycetoma in a cat. *JAVMA* 161:500-503, 1972.

4. Miller WH Jr and Goldschmidt MH: Mycetomas in the cat caused by a dermatophyte. *JAAHA* 22:255-260, 1986.

5. Mishra SK et al: Identification of *Nocardia* and *Streptomyces* of medical importance. *J Clin Microbiol* 11:728-736, 1980.

6. Poenaru ID: Les mycetomes actinomycosiques chez le chat. *Archiva Vet* 29:104, 1937.

7. Reinke SI et al: Actinomycotic mycetoma in a cat. *JAVMA* 189:446-448, 1986.

8. Tuttle PA and Chandler FW: Deep dermatophytosis in a cat. *JAVMA* 183:1106-1108, 1983.

9. Van den Akker S: Een schimmelinfectie (*Cephalosporium patronii*) in de mondholte van een kat. *Tijdschr Diergeneeskd* 77:515-516, 1952.

Chapter 52

Protothecosis

Etiologic Agent

Prototheca wickerhamii is an alga that does not contain chlorophyll. Like other algae, it is a saprophyte found in moist environments. It reproduces by endosporulation, rather than by budding.

Pathogenesis

Prototheca is a very rare disease of mammals, including people and cats. The organism apparently enters skin abrasions, causing a localized subcutaneous pyogranulomatous inflammatory response.

Clinical Features

Localized, dissecting, subcutaneous masses have been observed on the tarsus and forehead of affected cats.[2-4] The author consulted on a cat with chronic, deforming rhinitis and a metatarsal pad lesion caused by *Prototheca*. The overlying skin is usually unbroken, and the subcutaneous masses are often soft and pliable. Affected cats tend to be older and otherwise healthy. The disease course is usually long, with slow progression to adjacent bones and tendons.

Pathologic Features

Subcutaneous protothecal infections are grossly characterized by local invasion of adjacent tendons and bones, and microscopically by pyogranulomatous inflammation, with macrophages predominating (Fig 1).[2-4] Numerous ovoid, crescent-shaped, nonbudding organisms 2-20 μ in diameter are seen within the inflammatory reaction (Fig 2). The organisms often contain 2-8 or more endospores.[4] Organisms are found within and outside of epithelioid giant cells, which are most abundant around blood vessels. In 1 cat the infection spread to regional lymph nodes.[2]

Clinicopathologic Features

The organisms can be readily identified in tissue sections or on impression smears stained with common stains. They can be grown on such media as Sabouraud's dex-

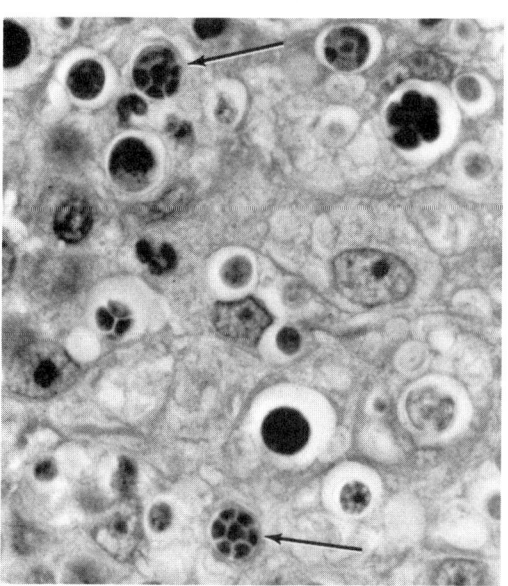

Fig 1. Photomicrograph of tissue from a cat with nasal and pedal prototheocosis shows numerous *Prototheca* organisms (arrows) and macrophages. The organisms are typical in appearance, with compartments and 2-8 endospores. Hematoxylin and eosin stain, 1000X. (Courtesy of Dr. Kerry Levin-Smith, Willits, California)

Fig 2. Fleshy mass protruding from the right naris of a cat with unilateral rhinitis of several months' duration. Biopsy of the mass revealed *Prototheca* organisms. The cat also had a fluctuant mass on the metacarpal pad that eroded through the overlying skin. (Courtesy of Dr. Kerry Levin-Smith, Willits, California)

trose agar with chloramphenicol.[4] The colonies are creamy-white and yeast-like.

Treatment and Prevention

Affected people have been treated with IV amphotericin B and ketoconazole.[4] One cat failed to respond to ketoconazole at 10 mg/kg daily, but another cat responded to a ketoconazole dosage of 28 mg/kg divided BID. *Prototheca* is resistant to flucytosine. Excision of the mass or amputation of the affected limb has been the usual treatment in animals.

Infection and Immunity

Though protothecosis seems to be an opportunistic infection, infected cats have been otherwise healthy. One affected cat was negative for both FeLV and FIV infections. Lesions do not resolve once they become clinically apparent.[1]

Animal and Public Health Considerations

Affected cats are not infectious to people and other cats. The infection is usually acquired from the environment, where the organism is ubiquitous.

References

1. Bennett JE, in Mondell GL *et al*: *Principles and Practice of Infectious Disease*. Wiley & Sons, New York, 1985. p 1503.

2. Coloe PJ and Allison JF: Protothecosis in a cat. *JAVMA* 180:78-79, 1982.

3. Finnie JW and Coloe PJ: Cutaneous protothecosis in a cat. *Aust Vet J* 57:307-308, 1981.

4. Kaplan W *et al*: Protothecosis in a cat: First recorded case. *Sabouraudia* 14:281-286, 1976.

Chapter 53

Miscellaneous Fungal Infections

Paecilomycosis

Paecilomyces fumosoroseus has been isolated antemortem from an adult, spayed-FeLV negative cat with a localized paw lesion that disseminated to the nasal passages, liver and mesenteric lymph nodes over a 9-month period or longer.[1] The infection failed to respond to high daily dosages of ketoconazole (40 mg/kg) and the cat was euthanized.

Fungal infections caused by these organisms respond poorly to therapy. Amphotericin B, potassium or sodium iodide, and excision have all failed to cure infections in dogs.

Reference

1. Elliot GS et al: Antemortem diagnosis of paecilomycosis in a cat. *JAVMA* 184:93-94, 1984.

Section V

Parasitic Diseases

A parasite is an organism that requires a host animal or plant for all or part of its life cycle. The host may serve as a source of environmental protection, a transport medium or, more frequently, as a source of food. The relationship between host and parasite can be symbiotic, or mutually beneficial. In other cases, the relationship is indifferent to the host; the parasite does not measurably interfere with any host activity. In the strictest sense, true parasitism is either beneficial or of no consequence to the host. Only in this way is the parasite always assured of an adequate and continual supply of hosts for its survival. If the parasite destroyed the host, it would prevent its own survival.

Parasites are found mainly in the phyla Nemathelminthes (roundworms), Platyhelminthes (flatworms and tapeworms), Acanthocephala (spiny-headed worms) and Arthropoda. The last is a phylum of invertebrate animals that have chitinous skeletons, segmented bodies and jointed paired appendages. This phylum includes a number of classes that are important parasites of cats, such as insects (6-legged arthropods) and arachnids (8-legged arthropods). Many intermediate and definitive hosts for various types of worms are also found within the phylum Arthropoda (crustaceans, myriapods, etc).

Parasites within these phyla have domestic cats as either true or spurious hosts. A true host is required by the parasite for some stage of its life cycle. Without this true host-parasite relationship, the parasite would not survive. A spurious, incidental or accidental host is not required by the parasite for its life cycle. In contrast to true parasites, spurious parasites have not evolved closely with their hosts and are more apt to cause disease.

Some parasites have complex life cycles and utilize a number of hosts during their development. The definitive host supports the sexual stages of the parasite. The dog is the definitive host for the heartworm. Nonsexual developmental stages occur in intermediate hosts. The mosquito is the intermediate host of the heartworm. A transport host provides a haven for the parasite, but is not essential for the life cycle. If the transport host is eaten by the intermediate or definitive host, it is called a paratenic host. Rodents are paratenic hosts for ascarids of cats, which are the definitive host.

Disease is usually a consequence of over-parasitism of the host. Over-parasitism results from changes in the environment of the parasite or host that favor an increase either in parasite numbers or host exposure. Over-parasitism can also be caused by a lack of host resistance, thus allowing parasite numbers to increase on or within the animal. An example of environmentally induced over-parasitism is the introduction of large numbers of cats into warm and humid climates that favor larval development of cat fleas. In this example, both the nature of the environment and introduction of large numbers of the host species favor over-parasitism. An example of over-parasitism due to reduced host resistance is seen in cats that become ill and stop grooming.

Sick cats become very attractive targets for fleas and can become severely infested.

The parasites discussed here are found worldwide or only in certain geographic areas. The list in Table 1 is by no means complete but covers the majority of parasites detected by veterinarians in practice. The diseases described in this section also provide many different examples of the host-parasite relationship and how it can lead to disease.

Table 1. Common parasites of domestic cats.

Roundworms
Ascarids
  Toxocara cati
Heartworms
  Dirofilaria immitis
Lungworms
  Aelurostrongylus abstrusus
  Troglostrongylus subcrenatus
Trichurids
  Trichuris campanula
  T serrata
  Capillaria putorii
  C erinacea
  C hepatica
  C aerophila
  C feliscati
  C plica
Hookworms
  Ancylostoma tubaeforme
  A braziliense
  A ceylanicum
  Uncinaria stenocephala
Stomach Worms
  Ollulanus tricuspis
  Cyathospirura dasyuridis
  Cylicospirura felineus
  Physaloptera praeputialis
  P felidis
  P pseudopraeputialis
  P canis
Large Intestinal Worms
  Strongyloides tumefaciens
  S planiceps

Flatworms
Lung Flukes
  Paragonimus kellicotti
  P westermani
  P ohihari
  P iloktsuensis
  P africanus
  P uterobilateralis
  P caliensis
  P peruvianus
  P mexicanus
Liver Flukes
  Platynosomum fastosum
Pancreatic Flukes
  Eurytrema procyonis
Miscellaneous Liver and Pancreatic Flukes
  Opisthorchis tenuicollis
  O viverrini
  Clonorchis sinensis
  Pseudamphistomum truncatum
  Metorchis albidus
  M conjunctus
  Parametorchis complexus
  Amphimerus pseudofelineus
Tapeworms
  Dipylidium caninum
  Joyeuxiella pasqualei
  J echinorhynchoides
  Taenia taeniaeformis
  T pisiformis
  Diphyllobothrium latum
  Spirometra mansonoides
  S mansoni
  S erinacei

Thorny-Headed Worms
  Oncicola canis
  O campanulatus

Arthropods
Mites
  Otodectes cynotis (ear mite)
  Cheyletiella yasguri
  C blakei
  Demodex cati
  Demodex spp
  Notoedres cati
Fleas
  Ctenocephalides felis
  C canis
  Pulex irritans

Chapter 54

Roundworm Infections

TOXOCARIASIS

Etiologic Agent

Toxocara cati is the principal ascarid that infects cats. It is found as an adult in the small intestine of domestic and wild Felidae.[7] Adult male worms are 3-6 cm long, while females are 4-10 cm long. Eggs laid by female worms are 65-75 μ in diameter and shed in the feces in relatively large numbers. Ascarid eggs can survive several months or longer in the environment.

Cats are infected directly or by way of intermediate (paratenic) rodent hosts. Eggs passed in the feces contain infectious second-stage larvae. Following ingestion by the cat, second-stage larvae are released and enter the stomach wall, where they remain for 1-2 days. Larvae migrate to the liver in the mesenteric veins, and then enter the bloodstream and are carried to the lungs. They exit the pulmonary vasculature and enter the alveoli, bronchioli and trachea, where they form third-stage larvae. Then they are coughed up and swallowed, and re-enter the stomach wall. Following further maturation, they migrate to the lumen of the small intestine, where egg laying occurs. This entire migration can take place in as short a time as 10 days.

Transmission of *T cati* through ingestion of intermediate hosts is important for hunting cats. Eggs passed by the cat are ingested by rodents, and second-stage infectious larvae are released in the intestinal tract and migrate to various tissues, particularly the liver. Because rodents are not the natural definitive hosts, larval development is arrested and encystation occurs. Rodents are referred to as paratenic hosts because no essential developmental stages occur in them. Encysted second-stage larvae can remain alive for months in rodent tissues. When a cat eats the rodent, second-stage larvae are released from the cysts by digestive enzymes and enter the stomach wall, where they develop to third-stage larvae over a 6-day period. They then re-enter the stomach, where they become fourth-stage larvae. These make their way to the small intestine, where they become adults. Following ingestion of paratenic hosts, the entire cycle takes about 3 weeks. Larval migration through the liver and lungs does not occur in cats infected in this manner.

In addition to being infected by eggs or encysted second-stage larvae, kittens can be infected through nursing. Larval forms encysted in the queen or migrating during pregnancy find their way to the mammary glands and are secreted in the milk. Larvae ingested by the kittens while nursing develop in the same manner as larvae acquired by eating infected rodents.

Pathogenesis

Toxocara cati is found throughout the world. As in other infectious diseases, ascarid infections are most severe in high-density environments where fecal contamination is high, conditions are favorable for survival of ascarid eggs, and many young cats are present. In Iowa, Lightner and co-workers found the proportion of infected cats was 0% in newborns, 4.3% in 0.5- to 2-week-old kittens, 5.8% in 2- to 6-week-old kittens, 1.9-2.1% in 0.5- to 4-year-old cats, and 0.8-1.3% in 4- to 15-year-old cats. No infections were seen in cats over 15 years of age.[4] These percentages are considerably lower than those reported in other studies. In Missouri, Visco and associates reported 24.4% infection.[9] Australian studies reported 20.3% infection among urban cats in western Australia, 24.5% infection in Brisbane and 21.9% infection in New South Wales.[5,6,11] In southwest England, 63% of farm cats were infected.[12]

Fecal shedding and fecal-oral exposure are the predominant forms of cat-to-cat transmission. Transmammary infection is a continuous phenomenon; larval ascarids are present in the milk throughout lactation, not just in colostrum.[8]

Clinical signs of *T cati* infections are mainly caused by visceral migration. Pulmonary parenchymal and arterial changes occur over a 2-month period or longer following exposure.[10] Irritation to gastric and intestinal walls, aberrant migrations into such sites as the bile ducts, and mechanical obstruction of the bowel can also cause clinical signs.

Clinical Features

Clinical signs associated with *T cati* infections are limited mainly to kittens and to environments in which exposures and worm loads are high. The most prominent feature of severe infections is generalized unthriftiness manifested by delayed growth, a poor haircoat, and a pot-bellied appearance due to generalized muscle thinning caused by relative malnutrition. Acute colic, peritonitis and death have been associated with intestinal blockage by masses of adult worms. In kittens, this can be associated with perforation of the proximal small intestine. Pulmonary changes due to visceral larval migrans, though grossly and histologically severe at times, usually are not clinically apparent.

Pathologic Features

Pathologic features within the intestinal tract are absent or mild. Reddening of the gastric and small intestinal walls is the predominant gross change. Likewise, changes in the liver are usually not grossly apparent or consist only of subcapsular scarring. Pulmonary changes can be severe in some animals and occur within 2 weeks of infection.[10] Multiple tan lesions 1-2 mm in diameter may be observed throughout the lung parenchyma, particularly on the pleural surfaces. Some foci may be hemorrhagic. A marked leukocytic infiltrate with eosinophils may be seen around pulmonary arterioles and bronchioli. However, migrating larvae are rarely identified.

Medial hypertrophy and hyperplasia of pulmonary arteries can be observed as soon as 2 weeks following infection; such changes can become progressively more severe over the next 6 weeks. During the latter course of disease, eosinophils and lymphocytes can be found in considerable numbers in the adventitia of many larger pulmonary arterioles. This is often associated with muscularization of arteriolar walls and intimal proliferation. Such changes can be severe enough to virtually occlude some vessels. Larval migration from pulmonary vessels to the airways evokes both tissue eosinophilia and increased numbers of mast cells. Lungs of experimentally infected kittens contain 3-4 times more mast cells than normal from weeks 2-8 postinfection.[10] This was associated with a 50% increase in lung histamine content by week 6.

Clinicopathologic Features

Ascarid infections are diagnosed by examination of feces for typical eggs (Fig 1). In kittens with visceral larval migrans, eosinophilia may be pronounced.

Treatment and Prevention

Prevention of ascarid infections is routine in many catteries. Regular deworming of kittens and adult cats, coupled with frequent removal of litter, is effective when performed continuously. It is important to note that many queens can serve as reservoirs for reintroduction of infection into the cattery. Queens with encysted larval forms of *T cati* in their tissues can infect several generations of their kittens by transmammary infection. Periodic deworming of such queens does not eliminate this problem because most anthelmintics only kill adult worms within the intestinal tract. However, routine deworming slowly reduces the number of new infected queens.

Prevention of environmental egg contamination is an essential part of disease control. To minimize egg accumulation, cattery surfaces should be as impervious as possible to allow for thorough cleaning with soap and water.

Fig 1. *Toxocara cati* ovum in the stool of a cat. The egg is about 65 x 75 μ in size. (Courtesy of Dr. Norman Baker, University of California, Davis)

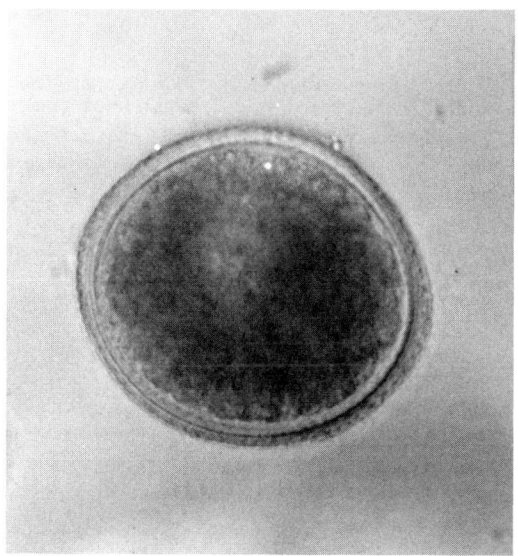

Numerous drugs are effective against adult and immature intestinal stages of the worm. The most popular are various piperazine salts. A single oral treatment with piperazine adipate at 200 mg/kg removes both immature and adult forms from the intestine. Dichlorvos is also highly effective but has been associated with severe diarrhea and, occasionally, rectal prolapse in some kittens. Fenbendazole at 10 mg/kg PO BID for 2 days or at 100 mg/kg PO as a single treatment, and pyrantel pamoate at 5 mg/kg PO as a single treatment, are also effective. Dubey found that fenbendazole may also reduce the number of larvae in tissues of bitches with *T canis* infections.[2] The efficacy of fenbendazole against tissue stages in cats is unknown. Ivermectin, given once SC at 200 μg/kg, has also eliminated all egg shedding in infected cats.[3] Its effect against the larval stages is unknown.

Infection and Immunity

Immunity to ascarid infection develops over time. Wilson-Hanson and Prescott found an infection rate of 39.9% in 6- to 8-week-old kittens, 41.2% in 5- to 8-month-old kittens, 21.1% in 10- to 15-month-old cats and 4.6% in cats over 2 years of age.[11] This immunity is directed against both tissue-migrating forms and stages confined to the intestinal tract. As in many complex parasitic infections, immunity probably involves type-I, -III and -IV mechanisms. Immunity may explain why ascarids are much more common in cats younger than 6 months of age than in older animals. Neutered cats also appear to have about half the ascarid load of intact cats, perhaps because of some hormonal influence on immunity.[9]

Animal and Public Health Considerations

Cats that shed *Toxocara* eggs are the principal reservoir for infection of other cats. However, when cats hunt freely, paratenic hosts (rodents) also constitute an important reservoir.

Visceral larval migrans is a potentially serious disease that occurs mainly in children. *Toxocara canis* is a far more common cause of this disease than *T cati*.[7] Nevertheless, a wide range of roundworms has been incriminated at times with the human syndrome. These include *Toxascaris leonina* and *Toxocara cati*. Visceral larval migrans in children is similar to the somatic infection seen in rodents infected with *T cati*. Larval forms are apt to migrate to the liver, lungs, brain and eyes. Encysted or dying organisms in human tissues provoke an eosinophilic granulomatous response and, if sufficiently severe, clinical signs. Clinical signs include fever, coughing, asthma-like wheezing, malaise, weight loss, hepatomegaly, CNS disturbances and eye disease ranging from retinal granulomas to severe exudative enophthalmitis.[1] Eosinophilia is very pronounced. The ocular lesions can be particularly severe in people and lead to blindness or enucleation because of misdiagnosis as an ocular tumor.

MISCELLANEOUS ASCARID INFECTION

Toxascaris leonina is found occasionally in the small intestine of cats.[11] It is much more common in dogs and wild Felidae and Canidae, and is worldwide in distribution. The life cycle is direct; embryonated eggs pass in the stool (Fig 2).[7] Following ingestion, second-stage larvae are released and burrow into the intestinal wall. They remain there for about 2 weeks while molting to fourth-stage larvae and then re-enter the intestinal lumen. Fifth-stage larvae are produced about 6 weeks postinfection and mature to egg-laying adults by week 10 or later. Mice can serve as paratenic hosts for *T leonina*.[7] Therefore, mice may be important reservoir hosts for cats.

The treatment of infected cats is the same as for *T cati* infections.

References

1. Blumenthal DS, in Wyngaarden JB and Smith LH Jr: *Cecil's Textbook of Medicine*. Saunders, Philadelphia, 1985. pp 1823-1824.

2. Dubey JP: Effect of fenbendazole on *Toxocara canis* larvae in tissues of infected dogs. *Am J Vet Res* 40:698-699, 1979.

3. Kirkpatrick CE and Megella C: Use of ivermectin in treatment of *Aelurostrongylus abstrusus* and *Toxocara cati* infections in a cat. *JAVMA* 190:1309-1310, 1987.

4. Lightner L et al: Epidemiologic findings on canine and feline intestinal nematode infections from records of the Iowa State University Veterinary Clinic. *JAVMA* 172:564-567, 1978.

5. Ryan GE: Gastro-intestinal parasites of feral cats in New South Wales. *Aust Vet J* 52:224-227, 1976.

6. Shaw J et al: Prevalence of some gastrointestinal parasites in cats in the Perth area. *Aust Vet J* 60:151-152, 1983.

7. Soulsby EJL: *Helminths, Arthropods and Protozoa of Domesticated Animals*. Lea & Febiger, Philadelphia, 1982. pp 152-155.

8. Swerczek TW et al: Transmammary passage of *Toxocara cati* in the cat. *Am J Vet Res* 32:89-92, 1971.

9. Visco RJ et al: Effect of age and sex on the prevalence of intestinal parasitism in cats. *JAVMA* 172:797-800, 1978.

10. Weatherly AJ and Hamilton JM: Possible role of histamine in the genesis of pulmonary arterial disease in cats infected with *Toxocara cati*. *Vet Record* 114:347-349, 1984.

11. Wilson-Hanson SL and Prescott CW: A survey for parasites in cats. *Aust Vet J* 59:194, 1982.

Additional Reference

12. Gethings PM et al: Prevalence of *Chlamydia, Toxoplasma, Toxocara*, and ringworm in farm cats in south-west England. *Vet Record* 121:213-216, 1987.

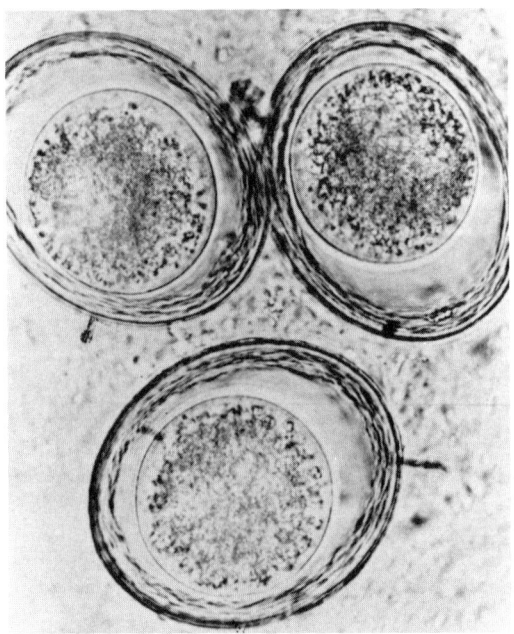

Fig 2. Ova of *Toxocara leonina* in the stool of a dog. These eggs average about 80 x 77 μ in size. (Courtesy of Dr. Norman Baker, University of California, Davis)

HEARTWORM DISEASE (DIROFILARIASIS)

Etiologic Agent

Dirofilaria immitis is a filarid worm that has its sexual stages in dogs and, to a lesser extent, in cats. Its intermediate developmental stages are in the mosquito. *Dirofilaria immitis* is found throughout the world in humid temperate and tropical regions that favor mosquito growth. Over 65 species of mosquitoes serve as intermediate hosts.[17,21] Appropriate mosquito vectors are also present in cooler regions; infection has spread rapidly into these areas over the last few decades. For instance, dirofilariasis was largely limited to the American southeast but has moved rapidly over the last 20 years into virtually every state as well as Canada.[28] In colder or hotter and dryer regions, however, infected mosquitoes and animals are found in pockets of high incidence. These pockets are more common in foothill regions than valley floors, and may be small enough to comprise only a part of a city.

A discussion of dirofilariasis in cats must be prefaced with a description of the infection in dogs. Dogs are the definitive hosts and the main reservoir for most feline infections. The adult form of *D immitis* is found in the right heart and pulmonary arteries. If both male and female worms are present, mating occurs. Females produce numerous embryonic worms called microfilariae, which circulate in the bloodstream until they are ingested by a mosquito or die, a process that can take as long as 2 years. Microfilariae ingested by the mosquito with the blood meal migrate to the malpighian tubules, where they enter the lining cells and molt twice to become third-stage infectious larvae. The transformation from microfilariae to third-stage infectious larvae can take 10-48 days. Infectious larvae leave the cells of the malpighian tubules, migrate to the proboscis of the mosquito and are deposited on the dog's skin when the mosquito feeds. The larvae penetrate the skin at the puncture site and spend the next 10 weeks of their life cycle in the subcutaneous tissues. During this time, they molt twice and grow 0.1-2.5 cm long in the process. They then penetrate local veins and are carried to the heart and pulmonary arteries, growing to 10-24 cm over the next 3 months. Mating occurs and microfilariae are produced. The entire life cycle from infection to production of microfilariae takes about 7 months (191-285 days) in dogs. Adult worms can live 5 years or longer in dogs and produce microfilariae almost continuously.

Two types of infection occur in dogs: patent and occult. In a patent infection, the life cycle is complete and circulating microfilariae are present. Two-thirds of dogs have patent infections in highly enzootic areas.[18] Clinical signs associated with patent infections are generally mild or inapparent; many dogs are microfilaremic for months or years without showing noticeable signs. When clinical signs are seen, they usually include fatigue on exercise, slight unthriftiness and a mild cough.

Occult infections are characterized by the presence of adults in the heart but no circulating microfilariae. Occult infections occur in less than one-third of dogs and are caused by development of immunity to the circulating microfilariae. Immune responses destroy the microfilariae as they enter the bloodstream. Dead and dying microfilariae are trapped in blood vessels in the lungs, where they elicit a severe vascular and perivascular inflammatory response. Therefore, dogs with occult disease are usually much sicker than dogs with patent infections.

In hosts other than dogs, vigorous immune responses are generated against all stages of the parasite. In people, this immune response is so effective that most larvae are destroyed in the subcutaneous tissues or at some other site outside the heart. Cats have an intermediate type of immunity between that of people and dogs. A much smaller percentage of migrating larvae reach the heart in cats than in dogs. Many migrating worms end up in spurious sites in the body, where they die and elicit local inflammatory responses. If adult worms reach the heart of cats, microfilariae are usually seen in the blood for only a few weeks.

Incidence of feline dirofilariasis parallels that of canine cases in a given area but is generally much lower. In areas of the world where 5-59% (average 44%) of dogs were infected, only 0-10% (average 2.6%) of cats examined at necropsy had adult worms in their heart or pulmonary arteries.[24] The highest reported incidence of dirofilariasis in cats was 32% in a study of 50 cats from Papua, New Guinea.[1] Feline dirofilariasis is most apt to occur in cats around 3 years of age, though animals as young as 9 months and as old as 9 years have been affected. There is no breed predisposition. Males with dirofilariasis outnumber females 2.6:1.[8] Cats that develop heartworm disease usually spend considerable time outdoors.

Pathogenesis

The pathogenesis of feline dirofilariasis differs from that of the canine disease mainly in the greater immunologic responsiveness of cats and the tendency of infected cats not to show many clinical signs. The greater immunologic responsiveness of cats to worm migration results in fewer infectious larvae reaching adulthood (2-30% in cats vs 40-90% in dogs), a slower rate of development to adulthood (8 months or longer in cats vs 6-7 months in dogs), shortened life span of adults (<18 months in cats vs 5 years in dogs), and a lower incidence and severity of microfilaremia (<18% of cats exhibit a low level of microfilaremia vs ≥75% incidence of pronounced microfilaremia in dogs).[10,14,36]

The greater immunologic responsiveness of cats leads to some essential differences between the forms of disease in cats and in dogs. Infection in cats is usually occult, pulmonary vascular lesions are more severe on radiographic and histopathologic examination, and disease caused by spurious worm migrations is more common. Spurious worm migrations in cats are probably associated with 2 factors: the inappropriateness of cats as definitive hosts, together with physiologic and anatomic differences that make it more difficult for migrating worms to reach the heart and pulmonary vessels; and a sustained immunologic attack on migrating worms, leading to abnormalities in parasite metabolism and migratory habits.

Actual disease due to heartworm infection is caused by mechanical and immunologic mechanisms. Mechanical damage due to the physical presence of the worms is less important. Rupture of a large vein with fatal hemorrhage into the brain was associated with spurious heartworm migration in a cat.[11] Knight has associated 2 types of lesions due to the physical presence of heartworms in blood vessels downstream of fifth-stage worms in the heart and pulmonary arteries: an intimal proliferative response to live worms; and embolization of pulmonary vessels with dead parasites.[19] He was unable to determine the contribution of mechanical, immune-mediated or other unknown factors to lesion development. However, it is certain that the worms cause vascular lesions that are limited to tributaries of vessels containing living worms.[19]

Clinical Features

Three basic syndromes are seen in feline dirofilariasis: asymptomatic and self-limiting infections; clinically apparent pulmonary disease; and miscellaneous conditions, often neurologic, associated with spurious heartworm migration.

Asymptomatic and self-limiting infections are seen in 40% of experimentally infected cats.[10,12] They are probably even more common among naturally exposed cats, which seldom receive the dose of infectious second-stage larvae (20-100 or more) used in experimentally created disease. Asymptomatic infections occur when larvae never migrate beyond the subcutaneous tissues or when adults reach the heart but are subsequently destroyed. Cats rarely show outward signs of heartworm disease, though thoracic radiographs might demonstrate pronounced abnormalities.

The pulmonary form of feline dirofilariasis is usually associated with small numbers of adults (usually 1-7) in the right ventricle, right atrium or mainstem pulmonary arteries. The relative incidence of this form of disease in nature is unknown, though 60% of cats experimentally infected with large numbers of third-stage larvae develop pulmonary signs.[12] The relative incidence of pulmonary to asymptomatic disease is probably lower in natural infections in which cats are infected with lower numbers of larvae. Infection is occult in 80-90% of cases due to a lack of mating pairs or immune-mediated destruction of microfilariae. One-third or less of cats with this form of disease die suddenly or develop acute and usually fatal respiratory distress.[3,23,27,29,31,33] Cats with acute respiratory distress are severely depressed, dyspneic, cyanotic, and often frothing from the mouth and nostrils. Death occurs within minutes or hours after onset. However, most cats with the pulmonary form have a more chronic course of disease lasting several weeks to a year or longer.[23,25,29-31,33,34] The most common clinical signs include a chronic or episodic cough that is usually mild in nature, gagging and dysphagia, vomiting, weight loss and listlessness. The common occurrence of vomiting among cats with dirofilariasis cannot be readily explained. Paradoxically, vomiting has been recognized as a more common sign of pulmonary dirofilariasis than coughing.[7]

Disease caused by spurious heartworm migration is relatively common in cats as compared to dogs. The most common site for spurious migration is the brain and, to a lesser extent, the spinal cord. Of 10 experimentally infected cats studied, 2 died from cerebral dirofilariasis.[24] About 25% of cats reported in the literature suffered from cerebral dirofilariasis. [2,5,8,13,15,20,22,23,29] Clinical signs of CNS dirofilariasis usually result from 1 or 2 adult worms in the cerebral arteries, lateral ventricle or subdural spaces of the cerebellum, brainstem or spinal cord. The most common clinical signs include sudden depression, circling, head tilt, nystagmus, muscle fasciculations, anisocoria, dementia, convulsions, profuse salivation, ataxia and paralysis. Spurious migration to the perirenal fascia and subcutaneous tissues has also been observed. Several cats in an experimental study developed chylothorax.[10,12] Though no worms were observed in the major lymphatic trunks, spurious migrations to such sites has been observed with other filarid diseases of people and animals. Solitary granulomas associated with dead worms have also been observed occasionally in the lungs of cats without worms in the heart or pulmonary arteries.

Pathologic Features

The pulmonary vasculature and surrounding tissues are the most severely affected tissues in cats with classical dirofilariasis (Fig 3). Vascular changes are concentrated in vessels and their tributaries that harbor adult worms. The most common lesions are muscular hypertrophy of pulmonary arterial walls, and thickening of the intima from villus hyperplasia and cellular infiltrates that consist of neutrophils and eosinophils in the adventitia. Such changes can occur within 1 week of experimental transplantation of adult worms to the pulmonary arteries.[7] Thrombosis of vessels due to embolization of worms or worm fragments, or from vasculitis, is sometimes observed. Changes within involved vessels lead to gradual narrowing of the pulmonary arteries and pulmonary hypertension. Hypertension leads to an increase in the smooth muscle mass in the walls of larger vessels and right cardiac hypertrophy. Cardiac changes are much less severe in cats than dogs, especially considering the intensity of pulmonary vessel disease.

Lesions of cerebral dirofilariasis are often much more diffuse than expected from the mere presence of adult worms in the cerebral arteries, subdural spaces or ventricles.[15] Changes in tissues of the brain bear a basic resemblance to those in the lungs. Dying worms are often surrounded by a granulomatous process involving numerous lymphocytes, eosinophils and macrophages. Areas of focal necrosis with malacia and hemorrhage are common in areas adjacent to or surrounding living or dying worms. Lymphocytic perivascular cuffing around blood vessels in the subependymal space and meninges distant from sites of worm infection is common. Massive hemorrhage into the lateral ventricle has been associated with rupture of a parasitized subependymal vein.[11]

Clinicopathologic Features

Heartworm disease in cats is often diagnosed from characteristic findings on thoracic radiographs, serologic tests or necropsy. The Knott's test for detection of circulating microfilariae is negative in 80-90% of cats; therefore, it is not of great diagnostic value. Hematologic changes are relatively nonspecific and consist mainly of eosinophilia that begins about 10 weeks postinfection. Cats with unisex infections have lower levels of circulating eosinophils, while cats harboring more than 10 worms of both sexes often have 40% eosinophils or more.[35] However, eosinophilia fluctuates greatly and absence of eosinophilia does not rule out the infection. Eosinophilia may also be present in syndromes manifested in similar ways, such as lungworm infection and chronic allergic bronchiolitis.

Radiographic changes of heartworm infection in cats mainly involve the pulmonary vasculature. Cardiac enlargement is often not pronounced. Proximal pulmonary arteries are enlarged and exhibit increased tortuosity with a sudden loss of smaller arteriolar branching (pruning of pulmonary arteries). The loss of definition of smaller caliber arteries is due to narrowing and occlusion of these vessels as part of the parasite-induced endarteritis. Vascular changes are most pronounced in the caudal lung lobes and on ventrodorsal projections. Parenchymal changes consisting of diffuse or coalescing perivascular densities and atelectasis are also frequently seen in severely affected animals. Pulmonary vascular abnormalities tend to persist to some extent following self-limiting disease or treatment. Therefore, sometimes it is difficult to state whether or not the disease is active, based on radiographs alone.

Serologic tests are becoming more popular for diagnosis of heartworm infection in dogs. Some of these same procedures are being applied to cats. Thilsted and co-workers studied both the sensitivity and specificity of several of these tests in

Fig 3. Adult *Dirofilaria immitis* in the right ventricle and pulmonary artery of a cat experimentally infected with heartworms. (Courtesy of Dr. Ming Wong, University of California, Davis)

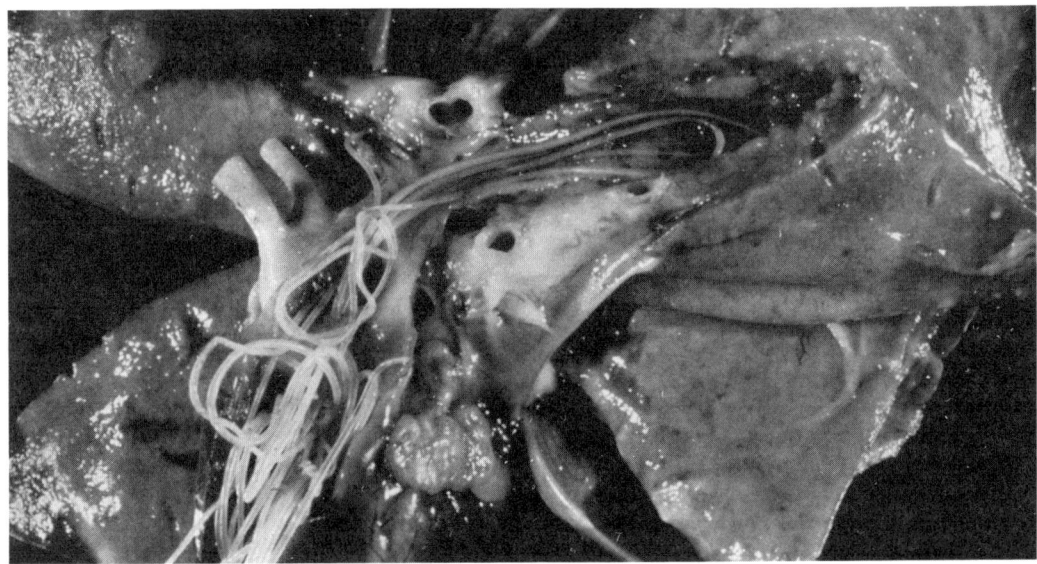

detecting patent and occult infections in dogs.[32] They found that enzyme-linked immunosorbent assays (ELISA) for detection of heartworm antibodies in canine serum were 70-95% sensitive and 77-87% specific. Indirect immunofluorescent antibody (IFA) tests for adult worms were 100% accurate in detecting occult infections and 91% accurate in detecting patent infections. Immunofluorescent antibody tests against microfilariae were 67% accurate in detecting occult infections and 73% accurate in detecting patent infections. Enzyme-linked immunosorbent assays to detect dirofilarial antigen in canine serum were 75% sensitive and 99% specific. The ELISA for heartworm antigens appears to be applicable to cats. However, it is usually not positive until 5-8 months postinfection. This is not of diagnostic concern because cats with heartworm infection usually do not develop clinical signs until after this time anyway. Similar comparative studies need to be done in cats.

Wong and co-workers used an IFA test to study occult and patent infections in cats.[36] They found that antibodies to microfilarial cuticular antigens were not generated in animals with unisex or sterile infections. Cats that tested positive to the microfilarial cuticular antigens almost always had occult infections, with substantial pathologic changes in the lungs and heart.

Treatment and Prevention

Cats with heartworm disease are treated in the same manner as dogs. Animals with severe pulmonary vascular disease should be pretreated with prednisolone (or equivalent) at 2 mg/kg PO daily for at least 2 weeks before being treated with arsenical adulticides. Prednisolone use should be discontinued several days before arsenical therapy because it tends to decrease the toxicity of arsenic to adult worms and increase their survival. Such pretreatment greatly decreases the extent of pulmonary complications and improves the chances of surviving treatment. Thiacetarsamide is given IV as an adulticide at 2.2 mg/kg daily for 2 days. Toxic effects of the drug are greater in cats than dogs but are still not significant enough to forfeit treatment in cats showing obvious clinical signs. The main complication of therapy arises 7-14 days after the end of treatment, when adult worms begin to die. Death of adult worms can lead to considerable embolization and inflammatory thrombosis of pulmonary vessels, and acute mortality. Up to 30% of treated cats can develop such complications, especially if not pretreated with corticosteroids or kept strictly confined. Cats that become dyspneic during this critical period should be cage-rested, given oxygen if necessary, and treated immediately with high levels of corticosteroids for several days. Successful elimination of adult worms with a single arsenical treatment is achieved in 75-100% of cats.

Treatment of cats with microfilaricides following successful arsenical therapy is only indicated in animals with patent infections. The value of routinely treating cats with heartworm preventives, such as diethylcarbamazine citrate or ivermectin, is debatable. The incidence of heartworm infection in cats, even in highly enzootic areas, is seldom >5-10% at any given time, and most of these animals recover spontaneously. Nevertheless, routine preventive treatment is recommended by some veterinarians for outdoor cats in areas of high incidence.

Infection and Immunity

Immunity to heartworms is due to type-I (IgE-mediated), type-III (precipitating antibodies or immune-complex formation) and type-IV (cell-mediated) immune mechanisms. Immune responses are directed mainly at the cuticular proteins of the parasite, which are largely stage specific. This means that worm migration can be halted at various stages, including third-stage larvae, adults and microfilariae. Immunity to migrating pre-adult forms appears considerable in cats. Immunity to adult forms appears to be the slowest to develop, though over time it can become quite intense. Donahoe found that most of the radiographic and hematologic changes (eosinophilia) occurred 3-9 months after inoculation of cats with infectious larvae and that these abnormalities tended to disappear by 6-14 months postinoculation.[9]

The most severe form of heartworm disease in cats and dogs is associated with microfilariae production by mating pairs of worms and concurrent microfilarial immunity (occult dirofilariasis). If the immune response to the microfilariae is intense enough, most microfilariae are attacked as soon as they are produced. Dead and dying microfilariae are trapped within the vasculature of the lungs and elicit localized inflammatory reactions. Such reactions contribute greatly to the total disease process and may explain why occult dirofilariasis is much more devastating than patent infections. In patent infections, microfilariae are free to circulate without being attacked by the host, and elicit minimal tissue reaction.

Pulmonary and vascular lesions cannot always be attributed to immune responses against microfilariae. Significant pulmonary changes have sometimes been seen in cats before the worms reach sexual maturity and in cats with unisex or sterile adult worm infections.[9] This suggests that products of immature or sterile adults may also lead to disease in pulmonary vasculature through immune-mediated or metabolic mechanisms.

Animal and Public Health Considerations

Cats are a limited health hazard to other animals. Patent infections are relatively uncommon, making cats a poor reservoir as compared to dogs.

People are susceptible to infection with *D immitis* from carrier mosquitoes. Direct cat- or dog-to-person transmission does not occur. Most mosquito-borne infectious larvae are killed rapidly within the subcutaneous tissues of people by vigorous host immunity. An occasional worm develops for some time before being destroyed. Uncommonly, adult worms may be found in the heart and related vessels.[24] Larger dying worms are often encircled by a granulomatous reaction of some magnitude. Such nodules can be found subcutaneously or, more commonly, as "coin-like" lesions in the lungs.[24] None of these nodular reactions is of clinical significance, but coin lesions in the lung may be mistaken for early tumors or tubercular granulomas. Therefore, human dirofilariasis is of more diagnostic importance than clinical significance.

References

1. Abbott PK: Feline dirofilariasis in Papua. *Aust Vet J* 42:247-249, 1966.

2. Ader P: Heartworm (*Dirofilaria immitis*) in the brain of a cat-review and case report. *Calif Vet* 33:23-28, 32, 1979.

3. Bernard MA: Feline dirofilariasis. *Can Vet J* 11:190-191, 1970.

4. Calvert CA and Mandel CP: Diagnosis and management of feline heartworm disease. *JAVMA* 180:550-552, 1982.

5. Cusick PK et al: *Dirofilaria immitis* in the brain and heart of a cat from Massachusetts. *JAAHA* 12:490-491, 1976.

6. Dillon R et al: Indirect immunofluorescence testing for diagnosis of occult *Dirofilaria immitis* infection in three cats. *JAVMA* 180:80-82, 1982.

7. Dillon R: Feline dirofilariasis. *Vet Clin No Am* 14:1185-1198, 1984.

8. Donahoe JMR: Clinical aspects of feline dirofilariasis. *Proc Am Heartworm Soc Symp*, 1974. pp 59-65.

9. Donahoe JMR et al: Hematologic and radiographic changes in cats after inoculation with infective larvae of *Dirofilaria immitis*. *JAVMA* 168:413-417, 1976.

10. Donahoe JMR: Experimental infection of cats with *Dirofilaria immitis*. *J Parasitol* 61:599-605, 1975.

11. Donahoe JMR and Holzinger EA: *Dirofilaria immitis* in the brains of a dog and a cat. *JAVMA* 164:518-519, 1974.

12. Donahoe JMR et al: Chylothorax subsequent to infection of cats with *Dirofilaria immitis*. *JAVMA* 164:1107-1110, 1974.

13. Faries FC et al: Incidental findings of *Dirofilaria immitis* in domestic cats. *VM/SAC* 69:599-600, 1974.

14. Fowler JL et al: Experimental infection of the domestic cat with *Dirofilaria immitis*. *JAAHA* 8:79-80, 1972.

15. Fukushima K et al: Aberrant dirofilariasis in a cat. *JAVMA* 184:199-201, 1984.

16. Hawe RS: The diagnosis and treatment of occult dirofilariasis in a cat. *JAAHA* 15:577-582, 1979.

17. Hendrix CM et al: Natural transmission of *Dirofilaria immitis* by *Aedes vexans*. *Am J Vet Res* 41:1253-1255, 1980.

18. Hoskins JD et al: Heartworm disease in dogs from Louisiana: Pretreatment clinical and laboratory evaluation. *JAAHA* 20: 205-210, 1984.

19. Knight DH, in Ettinger SJ: *Textbook of Veterinary Internal Medicine.* Saunders, Philadelphia, 1983. pp 1097-1120.

20. Lindquist WD and Winters KD: Cerebral feline dirofilariasis. *Feline Pract* 11(2):37-40, 1981.

21. Ludlam KW et al: Potential vectors of *Dirofilaria immitis*. *JAVMA* 157:1354-1359, 1970.

22. Mandelker L and Brutus RL: Feline and canine dirofilarial encephalitis. *JAVMA* 159:776, 1981.

23. Anon: Feline dirofilariasis: Seek and you shall find. *Norden News*, Summer, 1985. pp 18-26.

24. Otto GF: Occurrence of the heartworm in unusual locations and in unusual hosts. *Proc Am Heartworm Soc Symp*, 1974. pp 6-13.

25. Schwartz A: Two cases of feline heartworm disease. *Feline Pract* 5(4):20-28, 1975.

26. Seymore DN: Dirofilariasis in a cat. *Mod Vet Pract* 61:251, 1980.

27. Sherman WA and Wechsler SJ: Unusual case of heartworm disease in a cat. *VM/SAC* 70:1320, 1975.

28. Slocombe JOD and McMillan I: Heartworm in dogs in Canada in 1978. *Can Vet J* 20:284-287, 1978.

29. Smith F: Feline heartworm disease. *Cornell Feline Health Center Vet News*, Summer, 1985.

30. Soifer FK: Dirofilariasis in a cat. *VM/SAC* 71:484-486, 1976.

31. Stackhouse LL and Clough E: Five cases of feline dirofilariasis. *VM/SAC* 67:1309-1310, 1972.

32. Thilsted JP et al: Comparison of four serotests for the detection of *Dirofilaria immitis* in dogs. *Am J Vet Res* 48:837-841, 1987.

33. Todd KS et al: Heartworm infections in Illinois cats. *Feline Pract* 6(2):41-44, 1976.

34. Tornes WA and Sambol RM: Heartworm infection in a cat. *Allied Vet* 30:150-152, 1959.

35. Wong MM et al: Dirofilariasis in cats. *JAAHA* 19:855-864, 1983.

36. Wong MM and Suter PF: Indirect fluorescent antibody test in occult dirofilariasis. *Am J Vet Res* 40:414-420, 1979.

LUNGWORM INFECTION

Etiologic Agent

Aelurostrongylus abstrusus is the principal lungworm of domestic cats.[15] A closely related and morphologically similar worm, *Troglostrongylus subcrenatus*, has been found in the lungs of domestic and wild Felidae in Africa, Italy and the United States.[2,15] *Metathelazia californica* and *M vogeloides* are filarid lungworms of domestic cats from California and the USSR, respectively.[15] *Aelurostrongylus* adults live in the lungs of cats. They are worldwide in distribution. The male worm is about 7.5 mm long and the female about 10 mm long.

The life cycles of all filarid lungworms are probably similar. More is known, however, about the life cycle of *A abstrusus*. Adult worms live in the terminal respiratory bronchioli and alveolar ducts. Concentrations of eggs form small nodules in the alveolar ducts and alveoli. Larvae hatch from the eggs, ascend the airways and are swallowed. Larvae are passed in the feces and live in the environment for as long as 5 weeks, especially in damp conditions. The larvae die unless taken up by snails and slugs. They molt twice in snails or slugs before becoming infectious third-stage larvae. Rodents, frogs, lizards and birds also act as transport hosts and become infected themselves if they eat infected slugs and snails. Larvae migrate to the tissues and encyst.

Cats are infected either by eating slugs and snails carrying infectious lungworm larvae or, more commonly, by eating 1 of the numerous transport hosts. Larvae penetrate the esophageal, gastric or small intestinal walls and are carried in the bloodstream to the lungs. There, they become adults, mate and begin the egg-laying cycle. The prepatent period in cats is about 6 weeks; peak egg output occurs between the third and seventh month. After that, egg production usually declines rapidly due to immune destruction of adults.

The occurrence of patent lungworm infection in a 9-week-old kitten suggests the possibility of *in-utero* or transmammary infection.[1]

Pathogenesis

The incidence of lungworm infection varies considerably among localities, depending on the population of cats and availability of water and intermediate and transport hosts. Hamilton found the incidence of lungworm infection of cats in Scotland was 9.4%, while incidences of 2-26% were common in other parts of the world.[3] Willard and associates found that nearly 20% of mature stray cats from an animal shelter in Alabama were infected.[16] Wilson-Hanson and Prescott isolated *A abstrusus* from 3.8% of cats in Brisbane, Australia.[17] There is no known breed or sex predisposition. Lungworm infection appears to be more common in cats 1-3 years of age, though cats as young as 9 weeks and as old as 15 years have been affected. In 1 study, *A abstrusus* was found only in cats >10 months of age.[17]

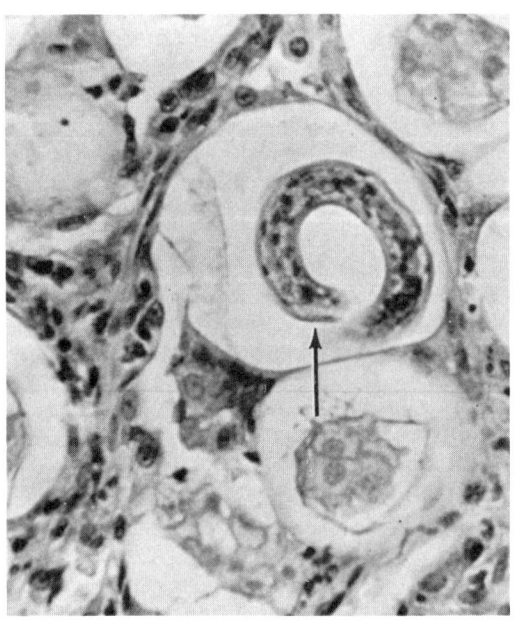

Fig 4. Photomicrograph showing an adult *Aelurostrongylus abstrusus* (arrow) in the lung of a cat with a natural lungworm infection. Hematoxylin and eosin stain, 1000X. (Courtesy of Dr. Norman Baker, University of California, Davis)

The pathogenesis of lungworm disease in cats is intimately associated with host immune responses to eggs and adult worms in the lungs. Therefore, clinical signs are most apt to be seen 1.5-7 months after initial infection.

Clinical Features

Most cats infected with lungworms show no clinical signs of illness. Even in cats with severe infections, clinical signs are usually mild. Predominant clinical signs include a chronic mild cough, wheezing and, on occasion, exertional dyspnea and fatigue.[3,12,13] Mild ocular and nasal discharges, sometimes associated with sneezing, have been described.[3] Weight loss and anorexia are usually absent or minimal. Dyspnea is seen at rest in relatively few severely infected cats.

Lungworm infections reported in the literature have been frequently complicated by other more serious conditions, such as feline infectious peritonitis, lymphosarcoma, cryptococcosis, trauma, poisoning, abscesses and enteritis.[3,7] Whether these concurrent conditions decrease the animal's ability to respond to lungworm infection has not been addressed. More likely, the lungworm infections were subclinical and only discovered in the process of diagnosing the concurrent disease.

Pathologic Features

Gross lesions are limited to the lungs and consist of multiple grayish foci that range in size from pinpoint to 10 mm in diameter.[3] Nodules are scattered throughout the lungs but tend to concentrate in subpleural sites. The lungs are firmer than normal on cut section. Pleural effusion, either chylous or opaque in nature, has been seen in a few cats.[3,10]

Histopathologic changes are concentrated around alveoli, bronchioli and bronchi. Foci of lymphocytes, plasma cells, eosinophils, macrophages and giant cells surround clusters of eggs in dilated alveoli and bronchioli. These granulomatous reactions are associated with central necrosis, though calcification is infrequent. Adult worms appear in cross-section within smaller airways and are associated with considerable eosinophil and macrophage infiltration (Fig 4). Diffuse and follicular peribronchial and peribronchiolar lymphoid hyperplasia is conspicuous in sites distant to eggs and adults. The mucosa of bronchioli is frequently hyperplastic, with increased mucous cell activity and hypersecretion. Hypertrophy of the smooth muscle layers of the bronchioli and alveolar ducts is evident. Emphysematous alveolar changes and filling of alveolar spaces with macrophages occur in areas adjacent to parasitized lung tissue.

Vascular changes can be pronounced in lungworm infection. Vessel changes consist of hypertrophy and hyperplasia of pulmonary arterial and arteriolar smooth muscle. Vascular lesions are frequently associated with infiltration of eosinophils into the subendothelial tissues, splitting and reduplication of the internal and external elastic membranes, subendothelial fibrosis, endothelial-cell hyperplasia and perivascular lymphoid-cell hyperplasia. These changes, though seldom severe enough to lead to vascular occlusion, are reminiscent of those associated with dirofilariasis in cats.

Clinicopathologic Features

Lungworm infection is diagnosed by clinical signs, radiographic appearance of the lungs, detection of eosinophils in tracheal washes, peripheral eosinophilia, and identification of first-stage larvae in tracheal exudates or feces.

Willard and co-workers found that the Baermann fecal flotation technique was more sensitive than gross necropsy or histopathologic examination in diagnosing lungworms.[16] It was both more sensitive and specific than radiographic examination.

Radiographic changes are highly suggestive of the disease but not pathognomonic. They must be differentiated from changes caused by dirofilariasis and chronic allergic bronchiolitis. Radiographic changes appear as soon as 2-3 weeks after experimental infection and consist of mixed patchy bron-

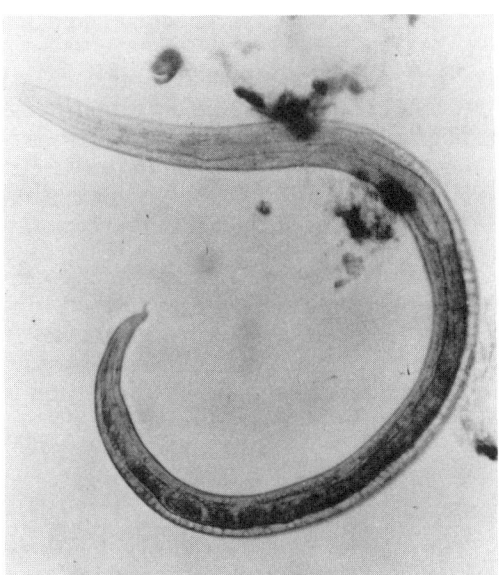

Fig 5. Larva of *Aelurostrongylus abstrusus* in the feces of a cat with a chronic cough and radiographic pulmonary densities suggestive of lungworm infection. Lungworm larvae are about 360 μ long and have an S-shaped caudal appendage. (Courtesy of Dr. Norman Baker, University of California, Davis)

chial and alveolar densities.[7,8] During the most severe stage of disease, which occurs 5-21 weeks after infection, alveolar changes become more predominant. In a study of naturally occurring disease, Losonsky and associates observed patchy alveolar densities in 87% and increased peribronchial densities in 57% of cats <1 year of age.[6] Interstitial and bronchial changes predominate in older cats. Radiographic enlargement of the pulmonary arteries was apparent in about 50% of infected animals. Pulmonary densities often obscured vascular details. Alveolar disease slowly resolves as the worms are destroyed by host immune responses, a process that usually occurs 17-40 weeks after experimental infection.[7] As alveolar densities disappear, bronchial and miliary pulmonary interstitial densities become more pronounced.

Lungworm infection is confirmed by identifying first-stage larvae in the tracheal wash or feces. However, tracheal washing is much less sensitive than fecal analysis. Numbers of larvae are relatively small, especially during the later stages of disease, and are unlikely to be seen in the small amount of dilute tracheal fluid taken at a single collection. Fecal analysis, using Baermann fecal flotation procedure, is considerably more accurate because total larval output over several hours or more is concentrated. Larval forms are 0.36 mm long and have an S-shaped caudal appendage (Fig 5). Larvae are most likely to be seen over a 2- to 3-month period. After that, egg output decreases dramatically even though radiographic and clinical signs of disease persist. It is very difficult in these circumstances to differentiate lungworm infection from chronic allergic bronchiolitis.

About 35% of confirmed heartworm-free, lungworm-infected cats test positive ELISA tests for *Dirofilaria* antibodies.[16] The heartworm antigen ELISA appears to be specific for *Dirofilaria*, however, and is not positive in lungworm-infected cats.

Treatment and Prevention

The success of drug therapy for lungworm infection of cats is debatable. Fenbendazole at 20 mg/kg PO daily for 5 days has reportedly cleared larvae from the feces of 6 of 6 experimentally infected cats.[5] Adults and eggs were degenerating (3 of 6) or absent (3 of 6) 4 weeks after treatment. Roberson and Burke observed marked degenerative changes in eggs and adults in cats treated with fenbendazole at 50 mg/kg daily for 3 days.[11] However, they were unable to conclude whether this degeneration was significant. Some clinicians give fenbendazole every 2 weeks for 4-8 weeks.

Albendazole and mebendazole are highly efficacious against lungworm infections of rats but have not been well studied in cats.[14] Levamisole decreases larval shedding but is probably not effective as an adulticide.[15] Tetramisole has also been used to successfully treat lungworm infections in cats but produces signs of organophosphate toxicity in some animals. The recommended dosage is 45 mg/kg PO every other day for 5 treatments.[4,14] Atropine can be given if salivation becomes noticeable. Though 2 studies of tetramisole showed the drug to be quite effective, Schalm and associates were only partially successful with a larger dose given to 2 cats.[4,12-14] A single injection of ivermectin, SC at 400 μg/kg, eliminated shedding of lungworm larvae in a cat.[6] A dosage of 200 μg/kg was ineffective.

Infection and Immunity

Immunity to lungworm infection probably begins 2-6 weeks after infection, when eosinophilia is first detected. Immunity involves type-I, -III and -IV reactions and takes several months to effectively eliminate adult worms from the lungs. The peribronchial, interstitial, alveolar and vascular abnormalities that occur in lungworm disease are probably directly attributable to host immunity against adult worms, eggs and soluble products.

Animal and Public Health Considerations

Because of the complex life cycle of the organism, there is no direct cat-to-cat transmission of lungworms. Cat lungworms do not cause disease in people.

References

1. Clinton RL et al: Lungworm in a nine-week-old kitten. *Feline Pract* 6(2):45-46, 1976.

2. Fitzsimmons WM: *Bronchostrongylus subcrenatus*, a new parasite recorded from the domestic cat. *Vet Record* 73:101-102, 1961.

3. Hamilton JM: *Aelurostrongylus abstrusus* infestation of the cat. *Vet Record* 75:417-422, 1963.

4. Hamilton JM: The treatment of lungworm disease in the cat with tetramisole. *J Small Anim Pract* 8:325, 1967.

5. Hamilton JM et al: Treatment of lungworm disease in the cat with fenbendazole. *Vet Record* 114:40-41, 1984.

6. Kirkpatrick CE and Megella C: Use of ivermectin in treatment of *Aelurostrongylus abstrusus* and *Toxocara cati* infections in cats. *JAVMA* 190:1309-1310, 1987.

7. Losonsky JM et al: Radiographic findings in *Aelurostrongylus abstrusus* infection in cats. *JAAHA* 14:348-355, 1978.

8. Losonsky JM et al: Radiographic evaluation of pulmonary abnormalities after *Aelurostrongylus abstrusus* inoculation in cats. *Am J Vet Res* 44:478-482, 1983.

9. Mahaffey MB: Radiographic-pathologic findings in experimental *Aelurostrongylus abstrusus* infection in cats. *Proc Am College Vet Rad.*, 1978. p 81.

10. Miller BH et al: Pleural effusion as a sequel to aelurostrongylosis in a cat. JAVMA 185:556-557, 1984.

11. Roberson HL and Burke TM: Evaluation of granulated fenbendazole (22.2%) against induced and naturally occurring helminth infections in cats. Am J Vet Res 41:1499-1502, 1980.

12. Schalm OW et al: Lungworm infection in cats. Feline Pract 4(6):41-45, 1974.

13. Scott DW: Current knowledge of aelurostrongylosis in the cat. Cornell Vet 63:483-500, 1973.

14. Scott DW: Treatment of aelurostrongylosis in a cat. VM/SAC 68:134-135, 1973.

15. Soulsby EJL: *Helminths, Arthropods and Protozoa of Domesticated Animals.* Lea & Febiger, Philadelphia, 1982. pp 278-283.

16. Willard MD et al: Diagnosis of Aelurostrongylus abstrusus and Dirofilaria immitis infections in cats from a humane shelter. JAVMA 192:913-916, 1988.

17. Wilson-Hanson SL and Prescott CW: A survey for parasites in cats. Aust Vet J 59:194, 1982.

NASAL WORM (GAPEWORM) INFECTION

Etiologic Agent

Mammomonogamus ierei is a nematode belonging to the family Syngamidae.[5] Adult worms are found attached by their large buccal cavities to the nasal mucosa, from the nares to the pharynx.[1-4] Infected cats have been observed in the Caribbean region and Nigeria.[1-4] A closely related species, *Syngamus felis*, has been isolated from the Indian tiger.[1]

The life cycle of *M ierei* is unknown but is probably similar to that of closely related worms of fowl, such as *Syngamus trachea* and *S skrjabinomorpha*.[5] The life cycle of *Syngamus* spp begins with adults in the trachea. *Syngamus* adults, like adult *Mammomonogamus*, are in permanent copulation. The smaller male (5 mm long) attaches itself with its caudal alae to the vulva of the larger female (20 mm long). Eggs are passed into the host's respiratory tract and coughed up into the pharynx and swallowed. In the case of *M ierei*, eggs pass directly into the host's oropharynx.

The eggs of *M ierei* are passed in the feces in the 4- to 6-cell stage.[1] Larvae form in culture within 20 days, going through 3 developmental stages before hatching. The events that occur in nature are less certain. The eggs of *Syngamus* are ingested by earthworms, snails, slugs, flies, and other arthropods. The larvae penetrate the tissues of the intermediate host and encyst. The definitive host is infected through the ingestion of the parasitized intermediate host. *Syngamus* spp of fowl penetrate the intestine and reach the lungs via the bloodstream or by migrating through the peritoneal cavity, into the airsacs and then to the lungs. The larvae then migrate up the respiratory passages. Evidence that intermediate hosts are also important for *Mammomonogamus ierei* has been provided by Buckley.[1] As the larvae migrate to the proximal respiratory passages, adulthood is reached and mating occurs. The adults attach themselves to the mucosa by their buccal capsule (Fig 6). The adults probably feed on body fluids.

Pathogenesis

Mammomonogamus ierei infection is common in areas of the Caribbean, with up to 50% of cats being parasitized.[1] One-third of 40 adult cats in Puerto Rico were also infected.[2] In the only account of experimental *M ierei* infection, 3 cats were orally infected with several hundred larvae that were propagated *in vitro* from eggs teased out of adult worms.[1] Only 1 cat became infected, as evidenced by the appearance of eggs in the feces 14 days after infection. The low infectivity of *in-vitro* cultivated larvae was attributed to the fact that they had not matured in an invertebrate host.

Naturally infected cats have as many as 14 copulating pairs of worms (average, 4 pairs).[2] Worms are restricted to the nasal passages; no worms have been observed in the trachea.[1]

Clinical Features

Infected cats may be asymptomatic or show mild to moderately severe sneezing, coughing, nasal congestion and open-mouth breathing.[1-4] Worms may be passed from

Fig 6. Cross sections of an adult male (left arrow) and female (right arrow) *Mammomonogamus ierei* attached to the the nasopharyngeal mucosa of a naturally infected cat from Puerto Rico. The adult worms fill their buccal cavity with host mucosa. Hematoxylin and eosin stain, 85X. (Courtesy of Dr. R. Cuadrado and *Journal of the American Veterinary Medical Association*)

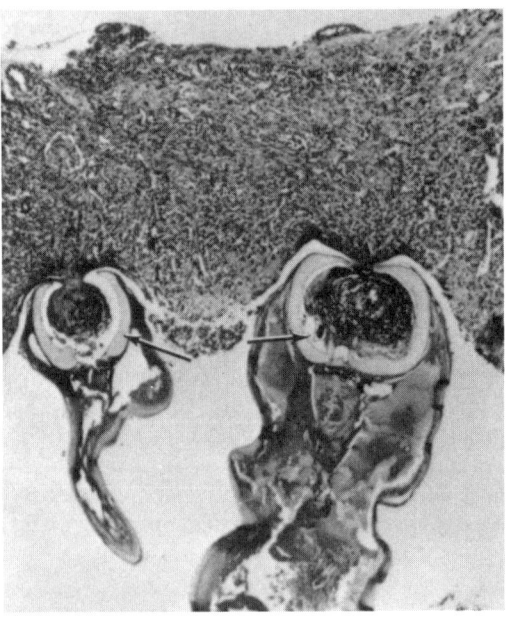

Fig 7. Ova of *Ancylostoma* (A) and *Mammomonogamus* (B) in cat feces. The *M ierei* egg resembles that of *Ancylostoma* but is larger and has a thicker shell that is usually surrounded by debris. 1000X. (Courtesy of Dr. R. Cuadrado and the *Journal of the American Veterinary Medical Association*)

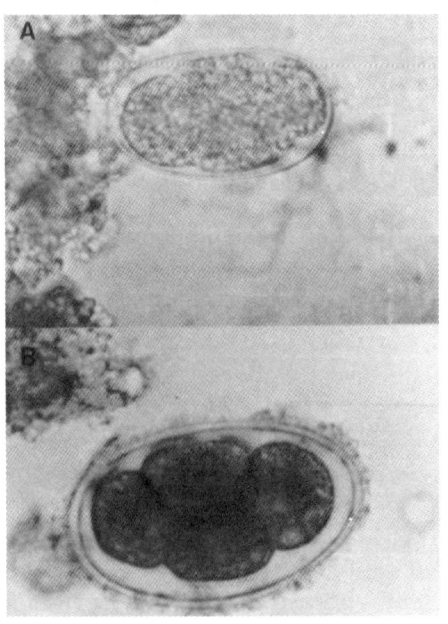

the nasal cavity during bouts of sneezing.[4] Worms passed in this manner are reddish-brown.

Pathologic Features

In the only histopathologic description of gapeworm infection in domestic cats, the adult worms were attached to a small polypoid mass of mucosa (Fig 6).[2] Mucosal tissue in the attachment site was often denuded and covered with a mucopurulent exudate, with occasional eosinophils. Mucosal fibrosis in the area of attachment was slight, plasma-cell infiltrates were abundant, and neutrophils and eosinophils scant.

Clinicopathologic Features

Diagnosis is made most commonly by observing adult worms in the nasal exudate or in the nasal passages, or by identification of eggs in the stool. The eggs average 92 x 50 μ and closely resemble those of *Ancylostoma* spp (Fig 7).[1,2] The shell is marked by fine irregular transverse striations, giving it a pitted appearance. Polar caps are absent and the enclosed embryo is typically in the 4- to 6-cell stage.

Treatment and Prevention

Infections can usually be treated with oral mebendazole or fenbendazole. Tetramisole has also been advocated as a possible treatment.[4]

Infection and Immunity

Nothing is known about the survival of *M ierei* in domestic cats. The presence of eosinophils and plasma cells at the site of attachment of adult worms suggests that some sort of immunity is evoked to mature worms.

Animal and Public Health Considerations

Infected cats are probably not infectious to other cats. There are no reports of human infection.

References

1. Buckley JJC: On *Syngamus ierei* sp. nov. from domestic cats, with some observations on its life-cycle. *J Helminthol* 12:89-98, 1934.

2. Cuadrado R et al: Gapeworm infection of domestic cats in Puerto Rico. *JAVMA* 176:996-997, 1980.

3. Guillbride PDL: *Syngamus ierei, Physaloptera praeputialis* and *Platynosomum fastosum* from a cat in Jamaica. *Vet Record* 65:220, 1953.

4. Lindquist WD, Austin ER: Exotic parasitism in a Siamese cat. *Feline Practice* 11(5):9-11, 1981.

5. Soulsby EJL: *Helminths, Arthropods and Protozoa of Domesticated Animals*. Lea & Febiger, Philadelphia, 1982. pp 195-198.

TRICHURID WORM INFECTION

Etiologic Agents

Trichurid worms are nematodes belonging to the superfamily Trichuroidea, families Trichuridae and Capillaridae.[18] Two major genera infect cats: *Trichuris* spp and *Capillaria* spp. Species of importance include *T campanula, T serrata, C putorii, C erinacea, C hepatica, C aerophila, C plica* and *C feliscati*. They are considered as a group herein because of the great similarity in their ova, which cannot be easily differentiated by untrained eyes. Infection with various trichurid worms is often asymptomatic, and veterinarians usually identify infections by routine fecal examinations done on healthy animals or animals with other diseases. In some regions, 2-10% of cats shed trichurid eggs in their feces. Veterinarians that often see whipworm infections of dogs often diagnose "whipworms" in cats that have ova of *Trichuris* spp or *Capillaria* spp in their feces. However, there is some controversy on the prevalence of "whipworm" infections in cats.[9,10] Studies correlating trichurid ova in cat feces with worms in the intestinal tract have been conducted infrequently, and results have often been negative. This suggests that some trichurid worm eggs originate from the ingested prey and are merely being transported through the cat's digestive tract.

Trichuris campanula and *T serrata* infect a low percentage of cats in South America, the Caribbean nations, the United States and Australia.[2,6,7,13,16] Adult worms are 21-31 mm long and the cranial two-thirds of their bodies is threadlike (Fig 8). This is a characteristic of all *Trichuris* spp and is the reason they are called "whipworms." Ova shed in the feces can become infectious after several weeks in optimum conditions. Cats are infected when they ingest embryonated ova. Larvae emerge in the proximal small intestine and burrow into the mucosa, where they remain for several days. They then re-enter the lumen and reside in the cecum and colon, where they become adults and begin laying eggs within 2-3 months. The cranial end of the worm burrows into the mucosa. Worms feed on blood and tissues.[18]

Capillaria putorii is found in the small intestine of Mustelidae and cats in Europe and the USSR.[18] However, the exact site of infection in cats in not known. Greve and Kung found the largest number of worms in the gastric mucus.[10] They were not able to determine whether the adults inhabited the stomach or were refluxed from the small intestine. Adult worms are 5-15 mm long. *Capillaria erinacea* is a similar worm found in New Zealand.[3,4] The life cycle of these worms appears to be direct, similar to that of *Trichuris* spp.

Capillaria hepatica is principally a parasite of small rodents and is found throughout the world. Adult worms are found in the liver, and eggs are laid directly in the surrounding parenchyma. Eggs are released when the rodent dies and the carcass decomposes, or when liver tissue is ingested by carnivorous or cannibalistic hosts. Eggs released from infected tissues pass

Fig 8. Adult female *Trichuris* from the intestine of a cat from Puerto Rico. Adult whipworms are 21-31 mm long. (From *Parasitology for Veterinarians*, courtesy of Dr. J. Georgi and W.B. Saunders Co.)

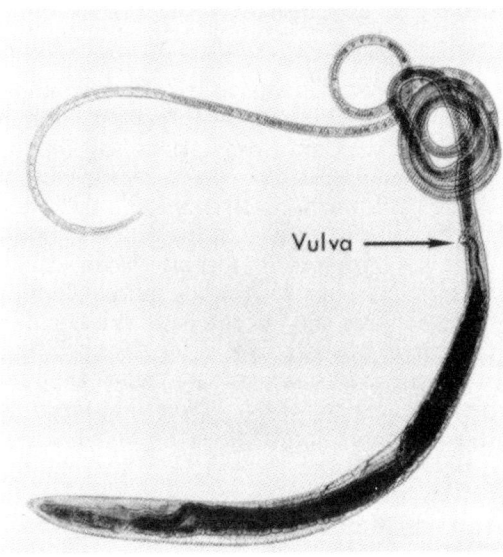

Fig 9. Pine pollen (top) and *Capillaria* ovum (bottom) in cat feces. *Capillaria* eggs are typically 30 x 60 μ in size. (Courtesy of Dr. Norman Baker, University of California, Davis)

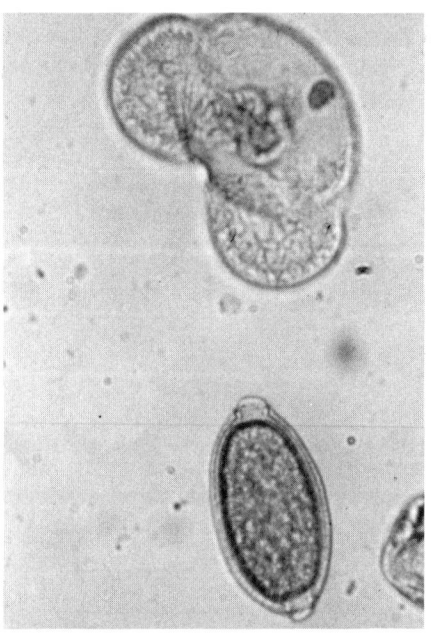

through the intestinal tract of carnivorous hosts, such as cats, and are shed in the feces (Fig 9). Cats are not infected *per se*. This process may explain the presence of trichurid eggs in cat feces in the absence of adult worms in the body.[15] Eggs within decomposing rodents or cat feces embryonate within 4 weeks under optimum conditions. Definitive rodent hosts are infected when they ingest embryonated ova. Larvae migrate from the intestinal tract to the liver, where they become adults.

Capillaria aerophila is found in the tracheal and bronchial mucosa and, rarely, in the nasal passages and frontal sinuses of dogs, foxes and several other species including cats.[18] It has been reported in the United States and Australia.[14,18] Adult worms are 25-32 mm long. Eggs are laid in the respiratory tract, coughed up, swallowed and passed in the feces. Eggs become infectious after 5-7 weeks under optimal conditions and remain viable for some time. Larvae emerge upon ingestion by definitive hosts, penetrate the intestine and migrate in the bloodstream to the lungs over a 7- to 10-day period. Eggs appear in the feces after about 40 days.

Capillaria plica and *C feliscati* are found as adults in the urinary bladder and occasionally the renal pelves of cats. *Capillaria plica* is more commonly found in dogs and foxes, while *C feliscati* is found mainly in cats. They occur in many parts of the world, though the incidence of infection in cats is generally low. There are exceptions, however. Waddell found 31 of 100 adult cats in Brisbane, Australia, infected with *C feliscati*.[20] In a follow-up study in Brisbane, Wilson-Hanson and Prescott found 18.3% of cats infected with *C feliscati*.[21] In 1 cat they also identified larger trichurid worms that did not appear the same as *C feliscati*. The identity of this worm is not known. Adult worms are 30-60 mm long.

The life cycle appears to be direct, though Enigk has implicated earthworms as possible intermediate hosts.[8,18] Eggs are shed in the urine and become infectious within a few weeks in the environment (Fig 10). Following ingestion by cats, larvae emerge, penetrate the intestine and migrate to the kidney via the peritoneal cavity. Larvae usually become adults in the urinary bladder and eggs appear about 60 days after infection. Waddell indicated that adult worms were present immediately under the thin transitional-cell mucosa of the bladder and presented histologic evidence for his findings.[20] Wilson-Hanson and Prescott found most of the worms free in the lumen, not attached to the bladder wall.[21] The numbers of worms found in infected bladders can be as high as 25.[21]

Pathogenesis

No lesions have been described in *Trichuris campanula*, *T serrata*, *C putorii* and *C erinacea* infections. This is probably because cats are not generally kept in environments that favor accumulation of infectious eggs. Therefore, infections in cats tend to be infrequent and mild.

Capillaria hepatica can be highly pathogenic to rodents as well as to aberrant definitive hosts, such as people and some domestic animals. Cats serve as intercalary hosts and ova do not usually hatch within the intestinal tract. On rare occasions, larvae may migrate to the liver and cause focal lesions.

Capillaria aerophila can cause severe respiratory disease in dogs and foxes, especially when they are kept in high-density kenneling situations in which husbandry is poor. Infection in cats, even in catteries, is usually infrequent and seldom of massive proportions. A coughing cat was found to be infected upon routine fecal examination.[17] Infected stray cats in Australia were asymptomatic.[14]

Capillaria plica and *C feliscati* apparently exist in the bladder of many cats without causing extensive changes in the bladder wall.[20,21] Infection is almost always seen in cats >8 months of age.

Clinical Features

Infections with various trichurid worms are usually asymptomatic. Though it is conceivable that massive intestinal infections

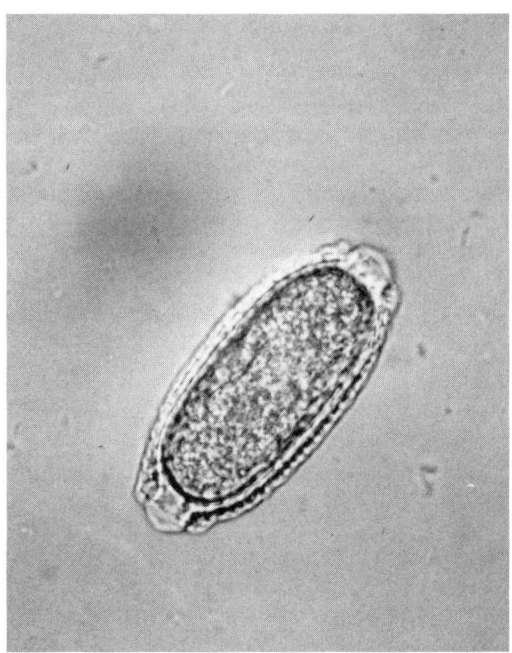

Fig 10. Ovum of *Capillaria plica* in urine from a dog. (Courtesy of Dr. Norman Baker, University of California, Davis)

with *T campanula*, *T serrata*, *C putorii* and *C erinacea* could cause signs of diarrhea and unthriftiness, it has not been reported. Likewise, clinical disease caused by aberrant *C hepatica* infections has not been reported in cats. *Capillaria aerophila* may be the most pathogenic trichurid worm, though clinical signs have been negligible, except for a cough.

Capillaria plica and *C feliscati* infections are seldom severe enough to cause clinical signs.[20,21] It is possible that massive chronic infections could cause cystitis, with signs of dysuria, pollakiuria and hematuria.

Pathologic Features

Only a few reports of pathologic lesions from trichurid worm infections of cats are available. Greve and Kung were not able to show any gross or histopathologic changes in the gastric or intestinal mucosa of cats with *C putorii* infections.[10] Lesions caused by *C aerophila* are often difficult to see grossly, and worms are found as coiled masses surrounded by eggs, deeply embedded in the tracheal mucosa. Tissues adjacent to worm and egg masses are infiltrated with large numbers of lymphocytes, plasma cells, macrophages and eosinophils.[14]

Capillaria feliscati infections produce minimal changes in the bladder. A brownish-pink discoloration of serosal surfaces has been observed in cats with larger numbers of worms. No mucosal inflammation was noted in cats with <3 worms. Mild mucosal changes consisted of a lifting of the transitional epithelium, hyperemia, and some extravasations of blood.[21] Waddell observed no macroscopic or microscopic inflammatory changes in infected bladders.[20]

Clinicopathologic Features

Trichurid worm infections are diagnosed by identifying eggs in feces (*T campanula, T serrata, C putorii, C erinacea, C aerophila* and *C hepatica*) or urine (*C plica, C feliscati*). Eggs of *C aerophila* may also be seen in sputum, tracheal exudate or, at times, in nasal exudate. Trichurid eggs are barrel-shaped, plugged at both ends and about 30 x 60 μ (Figs 9,10). Eggs of various species are difficult to differentiate by untrained personnel or without the aid of accurate measuring devices.

In addition to eggs in the urine, slight proteinuria and increase in bladder epithelial cells have been reported in cats with larger numbers of bladder worms.[20,21]

Treatment and Prevention

Intestinal forms of *Trichuris* spp respond to mebendazole, phthalofyne, glycobiarsol and dichlorvos.[18] Treatment of intestinal forms of *Capillaria* spp in cats has not been described. Mebendazole, fenbendazole and pyrantel have proven effective against *Capillaria* spp infections in other species. *Capillaria aerophila* infections appear to respond to levamisole at 5 mg/kg PO daily in 3 5-day treatment cycles 9 days apart.[18] Treatment of *C plica* and *C feliscati* infections has not been described. *Capillaria* spp infections in cats have not been susceptible to treatment with febantel/praziquantel paste.[5]

Infection and Immunity

Immunity to *Trichuris* spp and *Capillaria* spp infections of cats has not been studied.

Animal and Public Health Considerations

Cats infected with intestinal forms of *Trichuris* spp and *Capillaria* spp are infectious mainly for other cats but not for people. People can be infected with *Capillaria philippinensis* and, less commonly, with *C hepatica* by ingesting meat from infected hosts. The role of shedding cats in this transmission has not been determined. Capillariasis in people is manifested by a severe protein-losing enteropathy due to adult worms in the intestines. *Capillaria aerophila* is only infectious among foxes, dogs and cats. *Capillaria feliscati* is apparently confined to felids.

References

1. Blumenthal DS, in Wyngaarden JB and Smith LH Jr: *Cecil's Textbook of Medicine.* Saunders, Philadelphia, 1985. p 1820.

2. Clarkson MJ and Owen LN: The species of *Trichuris* in the domestic cat. *J Helminthol* 34:319-322, 1960.

3. Collins GH: A limited survey of gastro-intestinal helminths of dogs and cats. *New Zeal Vet J* 21:175-176, 1973.

4. Collins GH and Charleston WAG: *Ollulanus tricuspis* and *Capillaria putorii* in New Zealand cats. *New Zeal Vet J* 20:82, 1972.

5. Corwin RM *et al*: Anthelmintic effect of febantel/praziquantel paste in dogs and cat. *Am J Vet Res* 45:154-155, 1984.

6. Diaz-Ungria C: Nematodes parasites nouveaux ou interessants du Venezuela. *Ann Parasitol* 38:893-914, 1963.

7. Diaz-Ungria C: Nematodes gastrointestinales de carnivoros Venezolanos. *Soc Venezolano de Ciencias Naturales Boletin* 27:114-128, 1967.

8. Enigk K: Die Biologie von *Capillaria plica* (Trichuroidea, Nematoda). *Z Tropenmed Parasitol* 1:560-571, 1950.

9. Enzie FD: Do whipworms occur in domestic cats in North America? *JAVMA* 119:210-213, 1951.

10. Greve JH and Kung FY: *Capillaria putorii* in domestic cats in Iowa. *JAVMA* 182:511-513, 1983.

11. Guterbock WM and Levine ND: Coccidia and intestinal nematodes of east central Illinois cats. *JAVMA* 170:1411-1413, 1977.

12. Hass DK: Do whipworms occur in cats? *Feline Pract* 3(4):36-37, 1973.

13. Hass DK and Meisels LS: *Trichuris campanula* infection in a domestic cat from Miami, Florida. *Am J Vet Res* 38:1553-1555, 1978.

14. Holmes PR and Kelly JD: *Capillaria aerophila* in the domestic cat in Australia. *Aust Vet J* 49:472-473, 1973.

15. Newcomb KM et al: Polar plugged eggs in a feline fecal specimen. *Feline Pract* 14(5):19-20, 1984.

16. Ng BKY and Kelly JF: Isolation of *Trichuris campanula* from Australian cats. *Aust Vet J* 51:450-451, 1975.

17. Norsworthy GD: Feline lungworm treatment case report. *Feline Pract* 5(3):14, 1975.

18. Soulsby EJL: *Helminths, Arthropods and Protozoa of Domesticated Animals*. Lea & Febiger, Philadelphia, 1982. pp 333-337.

19. Visco RJ et al: Effect of age and sex on the prevalence of intestinal parasitism in cats. *JAVMA* 172:797-800, 1978.

20. Waddell AH: Further observations on *Capillaria feliscati* infections in cats. *Aust Vet J* 44:33, 1968.

21. Wilson-Hanson S and Prescott CW: *Capillaria* in the bladders of the domestic cat. *Aust Vet J* 59:190-191, 1982.

TRICHINELLOSIS

Etiologic Agent

Trichinella spiralis is a nematode belonging to the family Trichinellidae of the superfamily Trichuroides.[5] It is found mainly in temperate regions of the world. About 75% of the infected people reside in the United States.[4] The tiny adults (males 1.5 mm and females 3-4 mm) are found embedded in the small intestinal mucosa of swine, carnivores and people. Larvae are encysted in the muscles.

The life cycle of *T spiralis* is intimately associated with predation.[1,5] Predators are infected when they ingest muscle containing encysted larvae. Larvae are released by proteolytic enzymes in the stomach and proximal small intestine and invade the intestinal villi. The larvae molt once and reach adulthood in about 2 days. The male worms die shortly after mating and the viviparous female worms burrow deeper into the intestinal wall and begin producing prelarvae. The prelarvae (0.1 mm long) enter the intestinal lymphatics and are carried into the blood. They then invade individual muscle cells, first lying perpendicular to the long axis of the myofibers. They expand about 10-fold in size over the next few weeks and assume a coiled shape, then become encapsulated by a cyst wall of muscle origin. The capsules tend to calcify within 6-24 months. The larvae remain viable within the cysts for many years and may survive in the decomposing carcass for an extended period.

Pathogenesis

The source of trichinellosis in cats has not been determined but it is most likely associated with predation. Clinical signs may be associated with 2 phases of infection: the intraintestinal phase, in which adult worms actively invade the mucosa and produce prelarvae; and the phase of muscle invasion and encystation. The initial intraintestinal phase develops several days after ingestion of infected muscle and terminates when host immune responses to the adults develop, about 2-4 weeks after prelarvae begin to appear.

Clinical Features

The primary intestinal and secondary muscular phases of infection are usually asymptomatic. Clinical signs referable to the intestinal and muscular phases of infection are most likely to occur under conditions of massive larval ingestion. Poorly understood host factors may also delay development of host immunity to adults and may prolong the duration of prelarval production. Holzworth and Georgi described transient bloody diarrhea in a cat that had been acutely infected with *Trichinella*.[3] Adults and larvae were seen in the stool and prelarvae were observed in the blood. The cat was otherwise fairly normal and the diarrhea disappeared in a few days. No signs were associated with the subsequent muscle-invasion stage, though eosinophilia persisted for 3 months.

Clinical signs associated with the muscular phase of infection begin 7-21 days or more after commencement of prelarval production and last 3-6 weeks or more, depending on the severity of infection. Clinical signs during this phase consist of fever, eosinophilia, muscle pain and weakness. Hemmert-Halswick and Bugge described a kitten in the muscular phase of infection.[2] The kitten was found laterally recumbent, with limbs extended, painful to palpation, salivating, polypneic and crying constantly.

Pathologic Features

There are no pathologic descriptions of the various forms of trichinellosis in cats. Tissue findings tend to be rather stereotyped, however, from species to species.

Mucosal ulceration and hyperemia, localized edema, punctate hemorrhages and inflammation have been observed in the intestinal phase of trichinellosis in people. Prelarvae produce basophilic granular alterations of muscle fibers within 48 hours of invasion. The fibers enlarge to incorporate the growing larvae, and edema, nuclear proliferation and interstitial inflammation ensue. This is followed later in the course of disease by muscle atrophy and fibrosis. A cyst wall rapidly appears around the growing larvae; calcification of the cyst wall may occur with time. Inflammatory changes tend to subside as encystation becomes complete.

Clinicopathologic Features

Characteristic adults and larvae have been observed in the bloody stools of a naturally infected cat.[1] Prelarvae were seen in the blood of this animal during the acute phase of intestinal infection (Fig 11).[1] Eosinophilia, persisting for up to 3 months, has been reportedly associated with the muscle-invasion phase in a cat.[1] Encysted organisms are occasionally seen in the muscles, especially the diaphragm, of animals being necropsied for other reasons.

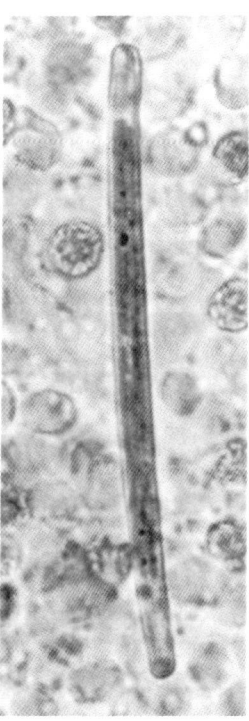

Fig 11. Prelarva of *Trichinella spiralis* in blood from a cat with acute diarrhea. Knott's technique, 1470X. (From *Parasitology for Veterinarians*, courtesy of Dr. J. Georgi and W.B. Saunders Co.)

Treatment and Prevention

The intestinal phase of infection can be successfully treated with mebendazole given PO for 4 days at the usual anthelmintic dose. The muscular phase in people is usually treated with a combination of corticosteroids and anthelmintics.

Immunologic Features

Nothing is written about the immunity to *T spiralis* in cats. The clinical form and course of the infection in cats resemble those in people. There is reason to believe, therefore, that immunity in cats is similar to that in people. Immunity to the adult females develops in the intestinal mucosa after 2-4 weeks. This leads to disappearance of adults from the intestine and prelarvae from the blood. The appearance of immunity to adult forms probably coincides with the developing immunity to larvae in the muscles. This immunity is related in part to development of a host-derived cyst around the larvae and cessation of larval growth. Immunity to trichinellosis resembles that to intestinal and tissue phases of *Toxoplasma gondii.*

Animal and Public Health Considerations

Trichinellosis is diagnosed in about 100 people in the United States each year.[4] Most of these infections come from eating uncooked or poorly cooked pork, bear and walrus meat.[4] Since cats do not constitute a food source for people in most countries, infected cats are not a health hazard to people. The clinical appearance of trichinellosis in people is similar to that observed in animals; both intestinal and muscle-invasion stages of infection have been recognized.[4] Myocardial, CNS, ocular and skin disease may be additional features of the disease in people.

References

1. Georgi JR: *Parasitology for Veterinarians.* 4th ed. Saunders, Philadelphia, 1985. pp 134-136.

2. Hemmert-Halswick A and Bugge G: Trichinen und Trichinose. *Ergebn Allegem Path u Path Anat* 28:313-392, 1934.

3. Holzworth J and Georgi JR: Trichinosis in a cat. *JAVMA* 165:168-191, 1974.

4. Hoskins DW, in Wyngaarden JB and Smith LH: *Textbook of Medicine.* Saunders, Philadelphia, 1985. pp 1825-1826.

5. Soulsby EJL: *Helminths, Arthropods and Protozoa of Domesticated Animals.* Lea & Febiger, Philadelphia, 1982. pp 330-333.

HOOKWORM INFECTION

Etiologic Agents

Hookworms are nematodes that parasitize the small intestine. They get their name from the dorsal bend of their cranial extremities. Unlike other intestinal helminths, they are voracious blood suckers. Hookworms belong to the order Strongylidae, family Ancylostomidae. Species pathogenic to cats include *Ancylostoma tubaeforme, A braziliense, A ceylanicum,* and *Uncinaria stenocephala.*[10]

Ancylostoma tubaeforme is found throughout most of the world but is reportedly absent in Great Britain.[10] *Ancylostoma braziliense* is found mainly in tropical and subtropical regions, while *A ceylanicum* is enzootic in Sri Lanka, Malaysia and part of Asia. *Ancylostoma caninum* is infrequently found in cats.[12] *Uncinaria stenocephala* is a common hookworm of cats in Europe and North America. Hookworms vary somewhat in size according to species; males are 5-11 mm and females 10-15 mm long.

The life cycle of hookworms is direct. Adult worms mate in the intestinal tract of cats and produce myriad embryonated eggs daily. Eggs hatch in the environment and larvae survive in moist environments. Optimal hatching and development occurs at ambient temperatures between 23 C and 30 C. Larvae become infectious in as short a time as 7 days in warmer environments, and longer in cooler weather. Infection of other cats occurs when infectious larvae are ingested, penetrate the mucous membranes of the oral cavity, or penetrate intact skin. Intrauterine infection, as in *A caninum* of dogs, has not been recognized. Likewise, colostral infection has also not been identified for species of hookworms that infect cats.[10]

The role of paratenic or transport hosts, such as small rodents, has not been evaluated. It is known that rodents may accumulate third-stage larvae that develop to adults when ingested by definitive hosts.[5] Infectious larvae that enter the body through the skin or mucous membranes are carried by blood vessels and lymphatics to the heart. They exit vessels in the lungs, pass into the alveoli and migrate retrograde up the airways to the pharynx. They are swallowed and mature into adults in the small intestine within 2-3 weeks. Infectious larvae that are ingested transform directly into adults without further migration from the intestinal tract.

Pathogenesis

Hookworms are reportedly common in cats in the southern and central United States.[1] *Ancylostoma* spp were found in 19-23.3% of cats in several areas of Australia and 6.4% of cats in Missouri.[3,11,12] Hookworm infections of cats have been observed more commonly in cats 1-5 years of age.[12] This is in contrast to ascarids, which are more prevalent in cats <6 months of age.[11,12] Ryan found an average of 3-5 *Uncinaria stenocephala* and 26-437 *Ancylostoma* spp worms per infected feral cat in Australia.[9]

Hookworm infections are more severe in warm, moist environments that favor larval accumulations. Catteries are much less apt to be affected than dog kennels, in which infections can be particularly severe. Catteries are more apt to be indoors, "hosing down" cages is less common, and favorable ground conditions for larval survival are lacking.

Blood loss associated with hookworms of dogs has been calculated to be as high as 0.01-0.09 ml per worm each day, depending on severity of infection. Loss of blood elements, if excessive, can debilitate the host.

Clinical Features

Recurrent diarrhea, poor growth and roughness of the coat are more common features of severe infections in cats. Heavy infections of hookworms are less likely to cause severe anemia in cats than puppies.[10]

Pathologic Features

Pathologic changes associated with larval migration through the skin, mucous membranes and lungs are not readily apparent. Mild inflammatory changes in the small intestinal mucosa may be associated with adult worms.

Clinicopathologic Features

Hookworm infections are diagnosed by identifying characteristic eggs in fecal flotations. Eggs are of the strongyloid type, 45-75 μ in dimension and embryonated (Figs 7,12).

Treatment and Prevention

Mebendazole, fenbendazole, nitroscanate, tetramisole, disophenol and dichlorvos are all effective against hookworms.

Changes in husbandry procedures and environmental treatment to kill infectious larvae are essential steps to prevent hookworm infections in dog kennels. This is seldom necessary or practical in catteries. Prevention is by limiting environmental contamination by routine deworming and keeping the premises dry and clean of feces. Formalin solutions have been used to kill larval forms in the soil.

Infection and Immunity

Very little is known about immunity to hookworm infections in cats. Immunity to hookworm infections in dogs was first reported by McCoy in 1931.[4] It was noticed that fecal egg counts increased up to 2 months after initial infection and then decreased rapidly, with an associated passage of large numbers of adult worms in the feces. Vaccines composed of irradiated infectious larvae have provided up to 7 months' protection against heavy challenge-exposure in dogs.[6,7] Therefore, it

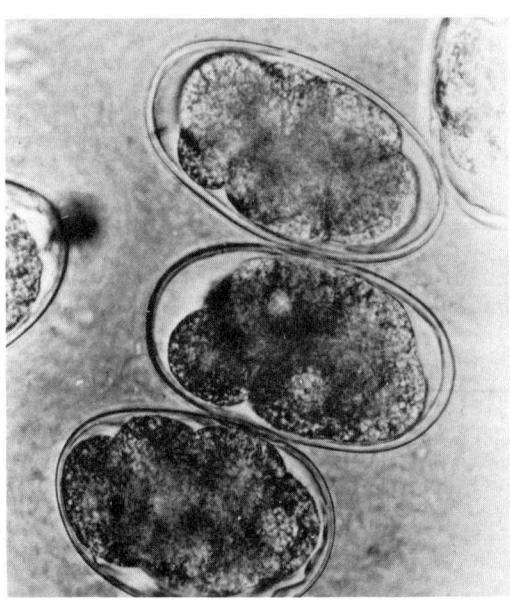

Fig 12. *Ancylostoma caninum* ova in feces from a dog. The eggs measure 77-88 x 43-48 μ. (Courtesy of Dr. Norman Baker, University of California, Davis)

is likely that cats also produce a similar immunity.

Animal and Public Health Considerations

With the exception of *A tubaeforme*, hookworms of cats are also infectious for dogs. Hookworms have a direct life cycle, so infected animals are infectious to other cats and dogs.

Infectious larvae of *A braziliense* and, to a lesser extent, those of *U stenocephala* are responsible for a disease of people called cutaneous larval migrans.[10] Larvae penetrate the skin of people, usually as a consequence of swimming or walking barefooted in moist environments. The larvae cause papules and inflamed dermal tracks. Lesions are pruritic and the involved skin can become thickened. Skin reactions are due to host immune attacks on the migrating larval forms. Lesions tend to become more intense with repeated exposures. Larvae are usually destroyed in the skin of people, but some occasionally reach the lungs and cornea.[2,8]

References

1. Anonymous: Endoparasites in cats: Current practice and opinions. *Feline Pract* 3(4):21-34, 1973.

2. Beaver PC, in Soulsby EJL: *Biology of Parasites*. Academic Press, New York, 1966. pp 215-225.

3. Coman BJ et al: Helminth parasites and arthropods of feral cats. *Aust Vet J* 57:324-327, 1981.

4. McCoy OR: Immunity reactions of the dog against hookworm (*Ancylostoma caninum*) under conditions of repeated infection. *Am J Hyg* 14:268-303, 1983.

5. Miller TA: Potential transport hosts and the life cycles of canine and feline hookworms. *J Parasitol* 56 (suppl):238, 1970.

6. Miller TA: Vaccination against the canine hookworm diseases. *Adv Parasitol* 9:152-183, 1971.

7. Miller TA: Industrial development and field use of the canine hookworm vaccine. *Adv Parasitol* 16:333-342, 1978.

8. Nadbath BP and Lawlor PP: Nematode (*Ancylostoma*) in the cornea. *Am J Ophthalmol* 59:486-490, 1965.

9. Ryan GE: Gastro-intestinal parasites of feral cats in New South Wales. *Aust Vet J* 52:224-227, 1976.

10. Soulsby EJL: *Helminths, Arthropods and Protozoa of Domesticated Animals*. 7th ed. Lea & Febiger, Philadelphia, 1982. pp 198-211.

11. Visco RJ et al: Effect of age and sex on the prevalence of intestinal parasitism in cats. *JAVMA* 172:797-800, 1978.

12. Wilson-Hanson SL and Prescott CW: A survey for parasites in cats. *Aust Vet J* 59:194, 1982.

STOMACH WORM INFECTION

Etiologic Agents

At least 8 nematodes parasitize the stomach of domestic cats. These include the trichostrongyloid worm *Ollulanus tricuspis*, the spiruroid worms *Cyathospirura dasyuridis* and *Cylicospirura felineus*, the physalopterid worms *Physaloptera praeputialis*, *P felidis*, *P pseudopraeputialis* and *P canis*, and *Gnathostoma spinigerum*.

Ollulanus tricuspis has been recognized in Europe, North America, Australia and Chile.[23] Male worms are 0.7-0.8 mm and females are 0.8-1.0 mm long (Fig 13). In addition to domestic cats, they also infect wild Felidae, foxes and pigs. Adult worms are found in the mucous layer and acini of secretory glands in the stomach, and do not penetrate or firmly attach to the mucosa (Fig 14).[5] In severe infections, worms may also be found in the most proximal inch of duodenum. The female worm is viviparous. Large eggs formed in the single uterus hatch within the reproductive tract and develop through first and second stages before being released as third-stage larvae into the gastric lumen. Third- and fourth-stage larvae develop free in the stomach. Sexual differentiation is complete in fourth-stage larvae, which rapidly mature to adults within the stomach. Third- and fourth-stage larvae that pass into the intestinal tract are rapidly destroyed by digestive processes and intact worms are not seen in the feces except when transit time is decreased. However, infectious third- and fourth-stage larvae are

Fig 13. Adult male and female *Ollulanus tricuspis*. The male worm (left) has a well-formed bursa, while the female has a tricuspid tail (arrow). (Courtesy of Dr. A. Hargis and *Veterinary Pathology*)

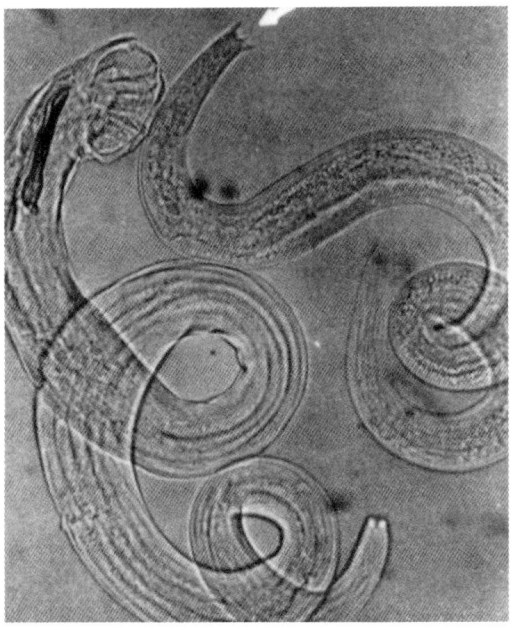

present in vomitus. Susceptible animals are apparently infected when they ingest infectious larvae that have been expelled in this manner into the environment.

Cyathospirura dasyuridis and *Cylicospirura felineus* infections have only been reported in cats in India and areas of Australia from Tasmania to Queensland.[7,9,10,12,25] The life cycle of these worms is unknown. However, most spiruroid worms have arthropods as intermediate hosts.[28] Adult worms are 1-4 cm long and live in the gastric lumen (*Cyathospirura dasyuridis*) or as coiled groups within pyloric granulomas (*Cylicospirura felineus*). Eggs are shed in the feces of cats and other definitive hosts.

Physaloptera praeputialis has been observed in Asia, Africa, Brazil, the Caribbean and the United States. *Physaloptera felidis* has been reported in cats in the United States, while *P pseudopraeputialis* has been recognized in both the United States and the Philippines.[28] *Physaloptera canis* has been recognized in cats in South Africa. Male worms are 13-40 mm long and females 15-48 mm long; they grossly resemble as-

carids (Fig 15).[14] Adult worms firmly attach to the gastric mucosa, on which they feed. They may also suck blood. Eggs are passed in the feces, and larval development occurs in several species of cockroaches, crickets and beetles. Snakes, frogs and mice may act as transport or paratenic hosts. Cats can be infected by eating infected insects or paratenic hosts.

Gnathostoma spinigerum is found in the stomach of cats, dogs, mink, polecats and several other wild carnivores.[28] Infections have been reported in cats in Australia and southeast Asia.[3,11,30,31] Males are 10-25 mm and females 9-31 mm long. Adult worms anchor into the tissues of the stomach by a barbed bulbous head appendage (Fig 16). Embryonated eggs (210,000-767,000/day) are passed in the feces and hatch in water within 4 days or longer. Motile larvae are ingested by a cyclopid. The infected cyclopid is then eaten by freshwater fish, frogs or reptiles, and the infectious third-stage larvae encyst in the tissues. Third-stage larvae may also encyst in the tissues of mice, rats and other small rodents. Cats are infected by ingestion of in-

Fig 14. Scanning electron micrograph of a male *Ollulanus tricuspis* in the gastric mucosa. Note the cuticular ridges and embedded head. (Courtesy of Dr. A. Hargis and *Veterinary Pathology*)

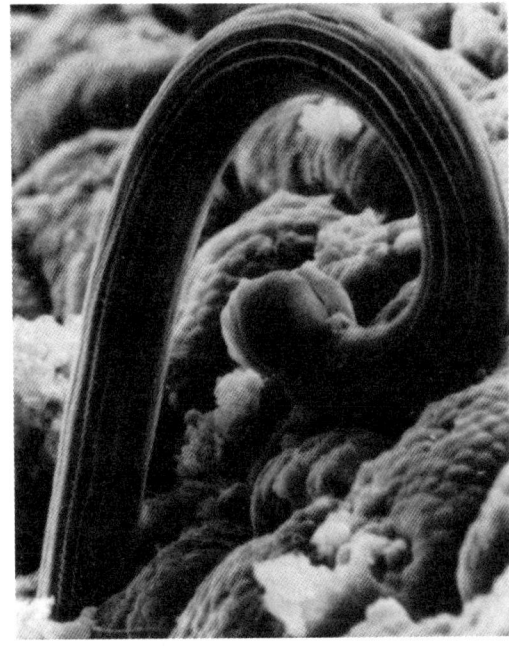

fected prey animals. The life cycle after this point is not completely understood. The third-stage larvae excyst and embed themselves in the gastric wall, where they mature. Eggs appear in the feces after 81-363 days (Fig 17).[11] Infectious larvae occasionally migrate through the liver, mesentery, diaphragm and pleural cavity.[8,30] Whether this is a normal or aberrant part of the migration path from intestine to stomach is not known.

Pathogenesis

Ollulanus tricuspis is the most common stomach worm that infects cats. The incidence of infection has been reported as 6.1% in indoor pet cats and about 40% in free-roaming outdoor cats in Germany, 42.8% in feral cats in Australia, 30% in outdoor cats in Greece, 18.3% in Turkey, and 27% in cats in the United States.[9,19,22,23] The overall infection rate is reportedly higher in cattery-housed cats than among individual pet and free-roaming animals.[2,21,26]

Fig 15. Two views of the cranial extremity of *Physaloptera*. Adult worms are found firmly attached to the gastric mucosa. They grossly resemble ascarids and are 13-48 mm long. (From *Parasitology for Veterinarians*, courtesy of Dr. J. Georgi and W.B. Saunders Co.)

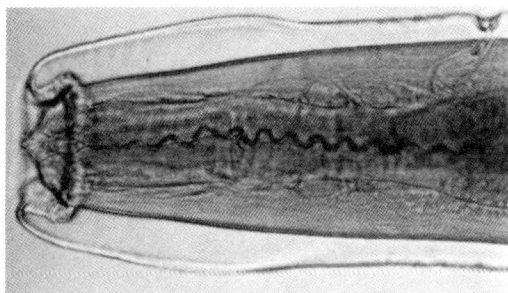

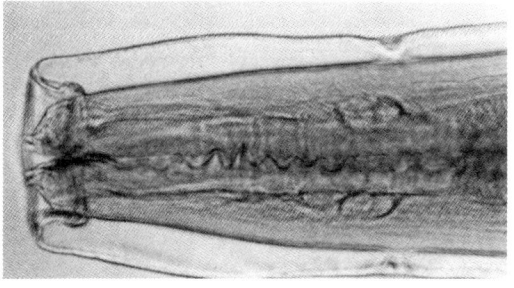

Fig 16. Mouth (upper) and caudal extremity (lower) of an adult male *Gnathostoma spinigerum*. Adults are 10-30 mm long and found in cysts embedded in the gastric wall. (From *Parasitology for Veterinarians*, courtesy of Dr. J. Georgi and W.B. Saunders Co.)

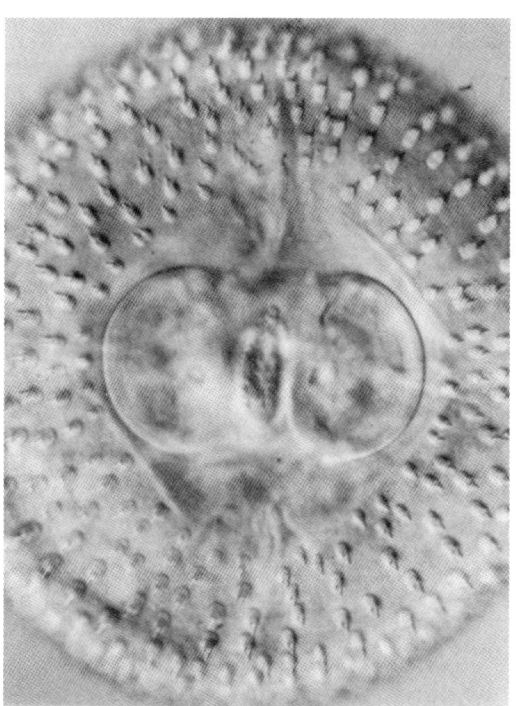

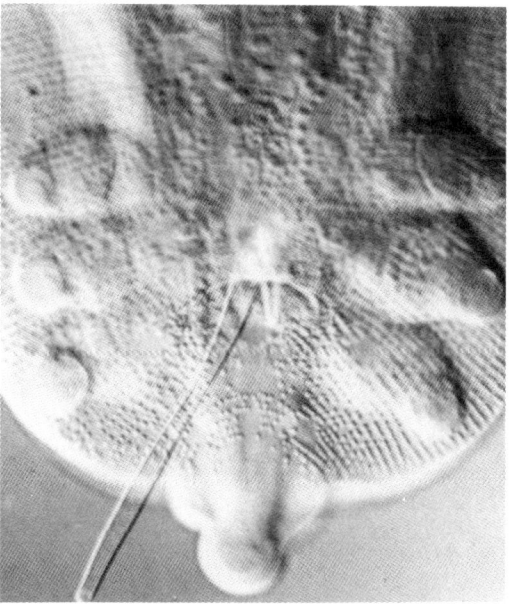

The exact pathogenic effect of *Ollulanus* spp infection of cats is debatable. It is probably related to the degree of infection and chronicity. Hasslinger and Trah found an average of 1500 worms per cat in a study of rural cats in Germany.[24] Even with such worm burdens, infection was often asymptomatic. When clinical signs occur, they are usually associated with chronic irritation, inflammation, increased mucus secretion and vomiting associated with the presence of worms adjacent to the mucosa and in gastric glands.

Cyathospirura dasyuridis is relatively common in most areas of the world, though *Cylicospirura felineus* is relatively uncommon. In certain geographic areas, they can be quite prevalent. For instance, the infection rate in feral cats in New South Wales, Australia, was 15-17%, while it was 57% in feral cats in north-central Victoria.[10] *Cylicospirura felineus* worms usually occur in tightly coiled groups within large granulomas in the pyloric region. Lesions are bullous and mucosa-covered, and the dorsal opening is very small.[3] Adult worms do not protrude from the opening. In each cat there are usually 1-6 lesions, each 0.5-2.5 cm in diameter.[9]

Cyathospirura dasyuridis, similar to *Ollulanus* spp, is more apt to be found in the gastric lumen. It can also coexist in gastric nodules with *Cylicospirura felineus*.[12] Pence and co-workers have observed a similar association of *C felineus* with a related worm, *Cyathospirura chevreuxi*, in wild Felidae in North America.[27] Though pyloric granulomas associated with *C felineus* can be quite large, lesions have only been rarely observed in cats. This suggests that either the lesions are usually clinically inapparent and unlikely to be noticed, or that infection is uncommon.

Physaloptera spp can cause severe inflammation, mucosal erosions and hypersecretion of mucus in the stomach of cats and other definitive hosts.[28] Clinical signs, except in massive infections, are uncommon.[14]

Gnathostoma spinigerum is the most pathogenic of stomach worms. Naturally infected cats are almost always adults.[31] Natural and experimentally induced infections in cats have been studied by Daengsvang and co-workers.[11] Adult worms are found in groups of 1-4 within nodules in the gastric fundus. Unlike the more bullous and flattened nodules seen in *C dasyuridis* and *C felineus* infections, *Gnathostoma* spp nodules are conical, with a central crater.[3] They are 1-2 cm or more in diameter and project an equal distance above the mucosa. The caudal end of adult worms protrudes from a small opening in the center of the crater. Nodules are lined by fibrous tissue and contain serosanguineous fluid, adult worms, eggs and inflammatory cells. Lesions are usually clinically apparent only when they break through the serosal surface of the stomach.[30]

Chandler described a more severe form of gnathostomiasis in cats experimentally infected with infectious larvae from a snake.[7] Most cats died 2-10 days after infection. Immature worms were found curled up between the parietal peritoneum and abdominal muscles as well as burrowing beneath the capsule of the liver. *Gnathostoma* spp migration was the presumed cause of death in these cats, though the type and severity of lesions did not sup-

Fig 17. Ova of *Gnathostoma spinigerum* in feces from a dog. 1100X. (From *Parasitology for Veterinarians*, courtesy of Dr. J. Georgi and W.B. Saunders Co.)

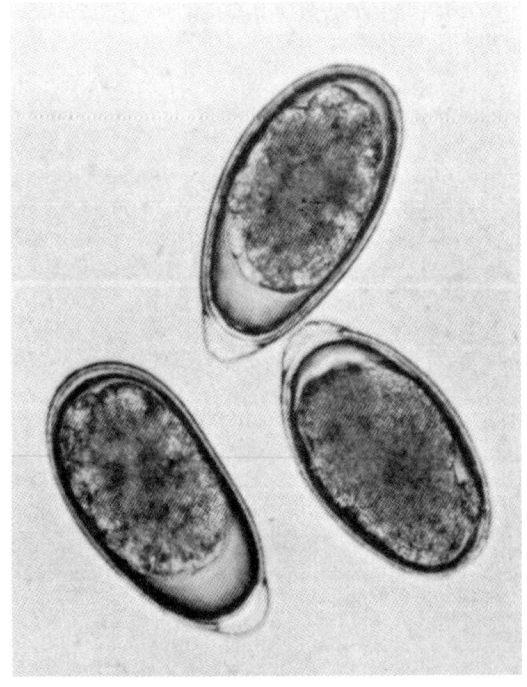

port such assumptions. A few worms were found under the peritoneal lining of the diaphragm. In surviving cats, all of the worms were in the liver and the peritoneal wall 2-4 weeks later. The surface of the liver had a yellowish mosaic pattern associated with the burrowing tracts of immature gnathostomes. None was in the stomach. In a study of naturally infected cats in the same area, Chandler found that about 10% had 3-25 immature gnathostomes in the liver and peritoneal wall.[7] However, only 1 cat had gastric lesions. Chandler concluded that this form of infection was associated with aberrant migration of another gnathostome, possibly *G pelicans*.[7] However, it is interesting that two-thirds of the cats with gastric nodules containing *G spinigerum* also had yellowish burrow marks under the hepatic capsule.[30] Therefore, it appears that some immature *G spinigerum* larvae undergo some sort of intrahepatic migration. Whether or not immature worms in the liver eventually migrate to the stomach has not been determined.

Clinical Features

Infection with *O tricuspis* is widespread and often asymptomatic.[19,21] Periodic vomiting is the most frequent clinical sign.[2,5,13,21,29] Vomiting is first seen within 4 months of infection and correlates within a week or so to detection of worms in gastric contents.[27] Vomiting is usually intermittent, occurring every 1-93 days (mean of 12 days).[29] Vomiting usually occurs 10-15 minutes after eating. A mild intermittent diarrhea has been seen in several cases, though whether the infection was the cause was not determined.[2,18]

A more severe fibrosing or sclerosing gastritis has been associated with *O tricuspis* infection in both wild and domestic Felidae.[16,20,23] Clinical signs include vomiting, chronic weight loss, poor coat condition and, in some instances, death.

Physaloptera spp infections are also often inapparent. However, severe infections may be associated with chronic vomiting, melena, roughening of the coat and weight loss. Fatalities are unusual.

Infections with *Cyathospirura dasyuridis* and *Cylicospirura felineus* are usually subclinical.[10,12,25] Variable signs of vomiting, chronic weight loss, and roughening of the coat may occur with more massive infections. However, massive infections are uncommon; usually no more than 1-6 nodules are found per animal.[9]

Gnathostomes are the most pathogenic of stomach worms and are most likely to cause clinical signs. Though lesions can be quite large, no apparent signs are associated with lesions opening into the gastric lumen.[3,11,30] An exception is a case described by Beveridge.[3] Partial perforation of the lesion into the peritoneal cavity caused localized peritonitis, anorexia and weight loss. Complete perforation of the stomach resulted in generalized serofibrinous peritonitis and death.[30] Chandler reported high acute mortality in cats experimentally infected by feeding immature *Gnathostoma* obtained from tissues of a snake.[7] There was severe extraintestinal migration into the liver and abdominal musculature. However, from descriptions of the lesions and other circumstances, it is doubtful whether the cats actually died from the parasites. Panleukopenia would be a more plausible explanation for these acute deaths.

Pathologic Features

Gross and microscopic lesions of *O tricuspis* infection have been well documented.[2,16,19,21,23] Gross lesions are seen in <5% of infected cats. The gastric wall in such cases appears thickened and the rugal folds much more prominent. Mucosal fibrosis that progresses at times to sclerosis may be evident in severe cases. More mildly affected cats may show some mucosal reddening, with excessive mucus production. Histopathologic changes include reactive mucosal hyperplasia, increased mucosal fibrous tissue, and glandular atrophy. Enlarged lymphoid nodules with prominent germinal centers may be seen. Adult worms are usually apparent in sections within the mucous layer with their heads embedded in gastric glands. The worms have numerous cuticular projections that represent longitudinal ridges when viewed in cross-section.

Nodules of *Cylicospirura felineus* are bullous and do not protrude very far into the lumen.[3] They usually number 1-6 per animal and are 0.5-2.5 cm in diameter.[9] They tend to concentrate in the pyloric region. Several worms are often found as tightly coiled masses within the nodules. Walls of the nodules are fibrous and surrounding tissue is often involved in a granulomatous inflammatory response. *Cyathospirura dasyuridis* may be present within the same nodules as *C felineus* in mixed infections; in single infections, it is more often a luminal parasite. Pure *C dasyuridis* lesions have not been described.

Only rudimentary descriptions of lesions of *Physaloptera* infections are available.[28] By their feeding activity, the worms can cause severe inflammation and erosion of the gastric mucosa, with increased mucus secretion. Such lesions are caused by damage done at the attachment and feeding site. The worms move actively from 1 feeding site to another, and wounds may bleed for considerable periods.

Gnathostoma spinigerum nodules are 1-2 cm or more in diameter and concentrate in the gastric fundus.[3] Adult worms are found in cystic cavities within nodules. Walls of the lesions are fibrous and surrounded by a granulomatous host response. The major host reaction is in the submucosa and consists of increased fibrous tissue, interconnecting foci of inflammation, and necrotic tracts. Vascular inflammatory foci are seen around intact or degenerating eggs. Inflammatory exudates consist of lymphocytes, macrophages, neutrophils and a few eosinophils. Adult worms are bathed in serosanguineous fluid that contains many eggs and inflammatory cells. The worms appear red due to ingested blood. Numerous bacteria are sometimes observed within the fluid.

Yellowish subcapsular tracts are frequently seen in the liver.[30] They have a mosaic pattern and represent earlier paths of migrating worms. The tracts are filled with necrotic debris, fibrin, hemorrhagic blood and inflammatory cells. In more seriously ill animals, it is not uncommon to observe serosal ulceration over the nodules. In mild cases, this may cause focal peritonitis, with adhesion of the omentum. If the perforation is large enough and not successfully sealed off, more widespread peritonitis may result. This is usually serofibrinous and associated with visible edema, hyperemia, hemorrhage, and fibrinous exudation of the visceral and parietal serosa and omentum.

Clinicopathologic Features

Diagnosis of *Ollulanus tricuspis* infection requires a high index of suspicion. Larvae of the parasite are destroyed by digestive enzymes in the intestines and do not usually appear in the feces. An exception is when transit time decreases, such as in diarrhea.[18] Adult female worms are about 1 mm long and have 3 major cusps or projections on their caudal end. Males are slightly smaller and have a caudal bursa. Larvae can be very small and difficult to visualize. Larvae can only be observed in the gastric mucosa, gastric contents or vomitus.[15,23]

Guy, in comparing 3 standard diagnostic procedures, found that pepsin-hydrochloric acid digestion of the gastric mucosa was 71% accurate, punch biopsy only 29% accurate, and examination of stomach contents and mucosal washings was 100% accurate.[15,23] Antemortem diagnosis of *Ollulanus* infection using the last procedure has been well described by Hargis and co-workers.[17] Cats are usually induced to vomit 1-2 hours after feeding using xylazine at 2.2 mg/kg IM. If vomiting cannot be induced, a stomach wash is obtained with a large tube. Gastric contents are strained through coarse gauze or a kitchen strainer to remove particulate debris and examined under a dissecting microscope. Guy described a sedimentation concentration procedure that is slightly more accurate but much more cumbersome.[15]

Infections with *Cyathospirura dasyuridis*, *Cylicospirura felineus*, *Physaloptera* spp and *Gnathostoma spinigerum* are diagnosed by identifying typical eggs in the feces using standard flotation procedures, or by finding adult worms at necropsy or on gastroscopy.

Treatment and Prevention

Ollulanus spp infection has reportedly responded to a single dose of tetramisole at 5 mg/kg PO or dichlorvos at 11 mg/kg.[13,23]

Drug therapy for other stomach worms has not been extensively studied. Soulsby suggests use of dichlorvos and benzimidazole-type anthelmintics for *Physaloptera* spp infection.[28] Similar drugs would probably be effective against *G spinigerum*. Treatment of *C dasyuridis* and *C felineus* has not been reported. Experience with similar gastric granulomas caused by related *Habronema* spp of horses has shown piperazine and phenothiazine to be ineffective, fenbendazole probably ineffective, and trichlorfon and dichlorvos possibly effective.[28] The efficacy of broad-spectrum systemic anthelmintics, such as ivermectin, has not been evaluated.

Prevention of *Ollulanus* infection in catteries and closely confined groups of cats can be attempted in enzootic environments. Thorough deworming of all animals, coupled with increased cleanliness and reduced population density, greatly reduces the problem. Special attention should be paid to cats that vomit more frequently than expected; such animals are the main source of environmental contamination with infectious larvae.

Infection and Immunity

Nothing is known about immunity to *O tricuspis*, *Cyathospirura dasyuridis*, *Cylicospirura felineus* and *Physaloptera* spp infections. However, immunity to *Ollulanus* spp appears quite minimal. Some groups of cats develop many chronic infections, and average worm burdens are often very large.

In a study of immunity to *Gnathostoma* infection, egg excretion lasted 37-223 days after experimental infection.[11] Cats necropsied 10-30 days after egg excretion stopped had only 1-3 living adult worms. No worms were found 40-64 days after eggs disappeared from the stool. Spontaneous cures were observed in 12 of 16 naturally and experimentally infected cats. The time for spontaneous cures from the day of infection was 235-554 days.

Animal and Public Health Considerations

Cats infected with *O tricuspis* are only health hazards to other cats. Among the various stomach worm infections, only *G spinigerum* is also infectious for people.[4] People are infected by eating raw or undercooked fish infected with intermediate stages of the worm. People are not infected by eggs, so cats are not direct health hazards to people. Larvae undergo an aberrant migration through human tissues and most commonly end up as granulomatous reactions in the subcutaneous tissues. Fever, vomiting and abdominal pain may occur shortly after fish consumption due to migration of immature worms from the intestinal tract. Central nervous system and ocular involvement are less common but more severe sequelae of infection.

References

1. Bearup AJ: Parasitic infection in cats in Sydney, with special reference to the occurrence of *Ollulanus tricuspis*. *Aust Vet J* 36:352-354, 1960.

2. Bell AG: *Ollulanus tricuspis* in a cat colony. *New Zeal Vet J* 32:85-87, 1984.

3. Beveridge I *et al*: *Gnathostoma spinigerum* infection in a feral cat from New South Wales. *Aust Vet J* 54:46, 1978.

4. Blumenthal D, in Wyngaarden JB and Smith LH Jr: *Cecil's Textbook of Medicine*. Saunders, Philadelphia, 1985. p 1822.

5. Cameron TWM: Observations on the life history of *Ollulanus tricuspis*, the stomach worms of the cat. *J Helminthol* 5:67-80, 1927.

6. Cameron TWM: On the pathogenicity of the stomach and lung worms of the cat. *J Helminthol* 10:231-234, 1932.

7. Chandler AC: Helminthic parasites of cats in Calcutta. *Indian J Med Res* 13:213-227, 1925.

8. Chandler AC: A contribution to the life-history of a gnathostoma. *Parasitol* 3:237-244, 1925.

9. Coman BJ: A survey of the gastrointestinal parasites of the feral cats in Victoria. *Aust Vet J* 48:133-136, 1972.

10. Coman BJ *et al*: Helminth parasites and arthropods of feral cats. *Aust Vet J* 57:324-327, 1981.

11. Daengsvang S et al: Spontaneous cure of the natural and induced *Gnathostoma spinigerum* infection in cats. *Ann Trop Med Parasitol* 63:489-491, 1969.

12. Gregory GG and Munday BL: Internal parasites of feral cats from the Tasmanian midlands and King Island. *Aust Vet J* 52:317-320, 1976.

13. Greve JH: A nematode causing vomiting in cats. *Feline Pract* 11(4):17-18, 1981.

14. Guillbride PDL: *Syngamus ierei, Physaloptera praeputialis* and *Platynosomum fastosum* from a cat in Jamaica. *Vet Record* 14:220, 1953.

15. Guy PA: *Ollulanus tricuspis* in domestic cats—prevalence and methods of post-mortem diagnosis. *New Zeal Vet J* 32:81-83, 1984.

16. Hanichen Von T and Hassingler MA: Chronische Gastritius durch *Ollulanus tricuspis* bei einer Katze. *Berl Munich Tierarztl Wschr* 90:59-62, 1977.

17. Hargis AM et al: Diagnosis of *Ollulanus tricuspis* infection in living cats. *Feline Pract* 13(3):16-19, 1983.

18. Hargis AM et al: *Ollulanus tricuspis* found by fecal flotation in a cat with diarrhea. *JAVMA* 182:1122-1123, 1983.

19. Hargis AM et al: Prevalence, lesions, and differential diagnosis of *Ollulanus tricuspis* infection in cats. *Vet Pathol* 20:71-79, 1983.

20. Hargis AM et al: Chronic fibrosing gastritis associated with *Ollulanus tricuspis* in a cat. *Vet Pathol* 19:320-323, 1982.

21. Hargis AM et al: A gastric nematode (*Ollulanus tricuspis*) in cats in the Pacific Northwest. *JAVMA* 178:475-478, 1981.

22. Hasslinger MA: Zum Vorkommen von *Ollulanus tricuspis* bei Hauskatzen. *Berl Munich Tierarztl Wschr* 92:316-318, 1979.

23. Hasslinger MA: *Ollulanus tricuspis*, the stomach worm of the cat. *Feline Pract* 14(5):22-35, 1984.

24. Hasslinger MA and Trah M: Studies on the distribution and the demonstration of the stomach worms of the cat, *Ollulanus tricuspis*. *Berl Munich Tierarztl Wschr* 94:235-238, 1983.

25. Mawson PM: Two species of nematoda (*Spirurida*) from Australian dasyuridis. *Parasitol* 58:75-78, 1968.

26. Pavlov PM and Howell MJ: Helminth parasites of Canberra cats. *Aust Vet J* 53:599-600, 1977.

27. Pence DB et al: Spirocerid stomach worms from wild felids in North America. *Can J Zool* 56:1032-1042, 1978.

28. Soulsby EJL: *Helminths, Arthropods and Protozoa of Domesticated Animals*. 7th ed. Lea & Febiger, Philadelphia, 1982. pp 302-305.

29. Tiberio SR et al: A report of *Ollulanus tricuspis* and vomiting in cats from Florida. *JAAHA* 19:887-890, 1983.

30. Trueman KF and Ferris PBC: Gnathostomiasis in three cats. *Aust Vet J* 53:498, 1977.

31. Wilson-Hanson SL and Prescott CW: A survey for parasites in cats. *Aust Vet J* 59:194, 1982.

LARGE INTESTINAL WORM INFECTION

Etiologic Agents

Strongyloides tumefaciens and *S planiceps* have been associated with chronic colon infections in domestic cats. *Strongyloides planiceps* is also referred to as *S cati* in some literature. *Strongyloides stercoralis*, an important pathogen of the upper small intestine of dogs and man, causes a mild and self-limiting experimental infection in cats.[11] However, no naturally occurring infections with *S stercoralis* have been reported in cats.

Strongyloides tumefaciens and *S planiceps* are nematodes (roundworms) belonging to the family Strongyloididae. *Strongyloides tumefaciens* has been identified in cats along the southeastern coast of the United States from Texas to Florida.[5,6,8,9] *Strongyloides planiceps* is widespread in Japan.[1-4,7] The incidence of infection in cats in the United States appears to be low. About 4% of domestic cats in some prefectures of Japan have been infected with *S planiceps*.[1,2]

Cats are apparently not the main reservoir of *S planiceps*. A very high rate of natural infection has been observed in raccoon dogs and red weasels in Japan.[4] The very low incidence of *S tumefaciens* infection in cats and the absence of the worm from other domestic species also suggest that wildlife reservoirs probably exist.

The life cycles of *S tumefaciens* and *S planiceps* are unknown. However, it is suspected they are similar to that of *S stercoralis*, based on observations that infectious larvae of *S stercoralis* can reach the large intestine of cats following skin exposure.[11]

The life cycle of *S stercoralis* in dogs begins with ingestion or skin penetration of female infectious third-stage larvae. Larvae then enter the bloodstream, migrate to the lungs and enter the air passages. They are then coughed up, swallowed and carried to the intestinal tract. Larvae burrow into the intestinal mucosa and induce a somewhat raised cyst-like structure with a central depression or pore. Larvae transform into adult parthenogenic females within the cyst and begin to lay eggs. Eggs hatch into first-stage larvae, which then enter the intestinal tract. Development to third-stage larvae or adults can occur within the intestinal tract of dogs. Some larvae can transform into free-living adults in the environment while others remain as female third-stage infectious larvae.[13] Sexual reproduction occurs mainly in the free-living stage.. In *S tumefaciens* infection, the infectious third stage may not develop until 36-72 hours after being voided in the stool.[6] The prepatent period from larval infection to the appearance of larval forms in the feces is 9-11 days for cats.[3]

Pathogenesis

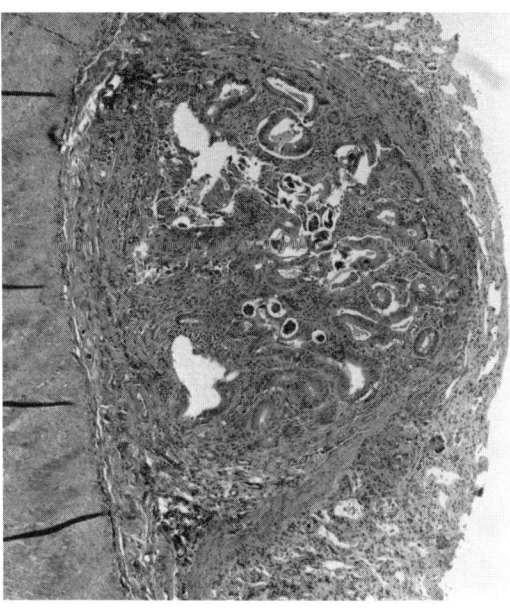

Fig 18. Section of the colon of a cat with *Strongyloides tumefaciens* infection. A parasitic nodule containing an adult worm is seen below the muscularis mucosae and protruding into the lumen. Hematoxylin and eosin stain, 25X. (Courtesy of Dr. Jack Malone, Louisiana State University, Baton Rouge)

Incidence of exposure of cats to *S tumefaciens* and *S planiceps* appears low. *Strongyloides planiceps* infects virtually all experimentally exposed cats, yet incidence of natural infection in cats within highly enzootic areas appears low.[1-4] The proportion of infected cats that show clinical signs is probably also low.[1-4,7] Clinical disease is most likely to be associated with massive and chronic infections. Disease is directly attributable to inflammatory reactions evoked by the adults, eggs and larvae.

Clinical Features

Clinical *Strongyloides* spp infections in domestic cats usually cause mild to severe diarrhea that lasts for weeks or months. Mild to severe debilitation and death have also been observed in severely affected animals.[5,6,9]

Pathologic Features

Adult parthenogenic female worms are 2-3 mm long and found within spherical, 2- to 10-mm nodules that lie between the muscularis mucosae and muscular coats of the intestinal wall (Fig 18). Nodules have a whitish glistening appearance and are slightly raised from the mucosa of the descending colon. Mucosa overlying and adjacent to the nodules is covered with a moderate amount of mucus. Parasitic nodules are not apparent from serosal surfaces; edema and hyperemia of surrounding tissues are not seen. Larger nodules may sometimes appear hemorrhagic. Each nodule has a central depression, which represents an epithelial cell-lined communication between the lumen and inside of the nodule. Nodules may become quite large and coalesce, giving the appearance of adenomatous tumors.[8,9]

Parasitic nodules are made up of tortuous interconnecting passageways lined by proliferating columnar epithelial and goblet cells supported by a fine connective tissue stroma.[5,6,8,9] Cross-sections of adult worms can be seen throughout the lumen of the nodules. Eggs and larvae are frequently observed in the lumen of nodules adjacent to adult worms. Eggs and larvae, but not adult worms, are occasionally seen in sub-

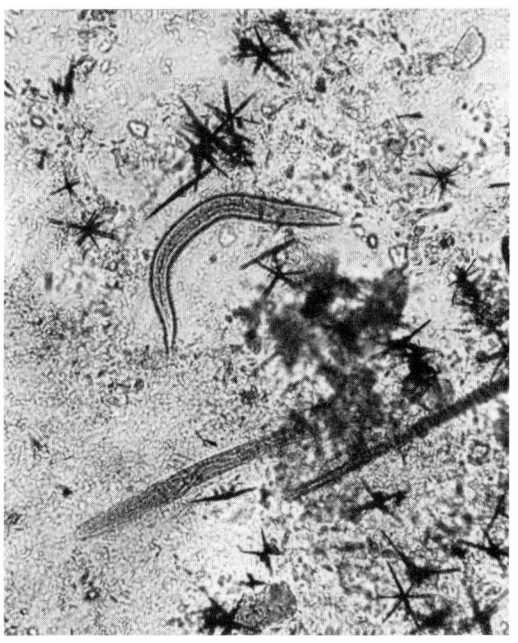

Fig 19. First-stage larva of *Strongyloides tumefaciens* in a direct fecal smear from a cat. The larva is about 0.5 mm long. Lugol's iodine stain. (Courtesy of Dr. Jack Malone, Louisiana State University, Baton Rouge)

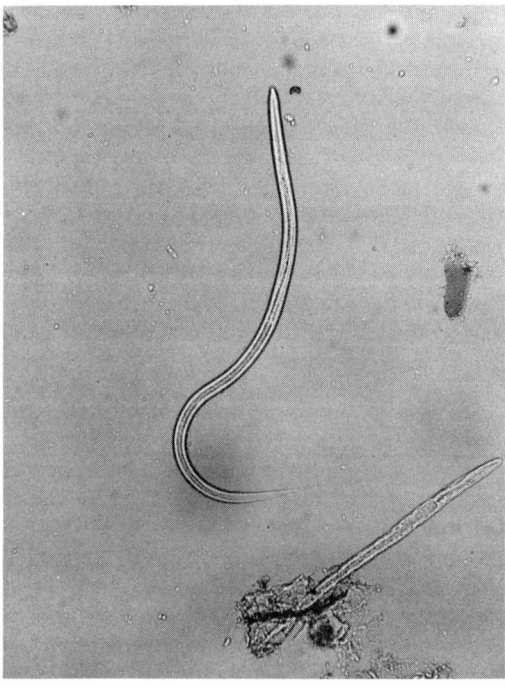

Fig 20. Third-stage (infective) larva of *Strongyloides tumefaciens*. The larva has now acquired the typical long, filariform esophagus, and is about 1 mm long. (Courtesy of Dr. Jack Malone, Louisiana State University, Baton Rouge)

mucosal tissues underlying the epithelial lining. A pronounced inflammatory response, composed of polymorphonuclear neutrophils, lymphocytes and plasma cells, is observed in submucosal tissues underlying the nodular epithelium. Eosinophils are surprisingly sparse.[9]

Clinicopathologic Features

A fecal analysis is warranted on any cat with a history of chronic diarrhea. Characteristic strongyloid larvae are observed both on direct smears and by sodium nitrate or analogous flotation techniques (Fig 19).[6] Larvae of *S tumefaciens* and *S planiceps* can be differentiated from those of *Aelurostrongylus* spp by their lack of a hooked tail. If larvae are allowed to develop for 36-72 hours in a Baermann apparatus, they demonstrate the elongated filariform esophagus and split tail typical of *Strongyloides* spp (Fig 20).[6]

Adult worms can often be speciated upon cross-section on microscopic examination.[3] *Strongyloides tumefaciens* is about 105 μ in diameter, with meromyarian-platymyarian muscle cells, an intestine composed of cuboidal uninucleate cells with a low microvillus brush border, a uterus with thin-shelled darkly staining eggs, and a smooth cuticle.[5] *Strongyloides planiceps* is similar but several internal and external measurements are characteristically different.[3]

Infection and Immunity

Cats exposed to larvae of *S planiceps* are easily infected.[3] Natural infections with both *S tumefaciens* and *S planiceps* appear to persist for many months.[6] Cats have a much greater immunity to *S stercoralis*.[12] Far fewer *S stercoralis* larvae reach the intestine of cats as compared to dogs, and clinical signs of diarrhea occur in only about 20% of infected individuals. Duration of *S stercoralis* larval shedding is also quite short: 1-6 weeks in cats vs 2-10 months or longer in dogs.[12]

The relative absence of eosinophils and predominance of plasma cells and lymphocytes suggest that cats respond to strongyloid infections mainly with cell-mediated immunity. The duration of natural infections is unknown. However, some cats may resolve infections quite rapidly, while others maintain infections for months.

Treatment and Prevention

Adult cats with intestinal strongyloidosis have been successfully treated with thiabendazole at 125 mg daily for 3 days.[6] The success of treatment is reflected by disappearance of larvae from feces, correction of diarrhea and weight gain.[6]

Animal and Public Health Considerations

Strongyloides tumefaciens and *S planiceps* are not infectious for people. Infectivity of affected cats for other cats has not been determined. Two sequentially infected cats have been observed in an outbreak, but the source of infection for each of these animals was not determined.[6]

References

1. Fukase T et al: *Strongyloides planiceps* from cats in Kanagawa Prefecture, Japan. *J Jpn Vet Med Assn* 36:589-592, 1983.

2. Fukase T et al: Helminthic parasites of stray domestic cats in Kanagawa Prefecture, Japan. *J Jpn Vet Med Assn* 37:15-19, 1984.

3. Fukase T et al: *Strongyloides planiceps* in some wild carnivores. *Jpn J Vet Sci* 47:627-632, 1985.

4. Horie M et al: Studies on *Strongyloides* sp isolated from a cat and raccoon dog. *Jpn J Parasitol* 30:215-223, 1981.

5. Lindsay DS et al: *Strongyloides tumefaciens* infection in a cat. *Companion Anim Pract* 1(1):12-13, 1987.

6. Malone JB et al: *Strongyloides tumefaciens* in cats. *JAVMA* 171:278-280, 1977.

7. Miyamoto D and Kutsumi H: Studies on zoonoses in Hokkaido, Japan. IV. A survey on parasites of cats in Asahikawa. *Jpn J Parasitol* 29:74-75, 1980.

8. Price EW and Dikmans G: Multiple adenomata of the large intestine of a cat caused by a species of *Strongyloides*. *J Parasitol* 16:104, 1929-30.

9. Price EW and Dikmans G: Adenomatous tumors in the large intestine of cats caused by *Strongyloides tumefaciens*. *Helminthol Soc Washington Proc* 8:41-44, 1941.

10. Rogers WP: A new species of *Strongyloides* from the cat. *J Helminthol* 17:229-238, 1939.

11. Rogers WP: *Strongyloides planiceps*, new name for *S cati* Rogers. *J Parasitol* 29:160, 1943.

12. Sandground JH: The role of *Strongyloides stercoralis* in the causation of diarrhea. Some observations on the condition of dogs and cats experimentally infected with this parasite. *Am J Trop Med* 6:421-432, 1926.

Additional Reference

13. Little MD: Experimental studies on the life cycle of *Strongyloides*. *J Parasitol* 48:41, 1962.

Chapter 55

Flatworm Infections

PARAGONIMIASIS (LUNG FLUKE INFECTION)

Etiologic Agent

Lung fluke infection of cats is caused by a number of species of trematodes belonging to the genus *Paragonimus*. Each species has a somewhat limited geographic range. Species include *P kellicotti* (North America), *P westermani* (Asia), *P ohihari* (China), *P iloktsuensis* (Japan), *P africanus* (Africa), *P uterobilateralis* (Africa), *P caliensis* (Colombia), *P peruvianus* (Peru) and *P mexicanus* (Mexico).[13]

Paragonimus spp infect a wide range of animals, including dogs, cats, pigs, rodents, mongooses, mink and others.[13] They are ovoid, 8-16 mm long and 4-8 mm wide (Fig 1).[13] Adults live in pairs in cystic structures within the lungs of mammalian hosts. Eggs escape into bronchioli through connecting air channels in the cyst wall and appear in the sputum. They are swallowed and shed in the feces at a rate of 920-1350 per day.[5] After development for 2-7 weeks, preferably in moist environments or free-standing water, miracidia are released. Miracidia penetrate aquatic snails. Sporocyst, redial and cercarial stages form in the snail over a 2- to 3-month period. Cercarial stages are freed from the snail and are free-swimming before penetrating a suitable crustacean host (crab, crayfish). Cercariae change to metacercariae over a 6- to 7-week period within the crustacean, and are particularly abundant in the heart, liver and muscles. Definitive hosts, including cats, are infected by eating crustaceans. After being ingested, young flukes are liberated in the intestine. They penetrate the intestine and migrate to the lungs via the peritoneal cavity and diaphragm. Transit time from intestine to lung is 5-23 days. Eggs first appear in the sputum 5-6 weeks postinfection.

Pathogenesis

Lung fluke infection of cats is uncommon and seen mainly in outdoor cats with access

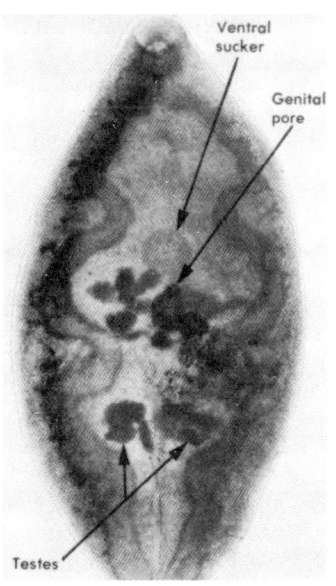

Fig 1. Adult male *Paragonimus kellicotti*, the lung fluke of cats. Adult flukes are 8-16 mm long and 4-8 mm wide. (From *Parasitology for Veterinarians*, courtesy of Dr. J. Georgi and W.B. Saunders Co.)

to intermediate crustacean hosts. The fact that crustaceans are not an important part of feline diets probably also limits the importance of the disease to domestic cats.

Paragonimiasis has been experimentally studied in some detail.[5,8] Cats can be readily infected with as few as 15-50 metacercariae of *P kellicotti* given PO. The migration path of the immature flukes through the intestine, peritoneal cavity, diaphragm and lungs is both grossly and histologically apparent. Lesions appear within lung parenchyma by the second week of infection and become progressively larger and more developed up to the ninth week. They remain highly visible but static after that time.

Clinical Features

Infected cats often show no or only minimal clinical signs.[6,7,11] In more severely infected cats, clinical signs include a chronic soft cough, wheezing, exertional dyspnea and fatigue, hemoptysis, excessive salivation, and minimal weight loss and deterioration of the coat.[1,7,9-11,14] Acute and recurrent pneumothorax has been observed in 4 of 28 experimentally infected cats but has not been described in natural infections.[5]

Clinical expression of experimentally induced paragonimiasis is the same as in the naturally occurring disease.[5] Clinical signs are mild until the fourth week of infection. At this time, some experimentally infected cats develop a soft cough and lose weight and their haircoats become rough.

Pathologic Features

Cats with naturally occurring lung fluke infections are usually necropsied only after the infection has become patent.[1,7,11] However, gross and histopathologic changes are seen much earlier in the course of infection.[8] The earliest gross lesions appear at 7-10 days and consist of superficial hemorrhagic foci, with overlying fibrinous exudation on the pleural surfaces. Such lesions are associated with penetrating immature flukes. By week 2, hemorrhagic foci are apparent in the subpleural areas, usually in the diaphragmatic lobes. Such foci become progressively larger and more encapsulated over time, reaching sizes of 1-2 cm by week 9.

Early histopathologic changes consist of eosinophilic inflammation, hemorrhage and edema along the migratory path of the immature flukes in the intestinal and diaphragmatic muscles and pleura. Flukes penetrating deeper into the pulmonary parenchyma are surrounded by a serosanguineous eosinophilic exudate. By week 2 postinfection, subpleural cavities are considerably larger and contain single and paired immature flukes. By week 4 or 5, the parasitic nodules take on a more cystic appearance, changing color from bright red to reddish brown. At this point, virtually all cystic lesions contain pairs of mating flukes. Ova production begins near week 6; ova are found in masses adjacent to the flukes within parasitic nodules. At this point, cyst walls are still comprised of inflamed lung tissue and loosely organized connective tissue, and the parasites are surrounded by a sanguineous eosinophilic exudate. Communicating tracts begin to develop between the cysts and bronchioli. Over time, bronchiolar epithelium moves into these communicating tracts and the cyst walls become more and more fibrous. Some areas of the cyst walls are lined with squamous epithelium that appears to originate from bronchiolar epithelium. However, the majority of the cyst interior is lined by a mixed leukocytic exudate comprised of neutrophils, eosinophils and macrophages. Alveolar tissue adjacent to cystic lesions is infiltrated with plasma cells, lymphocytes, macrophages, eosinophils and neutrophils. Fluke eggs that are often degenerating may be observed free within alveoli adjacent to parasitic cysts. Fluke ova surrounded by inflammatory exudates are seen within the lumens of hyperplastic bronchioles. Hyperplasia of peribronchiolar glands and lymphoplasmacytic infiltration are pronounced. Cystic lesions contain pairs of mature flukes.

Clinicopathologic Features

Hematologic changes in cats with natural and experimental *P kellicotti* infections are surprisingly mild for such a tissue-invasive parasitic infection. Two major peaks of eosinophilia are seen.[5] The first occurs about 2 weeks postinfection and the second about 8 weeks postinfection. The first peak is probably associated with penetration of flukes into lung parenchyma and the beginning development of host immunity. The second peak corresponds with ova production.[5] However, the eosinophil count declines, and is only mildly increased after week 12.

Fig 2. Ovum of *Paragonimus kellicotti* in the feces of a cat with lung fluke infection. Ova are 75-120 μ long and 50 μ wide. (Courtesy of Dr. P. Stewart and *Feline Practice*)

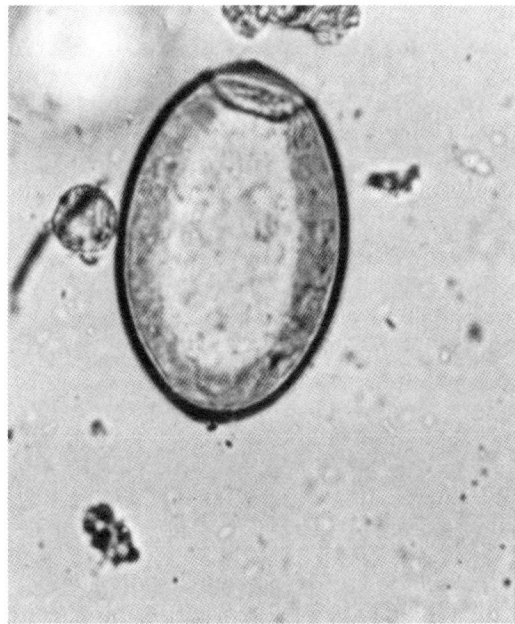

Radiographic signs of experimental infection appear 2-3 weeks postinoculation and are concentrated in the caudal lung lobes.[5] Early lesions consist of 2- to 4-cm, indistinct nodular densities with radiolucent centers that are crisscrossed with thin septa. Lesions tend to become larger and more distinctly cyst-like as the disease progresses. However, radiographic appearances do not change appreciably after day 63.[5] At this time, the flukes are mature and the surrounding cystic structure is fully developed. The radiographic appearance of naturally occurring cases of paragonimiasis in cats is similar.[11] The hilar to mid-zone of the right diaphragmatic lung lobe tends to be most severely involved. Parasitic cysts appear as circumscribed soft tissue densities several centimeters in diameter, with radiolucent centers and well-defined but sometimes irregular borders. Adjacent areas of lung often contain diffuse alveolar densities corresponding to inflammatory reactions to eggs and parasitic secretions. Pulmonary arteries sometimes appear more distinct than normal.

Lung fluke infection is confirmed by fecal examination. Sedimentation procedures detect eggs a week or more earlier than salt or sugar flotation procedures.[5] *Paragonimus* spp eggs are capped (operculate) at 1 end and gold-brown, and average about 50 x 90 μ (Fig 2).

Treatment and Prevention

Albendazole at 50-100 mg/kg PO daily for 14-21 days has killed mature lung flukes in experimentally infected cats.[3] Rim and co-workers have also described the efficacy of niclofolan at 1 mg/kg PO daily for 3 days or 2 mg/kg every other day for 2 treatments.[12] Bithionol at 100 mg/kg PO daily for 7 days is also effective, as is niclosamide.[6,10,13] Fenbendazole at 50-100 mg/kg PO divided BID for 10-14 days is equally effective.[4] Praziquantel and febantel have not proven effective against *P kellicotti* in cats.[2]

If fluke infection is limited to a single lung lobe, as in many cases, excision of the involved lobe has been curative.[1] However, given the efficacy of current drugs, this approach seems unwarranted.

Infection and Immunity

Cats appear much less capable of mounting an effective immune response to lung flukes than to other systemic parasitic diseases. Once the infection is established and adult mating pairs are well encysted, the main inflammatory response appears to be against egg masses surrounding the flukes and eggs that have escaped to lung tissues. The length of time cats remain infected under natural circumstances is unknown. In experimentally infected cats followed for as long as 263 days, there was no change in fluke viability or egg production during this entire period.[8] Therefore, it appears that cats are good definitive hosts for lung fluke infection and that flukes cause minimal clinical signs in spite of severe radiographic and pathologic lesions. This is probably because fluke cysts tend to be limited to only 1 or 2 lung lobes, leaving the remaining lobes free to function normally.

Animal and Public Health Considerations

Due to the complex life cycle of *Paragonimus* spp, cats are not directly infectious to other cats or other susceptible species of animals. Some *Paragonimus* spp are also infectious to people but these infections are contracted from ingestion of crustaceans and not from cat contact.

References

1. Bisgard GE and Lewis RE: Paragonimiasis in a dog and a cat. *JAVMA* 144:501-507, 1964.

2. Corwin RM et al: Anthelmentic effect of febantel/praziquantel paste in dogs and cats. *Am J Vet Res* 45:154-155, 1984.

3. Dubey JP et al: Albendazole therapy for experimentally induced *Paragonimus kellicotti* infection in cats. *Am J Vet Res* 39:1027-1031, 1978.

4. Dubey JP et al: Fenbendazole for treatment of *Paragonimus kellicotti* infection in dogs. *JAVMA* 174:835-837, 1979.

5. Dubey JP et al: Induced paragonimiasis in cats: clinical signs and diagnosis. *JAVMA* 173:734-742, 1978.

6. Eliasoff LB and Harden CR: Treatment of *Paragonimus kellicotti* infestation. *Feline Pract* 7(5):45-47, 1977.

7. Herman LH and Helland DR: Paragonimiasis in a cat. *JAVMA* 149:753-756, 1966.

8. Hoover EA and Dubey JP: Pathogenesis of experimental pulmonary paragonimiasis in cats. *Am J Vet Res* 39:1827-1832, 1978.

9. Majure TV and Moore WT: Clinical observations on lung flukes in the cat. *VM/SAC* 70:852-853, 1975.

10. Nance HW and Bailey WS: Feline paragonimiasis: A case report. *Auburn Vet* 31:101-104, 1975.

11. Rendano VT Jr: Paragonimiasis in the cat: a review of five cases. *J Small Anim Pract* 15:637-644, 1974.

12. Rim HJ et al: Experimental chemotherapeutic effects of niclofolan in animals infected with *Paragonimus westermanii* or *P iloktsuensis*. *Korean J Parasitol* 14:140-146, 1979.

13. Soulsby EJL: *Helminths, Arthropods and Protozoa of Domesticated Animals*. Lea & Febiger, Philadelphia, 1982. pp 64-66.

14. Stewart P et al: Paragonimiasis in a cat. *Feline Pract* 11(3):37-38, 1981.

PLATYNOSOMIASIS (LIVER FLUKE INFECTION)

Etiologic Agent

The fluke *Platynosomum fastosum* (*P concinnum*) is a common parasite of the biliary tract of domestic and wild cats in Papua-New Guinea, Australia, Malaysia, Central and South America, the Caribbean, West Africa, the American Southeast, and the South Pacific region, including Hawaii.[1-3,5-10,13] Adult flukes measure 4-8 mm by 1.5-2.5 mm (Fig 3).

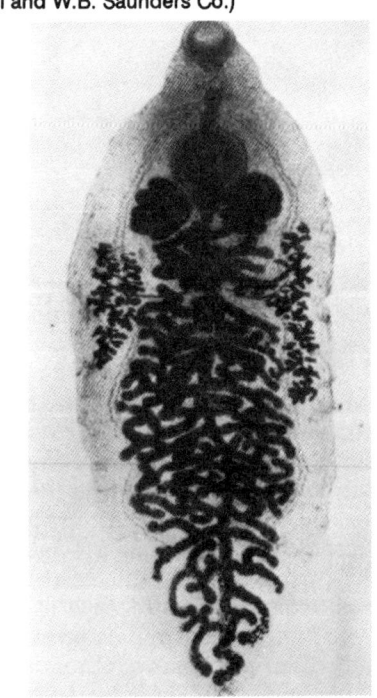

Fig 3. Adult *Platynosomum fastosum*, the liver fluke of cats. Adult flukes are 4-8 mm long and 1.5-2.5 mm wide. (From *Parasitology for Veterinarians*, courtesy of Dr. J. Georgi and W.B. Saunders Co.)

The life cycle of *P fastosum* is complex.[16] Eggs are passed from the bile ducts and gall bladder of infected cats and are shed in the feces. Free-swimming miracidia hatch from the eggs and penetrate snails. Cercariae are eventually produced. Snails are eaten by a number of different transport hosts, including crustaceans, lizards and toads. Cercariae migrate through the tissues of the transport host and encyst in large numbers in the liver, where they become metacercariae. Cats are infected by eating transport hosts. After ingestion, the metacercariae migrate proximad up the common bile ducts and reside in the gall bladder and larger ducts from the liver. Mating and egg production occur 8-12 weeks after infection. Maximum egg production (100-255 eggs/g feces) occurs 3-4 months after infection and declines slowly thereafter.[17]

Pathogenesis

The incidence of liver fluke infection in domestic cats is often quite high in enzootic areas. The infection rate in randomly necropsied cats was 15-62% in Hawaii.[1,3,10] Infection rates approaching this can be found in other parts of the world where flukes are found.[6] There appears to be a male sex predisposition to infection and no correlation with other types of parasitism. Older cats are more commonly infected than younger ones.[10]

The pathogenesis of *P fastosum* infection in domestic cats has been studied experimentally by Taylor and Perri.[17] Cats in this study were fed fresh liver tissue from toads (*Bufo marinus*) and followed for up to 21 months. All of the cats given a small number (125) of metacercariae and 40% of the cats given a large number (1000) remained asymptomatic. Of the cats given larger numbers, 60% became clinically ill 7-16 weeks after infection with mild signs of inappetence, lethargy, weight loss and abdominal tenderness. Clinical signs tended to disappear by the sixth month. The proportion of naturally infected cats with clinical illness is unknown, though various reports cite clinical signs in several to 50% or more of affected cats.[3,8] Considering the high percentage of cats infected in such areas as Hawaii and south Florida, the percentage of infected cats showing clinical signs must be low.

Clinical Signs

Clinical signs of liver fluke infection are usually absent as determined by experimental studies and routine necropsies of pound animals. Therefore, cats with clinical illness described in the literature represent only the small proportion of cats with particularly severe infections or concurrent illnesses. Chronic weight loss, anorexia, intermittent vomiting, abdominal distension and jaundice are among the most severe signs described in naturally occurring cases.[2,5,6,9,12] Platynosomiasis appears to be particularly severe in the Caribbean area, where it is referred to as "lizard poisoning."[8]

Pathologic Features

Gross features of platynosomiasis include some degree of hepatomegaly, enlargement and fibrosis of the gall bladder and large bile ducts, and a honey-like exudate containing numerous small adult flukes in the gall bladder.[17] Histopathologic changes include adenomatous hyperplasia of bile duct epithelium, with periductal eosinophilic inflammation and fibrosis.[6,17] Gross and histologic changes usually are not seen within the hepatic parenchyma itself.

Clinicopathologic Features

Eosinophilia is mild to moderate in most naturally infected animals. In experimentally infected animals, eosinophilia became apparent 3-14 weeks after infection but was never pronounced.[17] A small rise in serum AST activity and total serum bilirubin levels and the icterus index occurs at about this same time in experimental disease. Much more pronounced changes are likely to be seen with severe naturally acquired infections.

The most accurate method for detecting ova in the feces is the Ritchie formalin-ether sedimentation technique.[14,17] Direct smears and detergent sedimentation procedures are less accurate.[11] Even using this procedure, however, eggs might be identified in only one-third of infected cats.[13]

Treatment and Prevention

Infection can be prevented by not allowing cats to hunt in enzootic areas. However, this is difficult and often impractical. Infection can usually be eliminated by 1 treatment with either nitroscanate at 100 mg/kg or praziquantel at 20 mg/kg.[4]

Infection and Immunity

As in lung fluke infection, cats appear relatively incapable of terminating the infection over a long period. This may be because both infections are limited mainly to the lumen of ducts or duct-like structures. Also, both liver and lung fluke infections evoke comparatively mild eosinophilic responses. Eosinophilia is a measure of the intensity of tissue invasion by the parasites and of type-I immunity. The duration of untreated liver fluke infection is unknown. The fact that liver fluke infection is much more common in older cats, and the unaltered course of egg shedding is at least 21 months, indicates that it is very long.[10,17]

Animal and Public Health Considerations

Due to the complex life cycle of the organism, which requires both intermediate and transport hosts, infected cats are not infectious to other cats. *Platynosomum fastosum* is not infectious for people.

References

1. Ash LR: Helminth parasites of dogs and cats in Hawaii. *J Parasitol* 48:63-65, 1964.

2. Barriga OO *et al*: Liver flukes (*Platynosomum concinnum*) in an Ohio cat. *JAVMA* 179:901-903, 1981.

3. Chung NY *et al*: The prevalence of liver flukes in the city and county of Honolulu. *JAAHA* 13:258-262, 1977.

4. Evans JW and Green PE: Preliminary evaluation of 4 anthelmintics against the cat liver fluke *Platynosomum concinnum*. *Aust Vet J* 54:454-455, 1978.

5. Greve JH and Leonard PO: Hepatic flukes (*Platynosomum concinnum*) in a cat from Illinois. *JAVMA* 149:418-420, 1966.

6. Hitt ME: Liver fluke infection in south Florida cats. *Feline Pract* 11(3):26-29, 1981.

7. Ikede BO and Losos GJ: *Platynosomum concinnum* infection in cats in Nigeria. *Vet Record* 89:635-638, 1971.

8. Leam G and Walker IE: The occurrence of *Platynosomum fastosum* in domestic cats in the Bahamas. *Vet Record* 75:46-47, 1963.

9. Levine ND and Beamer PD: *Platynosomum fastosum* in an Illinois cat. *J Parasitol* 43:29-30, 1957.

10. Palumbo NE *et al*: Cat liver fluke, *Platynosomum concinnum*, in Hawaii. *Am J Vet Res* 35:1455, 1974.

11. Palumbo NE *et al*: Evaluation of fecal examination techniques for the diagnosis of cat liver fluke infection. *Lab Anim Sci* 26:490-493, 1976.

12. Powell KW: Liver fluke infection in a cat. *JAVMA* 156:218, 1970.

13. Retnasabapathy A and Prathap K: The liver fluke *Platynosomum fastosum* in domestic cats. *Vet Record* 88:62-65, 1971.

14. Ritchie LS: An ether sedimentation technique for routine stool examinations. *Bltn US Army Med Dept* 8:326, 1948.

15. Robinson VB and Ehrenford FA: Hepatic lesions associated with liver fluke (*Platynosomum fastosum*) infection in a cat. *Am J Vet Res* 23:1300-1303, 1962.

16. Soulsby EJL: *Helminths, Arthropods and Protozoa of Domesticated Animals*. Lea & Febiger, Philadelphia, 1982. pp 26-27.

17. Taylor D and Perri SF: Experimental infection of cats with the liver fluke *Platynosomum concinnum*. *Am J Vet Res* 38:51-54, 1977.

PANCREATIC FLUKE INFECTION

Etiologic Agent

Eurytrema procyonis (*Concinnum procyonis*) is a fluke that inhabits the major pancreatic ducts of cats, raccoons and foxes.[5] Eggs are passed in the feces and emerging miracidia penetrate snails, in which sporocyst, redial and cercarial development occurs. A second intermediate host has not yet been identified but is probably a grasshopper or similar arthropod.[5]

Pancreatic fluke infection of domestic cats has been recognized mainly in the United States in the Mississippi, Ohio, Tennessee and Missouri River valleys and surrounding areas. Infection is fairly common within enzootic areas. Sheldon found 5 of 36 cats from Kentucky infected.[4] Fox and associates found almost 11% of cats from the St. Louis, Missouri, area infected.[2]

Pathogenesis

No age, sex or breed predisposition has been reported. The highest incidence of infection appears to be in stray domestic cats, which live most of their lives outdoors and depend more on small game for survival. Definitive mammalian hosts are apparently infected when they ingest second intermediate hosts. The life cycle within cats has not been extensively studied. Immature flukes probably exit tissues of the arthropod host in the proximal small intestine of cats and migrate proximad up the pancreatic ducts. They attach themselves to walls of larger ducts by their ventral sucker.[2,4]

Clinical Features

Pancreatic fluke infections are usually asymptomatic or coincidental to other illness.[2,4] Anderson and associates described an infected cat with vomiting and weight loss over a 2-year period.[1] Though they attributed the clinical signs to pancreatic disease, the terminal incoordination was unrelated to chronic parasitic pancreatitis. However, Fox and co-workers described mild to moderate impairment of both bicarbonate and enzyme secretions from severely affected pancreas.[2] Clinical signs of pancreatic insufficiency were not noted even in cats with exocrine function <25% of normal. Though most infected cats are clinically normal, a few with severe pancreatic infection and fibrosis show some signs of pancreatic insufficiency.

Pathologic Features

Gross and histopathologic changes of pancreatic fluke infection have been described.[1,2,4] The most prominent gross lesion is a 3- to 5-fold increase in the size of the larger pancreatic ducts, with ductal and periductal fibrosis. Involvement of pancreatic acinar tissue is generally mild, but entire lobules may be fibrotic in some animals. Numerous adult flukes 1-2 mm long can be expressed from the cut surface of the pancreas. Histopathologic lesions are likewise mild. Attachment of flukes to duct walls elicits little change in the epithelium *per se*. Thickening of the duct wall with mucosal proliferation and periductal fibrosis is often apparent in surrounding tissues. Destruction of acinar tissue with fibrosis can be severe in isolated lobules. Islet cells are unaffected.

Clinicopathologic Features

The major, and often sole, clinicopathologic feature of pancreatic fluke infection is fluke eggs in the feces. Fluke eggs are operculated on 1 end and average 34-50 μ in size. Tissue and blood eosinophilia is absent.

Treatment and Prevention

Fenbendazole, PO at 30 mg/kg daily for 6 days, eliminated eggs from the feces of a naturally infected cat.[3]

Infection and Immunity

As in lung and liver fluke infections, cats seem to be ideal definitive hosts. The host response appears minimal and largely ineffective in eliminating flukes from within pancreatic ducts. Very little inflammatory response is elicited either by attached adult flukes or eggs.

Animal and Public Health Considerations

Due to the complex life cycle involving several intermediate hosts, infected cats are not health hazards to other animals. People are apparently not infected by feline pancreatic flukes.

References

1. Anderson WI *et al*: Pancreatic atrophy and fibrosis associated with *Eurytrema procyonis* in a domestic cat. *Vet Record* 120:235-236, 1987.

2. Fox JN *et al*: Pancreatic function in domestic cats with pancreatic fluke infection. *JAVMA* 178:58-60, 1981.

3. Roudebush P and Schmidt DA: Fenbendazole for treatment of pancreatic fluke infection in a cat. *JAVMA* 189:545-546, 1982.

Table 1. Miscellaneous flukes that cause infections of the liver and pancreas.

	Intermediate Hosts		Geographic	Sites of Infection	
	First	Second	Location	Principal	Secondary
Opisthorchis tenuicollis (O felineus)	snail	fish	eastern Europe Siberia, Asia	bile duct	pancreatic duct, small intestine
O viverrini	snail	fish	southeastern Asia	bile duct	pancreatic duct, small intestine
Clonorchis sinensis	snail	fish	southeastern Asia, China, Japan	bile duct	pancreatic duct, small intestine
Psuedoamphistomum truncatum	snail	fish	Europe, USSR, India	bile duct	
Metorchis albidus	snail	fish	Europe, USSR, North America	gall bladder, bile duct	
Metorchis conjunctus	snail	fish	North America	bile duct	
Parametorchis complexus	snail	fish	northeastern US	bile duct	
Amphimerus pseudofelineus	snail	fish	US	bile duct	pancreatic duct

MISCELLANEOUS LIVER AND PANCREATIC FLUKE INFECTIONS

Several species of flukes belonging to the family *Opisthorchiidae* can infect a number of mammalian, reptilian and avian hosts including wild and domestic cats.[1-7] They are small to medium-sized flukes with long, extremely flattened bodies. The principal genera and species of these flukes are given in Table 1.

The pathogenesis, clinical aspects, management and public health considerations for these various fluke infections are essentially the same as those described for liver and intestinal fluke infections.

4. Sheldon WG: Pancreatic flukes (*Eurytrema procyonis*) in domestic cats. *JAVMA* 148:252-253, 1966.

5. Soulsby EJL: *Helminths, Arthropods and Protozoa of Domesticated Animals*. Lea & Febiger, Philadelphia, 1982. p 28.

References

1. Dikmans G: Check list of the internal and external parasites of domestic animals in North America. *Am J Vet Res* 6:211-241, 1945.

2. Essex EH and Bollman JL: Parasitic cirrhosis of the liver in a cat infected with *Opisthorchis pseudofelineus* and *Metorchis complexus*. *Am J Trop Med* 10:65-70, 1930.

3. Koutz FR: The liver fluke (*Amphimerus pseudofelineus*) from a cat in Ohio. *JAVMA* 116:127, 1950.

4. Levine ND et al: Hepatitis due to *Amphimerus pseudofelineus* in a cat. *Illinois Vet* 1:47-49, 1958.

5. Okaeme AN: Zoonotic helminths of dogs and cats at the New Bussa, Kainji Lake area, Nigeria. *Intl J Zoonoses* 12:238-240, 1985.

6. Rothenbacher H and Lindquist WD: Liver cirrhosis and pancreatitis in a cat infected with *Amphimerus pseudofelineus*. *JAVMA* 143:1099-1102, 1963.

7. Soulsby EJL: *Helminths, Arthropods and Protozoa of Domesticated Animals*. Lea & Febiger, Philadelphia, 1982. pp 35-38.

8. Turk RD: Liver flukes from a cat. *JAVMA* 115:23, 1949.

TAPEWORM INFECTION

Etiologic Agent

Tapeworms have ribbon-like bodies and lack an alimentary canal.[1-8] They are composed of tens to thousands of connected segments. The head segment, or scolex, attaches to the mucosa of the small intestine. The adjacent neck segment serves as the germinative center for subsequent reproductive segments, called proglottids. As new proglottids are formed from the neck segment, older proglottids move caudad. Terminal proglottids break off and are shed in the feces.

Tapeworms are hermaphroditic; each proglottid has both testes and ovaries. Mature proglottids contain from 10 to several thousand elongated operculated eggs that are 25-75 μ wide or long. In some cases, all of the eggs are released through the lateral pores of the proglottids during passage down the intestine and intact proglottids are not seen in the feces (Cotyloda). In other cases, only part of the eggs are released and eggs appear both free and within mobile proglottids in the stool (Eucestoda). Tapeworms can live 2-3 years and reach 50 cm to several meters in length.

Though some species of tapeworms have cats as their definitive hosts, only 9 have been commonly described in the literature (Table 1). Several other species of tapeworms can have cats as aberrant intermediate hosts. The life cycles, geographic distribution and incidence of infection for tapeworms of domestic cats are quite variable.

Dipylidium caninum is the most common tapeworm of cats and dogs found throughout the world. It is one of the few feline tapeworms found more commonly in urban areas than among rural populations.[4,14,16] The infection rate is intimately related to the numbers of fleas on or near the cat and to other host animals, such as dogs. Shaw and associates found one-third of the urban cats in Australia to be infected,[16] while the infection in feral cats in Australia was only 2-11.6%.[4,14]

Dipylidium spp adults are up to 50 cm long and attach to the wall of the small intestine. The average worm burden in heavily infected cats is 46-256.[14] A dozen or more proglottids, each containing 30 or more eggs, are passed in the feces each day. Proglottids are initially quite active and appear as small whitish-tan pumpkin seed-like structures on the skin and hair around the anus and on the surface of droppings. They rapidly become dry and immobile, and tend to resemble grains of rice. Eggs are released during passage of proglottids down the intestine or from desiccated proglottids on the ground. Eggs are ingested by the larvae of several species of fleas (*Ctenocephalides canis*, *C felis*, *Pulex irritans*) or lice (*Trichodectes canis*).[18] Cysticercoids develop within larval fleas and lice, and are present in the adults. Cats are usually infected when they ingest adult fleas during grooming. The cysticercoid is released in the digestive tract, attaches itself to the

---

Table 1. Some species of tapeworms with adult forms in the intestinal tract of domestic cats.

Phylum: Platyhelminthes
Class: Eucestoda
  Order: Dilepididea
    Family: Dipylidiidae
      Genus: *Dipylidium caninum*
      Genus: *Joyeuxiella pasqualei*
  Order: Taeniidea
    Family: Taeniidae
      Genus: *Taenia taeniaeformis*
             T pisiformis
Class: Cotyloda
  Order: Diphyllidea
    Family: Diphyllobothriidae
      Genus: *Diphyllobothrium latum*
      Genus: *Spirometra mansonoides*
         S mansoni
         S erinacei

small intestinal mucosa and develops to an adult in several weeks.

Several *Joyeuxiella* spp infect domestic cats; the 2 most common are *J pasqualei* and *J echinorhynchoides*.[2,10] Infection with these tapeworms may be common in some areas of the Middle East, Africa, the Caribbean and Australia.[2,10,18,21] Cats and dogs are common definitive hosts. The first intermediate hosts are beetles and cockroaches. The second, or transport, hosts are small reptiles and rodents. Cats are usually infected by eating small prey animals.

Taenia taeniaeformis is found throughout the world, but the incidence of infection varies greatly. Morbidity tends to be much greater in rural than urban areas. As many as 22-60% of cats in Australia have been infected, though incidence has not been nearly as high in other areas.[4,14,16] *Taenia pisiformis* is only rarely found in cats.[18]

Taenia taeniaeformis adults can reach lengths of 60 cm and are found in the small intestine of cats and related carnivores.[18] The average worm burden in infected cats tends to be low, ranging from 2 to 10.[14] Rodents, and occasionally rabbits, serve as intermediate hosts. Eggs ingested by intermediate hosts develop in the tissues into strobilocerci, which are bladder-like structures containing a short segmented strobila. The strobila is released during digestion within the intestine of the cat and the scolex attaches itself to the intestinal wall. Gravid proglottids first appear in cat feces within 36-42 days, and adult worms may live for 1-3 years.[19] About 4 proglottids are shed in the feces every day, each containing an average of 1600 eggs.[19]

Diphyllobothrium latum is one of the largest of the tapeworms that infect cats, reaching lengths of 2-12 m. Adult worms live in the small intestine of people, dogs, cats and many fish-eating mammals.[18] It is most prevalent in the Baltic regions, USSR and the Great Lakes area of North America. Even within enzootic areas, however, the incidence of infection in cats is sporadic and quite low. Eggs shed in the feces hatch into motile coracidia in water.

Coracidia are ingested by immature cyclopids or diaptomid copepods (crustaceans).[18] The next larval stage, called a procercoid, is found within the body cavity of the crustacean. Further development to a plerocercoid occurs within predatory freshwater fish that feed upon the cyclopids and copepods. Plerocercoids are found within the viscera and musculature of the fish and are very long-lived. Cats become infected when they prey upon fish or when fed fresh, improperly cooked or pickled fish. Plerocercoids develop to adults within the intestinal tract of cats within 3-4 weeks.

Spirometra spp are found throughout the world and are very common in some geographic areas. They have been found in 33-61% of feral cats in Australia.[4,14] As in infection with *Taenia* spp, the infection rate for *Spirometra* appears higher in rural cats that are free to hunt than in urban animals. *Spirometra mansonoides* is the most common species found in North America and parts of South America, *S mansoni* in the Far East and South America, and *S erinacei* in Australia and the Far East.[9,18] *Spirometra* spp are small to medium-sized tapeworms that are morphologically similar to *Diphyllobothrium* spp.

Wild carnivores, dogs and feral and domestic cats serve as definitive hosts for adult worms. Worm burdens in infected cats range from 20 to 625.[14] Eggs embryonate in water, and the resultant free-swimming coracidia are ingested by small crustaceans of the genus *Cyclops*.[18] Procercoids develop within crustacean hosts and transform to plerocercoids upon ingestion by water snakes, birds, tadpoles, alligators and other amphibians. Feral pigs may also serve as paratenic or transport hosts for *S erinacei*.[1] Pigs are apparently infected by ingesting reptiles or amphibians containing plerocercoids. Plerocercoids migrate to muscle tissues, where they remain viable for long periods. Cats are infected by ingesting prey animals or infected meat. Eggs and proglottids are shed within 10-30 days following infection. Adult worms may live for several years in the intestinal tract and produce eggs almost continuously.

Pathogenesis

Tapeworms attach themselves by the scolex to the small intestinal mucosa and obtain nutrients by diffusion from intestinal contents. They do not usually cause clinical signs in the host. If infection is massive, there is significant competition for nutrients between the host and worms. This can lead to nutritional deficiencies in the host. Irritation and inflammation in the intestinal wall are occasionally severe enough to cause diarrhea.

Severe and often fatal disease can be associated with extraintestinal tapeworm infections. In these circumstances, cats act as aberrant intermediate hosts, usually for some avian *Mesocestoides* spp.[18] Cats are usually infected when they ingest arthropod intermediate hosts that contain cysticercoids. Cysticercoids are released by digestive enzymes of cats and penetrate the intestinal wall. Tetrathyridia are formed in the serous cavities, liver and, sometimes, lungs of cats. Tetrathyridia multiply asexually within these tissues by longitudinal splitting; massive internal infections can result over time.

Cystic, or coenuric, larvae of *Taenia* spp have also been recognized uncommonly in extraintestinal sites in cats.[7,22] As in human cysticercosis and echinococcosis, this form of infection is usually due to systemic migration of immature tapeworms and formation of large cysts in such vital structures as the brain, lung or liver.[20] Cysts may also form in subcutaneous and muscular areas of the body.

Clinical Features

Adult tapeworms in the intestinal tract of cats usually do not cause clinical signs. However, diarrhea attributable to tapeworm infection has been described.[8] Owners usually notice mobile or desiccated proglottids around the anus of the cat and in the stools, which is aesthetically displeasing. Massive infections may cause cats to be nutritionally deprived and somewhat thin and rough in appearance.[18] Infection with *D latum* has also been rarely associated with vitamin B_{12} deficiency. If several large worms are present in absorptive areas of the digestive tract, they effectively compete with the host for vitamin B_{12} and cause macrocytic hypochromic anemia.[18,20]

Systemic tapeworm infections are relatively rare. Within specific small geographic areas, however, veterinarians may see a number of cases during their careers. The most common site for infection with *Mesocestoides* spp is the peritoneal cavity. Infected cats have chronic weight loss ending in cachexia and death. Peripheral eosinophilia and abdominal distension due to ascites are common. Ascitic fluid is often yellowish and blood-tinged, and contains myriad tetrathyridia that appear like rice grains.

Pathologic Features

Intestinal tapeworms cause minimal gross microscopic changes in the intestinal wall. However, such is not the case with extraintestinal tapeworm infections. Cats with mesocestoidiasis usually have severe peritonitis, with reddening and thickening of the serosa and omentum. Abdominal fluid often contains copious to slight amounts of a thick reddish-yellow fluid containing numerous tetrathyridia that appear like rice grains. Coenurosis is associated with progressive neurologic signs.[8,22]

Tapeworm cysts, usually associated with *Taenia* spp, are more focal and less associated with violent host inflammatory reactions.[22] Cysts are often clear to semiopaque, fluid-filled, and 1-2 cm or more in diameter.[8,22] Host tissue surrounding the cysts is sometimes fibrous and contains an eosinophilic inflammatory reaction.

Clinicopathologic Features

Intestinal tapeworm infections are usually diagnosed by identifying proglottids around the anus or on the feces. Tapeworm eggs are also present in the feces, having been released from proglottids during their passage down the digestive tract. The genus of tapeworm can usually be determined by the characteristic size and appearance of

Fig 4. Individual ovum (A), 28 μ in diameter, and egg packet (B), 100 x 175 μ, of *Dipylidium caninum* in cat feces. (Courtesy of Dr. Norman Baker, University of California, Davis)

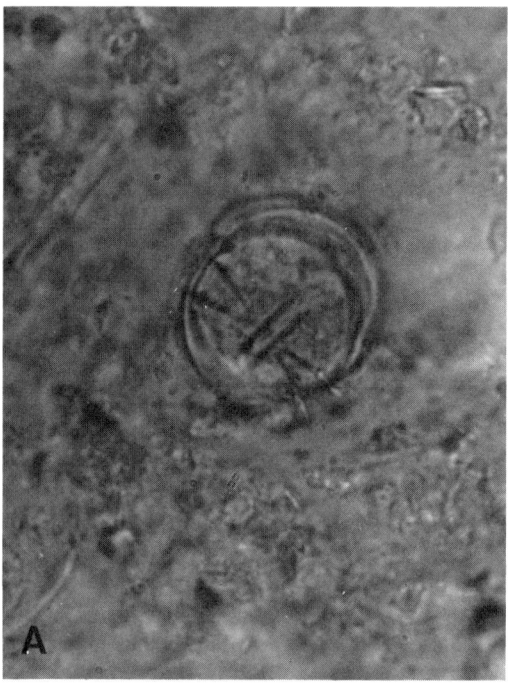

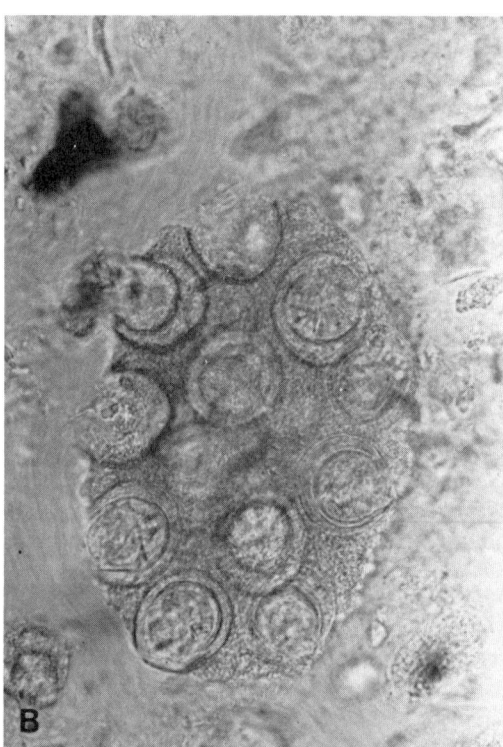

the eggs or egg packets, but speciation can sometimes be difficult (Figs 4-7).

Cats with extraintestinal tapeworm infections usually have mild to severe eosinophilia. Examination of ascitic fluid from cats with peritonitis caused by *Mesocestoides* spp can confirm tapeworm infection. The fluid is rich in eosinophils and tetrathyridia. However, speciation of the organism is seldom possible without differentiating the adult form. This requires feeding the organisms to a large number of potential definitive hosts.

Treatment and Prevention

Prevention of tapeworm infection involves eliminating intermediate hosts from feline habitats or preventing cats from entering environments where intermediate hosts are found. With the exception of flea control for prevention of *D caninum* infection, this is difficult to achieve and sustain.

Several drugs are effective against intestinal tapeworms. Perhaps the safest and most effective is praziquantel.[15,17] Oral or SC dosages of 4.2-12.7 mg/kg given once are safe and effective; 5 mg/kg is the recommended dosage. *Spirometra* spp require

Fig 5. Ovum of *Taenia*, 32 μ in diameter, in cat feces. (Courtesy of Dr. Norman Baker, University of California, Davis)

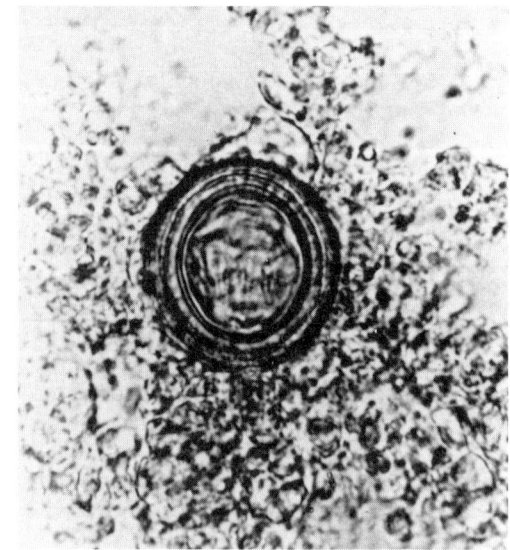

about twice the dosage as other species (7.5 mg/kg daily for 2 days).[6,15] *Spirometra* spp, as well as other tapeworms, are also susceptible to a single treatment of bunamidine hydrochloride at 25 mg/kg PO.[3,8] Alternative drugs commonly used to treat intestinal tapeworm infections include a single treatment of niclosamide at 100-150 mg/kg PO or dichlorophene at 0.1-0.2 mg/kg PO. Niclosamide and bunamidine are not highly effective against *Joyeuxiella*.[2] Mebendazole is also used at 100-200 mg PO BID for 5 days.

Treatment of extraintestinal cestode infections has proven more difficult. Usually the infection is not diagnosed until necropsy or is recognized only in an advanced state. Therefore, there is very little experience with treatment. Praziquantel has been successful against human cysticercosis, but its efficacy against extraintestinal tapeworm disease in cats has not been determined.[20] A dose 10 times that generally recommended was effective in a dog with peritoneal cestodiasis. Repeated treatment with mebendazole should be considered in animals with peritonitis caused by *Mesocestoides* spp. Glucocorticoid therapy should also be used to reduce tissue reactions to dead and dying organisms.

Fig 6. Individual ovum (A) and egg packet (B) of *Joyeuxiella* from a cat. Eggs are 30 μ in diameter. (Courtesy of Dr. W. Lindquist and *Feline Practice*)

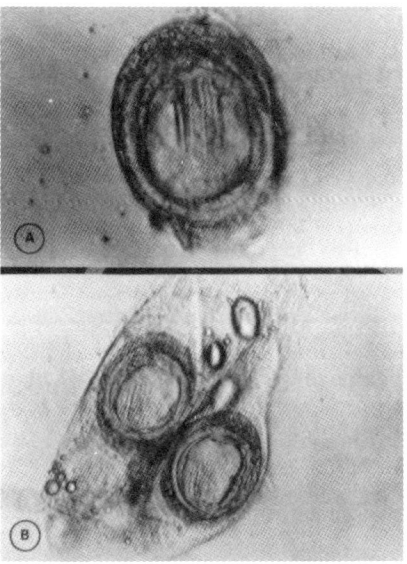

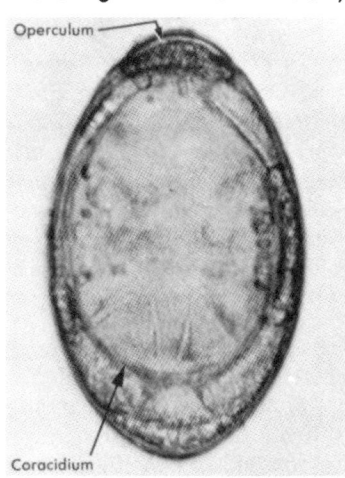

Fig 7. Ovum of *Spirometra mansonoides*. The egg is operculated and 30 x 60 μ, and contains a developing coracidium. (From *Parasitology for Veterinarians*, courtesy of Dr. J. Georgi and W.B. Saunders Co.)

Infection and Immunity

Cats mount very little immunity to adult forms in the intestine, and worms appear to die within 1-3 years from natural aging. No or only minimal immunity to reinfection develops after natural or drug-induced death of worms.[19] However, it appears that some mechanism prevents massive accumulations of organisms associated with continuous re-exposure. Numbers of tapeworms found in intestines of cats remain fairly constant even though animals in certain environments are continuously re-exposed to infected intermediate hosts.[14] A similar phenomenon may explain why animals cannot be superinfected. Immunity may vary greatly from 1 cat to another, similar to strain variations that have been recognized in rodents.[11] Acquired immunity has been recognized in dogs and appears to interfere with development during the parasite's rapid growth stage. It has less effect on the more stable adults.[5] Immunity to systemic forms of tapeworms appears relatively strong because few cats develop extraintestinal disease despite frequent exposures to infected prey.

Animal and Public Health Considerations

Cats infected with various species of tapeworms are not directly infectious for other cats. Eggs shed by cats must first be ingested by appropriate intermediate hosts, in which essential developmental stages occur.

A number of tapeworms of cats are infectious to people, including *Spirometra mansonoides*, *S erinacei*, *Diphyllobothrium latum* and *Dipylidium caninum*. Adult tapeworms of the last 2 species are found occasionally in the alimentary tract of people, particularly children. Infection is by eating infected intermediate hosts and not eggs.

Human infection with *Spirometra* spp is responsible for a condition called sparganosis, in which larvae (plerocercoids) from infected flesh of reptiles or amphibians penetrate the skin (raw flesh from such animals is used as poultices for ocular and skin lesions by some cultures in the Far East) or intestinal tract after ingestion.[18,20] Infection can also occur when people ingest water-borne crustacea containing procercoids. *Spirometra erinacei* plerocercoids have also been found in feral pigs in Australia; this has been a source of human infection.[1,18] Plerocercoids that enter the body through the skin or intestinal mucosa migrate to subcutaneous tissues and muscles, where they produce slow-growing pruritic nodules. Some nodules may reach a size of 3 cm or more over a 3- to 10-month period. In addition to local signs from the nodules, systemic urticarial and erythemic reactions, chills, fever and marked eosinophilia may accompany infection. People are not infected by ingestion of eggs, so cats are not direct health hazards.

References

1. Bearup AJ: Life history of a spirometrid tapeworm, causing sparganosis in feral pigs. *Aust Vet J* 29:217-224, 1953.

2. Blagburn BL and Todd KS Jr: Exotic cestodiasis (*Joyeuxiella pasqualei*) in a cat. *Feline Pract* 16(2):8-11, 1986.

3. Burrows RB and Lillis WG: Treatment of canine and feline tapeworm infections with bunamidine hydrochloride. *Am J Vet Res* 27:1381-1384, 1966.

4. Coman BJ et al: Helminth parasites and arthropods of feral cats. *Aust Vet J* 57:324-327, 1981.

5. Gemmell MA: Natural and acquired immunity factors interfering with development during the rapid growth phase of *Echinococcus granulosus* in dogs. *Immunol* 5:495-503, 1962.

6. Georgi JR: *Parasitology for Veterinarians*. 4th ed. Saunders, Philadelphia, 1985.

7. Hayes MA and Creighton SR: Tapeworm-induced nervous disorder in a cat. *JAVMA* 179:387, 1979.

8. Kirkpatrick CE and Sharninghausen F: *Spirometra* sp in a domestic cat in Pennsylvania. *JAVMA* 183:111-112, 1983.

9. Lillis WG and Burrows RB: Natural infections of *Spirometra mansonoides* in New Jersey cats. *J Parasitol* 50:680, 1964.

10. Lindquist WD and Austin ER: Exotic parasitism in a Siamese cat. *Feline Pract* 11(2):9-11, 1981.

11. Olivier L: Natural resistance to *Taenia taeniaeformis*. I. Strain differences in susceptibility of rodents. *J Parasitol* 48:373-378, 1962.

12. Olsen OW and Haas WR: A new record of *Spirometra mansoni*, a zoonotic tapeworm, from naturally infected cats and dogs in Hawaii. *Hawaii Med J* 35:261-263, 1976.

13. Read CP: *Spirometra* from Texas cats. *J Parasitol* 34:71-72, 1948.

14. Ryan GE: Gastro-intestinal parasites of feral cats in New South Wales. *Aust Vet J* 52:224-227, 1976.

15. Sakamoto T: The anthelmintic effect of Droncit on adult tapeworms of *Hydatigera taeniaeformis*, *Mesocestoides corti*, *Echinococcus multilocularis*, *Diphyllobothrium erinacei*, and *D latum*. *Vet Med Rev* 1:64-74, 1977.

16. Shaw J et al: Prevalence of some gastrointestinal parasites in cats in the Perth area. *Aust Vet J* 60:151-152, 1983.

17. Shmidl JA et al: Summary of safety evaluations for praziquantel in cats. *VM/SAC* 77:771-773, 1982.

18. Soulsby EJL: *Helminths, Arthropods and Protozoa of Domesticated Animals*. 7th ed. Lea & Febiger, Philadelphia, 1982. pp 87-136.

19. Williams JF and Shearer AM: Longevity and productivity of *Taenia taeniaeformis* in cats. *Am J Vet Res* 42:2182-2183, 1981.

20. Wolfe MS, in Wyngaarden JB and Smith LH Jr: *Cecil's Textbook of Medicine*. Saunders, Philadelphia, 1985. pp 1804-1809.

Additional References

21. Agrawal RD: Infective stages of two helminth parasites from intermediate-paratenic hosts with notes on their partial life cycles in experimental mammals. *Agra Univ J Res* 20:137-138, 1971.

22. Smith MC et al: Cerebral coenurosis in a cat. *JAVMA* 192:82-84, 1988.

Chapter 56

Thorny-Headed Worm Infection
(Acanthocephaliasis)

Etiologic Agent

Acanthocephalans are commonly referred to as thorny-headed worms.[3] They have a cylindric body, lack an alimentary tract and absorb nutrients through the body wall. They get their name from a hollow, cylindric head appendage (proboscis) armed with rows of hooks. In the genus *Oncicola* are 2 species that may infect domestic and wild Felidae and Canidae: *O canis* and *O campanulatus*.[3] Both species occur in North America; the former also occurs in South America. Unidentified *Oncicola* spp have also been commonly recognized in Australian cats; Australian isolates appear very similar to *O canis*.[1,2]

The life cycles of *Oncicola* spp have not been determined. As in *Acanthocephala*, however, arthropod intermediate hosts are probably required.[3] Arthropod hosts for acanthocephalans that parasitize land animals are usually insect larvae, beetles and cockroaches. Eggs are ingested by an appropriate arthropod host and larvae are released. Encystation as a cystacanth occurs in the hematocele. Cystacanths become infectious in 1-3 months. Infected arthropods can directly infect definitive hosts or they may be ingested by paratenic hosts. No further development occurs within tissues of paratenic hosts, which act only as reservoirs for the infectious form. Armadillos and turkeys have been identified as paratenic hosts in Texas.[3]

Cats are probably infected by eating infected arthropods or paratenic hosts. Infectious larvae are liberated from the body of the intermediate or paratenic host and develop into adults in the intestine. Adult male worms are 6-13 mm long, while females are 7-14 mm.[3]

Pathogenesis

Oncicola spp are fairly common in some areas of the world, especially among feral cat populations. Ryan found the parasite in the intestines in 29.5% of all feral cats from New South Wales.[2] Infection rates varied from 0-79.2% within the region. Cats in the more populous Sydney area had the lowest morbidity. Infection rates of cats in Victoria were similar to those of feral cats in New South Wales.[1] Morbidity figures for North America are not available but seem considerably lower than those observed in Australia.

The adult worm attaches itself deeply in the intestinal mucosa by its hooked proboscis. Though clinical signs have occasionally been seen in infected dogs, all infected cats have been asymptomatic.[3] There has been no evidence that *Oncicola* spp infection causes any pathologic changes within the mucosa. This may be due to the relatively low worm burden (15-131 worms) in the individual cats surveyed.[2]

Clinical Features

There have been no descriptions of clinical illness associated with *Oncicola* infection of domestic cats.

Pathologic Features

Eggs are passed in the feces. They are oval and brown, and measure 59-71 x 40-50 μ.

Treatment and Prevention

There have been no reports on treatment of infected animals. The efficacy of anthelmintics has not been determined.

Infection and Immunity

Nothing is known about immunity to infection or immunopathologic mechanisms.

Animal and Public Health Considerations

Infected cats are not directly infectious for other cats or dogs. *Oncicola* spp are not human pathogens.

References

1. Coman BJ et al: Helminth parasites and arthropods of feral cats. *Aust Vet J* 57:319-323, 1981.

2. Ryan GE: Gastro-intestinal parasites of feral cats in New South Wales. *Aust Vet J* 52:224-227, 1976.

3. Soulsby EJL: *Helminths, Arthropods and Protozoa of Domesticated Animals*. Lea & Febiger, Philadelphia, 1982. pp 347-352.

Chapter 57

Arthropod Infestations

EAR MITE INFESTATION

Etiologic Agent

Otodectes cynotis commonly infests the external ear canals of dogs, cats, foxes, raccoons, ferrets and other carnivores.[4] The mite is found throughout the world and is particularly prevalent among cats kept in cattery-type environments.

Adult mites live mainly in the middle to proximal portion of the external ear canals and inner pinnae, where they feed on epidermal debris and inflammatory exudate. Eggs are laid singly and hatch in 1-3 days.[4] Larval mites molt at least twice during a 5- to 7-day period and become sexually competent young adults. Mating occurs shortly after the second molt. Gravid young female mites molt a third time 2 days after mating and begin to lay eggs 1 day later. Therefore, the period from hatching to egg laying is as short as 9 days. Adult mites live for a month or more and lay 2-3 eggs per day.

Pathogenesis

Ear mite infestations are very common among cats, especially those housed in catteries or cattery-like environments. The extent and severity of infestation within a closely confined group of cats are usually directly proportional to incidence of other common cattery problems, such as fleas, ringworm and viral upper respiratory diseases. Stress, environmental contamination and husbandry practices that favor respiratory disease also appear to favor large mite accumulations.

The route of transmission from cat to cat has not been precisely determined. Infestation is much more severe when multiple animals are kept closely confined. This indicates that transmission is direct and by close contact. Mites may then transport themselves from host to host, or from environment to host, and migrate to the external ear canals.

Mites feed on inflammatory products stimulated by the mites themselves.[2] Low-grade inflammatory reactions elicited by the mites may be due to host immunity, *ie*, hypersensitivity.[3] Inflammation of feline ear canals, regardless of etiology, also causes eventual exhaustion of sebaceous glands, hypersecretions of apocrine glands, and increased secretions of acidic lipids, acid mucopolysaccharides, protein-bound lipids and carbohydrates.[2] Such inflammatory products are probably more desirable for mite nutrition than normal sebaceous gland secretions (cerumen).

Mite infestations are first noticed in 2- to 6-week-old kittens. Infestation is usually less severe in adult cats than in kittens and adolescent animals. It is also less severe in females than males. The severity of infestations also varies greatly from animal to animal within the same environment. Certain animals have severe infestations, while others have light infestations or are completely free of mites.

Ear mites occasionally cause pruritic miliary lesions distant to the ears. In a study of cats with miliary dermatitis, Scott observed, 4/133 to have ear mite infestations.

Clinical Features

Cats with ear mite infestations may show no outward signs or may scratch at their ears. Close examination of the proximal part of the external ear canals and inner pinnae often demonstrates a darkening and thickening of the epidermis and greatly increased amounts of blackish, flaky or granular sebaceous exudate. Scratch marks and small sores may be seen on the more sparsely haired region rostral to the ears and on the inner pinnae. If secondary bacterial infection occurs, the exudate may be purulent and the ear canals will be much more inflamed.

Pathologic Features

In addition to the gross changes described above, characteristic changes are observed on microscopic examination of the affected aural epidermis. Squamous epithelial cell hypertrophy, acanthosis, hyperplasia of sebaceous glands, and hyperemia and edema of the dermis are prominent microscopic features.[5] Inflammatory cells within the dermis include mast cells, lymphocytes and plasma cells.

Clinicopathologic Features

A presumptive diagnosis of ear mite infestation can be made on the basis of the characteristic appearance of involved tissues of the ear and associated exudate. Ear mites are often seen grossly within the exudate, appearing as small whitish specks that move slowly under bright light and low magnification with a hand lens. Exudate can also be smeared onto a slide and examined microscopically under low power. Eggs and adult, nymphal and larval mites are readily observed in most cases (Fig 1).

Treatment and Prevention

Infested ears should be cleansed of exudates by instilling a few drops of warm mineral oil or ceruminolytic ear drops into each ear canal and gently massaging the base of each ear. This loosens the exudate, which can then be gently removed with cotton swabs. Following exudate removal, the ears are treated daily for 10-14 days with mineral oil, commercial oil-based acaricidal preparations, or a 20% suspension of benzyl benzoate. A short repeat treatment is often done 9-10 days later. Organophosphate-impregnated flea and tick collars are not effective against ear mites.[5]

Ivermectin is effective in treatment of ear mites in dogs and cats and is probably the treatment of choice.[1,6] A single SC dose of ivermectin at 200-1330 µg/kg (400 µg/kg preferred) has been effective in several cats. Topical antibacterial medications are sometimes required for ear infestations with a secondary bacterial component.

With repeated usage, ear medications can elicit hypersensitivity reactions that may mimic the original mite infestation.

Fig 1. Adult male (A) and female (B) *Otodectes cynotis* in exudate from the ear of a cat. (Courtesy of Dr. Norman Baker, University of California, Davis)

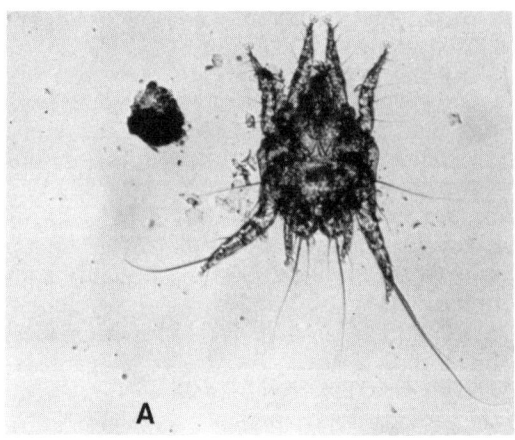

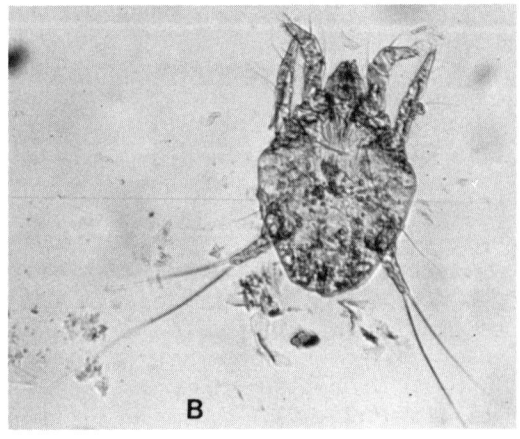

With ear mite infestations that appear refractory to treatment or recur despite continuous therapy, such reactions should be suspected. If the true etiology of the otitis is doubtful, therapy should be discontinued for several weeks. Otitis externa rapidly resolves following discontinuation of treatment if drug hypersensitivity is causing the problem.

Elimination of ear mites from catteries is difficult with topical medications. The mites persist on normal untreated parts of the body and in the environment. Use of ivermectin has facilitated eradication. All cats should be treated as described for individual infestations, with treatment repeated in 2-4 weeks. The cats are then monitored at monthly intervals and treated again if new mite infestations are detected.

Infection and Immunity

Cats vary greatly in their resistance to ear mite infestations. However, the nature of this resistance is not clearly understood. Ear mite infestations are more common among some litters of kittens than others. The level of infestation peaks in adolescent kittens and declines as they become older.[3]

The possible nature of mite immunity has been studied by Weisbroth and co-workers and Powell and associates. Infested cats respond to mites by producing precipitating and reaginic antibodies.[3,5] Both immmediate and Arthus-type hypersensitivity reactions can also be elicited in diseased cats by intradermal injections of mite antigen.

Elicitation of immediate skin hypersensitivity reactions may be a way in which feeding mites ensure their food supply. Histopathologic studies of the skin in areas of feeding mites show squamous epithelial cell hypertrophy, acanthosis, hyperplasia of sebaceous glands, and hyperemia and edema of the dermis associated with an infiltration of mast cells, lymphocytes and plasma cells.[5] The exudate produced by this type of reaction appears ideally suited for mite sustenance.

Immunologic influence on mite populations could occur by 2 means. First, cats that are more prone to hypersensitivity may provide mite populations with a greater food supply; animals that do not respond, would not. Mites may also be damaged by ingesting lymph that presumably contains antibodies, as well as living immunocytes and macrophages.

Animal and Public Health Considerations

Otodectes cynotis can be transmitted between dogs and cats. However, people cannot become infested.

References

1. Chauve C and Reynaud MC: Traitement parenteral de l'otoacariose du chat efficacite de l'ivermectine. *Sci Vet Med Comp* 86:41-43, 1984.

2. Fernando SDA: Certain histopathologic features of the external auditory meatus of the cat and dog with otitis externa. *Am J Vet Res* 28:278-286, 1967.

3. Powell MB et al: Reaginic hypersensitivity in *Otodectes cynotis* infestation of cats and mode of mite feeding. *Am J Vet Res* 41:877-882, 1980.

4. Soulsby EJL: *Helminths, Arthropods and Protozoa of Domesticated Animals*. Lea & Febiger, Philadelphia, 1982. pp 488- 492.

5. Weisbroth SH et al: Efficacy of Vapona-containing "flea collar" for control of *Otodectes cynotis*. *Cornell Vet* 64:549-558, 1974.

6. Yazwinski TA et al: Efficacy of ivermectin against *Sarcoptes scabei* and *Otodectes cynotis* infestation in dogs. *VM/SAC* 76:1749-1751, 1981.

7. Scott DW: Feline dermatology 1983-1985: "The secret sits." *JAAHA* 23:255-274, 1987.

CHEYLETIELLOSIS

Etiologic Agent

Cheyletiella spp are mites belonging to the family Cheyletiellidae, suborder Trombidiformes, class Arachnida.[16] There is some confusion in the literature on the species that infest cats.[15] Most reports of cheyletiellosis is cats refer to the mite as *Cheyletiella parasitivorax*. The genus has recently been divided into several species: *C yasguri*, which infests mainly dogs; *C blakei*, which is a feline pathogen and *C strandtmanni, C parasitivorax, C furmani, C takahashi, C ochotanae* and *C johnstoni*, which are pathogens of rabbits, pikas and hares.[2,3,15] *Cheyletiella parasitivorax* and *C blakei* are the main species found on cats.[9,10] *Cheyletiella yasguri* is the main species found on dogs and infests cats only when they are in close contact with infested dogs.

Adult mites live in the surface layers of the skin. Larvae hatch about 4 days after eggs are laid. Eggs are attached to the base of hair shafts similar to louse nits. The 6-legged larval stage is followed by 2 nymphal stages, and adults appear about 1 month after eggs are laid.[9,10]

Pathogenesis

Cheyletiellosis has been recognized in cats in many areas of the world. Similar to notoedric mange, however, infestations are relatively uncommon. Mites apparently do not penetrate the skin. Rather, there is pronounced reactive hyperkeratosis, with desquamation of cornified epithelium. Mites live and feed on this epithelial debris. Lesions are superficial and usually not highly pruritic. Larvae, nymphs and adult males die within 48 hours off the host, while adult females may survive several days longer.[9,10]

Clinical Features

Most infested cats appear asymptomatic and without visible lesions.[3] When lesions occur, they are usually focal and concentrated about the dorsum of the head and spine. They appear mainly as slight to moderate accumulations of dandruff or as a mild miliary dermatitis with papular eruptions.[3,8-12] Pronounced dandruff-laden lesions are not as common in cats as in dogs. Pruritus and self-mutilation of lesions are not usual features in cats. Lesions are more apt to be severe in younger cats than older animals.

Pathologic Features

Histologic changes include hyperkeratosis, with marked desquamation of epithelial cells. A mild plasmacytic and lymphocytic infiltrate is seen within the dermis. Tissue eosinophilia is usually mild.

Clinicopathologic Features

Dandruff collected from lesions contains numerous mites. This material appears to move when closely observed, the so-called "walking dandruff." Mites can be readily identified under low-power microscopy (Fig 2). Mite eggs are sometimes seen in fecal flotations, probably because they were ingested during grooming and biting of the skin.[3]

Treatment and Prevention

A single dip with 0.2% malathion in water has been curative.[14] Lime-sulfur (1.6%) dips performed 3 times at 1-week intervals have also proven satisfactory, as have pyrethrins.[9,10]

Animal and Public Health Considerations

Infested cats are infectious for other cats. Canine and feline *Cheyletiella* spp are also highly infectious for people.[6] Lesions on people are usually not seen upon initial exposure or, at best, are only small (1-2 mm),

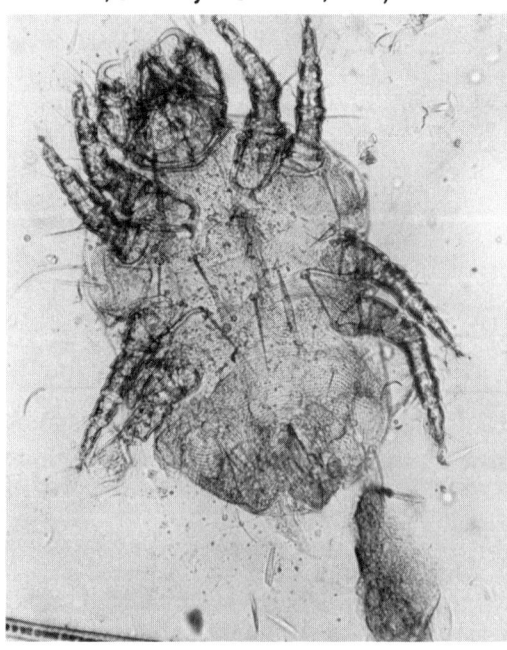

Fig 2. Adult female *Cheyletiella* mite in a skin scraping from a cat with generalized scurfiness. (Courtesy of Dr. Peter Ihrke, University of California, Davis)

transient erythematous maculae or papules on the arms, legs and trunk. Lesions in sensitized people are pruritic and 4-20 mm in diameter. They are papular, papulovesicular or papulourticarial, and may persist for days to weeks. Cats living in proximity to infested people are frequently asymptomatic carriers. Therefore, it is important not to exclude cats as a source of infection merely because they do not have lesions.

CHIGGER MITE INFESTATION

"Chigger" mite infestations have been rarely observed in cats.[1,4,5,7,13] The most common species include *Eutrombicula alfreddugesi*, *Neotrombicula autumnalis* and *Walchia americana* (Fig 3).[4] Chiggers are free-living in grasses and shrubs. Only the 6-legged larval stages are parasitic to animals. Snakes, lizards, rabbits and birds are the usual hosts; cats are only incidentally infested. Accumulation of larval mites causes multifocal orangish crusts, usually on the head, ears, ventrum and interdigital areas. Lesions result from the feeding activities of mites and liquefaction of superficial tissues by their saliva. Larvae feed for 1-2 weeks and then fall to the ground to complete their life cycle. Larval mites are easily identified on skin scrapings.

Treatment is identical to that for cheyletiellosis. Infested cats are not contagious for people.

References

1. Bullman CC *et al*: Feline trombiculiasis. *Feline Pract* 6(2):36, 1976.

2. Carroll HF and Theis JH: *Cheyletiella* mite dermatitis: A review. *JAAHA* 9:573-576, 1973.

3. Fox JG and Hewes K: *Cheyletiella* infestation in cats. *JAVMA* 169:332-333, 1976.

4. Greene RT *et al*: Trombiculiasis in a cat. *JAVMA* 188:1054-1055, 1986.

5. Hardison JL: *Eutrombicula alfreddugesi* (chiggers) in a cat. *VM/SAC* 1:47, 1977.

6. Krinsky WL, in Wyngaarden JB and Smith LH Jr: *Cecil's Textbook of Medicine*. Saunders, Philadelphia, 1985. pp 1833-1834.

7. Lowenstine LJ *et al*: Trombiculiasis. *JAVMA* 175:289-292, 1979.

8. McKeever FJ and Allen SK: Dermatitis associated with *Cheyletiella* infestation in cats. *JAVMA* 174:718-720, 1979.

9. Muller GH *et al*: *Small Animal Dermatology*. 3rd ed. Saunders, Philadelphia, 1983. pp 324-330.

10. Ibid. pp 319-321.

11. Niiyama M and Ohbayashi M: *Cheyletiella blakei* in a cat. *Jpn J Vet Sci* 41:395-399, 1979.

12. Ottenshot TRF and Gil D: Cheyletiellosis in long-haired cats. *Tijdschr Diergeneesk* 103:1104-1108, 1978.

13. Scott DW: Feline dermatology 1900-1978. A monograph. *JAAHA* 16:365-375, 1980.

14. Skerman KD *et al*: *Psoroptes ovis*, the itch mite of the sheep. *Aust Vet J* 36:317-321, 1960.

15. Smiley RL: A review of the family Cheyletiellidae (acarina). *Ann Entomol Soc Am* 63:1056, 1970.

16. Soulsby EJL: *Helminths, Arthropods and Protozoa of Domesticated Animals*. 7th ed. Lea & Febiger, Philadelphia, 1982. pp 475-482.

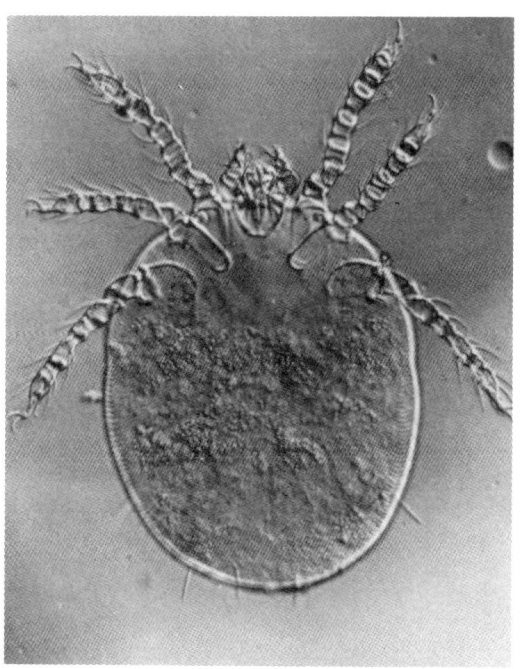

Fig 3. Ventral view of an adult chigger mite, *Walchia americana*. These mites are about 0.3 mm long. (From *Parasitology for Veterinarians*, courtesy of Dr. J. Georgi and W.B. Saunders Co.)

DEMODECTIC MANGE

Etiologic Agent

The genus *Demodex* belongs to the suborder Trombidiformes, class Arachnida.[9] Two or more species of *Demodex* infest cats. The earliest recognized species was *D cati*.[3,5] *Demodex cati* resembles *D canis*, having an elongated body but being somewhat smaller.[3] A second species, with a wider and more blunt-ended body, has also been recognized but is yet unnamed.[2,11,13] This latter organism is similar but not identical in appearance to *D criceti*, which infests hamsters.[2,6]

The life cycle of *D cati* resembles that of *D canis* and is spent entirely on the host.[3,9] Adults, eggs, larvae and 2 nymphal stages are found in hair follicles and sebaceous glands. The life cycle is completed in 18-24 days. The life cycles of the more newly recognized species are unknown. Similar to *D criceti*,[6] the unnamed cat organism appears to replicate within pits in the stratum corneum of the skin and is not found within hair follicles or sebaceous glands.[2,13]

Pathogenesis

Similar to *Demodex* spp of other animals, demodectic mites of cats probably inhabit a substantial proportion of normal cats throughout the world. Infestation probably occurs shortly after birth from maternal contact.[9] Cats of all ages have been clinically affected.

Clinical Features

Most cats that harbor *Demodex* spp apparently have no lesions or clinical signs. Clinically apparent infestations are uncommon and conditions leading to disease in a small proportion of cats are unknown. More severely affected animals appear to have predisposing hormonal or debilitating disorders that lower resistance or change the microenvironment of the skin.[13]

Lesions of demodicosis are manifested by focal areas of partial alopecia that are sometimes bilaterally symmetric.[1-4,7,8,10-14] The ears, periorbital areas and bridge of the nose are commonly involved. Lesions may also be seen on the chin, thorax, abdomen, inner thighs, flanks, perineum and tail. Ear lesions can extend proximad down the external canals and cause an otitis-like condition.[3,11] Skin underlying areas of partial alopecia ranges from normal in appearance to slightly erythematous, with papular eruptions and crusting.

More severe and chronic lesions may be hyperpigmented. Pruritus is absent or mild.[13] Hairs within lesions are shed completely or broken and retained as a short stubble. *Demodex* spp lesions, especially if bilaterally symmetric and widespread on the trunk, may resemble those described for feline neurodermatitis or feline endocrine alopecia.[8] Occasionally, lesions are more pruritic and crusty, and resemble those of notoedric mange.[11] Lesions tend to remain localized or spread slowly with time. Spontaneous resolution after several weeks has been described in younger animals.[7] However, most cases described in the literature have tended to be persistent.

Pathologic Features

No detailed descriptions of histopathologic lesions have been reported. *Demodex cati* is seen microscopically within hair follicles and sebaceous glands,[13] while feline species resembling *D criceti* are found mainly within the stratum corneum.[2,13]

Clinicopathologic Features

Superficial scrapings are adequate to detect *Demodex* spp resembling *D criceti* (Fig 4). Deep scrapings are necessary to detect *D cati* (Fig 5). Scrapings should be diluted with glycerin or mineral oil and viewed under low-power (100X) magnification.

Treatment and Prevention

Lime-sulfur (1.6%) baths once weekly for 3-8 weeks have proven effective by themselves or in combination with phosmet.[2,8,13] Topical amitraz (0.0125-0.025%) dips applied once or twice weekly for 3-8 weeks have proven effective.[8,11,12] Mild signs of toxicity, especially at the start of therapy, are common with such products as amitraz.

Fig 4. Adult *Demodex* sp in a skin scraping from a cat. This unnamed species of *Demodex* resembles *D criceti* of hamsters, and is found in the stratum corneum rather than in hair follicles and sebaceous glands. Note the wide, blunt body. (Courtesy of Dr. N. Gabbert and *Feline Practice*)

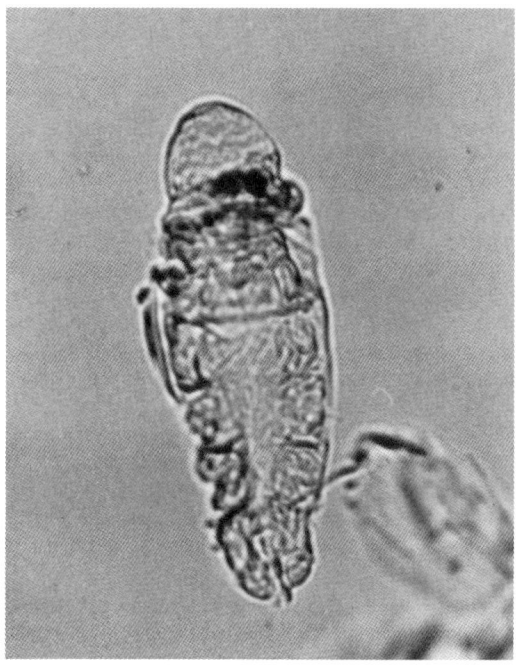

Fig 5. Adult male (A) and female (B) *Demodex cati* mites. Males are 182 μ long and females 219 μ long. (Courtesy of Dr. C. Desch and *Cornell Veterinarian*)

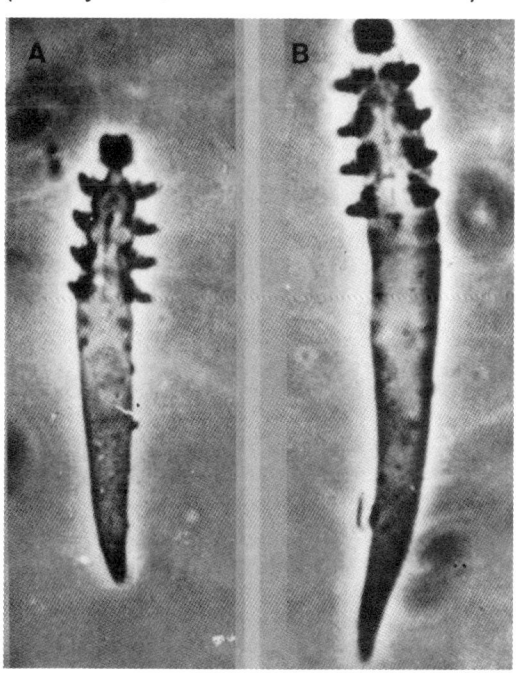

Otitis externa associated with *Demodex* has been treated successfully with ear drops composed of mineral oil and rotenone.[7] Rotenone has also proven effective on focal lesions on the pinnae but not on more generalized disease.[4,8,13] Focal lesions on younger animals often spontaneously regress, making evaluation of any treatment difficult.[7] Ivermectin is highly effective against notoedric and sarcoptic mange but has proven ineffective against demodectic mange.

Infection and Immunity

It has been suggested that virtually all cats are infested with *Demodex* spp when very young.[7] The question then arises as to why relatively few cats develop lesions. Small focal and self-limiting lesions in young cats can be explained by the relative immune incompetence of young animals as compared to older cats. Demodicosis in older cats has been often linked to concurrent or more serious disorders, such as diabetes mellitus and feline leukemia virus infection, feline endocrine alopecia, FIV infection or other debilitating conditions.[1,7,8,13,14] Such disorders can either potentiate infection by lowering immune competence or altering the microenvironment of the skin to favor mite growth.

Animal and Public Health Considerations

Demodex spp mites are apparently readily transmitted from adult to young animals shortly after birth. Very few infestations occur after kittenhood. The fact that most cats are asymptomatically infested limits the importance of clinically apparent carriers as sources of mites. There is no evidence that feline *Demodex* spp can infest people, who have their own resident species of mites.

References

1. Batey RG and Thompson RCA: Demodectic mange in a cat. *Aust Vet J* 57:49, 1981.

2. Conroy JD et al: New *Demodex* sp infesting a cat: A case report. *JAAHA* 18:405-407, 1982.

3. Desch C and Nutting WB: *Demodex cati* Hirst, 1919: A redescription. *Cornell Vet* 69:280-285, 1979.

4. Gabbert N and Feldman BF: Feline *Demodex*. *Feline Pract* 6(2):32-33, 1976.

5. Leydig F: Ueber Haarsackmilben und Krätzmilben. *Arch Natur Berlin* 1:338-354, 1859.

6. Nutting WB and Rausch H: *Demodex criceti*, with notes on its biology. *J Parasitol* 44:328-333, 1958.

7. Scott DW: Feline dermatology 1900-1978: A monograph. *JAAHA* 16:331-459, 1980.

8. Stogdale L and Moore DJ: Feline demodicosis. *JAAHA* 18:427-432, 1982.

9. Soulsby EJL: *Helminths, Arthropods and Protozoa of Domesticated Animals*. Lea & Febiger, Philadelphia, 1982. pp 482-486.

10. Trimmier BR: Demodicosis in a cat. *Southwestern Vet* 21:57-58, 1966.

11. Wilkinson GT: Demodicosis in a cat due to a new mite species. *Feline Pract* 13(6):32-41, 1983.

Additional References

12. Cowan LA and Campbell K: Generalized demodicosis in a cat responsive to amitraz. *JAVMA* 192:1442-1444, 1988.

13. Medleau L et al: Demodicosis in cats. *JAAHA* 24:85-91, 1988.

14. White SD et al: Generalized demodicosis associated with diabetes in two cats. *JAVMA* 191:448-450, 1987.

NOTOEDRIC MANGE

Etiologic Agent

Notoedric mange of cats is caused by a minute mite called *Notoedres cati*.[10] The mite belongs to the family Sarcoptidae, suborder Sarcoptiformes, class Arachnida. The life cycle of the mite resembles that of *Sarcoptes scabiei*. Cats are the primary host, but foxes, dogs and rabbits can also be infested.

Notoedres spp adults are 200-600 μ in diameter and females are about 50% larger than males (Fig 6). Female mites burrow into the skin and lay clutches of eggs along the burrow path (Fig 7). Eggs hatch in several days and produce 6-legged larvae that may move about in the skin and appear on the surface. Most larvae burrow into the stratum corneum, where they form so-called molting or larval pockets. Larvae transform to nymphs during molting. Nymphs can be differentiated from larvae by the presence of 8 legs and from adults by the absence of genital apertures. Adult mites appear 2-3 weeks after the eggs. Following mating, which usually occurs within molting pockets, females burrow out of the pockets and begin laying several eggs per day along the burrow path (Fig 7). Adult mites probably live 3-4 weeks. Adult, larval and nymphal mites feed on lymph and young epidermal cells.

Pathogenesis

Notoedric mange has been seen in cats in many areas of the world. However, it is sporadic or highly localized, even in enzootic areas. Infestation spreads mainly via wandering larvae, nymphs and young fertilized females. Mature and immature mites are short-lived off the host, probably surviving no more than several days. However, under proper conditions of humidity and temperature, they may survive several weeks.

Lesions of notoedric mange are caused by burrowing and feeding activities of mature

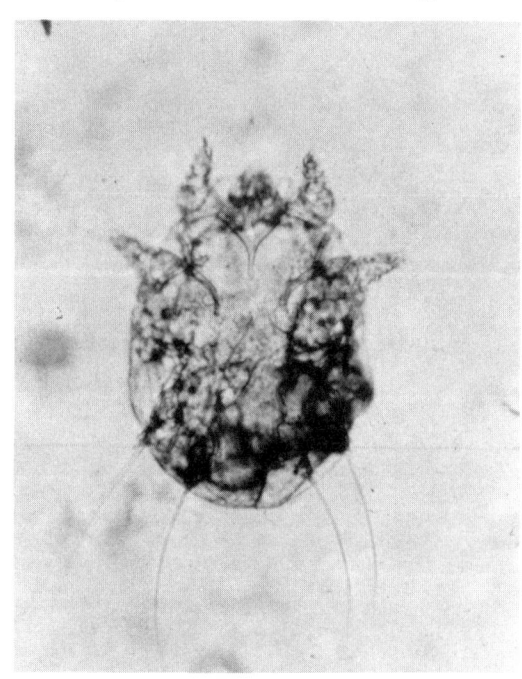

Fig 6. Adult *Notoedres cati* in a skin scraping from a cat. Adult mites are 0.2-0.6 mm long. (Courtesy of College of Veterinary Medicine, Texas A&M University)

and immature mites and host immune responses to mite proteins. Lesions are worsened by itching and scratching, especially several weeks after initial infestation, when immunity begins to develop.

Clinical Features

Lesions of notoedric mange occur initially on the medial tips of the ears and the back of the neck, then spread slowly to the face and eyelids. In severely affected animals, lesions may also be seen on the perineum and paws.[5] The whole body may be involved in young cats.[10] Affected skin is alopecic, thickened, wrinkled and covered with a yellowish to grayish crust. Lesions range from nonpruritic to highly irritating. Pruritus leads to a great deal of scratching, biting and self-mutilation, with secondary bacterial infections of the skin.

Pathologic Features

Microscopic changes include hyperkeratinization of the skin, with connective tissue proliferation. Sections of mites and eggs are frequently observed in the cornified layer of the epidermis. Lymphocytes, plasma cells, neutrophils, eosinophils and mast cells infiltrate the dermis and are usually associated with blood vessels.

Clinicopathologic Features

Notoedric mange is diagnosed by detecting eggs and immature and mature mites in skin scrapings (Figs 6,7). Scrapings should be as deep as possible without causing bleeding and should cover a wide area. Material is usually placed on a slide and mixed with water, glycerin or mineral oil before low-power (100X) microscopic examination.

Treatment and Prevention

Malathion dips have been recommended for treatment of cats with notoedric mange.[1] Cats are immersed for several seconds in a 0.25-1.25% suspension of malathion in water. This usually is repeated several times at 2-week intervals as long as lesions persist. Lime-sulfur (2.5%) shampoos repeated every 10-20 days for a month or so may also be effective. Fenchlorphos dips have also been effective in cats.[14] Clipping to remove hair, followed by a brief soap shampoo, helps remove scale and other impediments to drug penetration. Localized lesions may be treated topically with insecticide or sulfur-containing ointments or suspensions. A single topical treatment with amitraz (0.025%) has also been effective.[11] Ivermectin, given SC at 1000 µg/kg for 1-3 treatments 15-20 days apart, has been safe and effective for treating notoedric mange in cats.[7] Bigler and associates found a similar dose of ivermectin to be safe and efficacious in 17 cats treated only once.[13]

Infection and Immunity

Immune phenomena involved with notoedric mange in cats have not been reported. Cats appear to develop immunity to the mites over time because lesions often fail to progress beyond a certain point. In many cases lesions may actually regress. The shallow burrowing habits of the mites protect them from immune attack. Due to the nature of the stratum corneum, it is difficult for immune cells and antibodies to come into direct contact with mites.

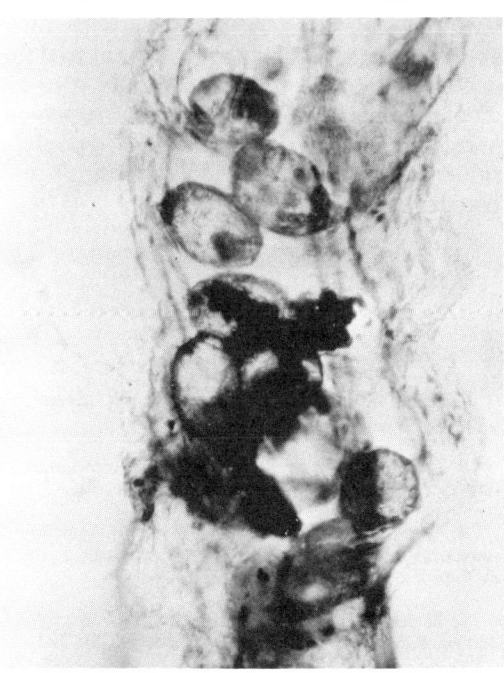

Fig 7. *Notoedres cati* eggs in a burrowed tunnel in a skin scraping from an infested cat. (Courtesy of College of Veterinary Medicine, Texas A&M University)

Lesions of notoedric mange appear to be caused by host immunity to mite antigens. Studies on sarcoptic mange in people and pigs demonstrate an absence of pruritus for the first 2-6 weeks.[4,7] After this time, urticarial reactions appear in the skin and pruritus becomes evident. The intensity of urticarial reactions appears related to the course of infestation. Animals with more severe urticarial reactions often recover more quickly than those with mild responses.[9]

Animal and Public Health Considerations

Notoedres cati is infectious mainly for cats and, to a lesser extent, rabbits.[10] People are not infested with the mite.

MISCELLANEOUS MANGE MITE INFESTATIONS

Sarcoptic Mange

Sarcoptes scabiei infestations are common in dogs but very rare in cats. The life cycle of the mite is similar to that of *Notoedres cati*.[10] Only 3 cases have been reported in the literature, 2 of which were clearly *S scabiei* infestations.[2,3,6] One of these cases involved an 8- to 10-week-old stray kitten with extensive hair loss over the ears, head, neck, abdomen, proximal limbs and tail.[3] The skin on the abdomen was scaly, thickened and wrinkled. The kitten was euthanized after *S scabiei* mites were identified on skin scrapings. Of 6 people in contact with the kitten, 4 developed sarcoptic-like lesions on the skin that responded to insecticidal medications.

The second case involved an emaciated, shocky and dehydrated female cat that was at least 6 years of age. The cat had a progressive skin disease of at least 12 months' duration but was only presented for examination when it became acutely ill. Yellowish-gray crusty lesions were present on the tail, caudal thighs and all of the feet. The nail beds were involved and the nails were deformed. Skin scrapings for parasites were unrewarding and the cat tested negative for feline leukemia virus (FeLV) by enzyme-linked immunosorbent assay (ELISA). The cat was rehydrated, given supportive treatment and sent home with prednisolone. Several days later, 2 people that handled the cat while it was in the hospital developed typical pruritic lesions of sarcoptic mange. The owner then also reported a history of a similar chronic skin disease. The cat was readmitted and *S scabiei* mites were found on both skin scrapings and biopsy. The cat failed to respond to treatment and was euthanized.

The highly generalized nature and rarity of sarcoptic mange in cats suggests that it occurs mainly in predisposed or immunosuppressed hosts.

The treatment of choice is lime-sulfur dips, or SC ivermectin at 400-1000 μg/kg for 3 treatments 15-20 days apart.

Poultry Mite Infestation

The red poultry mite, *Dermanyssus gallinae*, may occasionally prey on cats.[8] These mites live in poultry houses and feed mainly at night. In cats, the mites cause a papular and crusty type of pruritic dermatitis, usually about the face and lips.[8] Encrustations may resemble those associated with cheyletiellosis. Treatment is with lime-sulfur or other miticidal dips formulated for use on cats. The premises should also be treated because it is the primary reservoir of infestation and reinfestation. Red poultry mites occasionally infest dogs, pet birds and people.

References

1. English PR: Notoedric mange in cats with observations on treatment with malathion. *Aust Vet J* 36:85-88, 1960.

2. Hawkins JA *et al*: *Sarcoptes scabiei* infestation in cats. *JAVMA* 190:1572-1573, 1987.

3. Lindquist WD and Cash WC: Sarcoptic mange in a cat. *JAVMA* 162:639-640, 1973.

4. Mellanby K: The development of symptoms, parasitic infection and immunity in human scabies. *Parasitol* 35:197-206, 1944.

5. Muller GH *et al*: *Small Animal Dermatology*. 3rd ed. Saunders, Philadelphia, 1983. pp 360-363.

6. Orkin M et al, in Orkin M: *Scabies and Pediculosis.* Lippincott, Philadelphia, 1977. pp 108-116.

7. Quintavalla F et al: L'impegio della ivermectina nella rogna notoedrica del gatto. *Obiet Doc Vet* 6:85-86, 1985.

8. Scott DW, in Holzworth J: *Diseases of the Cat.* Saunders, Philadelphia, 1987. pp 619-675.

9. Sheahan BJ: Experimental *Sarcoptes scabiei* infection in pigs: Clinical signs and significance of infection. *Vet Record* 94:202-209, 1974.

10. Soulsby EJL: *Helminths, Arthropods and Protozoa of Domesticated Animals.* Lea & Febiger, Philadelphia, 1982. pp 482-486.

11. Wilkinson GT: An overview of feline skin diseases in Australia. *Proc Univ Sydney Postgrad Comm Vet Sci* 57:277, 1981.

12. Yazwinski TA et al: Efficacy of ivermectin against *Sarcoptes scabiei* and *Otodectes cynotis* infestation in dogs. *VM/SAC* 76:1749-1751, 1981.

Additional References

13. Bigler B et al: Erste er folguersprechende ergebnisse in der behandlung von *Notoedres cati* mit ivermectin. *Schweiz Arch Tierheilk* 126:365-367, 1984.

14. Sakaki S and Sakaki I: Treatment of scabies in cats and dogs with Fenchlorphos. *J Jpn Vet Med Assoc* 35:712-714, 1982.

FUR MITE INFESTATION

Etiologic Agent

The cat fur mite (*Lynxacarus radovski*) belongs to the family Listrophoridae, class Arachnida. It is the only member of the genus found on domestic cats. However, whether or not domestic cats are the true host of the mite has not been determined. It has not been found on rodents in areas where infested cats are found.[5] Infested cats have been reported from Puerto Rico, Florida, the Hawaiian Islands, Fiji and more tropical regions of Australia.[1-5] Adult, nymphal and egg stages of the mite are all found on the cat.[3,5] Adult mites attach themselves to the base of the hairs with paddle-like sternal appendages (Fig 8).[3] Adult and larval mites probably feed on secretions and exfoliations of the skin and hairs.

Cats apparently contact the fur mite through interactions with infested individuals. Pockets of infested cats have occurred in certain localities and on the same parcel of land.[1,5] In some situations, however, heavily infested cats have lived in the same households as uninfested individuals.[1]

Pathogenesis

Cat fur mites do not burrow into the skin. Lesions are found mainly on the coat.[1,2,3,5] There are exceptions, however. Cat fur mite infestations in cats in Fiji have reportedly been associated with scab-like skin lesions.[4]

Clinical Features

Mite infestations are usually generalized when first recognized.[1-5] The coat of infested cats is dry and lusterless, and affected hairs are easily epilated. The characteristic feature of mite infestation is a generalized "scurfiness" caused by a heavy "salt and pepper" deposition among the hairs. The salt and pepper-like flecks in the coat represent the actual mites. Pruritus and skin lesions have been largely absent from infested cats in Puerto Rico, Florida, Hawaii and Australia.[1-3,5]

Infestations of cats from Fiji appear somewhat more pathologic than infestations of cats from other countries.[5] Munro and Munro described cats with much less massive infestations of fur mites than reported for other areas.[4] However, the mites appeared identical to *L radovski*. Mites tended to concentrate around the tail, tailhead, perianal regions and thighs. In addition to the characteristic coat changes described in other reports, well-circumscribed scabby lesions of the adjacent skin were seen often. The condition was highly pruritic in cats from Fiji. Careful examinations for other parasites or concomitant skin diseases were unrewarding, and lesions disappeared after treatment of the mites.

Pathologic Features

Gross pathologic lesions are limited mainly to the coat. Secondary excoriations

Fig 8. Lateral (A) and ventral (B) views of the cat fur mite, *Lynxacarus radovski*, adhered to feline hair shafts. (Courtesy of Dr. J. Greve and *Feline Practice*)

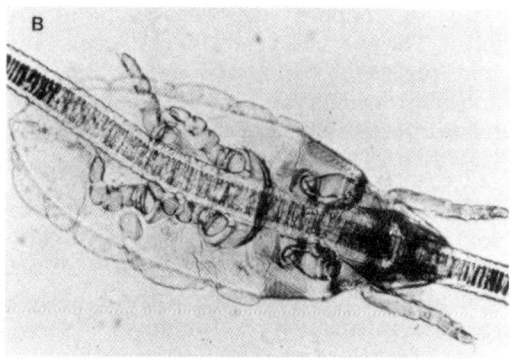

and bacterial infections of the skin may accompany the disease in pruritic animals.

Clinicopathologic Features

Characteristic mites can be seen under low-power (100X) magnification at the base of affected hairs (Fig 8).[1,3,5]

Treatment and Prevention

Mites appear sensitive to 5% carbaryl powder or lime-sulfur dips.[1,5] Other insecticidal dips commonly used on cats would probably also be effective. Several dips may be required to kill all of the mites.[1,5]

Infection and Immunity

The mites do not invade the epidermis, so probably very little immunity is elicited against them. However, there is some indication that cats debilitated with other illnesses may be more susceptible to infestations. Two infested cats from Florida also had chronic debilitating diseases (pyothorax and congestive heart failure).[3] The epidemiology of the disease in Hawaii resembles that of FIV infection, suggesting a possible relationship between the two diseases.

Animal and Public Health Considerations

Cat fur mites do not infest people. The ability of the mite to spread readily from cat to cat is also uncertain. Cases within a locality or premises are sporadic at best, and housemates of some severely infested individuals have not been infested.[1,3,5]

References

1. Bowman WL and Domrow R: The cat fur mite (*Lynxacarus radovski*) in Australia. *Aust Vet J* 54:403-404, 1978.

2. Fox I: *Felistrophorus*, a new genus of mites on cats in Puerto Rico. *Proc Entomol Soc Wash* 79:242-244, 1977.

3. Greve JH and Gerrish RR: Fur mites (*Lynxacarus*) from cats in Florida. *Feline Pract* 11(6):28-30, 1981.

4. Munro R and Munro HMC: *Lynxacarus* on cats in Fiji. *Aust Vet J* 55:90, 1979.

5. Tenorio JN: A new species of *Lynxacarus* from *Felis catus* in the Hawaiian Islands. *J Med Entomol* 11:599-603, 1974.

PEDICULOSIS
(LICE INFESTATION)

Etiologic Agent

Felicola subrostratus is the principal louse of cats. It belongs to the class Insecta, order Mallophaga, suborder Ischnocera.[3] It is a relatively small wingless insect with a dorsoventrally flattened body (Fig 9). *Trichodectes canis*, the dog louse, may also rarely parasitize kittens and aged cats in poor condition.[4]

The life cycle of *F subrostratus* is direct. Adults live on the host and feed on superficial secretions and layers of the epidermis with the aid of biting mouthparts. Eggs, or nits, are attached to the base of hair shafts. After hatching, the nymphal mites undergo 3 molts before becoming adults. Nymphal mites resemble smaller versions of the adults. The period between hatching and adulthood is about 3-4 weeks.

Pathogenesis

Infestations of cats with biting lice are very uncommon. When they occur, they usually involve older, anemic or debilitated animals.[2] Biting lice spread from cat to cat by close contact, or on such fomites as hair, combs or brushes.

Clinical Features

Affected cats may be asymptomatic or mildly to intensely pruritic. Nits and adult lice appear as fine dandruff in the coat. Pruritus is often accompanied by hair loss, excoriations and hyperkeratosis.

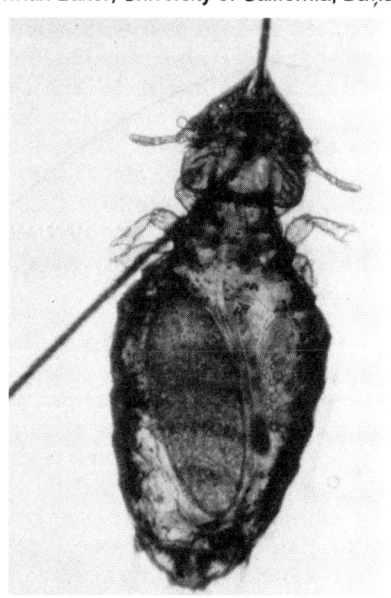

Fig 9. Adult female biting louse, *Felicola subrostratus*, from an infested cat. Note the ovum within the mite's abdomen. Adults are about 0.1 mm long. (Courtesy of Dr. Norman Baker, University of California, Davis)

Pathologic Features

Skin lesions are largely secondary to scratching and biting.

Clinicopathologic Features

Biting lice are difficult to visualize without magnification. When magnified, they are of characteristic morphology (Fig 9).

Treatment and Prevention

Biting lice of cats are easily killed with carbaryl- or dioxathion-based sprays, powders or shampoos.[1]

Infection and Immunity

Massive and clinically significant infestations often occur on animals that are debilitated from other disease.[2,4] This is the general pattern for all ectoparasitic infestations of cats. It appears, therefore, that grooming or immunologic factors may play a role in resistance.

Animal and Public Health Considerations

Felicola subrostratus is infectious mainly for cats. It is not a normal pathogen of people or other domesticated animals.

References

1. Georgi JR: *Parasitology for Veterinarians.* Saunders, Philadelphia, 1985. p 145.

2. Scott DW, in Holzworth J: *Diseases of the Cat.* Saunders, Philadelphia, 1985. p 665.

3. Soulsby EJL: *Helminths, Arthropods and Protozoa of Domesticated Animals.* Lea & Febiger, Philadelphia, 1982. pp 365-370.

4. Wilkinson GT: *Diseases of the Cat and Their Management.* Blackwell Scientific Publications, Melbourne, 1983.

FLEA INFESTATION

Etiologic Agent

Fleas are wingless insects belonging to the order Siphonaptera, class Insecta. They are about 1.5-4 mm long and have a chitin-

Fig 10. Various stages in the life cycle of the cat flea, *Ctenocephalides felis*. Maggot-like larvae (A) are found free in the cat's environment. The pupa (B) is very sticky and accumulates a coating of debris, which makes it difficult to distinguish from house dust. The adult (C) is the most likely form to be found on an infested cat. (Courtesy of Dr. Lorry Dunning, University of California, Davis)

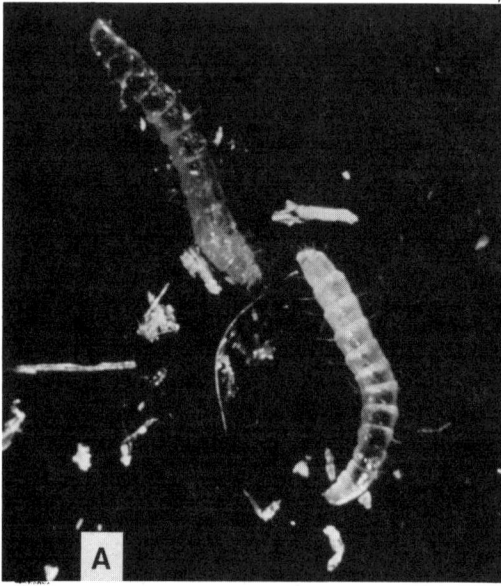

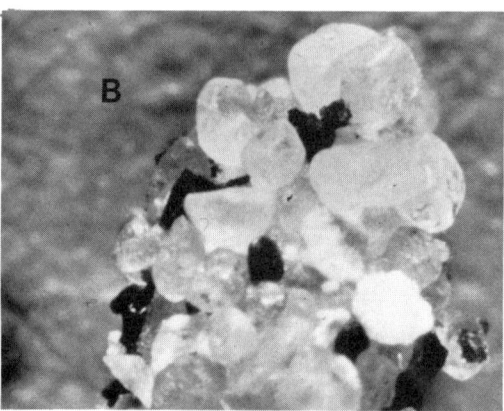

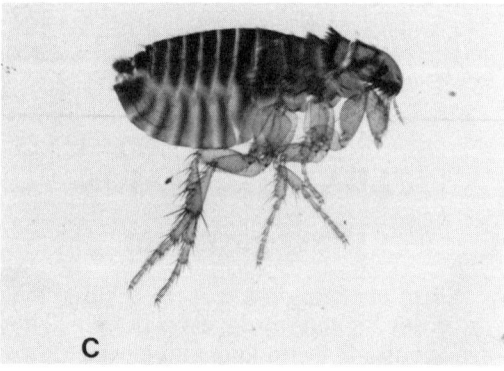

ous covering. Their long strong legs are well adapted to jumping and for continuous movement between their hosts and the environment.

Ctenocephalides felis is the principal flea of cats. This species is composed of 4 subspecies: *C felis felis*, which occurs on cats, dogs and occasionally people, mice, rats and primates; *C felis strongylus*, which occurs in Africa; *C felis damarensis*, which occurs in southwestern Africa; and *C felis orientalis*, which is found mainly in India, Sri Lanka and southeast Asia.[14] Cats may also be infested with the dog flea (*C canis*) and human flea (*Pulex irritans*).

Adult fleas live on the skin of the cat and obtain nutrients by sucking blood. Most of the adult fleas' life is spent on the animal.[2] After mating, female fleas lay 400-500 eggs during their lifetime. Eggs are laid in clutches of 20 or more while the females are off the host. After egg laying, fleas return to the cat for feeding until the next egg-laying cycle. Adult fleas live 58 days off the host if fed, and 234 days if unfed.[14] Eggs are usually laid in the dust and dirt in carpeting, bedding or yards. Larvae hatch in 2-16 days, depending on temperature and humidity. Larval fleas are maggot-like and feed on organic matter (Fig 10). Flea feces, which are rich in nutrients and continually shed from the coat of infested animals, may be a particularly good source of nutrition. Within about 10 days, mature maggots spin a cocoon that quickly becomes camouflaged by dust and debris adhering to its sticky surface (Fig 10). The pupal stage lasts from 10-17 days to several months, depending on temperature and humidity. Young fleas then emerge and jump onto a cat, where they feed and complete their life cycle (Fig 10). The remainder of their lives is spent on and off the cat.

Pathogenesis

Fleas are found throughout the world but are particularly prevalent in warmer and more humid climates. Extremely cold or hot and dry climates limit accumulations of fleas by killing or impeding development of both adult and immature forms. Fleas have adapted for survival and reproduction both within dwellings and in the environment. Seasonality may be less evident when animals are continuously kept in air-conditioned environments. Extremely large flea accumulations can occur when climate, humidity and host numbers are favorable. Therefore, fleas are more apt to be a problem within catteries, multiple-cat households, or urban and suburban environments where climate and humidity are favorable and the feline population is dense.

Clinical Signs

Clinical signs associated with flea infestations vary greatly, depending on numbers of fleas and whether or not the animal becomes hypersensitized (allergic) to flea saliva. Severe anemia and death have been associated with massive flea infestations in kittens. Such infestations are more apt to be seen among confined cat populations. The anemia in such infestations is of the blood-loss type and is associated with the feeding of adult fleas.

Fig 11. Back of a cat with severe, chronic flea-bite hypersensitivity dermatitis. The skin is thickened, darkly pigmented, scabby and depilated. Secondary bacterial infection may be manifested as pustules.

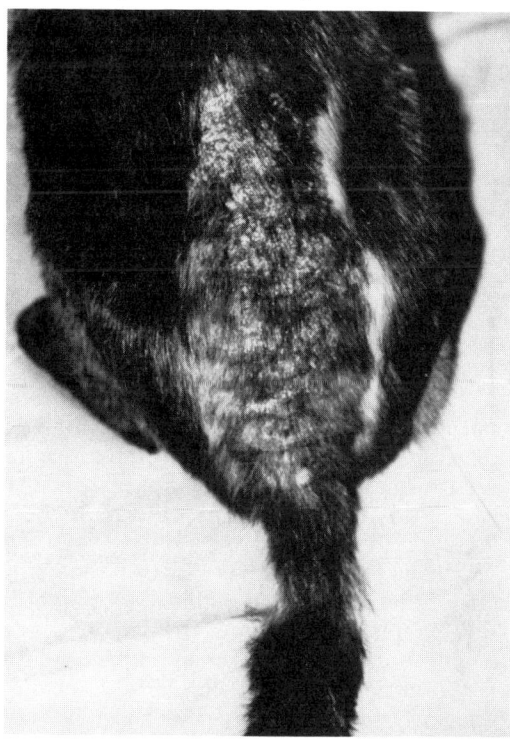

Most healthy cats that are infested with fleas maintain a small and relatively stable resident population and do not show adverse clinical signs. The natural grooming behavior of cats usually keeps numbers of fleas at a minimum, providing that the flea population in the environment is not overwhelming. However, if cats become sick for any reason and stop grooming, flea numbers on the cat can greatly increase. Excessive numbers of feeding fleas can further drain an ill cat of energy and contribute to the overall disease.

Cats that become allergic to flea bites show considerably more clinical signs, the severity of which depends on the degree of hypersensitivity and numbers of feeding fleas. Flea allergies usually develop in cats after 3 years of age.[16] Initial lesions consist of small erythematous papules on the skin at the site of flea bites. These are most prevalent around the tailhead, inner thighs, abdomen, and head and neck. Lesions are usually pruritic. Lesions resemble those described for miliary dermatitis; 55% of cats presented with miliary dermatitis in one study were suffering from flea-bite hypersensitivity.[16] Appearance of the lesion can be greatly altered by self-excoriation and secondary bacterial infection due to chewing, biting and scratching. In severe and chronic infestations on sensitized animals, the involved skin becomes thickened, crusty, scabby, darkened and alopecic (Fig 11). Peripheral lymphadenopathy is common in such animals.[16]

Pathologic Features

Gross and histologic lesions are seen only in cats that have developed allergic dermatitis. The most consistent microscopic lesions are hyperkeratosis and dermal infiltrates of lymphocytes, plasma cells, eosinophils and mast cells. The lymphadenopathy of flea-bite hypersensitivity is characterized by lymphoid and plasma cell hyperplasia and eosinophilic cell infiltrate.[16]

Clinicopathologic Features

Flea infestations are easily diagnosed by close examination of the skin and coat for adult fleas or flea feces. In mild infestations, fleas and flea feces may be hard to visualize. Diagnosis can be facilitated by vigorously rubbing the coat while the animal is standing over a moistened white paper towel. After 30 seconds or so, the paper towel is examined for small black specks, which are flea feces. Within a minute or longer, reddish discoloration emanates from the specks due to dissolution of the blood in the flea feces.

Cats with severe flea allergic dermatitis often have mild to severe eosinophilia that is proportional to the chronicity and severity of the skin lesions.[16] Polyclonal hypergammaglobulinemia may be seen in severely affected animals.

The use of intradermal skin testing for flea allergic dermatitis has been reviewed by Scott.[16] It appears to have more value for diagnosing flea allergies in cats than it does for desensitization.

Treatment and Prevention

Treatment and prevention of flea infestations require patience, persistence and expense. Control of fleas on premises should be directed to 4 areas: controlling flea populations by environmental manipulation; killing adult fleas on all host animals; destroying adult and larval flea populations within the home; and killing adult fleas in surrounding yards.

Several studies have dealt with survival of adult and immature fleas in the environment and how environmental factors apply to flea control. Temperature and relative humidity are the 2 most important environmental variables for flea growth and survival. Adults and immature forms survive best in warm, but not exceptionally hot, environments with high relative humidity. Bruce reported 90-99% survival of cat fleas at ambient temperatures of 21-32 C (70-89 F) and 80% relative humidity.[5] Adult emergence from pupae was almost totally inhibited when relative humidity fell below 45% and ambient temperatures were ≥ 32.2 C (≥ 89 F). Silverman and co-workers found that the lower and upper ambient temperature limits for optimal flea development were 13 C (55 F) and 32 C (89 F), respectively.[13] Relative humidities from 50% to 92% within this temperature range resulted in >80% flea egg hatch, 100% larval development and 90% pupal survival.

However, these findings on optimum temperature and humidity do not explain flea survival in semi-arid climates. In a second study, Silverman and Rust found that pupae survived outdoors most of the year in semi-arid southern California, except for July and August, when ambient temperatures often exceeded 35 C (96 F) and relative humidities were low.[12] They also found that pupal survival decreased dramatically at ambient temperatures as low as 27 C (81 F) when relative humidities fell below 33%. At 27 C (81 F), relative humidities of 12% and 33% killed 97% and 100% of pupae, respectively, over a period as short as 16 hours. However, larval survival at warmer ambient temperatures was greatly increased when humidity of the air or microenvironment rose above 50%. Larvae could also survive in the ground at high temperatures and low relative humidity if soil moisture was 1-10%. However, soil moistures from 20% to 50% were deleterious. Exposure to ambient temperatures from -1 C (30 F) to 3 C (37 F) killed all immature stages of the flea within 5-10 days, respectively.

Osbrink and co-workers also studied flea populations in southern California.[15] They found more fleas in living rooms and bedrooms, and in carpeted rooms more than in uncarpeted rooms. Fleas were found in the yards of only 8/50 infested residences. Flea control should be concentrated in areas where most fleas are found.

Knowledge of the optimum ambient temperatures and relative humidity for flea development can be used in some areas for environmental flea control. For instance, in semi-arid and arid regions, catteries should be kept dry. Yards around the catteries should be planted with vegetation requiring as little irrigation as possible. Lawns should not be planted around the cattery, and swamp water coolers should not be used for air-conditioning. Cats should be kept outdoors in open catteries rather than indoors. Indoor environments are often cooler and more humid because of air conditioning and other factors (running water, washing, cooking, toilets, baths, poor ventilation, respiration, etc).

In cooler regions, the ambient temperature in the cattery should be maintained as low as possible. Cats easily acclimate to ambient temperatures as low as 55 F, which inhibit flea growth. However, flea control by environmental manipulation is virtually impossible if cats are maintained in homes. People usually maintain the home environment at a temperature and humidity that is comfortable to them and ideal for flea development, thus negating any beneficial effect of outside temperature and humidity.

Fleas on host animals can usually be killed with appropriate insecticidal powders, sprays or shampoos. Active ingredients within these preparations vary greatly. New insecticides are also continuously being developed and incorporated into flea-control products. Preparation changes are mandated mainly by safety to cats and developing drug resistance of fleas. Drug resistance occurs commonly, thus necessitating incorporation of new insecticides.

Insecticides are generally active against adult fleas (adulticides) or larvae (larvicides). Adulticides currently used belong to 1 of 4 groups of drugs: carbamates, organophosphates, chlorinated hydrocarbons and botanical compounds.[8] Carbamates are cholinesterase inhibitors, which fortunately are more toxic to fleas than to host animals. The 2 most commonly used carbamates in cats are carbaryl and propoxur. Carbaryl is a common insecticide in garden powders. It has a relatively low toxicity for cats but tends to stain the fur, furniture and rugs. Propoxur is popular in many commercial flea preparations and has a good residual action.

Organophosphates are also cholinesterase inhibitors. Organophosphates used in cats include dichlorvos (a component of many flea collars), dioxathion, malathion, naled, phosmet, ronnel, temephos and tetrachlorovinphos. Organophosphates tend to be much more toxic to cats than carbamates, even though their mode of action is similar. Though they are used routinely in cats, careful attention must be given to concentration of the compounds used, total amount applied, and amount of residual insecticide on the fur. Toxic signs include vomiting, diarrhea, sweating, dyspnea, miosis and, in severe cases, death. Atropine sulfate at 0.2 mg/kg IM is considered the best of readily available antidotes for organophosphate or carbamate poisoning. Poisoned cats should also be thoroughly washed to remove residual insecticide on the fur.

Fenthion (20%) is being increasingly used for flea control in cats. About 0.3 ml is applied to the top of the head, behind the ears, or in the ears. This is repeated every 1-2 weeks initially, then every 4-6 weeks as needed to keep the cats flea free. The use of such a potent organophosphate in cats is questionable. Signs of organophosphate poisoning are subtle at this dosage but nevertheless common. Deaths have been reported in catteries using fenthion in this manner. These may have resulted, however, from incorrect dosage of the drug. Chronic neurotoxicity has been reported in people exposed to fenthion, as well as other potent organophosphates. Dogs may develop a similar syndrome after brief or prolonged use of fenthion.

Chlorinated hydrocarbons are selectively more neurotoxic to fleas than to host animals. Many forms of chlorinated hydrocarbons, such as DDT or chlordane, are no longer permitted in many countries because of environmental hazards. Lindane and methoxychlor are 2 chlorinated hydrocarbons that are still used for flea control in cats. Other environmentally acceptable chlorinated hydrocarbons are considered too toxic for animals. Similar to organophosphates, chlorinated hydrocarbons have a lower safety margin for cats than other species. Serious toxicities have even been seen in some cats following use of approved products. Toxic signs include hyperexcitability, inappetence, muscle weakness, tremors, convulsions, paralysis and death. Mildly toxic animals should be treated with diazepam; more severely affected animals should be treated with phenobarbital. The fur should also be thoroughly washed to eliminate drug residues.

Botanical compounds are of plant origin and include rotenone, d-limonene and pyrethrin. D-limonene has not proven nearly as efficacious as have the pyrethrins.[16] Synthetic pyrethrin-like compounds include allethrin, d-trans allethrin, fenvalerate, d-phenothrin, resmethrin and tetramethrin. Both natural and synthetic compounds in this class have a high margin of safety. Potency and residual effect of natural pyrethrins can be "potentiated" by addition of piperonyl butoxide. Some synthetic pyrethrins are naturally potentiated.[8]

The effectiveness of many adulticides has been limited by emergence of drug-resistant strains of fleas. This is especially true for carbamates and chlorinated hydrocarbons. Pyrethrins and pyrethrin-like compounds are much less likely to evoke drug resistance. Resistant strains of fleas are usually found in areas where flea populations accumulate all year and use of insecticides is heavy. Due to problems with low drug resistance of and toxicity to cats, natural and synthetic pyrethrins are preferred. Their organic or "natural" composition also makes them much more acceptable to people concerned with environmental accumulation of toxic chemicals. A potentiated or long-acting pyrethrin compound should be applied to infested cats every 3-7 days during the flea season in temperate climates and throughout the year in more tropical areas.

Adult and larval fleas that are living in the environment, usually in carpeting, bedding and dusty areas, should also be eliminated with appropriate insecticides. If possible, this should be done by experienced pest exterminators. Nevertheless, various compounds incorporating both adulticides and larvicides are available as over-the-counter preparations for home use. These various preparations are administered as powders, sprays or aerosol "bombs" that can be set off after the house is temporarily vacated of people and animals. Adulticides used indoors usually kill fleas quickly but have a short residual action. However, the larvicide portion of such preparations usually has a very long residual effect. The most popular larvicide is a synthetic hormone called methoprene.[4] This compound has a residual effect of 75-90 days and prevents pupation of fourth-stage larvae. Methoprene is virtually nontoxic for other living organisms, including adult fleas and flea eggs. Home environments should be retreated with adulticide-larvicide combinations every 75 days during the flea season in seasonal areas and all year in more tropical climates. Methoprene combined with pyrothins has proven completely effective in controlling fleas within homes.[15]

Fleas in surrounding yards can be killed with chlorpyrifos or diazinon. Both have relatively long residual effects. Diazinon is also available in microencapsulated form. Malathion is also effective against fleas but has a very short residual effect. Yards should be treated 3 times at 10- to 14-day intervals during the height of flea season or all year in more tropical climates.

Flea repellents have emerged again as a popular means to control fleas. Early preparations were not highly effective and quite messy to use. Recently, however, more effective and aesthetically pleasing preparations have been developed. Contrary to common myths, fleas are not repelled by feeding brewers' yeast or thiamin.[1,6] Use of flea repellents in a good flea-control program is questionable. The object of flea control is to lower numbers, not merely redistribute fleas from 1 animal to another. It is also highly unlikely that any flea repellent will be 100% effective, especially in areas with large flea numbers. Repellents may be most helpful in limiting the numbers of fleas that cats bring into the home from outside.

Persistent treatment of fleas on the animals and in the home and environment can greatly reduce flea problems. In more temperate climates, such methods may effectively eliminate the problem. In more tropical areas, where fleas are rampant and drug resistance is high, control is less successful even when rigorously applied. Moreover, many people are not prepared to expend the time and money required to continuously control fleas in highly enzootic areas. In these areas, it is important to prevent fleas from initially entering the environment. Cat owners moving into flea-free homes and environments should maintain flea control at all times and not wait until infestation occurs. This is especially true in tropical climates where flea problems can sometimes be overwhelming. The problem of flea control in these areas is compounded by cats roaming outside and large flea-infested feral cat populations.

When it is impossible to eliminate fleas from the environment of animals suffering from flea-bite allergies, the skin itself may require direct treatment. This has been approached in 2 ways: treatment of the allergy with drugs, usually glucocorticoids; and desensitization of the animal with injections of flea proteins. Drug treatment usually consists of prednisolone or prednisone at an initial dosage of 2-4 mg/kg daily for 7-14 days, then 2 mg/kg every other day. Once the condition is under control, the lowest possible dosage of glucocorticoid should be used to maintain remission. Cats are reportedly much easier to desensitize with flea-antigen extracts than dogs.[10,11] However, such optimism has not been borne out by well-controlled double-blind hyposensitization trials in cats.[7,16] Therefore, desensitization should still be considered as an experimental approach to the control of flea allergic dermatitis in cats.

Infection and Immunity

The absolute number of fleas on any given animal often remains constant; however, flea numbers differ greatly from cat to cat. This implies that some cats are naturally more resistant to fleas than others; the nature of this immunity is not known. Flea numbers on cats increase dramatically when they become ill and stop grooming. Whether fleas are ingested during grooming or inhibited by proteinaceous products in saliva has not been determined.

Flea allergic dermatitis is caused by a hypersensitivity response to flea saliva. Haptens within flea saliva are apparently bound to dermal proteins.[9] Antigenically altered dermal proteins are immunogenic and elicit a host immune response. Studies on guinea pigs show that the earliest host immune response to flea antigens is of an immediate type and is probably mediated by reaginic (IgE) and precipitating (IgG) antibodies.[3] This is followed shortly thereafter by a cell-mediated, delayed-hypersensitivity response. With continued flea exposure, many guinea pigs become desensitized to flea antigens.[3] Whether or not cats go through a similar sequence of events has not been determined. Most cats do not become allergic to fleas. This suggests that most animals either do not initially respond immunologically or are desensitized by natural exposure. Factors that cause some animals, and not others, to become sensitized to fleas have not been determined.

Animal and Public Health Considerations

Cat fleas can be a major problem to dogs that live in the same environment. Dogs appear much more susceptible to flea-bite allergies than cats. Therefore, it is common to have households of animals in which the cats serve as reservoirs while the dogs suffer most with clinical disease. Cat fleas are also the principal intermediate host of the dog and cat tapeworm, *Dipylidium caninum*. Repeated infection with this

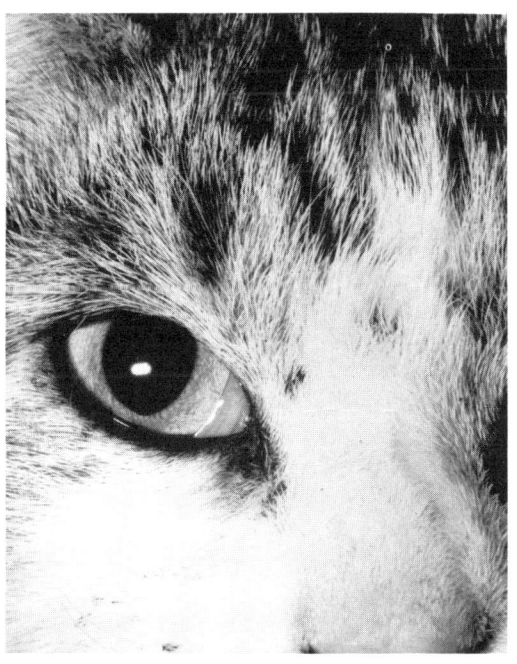

Fig 12. Stick-tight fleas near the medial canthus and over the bridge of the nose. Stick-tight fleas attach themselves firmly to the skin. Their blood-engorged bodies are readily apparent on close inspection. (Courtesy of Dr. Peter Ihrke, University of California, Davis)

tapeworm is inevitable as long as fleas exist in the same environment.

Cat fleas attack people when other suitable hosts are not available. Human bites most often occur when a flea-infested house has been left vacated of people and animals for several weeks or more. People returning from a vacation or moving into such a home or apartment may be greeted by a hungry population of fleas. Bites occur around the ankles and lower legs. People can also become sensitized to flea bites, and repeated exposure may elicit large and highly pruritic lesions.

STICK-TIGHT FLEA INFESTATION

Cats are occasionally infected with the "stick-tight" flea of poultry or birds, *Echidnophaga gallinacea*.[14] These large fleas often adhere to the skin in clusters on the face (Fig 12). Cats apparently become infested when they prey on birds or fowl. *Echidnophaga gallinacea* can be readily differentiated from common cat fleas because of their "stick-tight" nature when inspected and prodded. The fleas can be manually removed, or destroyed with an appropriate insecticidal powder or spray.

References

1. Baker NF and Farver TB: Failure of Brewer's yeast as a repellent to fleas on dogs. *JAVMA* 183:212-214, 1983.

2. Baker N: Musing the relationship between a dog and its fleas. *VM/SAC* 79:1037-1039, 1984.

3. Benjamini E *et al*: Skin reactivity in guinea-pigs sensitized to flea bites. The sequence of reactions. *Proc Soc Exp Biol Med* 108:700-702, 1961.

4. Bledsoe B *et al*: Current therapy and new developments in indoor flea control. *JAAHA* 18:415-422, 1982.

5. Bruce WW: Studies on the biological requirements of the cat flea. *Ann Entomol Soc Am* 61:346-352, 1948.

6. Halliwell REW: Ineffectiveness of thiamine (Vitamin B_1) as a flea repellent in dogs. *JAAHA* 18:423-426, 1982.

7. Kunkle GA and Milcarsky J: Double-blind flea hyposensitization trial in cats. *JAVMA* 186:677-680, 1985.

8. Melman SA and Hutton P: Flea control on dogs and cats indoors and in the environment. *Comp Cont Ed Pract Vet* 7:869-880, 1985.

9. Michaeli DI *et al*: The role of collagen in the induction of flea bite hypersensitivity. *J Immunol* 95:162-170, 1965.

10. Michaeli DI and Goldfarb S: Clinical studies on the hyposensitisation of dogs and cats to flea bites. *Aust Vet J* 44:161-165, 1968.

11. Reedy LM: Use of flea antigen in treatment of feline flea allergic dermatitis. *VM/SAC* 70:703-704, 1975.

12. Silverman J and Rust MK: Some abiotic factors affecting the survival of the cat flea, *Ctenocephalides felis*. *Environ Entomol* 12:490-495, 1983.

13. Silverman J *et al*: Influence of temperature and humidity on survival and development of the cat flea, *Ctenocephalides felis*. *J Med Entomol* 18:78-83, 1981.

14. Soulsby EJL: *Helminths, Arthropods and Protozoa of Domesticated Animals*. Lea & Febiger, Philadelphia, 1982. pp 378-384.

Additional References

15. Osbrink WLA *et al*: Distribution and control of cat fleas in homes in Southern California (Siphonaptera: Pulicidae). *J Econ Entomol* 79:135-140, 1986.

16. Scott DW: Feline dermatology 1983-1985: "The secret sits." *JAAHA* 23:255-274, 1987.

Chapter 58

Protozoal Infections

Protozoa are unicellular organisms that are 5-250 μ in size. They are structurally similar to animal cells, possessing a plasma membrane, mitochondria, endoplasmic reticulum, ribosomes and Golgi apparatus. Protozoa have made many structural adaptations. Some can change their plasma membrane into a thick, protective cyst wall. Many have acquired means to travel through their environment, which is usually fluid. Pseudopods are temporary extensions of the cell wall through which cytoplasm streams, thus propelling the organism slowly forward. Flagella and cilia are microtubular structures rooted in a basal body at one end of the organism and may be free or attached to the body wall, forming veil-like undulating membranes. Movement by use of flagella and cilia is very rapid.

Protozoa that are pathogenic to animals receive most of their nutrition from metabolic products of host cells. The exception is intestinal protozoal parasites that can use products of digestion. Protozoa receive their nutrients by pinocytosis or through mouth-like openings. Intracellular protozoal parasites receive nutrition through diffusion.

Most protozoa reproduce by binary fission. In some genera, internal division can occur without cytoplasmic separation, leading to large multinucleated structures. Sexual reproduction is also seen in some genera, accomplished by fusion of 2 diploid organisms, with rearrangement of genetic material during subsequent division of each member of the pair. Reduction division, leading to formation of haploid male and female gametes, is seen in some protozoa.

Most important protozoan parasites of domestic cats are in the phyla Sarcomastigophora and Apicomplexa. Sarcomastigophora contains the suborder Diplomonadina, genus *Giardia*. Apicomplexa contains the orders Eucoccidiida and Piroplasmida. Eucoccidiida contains the genera *Cystisospora, Toxoplasma, Sarcocystis, Hammondia, Cryptosporidium* and *Besnoitia*. Piroplasmida contains the genera *Babesia* and *Cytauxzoon*.

COCCIDIOSIS

Etiologic Agents

Coccidiosis is a term used to describe intestinal infections caused by a number of different coccidia. Species of coccidia infecting cats belong to the family Sarcocystidae, genera *Isospora, Hammondia, Besnoitia* and *Sarcocystis*. However, classification of these organisms changes rapidly over time. *Hammondia* spp and *Besnoitia* spp, along with *Toxoplasma* spp, have also been grouped together in a proposed family Toxoplasmatinae because of similarities in developmental stages and structure. Frenkel has also proposed that *Isospora* spp, such as *I felis*, be classified in a new genus called *Cystispora*.[8] Changes in names and classification can be expected as more is learned about individual coccidia. Table 1 lists the currently recognized species that have cats as their definitive host.[10]

Various species of intestinal coccidia are found in cats throughout the world. In a survey of cats in Illinois, Kansas, Missouri, Ohio and Hawaii, Dubey found 0-1.5% were infected with coccidia that appeared similar to *Toxoplasma* spp or *Hammondia* spp, 6-22% with *I felis*, 3-22% with *I rivolta*, and 0-0.8% with *Sarcocystis* spp. The infection rate within closely confined groups of cats is often much higher because of poor sanitation, overcrowding and stress. Wilkinson observed subclinical infection with *I felis* in 49 of 58 cats in a single colony.[15]

Cats are infected with *Isospora* spp by ingesting sporulated oocysts (shed by other cats) or by eating tissues of prey animals that contain encysted forms of the organism.[2,4,6,9] Infectivity and developmental stages are similar whether cats are infected by oocysts or cysts. However, when oocysts are the source of infection, organisms appear in the feces 12-48 hours later.[4] Infectious forms released from the cysts or oocysts infect intestinal mucosal cells and undergo several cycles of asexual replication. This is followed by sexual replication culminating in shedding of unsporulated oocysts. Oocysts sporulate in the environment within a day or less under optimum conditions. Extraintestinal spread to the liver, spleen, mesenteric lymph nodes, brain and muscle occurs in cats, but is not clinically significant.[5] Extraintestinal forms in cats consist of poorly staining bradyzoites. Mammalian intermediate hosts are infected upon ingestion of sporulated oocysts. Limited replication occurs and cysts are formed within the intestinal wall, mesenteric lymph nodes or other extraintestinal sites. Organisms cease replication upon encystation; each cyst contains a single large bradyzoite.

Besnoitia spp and *Hammondia* spp differ from *Isospora* spp in their absolute requirement for a nonfeline intermediate host.[2,13] Cats can only be infected by eating encysted forms of the organism and not by ingestion of sporulated oocysts. Tachyzoites are also not infectious to cats; only animals containing mature cysts are infectious.[6] Sporozoites of *Hammondia* spp invade cells within the lamina propria, muscularis mucosae and Peyer's patches of the intestine and mesenteric lymph nodes. Sporozoites of *Besnoitia* spp invade cells within the omentum, mesentery, ileum and cecum. The typical sexual stages of coccidial replication occur in the cat following ingestion of infected prey. Unsporulated oocysts appear in the feces 5-9 days after ingestion of cysts and are shed for 1-2 weeks or longer. An extraintestinal phase of replication leading to cyst formation does not occur to any extent in cats.

Sarcocystis spp differ from other species of coccidia because bradyzoites infect mucosal cells of cats and undergo gametogony without prior asexual replica-

Table 1. Species of coccidia with sexual stages in cats and intermediate other stages in species of animals.

Genus and Species	Recognized Intermediate Hosts
Besnoitia besnoiti	cattle
B wallacei	rodents
B darlingi	opossums, reptiles
Hammondia hammondi	rodents
H pardalis	rodents
Isospora felis	many species of mammals
I rivolta	many species of mammals
Sarcocystis bovifelis	cattle
S caniculi	rabbits
S fusiformis	buffalo
S gigantea	sheep
S horvathi	chickens
S leporum	rabbits
S medusiformis	sheep
S muris	rodents
S porcifelis	swine
S symruensis	rodents
Sarcocystis spp	gazelles, chickens

tion.[2] Oocysts contain 2 (rather than 4) sporocysts. Sporocysts are often released from oocysts within the alimentary tract of cats and are frequently found free in feces (Fig 1). Free sporocysts, each containing 4 sporozoites, are infectious for intermediate hosts immediately after being passed in the feces. Unlike other coccidia, shedding of oocysts is very prolonged, lasting 60 days or longer.[11,12] Infection of intermediate hosts can be particularly widespread and severe. Sporozoites are liberated in the intestine and asexual replication occurs in endothelial and periendothelial cells throughout the body. Second- and third-generation merozoites (tachyzoites) form cysts in the tissues of intermediate hosts. Immature cysts contain rapidly dividing merozoites that are sensitive to digestive enzymes. Over time, merozoites divide less rapidly and form more resistant bradyzoites.

Pathogenesis

Coccidiosis is probably one of the least understood yet most commonly diagnosed intestinal infections of dogs and cats. Diarrhea is common in cats, and coccidia are commonly found in the stool at the same time, especially in kittens. However, shedding of coccidia is usually totally unrelated to the presenting clinical syndrome.

Clinical coccidiosis has only been observed in very young animals infected with relatively large numbers of cysts.[4] *Isospora* spp are the only coccidia (in this group) that are also infectious for cats in the oocyst form. Severe coccidial enteritis has been experimentally induced in newborn kittens and immunosuppressed animals.[4,10]

Cats are infected with *Isospora* spp by ingesting oocysts or, as in *Besnoitia* spp, *Hammondia* spp and *Sarcocystis* spp, by ingesting prey animals that contain encysted forms of the organisms. Organisms are released from oocysts of tissue cysts during digestion and invade intestinal epithelial cells.

Clinical Features

Experimentally induced coccidiosis in weanling kittens is inapparent or relatively mild.[12] Clinical signs in natural infections consist mainly of diarrhea that lasts for several days. In severely affected animals, the stool is mucus laden and may contain some blood.[15] Rarely, intestinal infection is widespread and severe, and hemorrhagic diarrhea may develop.

Extraintestinal replication in cats does not occur to any extent with these species of coccidia. A small number of monozoic cysts is formed in intestinal and extraintestinal sites associated with *Isospora* spp infection of cats, but these are not clinically significant. The lack of significant extraintestinal replication and cyst formation in cats differs greatly from *Toxoplasma* spp infection. This also explains the great differences in clinical manifestations of toxoplasmosis and coccidiosis. In-utero transmission from the queen to fetus has not been observed with coccidia.[3]

Pathologic Features

Dubey described intestinal lesions of *I rivolta* in newborn kittens.[4] Microscopic lesions included desquamation of the cecum associated with replication of asexual and

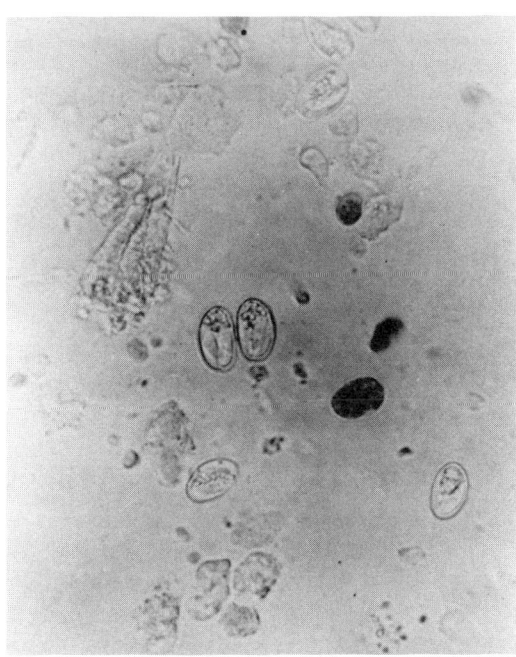

Fig 1. Oocysts of *Sarcocystis* in cat feces. *Sarcocystis* oocysts are 10-15 μ in diameter and easily distinguished from the oocysts of other coccidia. (Courtesy of Dr. Norman Baker, University of California, Davis)

Fig 2. Smear from fecal flotation from a cat infected with *Ancylostoma tubaeformes*, *Isospora felis* and *Hammondia*-like coccidia. The embryonated ova of *A tubaeformes* (A) are easily distinguished from the smaller oocysts of *I felis* (B). The *Hammondia*-like oocysts (C) are less than half the size (10 μ) of *I felis* oocysts (30-40 μ). (Courtesy of College of Veterinary Medicine, Texas A&M University)

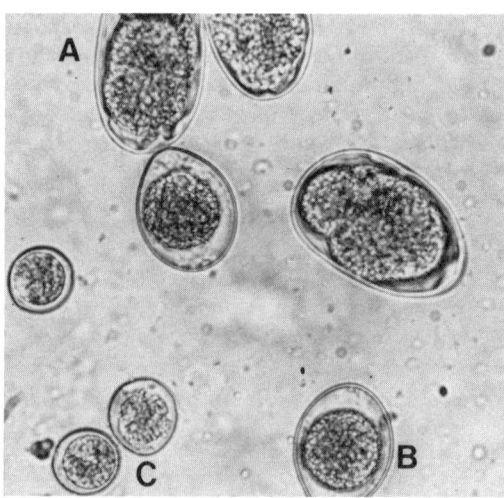

sexual stages. Replications of *Sarcocystis* spp in the intestines of carnivore hosts apparently elicits no host reactions.[12]

Clinicopathologic Features

Coccidiosis should not be automatically diagnosed in every cat that has diarrhea and organisms in the feces. Every attempt should be made to rule out other causes of diarrhea before diagnosing the condition as coccidiosis.

Coccidia are easily detected in fecal flotations. Some coccidia are of characteristic size or morphology and easily identified.[2] Others are difficult to distinguish from each other and can only be identified by experts or from animal inoculation studies. Coccidia are 10 μ (*H hammondi*) to 35-40 μ (*I felis*, *H pardalis*) long (Fig 2). Smaller forms of *Besnoitia* and *Hammondia* may be particularly hard to differentiate from oocysts of *Toxoplasma gondii* (Fig 3).

Treatment and Prevention

The usual treatment for coccidiosis in cats is sulfadiazine, sulfadimidine or sulfadimethoxine PO at 50 mg/kg daily or divided BID for 14 days.[15] Nitrofurazone at 15 mg/kg daily is an alternative treatment. All drugs that show activity against coccidia are coccidiostatic and not coccidicidal.

Total elimination of coccidia from a closed cattery by improved hygiene and sulfa treatment has been reported by Wilkinson.[15] However, dramatic or long-term successes with such approaches are uncommon.

Infection and Immunity

Immunity to coccidia is the same as described for toxoplasmosis. Immunity appears species specific. Cats infected sequentially with *T gondii*, *I felis*, *I rivolta* and *H hammondi* shed oocysts of the respective organism within 11 days post-inoculation.[3] Immunity to the intestinal stages is usually acquired within about 2 weeks. Immunity appears tenuous or short-lived because reinfections are common.[2] This differs from toxoplasmal immunity, which is usually more stable.[1]

Sarcocystis spp appear to elicit little or no immunity in carnivore hosts, which can

Fig 3. Unsporulated oocyst of *Toxoplasma gondii*. The oocyst is 10-12 μ in diameter and virtually impossible to distinguish from oocysts of *Hammondia* and *Besnoitia*. (Courtesy of Drs. Jerry Theis and Norman Baker, University of California, Davis)

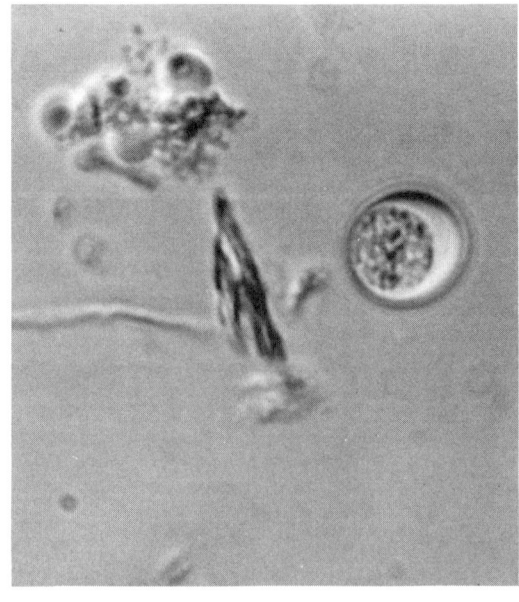

be infected repeatedly.[12] Immunity to *Besnoitia* spp appears similar. Of 5 previously infected cats, 3 shed oocysts after a second meal of cyst-infected mice, and 1 cat shed oocysts after a third meal.[14] Previous infection with *Toxoplasma* and *Sarcocystis* did not prevent infection with *Besnoitia*. Of 11 cats that had recovered from *H hammondi* infection 2-51 days earlier, 5 shed oocysts when reinfected. However, fewer oocysts were shed. One cat failed to shed oocysts after being reinfected 14 days after initial infection but shed oocysts when reinfected a third time on day 51. Oocysts were spontaneously shed in 3 of 3 cats that had been initially infected 14, 34 and 45 days earlier and then treated with methylprednisolone. However, earlier studies with *H hammondi* indicated that immunity to reinfection in cats was strong.[8] Of 14 cats, 13 failed to shed oocysts when reinfected. Cross-immunity to *T gondii* is observed in mice initially infected with *H hammondi*.[8] However, such cross-protection does not appear to exist in cats. The lack of cross-protection between *Sarcocystis* spp, *Toxoplasma* spp, *Isospora* spp and *Hammondia* spp has also been reviewed by Markus.[12]

Animal and Public Health Considerations

Only cats that shed *Isospora* spp are infectious to other cats. Oocysts of *Hammondia* spp, *Besnoitia* spp and *Sarcocystis* spp are only infectious for the appropriate intermediate hosts; cats are infected by eating tissues containing encysted organisms. Feline species of these coccidia are not pathogenic to people.

Cats may play an important role in the pathogenesis of sarcocystosis of cattle. Cats frequently defecate in barn litter and feed bunkers, and contaminate livestock forage with oocysts. A small number of *Sarcocystis* oocysts can cause severe systemic disease in calves. Systemic disease in cattle resemble systemic toxoplasmosis to some extent and is associated with massive proliferation of *Sarcocystis* spp merozoites (tachyzoites) in endothelial cells throughout the body. Disease in older cattle is often less fulminating and frequently goes unnoticed except for the presence of numerous cysts at slaughter.

References

1. Dubey JP: Immmunity to *Hammondia hammondi* infections in cats. *JAVMA* 167:373-377, 1975.

2. Dubey JP: A review of *Sarcocystis* of domestic animals and of other coccidia of dogs and cats. *JAVMA* 169:1061-1078, 1976.

3. Dubey JP: Attempted transmission of feline coccidia from chronically infected queens to their kittens. *JAVMA* 170:541-544, 1977.

4. Dubey JP: Life cycle of *Isospora rivolta* in cats and mice. *J Protozool* 26:433-443, 1979.

5. Dubey JP and Frenkel JK: Extra-intestinal stages of *Isospora felis* and *I rivolta* in cats. *J Protozool* 19:89-92, 1972.

6. Dubey JP and Streitel RH: Further studies on the transmission of *Hammondia hammondi* in cats. *J Parasitol* 62:548-551, 1976a.

7. Dubey JP and Streitel RH: *Isospora felis* and *I rivolta* infections in cats induced by mouse tissue or oocysts. *Brit Vet J* 132:649-651, 1976.

8. Frenkel JK: *Besnoitia wallacei* of cats and rodents, with a reclassification of other cyst-forming isosporoid coccidia. *J Parasitol* 63:611-628, 1977.

9. Frenkel JK and Dubey JP: Rodents as vectors for feline coccidia *Isospora felis* and *Isospora rivolta*. *J Infect Dis* 125:69-72, 1972.

10. Greene CE and Prestwood AK, in Greene CE: *Clinical Microbiology and Infectious Diseases of the Dog and Cat*. Saunders, Philadelphia, 1984. pp 824-858.

11. Levine ND: Nomenclature of *Sarcocystis* in the ox and sheep of fecal coccidia in the dog and cat. *J Parasitol* 63:36-51, 1977.

12. Markus MB: Sarcocystics and sarcocystosis in domestic animals and man. *Adv Vet Sci Comp Med* 22:159-193, 1978.

13. Smith DD and Frenkel JK: *Besnoitia darlingi*: Cyclic transmission by cats. *J Parasitol* 63:1066-1071, 1977.

14. Wallace GD and Frenkel JK: *Besnoitia* species (Protozoa, Sporozoa, Toxoplasmatidae): Recognition of cyclic transmission by cats. *Science* 188:369-371, 1975.

15. Wilkinson GT: Coccidial infection in a cat colony. *Vet Record* 100:156-157, 1977.

TOXOPLASMOSIS

Etiologic Agent

Toxoplasma gondii is a complex intracellular parasite and the only representative of its genus. It is a true coccidian belonging to the family Sarcocystidae, suborder Eimeriina, order Eucoccidia, subclass Coccidia, class Sporozoa, phylum Apicomplexa. It is worldwide in distribution.

Toxoplasma gondii is unique among coccidian parasites of cats and other animals. Though many different animals can serve as intermediate hosts, the entire life cycle can be completed within cats. In this regard, it resembles *Cryptosporidium* spp and *Isospora* spp. Unlike these latter organisms, however, an extensive extraintestinal phase of replication occurs and resembles that seen in *Hammondia* spp, Besnoitia spp and *Sarcocystis* spp. This extraintestinal phase of replication is limited to intermediate hosts in *Hammondia* spp, *Besnoitia* spp and *Sarcocystis* spp, whereas it occurs in both definitive and intermediate hosts in *T gondii*. In an evolutionary sense, the life cycle of *T gondii* is in transition between coccidia requiring only 1 host and those requiring 2 hosts for replication.

Pathogenesis

Cats are the only recognized definitive hosts for *T gondii*, in contrast to other coccidia, for which many fish, amphibians, birds and mammals serve as intermediate hosts. This large number of intermediate hosts makes *T gondii* the most important pathogenic coccidian of cats. *Toxoplasma gondii* occurs throughout the world and is responsible for clinical illness in a wide range of animals, both domestic and wild.

The incidence of toxoplasmal infection in cats varies greatly from country to country and from one subpopulation to the next. Morbidity also varies with age. Dubey found antibodies in < 10% of kittens younger than 10 weeks of age, 16.2% of 11- to 26-week-old domiciled kittens, 37.5% of adult house cats, and 57.9% of adult stray cats.[4] In Washington, the incidence of toxoplasmal antibodies was 31% in cats from animal pounds.[23] Morbidity was higher in house cats that owners relinquished than in strays. Incidences of this magnitude are common among domestic cats throughout the world.

The primary sources of infection for cats are probably small birds, rodents and reptiles containing encysted forms of the organism. Cats can also be infected by ingesting sporulated oocysts shed by other cats. However, a significantly lower percentage of cats sheds oocysts after having been infected with oocysts. The prepatent period is 20 days or longer.

The life cycle of *T gondii* in the definitive host is complex. It usually begins when cats ingest freshly killed prey or poorly processed meat containing encysted forms of the organism. Cats can also be infected with oocysts shed in the feces of other cats. However, this means of transmission is not nearly as effective. Encysted forms of *T gondii* are found in highest concentration in the muscle of intermediate hosts. Muscle cysts are composed of an outer fibroelastic capsule derived from the host's attempt to "wall off" the rapidly dividing tachyzoite stage of the parasite. Tachyzoites greatly decrease their replication rate during encystation and become slowly replicating bradyzoites. Proteolytic enzymes within the digestive tract of cats break down the cyst wall and release hundreds or thousands of bradyzoites. Subsequent stages in the life cycle, ending with shedding of oocysts by cats, can occur in as short a time as 3-10 days.

Bradyzoites released from muscle cysts in the digestive tract transform to rapidly dividing tachyzoites. Tachyzoites infect the small intestinal mucosal cells and are carried to the Peyer's patches, mesenteric lymph nodes and other organs of the body. Replication outside the intestinal tract occurs in many cell types; the endothelial cells of smaller blood vessels are severely affected. Therefore, during primary infection of cats, organisms replicate simultaneously in both intraintestinal and extraintestinal sites.

Sexual stages of the life cycle occur only within the small intestinal mucosal cells of cats. Sexual replication is generally preceded by 3 or more intraepithelial replicative stages in which tachyzoite numbers amplify greatly by asexual division. These tachyzoites can infect adjacent mucosal cells or spread systemically to contribute to the pool of organisms undergoing extraintestinal replication.

After several intraepithelial replication cycles, some tachyzoites within intestinal mucosal cells form microgametes (male) and macrogametes (female). Fertilization of macrogametes by microgametes leads to formation of zygotes, which transform in 1-4 days to oocysts. Oocysts are about 10 μ in diameter and are passed in the feces at up to 10,000 per day during initial infection. Oocysts generally appear in the feces after 3-10 days when cysts (bradyzoites) are ingested, or after 20 days or longer when oocysts are the source of infection. Cats usually shed oocysts for 5-14 days after primary infection.

Oocysts passed in the feces of cats are unsporulated. In this form, oocysts of *T gondii* are very difficult to differentiate from those of *Hammondia* spp and *Besnoitia* spp. Sporulation occurs outside the host in 1-21 days, depending on environmental conditions. Oocysts are relatively resistant and can survive in soil, especially if warm and moist, for at least 1 year.

Intermediate hosts are infected by ingestion of sporulated oocysts. Sporulated oocysts contain 2 sporocysts, each of which contains 4 sporozoites. Sporozoites infect intestinal mucosal cells and cells of the liver, lung and lymphoid organs. In the process, they transform to tachyzoites, which divide by budding within cellular vacuoles to form 8-32 progeny. Tachyzoites are released after eventual rupture of the cell and spread infection throughout the body. Replication of tachyzoites is eventually inhibited by developing host immunity, marking the transition from tachyzoites to bradyzoites. Aggregates of slowly replicating bradyzoites are surrounded by a cyst wall, where they remain for months or years. Cysts are most concentrated in the diaphragm, brain, lungs, abdominal muscles and heart. They are found less frequently in the stomach, small and large intestines, mesenteric lymph nodes, spleen and gall bladder.[22]

Clinical Features

Clinical signs related to *Toxoplasma* infection are infrequently observed in cats. When disease occurs, it is associated with different phases of infection: intestinal disease related to intraepithelial replication; systemic disease associated with extraintestinal replication during primary infection; disease associated with reactivation of encysted organisms; and neonatal infections associated with maternal transmission either *in utero* or at parturition.

Clinical signs related to primary intestinal replication (asexual and sexual) are uncommon in cats. Dubey and Frenkel induced severe diarrhea and death in neonatal kittens, a similar but less fatal illness in 2-week-old kittens, and no illness in adults that were fed *T gondii* cysts.[32] Greene and Prestwood produced severe enteritis in recently weaned kittens with concurrent viral respiratory disease.[17] Infection was inapparent in kittens without viral respiratory disease. Though intestinal signs can be experimentally induced in kittens with *Toxoplasma* spp, naturally occurring cases of enteritis have not been recognized.

Signs of systemic toxoplasmosis following primary infection are uncommon. The severity of this form of disease is proportional to the extent of extraintestinal proliferation of organisms after initial infection. This is age related. Cysts can be recovered by mouse inoculation from only about 10% of cats infected after 8 weeks of age but can be isolated from most kittens infected before this time.[10]

Petrak and Carpenter described 12 cats with acute toxoplasmosis among a series of 29 histopathologically confirmed cases.[28] Most of those 12 cats had negative *Toxoplasma* antibody titers. The ages of these cats ranged from 3 months to 15 years, and the most common presenting signs were anorexia, lethargy, fever and dyspnea. Cats with dyspnea had harsh bronchial lung sounds, tachypnea and deep abdominal breathing, but only a mild or inapparent cough. Two cats had signs similar to those of feline panleukopenia, *ie*, fever, vomiting or diarrhea, anorexia, abdominal pain on palpation, and enlarged mesenteric lymph nodes. Of the 12 cats, 2 had uveitis along with other signs, and 2 were obviously jaundiced. One cat aborted during the course of illness. The clinical course in these cats was 3-19 days (usually 3-8 days) and the disease was fatal in all 12 animals. Naturally occurring primary toxoplasmosis closely resembled the experimentally induced disease. Parker and co-workers induced systemic toxoplasmosis in specific-pathogen-free cats by IV inoculation of tachyzoites.[27] Inoculated cats became febrile within 2-4 days and were dead or moribund by day 6 or 7 postinfection. The most severe lesions were seen in the lungs, followed by the liver.

Secondary toxoplasmosis, resulting from recrudescence of encysted organisms, is probably the most common clinical form of the disease in cats. Evidence that this type of disease is caused by reactivation of latent organisms rather than primary extraintestinal infections is circumstantial and includes the following: the disease course is more apt to be chronic; toxoplasmal antibody titers are often high when animals are seen; it often occurs in conjunction with other debilitating or immunosuppressive diseases; both encysted and actively replicating forms of the organisms are often seen within the same animal; and many asymptomatic cats have subclinical foci of chronic inflammation associated with cysts in the brain.[32]

Recurrent or secondary toxoplasmosis, referred to as chronic toxoplasmosis by Petrak and Carpenter, has been reported on numerous occasions.[2,20,21,26,28,29] This form of toxoplasmosis is often associated with fever, abortion, vomiting, diarrhea, uveitis, anemia, myocardial disease, CNS signs, lymphadenopathy and respiratory signs of varying durations and intervals (weeks, months and sometimes years).

Respiratory involvement is common in cats with both primary and secondary forms of the disease. Cats with respiratory toxoplasmosis often have a fever and show signs of malaise, weight loss and anorexia. Dyspnea becomes more pronounced as the disease progresses. Gastrointestinal signs are also common among cats with secondary toxoplasmosis. The most frequent signs are fever, weight loss, vomiting, diarrhea, mesenteric lymph node enlargement and palpable thickening of the bowel wall. Clinical signs referable to CNS involvement include personality changes, incoordination, convulsions, anisocoria, blindness, plaintive crying, circling, ear twitching and impaired swallowing. Ocular involvement can be seen as a sole manifestation of the illness, or as a feature of a more systemic disease. Typically, the retina is involved; anterior uveal tract involvement is a late manifestation (Fig 4).[2] Chronic and healed lesions may coexist with active disease in the same eye. Healed lesions appear as focal areas of hyperreflective tapetum or mottled depigmented areas in the nontapetal retina. Active retinal lesions are deeper in the choroid and include diffuse or localized, dark, elevated lesions with poorly defined borders. Retinal hemorrhage may be associated with vascular involvement.

Fig 4. Chorioretinitis in a cat with systemic toxoplasmosis. (Courtesy of Dr. Ned Buyukmihci, University of California, Davis)

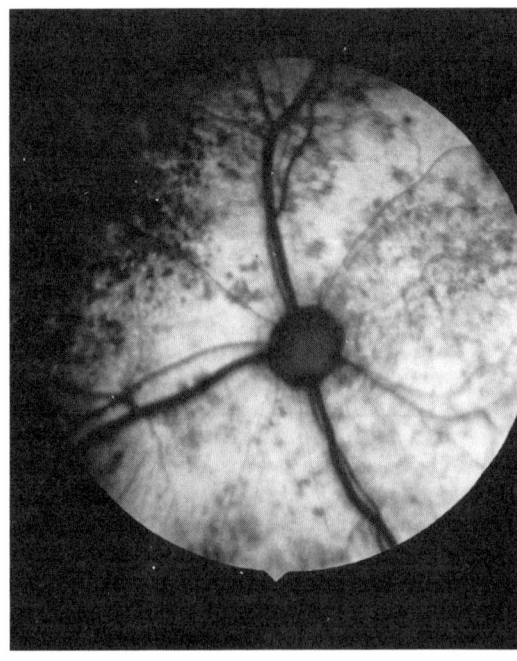

Recurrent toxoplasmosis is often associated with other underlying diseases. Feline leukemia virus (FeLV) and feline immunodeficiency virus (FIV) infections may predispose cats to secondary toxoplasmosis by their immunosuppressive effects. Holzworth described a cat with encephalitic toxoplasmosis that also had severe secondary bacterial pyelonephritis.[20] Concurrent hemobartonellosis and toxoplasmosis have been described in an FeLV-negative cat.[21] Concurrent feline infectious peritonitis and toxoplasmosis have also been recognized.[31]

Neonatal toxoplasmosis has been observed on several occasions, but whether the disease is transmitted *in utero* or shortly after birth has not been determined. Fetal infection is common in animals or people in which active intestinal replication of the organism occurs during gestation. In dogs, this can lead to abortion or progressive CNS and muscle disease manifested shortly after birth.[17] Human infants, depending on the stage of gestation in which they are infected and the dose of organisms, are born: healthy with protective immunity; with severe disease manifested at birth by ocular and CNS abnormalities; healthy but with disease signs developing during the first few weeks of life; or healthy but with low-grade chronic disease that can lead to disease signs as late as the third or fourth decade.[24] More severely affected fetuses are stillborn or aborted.

Queens appear much more resistant to maternal transmission than bitches or human mothers. Queens exposed to *T gondii* during weeks 1-7 of gestation did not have any infected fetuses or newborn kittens.[10] However, 3 kittens born to these queens developed neonatal toxoplasmosis. The route of transmission in this instance was not determined but was postulated to involve transfer of tachyzoites from mother to kitten in the milk. Milk-borne transmission of toxoplasmosis is also a serious problem in dairy goat kids. *In-utero* transmission of toxoplasmosis by queens was suggested by an outbreak.[11] Of 7 littermate kittens, 3 developed toxoplasmosis and died at 16-32 days of age with signs of dyspnea, mucopurulent nasal and ocular discharges, and progressive neurologic disease. Pneumonitis, hepatitis, myocarditis, retinitis and encephalitis were evident on microscopic examination of tissue. The presence of encysted organisms in the brain indicated that primary infection occurred before birth. Cell cultures from fetal kittens have occasionally contained *Toxoplasma* spp, again suggesting that toxoplasmosis can occur as an *in-utero* infection in cats.

Most cases of maternally transmitted toxoplasmosis manifest themselves before weaning. Hirth and Nielsen have reported the largest series of such cases.[19] They found that the most common sign of toxoplasmosis in kittens up to 3 weeks of age was sudden death or rapidly developing "sickness." Fever, depression, body tremors, dyspnea, paralysis and diarrhea were more apt to be seen in kittens between 5 and 8 weeks of age.

Pathologic Features

Lesions of active toxoplasmosis are widespread in the body but tend to be most concentrated in the lungs, followed by the liver and CNS.[19] Involvement of the alimentary tract is less frequent.

Gross lesions are most noticeable in the lungs. Lung lesions consist of edema and diffuse or focal firmness and reddening. Diffuse white and yellow foci are scattered throughout the parenchyma. Subpleural hemorrhages are sometimes seen, along with small amounts of free reddish pleural fluid or blood. The liver is often pale and mottled yellow-brown, or may contain small whitish foci. When involved, the pancreas is edematous and bordered by necrotic fat containing whitish or yellowish foci. Mesenteric lymph nodes are occasionally enlarged and edematous. Focal thickening of bowel walls has also been observed in some cats with predominantly GI disease. Likewise, the spleen is often enlarged and meatier than normal on cross-section.

Pulmonary lesions are characterized histopathologically by interstitial pneumonia with serofibrinous exudation. In some individuals, adenomatous changes of the alveolar cells occur due to hyperplasia and hypertrophy. Replicating *Toxoplasma* tachyzoites are frequently seen in alveolar cells that have been desquamated into the lumina. Interstitial inflammation is characterized by accumulations of fibrin, macrophages and collagenous connective tissue. Inflammation proceeding to necrosis is evident in focal areas of lung.

Histologic lesions in the liver consist mainly of disseminated foci of coagulation-type necrosis with little or sparse inflammatory response. Proliferating *Toxoplasma* tachyzoites are found intracellularly in Kupffer cells and, at times, in hepatocytes. Cyst forms are occasionally seen in liver parenchyma but are few in number and not associated with inflammatory reactions.

Central nervous system lesions are characterized by cystic forms, with little surrounding inflammatory reaction, or by significant encephalitis, with disseminated focal gliosis and perivascular cuffing with mononuclear cells. Though *Toxoplasma* can be seen in all areas of the brain, organisms concentrate in the cerebrum. Focal, suppurative meningoencephalitis, with cysts and replicating forms, is occasionally seen. Lesions in the choroid and retina are similar to those of the brain. Necrotic foci associated with *Toxoplasma* are sometimes observed in the cardiac muscle and pancreas. Mesenteric lymphadenopathy is associated with lymphoreticular hyperplasia or granulomatous lesions. Toxoplasmal organisms are also seen at times in the smooth muscles of blood vessel walls and endothelial cells.

Clinicopathologic Features

Toxoplasmosis should be suspected in younger cats dying of vague illnesses and in animals with disease involving the lungs, CNS or eyes. Toxoplasmosis should also be considered in cats with acute GI disease, especially if associated with mesenteric lymphadenopathy, pneumonia and hepatitis.

A diagnosis of toxoplasmosis is often suspected before death but almost always confirmed at necropsy. Cats with acute primary toxoplasmosis may have had insufficient time to produce serum antibodies;

antibody titers in cats with chronic or reactivated toxoplasmosis are often high. Cats with primary toxoplasmosis are often shedding oocysts when presented, while cats with recurrent disease are often nonshedders. Further, *T gondii* oocysts are not significantly different in appearance from those of *Hammondia* spp or *Besnoitia* spp (Fig 5). Accurate identification by inexperienced investigators is difficult. Examination of feces for toxoplasmal oocysts has been described by Dubey.[4] Unsporulated *T gondii* oocysts are about 10-12 μ in diameter and about one-quarter of the size of an *Isospora felis* oocyst, one-eighth the size of a *Toxocara* egg, and twice the size of an RBC. Definitive identification of oocysts is by mouse inoculation, after allowing time for oocyst sporulation. Oocysts may not be present in the feces of cats with chronic or maternally transmitted toxoplasmosis.

Serum antibodies appear within 7 days after primary infection.[30] These antibodies can be measured by the Sabin-Feldman dye exclusion test, indirect fluorescent antibody (IFA) procedure, indirect hemagglutination test, complement-fixation or enzyme-linked immunosorbent assay (ELISA). The Sabin-Feldman dye exclusion test is con-

Fig 5. Sporulated oocyst of *Toxoplasma gondii* in cat feces. The oocyst is 10-12 μ in diameter, and very difficult to distinguish from oocysts of *Hammondia* and *Besnoitia*. (Courtesy of Dr. Norman Baker, University of California, Davis)

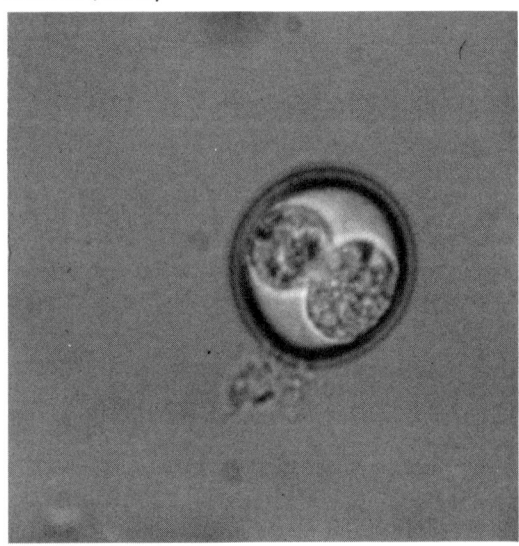

sidered the most reliable in all species, including cats, though the IFA test is the most widely used and an acceptable alternative. Antibody levels rise rapidly during the course of disease and reach levels somewhat proportional to the severity of extraintestinal replication and cyst formation. For instance, mouse-inoculation studies yield organisms from over 80% of the tissues of cats with Sabin-Feldman dye test antibody titers of $\geq 1:64$. Isolation of organisms from cats with lower titers is much less frequent.

A single antibody titer, regardless of magnitude, is of very little diagnostic value. As many as 60% of normal adult cats have positive antibody titers, some being very high. Therefore, it is important to use serologic test results wisely in making a diagnosis. A 4-fold rise in titer over a 2-week period has been used by some clinicians to diagnose toxoplasmosis. While this is acceptable in cats with active primary infections, it may not be diagnostic in cats with chronic or reactivated disease. Most active (acute or chronic) infections in man and animals are associated with IgM as well as IgG antibodies. The IgM antibodies disappear when the infection becomes quiescent. Therefore, the presence of IgM antibodies may be a more accurate measurement of disease activity.

The radiographic appearance of lung lesions of feline toxoplasmosis has been considered almost pathognomonic.[1] Radiographic changes mirror the focal alveolar nature of the infection. Ill-defined, coalescent, patchy densities throughout the lung parenchyma are due to interdigitation of fluid-filled alveoli with lesser involved or normal alveoli. Densities tend to adjoin bronchi. Air bronchograms become more noticeable as the disease progresses due to consolidation of parenchyma around air-filled bronchi. This reaction may extend down into the alveoli and lead to the appearance of air alveolograms.

Though variable blood and serum abnormalities are seen in cats with toxoplasmosis, none is specific for the disease. White blood cell numbers vary from low to high, the PCV is usually normal, liver enzymes are elevated with hepatic involvement, and urine and serum bilirubin levels are elevated in a few cats. Platelet counts are normal or decreased.

Cats showing signs compatible with toxoplasmosis should be tested for FeLV and FIV infections. About one-half or more of cats with toxoplasmosis may be FeLV or FIV positive. As in people, toxoplasmosis of cats is mainly an opportunistic disease.

Treatment and Prevention

The disease can be prevented by not allowing cats to eat raw and undercooked meat (especially from swine and sheep), hunt, or contact sporulated oocysts shed by other cats. These steps are seldom practical, so the disease cycle is difficult to break. Freezing meat at -20 C, a temperature not always achieved by home freezers, inactivates the organism, as does cooking meat at >60 C.

Treatment of cats with naturally occurring toxoplasmosis has had only limited success. This may partly be because many cases occur in immunocompromised hosts, in which treatment is not nearly as effective. Further, many cats are treated for toxoplasmosis because they have compatible signs and positive antibody titers when, in fact, they actually have other illnesses. The oldest treatment is a combination of pyrimethamine and sulfadiazine. Sulfadiazine is given PO at 100 mg/kg divided TID or QID. Pyrimethamine is given in conjunction at 1 mg/kg daily. Treatment is continued for 2 weeks. Folinic acid or baker's yeast are sometimes given to counteract the side effects of pyrimethamine without interfering with treatment. Trimethoprim-sulfa is similar to the above drug combination and has been used to treat some animals. Clindamycin IM at 5 mg/kg QID has been used to treat dogs with toxoplasmosis and is probably the treatment of choice.[16] The efficacy of this drug against toxoplasmosis has been established in experimental studies with mice and cats.[12,25]

Infections and Immunity

After primary infection, oocysts are shed for 4-16 days.[10] Oocyst production apparently ceases as a result of local immune mechanisms at about the same time that systemic immunity is developing and extraintestinal replication is halted. Even during the active shedding stage, oocyst production appears regulated to some extent by various host factors. Male cats appear to shed more oocysts after ingesting infected mice than females, and cats under 12 months of age shed more than older cats.[10] Even though oocyst production ceases with development of local immunity, some organisms remain inactive in the epithelium.

Actively replicating tachyzoites in extraintestinal sites are inhibited by developing systemic immunity. The host forms a cyst-like structure around the organisms, which turn into slowly replicating bradyzoites. Over time, each cyst contains <100 to several thousand individual organisms. Host reaction to the cysts is usually minimal, though in some cases a mild mononuclear-cell infiltrate is found around the periphery.

Immunity to reinfection occurs after initial recovery from oocyst shedding. This immunity is somewhat age dependent. About 60% of cats < 13 weeks of age when initially infected subsequently shed oocysts when fed infected mice; immunity in cats initially infected after 13 weeks of age is much better.[8] Oocysts are more apt to be shed after ingestion of cysts than sporulated oocysts, and oocysts are shed after a longer latent period and for a briefer duration than in primary infection.[8] Immunity to subsequent bouts of extraintestinal replication appears more solid than local immunity to oocyst shedding.

The nature of immunity to toxoplasmosis is not entirely understood. However, the level of serum antibody at challenge bears no relationship to the degree of immunity.[8] Cellular immunity appears to play an important role in recovery and maintenance of encysted organisms. Toxoplasmosis in people and cats is usually associated with immunosuppressive diseases, particularly those that profoundly affect cellular immunity. Infections with FeLV and FIV underly one-half or more of the cases of feline toxoplasmosis.

Recrudescence of latent organisms in intestinal and extraintestinal sites, resulting in oocyst reshedding and even clinical disease, has been induced in carrier cats with corticosteroid administration.[8] Such immunosuppression can result from a wide range of stressful and debilitating diseases in cats.

Certain manipulations have activated latent organisms in the intestinal tract. If a cat has not been previously infected with *Isospora*, infection with this organism causes transient shedding of *T gondii* oocysts as well.[6] Primary infection with *Isospora* apparently interferes with established local immunity to *T gondii*.

Artificially induced immunity to shedding of *Toxoplasma* oocysts was studied by Frenkel and Smith.[14] When reinfected later with bradyzoites, 94% of kittens infected initially with bradyzoites in cysts failed to shed oocysts. Tachyzoites produced immunity in 86%; primary infection with sporozoites alone produced immunity in only 11%. After administration of bradyzoites from nonoocyst-producing strains, only 9% of cats were immune. Killed tachyzoites given in Freund's complete or incomplete adjuvant produced immunity to subsequent challenge-exposure and oocyst shedding in only 1 of 24 kittens. When primarily infected with bradyzoites, 85% of kittens were immunized and given concurrent monensin or sulfadiazine combined with pyrimethamine therapy. Oocyst production was not seen in these animals after primary infection. Frenkel and Smith concluded that cats were immunized against oocyst shedding only by infections in which oocysts are produced or when developmental stages were suppressed by chemoprophylaxis.[14] Infections that failed to produce enteroepithelial stages also failed to induce immunity.

Animal and Public Health Considerations

Cats are much less infectious to other cats than to other species of animals. Cat-to-cat infection occurs exclusively by ingestion of sporulated oocysts, a relatively inefficient mode of infection. Since cats are the definitive host for the organism, they play an important role in transmitting the disease to many types of animals, particularly herbivores. Carnivorous and omnivorous animals are not only infected by ingesting oocysts from cats but also by ingestion of encysted forms in a multitude of intermediate hosts.

Farm cats are a common source of infection for cattle, sheep, goats and swine. Gethings and co-workers found that 77% of individual farm populations of cats in England had antibodies to *T gondii*.[33] Defecation in feed bunkers, barnyard litter and soil can lead to a large accumulation of oocysts. Cat-to-animal transmission of toxoplasmosis may be particularly severe in goat dairies where cats are an important source of infection. Maternal transmission to newborn goats via milk is an important link in the disease cycle.

People are infected with toxoplasmosis by ingesting sporulated oocysts from cats, raw goat milk, or uncooked or poorly cooked meat, especially lamb, pork and goat meat. In fact, in North America and Western Europe, where cats are kept more closely confined and fed processed foods, consumption of infected meat by people is probably of greater public health importance than contact with cats.[24]

The frequency of infection in the human population in the United States varies greatly according to sociologic, economic and environmental factors. Morbidity and seropositivity increase with age. Less than 1% of infants are congenitally infected, followed by an abrupt rise in the teens. Morbidity rises about 1% each year from the ages of 15 to 50.[24]

The most important form of human toxoplasmosis is associated with transplacental transmission. Such infection results from extraintestinal replication of organisms in the mother during pregnancy or just before conception. About 0.5-1% of women in the United States and Europe show rising titers during pregnancy. This indicates active infection, but only about 40% of these infections are transmitted to fetuses.[24] Moreover, only a small proportion of infected fetuses have significant clinical disease.

Veterinarians are frequently called upon to give advice to pregnant women with cats or to clients contemplating pregnancy. Medical advice to clients should be limited to steps needed to prevent cat-to-person transmission. Prenatal exposure advice is better left to experts on the human disease. Nevertheless, clients can be comforted that cats are only 1 of many reservoirs for toxoplasmosis, only a small fraction of infants are infected, and a much smaller percentage of infants are clinically affected.

Human exposure by cats to toxoplasmosis can be minimized by reducing the chances of infection of cats.[13,18] This can be done by confining cats to prevent hunting, feeding cats only processed meats, and changing litter boxes daily to prevent sporulation of oocysts. Litter should be discarded in a sealed plastic bag (not buried in the garden). People should eat only thoroughly cooked or processed meat, wash hands thoroughly after handling raw meat and uncooked home-raised vegetables, wear gloves when working in yards likely to be contaminated with cat feces, prevent cats from defecating in children's sand boxes, have someone other than the expectant mother change the litter box daily, and avoid raw milk (especially from goats).

Oocyst shedding by cats has been suppressed by feeding cats 0.02% monensin with their dried food.[14] Kittens appear to tolerate the medicated food well. However, use of such treatment to prevent oocyst shedding has not been widely applied in the field.

References

1. Bartels JE: *Toxoplasma* pneumonia in the cat. *Feline Pract* 2(3):11-13, 1972.

2. Campbell LH and Schiessl MM: Ocular manifestations of toxoplasmosis, infectious peritonitis, and lymphosarcoma in cats. *Mod Vet Pract* 59:761-764, 1978.

3. Dubey JP: Diagnosis of feline toxoplasmosis. *Feline Pract* 3(5):14-17, 1973.

4. Dubey JP: Feline toxoplasmosis and coccidiosis: A survey of domiciled and stray cats. *JAVMA* 162:873-877, 1973.

5. Dubey JP: Effect of immunization of cats with *Isospora felis* and BCG on immunity and reexcretion of *Toxoplasma gondii* oocysts. *J Protozool* 25:373-377, 1975.

6. Dubey JP: Reshedding of *Toxoplasma* oocysts by chronically infected cats. *Nature* 262:213-214, 1976.

7. Dubey JP: Fatal neonatal toxoplasmosis in cats. *JAAHA* 18:461-467, 1982.

8. Dubey JP and Frenkel JK: Immunity to feline toxoplasmosis; modification by administration of corticosteroids. *Vet Pathol* 11:350-379, 1974.

9. Dubey JP and Hoover EA: Attempted transmission of *Toxoplasma gondii* infection from pregnant cats to their kittens. *JAVMA* 170:538-540, 1970.

10. Dubey JP et al: Effect of age and sex on the acquisition of immunity to toxoplasmosis in cats. *J Protozool* 24:184-186, 1977.

11. Dubey JP and Johnstone I: Fatal neonatal toxoplasmosis in cats. *JAAHA* 18:461-467, 1982.

12. Dubey JP and Yeary RA: Anticoccidial activity of 2-sulfamoyl-4, 4-diaminodiphenylsulfone, sulfadiazine, pyrimethamine and clindamycin in cats infected with *Toxoplasma gondii*. *Can Vet J* 18:51-57, 1977.

13. Frenkel JK: Toxoplasmosis in cats and man. *Feline Pract* 5(1):28-41, 1975.

14. Frenkel JK and Smith DD: Immunization of cats against shedding of *Toxoplasma* oocysts by cats. *J Parasitol* 68:744-748, 1982.

15. Frenkel JK and Smith DD: Inhibitory effects of monensin on shedding of *Toxoplasma* oocysts by cats. *J Parasitol* 68:851-855, 1982b.

16. Greene CE et al: Clindamycin for treatment of *Toxoplasma* polymyositis in a dog. *JAVMA* 187:631-633, 1985.

17. Greene CE and Prestwood AK, in Greene CE: *Clinical Microbiology and Infectious Diseases of the Dog and Cat*. Saunders, Philadelphia, 1984. pp 824-858.

18. Hand PJ: Counseling clients on toxoplasmosis. *Mod Vet Pract* 66:710-713, 1985.

19. Hirth RS and Nielsen SW: Pathology of feline toxoplasmosis. *J Small Anim Pract* 10:213-221, 1969.

20. Holzworth J: Encephalitic toxoplasmosis in a cat. *JAVMA* 124:313-316, 1954.

21. Hoskins JD and Barta O: Concurrent *Haemobartonella felis* and *Toxoplasma gondii* infections in a cat. *VM/SAC* 79:633-637, 1984.

22. Katsube Y et al: Studies on toxoplasmosis. 2. Distribution of *Toxoplasma* in the organs of cat and dog cases of latent infection occurring naturally. *Jpn J Med Sci Biol* 22:319-326, 1969.

23. Ladiges WC et al: Prevalence of *Toxoplasma gondii* antibodies and oocysts in pound-source cats. *JAVMA* 180:1334-1335. 1982.

24. Masur H, in Wyngaarden SB and Smith LH Jr: *Cecil's Textbook of Medicine*. Saunders, Philadelphia, 1985. pp 1792-1796.

25. McMaster PRP et al: The effect of two chlorinated lincomycin analogues against acute toxoplasmosis in mice. *Am J Trop Med Hyg* 22:14-17, 1973.

26. Meier H et al: Toxoplasmosis in the cat—fourteen cases. *JAVMA* 1341:395-414, 1957.

27. Parker GA et al: Pathogenesis of acute toxoplasmosis in specific-pathogen-free cats. *Vet Pathol* 18:786-803, 1981.

28. Petrak M and Carpenter J: Feline toxoplasmosis. *JAVMA* 146:728-734, 1965.

29. Smart ME et al: Toxoplasmosis in a cat associated with cholangitis and progressive pancreatitis. *Can Vet J* 14:313-316, 1973.

30. Wallace GD: The role of the cat in the natural history of *Toxoplasma gondii*. *Am J Trop Med Hyg* 22:313-322, 1973.

31. Ward BC and Pedersen N: Infectious peritonitis in cats. *JAVMA* 154:26-35, 1969.

Additional References

32. Dubey JP and Frenkel JK: Cyst-induced toxoplasmosis in cats. *J Protozool* 19:155-177, 1972.

33. Gethings PM et al: Prevalence of *Chlamydia, Toxoplasma, Toxocara* and ringworm in farm cats in south-west England. *Vet Record* 121:213-216, 1987.

CRYPTOSPORIDIOSIS

Etiologic Agent

Similar to coccidia, *Cryptosporidium* spp belong to the order Eucoccidia, suborder Eimeriina.[1] However, they are classified in the family Cryptosporidiiae. Cross-species infection studies with a number of animal and human isolates indicate that all cryptosporidial organisms belong to the same or very similar species.[7,10-12,15]

Cryptosporidial infections are apparently common and widespread among animals and people throughout the world. Tzipori and Campbell detected antibodies in serum samples of 80-100% of all cats, people, dogs, domestic ruminants, pigs, horses, deer, mice and chickens tested.[12]

The morphology and life cycle of *Cryptosporidium* spp have been studied in chicken embryos and laboratory rodents.[3,10] Infection occurs by ingestion of thick-walled oocysts 4-8 μ in diameter. Sporozoites released from oocysts attach themselves to the surface of intestinal epithelial cells and displace the surrounding brush border. They undergo several cycles of asexual replication as merozoites before forming microgametes and macrogametes. Fusion of gametes results in 2 types of oocysts. Most are thick walled and shed intact in the feces. The remainder of the oocysts are thin walled and rupture easily during transit through the bowel. Sporozoites released from these thin-walled oocysts often reinfect new epithelial cells within the bowel of the same host.[3] Oocyst shedding in normal immunocompetent hosts begins as early as 5 days after infection and continues for a 2- to 3-week period.[7] Unlike other coccidia, many species of animals act as definitive hosts, cross-infection between species is common, extraintestinal replication does not occur, and both asexual and sexual division mainly occur extracellularly.

Pathogenesis

Infections are often limited to the ileum but can involve virtually the entire bowel in massive exposures in neonatal and immunocompromised individuals. Clinical signs are seen only when a substantial part of the brush border is displaced by organisms. Signs of disease apparently result from disruption of normal transport functions of the microvilli. Marked suppression of sucrase and lactase secretion has been observed in experimentally infected lambs.[12]

Clinical Features

The importance of *Cryptosporidium* spp in enteric diseases of cats is uncertain. Many cats shed organisms in the feces, kittens moreso than adults. However, oocyst shedding is often unrelated to concurrent intestinal disease. Adult cats fed large numbers of *Cryptosporidium* showed no signs of illness.[6] Current and co-workers were also unable to produce clinical disease in 6-week-old kittens.[4] Pavlasek induced a mild self-limiting enteritis in a 3-week-old kitten fed oocysts of calf origin.[15] Severe cryptosporidiosis has been described in an adult cat with chronic diarrhea, anorexia, weight loss and bowel thickening.[9] The disease in this cat was clinically and histopathologically similar to plasmacytic-lymphocytic enteritis, a disease of allergic or prelymphomatous etiology. Feline immunodeficiency virus (FIV) infection of cats produces a similar intestinal disorder. Barsanti observed a cat with severe intestinal cryptosporidiosis and concurrent feline leukemia virus (FeLV) infection.[1] A similar FeLV-infected cat with severe intestinal cryptosporidiosis was described by Monticello and associates.[14]

Pathologic Features

Most of what is known about cryptosporidiosis has come from experimental transmission studies in lambs or swine.[7,12] However, disease in these species is considerably more severe than naturally occurring infections of carnivores, which are usually inapparent. Cryptosporidial organisms in experimentally infected swine and lambs are found loosely attached to the apical borders of intestinal mucosal cells. Organisms are found mainly in the ileum, except in severe infections in which they are often widespread. The main abnormalities are stunting of villi, villus fusion, and a sparse neutrophil and macrophage infiltrate in the lamina propria. Squamous and cuboidal metaplasia of columnar epithelial cells is seen in severe infections.

Clinicopathologic Features

As in coccidiosis, every attempt should be made to eliminate other causes of enteritis before diagnosing cryptosporidiosis in cats with positive fecal examinations. This includes use of hypoallergenic diets to rule out food allergy, which is the single most common cause of diarrhea in cats. Older cats with chronic diarrhea and cryptosporidia in their stool should also be tested for FeLV and FIV infections.

The Sheather's sugar flotation method has been used to concentrate oocysts from fecal specimens.[5] Oocysts are slightly larger than RBCs, and one-sixth the size of

Isospora felis oocysts (Fig 6). Oocysts are difficult to visualize without phase microscopy or special contrast staining.

A serologic procedure has been described that uses immunofluorescent antibodies on infected lamb intestinal sections.[11] The procedure is sensitive enough to demonstrate postinfection titer rises in animals experimentally infected with *Cryptosporidium* spp. However, such a test has limited clinical use because preinfection serum samples are seldom available and the rate of spontaneous infection is high in normal animals.

Fig 6. Oocysts of *Cryptosporidium* in a fecal flotation of cat feces. The oocysts are about 5 μ in diameter. Sodium dichromate stain.

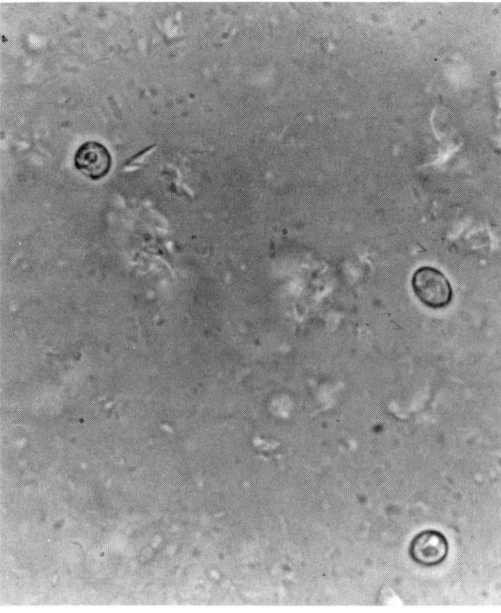

Treatment and Prevention

Standard anticoccidial drugs have no effect on *Cryptosporidium* spp. In fact, no single treatment has proven uniformly effective. Infection in healthy cats is usually subclinical or mild, and is self-limiting. For this reason, treatment is not generally recommended except in cats with particularly severe infections and there is a high likelihood that cryptosporidia are the cause of the enteritis.

Spiramycin, a derivative of clindamycin and lincomycin, has proven effective in some people with congenital or acquired immunodeficiency and severe cryptosporidiosis.[13] However, spiramycin is not available in the United States, and its efficacy against animal cases of cryptosporidiosis is unknown. Oral clindamycin and quinine have proven less effective in people and are associated with many more side effects.

Oocysts of *Cryptosporidium* spp are relatively resistant to disinfectants.[2] Cresylic acid (3%), hypochlorite (2-5%), benzalkonium chloride (5%), sodium hydroxide (0.02 M) and isophore (1-4%) failed to inactivate oocysts after 18 hours. However, oocysts are sensitive to ammonia (5-10%) and formaldehyde (10%).

Infection and Immunity

Immunity to *Cryptosporidium* appears within 1-2 weeks in normal individuals but is tenuous and short-lived. The poor postinfection immunity to cryptosporidiosis may be due to the superficial nature of infection in the bowel. Reinfection is common in normal animals. Debilitating diseases can lower resistance and further increase the incidence of recurrent infections. Moreover, animals that are debilitated or immunocompromised by other diseases often shed greater numbers of oocysts for a more prolonged period. If the infection is particularly severe and persistent, it can contribute to clinical signs. Barsanti observed an FeLV-infected cat that had acute signs apparently due to chronic cryptosporidiosis.[1] Another cat appeared to be suffering from concurrent cryptosporidiosis and lymphocytic-plasmacytic enteritis of unknown etiology.[9]

Animal and Public Health Considerations

Infected cats are hazards to human and animal health only in that they serve as 1 of hundreds of different mammalian, avian and human hosts. Cryptosporidiosis as a clinical entity is seen mainly in neonatal ruminants and immunocompromised people. Mild to moderately severe enteritis has been induced in neonatal lambs and there seems little doubt that cryptosporidiosis is an important natural cause of diarrhea in very young calves.[8,12] Cryptosporidiosis in calves is considered an important source of human infection.

Cryptosporidiosis in normal people is characterized by acute diarrhea and abdominal cramps lasting 1-10 days.[4] Clinical signs usually begin within 5 days or sooner after exposure. A severe and potentially fatal form of intestinal cryptosporidiosis has been seen in people with acquired or congenital immunodeficiency syndromes.[4] Opportunistic cryptosporidiosis appears particularly prevalent and severe among people with retrovirus-induced acquired immunodeficiency syndromes (AIDS).[13]

References

1. Barsanti JA, in Greene CE: *Clinical Microbiology and Infectious Diseases of the Dog and Cat.* Saunders, Philadelphia, 1984. p 854.

2. Campbell I et al: Effect of disinfectants on survival of *Cryptosporidium* oocysts. *Vet Record* 111:414-415, 1982.

3. Current WL and Long PL: Development of human and calf *Cryptosporidium* in chicken embryos. *J Infect Dis* 148:1108-1113, 1983.

4. Current WL et al: Human cryptosporidiosis in immunocompetent and immunodeficient persons. *New Engl J Med* 308:1252-1286, 1983.

5. Greene CE and Prestwood AK, in Greene CE: *Clinical Microbiology and Infectious Diseases of the Dog and Cat.* Saunders, Philadelphia, 1984. pp 824-858.

6. Iseki M: *Cryptosporidium felis* from the domestic cat. *Jpn J Parasitol* 28:285-307, 1979.

7. Moon HW et al: Experimental fecal transmission of human cryptosporidia to pigs and attempted treatment with ornithine decarboxylase inhibitor. *Vet Pathol* 19:700-707, 1982.

8. Pohlenz J et al: Cryptosporidiosis as a probable factor in neonatal diarrhea in calves. *JAVMA* 172:452-457, 1978.

9. Poonacha KB and Pippin C: Intestinal cryptosporidiosis in a cat. *Vet Pathol* 19:708-710, 1982.

10. Reese NC et al: Cryptosporidiosis of man and calf: a case report and results of experimental infections in mice and rats. *Am J Trop Med Hyg* 31:226-229, 1982.

11. Tzipori S and Campbell I: Prevalence of *Cryptosporidium* antibodies in 10 animal species. *J Clin Microbiol* 14:455-456, 1981.

12. Tzipori S et al: Experimental infection of lambs with *Cryptosporidium* isolated from a patient with diarrhea. *Gut* 23:741-743, 1982.

13. Whiteside M et al: Treatment of cryptosporidiosis in patients with acquired immunodeficiency syndrome (AIDS). *Morbidity Mortality Weekly Rpt* 33:117-119, 1984.

Additional References

14. Monticello TM et al: Cryptosporidiosis in a feline leukemia virus-positive cat. *JAVMA* 191:705-706, 1987.

15. Pavlasek I: Experimental infection of a cat and chicken with *Cryptosporidium* sp oocysts isolated from a calf. *Folia Parasitol (Praha)* 30:121-122, 1983.

BABESIOSIS

Etiologic Agent

Babesia spp are protozoan parasites classified with *Cytauxzoon* spp in the order Piroplasmida of the phylum Apicomplexa.[1] Numbers of poorly defined species differing somewhat in size and pathogenicity have been isolated from wild Felidae and associated domestic cats in Africa, India and South America, and from Felidae in zoos in many parts of the world. These species include *Babesia felis, B cati, B herpailuri, B pantherae, B pardus,* and *Nuttallia felis.* Based on current knowledge of these various species, it is perhaps premature to assign them different names. Feline isolates of *Babesia* spp are 1-3.4 μ in diameter and are observed mainly in peripheral RBCs, in which they assume annular or piriform shapes.

The first confirmed description of babesiosis in Felidae was in a Sudanese cat.[4] This isolate was successfully passed to domestic cats but was of low pathogenicity. Wenyon and Hamerton identified *Babesia* spp in a civet cat and North American lynx in the London zoo.[19] *Babesia* spp have also been isolated from domestic cats, a mountain lion in the Cairo zoo, an Indian leopard, an African leopard and the jaguarundi.[2,3,5,12,14,16] The first naturally occurring case of babesiosis in domestic pet cats was in South Africa.[11,13] Futter and Belonje reported 70 naturally occurring cases of babesiosis in domestic cats, also from South Africa.[7] Additional cases from South Africa have been reported.[17]

Pathogenesis

Babesia spp infections of domestic cats probably have their reservoir in wild Felidae. However, not all feline isolates are highly pathogenic for domestic cats. Mudaliar and co-workers could not infect domestic cats with *Babesia* spp from a feral Indian cat.[14] Davis successfully passed *Babesia* from a Sudanese wild cat to domestic cats, but the experimentally reproduced disease was very mild.[4] Futter and Belonje experimentally recreated severe disease in domestic cats with *Babesia* isolated from a naturally occurring case of babesiosis in a domestic cat living in a nature reserve in South Africa.[6]

The route by which domestic cats are infected is unknown but probably involves transmission by ticks of several genera. Carrier animals maintain a low level of RBC parasitemia at all times. Trophozoite forms in mammalian RBCs are released following ingestion by the tick and undergo a series of asexual replications. This leads to formation of the infectious form of *Babesia*, which can be passed from 1 generation of ticks to another by transovarial and interstadial transmission. Cats may then be infected when ticks feed. Infectious forms in the tick saliva enter the blood and parasitize RBCs, in which they replicate asexually.

Domestic cats inoculated IV with infectious whole blood become parasitemic within 24-48 hours.[7] Parasitemia is not associated with fever or other signs of illness during initial stages of the disease. Over a period of weeks, many cats become progressively more anemic. Depression, variable anorexia and weight loss, and fatigue on exercise and handling become more noticeable as the anemia worsens. Jaundice is not readily apparent in experimentally infected cats, but increased bile-staining of feces is common and indicates increased bile excretion.

Clinical Features

The best descriptions of naturally occurring babesiosis in domestic cats are from reports by Jackson and Dunning, McNeil, Futter and Belonje, and Steward and co-workers.[7,11,13,17] Cats with naturally occurring disease range from several weeks to 15 years or more of age; most are ≤ 2 years old. The usual presenting clinical signs are inappetence, weight loss, lethargy, weakness and roughening of the haircoat. Though the disease course is obviously chronic, many cats have had clinical signs for only a few days. Terminally ill cats are very depressed and often cry as if in pain. Fever is noticeable in $< 10\%$ of cats. Jaundice is uncommon. Changes in the stool color to bright yellow or orange occur in many animals. The mucous membranes are pale and the severity of clinical signs is proportional to the degree of anemia. Tachycardia and exertional dyspnea are noticeable in cats with a PCV $<15\%$, though some animals with lower values are still amazingly active. Death is common in untreated cats with a progressively decreasing PCV that drops below 15%.

Pathologic Features

Little information is available about gross or microscopic changes in feline babesiosis. Futter and co-workers described pallor of the tissues, hepatomegaly with centrilobular necrosis, bile stasis and extramedullary hematopoiesis.[9] Such findings are consistent with chronic anemia and are of no specific diagnostic value.

Clinicopathologic Features

Anemia is usually of the responsive type, with polychromasia and increased numbers of nucleated RBCs in the peripheral blood.[8] Though jaundice is often not clinically apparent, slight rises in the icterus index, total serum bilirubin level, and urinary and fecal bile pigments may occur in severely affected individuals. The diagnosis is confirmed by identifying organisms in peripheral RBCs. Giemsa blood stains readily demonstrate organisms in 1-50% of RBCs. The degree of parasitism is somewhat proportional to the PCV. Organisms appear as single annular (signet ring) or round forms, single and double teardrop forms, or rapidly dividing forms with the appearance of an "H" or Maltese cross (Fig 7).

Dogs with babesiosis usually have Coombs' antibodies on their RBCs, similar to cats with hemobartonellosis. This aspect of the disease in cats has not been studied, but it seems likely that the anemia of feline babesiosis is also Coombs' positive.

Treatment and Prevention

Domestic cats that spend great amounts of time in areas containing both infected animals and ticks are at highest risk. Therefore, restriction of the movement of cats in these areas limits the chance of infection.

The treatment of choice for babesiosis in cats is a single dose of primaquine phosphate given IM at 0.5 mg/kg. This is near the toxic level (1 mg/kg as a single dose).[1] Relapses occur in 5-15% of cats within 21-45 days. Quinine and clindamycin used in combination have proven effective in people but this treatment has not been evaluated in cats.[18] Whole-blood transfusions are sometimes required with drug treatment in clinically ill cats with a PCV < 15%.

Infection and Immunity

There is not a great deal of information on immunity of domestic cats to *Babesia* infection. However, immunity in babesiosis resembles that seen in hemobartonellosis.[20] Parasite levels are controlled by removal of infected RBCs by the reticuloendothelial system. Many infected cats are more or less successful in maintaining a low level of parasitemia and remaining relatively free of clinical signs. As in hemobartonellosis and canine babesiosis, immunity is probably one of premunition, ie, animals remain immune by virtue of a persistent low-grade infection that provides continuous stimulation to the reticuloendothelial system.[1]

A number of factors can apparently upset the balance of the chronic carrier state. Futter and Belonje observed 5 cats in their study group that had concurrent respiratory and oral infections.[7] Environmental stress, concurrent illnesses, immunodeficiency, splenectomy and immunosuppressive drug treatment have adversely affected the delicate normal carrier state in dogs with babesiosis.[10] The effect of splenectomy in cats was studied by Futter and Belonje.[7] They found no difference in the incubation period between splenectomized and nonsplenectomized cats, but the disease course was about twice as rapid in splenectomized animals.

Animal and Public Health Considerations

Cats that carry *Babesia* are a minimal health hazard to other cats. The organism can only be transmitted mechanically with whole blood or by way of ticks. People can be infected with *Babesia* spp, but infection is uncommon and almost always associated with murine (*B microti*) and occasionally bovine (*B bovis*, *B divergens*) strains.[8] The principal vector of human babesiosis in the United States is the northern deer tick (*Ixodes dammini*). Nymphal stages of this tick feed on rodents. The ability of feline *Babesia* spp to cause disease in people is unknown but appears to be negligible.

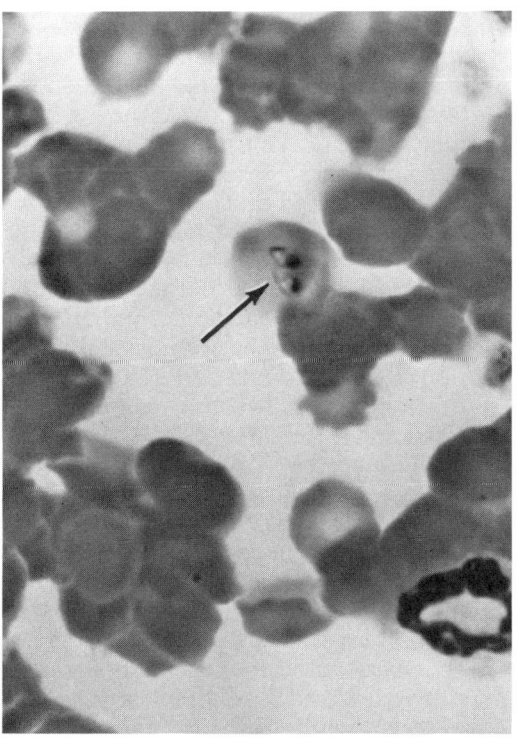

Fig 7. A pair of *Babesia* organisms (arrow) within an RBC of a naturally infected dog. Wright's-Giemsa stain, 2000X.

However, the human disease resembles the feline disease in most other respects.[18]

References

1. Breitschwerdt E, in Greene CE: *Clinical Microbiology and Infectious Diseases of the Dog and Cat.* Saunders, Philadelphia, 1984. pp 797-805.

2. Brocklesby DW et al: A *Babesia* species of the leopard *(Panthera pardus)* and its transmission to the domestic cat. *Proc 2nd Intl Conf Protozool,* Amsterdam, 1965. pp 177-178.

3. Carpano M et al: *Babesia pantherae,* nova piroplasm of the leopard *(Panthera pardus). Parasitol* 64:525-532, 1972.

4. Davis LJ: On a piroplasm of the Sudanese Wild Cat *(Felis ocreata). Trans Royal Soc Trop Med Hyg* 22:523-534, 1929.

5. Denning HK: Eine unbekannte Babesienard beim Jaguarundi *(Herpailurus yaguarundi). Kleintierpraxis* 12:146-152, 1967.

6. Futter GJ and Belonje PC: Studies of feline babesiosis: 1. Historical review. *J So Afr Vet Assoc* 51:105-106, 1980.

7. Futter GJ and Belonje PC: Studies of feline babesiosis: 2. Clinical observations. *J So Afr Vet Assoc* 51:143-146, 1980.

8. Futter GJ et al: Studies on feline babesiosis: 3. Hematological findings. *J So Afr Vet Assoc* 51:271-280, 1980.

9. Futter GJ et al: Studies on feline babesiosis: 4. Chemical pathology; macroscopic and microscopic postmortem findings. *J So Afr Vet Assoc* 52:5-14, 1981.

10. Hildebrandt PK, in Ristic R and Kreir JP: *Babesiosis.* Academic Press, New York, 1981. pp 459-473.

11. Jackson C and Dunning FJ: Biliary fever (nuttalliosis) of the cat. A case in the Stellenbosch district. *J So Afr Vet Assoc* 8:83-87, 1937.

12. Mangrulkar MY: On a piroplasm of the Indian cat *(Felis domesticus). Indian J Vet Sci Anim Husb* 7:243-246, 1937.

13. McNeil J: Piroplasmosis of the domestic cat. *J So Afr Vet Assoc* 8:88-90, 1937.

14. Mudaliar SV et al: On a species *Babesia* in an Indian wild cat *(Felis catus). Indian Vet J* 26:391-395, 1950.

15. Robinson EM: Biliary fever (nuttalliosis) of the cat. *J So Afr Vet Assoc* 34:45-47, 1963.

16. Shortt HE: *Babesia* in the Indian Leopard, *Panthera pardus fusca. Indian J Med Res* 28:277-278, 1940.

17. Stewart CG et al: An unidentified *Babesia* of the domestic cat *(Felis domesticus). J So Afr Vet Assoc* 51:291-321, 1980.

18. Swartz MN, in Wyngaarden JB and Smith LH Jr: *Cecil's Textbook of Medicine.* Saunders, Philadelphia, 1985. pp 1798-1799.

19. Wenyon CM and Hamerton EA: Piroplasms of the West African civet cat *(Viverra civetta)* and the bay lynx *(Felis rufa)* of North America. *Trans Roy Soc Trop Med Hyg* 24:7-8, 1930.

20. Zwart D and Brocklesby DW: Babesiosis: nonspecific resistance, immunologic factors and pathogenesis. *Adv Parasitol* 17:49-113, 1979.

CYTAUXZOONOSIS

Etiologic Agent

Cytauxzoon felis is a protozoan belonging to the order Piroplasmida, family Theileriidae.[7] Members of the genus *Cytauxzoon* infect mainly African ungulates, such as the duiker, springbok, kudu, eland and giraffe.[7] *Cytauxzoon* spp are small, round, oval, irregular or rod-shaped parasites of erythroid and reticuloendothelial cells. Carrier animals serve as reservoirs; the principal vectors, when identified, have been ixodid ticks.

Cytauxzoon felis infection was first reported in domestic cats living in heavily wooded, tick-infested areas of southwestern Missouri.[7] Subsequent cases have been reported from wooded areas of Arkansas, Mississippi, Georgia, Louisiana, Florida, Oklahoma and Texas.[1,3,5] The origin of *C felis* is obscure. Affected cats almost always die, suggesting that cats are merely dead-end hosts. Kier and co-workers could not infect dogs, cattle, goats, 9 different species of laboratory animals ranging from squirrel monkeys to rodents, or 15 species of local wildlife as varied as wild Canidae, raccoons, squirrels, opossum, bats and deer with *Cytauxzoon* spp from affected cats.[5] A Florida bobcat developed a fatal infection typical of the disease in domestic cats, but no overt signs associated with persistent parasitemia were seen in an eastern bobcat. Sheep developed a low level of persistent parasitemia without apparent illness. The possibility that organisms were imported to the United States with African wildlife destined for game parks and zoos cannot be excluded. The precise origin of the organism in the

United States will probably not be determined until the reservoir host is identified.

Pathogenesis

The disease has been extensively studied in the laboratory.[2,4,8,10] The infectious stage is the schizont.[11] The ring forms in RBCs are not pathogenic. Infection can be created with blood or tissue homogenates from infected cats given by virtually any route.[2] When blood is used, however, it must be from late in the disease course when schizonts are likely to be present.[11] The infection has been transmitted by ticks that have fed on parasitemic cats or bobcats.[11] *Cytauxzoon felis* has a predilection to grow in reticuloendothelial cells that line venous channels of the lungs, spleen, liver, lymph nodes, bone marrow and other organs (Fig 8).[2,4] Growth in lymphocytes is rare. Organisms (ring forms) are often seen in RBCs but do not appear to be replicating. Replication within reticuloendothelial cells occurs by serial binary fission (schizogony) leading to formation of schizonts. Host cells are rapidly destroyed by replicating organisms, releasing schizonts and numerous individual merozoites 0.1-0.2 μ in diameter. In turn, these are taken up by reticuloendothelial cells, in which schizogony occurs.

Clinical Features

Cats of all ages and sexes have been affected. Most animals come from rural heavily wooded areas of the American southeast.[7] The highest incidence is in the summer months when ticks are the most numerous. Clusters of cases are frequently observed at about the same time within enzootic areas.[7] Several cats in the same households have been simultaneously infected.[11] The incubation period of experimental disease is 5-7 days.[2,10] Initial signs include anorexia and depression followed by a gradual rise in rectal temperature to 40-41.1 C. The rectal temperature remains high for only 3-4 days, then drops precipitously to normal or subnormal levels before death. Most cats die by 9-15 days after exposure.[2] Survival is rare once clinical signs occur. Prominent features of the illness are jaundice, rapidly progressing hemolytic anemia, generalized lymphadenopathy, splenomegaly and dehydration.

Pathologic Features

Pathologic features of the disease have been well documented.[1,2,3,7] Fatally affected cats are often markedly dehydrated, pale and jaundiced. The spleen and lymph nodes are enlarged, congested and hemorrhagic. Numerous petechial and ecchymotic hemorrhages are often seen on the epicardium, serosal membranes of abdominal organs, visceral pleura of the lungs, and mucosa of the urinary bladder. The liver is frequently swollen and orange-brown. The pericardial sac often contains small to moderate amounts of icteric fluid.

Histopathologic lesions are concentrated in organs rich in reticuloendothelial tissue.[2,7] Parasitized reticuloendothelial cells accumulate in large numbers in venous channels in the spleen, lymph nodes, lungs and liver, and within capillaries of the kidney, heart, urinary bladder and bone marrow (Fig 8). Parasitized reticuloendothelial

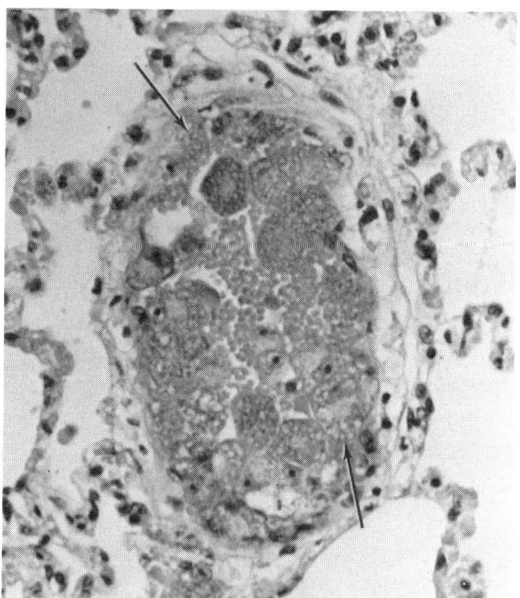

Fig 8. *Cytauxzoon felis* (arrows) within and outside reticuloendothelial cells in a pulmonary blood vessel of a naturally infected cat. The main form of the organism is the schizont, each of which contains numerous merozoites. The RE cells are engorged with replicating organisms. Infected cells and extracellular schizonts nearly occlude the vascular lumen. Hematoxylin and eosin stain, 125X. (Courtesy of Dr. Linda Lowenstine, University of California, Davis)

cells often partially or completely occlude venous channels in the spleen and liver. Thrombosis, edema and hemorrhage are common in heavily parasitized vessels.

Schizonts are common within reticuloendothelial cells in affected organs (Fig 8). Schizonts are relatively amorphous and basophilic on hematoxylin and eosin staining. They occupy most of the cytoplasm. The amorphous, foamy and somewhat vesicular appearance of the schizonts is due to the relative immaturity of individual merozoites. Some schizonts have a more granular appearance, indicating more mature merozoites. Ring forms of the organism are also apparent in RBCs within the lumens and blood vessels.

Clinicopathologic Features

Ring forms in the RBCs are usually seen in ≥ 50% of affected cats (Fig 9). They are usually present in 1-4% of the cells.[2] As many as 25% of the RBCs are parasitized in some cats.[9] *Cytauxzoon* organisms in RBCs appear as "signet-ring" bodies 1-1.5 μ in diameter or as bipolar, oval or safety pin-shaped bodies 1 x 2 μ.[9] The cytoplasm of the intraerythrocytic form of the organism stains light blue with Wright's or Giemsa stain, while the nucleus stains dark red to purple. These features usually allow ready differentiation from *Hemobartonella*.[9]

The PCV begins to fall by day 6, which is the time organisms are first seen in the RBCs.[10] The anemia is very acute and not associated with an increase in numbers of reticulocytes or mean corpuscular volume.[10] The platelet count is significantly depressed by day 8, and there is sometimes a terminal leukopenia.

Organisms have been detected in splenic reticuloendothelial cells by fluorescent antibody staining.[6] However, this procedure has not been applied to peripheral blood smears.

Cats with cytauxzoonosis often have hemolytic anemia. Total bilirubin, liver enzyme and BUN levels are often elevated in the terminal stages of the disease. The PT, PTT and FDP are normal during the entire disease course.[10]

Treatment and Prevention

Almost all experimentally or naturally infected cats have died. Likewise, no treatment has been found that alters the fatal course of the disease.[9] Drugs that have been tested include a number of antimalarials, and anti-theilerials, such as parvoquone and buparvoquone.[12]

Infection and Immunity

The disease appears to be extremely fulminating in domestic cats. Recovery has been seen only in a very small number of experimentally infected cats and never in naturally occurring cases.[4] The highly fatal nature of the disease in domestic cats appears to involve host-specific factors. Eastern bobcats inoculated with infectious material from cats develop parasitemia but do not become ill.[4] However, a Florida bobcat died from the infection. Sheep also become chronic low-level carriers of the organism without signs of illness.

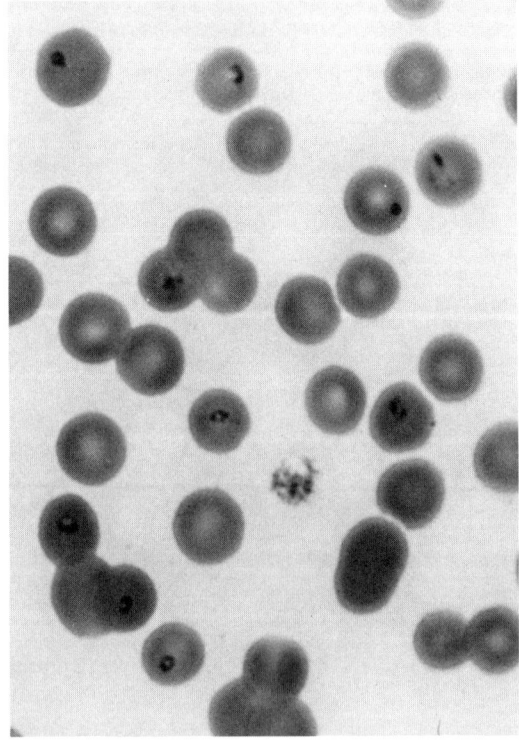

Fig 9. Piroplasmic forms of *Cytauxzoon felis* within erythrocytes in peripheral blood from a cat. Wright's-Giemsa stain. (Courtesy of Dr. John W. Harvey, University of Florida, Gainesville)

Passage of virulent *C felis* in eastern bobcats appears to attenuate or strain-select the organism.[4] Domestic cats inoculated with blood from an infected eastern bobcat developed chronic parasitemia but no clinical signs of illness. In turn, blood from such cats caused subclinical parasitemia in other cats. Cats that carried the avirulent bobcat strain of *C felis* were not immune to infection with the virulent cat-passaged organism.[4] Shindel and co-workers reported successful immunization of a cat with organisms attenuated in tissue culture.[6]

Animal and Public Health Considerations

Cats are apparently dead-end hosts for *Cytauxzoon felis*. Affected cats do not appear to be infectious to other cats, people or other animals.

References

1. Bendele RA et al: Cytauxzoonosis-like disease in Texas cats. *Southwestern Vet* 29:244-246, 1976.

2. Ferris DH: A progress report on the status of a new disease of American cats: Cytauxzoonosis. *Comp Immunol Microbiol Infect Dis* 1:269-276, 1979.

3. Hauck WN et al: Cytauxzoonosis in a native Louisiana cat. *JAVMA* 180:1472-1474, 1982.

4. Kier AB et al: Experimental transmission of *Cytauxzoon felis* from bobcats (*Lynx rufus*) to domestic cats (*Felis domesticus*). *Am J Vet Res* 43:97-101, 1982.

5. Kier AB et al: Interspecies transmission of *Cytauxzoon felis*. *Am J Vet Res* 43:102-105, 1982.

6. Shindel N et al: An indirect fluorescent antibody test for the detection of cytauxzoon-like organisms in experimentally infected cats. *Can J Comp Med* 42:460-465, 1978.

7. Wagner JE: A fatal cytauxzoonosis-like disease in cats. *JAVMA* 168:585-588, 1976.

8. Wagner JE et al: Feline cytauxzoonosis; a newly reported blood protozoan disease from southwestern Missouri. *Missouri Vet* 26:12-13, 1976.

9. Wightman SR et al: Feline cytauxzoonosis: clinical features of a newly described blood parasite disease. *Feline Pract* 7(3):23-26, 1977.

Additional References

10. Franks PT et al: Hematological findings in experimental feline cytauxzoonosis. *JAAHA* 24:395-401, 1988.

11. Harvey J, University of Florida, Gainesville: Personal communication, 1988.

12. Kocan A, Oklahoma State University, Norman: Personal communication, 1988.

GIARDIASIS

Etiologic Agent

The genus *Giardia* is comprised of 40 or more closely related or identical isolates from reptiles, birds and mammals.[16] Isolates vary greatly in pathogenicity and host specificity. Comparative isoenzyme studies of human, guinea pig and feline isolates showed that some were identical, while others were distinct.[5]

Giardia spp are protozoan parasites belonging to the phylum Sarcomastigophora, subphylum Mastigophora, class Zoomastigophorea, order Diplomonadidia and suborder Diplomonadina.[9] The organism is droplet shaped and averages 13 μ in length, 7 μ in breadth and 3 μ in width. Each organism is binucleated, and possesses 8 long flagella for movement and a large ventral circular disc for adhesion to epithelial cell surfaces. Organisms exist as motile trophozoites that divide by binary fission in the intestinal tract of their host and as hyaline-walled cysts containing 2 dormant trophozoites in the environment.

Giardia spp are found in many animal hosts throughout the world. Trophozoites are loosely attached to microvilli of the intestinal mucosa or free in the overlying mucus film. They are found most consistently in the dudodenum and jejunum of most animals. However, they are more common in the distal jejunum and proximal ileum in cats.[12,13] They do not invade mucosal cell surfaces, and obtain nutrients from intestinal contents by pinocytosis through the dorsal membranes.

The life cycle of *Giardia* is direct. Many trophozoites change to 7 x 10-μ cyst forms during passage through the large intestine. Encysted forms of the organism are quite resistant to environmental degradation and can survive for weeks or months under cool and moist conditions. Trophozoites die rapidly after being passed in the stool.

Pathogenesis

Surveys in different countries show an infection rate of 1-11% in cats.[11] Younger cats and kittens are more likely to be clinically infected than older cats.[11,15,22] Infection occurs by direct animal-to-animal transmission (fecal-oral) or contamination of drinking water with cyst forms. Fecal-oral transmission is probably the most important route in cats, while water-borne transmission is the most common route in people.

Ingested cysts are partially dissolved by stomach acids, and trophozoites are released into the small intestine. Trophozoites replicate rapidly and cysts appear in the feces within 5-16 days.[11]

Large numbers of organisms in the small intestine damage underlying epithelial cells. The mechanism of this effect is not understood but may include mechanical interference, elaboration of a yet-unidentified soluble toxin, competition between parasites and epithelial cells for essential nutrients, direct damage of epithelial cells by adherent organisms, changes in the microenvironment favoring bacterial overgrowth, and secondary damage to the epithelium caused by host immunity against the parasites.[25] Though the precise cause of muscoal damage is unknown, little doubt remains of its effect on normal intestinal function. Enterocyte disaccharidases, brush border alkaline phosphatase, glucose and amino acid transport, and lipid digestion all decrease significantly.[1,8] Therefore, intestinal disease caused by *Giardia* is of a malabsorption type.

Clinical Features

Giardial infections of cats are usually subclinical. Clinical signs are most often seen in younger animals from multiple-cat households and catteries. Outbreaks of disease are often associated with introduction of new animals into the environment. The introduced cat develops signs from exposure to the household cats, or is the vehicle for infecting the resident population. In its most severe form, infection is characterized by loose, mucoid and frequently foul-smelling stools, steatorrhea, flatulence, abdominal distension and poor haircoat.[4,6,11,13,15,18,23] The course of the disease in untreated individuals varies from less than a week to several months.

Pathologic Features

Pathologic changes are limited to the intestinal tract, mainly the jejunum. Gross anomalies are not seen and histopathologic changes vary from nonexistent to marked. Histopathologic abnormalities include subtotal villus atrophy characterized by reduced villus height, crypt elongation, and a mild submucosal inflammatory response. Blunting and deformation of individual microvilli are generally most noticeable in areas of large numbers of adherent trophozoites. *Giardia* trophozoites can be stained with hematoxylin and eosin, Giemsa or PAS stain.[13]

Clinicopathologic Features

Giardiasis is diagnosed by demonstrating cysts and trophozoites in the stool (Fig 10).

Fig 10. *Giardia* cyst in cat feces. These cysts are 8-10 μ in diameter. (Courtesy of Dr. Norman Baker, University of California, Davis)

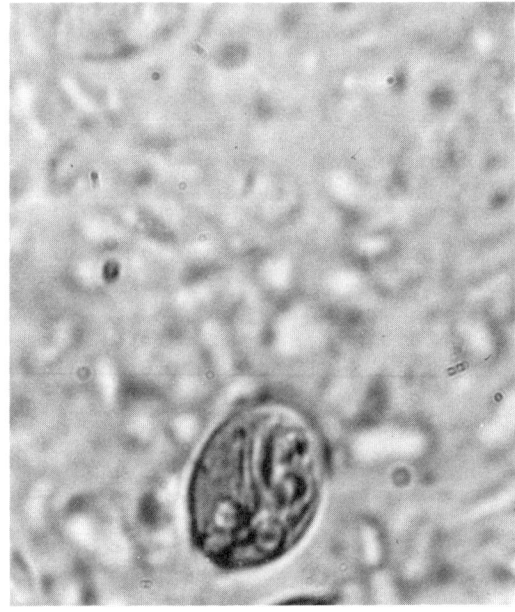

However, organisms are often shed sporadically and are not always easy to identify. Direct examination of fresh fecal smears is the simplest procedure. A small amount of feces is diluted with saline, mixed with a drop of Lugol's iodine solution and examined by conventional light microscopy. Cysts can be concentrated from feces by zinc sulfate centrifugal flotation but not with flotation procedures using sugar or other salts. Diagnosis of giardiasis is complicated by the cyclic nature of cyst shedding.[13] Therefore, at least 3 collections must be examined before declaring a fecal sample negative.

Treatment and Prevention

A favorable response to treatment is often the most accurate way to diagnose clinical giardiasis in animals and people. This is because some animals with giardiasis do not have demonstrable numbers of organisms in their stool, while others have demonstrable organisms but suffer from totally unrelated problems. Quinacrine hydrochloride, PO at 1.5 mg/kg TID for 10 days, is the treatment of choice for people. In cats, a dosage of 11 mg/kg daily for 12 days eliminated clinical signs but not shedding of trophozoites and cysts.[6] Metronidazole PO at 8 mg/kg BID for 10 days eliminated both clinical signs and fecal organisms in 2 cats.[18] Wolff and Eckert reported similar success in a cat given metronidazole at 25 mg/kg BID for 5 days.[28] Experimental studies in cats showed good results with metronidazole at 10 mg/kg BID for 5 days or furazolidone PO at 4 mg/kg BID for 5 days.[13]

Infection and Immunity

Immunity to *Giardia* is probably similar to that of *Cryptosporidium*. Both cellular and humoral immunity appear involved in resistance, as indicated by the high incidence of infection in people with either combined or specific IgA immunodeficiencies.[24] The role of both humoral and cellular immunity to *Giardia* has also been demonstrated in mice.[2,19,20,24] Lymphocytes have been observed adhered to trophozoites in the bowel lumen during the recovery stage of infection.[19] Granulocytes may also interact with antibody to remove parasites from the bowel.[26] Immunity in mice appears to be highly controlled by genetics.[4,20,21] Under normal circumstances, immunity to infection develops in several weeks. Infection can be greatly prolonged by stress and debilitating diseases. Glucocorticoid treatment has prolonged the course of primary infection and triggered recrudescence of low-grade or latent infection in mice.[17] Shedding of cysts increased more than 100-fold 2 days after an injection of glucocorticoids in 1 cat; other cats given lower daily oral dosages of prednisolone for 5 days did not shed more organisms until after therapy was stopped.[13] Once established, immunity is probably tenuous and short-lived. Therefore, reinfection with episodic shedding of organisms is probably common.

Animal and Public Health Considerations

Though cats apparently carry many strains of *Giardia* that antigenically resemble those found in other species,[27] feline strains are probably more pathogenic for cats than for other animals. Therefore, cats are the greatest health hazard to other cats. Human isolates of *Giardia* appear to be minimally infectious or noninfectious for cats.[14] The converse situation has not been studied, so the exact public health significance of infected cats is not known. Only 2 instances of concurrent human and feline giardiasis in the same households have been reported.[7] Until more information is obtained, infected cats should be considered as potential, but probably not important, reservoirs for human giardiasis.

References

1. Anand BS et al: Transport studies and enzyme assays in mice infected with human *Giardia lamblia*. Trans R Soc Trop Med Hyg 76:616-619, 1982.

2. Andrews JS and Hewlett EL: Protection against infections with *Giardia muris* by milk containing antibody to *Giardia*. J Infect Dis 143:242-246, 1981.

3. Belosevic M et al: Observations on natural and experimental infections with *Giardia* isolated from cats. Can J Comp Med 48:241-244, 1984a.

4. Belosevic M et al: Susceptibility and resistance of inbred mice to Giardia muris. Infect Immunity 44:282-286, 1984.

5. Bertram MA et al: A comparison of isoenzymes of five axenic Giardia isolates. J Parasitol 69:793-801, 1983.

6. Brightman AH and Slonka GF: A review of five clinical cases of giardiasis in cats. JAAHA 12:492-497, 1976.

7. Davies RB and Hibler CP, in Jakubowski W and Hoff JC: Waterborne Transmission of Giardiasis. US Env Prot Agency, Cincinnati, 1979. pp 104-125.

8. Gillon J et al: Features of small intestinal pathology (Epithelial cell kinetics, intraepithelial lymphocytes, disaccharidases) in primary Giardia muris infection. Gut 23:408-506, 1982.

9. Greene CE: Clinical Microbiology and Infectious Disease of the Dog and Cat. Saunders, Philadelphia, 1984. p 30.

10. Jarroll EL et al, in Erlandsen SL and Meyer EA: Giardia and Giardiasis: Pathogenesis, and Epidemiology. Plenum Press, New York, 1984. p 311.

11. Kirkpatrick CE: Feline giardiasis: a review. J Small Anim Pract 27:69-80, 1986.

12. Kirkpatrick CE and Farrell JP: Giardiasis. Comp Cont Ed Pract Vet 4:367-377, 1982.

13. Kirkpatrick CE and Farrell JP: Feline giardiasis: observations on natural and experimental transmission. Am J Vet Res 45:2182-2188, 1984.

14. Kirkpatrick CE and Green GA IV: Susceptibility of domestic cats to infections with Giardia lamblia cysts and trophozoites from human sources. J Clin Microbiol 21:678-680, 1985.

15. Kirkpatrick CE and Laczak JP: Giardiasis in a cattery. JAVMA 187:161-162, 1985.

16. Kulda J and Nohynkova E, in Kreier JP: Parasitic Protozoa. Vol 2. Academic Press, New York, 1978. p 1.

17. Nair KV et al: Corticosteroid treatment increases parasite numbers in murine giardiasis. Gut 22:475-480, 1981.

18. Nesvadba J: Giardiasis in a cat. Kleintier-Prax 24:177-179, 1979.

19. Owen RL et al: Ultrastructural observations on giardiasis in a murine model. I. Intestinal distribution, attachment, and relationship of the immune system of Giardia muris. Gastroenterol 76:757-769, 1979.

20. Roberts-Thomson IC et al: Genetic studies in human and murine giardiasis. Gut 21:397-401, 1980.

21. Roberts-Thomson IC and Mitchell GF: Giardiasis in mice. I. Prolonged infections in certain mouse strains and hypothymic (nude) mice. Gastroenterol 75:42-46, 1978.

22. Seiler M et al: Giardia und andere Darmparasiten bei Hund und Katze in der Schweiz. Schweiz Arch Tierheilk 125:137-148, 1983.

23. Shatto NL: Feline giardiasis: a case report. VM/SAC 76:1297-1298, 1981.

24. Stevens DP: Giardiasis: host-pathogen biology. Rev Infect Dis 4:851-858, 1982.

25. Stevens DP, in Wyngaarden JB and Smith LH Jr: Cecil's Textbook of Medicine. Saunders, Philadelphia, 1985. pp 1802-1803.

26. Smith DP et al: Human host response to Giardia lamblia. II. Antibody-dependent killing in vitro. Cell Immunol 82:308-315, 1983.

27. Visvesvara GS et al: Comparative antigenic analysis of Giardia from the human, the cat, and the guinea pig. J Protozool 27:38A, 1980.

28. Wolff K and Eckert J: Giardia infection of dogs and cats and its possible significance for man. Berl Munch Tierarztl Wochenschr 92:479-484, 1979.

TRYPANOSOMIASIS

Etiologic Agent

Trypanosoma spp are protozoa belonging to the phylum Sarcomastigophora, class Zoomastigophorea, order Kinetoplastida and family Trypanosomatidae.[23] They are leaf-like and 11-25 μ long, with a single flagellum attached to a lateral undulating veil-like membrane. Trypanosoma probably evolved from parasites of the alimentary tract of insects. Since many of these insects fed on blood, perhaps it is not surprising that some Trypanosoma spp have developed blood or tissue stages in the hosts of insects.

In domestic cats, 5 species of Trypanosoma have been reported to cause disease: T brucei, T gambiense, T congolense, T evansi and T cruzi.[5,6,8,9,13,17,18,20,22,24-26] At least 1 nonpathogenic trypanosome, T rangeli, can also infect cats.[15]

Trypanosoma brucei, T congolense and T gambiense are found mainly in equatorial Africa.[22,23] They all undergo cyclic development in the midgut and salivary glands of Glossina spp (blood-sucking flies).[23] Trypanosoma brucei has an extremely wide host range and is probably the most pathogenic of the species to domestic cats. It is an important pathogen of cattle. *Trypanosoma gambiense* causes disease mainly in people, but wild animals are the principal reservoir. *Trypanosoma congolense* infects a wide range of animals but is a principal cause of disease in cattle.

The infection cycle with this group of trypanosomes begins when the blood-sucking fly takes a blood meal from a carrier host.[23] Ingested forms multiply by binary fission in the distal midgut of the fly. This trypomastigote stage of replication lasts about 10 days. By 10-11 days, long slender forms of the organism appear. These migrate into the spaces around the peritrophic membrane and penetrate the proventriculus (forestomach). Many organisms are found in the proventriculus of the fly by days 12-20. Immature trypanosomes then migrate to the esophagus and pharynx, ultimately reaching the hypopharynx and salivary glands. The organisms undergo further multiplication and differentiation as epimastigotes. Ultimately, they become infectious metacyclic forms that are injected into the host's bloodstream when the fly bites.

Trypanosoma evansi is also very pathogenic to domestic cats.[5] It is found throughout the Indian subcontinent, Far East, Philippine Islands, Central and South America, and parts of North Africa.[23] It is mechanically transmitted by biting flies, such as *Tabanus* spp (tabanid horse flies), *Stomoxys* spp (stable flies) and *Lyperosia* spp (small biting flies of cattle and buffalo). Vampire bats have become important vectors for *T evansi* in South and Central America. Oral transmission from infected prey to predator has also been recognized.[27] No cyclic development occurs in the host flies.[23,27] *Trypanosoma evansi* is a major cause of disease in a wide range of animals, particularly horses, camels and dogs. Camels are an important reservoir in certain areas. In other areas, cattle and water buffalo are major host species. The blood form of *T evansi* is present on the palps (mouthparts) of flies after feeding and is mechanically transmitted among animals as the flies feed.[23,27]

Trypanosoma cruzi is the cause of American trypanosomiasis, or Chagas' disease of people.[4,14] It is found in South America from Argentina northward into Central America. It is also rarely found in regions of the American Southeast as far north as Maryland, and in pockets of the Sierra Nevada foothills in northern California.[4] Various animal species serve as reservoir hosts, including dogs, cats, pigs, foxes, ferrets, squirrels, opossum, monkeys, raccoons and skunks.[4] Though many animals serve as reservoirs and may develop minor forms of disease, young children and infants are the principal victims of Chagas' disease.[4,14] *Trypanosoma cruzi* is transmitted by a number of blood-sucking bugs belonging to the family Reduviidae. They are often referred to as triatomes, from the genus name *Triatoma*. After ingestion of infected blood by triatome hosts, development occurs in the lining cells of the stomach.[23] The trypomastigote stage divides rapidly and leads to rupture of the lining cells and release of organisms into the intestinal tract. The organisms pass to the distal intestine, where they firmly attach themselves to the lining cells. They undergo additional division to infectious metacyclic forms, which are passed in the feces. These forms are rubbed into the wound reduviid bugs make as they feed. Triatomes commonly defecate while feeding, which facilitates infection of animal or human hosts.

Pathogenesis

Most trypanosomes have reservoirs among wild species of animals, in which they do not cause severe disease.[23] Disease occurs when animal species are exposed to *Trypanosoma* spp to which they are highly susceptible. People, cattle, dogs and horses are unnatural hosts. This may explain why they suffer more from disease than enzootic species of wildlife.

What little is known about the pathogenesis of trypanosomiasis in cats has come from experimental studies with *T evansi* and observations of naturally infected cats.[5,6,8,9,13,17,20,24-26] A great deal of information can also be extrapolated from studies of natural and experimental disease in people and cattle.[22,23] After infection of cats with *T evansi*, parasitemia is first seen on day 14 or 15.[5] Cats that are 3-4 months of age or younger often succumb to the initial wave of parasitism. Older cats may survive the initial parasitemia and undergo cyclic disease corresponding to consecutive waves of parasitemia. Each wave of parasitemia usually lasts 4-5 days and occurs about 14 days apart. A similar pattern of disease is seen with *T congolense*, *T gambiense* and *T brucei*. Infection of cats with *T cruzi* is quite different. Most cats become relatively asymptomatic carriers following initial infection; clinical disease is relatively uncommon.[17]

Clinical Features

Clinical signs of *T brucei*, *T evansi*, *T congolense* and *T gambiense* infections usually correspond to periods of parasitemia. Cats often appear listless and anemic, and have rough coats. They are usually febrile and may breathe rapidly and shallowly. Edema and erythema are often seen around the face. Bilateral panophthalmitis is common.[5,8] In fact, blindness has been listed as a common sign of trypanosomiasis in cats.[12] Neurologic signs have also been seen in affected cats.[18] Cats with clinical disease usually die if untreated. The exact incidence of asymptomatic infections in cats with this group of trypanosomes is unknown. The ratio of asymptomatic to diseased cats is probably low as compared to that of *T cruzi* infections.

Trypanosoma cruzi infection in cats is reportedly similar to the infection in dogs but it is not as severe.[17] The disease in dogs is, in turn, milder than that in people. Chagas' disease in people occurs in acute and chronic forms.[4,14] Though the range of the trypanosome and its vector is great, most cases occur in economically underdeveloped countries. The acute stage of Chagas' disease occurs in about 1% of infected individuals, usually children under 10 years of age. A violet-hued edematous lesion is often seen at the site of the bite 4-12 days after infection.[14] If the bite is near the eye, conjunctivitis and periorbital edema, with periauricular lymph node enlargement, may be seen. Subsequent disease is due to widespread proliferation of the trypanosome in reticuloendothelial tissue.[14] This proliferation is usually accompanied by fever, lymphadenopathy, asthenia, edema of the face and legs, and hepatosplenomegaly. Transient severe myocarditis usually accompanies the disease but is often only recognized electrocardiographically. Meningoencephalitis is a rare occurrence in acute disease. The acute phase usually lasts 2-4 months and then disappears. Individuals that are asymptomatic or demonstrate the acute phase of disease often become latent carriers of the infection. Chronic Chagas' disease is manifested mainly by subclinical to severe right-sided cardiomyopathy and alterations in esophageal and colonic motility.[14] The cardiac, esophageal and colonic signs are due to inflammatory reactions against organisms within the musculature of these organs. Neurologic disease is uncommon.

Chagas' disease of dogs is similar to the human disease in most respects.[4] It is gen-

Fig 11. *Trypanosoma equiperdum* in the blood of a guinea pig. This organism has the typical appearance of trypanosomes infecting other species, such as cats. Wright's-Leishman stain, 2000X. (Courtesy of Dr. N. Jain, University of California, Davis)

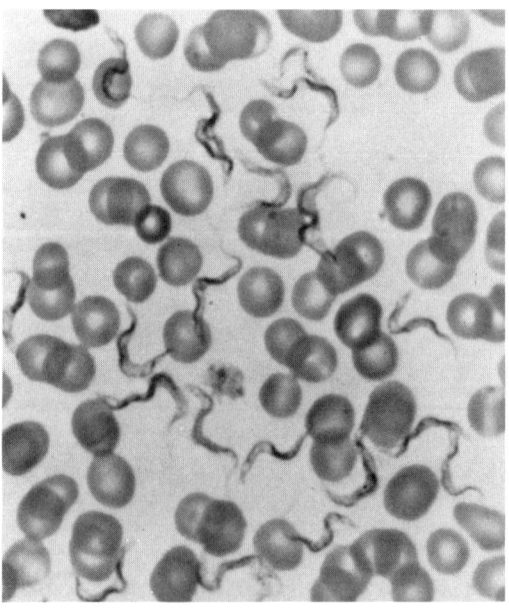

erally milder, however. For instance, intramural thrombosis of cardiac vessels was observed in 11% of experimentally infected dogs and 79% of people.[1] Likewise, thinning of the cardiac wall and intimal fibrotic plaques were observed in 42% of dogs and 72% of people.

Trypanosoma cruzi infection of cats is similar in frequency to infection of dogs and people in highly enzootic areas.[17] However, most cats are completely asymptomatic. No specific electrocardiographic or necropsy studies have been conducted on cats, so it is not known if infected cats have subclinical disease. Several cats infected with *T cruzi*, with signs resembling those of acute Chagas' disease, have been reported.[18,24] They manifested mainly fever, weight loss, edema and neurologic disturbances (convulsions, paresis).

Pathologic Features

There is very little information on the pathologic features of feline trypanosomiasis. The facial edema and panophthalmitis that are frequently seen in cats infected with *T brucei*, *T evansi*, *T congolense* or *T gambiense* suggest an immune-mediated host attack against organisms within vascular reticuloendothelial cells. The cause of the anemia that often accompanies infection with this group of trypanosomes has not been determined.[23] The anemia is ultimately associated with increased erythrophagocytosis and appears to be hemolytic. It has been postulated that trypanosomal antigens may attach themselves to RBCs and target them for immune destruction.[10] In support of this, both immunoglobulin and complement have been demonstrated on RBCs of cattle with *T congolense* infections and people with *T rhodesiense* infections.[11,28] Boreham suggested the anemia was due to disseminated intravascular coagulopathy and microangiopathy.[2] Degenerative changes reported in the heart and liver of infected cats are probably secondary to severe and chronic hypoxia associated with the anemia.

Lesions in cats infected with *T cruzi* have not been described.

Clinicopathologic Features

Trypanosomes can usually be identified in blood smears of clinically affected individuals (Fig 11). Blood smears should be as thick as possible. Heavy infections may demonstrate 2 or more organisms per high-power field. Lighter infections may require a careful search of the smear. Indirect fluorescent antibody tests have been used for serodiagnosis of Chagas' disease in people but have not been applied to dogs or cats.[17] Cats with asymptomatic *T cruzi* infections may demonstrate few organisms in blood smears. Infections in carrier animals, such as dogs and cats, are usually detected by allowing nymphal *Triatoma infestans* to feed on their blood. The feces of the bugs are examined for trypanosomes several days later.[17]

Immunologic Features

Trypanosoma brucei, *T congolense*, *T gambiense* and *T evansi* infections tend to be severe in susceptible hosts. Many other host species are susceptible to infection but not to disease. These animals apparently reach some sort of immune tolerance to the infection, similar to patent heartworm infection in dogs. When lesions occur, they are probably associated with the host's immune responses against the organisms. The chronic cardiovascular manifestations of *T cruzi* infection in people may also be caused by antibody- and cell-mediated immune responses against muscle-bound organisms. The organisms might also induce autoantibodies against an endocardial-vascular-interstitial factor.[23]

The cyclic waves of parasitism and disease seen in some highly susceptible species appear to be due to antigenic drift of coat antigens in the face of host immunity. As each wave of parasitism is contained by emerging immunity, existing organisms are largely destroyed. Surviving organisms appear with altered coat antigens that are not recognized by immunity to the preceding dominant forms. The 2-week interval between waves of parasitism mirrors the appearance of each new antigenic type of organism. Gray proposed that variants appear in predictable sequences and revert to the initial antigenic type on repassage in insect hosts.[7] Seed and Gram and McNeillage and associates showed that variants do not arise in an ordered sequence, though some variants seemed to occur more frequently than others.[16,21]

Treatment and Prevention

Information on treatment of cats with *T brucei*, *T evansi*, *T congolense* and *T gambiense* infections is scant. Hill treated a naturally infected cat with antrycide methylsulfate in a single treatment at 6-10 mg/kg IM or SC.[8] However, relapse occurred 4 times over a 6-month period and the animal was ultimately destroyed. Hutchinson reported successful treatment of a cat with a single dose of 25 mg of antrycide methylsulfate. Unsworth reported suramin to be effective when antrycide failed.[25] Soulsby reported the dose of suramin for dogs as 300 mg IV daily for 6 days.[23] Considering this an average dose for a 20-kg dog, the daily IV dose for a cat would be around 75 mg. Isometamidium chloride, at 0.5-1 mg/kg as a single deep IM injection, is also effective against some antrycide methylsulfate-resistant strains.[23] Drug resistance in people and cattle often develops rapidly, and it is not unusual for more than 1 drug to be used during the course of treatment.

Only 2 drugs have been effective against *T cruzi* infection: nifurtimox (Bayer 2502 or Lampit) and benznidazole (Rochagan R07-1051).[14] Nifurtimox is used in people at 8 mg/kg daily for 120 days. Benznidazole is used at 5 mg/kg daily for 60 days.

Animal and Public Health Considerations

Cats are not an important reservoir for *T gambiense*, a pathogen of people. However, the same may not be the case for *T cruzi* infection. Mott and co-workers found that 18% of dogs and 18% of cats in some areas of Brazil were infected, as determined by *Triatoma infestans* feeding assays.[17] While dogs are generally considered an important reservoir for the infection, the high morbidity in cats has gone unappreciated.

The high morbidity among domestic cats in enzootic areas has been recognized by Pedreira de Freitas.[20] Mott and associates found the rate of human infection was 5 times higher in homes in which dogs, cats and the triatome vector *Panstrongylus megistus* were infected than in homes in which neither animals nor vectors were infected.[17] They also recovered *T cruzi* from *P megistus* from homes in which infected dogs and cats were present, but not from homes with uninfected animals. The fact that *P megistus*, dogs and cats are cohabitants of many homes makes them important links in transmission of Chagas' disease in some areas.

References

1. Anselmi A et al: Myocardiopathy in Chagas' disease: Comparative study of pathologic findings in chronic human and experimental Chagas. *Am Heart J* 72:469-481, 1966.

2. Boreham PFL: Physiopathological changes in the blood of rabbits infected with *Trypanosoma brucei*. *Rev Elev Med Vet Pays Trop* 27:279-282, 1974.

3. Cameron TWM: *The Parasites of Domestic Animals*. 2nd ed. Lippincott, Philadelphia, 1951. p 26.

4. Chapman WL Jr and Hanson WL, in Greene CE: *Clinical Microbiology and Infectious Diseases of the Dog and Cat*. Saunders, Philadelphia, 1984. pp 757-763.

5. Choudhury A and Misra KK: Experimental infection of *T evansi* in the cat. *Trans Rev Soc Trop Med Hyg* 66:672, 1972.

6. Curson HH, as cited in Hill DH: *Trypanosoma brucei* in the cat. *Brit Vet J* 111:77-80, 1955.

7. Gray AR: Antigenic variation in a strain of *Trypanosoma brucei* transmitted by *Glossina morsitans* and *G palpalis*. *J Gen Microbiol* 41:195-214, 1965.

8. Hill DH: *Trypanosoma brucei* in the cat. *Brit Vet J* 111:77-80, 1955.

9. Hutchinson RA, as cited in Hill DH: *Trypanosoma brucei* in the cat. *Brit Vet J* 111:77-80, 1955.

10. Jennings FW, in Soulsby EJL: *Pathophysiology of Parasitic Infections*. Academic Press, New York, 1976. pp 41-67.

11. Kobayashi A et al: Studies on the anaemia in experimental trypanosomiasis. II. The pathogenesis of the anaemia in calves infected with *Trypanosoma congolense*. *Am J Trop Med Hyg* 25:401-406, 1976.

12. Laveran A and Mesnil F, in Masson et al: *Trypanosomas et Trypanosomiases*. Paris, Libraires de l'Academie de Medecin, 1904. pp 122-123.

13. Laveran A and Mesnil F, in Masson et al: *Trypanosomas et Trypanosomiases.* Paris, Libraires de l'Academie de Medecin, 1912. pp 435-436.

14. Macedo V, in Wyngaarden JB and Smith LH Jr: *Cecil's Textbook of Medicine.* Saunders, Philadelphia, 1985. pp 1783-1786.

15. Mansfield JM, in: *Parasitic Protozoology.* Vol I. Academic Press, New York, 1977. pp 297-327.

16. McNeillage GJC et al: Antigenic types of first relapse variants arising from a strain of *Trypanosoma (Trypanozoon) brucei. Exp Parasitol* 25:1-7, 1969.

17. Mott KE et al: *Trypanosoma cruzi* in dogs and cats and household seroreactivity to *T cruzi* in a rural community in Northeast Brazil. *Am J Trop Med Hyg* 27:1123-1127, 1978.

18. Neveu-Lemaire M: *Précis de Parasitologie Vétérinaire.* 2nd ed. Vigot Frères, Paris, 1952.

19. Paikne DL and Dhake PR: Trypanosomiasis in a domestic cat. *Indian Vet J* 51:387, 1974.

20. Pedreira de Freitas JL, as in Mott KE et al: *Trypanosoma cruzi* infections in dogs and cats and household seroreactivity to *T cruzi* in Northeast Brazil. *Am J Trop Med Hyg* 27:1123-1127, 1978.

21. Seed JR and Gram AA: Passive immunity to experimental trypanosomiasis. *J Parasitol* 52:1134-1140, 1966.

22. Soltys MA and Woo PTK, in: *Parasitic Protozoology.* Vol I. Academic Press, New York, 1977. pp 239-268.

23. Soulsby EJL: *Helminths, Arthropods and Protozoa of Domesticated Animals.* Lea & Febiger, Philadelphia, 1982. pp 514-543.

24. Talice RV: Primeros observaciones en el Uruquay de gatos espontaneamente infectados por el *Trypanosoma cruzi. Arch Urg Med* 13:61-64, 1938.

25. Unsworth K, as cited in Hill DH: *Trypanosoma brucei* in the cat. *Brit Vet J* 111:77-80, 1955.

26. Wenyon CM: *Protozoology.* Baillière, Tindall and Cox, London, 1926. p 1355.

27. Woo PTK, in: *Parasitic Protozoology.* Vol I. Academic Press, New York, 1977. pp 269-296.

28. Woodruff AW et al: Anaemia in African trypanosomiasis and (big spleen disease) in Uganda. *Trans Rev Soc Trop Med Hyg* 67:329-337, 1973.

MISCELLANEOUS PROTOZOAL INFECTIONS

Leishmaniasis

The genus *Leishmania* belongs to the family Trypanosomatidae.[18] Therefore, their structure, antigenicity and life cycle are similar to those of *Trypanosoma* spp. *Leishmania* spp are flagellated protozoa that are transmitted by biting sandflies of the genera *Phlebotomus* (Old World) and *Lutzomyia* (New World).[18] Tissue forms within mammalian hosts are nonflagellated. *Leishmania* spp are divided into New World and Old World species and varieties, and are the cause of either cutaneous (localized) or visceral (systemic) disease.[14,18] In most areas of the world, various types of rodents are the principal reservoirs. However, some species infect dogs and in these areas, dogs may play an important role in animal-to-person transmission. Dogs are highly susceptible to many *Leishmania* spp. Cats tend to be infected with the same *Leishmania* spp that infect dogs. However, infection in much less common in cats. Disease is rare and usually of the milder (cutaneous) form. In a study in Sicily, where dogs are commonly infected, no infection was seen in cats.[7]

Old World species causing visceral disease are variants of *L donovani*.[18] *Leishmania donovani* is found in the Indian subcontinent and Burma. Dogs are not a natural reservoir for this subspecies, though they can be experimentally infected. *Leishmania donovani sensu lato* is enzootic in Uganda, southern Ethiopia and Kenya. Naturally infected dogs have not been found in this area, nor have cases been reported in cats. A Sudanese variant of this subspecies is found in Sudan, western Ethiopia, Chad, Niger, the Central African Republic and Gabon. Though it infects some wild cats, no reports in domestic dogs or cats have been made. *Leishmania infantum*, another variant of *L donovani*, is found in North China, Asian portions of the USSR, Iran, Iraq, Syria, Jordan, Lebanon, Arabia, Turkey, Greece, Spain, Portugal and Algeria. Wild and domestic dogs are a major reservoir for this species. *Leishmania tropica* is an Old World species causing mainly cutaneous leishmaniasis. It is found in many of the same areas as *L donovani* and its variants. Dogs can be infected, though rodents are the principal reservoir.

The principal New World species causing visceral leishmaniasis is *L chagasi* and its variants.[18] They are found in the northern half of South America and regions of Central America. Dogs are important reservoirs for this group of organisms in some enzootic areas. Sporadic cases in dogs have also been seen in the United States. *Leishmania* spp associated with cutaneous leishmaniasis in the New World include *L mexicana*, *L braziliensis* and their variants. The *Leishmania mexicana* group rarely causes disease in dogs and cats; rodents are its reservoir. The *L braziliensis* group is found in Central and South America, and dogs may serve as a reservoir.

Visceral leishmaniasis is the most severe form of the disease in people and animals.[14] Sandflies deposit infectious forms of *Leishmania* in the bite wound. Organisms rapidly invade the lymphoid system throughout the body and are found mainly in macrophages. There is little resistance to replicating organisms, and host tissues become a mass of proliferating macrophages filled with leishmanial bodies. Proliferation is particularly intense in the liver, spleen and lymphoid tissues of the intestinal tract. Emaciation and death are almost inevitable within a year or less in untreated people. Dogs may survive for much longer periods, though the signs and clinical outcome are often similar to those in people. Sandflies become infected with organisms when they feed on reservoir hosts. In dogs, macrophages in many areas of the skin are filled with organisms, making infection of sandflies likely. Cutaneous leishmaniasis tends to occur from infection with *Leishmania* spp that are either less virulent or more prone to induce a partially effective immune response. Organisms are limited to areas of the skin where sandflies feed. Skin lesions tend to be crusty, tumor-like and ulcerated.

Leishmaniasis in cats, associated either with Old or New World species, is rare and usually of the cutaneous type. It is manifested by crusty ulcers on the lips, nose, eyelids, edges of the ears and, less commonly, the trunk.[1,2,11,13] Only 1 case of visceral leishmaniasis has been reported.[1] Even in this case, however, the principal lesion was on the skin, with secondary involvement only of the spleen. Reports of diseased cats in the New World are lacking. It has been reported that cats in the Americas harbor the agent without clinical disease.[6,17] However, it is likely that rare cases do occur in cats even in this part of the world. Organisms can usually be identified within macrophages, or in biopsies or impression smears of skin lesions (Fig 12). They stain well with Giemsa-type stains and measure about 2 x 5 μ. People are mainly treated with antimonial compounds.[10] Pentavalent antimony (stibogluconate sodium), given IM or IV at 0.1-0.2 mg/kg daily for 10-30 days, is generally used for initial infections.[14] Relapses occur in some human cases. Visceral leishmaniasis in dogs is virtually untreatable with these drugs. There is a report of 10 of 14 dogs being cured of leishmaniasis with ketoconazole.[22]

Though leishmaniasis is an important disease of people, infected cats are not considered health hazards. In 1 report, a child and a cat in the same household were infected.[7] This probably represented exposure to a common reservoir and not person-to-cat or cat-to-person transmission.

Fig 12. Bone marrow aspirate from a dog with visceral leishmaniasis shows *Leishmania donovani* bodies in the cytoplasm of a macrophage-like cell. Wright's-Giemsa stain, 2000X.

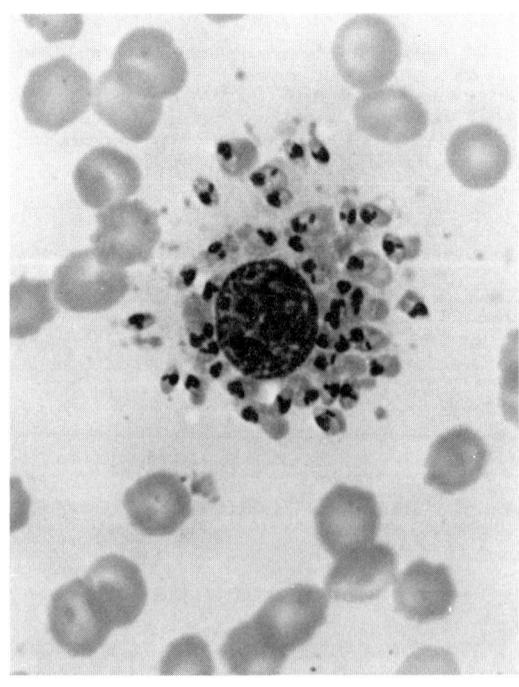

Encephalitozoonosis

Encephalitozoon spp belong to the phylum Microspora, class Microsporea. They are largely unrelated to most of the other protozoan parasites discussed.[18] They are obligate intracellular parasites that divide by binary and multiple fission. The principal species is *Encephalitozoon cuniculi*, a parasite of rodents, dogs and sometimes people.[18,19]

The life cycle begins with passage of spores in urine of the host species. The spores are then ingested by the same host species and somehow travel through the viscera to peritoneal macrophages, where they undergo asexual division (schizogony) to form sporants. Sporants give rise to paired sporoblasts, which then develop into spores. Macrophages may become filled with spores during this stage of replication. Spores eventually reach reticuloendothelial and nervous tissues, mainly the brain and kidneys. Spores are then passed in the urine, thus completing the cycle. When disease occurs, it is usually associated with host immune responses to spore-filled bodies in such areas as the brain, eyes and kidneys.

Experimental infection is most severe in dogs, in which it causes severe encephalomyelitis and nephritis.[19] Disease in rabbits is similar but much less severe. People are rarely affected. Kittens experimentally infected with *E cuniculi* under stressful conditions failed to develop signs of disease.[19] However, a clinically apparent nonsuppurative type of meningoencephalitis due to *Encephalitozoon* has been reported in older cats and in a litter of 4 kittens.[12,21] The 1 kitten that was necropsied from this litter had histopathologic lesions of meningoencephalitis and interstitial nephritis. Organisms were seen in many lymphoid organs and within the walls of some blood vessels. Localized unilateral keratitis has been associated with *Encephalitozoon* in an adult cat.[3] Schizonts are seen in the tissue of affected cats and must be differentiated from those of *Toxoplasma* spp.

Hepatozoonosis

Hepatozoon spp are protozoan parasites belonging to the class Sporozoa. They are distantly related to coccidian parasites.[18] *Hepatozoon canis* is a parasite of dogs, cats, jackals and hyenas.[4,18] It is found in the Far East, Central and North Africa, the Middle East, Italy and along the southeast coast of Texas in the United States. The geographic distribution of the organism parallels that of the brown dog tick, *Rhipicephalus sanguineus*.[4]

Dogs are infected when they ingest the tick host. Sporozoites in the tick are freed by digestive enzymes, penetrate the gut wall, and undergo division and differentiation in reticuloendothelial elements of the spleen, bone marrow, lungs, liver and muscles.[4] Schizogony in these cells results in production of macroschizonts and eventual release of macromerozoites. These reinfect reticuloendothelial cells and produce microschizonts and, ultimately, micromerozoites that escape and infect blood monocytes and neutrophils. When the tick feeds, gametocytes within monocytes or neutrophils are ingested and eventually differentiate to oocysts within the hemocele (blood cavity) of the tick. Oocysts become infectious for mammalian hosts as soon as sporulation occurs. *Hepatozoon canis* organisms have been seen in blood leukocytes of some cats in India and Nigeria.[9] Schizonts have also been seen in the lumina of blood capillaries in myocardial tissues of a large proportion of cats in Israel.[8,15] Granulomatous cholangiohepatitis, due to a host reaction against *Hepatozoon* schizonts, has been recognized in a cat originating from Hawaii.[5] Another cat with clinical hepatozoonosis was successfully treated with a combination of primaquine and oxytetracycline.[20] No drug has proven effective in treatment of hepatozoonosis in dogs, however.

Animal and Public Health Considerations

Hepatozoon canis infection is not considered a public health hazard.[4]

References

1. Bergeon P: Un cas de leishmaniose chez le chat. *Bltn Soc Sci Vet Lyon* 30:92-93, 1927.

2. Bosselut H: Un cas de leishmaniose générale du chat. *Arch Inst Pasteur Algér* 26:14, 1948.

3. Buyukmihci N et al: Encephalitozoon (Nosema) infection of the cornea of a cat. *JAVMA* 171:355-357, 1977.

4. Craig TM, in Greene CE: *Clinical Microbiology and Infectious Diseases of the Dog and Cat.* Saunders, Philadelphia, 1984. pp 771-780.

5. Ewing GO: Granulomatous cholangiohepatitis in a cat due to a protozoan parasite resembling *Hepatozoon canis*. *Feline Pract* 7(6):37-40, 1977.

6. Ferreira LC et al: Notas sobre a transmissao de leishmaniose visceral americana. *Hosp Rio de Jan* 14:1077-1087, 1938.

7. Giordano A: Le chat dans la transmission de la leishmaniose viscérale de la méditterranée. *Bltn Sez Ital Soc Internaz Microbiol* 5:330-332,1933.

8. Klopfer U et al: Hepatozoon-like parasite (schizonts) in the myocardium of the domestic cat. *Vet Pathol* 10:185-190, 1973.

9. Leeflang P and Ilemobade AA: Tick-borne diseases of domestic animals in northern Nigeria. *Trop Anim Prod* 9:211-218, 1977.

10. Levine ND: *Protozoan Parasites of Man and of Animals*. 2nd ed. Burgess Publishing, Minneapolis, 1973.

11. Machattie C et al: Naturally occurring oriental sore of the domestic cat of Iraq. *Trans Rev Soc Trop Med Hyg* 25:103-106, 1931.

12. Meier H et al: Toxoplasmosis in the cat—fourteen cases. *JAVMA* 133:395-414, 1957.

13. Mello GB: Verificacao de infeccao natural do gato (*Felix domesticus*) por um protozoario do genero *Leishmania*. *Brasil-Med* 54:180, 1940.

14. Neva FA, in Wyngaarden JB and Smith LH Jr: *Cecil's Textbook of Medicine*. Saunders, Philadelphia, 1985. pp 1786-1792.

15. Nobel TA et al: Histopathology of the myocardium in 50 apparently healthy cats. *Lab Ans* 8:119-125, 1974.

16. Schuster J: Uber eine Spontan bei Kaninchen auftretende encephalitische Erkrankung. *Klin Wochenschr* 4:550, 1925.

17. Sergent EE et al: La leishmaniose à Alger. Infection simultanée d'un enfant, d'un chien et d'un chat dans le même habitation. *Bltn Soc Path Exot* 5:93-98, 1912.

18. Soulsby EJL: *Helminths, Arthropods and Protozoa of Domesticated Animals*. Lea & Febiger, Philadelphia, 1982.

19. Szabo JR et al, in Greene CE: *Clinical Microbiology and Infectious Diseases of the Dog and Cat*. Saunders, Philadelphia, 1984. pp 781-790.

20. van Amstel S: Hepatozoönose in 'n kat. *J So Afr Vet Med Assoc* 50:215-216, 1979.

21. van Rensburg IBJ and du Plessis JL: Nosematosis in a cat: A case report. *J So Afr Vet Med Assoc* 42:327-331, 1971.

Additional Reference

22. D'Ambroso G et al: Trattamento della leishmaniore del cane. Impiego di un nuovo derivato dell'imidazole. *Obiettivi Doc Vet* 8(3):31-34, 1987.

Index

A

Acanthocephaliasis, 345-346
Actinomycosis, 161-164, 201-202
Actinomycetomas, 285-287
Aelurostrongylus abstrusus, 305-309
AIDS, feline, 115-123
Anaerobic infections, 161-164
Ancylostoma, 317-319
Ancylostomiasis, 317-319
Anemia, feline infectious, 225-230
    FeLV, 93-94
    trypanosomiasis, 392-397
Anisocoria, FeLV, 91
Anthrax, 149-150
Arthritis, 80-81, 93
Arthropod infestations, 347-366
    Cheyletiella parasitivorax, 349-351
    cheyletiellosis, 349-351
    chigger mite infestation, 351
    Ctenocephalides felis, 359-366
    demodectic mange, 352-353
    Demodex cati, 352-353
    Dermanyssus gallinae, 356
    ear mite infestation, 347-349
    Echidnophaga gallinacea, 366
    Felicola subrostratus, 358-359
    flea infestation, 359-366
    fur mite infestation, 357-358
    lice infestation, 358-359
    Lynxacarus radovski, 357-358
    Notoedres cati, 354-356
    notoedric mange, 354-356
    Otodectes cynotis, 347-349
    pediculosis, 358-359
    poultry mite infestation, 356
    Sarcoptes scabei, 356
    sarcoptic mange, 356
    stick-tight flea infestation, 366
Aspergillosis, 281-284
Astrovirus enteritis, 71-73
Aujeszky's disease, 29-32

B

Babesiosis, 383-386
Bacillary infections, 149-151
Bacterial diseases, 125-213
    Actinomyces, 161-164, 201-202
    Anaerobes, 161-164
    Anthrax, 149-150
    Bacillus, 149-151
    Bacteroides, 161-164
    Bordetella, 153-154
    Campylobacter, 129-132
    Cat scratch disease, 209-211
    Clostridium, 145-148, 161-164
    Corynebacterium equi, 203
    Dermatophilus, 187-188
    EF-4, 205-207
    Escherichia coli, 175-177
    Flavobacterium, 204
    Francisella tularensis, 159-160
    Fusobacterium, 161-164
    Leprosy, 194-197
    Leptospira, 179-181
    Listeria, 141-143
    Moraxella, 204
    Mycobacterium, 189-200
    Nocardia, 183-185
    Pasteurella, 155-157, 161-164
    Peptostreptococcus, 161-164
    Plague, 169-172
    Pseudomonas, 127-128
    Pseudotuberculosis, 172-174
    Rhodococcus equi, 203
    Salmonella, 165-167
    Serratia, 203
    Staphylococcus, 137-139
    Streptococcus, 133-136
    Tetanus, 145-147
    Tularemia, 159-160
    Tyzzer's disease, 150-151
    Yersinia, 169-174
Bacteroides, 161-164
Besnoitia, 367-371
Bladder worm infection, 312-315
Blastomycosis, 251-254
Bordetellosis, 153-154
Botulism, 147

C

Calicivirus, 61-68
Campylobacteriosis, 129-132
Candidiasis, 281-284
Capillaria, 311-315
Cat scratch disease, 209-211
Cell wall-deficient organisms, 237-240
Chagas' disease, 392-397
Cheyletiellosis, 349-351
Chigger mite infestation, 351
Chlamydia psittaci, 213, 231-236
Chlamydiosis, 213, 231-236
Chlamydial diseases, 213, 231-236
Chromomycosis, 277-280
Cladosporium, 277-280
Clostridium, 145-148, 161-164
Coccidioidomycosis, 243-245
Coccidiosis, 367-371

Colibacillosis, 175-177
Conjunctivitis
  chlamydial, 232-235
  mycoplasmal, 216-217
Coronaviruses, enteric, 41-44
Corynebacterium equi, 203
Coxiella burnetii, 221-224
Cryptococcosis, 92, 119, 255-261
Cryptosporidiosis, 380-383
Ctenocephalides felis, 359-366
C-type retrovirus, 101-102
Cyathospirura dasyuridis, 319-326
Cylicospirura felineus, 319-326
Cytauxzoonosis, 386-389

D

Demodectic mange, 352-353
Dermanyssus gallinae, 356
Dermatomycosis, 263-272
Dermatophilosis, 187-188
Dermatophytosis, 263-272
Diphyllobothrium latum, 339-344
Dipylidium caninum, 339-344
Dirofilariasis, 299-305
Distemper, 15-20

E

Ear mite infestation, 347-349
Echidnophaga gallinacea, 366
EF-4 infection, 205-207
Encephalitozoonosis, 399
Enteritis, astrovirus, 71-73
  colibacillosis, 175-177
  E coli, 175-177
  Salmonella, 165-167
  viral, 15-20, 41-44, 71-73, 75-76
Enzootic, 6
Epizootic, 6
Escherichia coli, 175-177
Eumycetomas, 285-287
Eurytrema procyonis, 336-337

F

Felicola subrostratus, 358-359
Feline infectious anemia, 225-230
Feline infectious peritonitis, 45-60, 91
Feline leukemia virus, 83-106
FeLV, 83-106
Fibrosarcoma, 109-114
FIP, 45-60, 91
Flatworm infections, 331-344
  Diphyllobothrium latum, 339-344
  Dipylidium caninum, 339-344
  Eurytrema procyonis, 336-337
  Joyeuxiella, 339-344
  liver fluke infection, 334-336, 338
  lung fluke infection, 331-334
  pancreatic fluke infection, 336-338
  paragonimiasis, 331-334
  Paragonimus kellicotti, 331-334
  Platynosomum fastosum, 334-336
  Spirometra, 339-344
  Taenia taeniaeformis, 339-344
  tapeworm infection, 339-344
Flavobacterium, 204
Flea infestation, 359-366
Francisella tularensis, 159-160
Fungal infections, see Mycoses
Fur mite infestation, 357-358
Fusobacterium, 161-164

G

Gangrene, 147
Gapeworm infection, 309-311
Giardiasis, 389-382
Gingivitis, FeLV, 92
Gnathostoma spinigerum, 319-326

H

Hammondia, 367-371
Heartworm disease, 299-305
Hemobartonellosis, 225-230
Hepatozoonosis, 399
Herpesvirus type-1, 21-28, 92
Histoplasmosis, 247-249
Hookworm infection, 317-319

I

Immunity, 3
Immunization, 5-6
Immunodeficiency virus, 115-123
Isospora, 367-371

J

Joyeuxiella, 339-344

L

Large intestinal worm infection, 326-329
L-form infections, 213, 237-240
Leishmaniasis, 397-398
Leprosy, 194-197
Leptospirosis, 179-181
Leukemia virus, 83-106
Lice infestation, 358-359
Listeriosis, 141-143
Liver fluke infection, 334-336, 338
Lung fluke infection, 331-334
Lungworm infection, 305-309
Lymphosarcoma, 88-95, 119
Lynxacarus radovski, 357-358

M

Mammomonogamus ierei, 309-311
Mange, demodectic, 352-353
　notoedric, 354-356
　sarcoptic, 356
Microsporum canis, 263-272, 285, 287
Moraxella, 204
Mucor, 281-284
Mucormycosis, 281-284
Mycetomas, 285-287
Mycobacteriosis, 119, 189-200
　atypical, 197-200
　leprosy, 194-197
　systemic, 189-194
Mycoplasmal diseases, 213-220
Mycoses, 241-291
　actinomycetomas, 285-287
　aspergillosis, 281-284
　Aspergillus, 281-284
　Blastomyces dermatitidis, 251-254
　blastomycosis, 251-254
　Candida, 281-284
　candidiasis, 281-284
　chromomycosis, 277-280
　Cladosporium, 277-280
　Coccidioides immitis, 243-245
　coccidioidomycosis, 243-245
　cryptococcosis, 255-261
　Cryptococcus neoformans, 255-261
　dermatomycosis, 263-272
　dermatophytosis, 263-272
　eumycetomas, 285-287
　Histoplasma capsulatum, 247-249
　histoplasmosis, 247-249
　Microsporum canis, 263-272, 285, 287
　Mucor, 281-284
　mucormycosis, 281-284
　mycetomas, 285-287
　Paecilomyces, 291
　paecilomycosis, 291
　penicilliosis, 281-284
　Penicillium, 281-284
　Prototheca wickerhamii, 289-290
　protothecosis, 289-290
　ringworm, 263-272
　Sporothrix schenckii, 273-276
　sporotrichosis, 273-276
　Streptomyces, 285-287
　Trichophyton mentagrophytes, 263-272

N

Nasal worm infection, 309-311
Nocardiosis, 183-185
Notoedric mange, 354-356

O

Ollulanus tricuspis, 319-326
Oncicola, 345-346

Otodectes cynotis, 347-349

P

Paecilomycosis, 291
Pancreatic fluke infection, 336-338
Panleukopenia, 15-20
Paragonimiasis, 331-334
Parasitic diseases, 293-400
Parvovirus enteritis, 15-20
Pasteurellosis, 155-157, 161-164
Pediculosis, 358-359
Penicilliosis, 281-282
Penicillium, 281-282
Peptostreptococcus, 161-164
Peritonitis, feline infectious, 45-60, 91
Physaloptera praeputialis, 319-326
Plague, 169-172
Platynosomiasis, 334-336
Pneumonia, *Bordetella*, 153-154
　chlamydial, 232-233
Pneumonitis, chlamydial, 232-233
Poultry mite infestation, 356
Pox virus, 11-14
Protothecosis, 289-290
Protozoal infections, 367-400
　Babesia, 383-386
　babesiosis, 383-386
　Besnoitia, 367-371
　Chagas' disease, 392-397
　coccidiosis, 367-371
　cryptosporidiosis, 380-383
　Cryptosporidium, 380-383
　Cytauxzoon felis, 386-389
　cytauxzoonosis, 386-389
　Encephalitozoon cuniculi, 399
　encephalitozoonosis, 399
　Giardia, 389-392
　giardiasis, 389-392
　Hammondia, 367-371
　Hepatozoon, 399
　hepatozoonosis, 399
　Isospora, 367-371
　Leishmania, 397-398
　leishmaniasis, 397-398
　Sarcocystis, 367-371
　Toxoplasma gondii, 372-380
　toxoplasmosis, 372-380
　Trypanosoma, 392-397
　trypanosomiasis, 392-397
Pseudomonas, 127-128
Pseudorabies, 29-32
Pseudotuberculosis, 172-174

Q

Q fever, 221-224

R

Rabies, 33-40

Reovirus, 69-73
Rhodococcus equi, 203
Rickettsial diseases, 213, 221-230
    Coxiella burnetii, 221-224
    Hemobartonella felis, 225-230
    hemobartonellosis, 225-230
    Q fever, 221-224
Ringworm, 263-272
Rotavirus, 75-76
Roundworm infections, 295-329
    Aelurostrongylus abstrusus, 305-309
    Ancylostoma, 317-319
    ancylostomiasis, 317-319
    bladder worm infection, 312-315
    Capillaria, 311-315
    Cyathospirura dasyuridis, 319-326
    Cylicospirura felineus, 319-326
    Dirofilaria immitis, 299-305
    dirofilariasis, 299-305
    gapeworm infection, 309-311
    Gnathostoma spinigerum, 319-326
    heartworm disease, 299-305
    hookworm infection, 317-319
    large intestinal worm infection, 326-329
    lungworm infection, 305-309
    Mammomongamus ierei, 309-311
    nasal worm infection, 309-311
    Ollulanus tricuspis, 319-326
    Physaloptera praeputialis, 319-326
    stomach worm infection, 319-326
    Strongyloides planiceps, 326-329
    Strongyloides tumefaciens, 326-329
    Syngamus, 309-311
    Toxascaris leonina, 298
    Toxocara cati, 295-298
    toxocariasis, 295-298
    Trichinella spiralis, 315-317
    trichinellosis, 315-317
    trichurid worm infection, 311-315
    Trichuris, 311-315
    Uncinaria, 317-319
    visceral larval migrans, 297-298
    whipworm infection, 311-315

S

Salmonellosis, 165-167
Sarcocystis, 367-371
Sarcoma virus, 107-114
Sarcoptic mange, 356
Serratia, 203
Spirometra, 339-344
Sporotrichosis, 273-276
Staphylococcus, 137-139
Stick-tight flea infestation, 366
Stomach worm infection, 319-326
Streptococcus, 133-136
Streptomyces, 285-287
Strongyloides, 326-329
Syncytium-forming virus, 77-82
Syngamus, 309-311

T

Taenia taeniaeformis, 339-344
Tapeworm infection, 339-344
Tetanus, 145-147
Thorny-headed worm infection, 345-346
Toxocariasis, 295-298
Toxoplasmosis, 92, 119, 372-380
Trichinellosis, 315-317
Trichophyton mentagrophytes, 263-272
Trichurid worm infection, 311-315
Trichuris, 311-315
Trypanosomiasis, 392-397
Tularemia, 159-160
Tyzzer's disease, 150-151

U

Uncinaria, 317-319

V

Viral diseases, 9-124
    Astrovirus, 71-73
    Aujeszky's disease, 29-32
    Calicivirus, 61-68
    C-type retrovirus, 101-102
    Coronaviruses, enteric, 41-44
    Enteric coronaviruses, 41-44
    Feline infectious peritonitis, 45-60, 91
    Feline leukemia virus, 83-106
    FeLV, 83-106
    FIP, 45-60, 91
    Herpesvirus type-1, 21-28, 91
    Immunodeficiency virus, 115-123
    Infectious peritonitis, 45-60, 91
    Leukemia virus, 83-106
    Panleukopenia, 15-20
    Parvovirus, 15-20
    Pox virus, 11-14
    Pseudorabies, 29-32
    Rabies, 33-40
    Reovirus, 69-73
    Rotavirus, 75-76
    Sarcoma virus, 107-114
    Syncytium-forming virus, 77-82
Visceral larval migrans, 297-298

W

Whipworm infection, 311-315

Y

Yersinia, 169-174

Date Due

SEP 29 1994			
NOV 20 1994			
MAR 27 2003			

BRODART, INC.   Cat. No. 23 233   Printed in U.S.A.